Table of Contents

D1504224

How The West Got

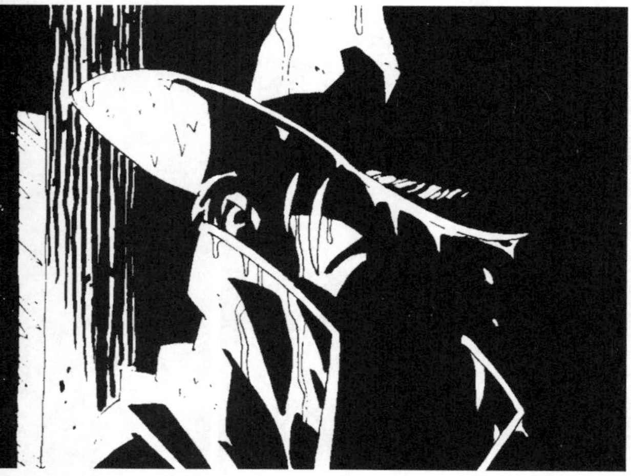

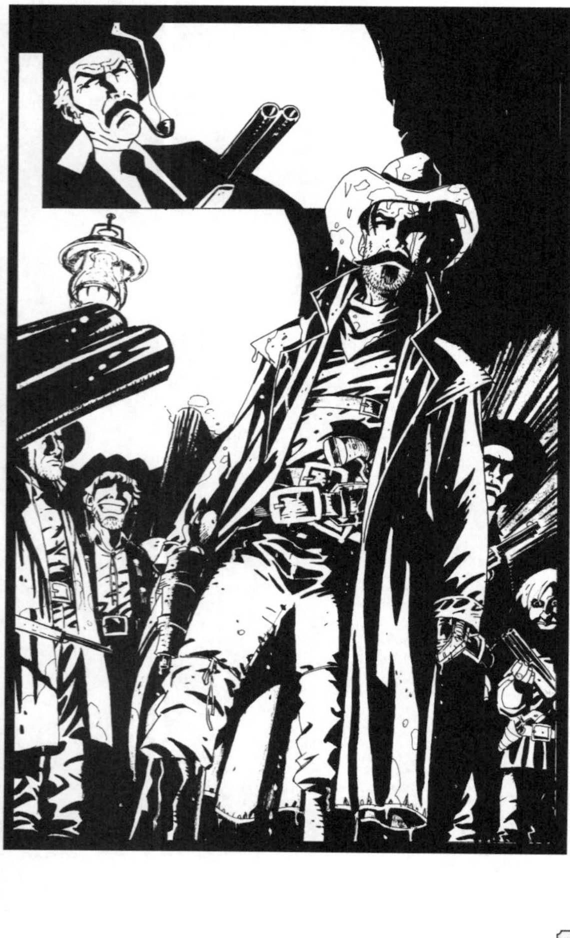

Sometimes things get out of hand. The book you're reading is a prime example of that truism. All we originally set out to do was create a follow-up to our graphic novel, THE WICKED WEST. But somewhere along the way, things got out of hand.

Let's go back to the beginning...

THE WICKED WEST marked the first appearance of Cotton Coleridge. Coleridge was a mysterious and contradictory fellow. At first glance he appeared to be just another dusty saddle tramp - admittedly a dangerous, dusty saddle tramp. Dangerous, we learned, when he took on nearly a dozen gunslingers in a lonely frontier saloon and killed them all. It was then that the contradictions set in as he proceeded to take a job teaching at the town school. Cotton, we learned, was an educated man. A veritable asset to the fledgling town of Javer's Tanks, way out on the 1870s Texas frontier.

And then those damned vampires showed up...

This didn't seem to surprise Cotton that much. Apparently, he was cursed. Really and truly, not just metaphorically, cursed. As a result, he was a lightning rod for the supernatural. The bad supernatural. Or as we say in ROAD TO JAVER'S (the short story that ran in the back of THE BLACK FOREST 2), "...bad shit happens to him for a very good reason." A reason we're not quite ready to share. But trust us - it really is a good one.

Anyway, the first story followed Cotton's efforts to save a town from an onslaught of the undead and at the same time dramatized a 1932 movie version of the so-called Massacre at Javer's Tanks. Fans loved the way the story moved back and forth between the "real" and the "reel." We loved it, too. So much so that we also included a text version of the "Penny Dreadful" that was the basis for the "movie" - TERROR OVER TEXAS. We threw in some awesome pin-ups, too.

As creators, putting these "DVD extras" in our books is fun, and we like to think it also makes the reading experience richer for you, our fans. We wanted to do more of that sort of thing the second time around, too.

Even Weirder...

Which is how things got out of hand...

As we set out to do the follow-up to the first book, events took an interesting turn. We had different stories, individually written, that we wanted to tell. Okay, no problem. But then we thought of another story we wanted to do together. Still okay - but wait - Neil doesn't have time to draw yet another story.

Well, let's just bring in a back-up artist, we thought. Why not? We already bring in other folks to do pin-ups. Then it occurred to us - why do pin-ups? Why not full-blown back-up stories? Just a couple...

So we invited a few writers and artists we admired to have a little fun in the world we created. Then we invited a few more. And more still. The next thing we knew, we had over twenty stories, written and drawn by some of the best creators in the business...and they were all fantastic.

At that point we had a full-blown anthology on our hands and there was no turning back. There was simply no way we were cutting out any of these great stories. Don't believe us? You try it. Read them and tell us which ones we should have cut, because we don't have a clue.

Our goal has always been to create better stories and deliver as much entertainment as possible. While reading the gems you're about to enjoy, we realized the bar has moved a few notches higher. It's incredibly flattering to see your character coming to life at the hands of others, and when you see them handled by such masterful talent like the posse we brought together, it's also invigorating and inspiring.

For you, the reader, we just hope it's a good time...

Enjoy.
L-T-V

The
WICKED WEST II

ABOMINATION

STORY BY
ROBERT TINNELL

ILLUSTRATED BY
NEIL VOKES

"I'M GOING TO SAIL TO CHINA SOMEDAY, GRANDFATHER."
"ALL THE WAY TO CHINA. AND ALL THE WAY BACK AGAIN."
"SAILING'S NOT TO BE FOR YOU, LADDIE."
YOUR FATHER'S PEOPLE ARE SOLDIERS. YOU'LL SOLDIER, TOO.
I SURE WISH I COULD DO BOTH.
MOTHER SAYS FATHER WILL BE HOME SOON.
I SAY WE JUST GO AND SEE HIM.
BEFORE YOU KNOW IT, THEY'LL HAVE THE MEXICANS WHIPPED AND WE'LL HAVE MISSED EVERYTHING.
IF YOU STILL HAD YOUR SHIP..
WE COULD SAIL TO MEXICO, COULDN'T WE?
WE COULD.
DO YOU MISS IT, GRANDFATHER?
OH, AYE.
I'D MISS IT.
I'D MISS ALL THOSE PLACES YOU'VE SAW.
SEEN. PLACES I'VE SEEN.
SEEN. YES, SIR.
I DO MISS 'EM. SO MANY PORTS. SO MANY PLACES.
THE SOUTH PACIFIC --
FILLED WITH WONDERS, IT WAS.
"BUT WHAT I MISS MOST IS THE SEA HERSELF.."
"BUT IT'S RIGHT THERE."
"AYE, 'TIS. RIGHT THERE. TAUNTING ME."
"REMINDING ME EVERY DAY OF EVERYTHING I'VE EVER LOVED AND LOST."

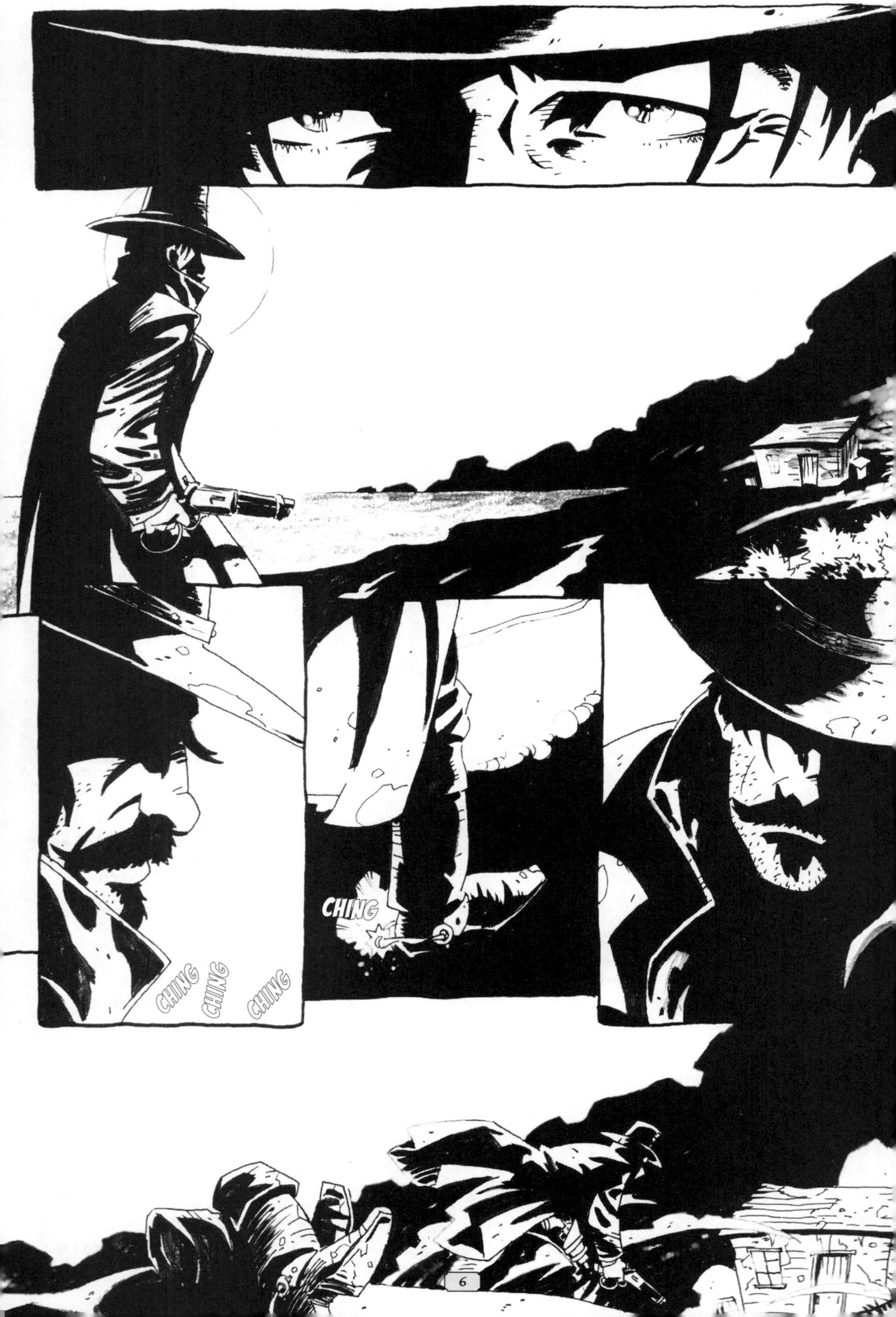
CHING
CHING
CHING
CHING

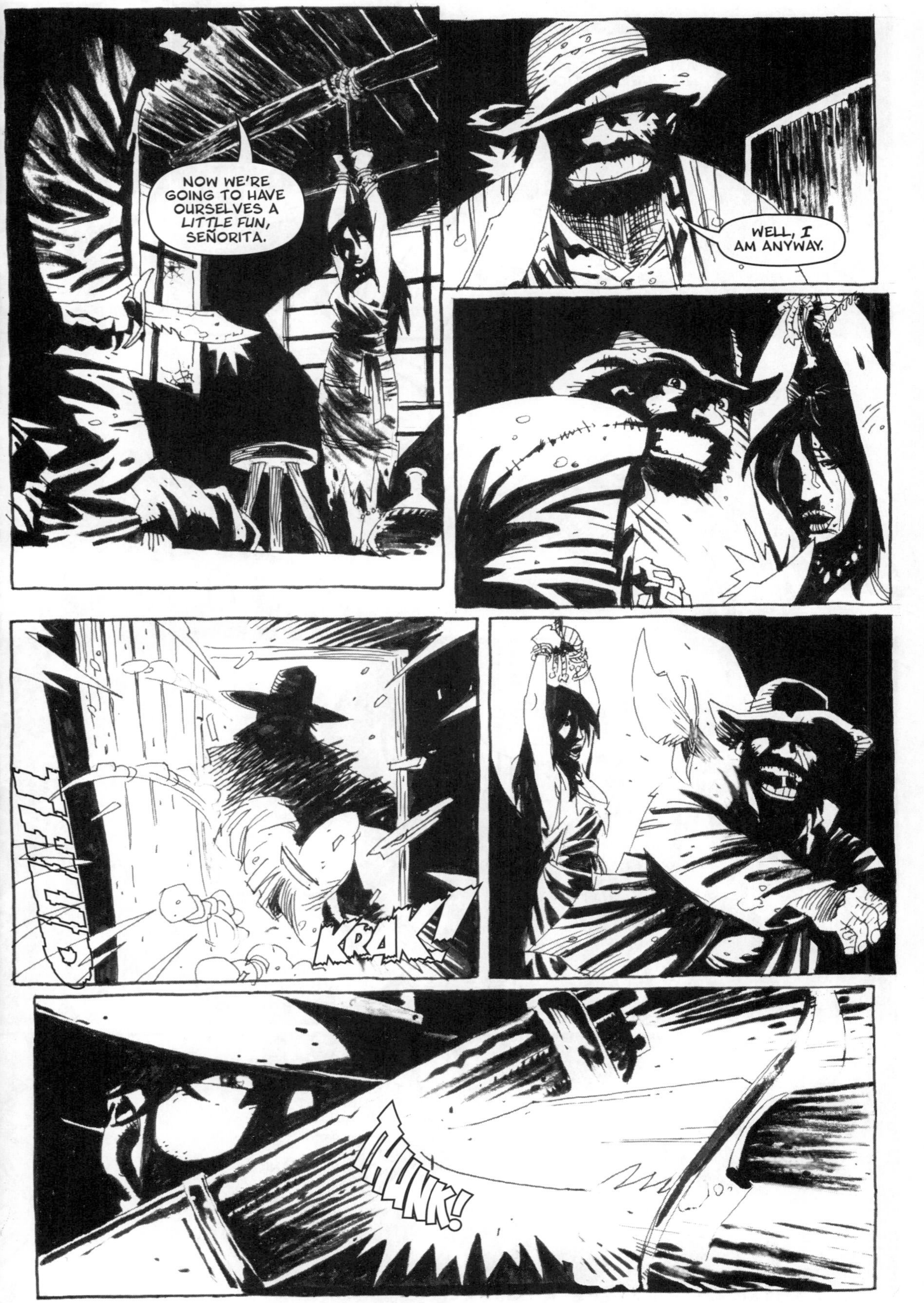
NOW WE'RE GOING TO HAVE OURSELVES A *LITTLE FUN,* SEÑORITA.
WELL, *I* AM ANYWAY.
KRAK!
THUNK!

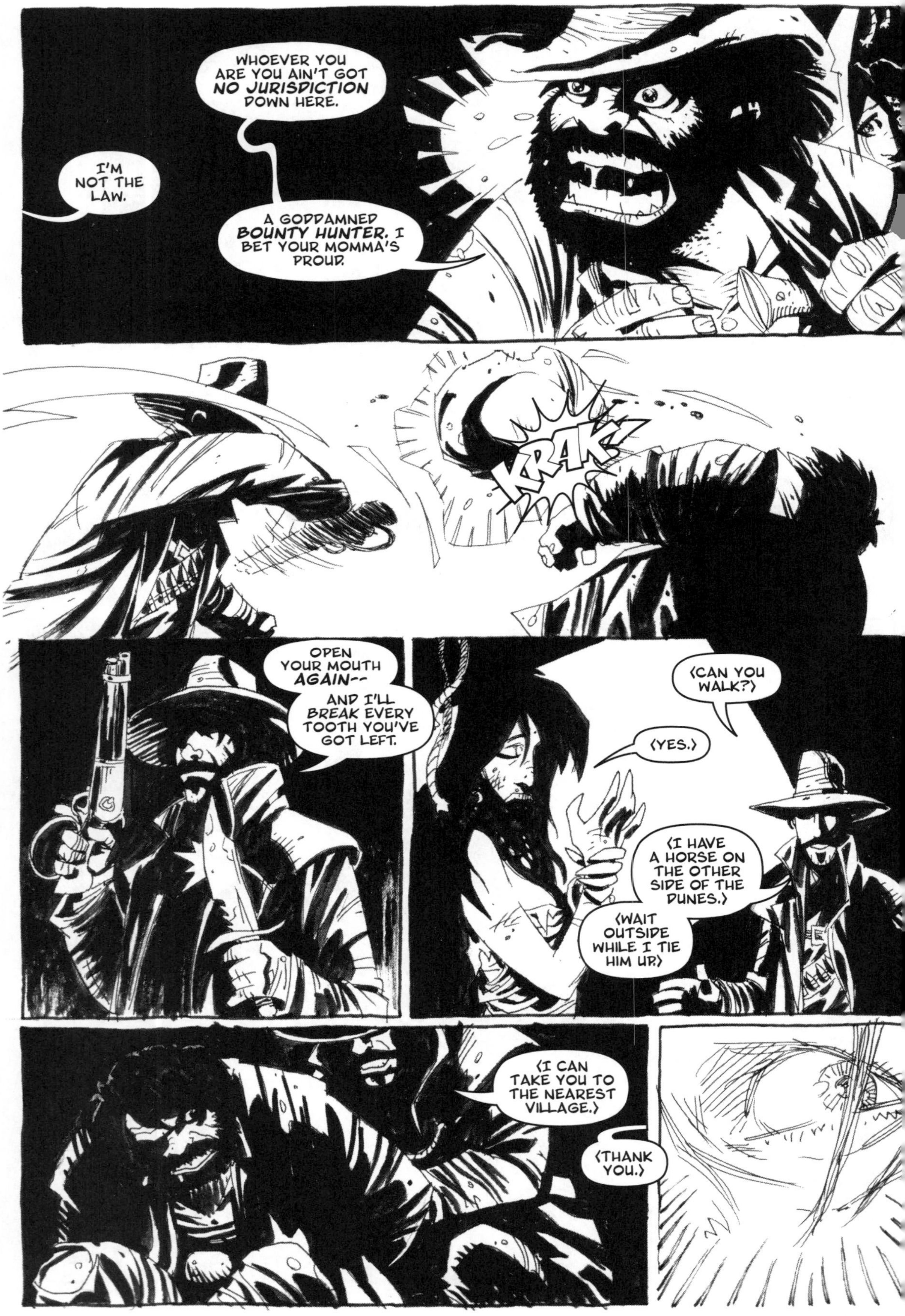

I'M NOT THE LAW.
WHOEVER YOU ARE YOU AIN'T GOT NO JURISDICTION DOWN HERE.
A GODDAMNED BOUNTY HUNTER. I BET YOUR MOMMA'S PROUD.
KRAK!
OPEN YOUR MOUTH AGAIN--
AND I'LL BREAK EVERY TOOTH YOU'VE GOT LEFT.
‹CAN YOU WALK?›
‹YES.›
‹I HAVE A HORSE ON THE OTHER SIDE OF THE DUNES.›
‹WAIT OUTSIDE WHILE I TIE HIM UP.›
‹I CAN TAKE YOU TO THE NEAREST VILLAGE.›
‹THANK YOU.›

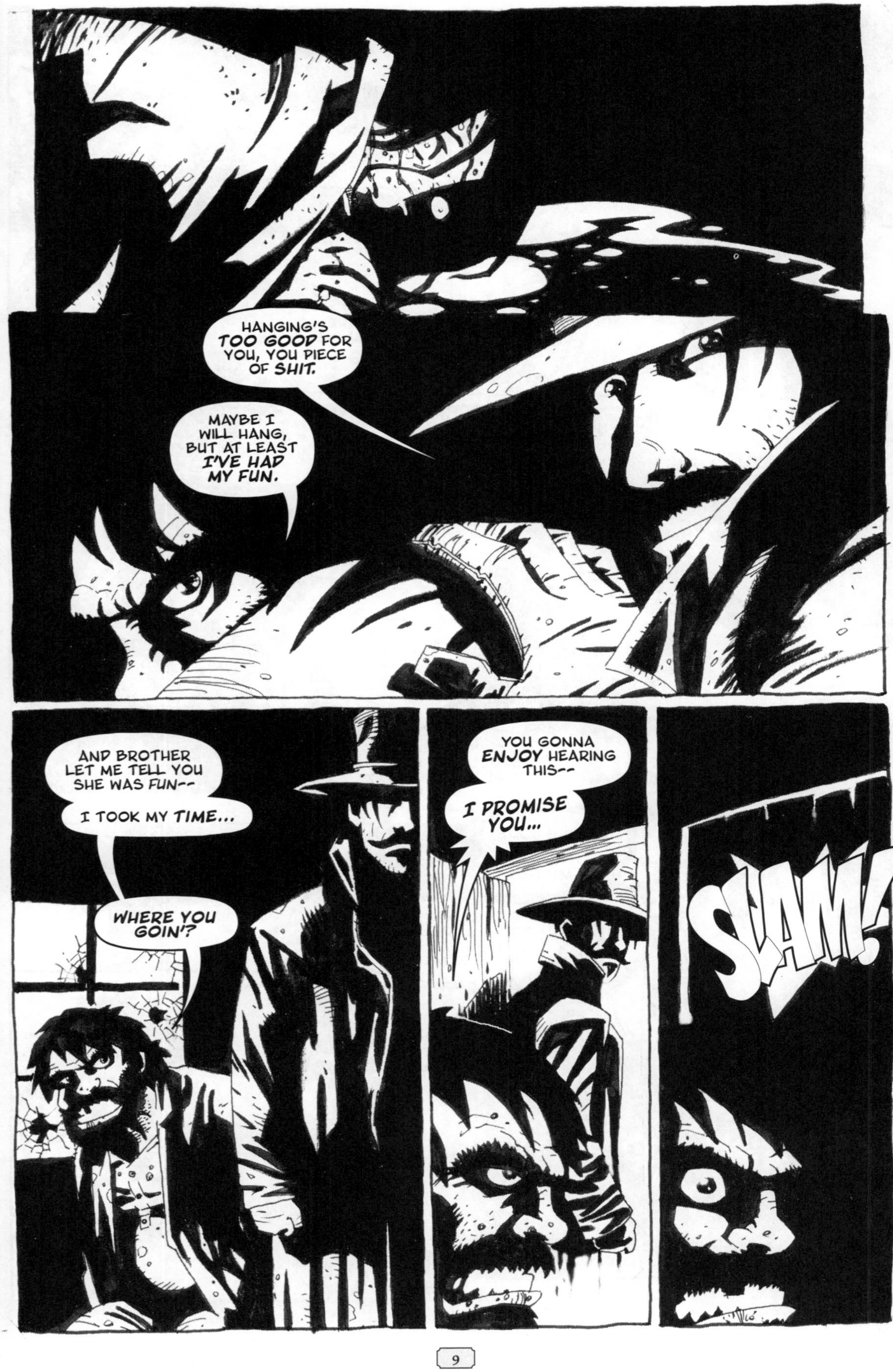

HANGING'S TOO GOOD FOR YOU, YOU PIECE OF SHIT.
MAYBE I WILL HANG, BUT AT LEAST I'VE HAD MY FUN.
AND BROTHER LET ME TELL YOU SHE WAS FUN--
I TOOK MY TIME...
WHERE YOU GOIN'?
YOU GONNA ENJOY HEARING THIS--
I PROMISE YOU...
SLAM!

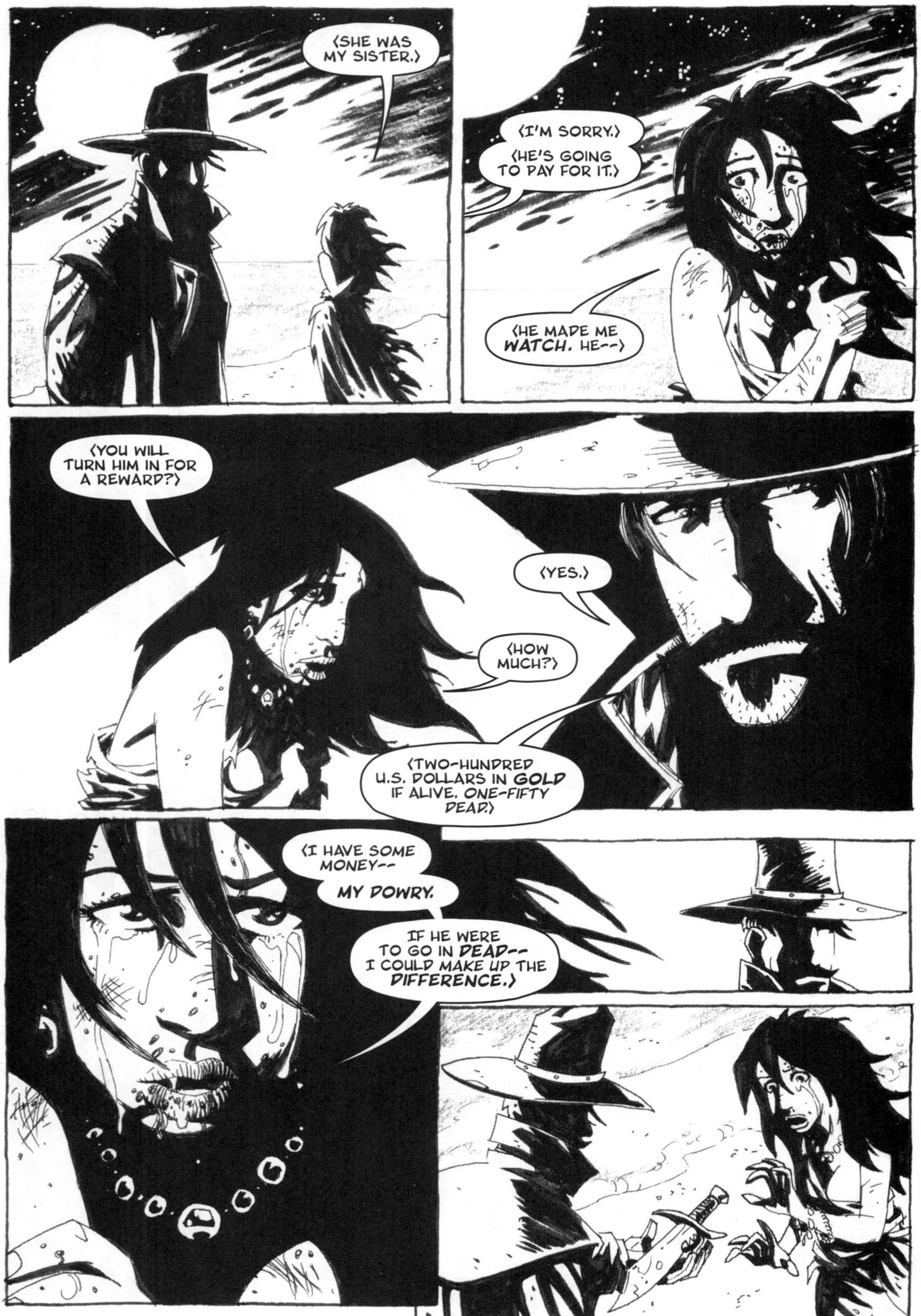
⟨SHE WAS MY SISTER.⟩
⟨I'M SORRY.⟩
⟨HE'S GOING TO PAY FOR IT.⟩
⟨HE MADE ME WATCH. HE--⟩
⟨YOU WILL TURN HIM IN FOR A REWARD?⟩
⟨YES.⟩
⟨HOW MUCH?⟩
⟨TWO-HUNDRED U.S. DOLLARS IN GOLD IF ALIVE. ONE-FIFTY DEAD.⟩
⟨I HAVE SOME MONEY--
MY DOWRY.
IF HE WERE TO GO IN DEAD-- I COULD MAKE UP THE DIFFERENCE.⟩

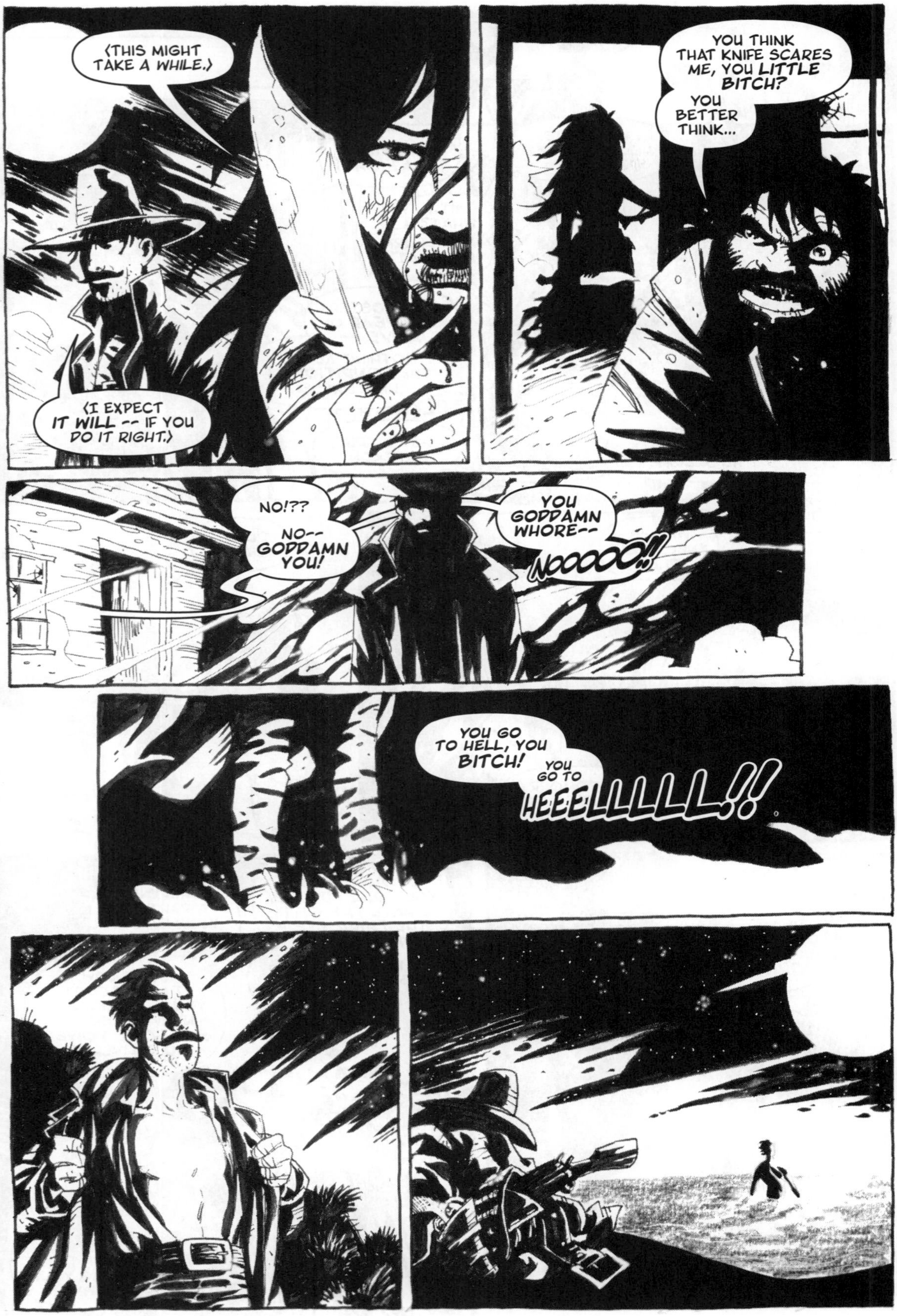
⟨THIS MIGHT TAKE A WHILE.⟩
⟨I EXPECT IT WILL -- IF YOU DO IT RIGHT.⟩
YOU THINK THAT KNIFE SCARES ME, YOU LITTLE BITCH?
YOU BETTER THINK...
NO!??
NO-- GODDAMN YOU!
YOU GODDAMN WHORE--
NOOOOO!!
YOU GO TO HELL, YOU BITCH!
YOU GO TO
HEEELLLLLL!!

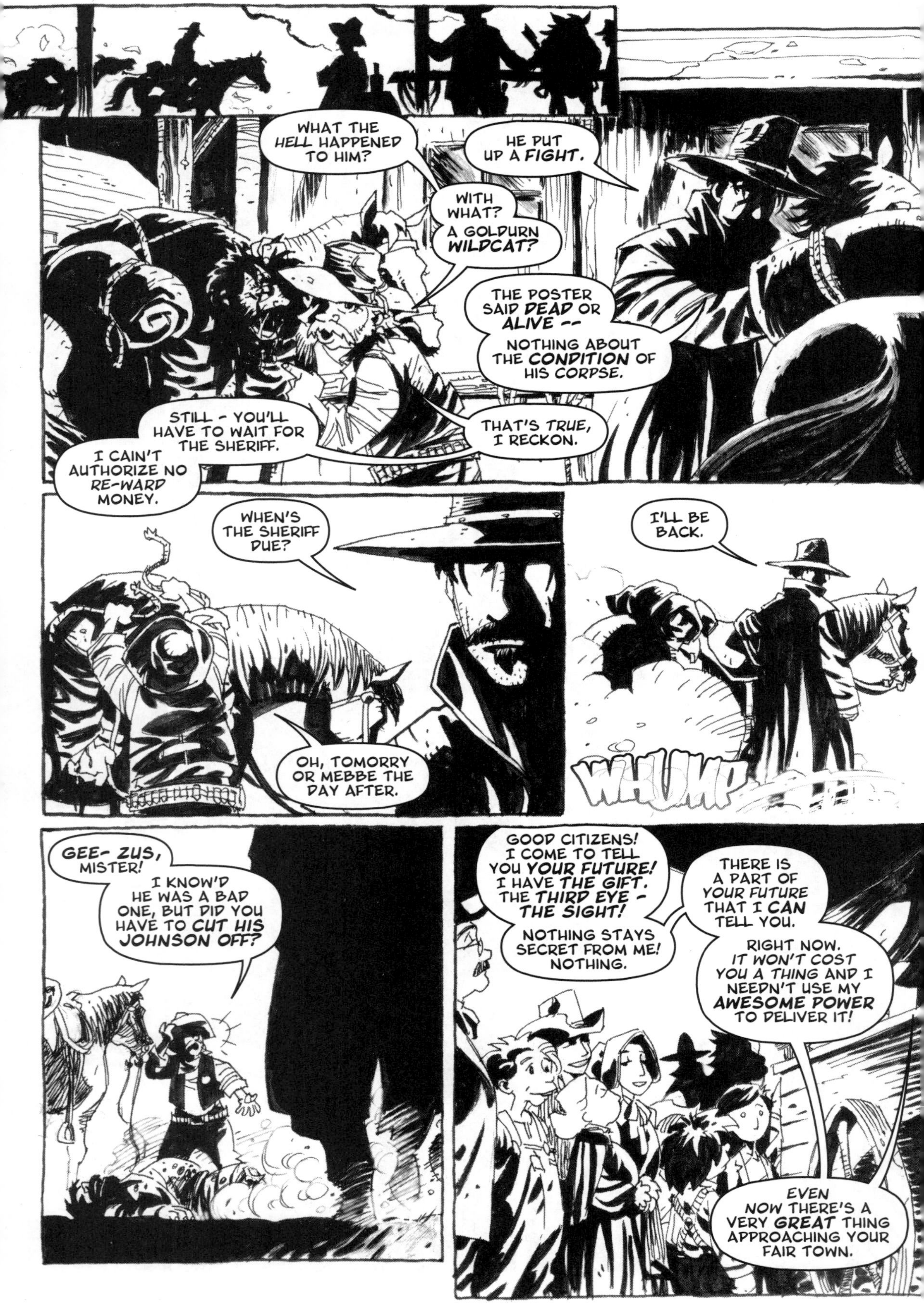
WHAT THE HELL HAPPENED TO HIM?
HE PUT UP A FIGHT.
WITH WHAT? A GOLDURN WILDCAT?
THE POSTER SAID DEAD OR ALIVE --
NOTHING ABOUT THE CONDITION OF HIS CORPSE.
THAT'S TRUE, I RECKON.
STILL - YOU'LL HAVE TO WAIT FOR THE SHERIFF.
I CAIN'T AUTHORIZE NO RE-WARD MONEY.
WHEN'S THE SHERIFF DUE?
OH, TOMORRY OR MEBBE THE DAY AFTER.
I'LL BE BACK.
WHUMP
GEE- ZUS, MISTER!
I KNOW'D HE WAS A BAD ONE, BUT DID YOU HAVE TO CUT HIS JOHNSON OFF?
GOOD CITIZENS! I COME TO TELL YOU YOUR FUTURE! I HAVE THE GIFT. THE THIRD EYE - THE SIGHT!
NOTHING STAYS SECRET FROM ME! NOTHING.
THERE IS A PART OF YOUR FUTURE THAT I CAN TELL YOU.
RIGHT NOW. IT WON'T COST YOU A THING AND I NEEDN'T USE MY AWESOME POWER TO DELIVER IT!
EVEN NOW THERE'S A VERY GREAT THING APPROACHING YOUR FAIR TOWN.

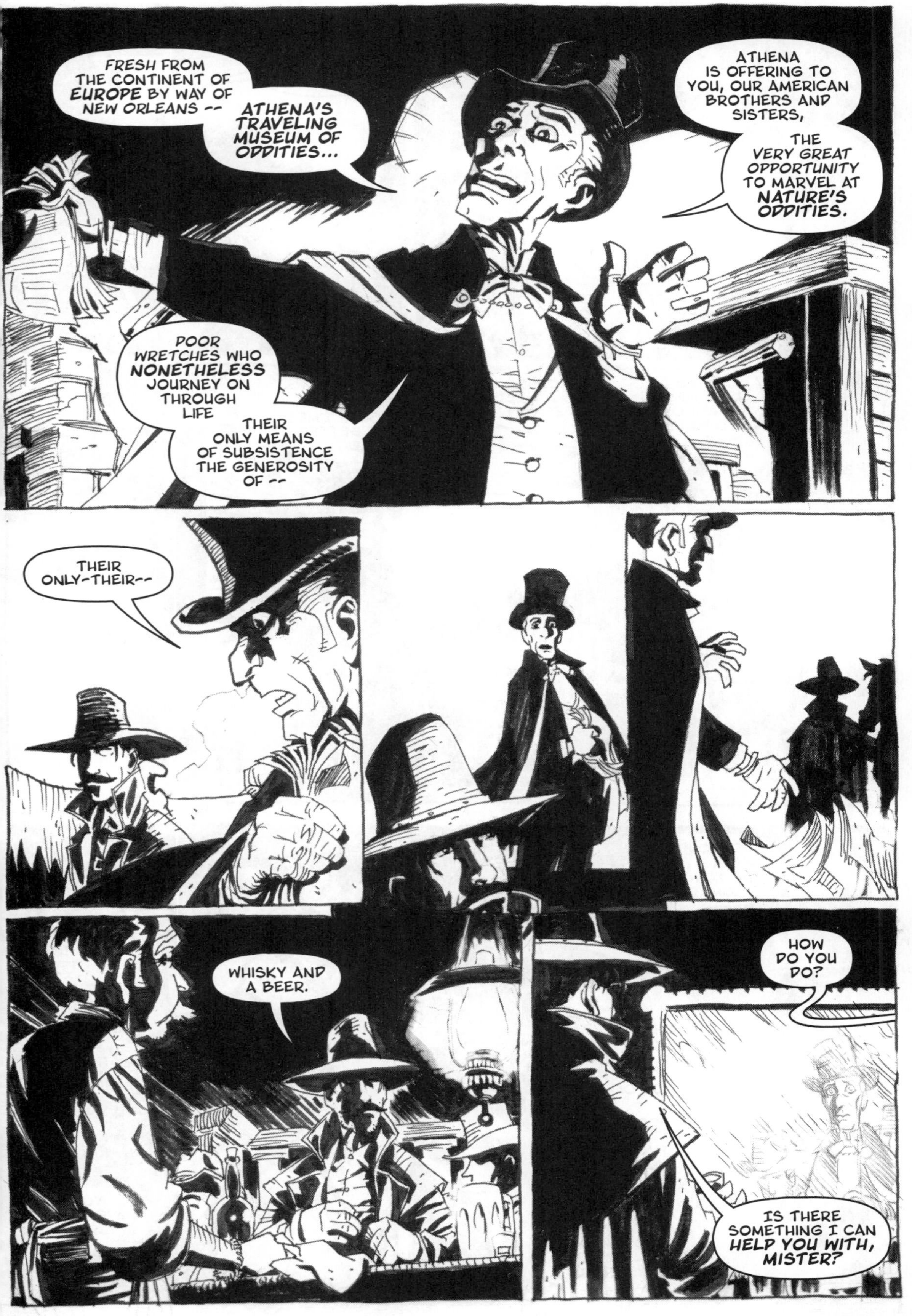
FRESH FROM THE CONTINENT OF EUROPE BY WAY OF NEW ORLEANS --
ATHENA'S TRAVELING MUSEUM OF ODDITIES...
ATHENA IS OFFERING TO YOU, OUR AMERICAN BROTHERS AND SISTERS,
THE VERY GREAT OPPORTUNITY TO MARVEL AT NATURE'S ODDITIES.
POOR WRETCHES WHO NONETHELESS JOURNEY ON THROUGH LIFE
THEIR ONLY MEANS OF SUBSISTENCE THE GENEROSITY OF --
THEIR ONLY-THEIR--
WHISKY AND A BEER.
HOW DO YOU DO?
IS THERE SOMETHING I CAN HELP YOU WITH, MISTER?

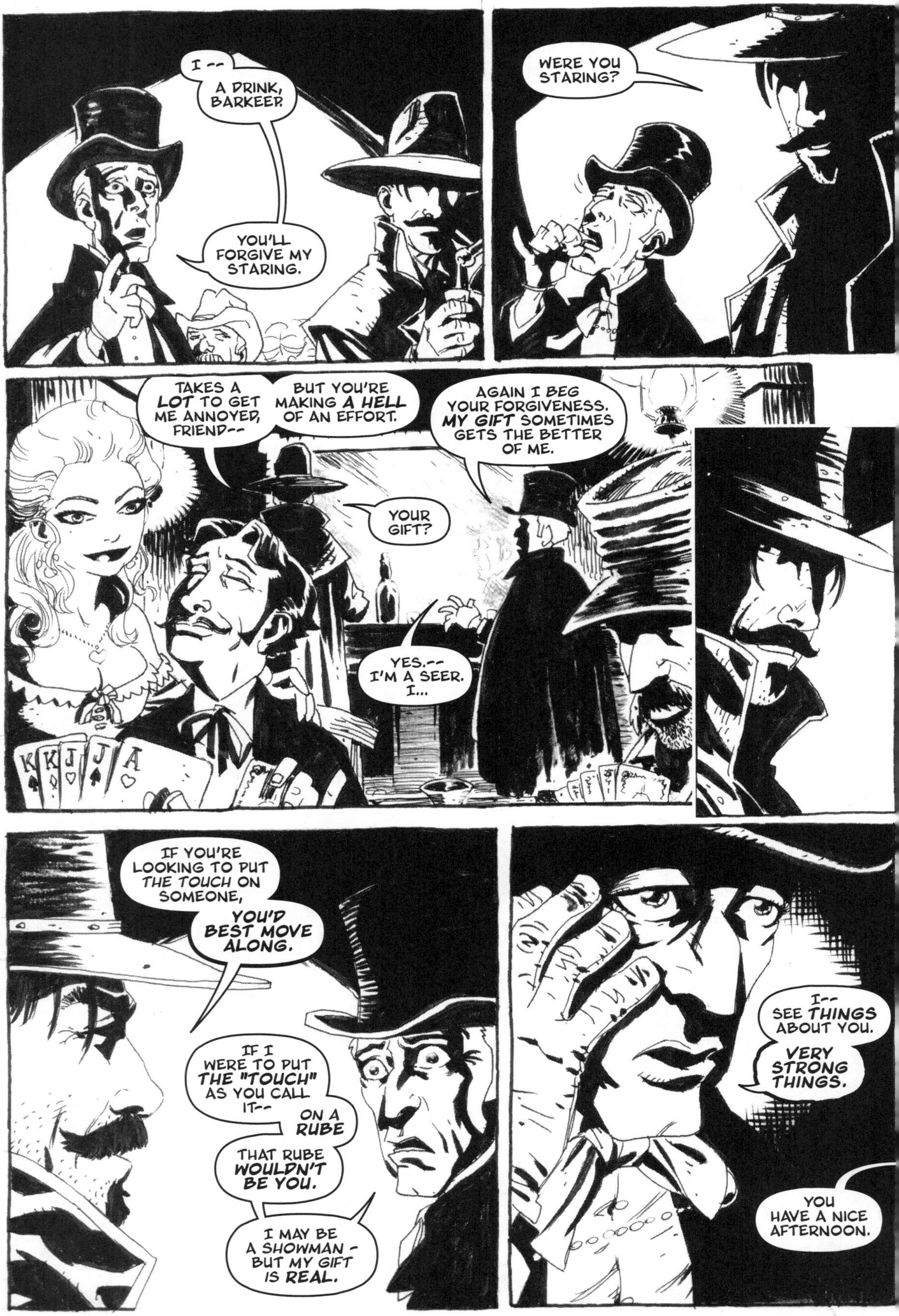
I --
A DRINK, BARKEEP.
YOU'LL FORGIVE MY STARING.
WERE YOU STARING?
TAKES A LOT TO GET ME ANNOYED, FRIEND--
BUT YOU'RE MAKING A HELL OF AN EFFORT.
AGAIN I BEG YOUR FORGIVENESS. MY GIFT SOMETIMES GETS THE BETTER OF ME.
YOUR GIFT?
YES.-- I'M A SEER. I...
IF YOU'RE LOOKING TO PUT THE TOUCH ON SOMEONE,
YOU'D BEST MOVE ALONG.
IF I WERE TO PUT THE "TOUCH" AS YOU CALL IT--
ON A RUBE
THAT RUBE WOULDN'T BE YOU.
I MAY BE A SHOWMAN - BUT MY GIFT IS REAL.
I-- SEE THINGS ABOUT YOU.
VERY STRONG THINGS.
YOU HAVE A NICE AFTERNOON.

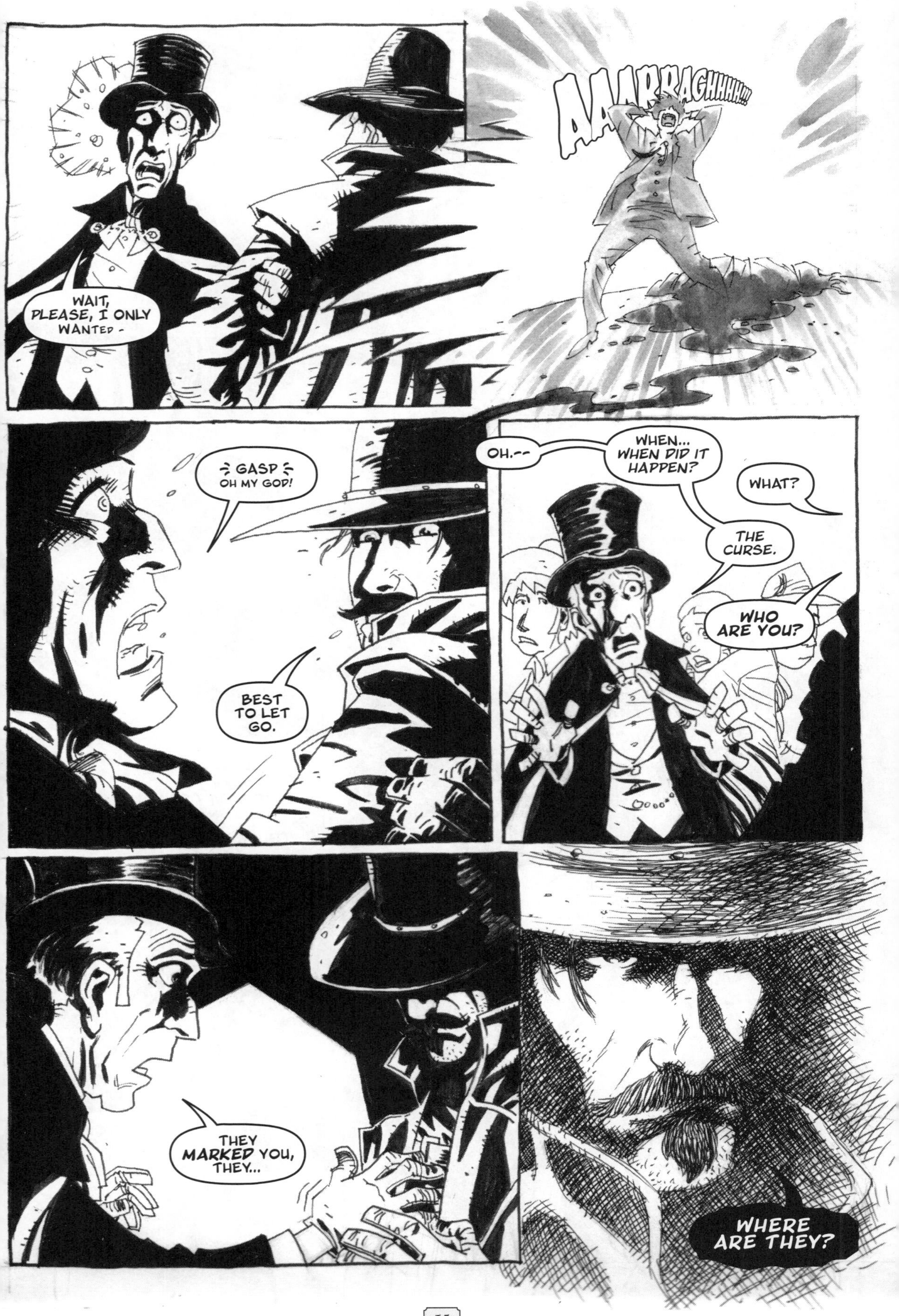
WAIT, PLEASE, I ONLY WANTED -
AAARRAGHHHH!!!
GASP OH MY GOD!
BEST TO LET GO.
OH.--
WHEN... WHEN DID IT HAPPEN?
WHAT?
THE CURSE.
WHO ARE YOU?
THEY MARKED YOU, THEY...
WHERE ARE THEY?

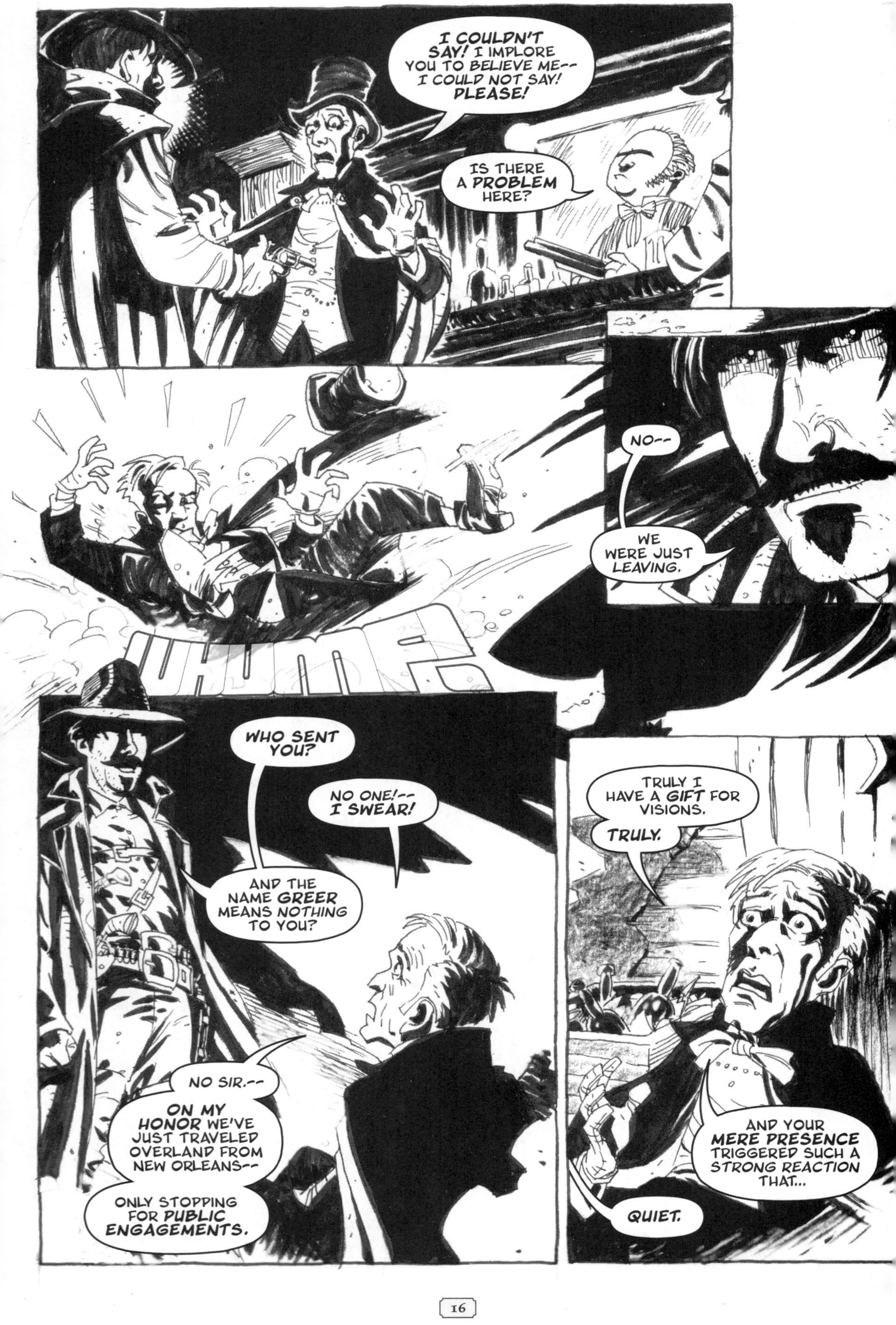
I COULDN'T SAY! I IMPLORE YOU TO BELIEVE ME-- I COULD NOT SAY! PLEASE!
IS THERE A PROBLEM HERE?
NO--
WE WERE JUST LEAVING.
WHUMP
WHO SENT YOU?
NO ONE!-- I SWEAR!
AND THE NAME GREER MEANS NOTHING TO YOU?
NO SIR.--
ON MY HONOR WE'VE JUST TRAVELED OVERLAND FROM NEW ORLEANS--
ONLY STOPPING FOR PUBLIC ENGAGEMENTS.
TRULY I HAVE A GIFT FOR VISIONS.
TRULY.
AND YOUR MERE PRESENCE TRIGGERED SUCH A STRONG REACTION THAT...
QUIET.

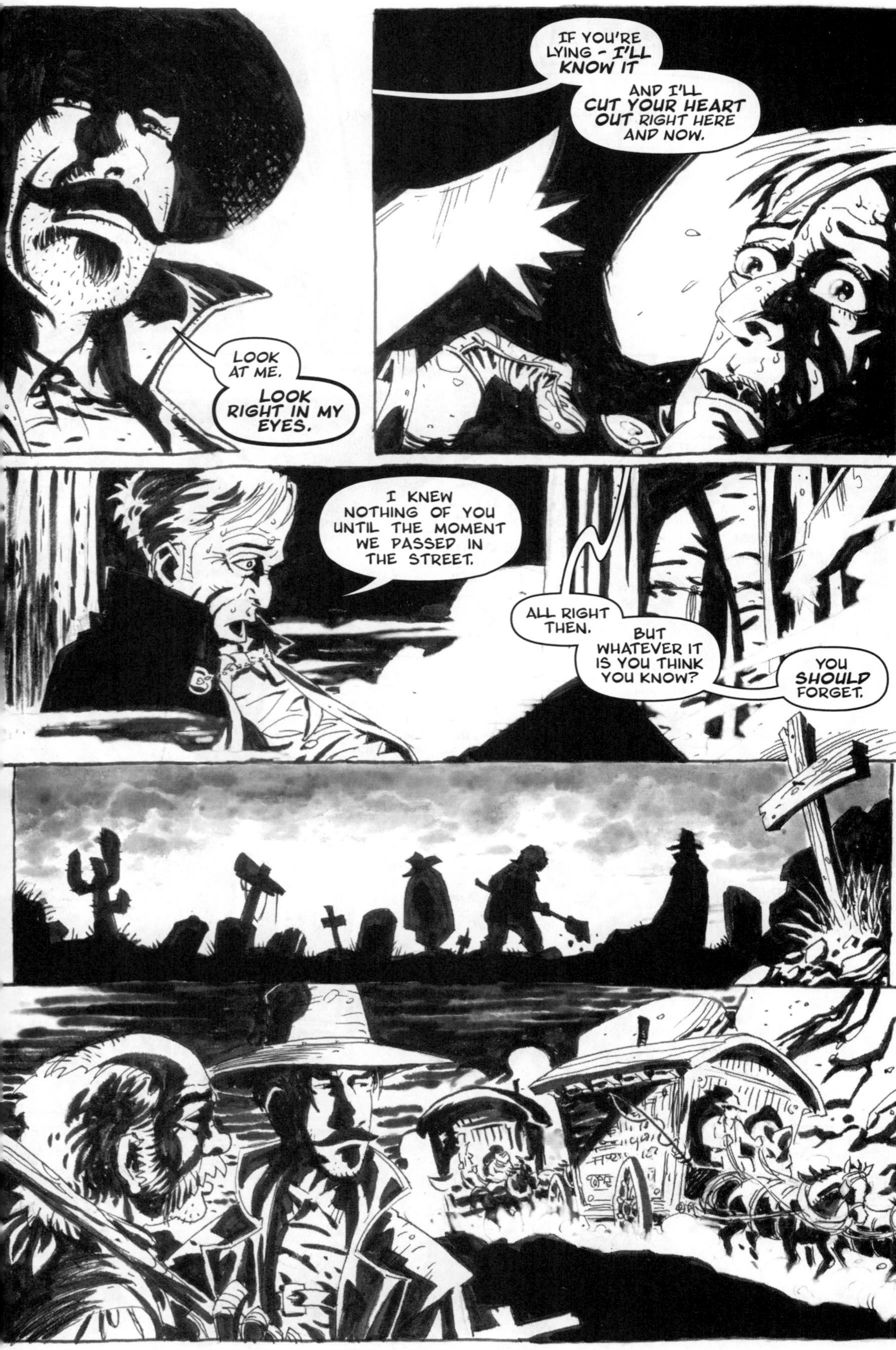

IF YOU'RE LYING - I'LL KNOW IT
AND I'LL CUT YOUR HEART OUT RIGHT HERE AND NOW.
LOOK AT ME.
LOOK RIGHT IN MY EYES.
I KNEW NOTHING OF YOU UNTIL THE MOMENT WE PASSED IN THE STREET.
ALL RIGHT THEN.
BUT WHATEVER IT IS YOU THINK YOU KNOW?
YOU SHOULD FORGET.

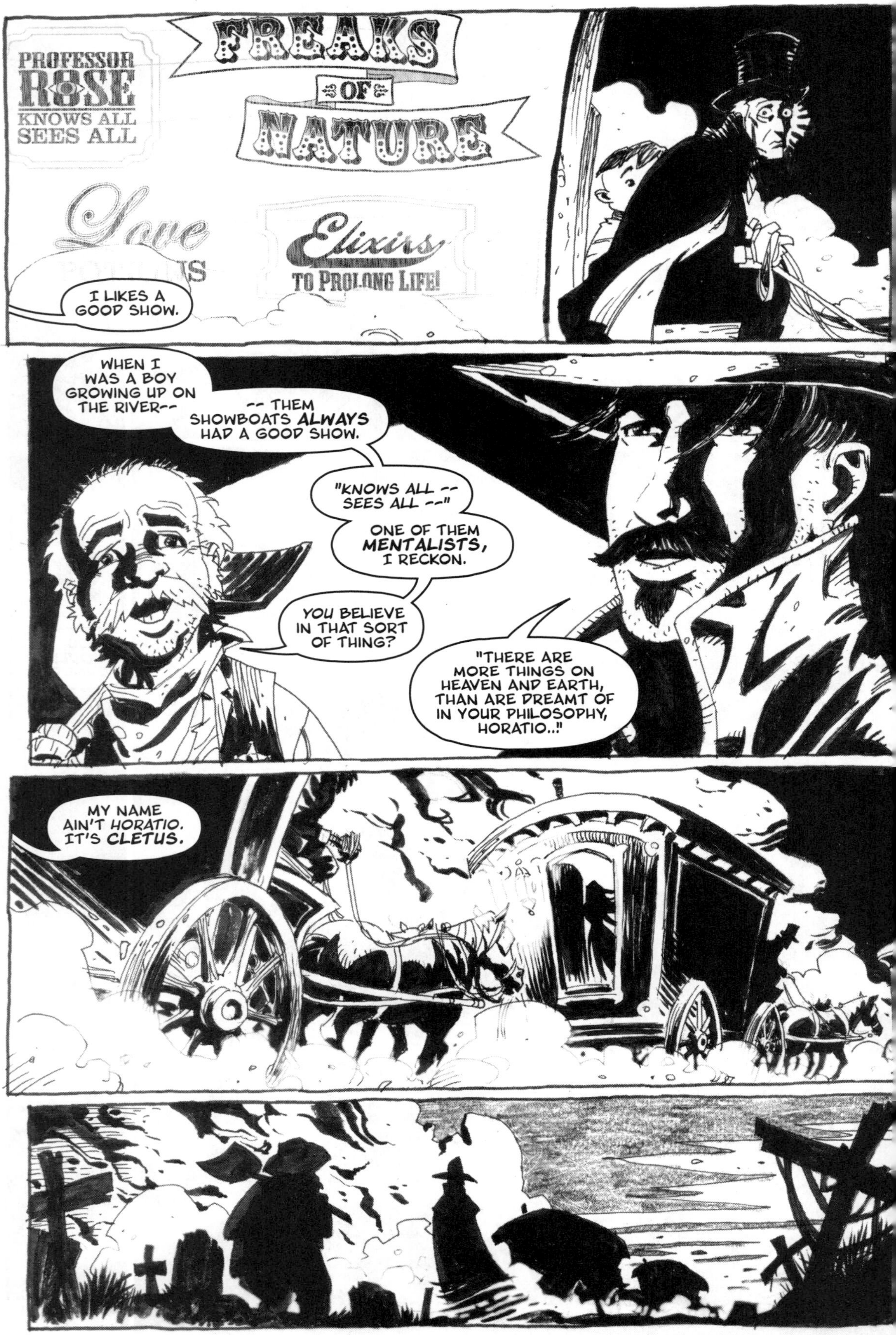

FREAKS OF NATURE
PROFESSOR ROSE KNOWS ALL SEES ALL
Love
Elixirs TO PROLONG LIFE!
I LIKES A GOOD SHOW.
WHEN I WAS A BOY GROWING UP ON THE RIVER--
-- THEM SHOWBOATS **ALWAYS** HAD A GOOD SHOW.
"KNOWS ALL -- SEES ALL --"
ONE OF THEM **MENTALISTS,** I RECKON.
YOU BELIEVE IN THAT SORT OF THING?
"THERE ARE MORE THINGS ON HEAVEN AND EARTH, THAN ARE DREAMT OF IN YOUR PHILOSOPHY, HORATIO..."
MY NAME AIN'T HORATIO. IT'S **CLETUS.**

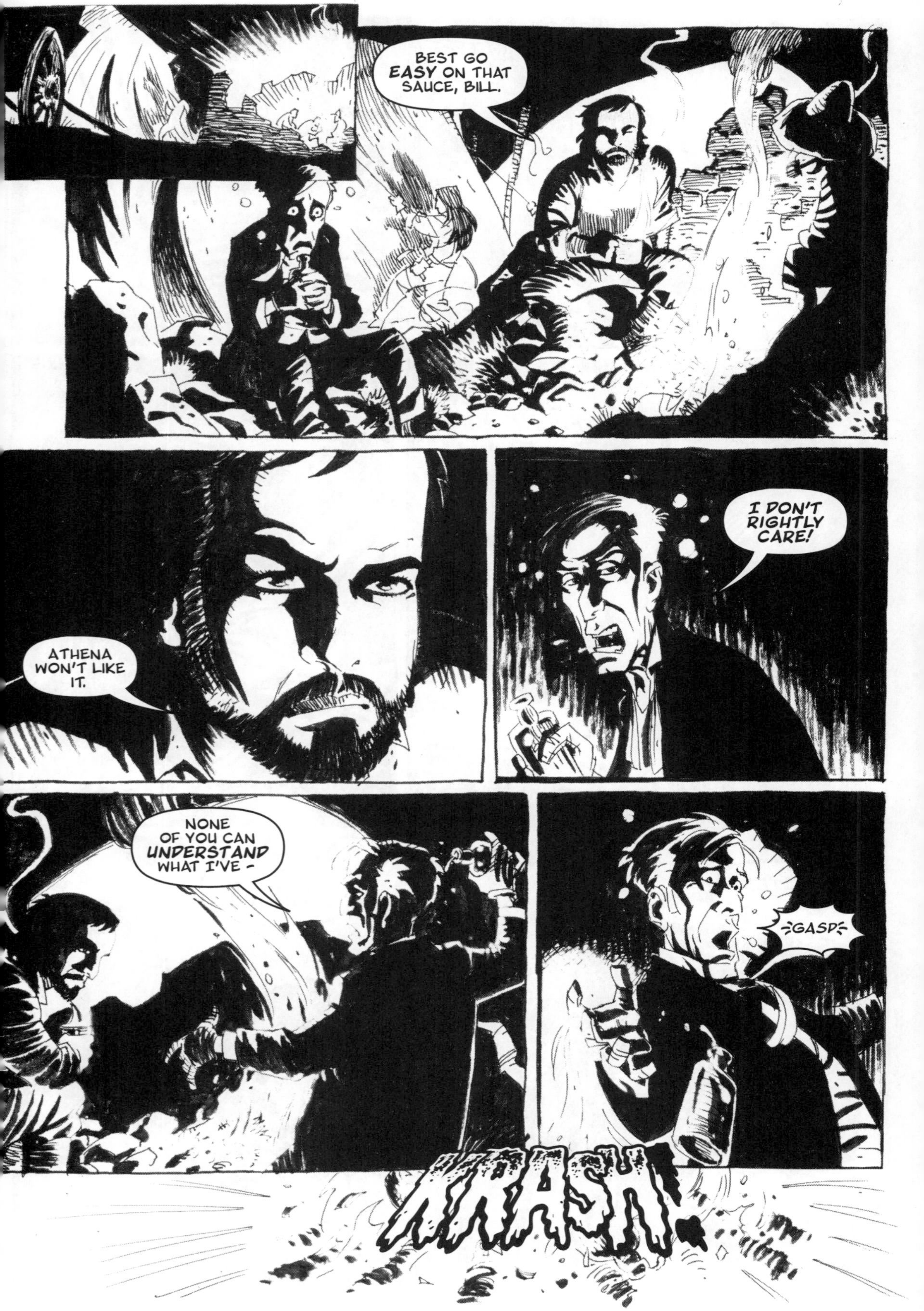
BEST GO EASY ON THAT SAUCE, BILL.
ATHENA WON'T LIKE IT.
I DON'T RIGHTLY CARE!
NONE OF YOU CAN UNDERSTAND WHAT I'VE -
GASP
KRASH!

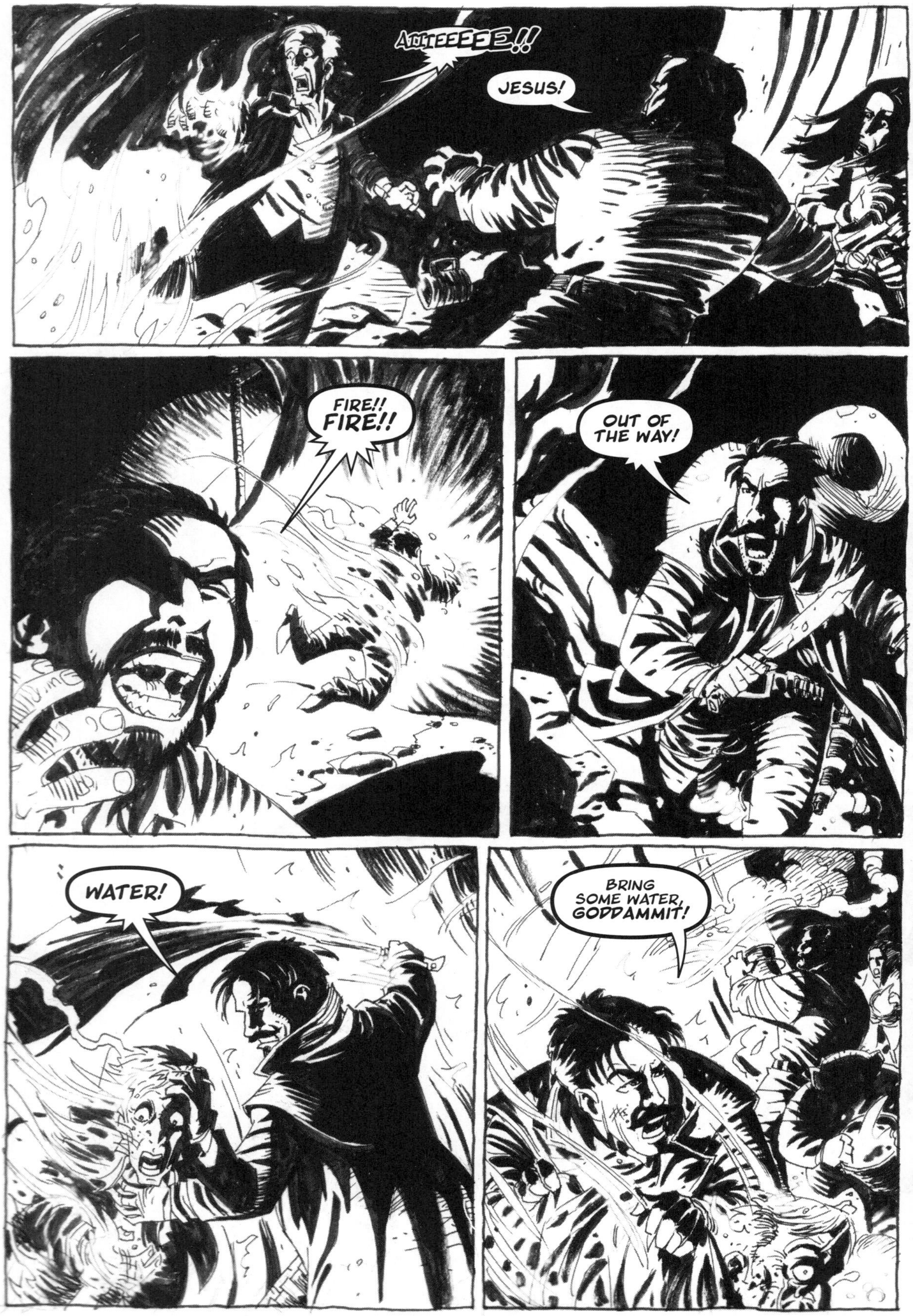
AIIIEEEEEE!!
JESUS!
FIRE!! FIRE!!
OUT OF THE WAY!
WATER!
BRING SOME WATER, GODDAMMIT!

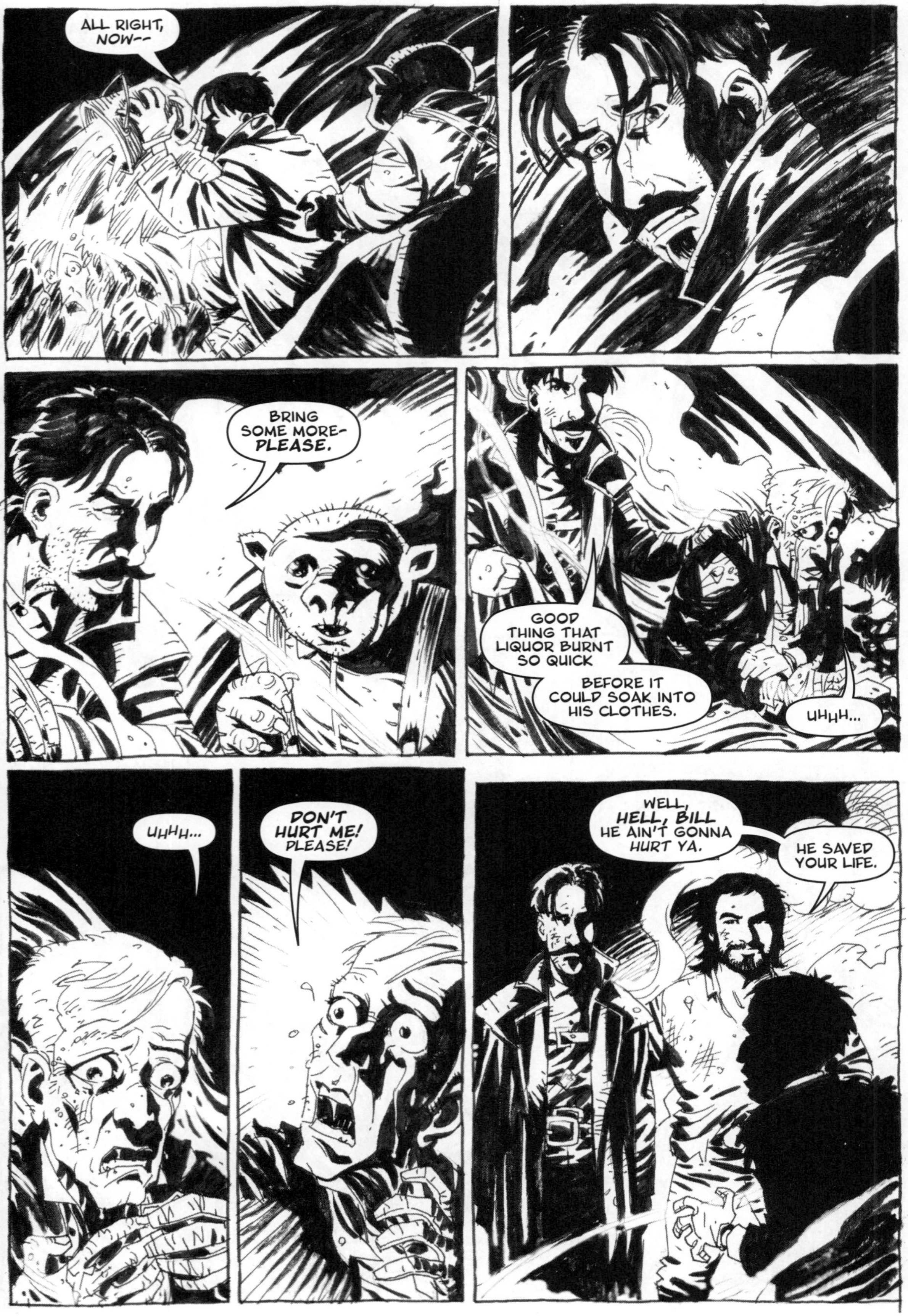
ALL RIGHT, NOW--
BRING SOME MORE- PLEASE.
GOOD THING THAT LIQUOR BURNT SO QUICK
BEFORE IT COULD SOAK INTO HIS CLOTHES.
UHHH...
UHHH...
DON'T HURT ME! PLEASE!
WELL, HELL, BILL HE AIN'T GONNA HURT YA.
HE SAVED YOUR LIFE.

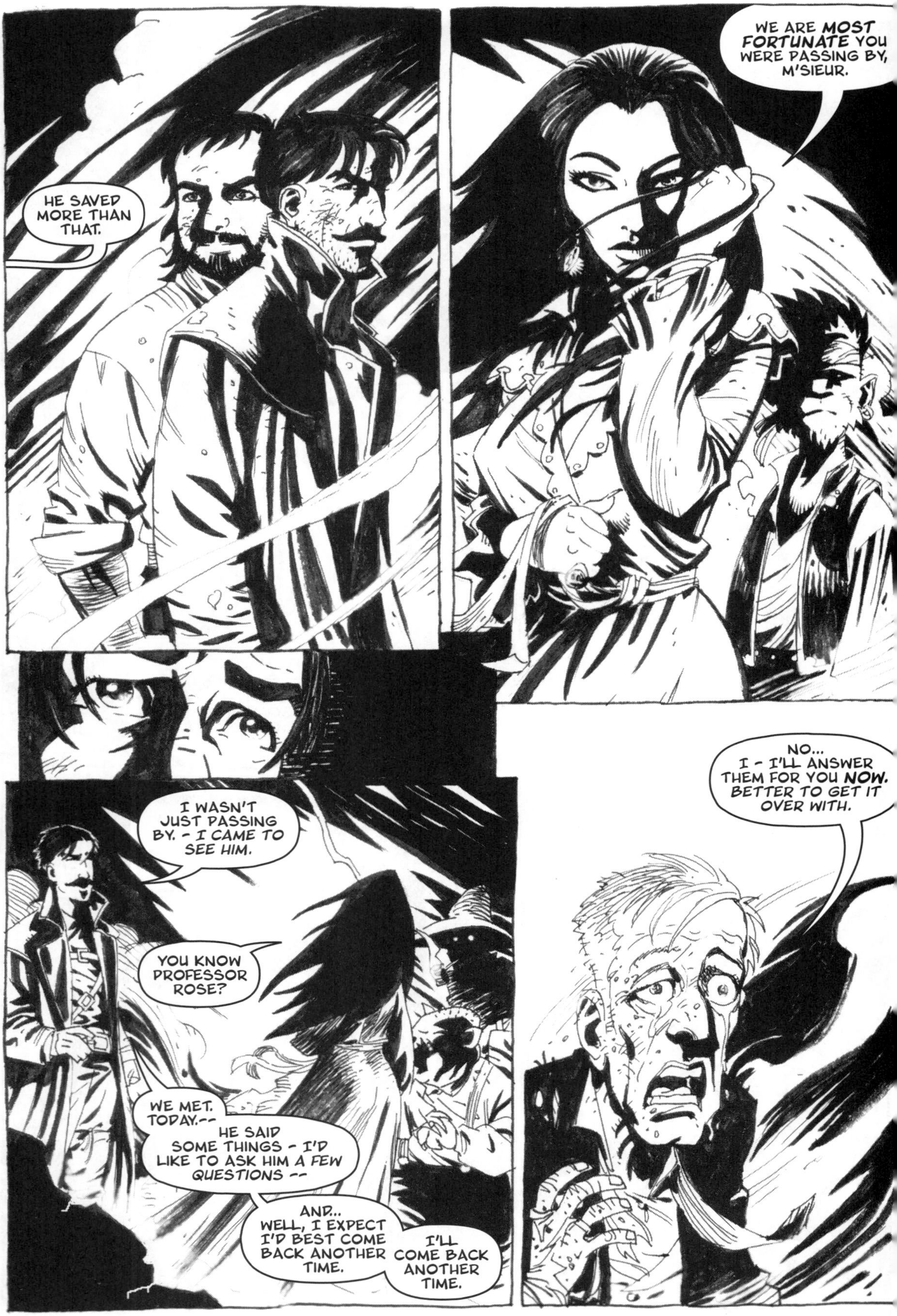
HE SAVED MORE THAN THAT.
WE ARE MOST FORTUNATE YOU WERE PASSING BY, M'SIEUR.
I WASN'T JUST PASSING BY. - I CAME TO SEE HIM.
YOU KNOW PROFESSOR ROSE?
WE MET. TODAY.--
HE SAID SOME THINGS - I'D LIKE TO ASK HIM A FEW QUESTIONS --
AND... WELL, I EXPECT I'D BEST COME BACK ANOTHER TIME.
I'LL COME BACK ANOTHER TIME.
NO... I - I'LL ANSWER THEM FOR YOU NOW. BETTER TO GET IT OVER WITH.

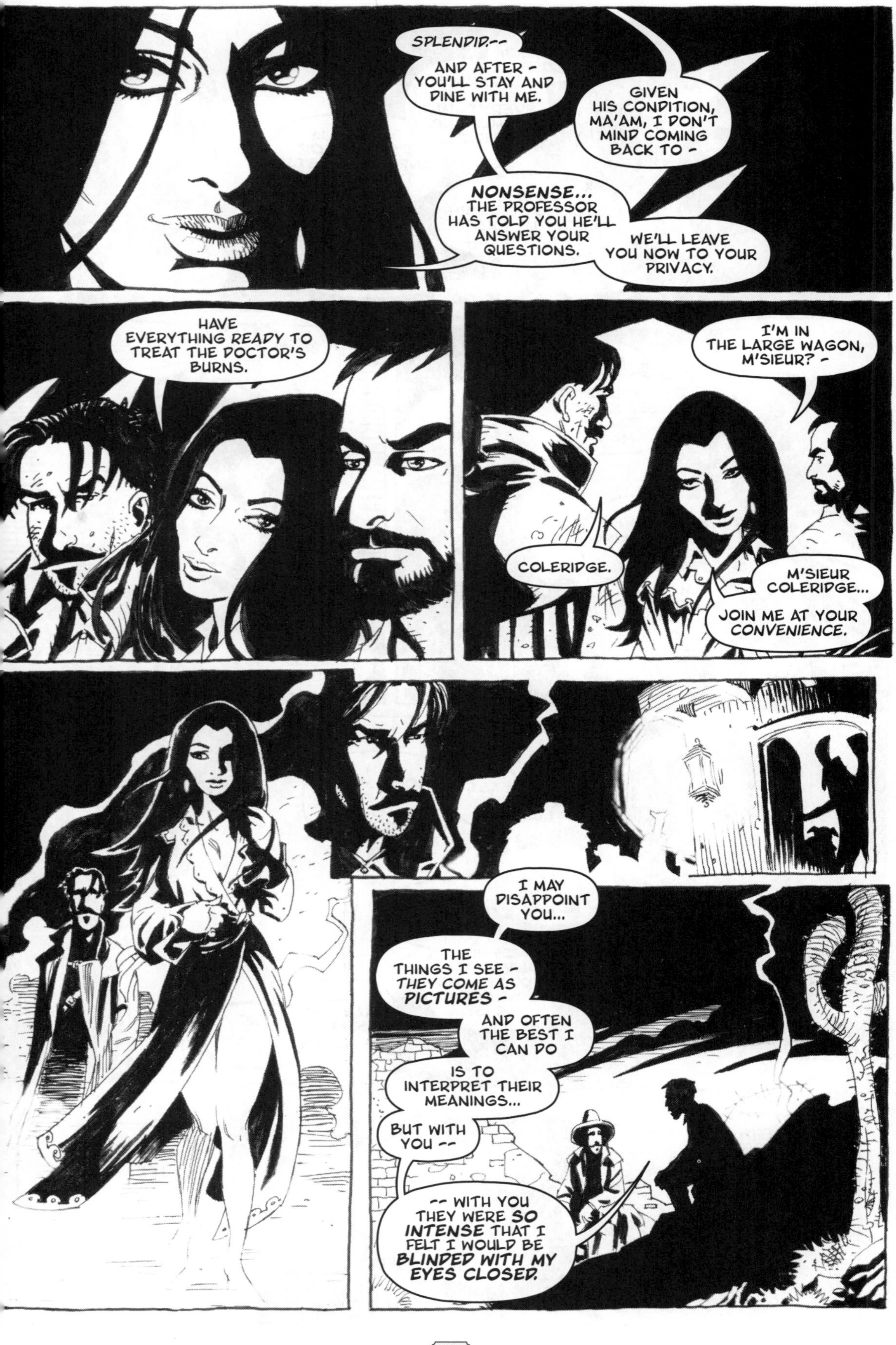
SPLENDID--
AND AFTER - YOU'LL STAY AND DINE WITH ME.
GIVEN HIS CONDITION, MA'AM, I DON'T MIND COMING BACK TO -
NONSENSE... THE PROFESSOR HAS TOLD YOU HE'LL ANSWER YOUR QUESTIONS.
WE'LL LEAVE YOU NOW TO YOUR PRIVACY.
HAVE EVERYTHING READY TO TREAT THE DOCTOR'S BURNS.
I'M IN THE LARGE WAGON, M'SIEUR? -
COLERIDGE.
M'SIEUR COLERIDGE...
JOIN ME AT YOUR CONVENIENCE.
I MAY DISAPPOINT YOU...
THE THINGS I SEE - THEY COME AS PICTURES -
AND OFTEN THE BEST I CAN DO
IS TO INTERPRET THEIR MEANINGS...
BUT WITH YOU --
-- WITH YOU THEY WERE SO INTENSE THAT I FELT I WOULD BE BLINDED WITH MY EYES CLOSED.

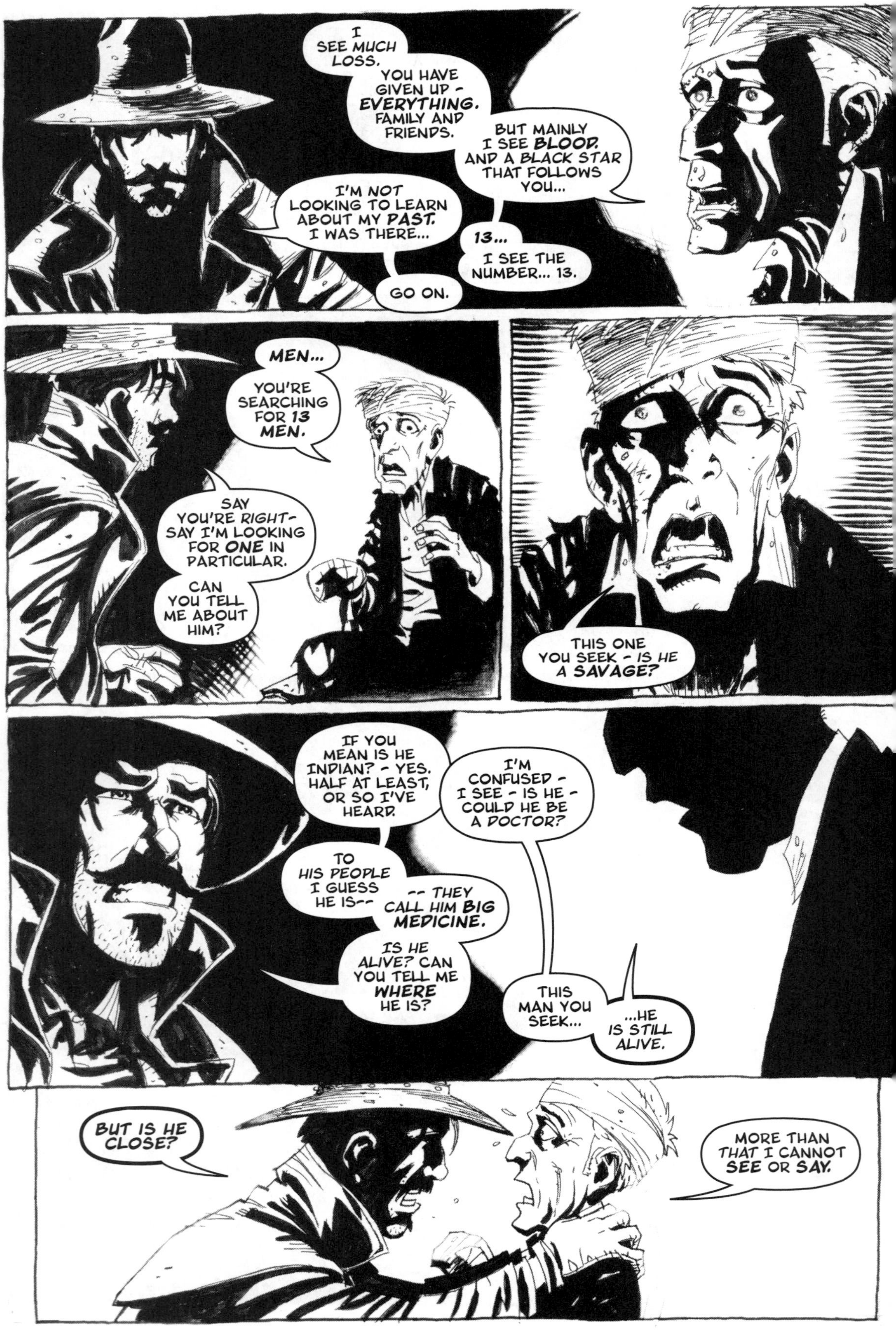
I SEE MUCH LOSS.
YOU HAVE GIVEN UP - EVERYTHING. FAMILY AND FRIENDS.
BUT MAINLY I SEE BLOOD. AND A BLACK STAR THAT FOLLOWS YOU...
I'M NOT LOOKING TO LEARN ABOUT MY PAST. I WAS THERE...
13...
I SEE THE NUMBER... 13.
GO ON.
MEN...
YOU'RE SEARCHING FOR 13 MEN.
SAY YOU'RE RIGHT- SAY I'M LOOKING FOR ONE IN PARTICULAR.
CAN YOU TELL ME ABOUT HIM?
THIS ONE YOU SEEK - IS HE A SAVAGE?
IF YOU MEAN IS HE INDIAN? - YES. HALF AT LEAST, OR SO I'VE HEARD.
I'M CONFUSED - I SEE - IS HE - COULD HE BE A DOCTOR?
TO HIS PEOPLE I GUESS HE IS--
-- THEY CALL HIM BIG MEDICINE.
IS HE ALIVE? CAN YOU TELL ME WHERE HE IS?
THIS MAN YOU SEEK...
...HE IS STILL ALIVE.
BUT IS HE CLOSE?
MORE THAN THAT I CANNOT SEE OR SAY.

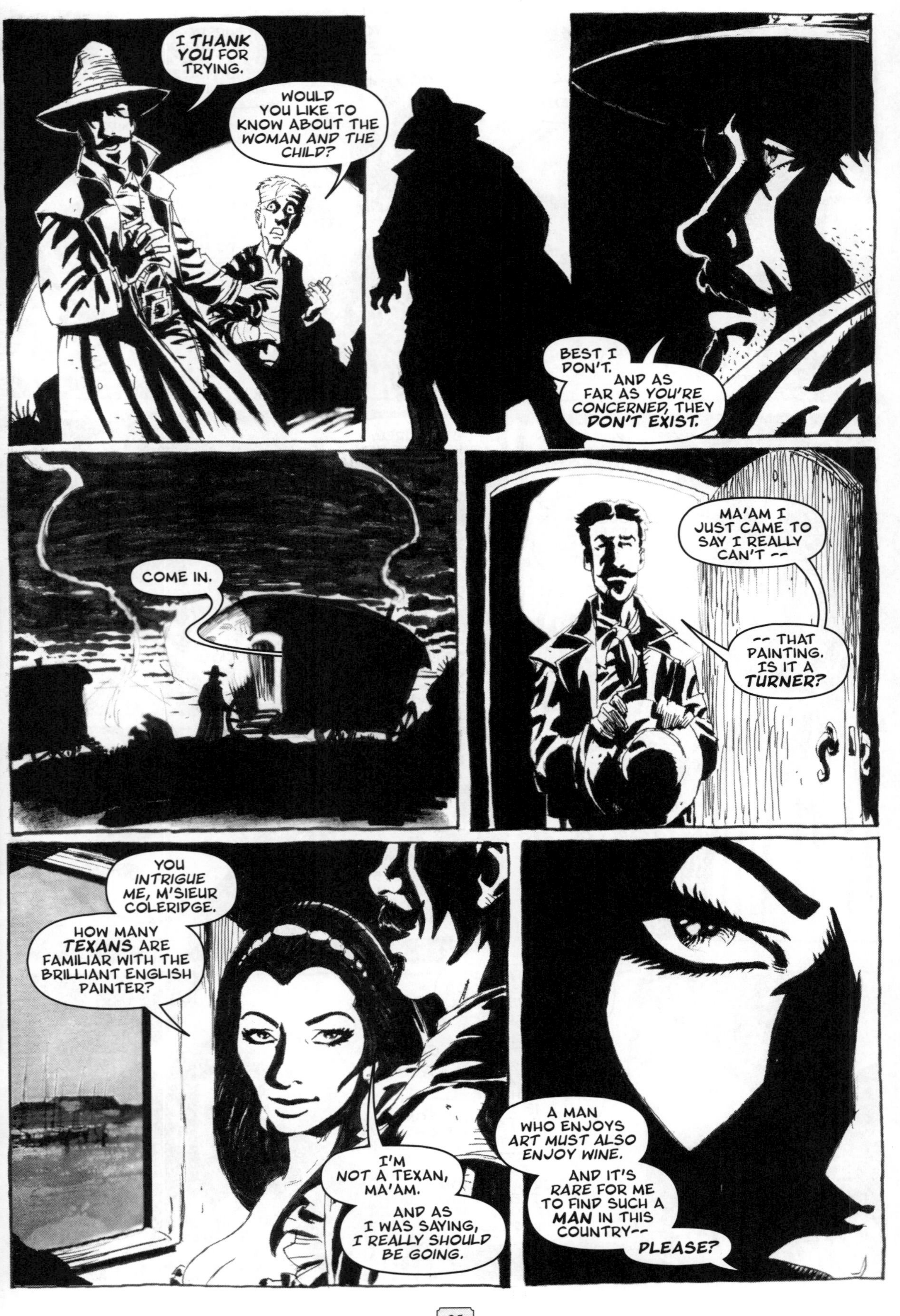

I THANK YOU FOR TRYING.
WOULD YOU LIKE TO KNOW ABOUT THE WOMAN AND THE CHILD?
BEST I DON'T.
AND AS FAR AS YOU'RE CONCERNED, THEY DON'T EXIST.
COME IN.
MA'AM I JUST CAME TO SAY I REALLY CAN'T --
-- THAT PAINTING. IS IT A TURNER?
YOU INTRIGUE ME, M'SIEUR COLERIDGE.
HOW MANY TEXANS ARE FAMILIAR WITH THE BRILLIANT ENGLISH PAINTER?
I'M NOT A TEXAN, MA'AM.
AND AS I WAS SAYING, I REALLY SHOULD BE GOING.
A MAN WHO ENJOYS ART MUST ALSO ENJOY WINE.
AND IT'S RARE FOR ME TO FIND SUCH A MAN IN THIS COUNTRY--
PLEASE?

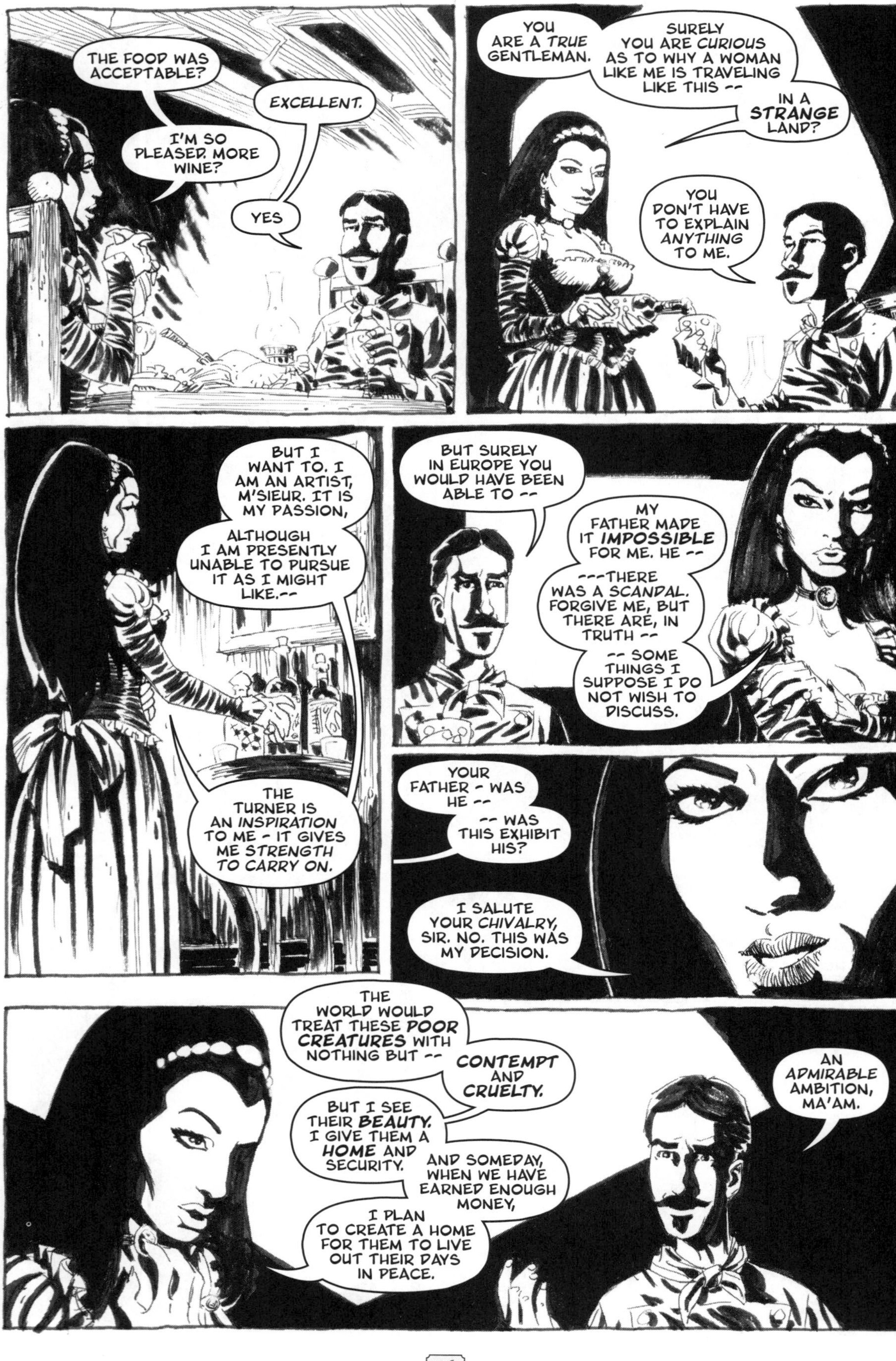
THE FOOD WAS ACCEPTABLE?
EXCELLENT.
I'M SO PLEASED. MORE WINE?
YES
YOU ARE A *TRUE* GENTLEMAN.
SURELY YOU ARE *CURIOUS* AS TO WHY A WOMAN LIKE ME IS TRAVELING LIKE THIS --
IN A **STRANGE** LAND?
YOU DON'T HAVE TO EXPLAIN ANYTHING TO ME.
BUT I WANT TO. I AM AN ARTIST, M'SIEUR. IT IS MY PASSION,
ALTHOUGH I AM PRESENTLY UNABLE TO PURSUE IT AS I MIGHT LIKE.--
THE TURNER IS AN *INSPIRATION* TO ME - IT GIVES ME *STRENGTH* TO CARRY ON.
BUT SURELY IN EUROPE YOU WOULD HAVE BEEN ABLE TO --
MY FATHER MADE IT **IMPOSSIBLE** FOR ME. HE --
---THERE WAS A SCANDAL. FORGIVE ME, BUT THERE ARE, IN TRUTH --
-- SOME THINGS I SUPPOSE I DO NOT WISH TO DISCUSS.
YOUR FATHER - WAS HE --
-- WAS THIS EXHIBIT HIS?
I SALUTE YOUR *CHIVALRY*, SIR. NO. THIS WAS MY DECISION.
THE WORLD WOULD TREAT THESE **POOR CREATURES** WITH NOTHING BUT --
CONTEMPT AND ***CRUELTY.***
BUT I SEE THEIR **BEAUTY.** I GIVE THEM A **HOME** AND SECURITY.
AND SOMEDAY, WHEN WE HAVE EARNED ENOUGH MONEY,
I PLAN TO CREATE A HOME FOR THEM TO LIVE OUT THEIR DAYS IN PEACE.
AN *ADMIRABLE* AMBITION, MA'AM.

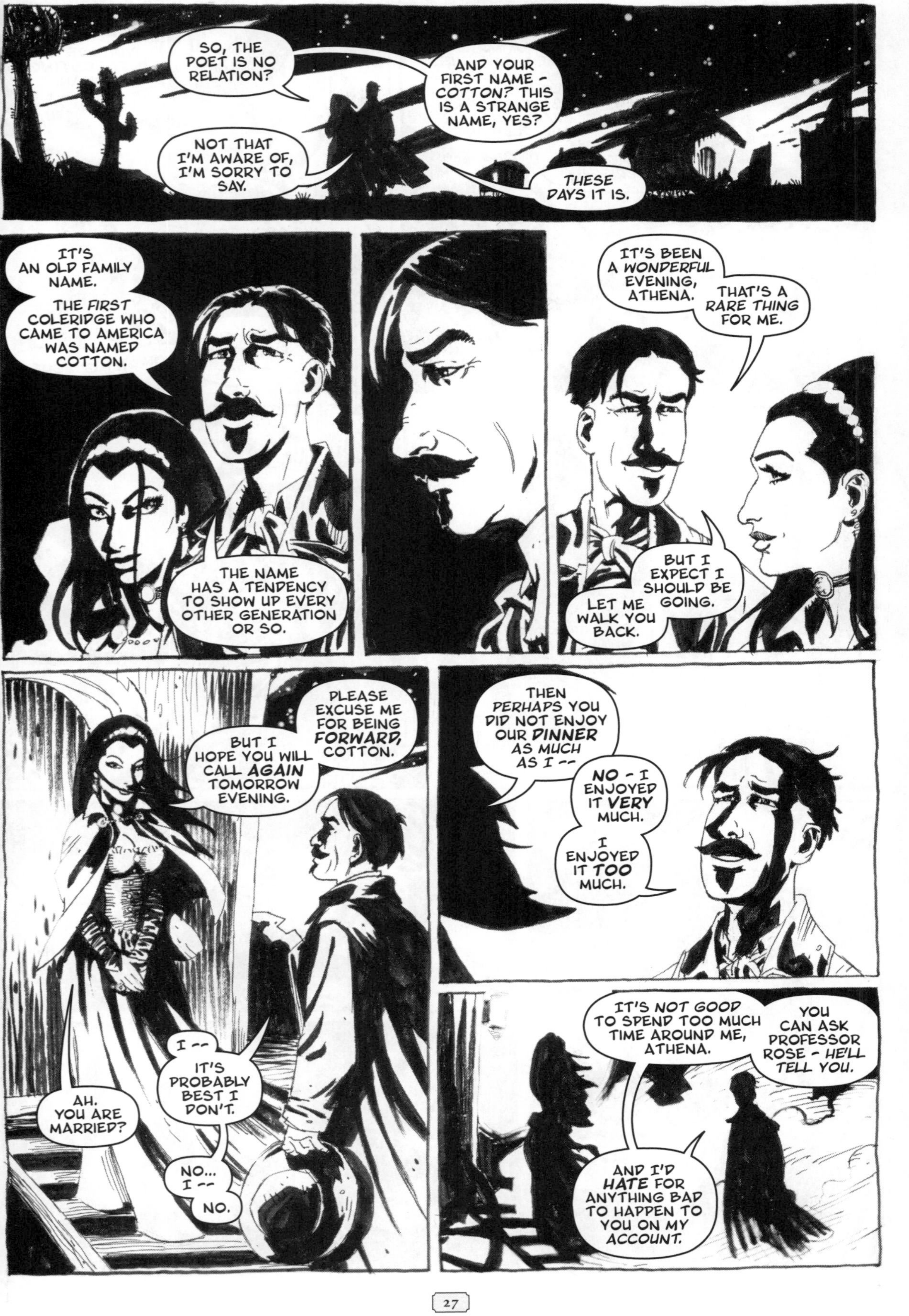
SO, THE POET IS NO RELATION?
NOT THAT I'M AWARE OF, I'M SORRY TO SAY.
AND YOUR FIRST NAME - COTTON? THIS IS A STRANGE NAME, YES?
THESE DAYS IT IS.
IT'S AN OLD FAMILY NAME.
THE FIRST COLERIDGE WHO CAME TO AMERICA WAS NAMED COTTON.
THE NAME HAS A TENDENCY TO SHOW UP EVERY OTHER GENERATION OR SO.
IT'S BEEN A WONDERFUL EVENING, ATHENA.
THAT'S A RARE THING FOR ME.
BUT I EXPECT I SHOULD BE GOING.
LET ME WALK YOU BACK.
PLEASE EXCUSE ME FOR BEING FORWARD, COTTON.
BUT I HOPE YOU WILL CALL AGAIN TOMORROW EVENING.
I --
IT'S PROBABLY BEST I DON'T.
AH. YOU ARE MARRIED?
NO... I --
NO.
THEN PERHAPS YOU DID NOT ENJOY OUR DINNER AS MUCH AS I --
NO - I ENJOYED IT VERY MUCH.
I ENJOYED IT TOO MUCH.
IT'S NOT GOOD TO SPEND TOO MUCH TIME AROUND ME, ATHENA.
YOU CAN ASK PROFESSOR ROSE - HE'LL TELL YOU.
AND I'D HATE FOR ANYTHING BAD TO HAPPEN TO YOU ON MY ACCOUNT.

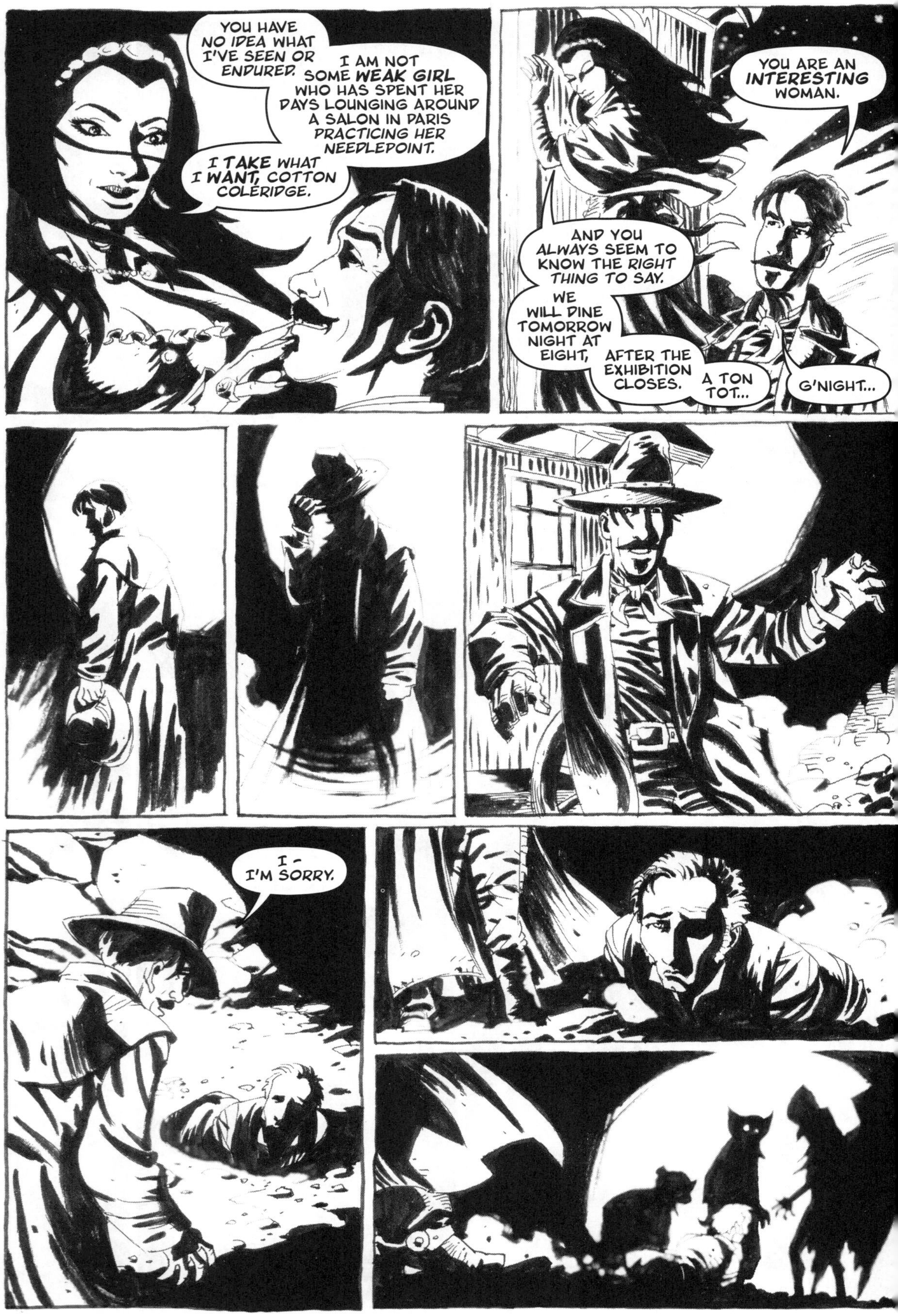
YOU HAVE NO IDEA WHAT I'VE SEEN OR ENDURED.
I AM NOT SOME WEAK GIRL WHO HAS SPENT HER DAYS LOUNGING AROUND A SALON IN PARIS PRACTICING HER NEEDLEPOINT.
I TAKE WHAT I WANT, COTTON COLERIDGE.
YOU ARE AN INTERESTING WOMAN.
AND YOU ALWAYS SEEM TO KNOW THE RIGHT THING TO SAY.
WE WILL DINE TOMORROW NIGHT AT EIGHT,
AFTER THE EXHIBITION CLOSES.
A TON TOT...
G'NIGHT...
I - I'M SORRY.

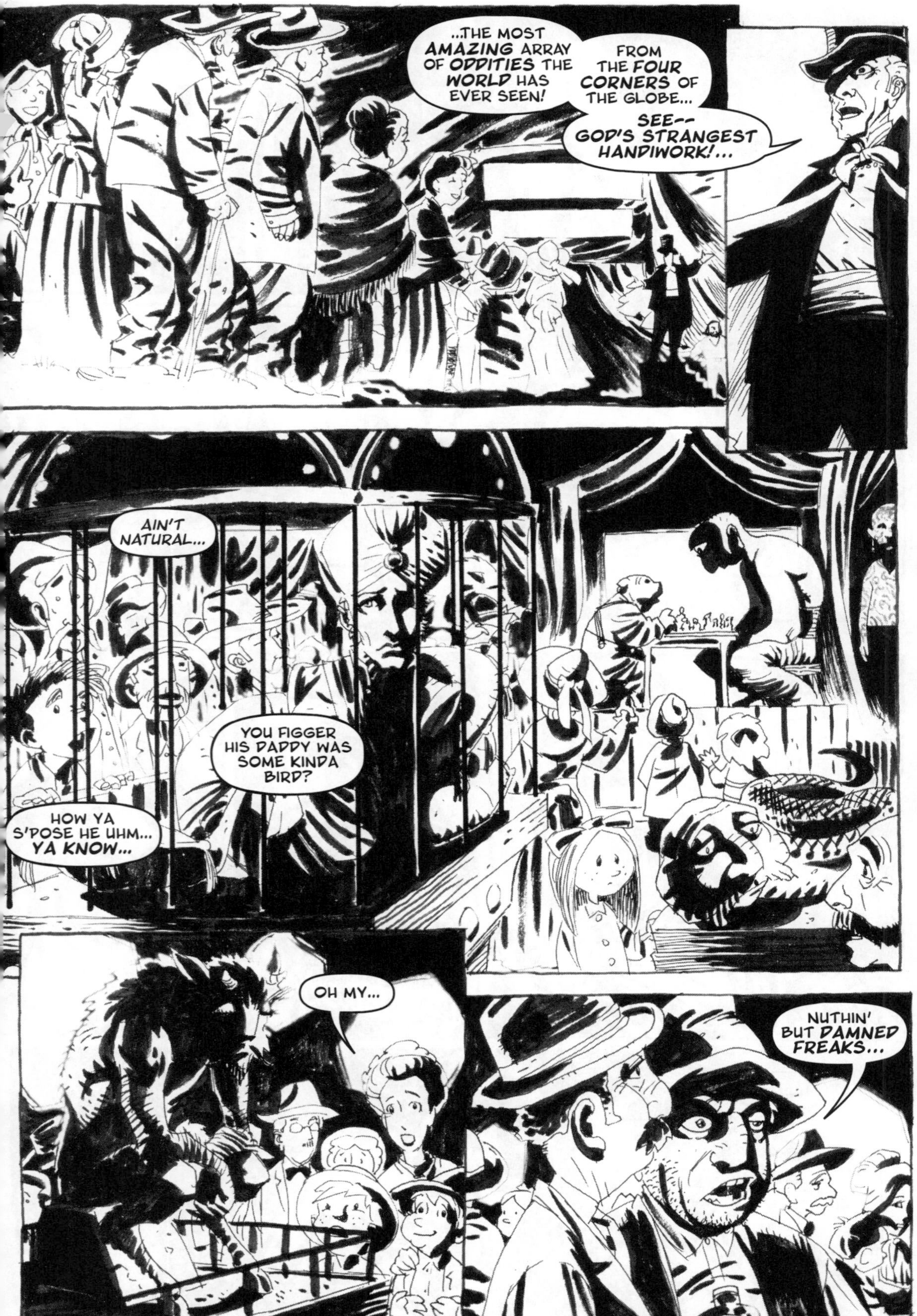

...THE MOST AMAZING ARRAY OF ODDITIES THE WORLD HAS EVER SEEN!
FROM THE FOUR CORNERS OF THE GLOBE...
SEE-- GOD'S STRANGEST HANDIWORK!...
AIN'T NATURAL...
YOU FIGGER HIS DADDY WAS SOME KINDA BIRD?
HOW YA S'POSE HE UHM... YA KNOW...
OH MY...
NUTHIN' BUT DAMNED FREAKS...

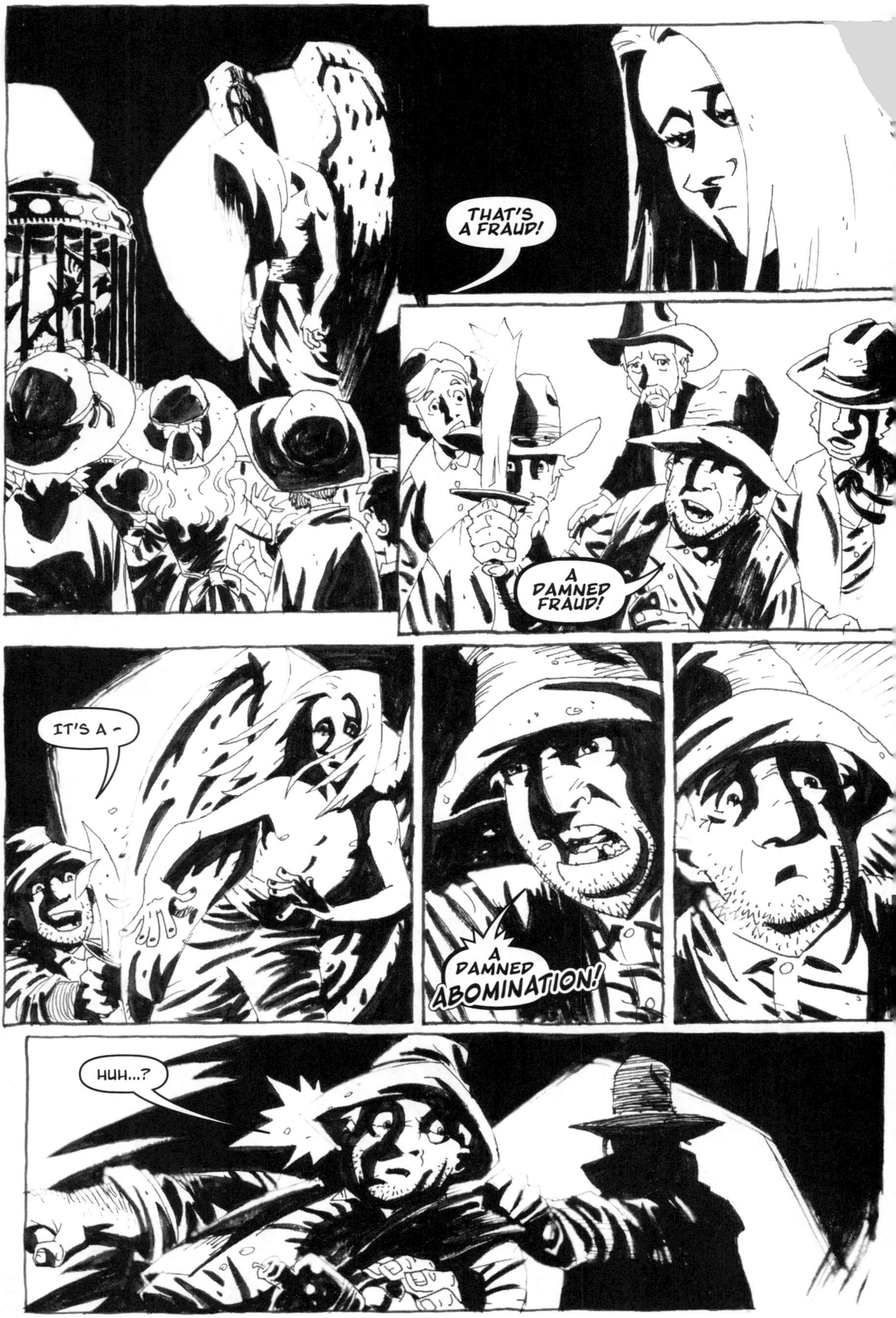
THAT'S A FRAUD!
A DAMNED FRAUD!
IT'S A -
A DAMNED ABOMINATION!
HUH...?

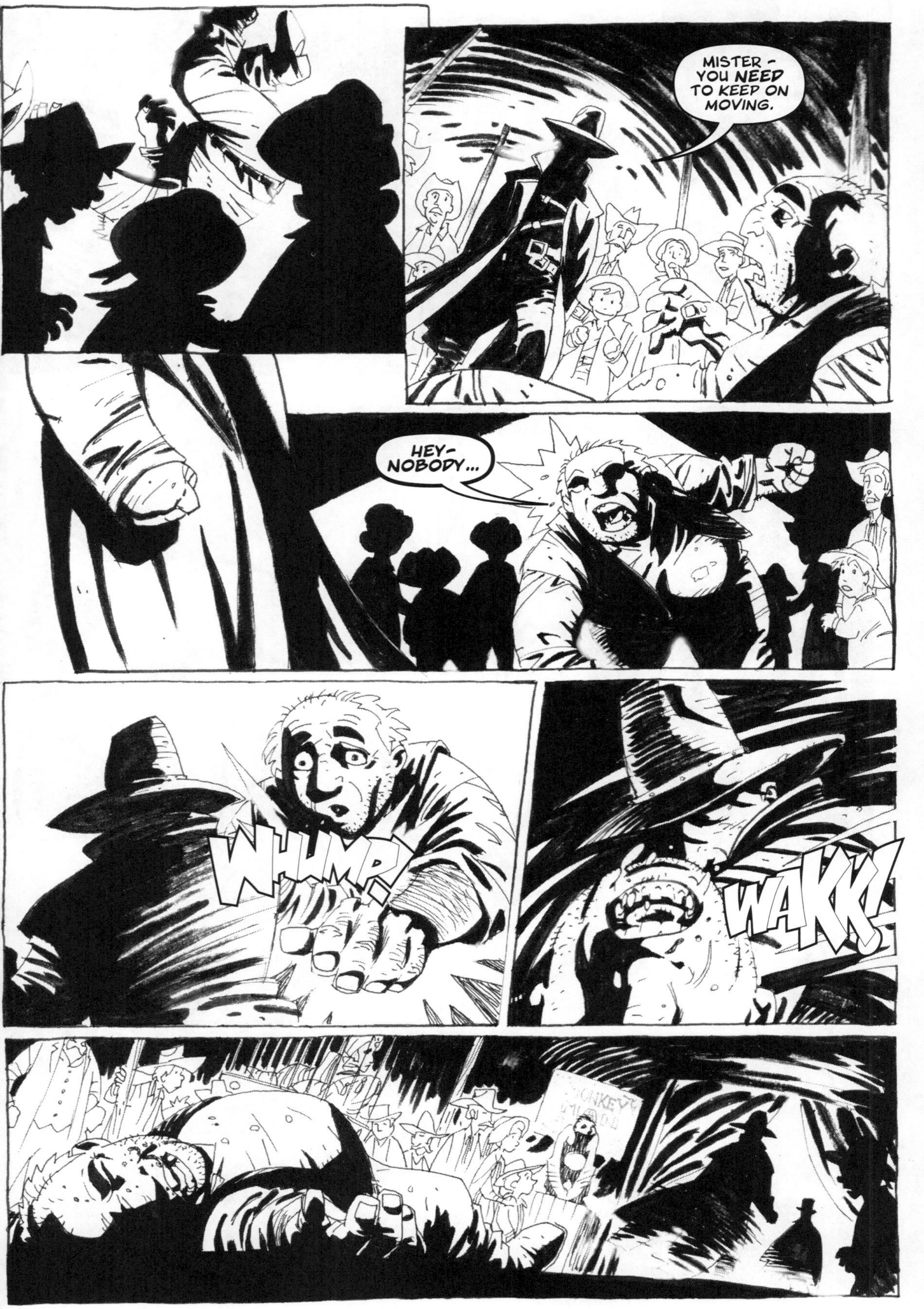
MISTER - YOU NEED TO KEEP ON MOVING.
HEY- NOBODY...
WHUMP!
WAKK!

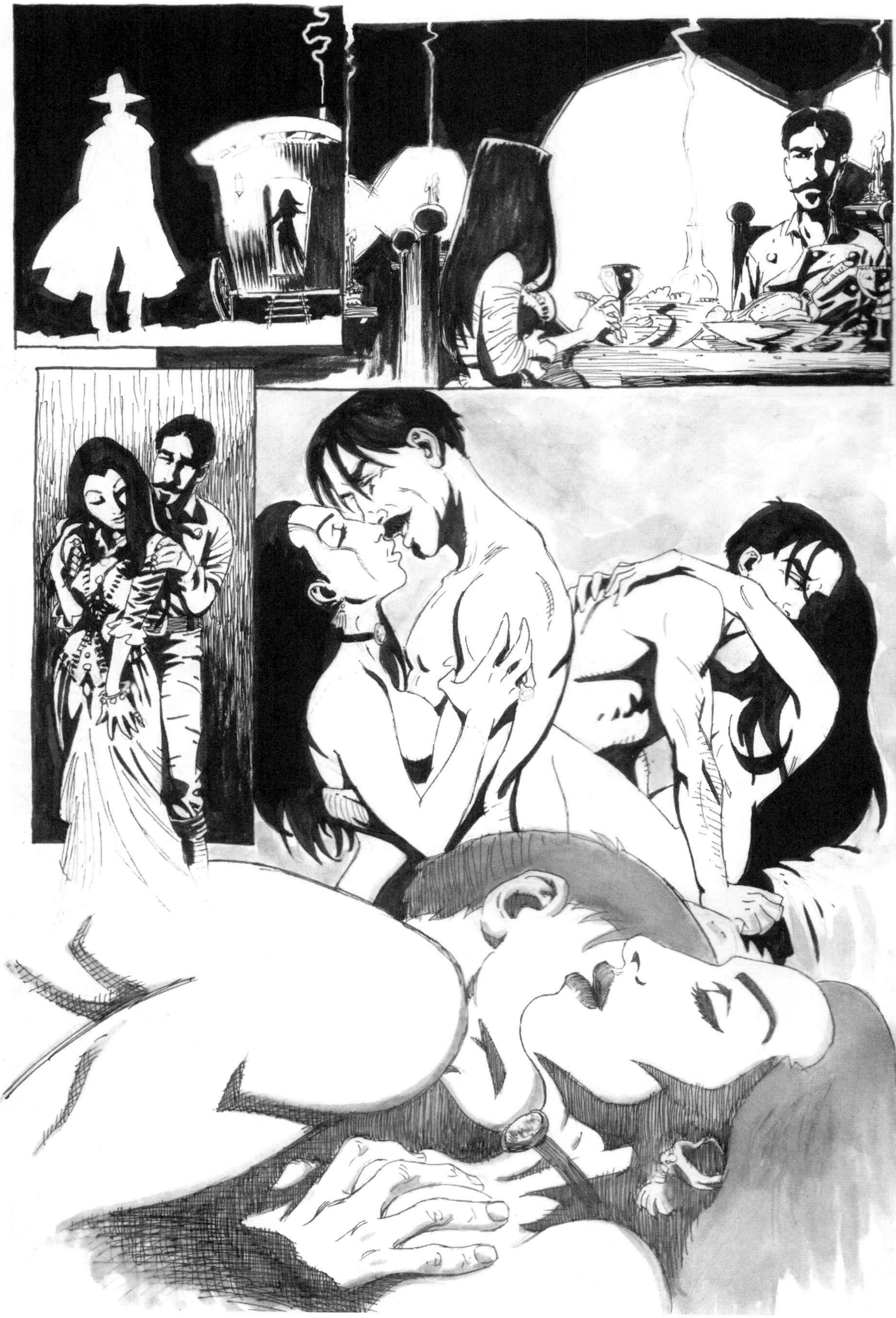

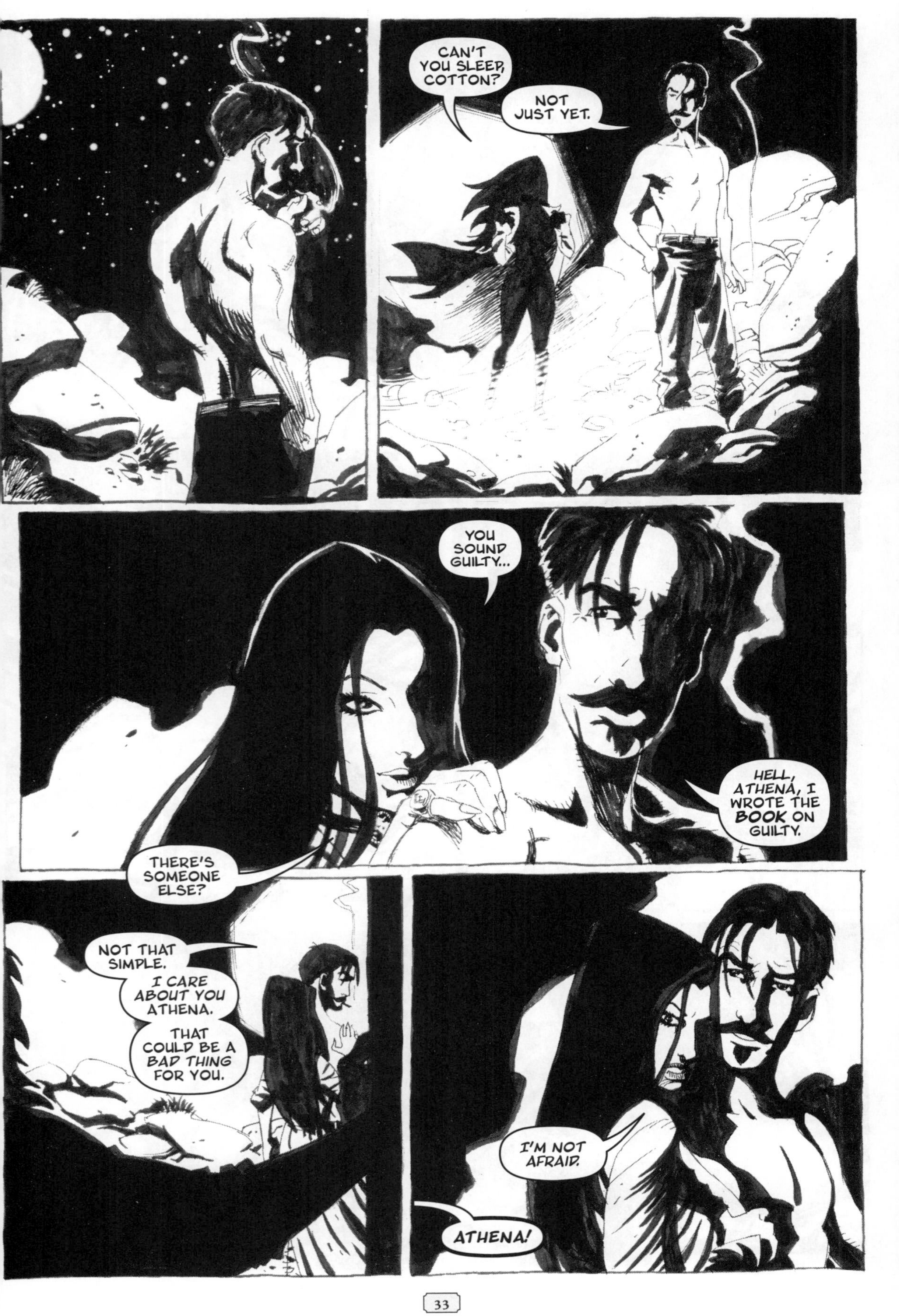
CAN'T YOU SLEEP, COTTON?
NOT JUST YET.
YOU SOUND GUILTY...
HELL, ATHENA, I WROTE THE BOOK ON GUILTY.
THERE'S SOMEONE ELSE?
NOT THAT SIMPLE.
I CARE ABOUT YOU ATHENA.
THAT COULD BE A BAD THING FOR YOU.
I'M NOT AFRAID.
ATHENA!

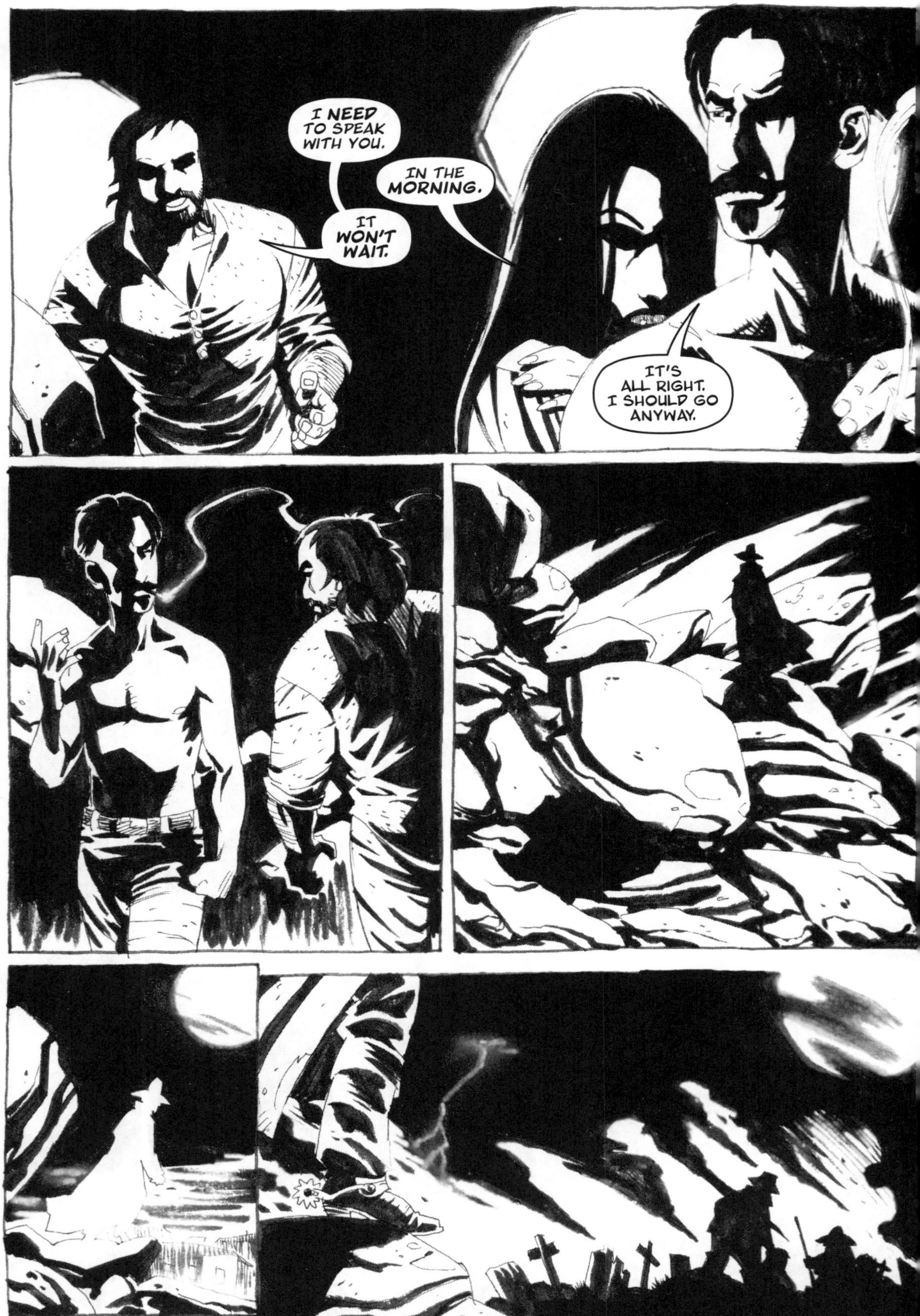
I NEED TO SPEAK WITH YOU.
IN THE MORNING.
IT WON'T WAIT.
IT'S ALL RIGHT. I SHOULD GO ANYWAY.

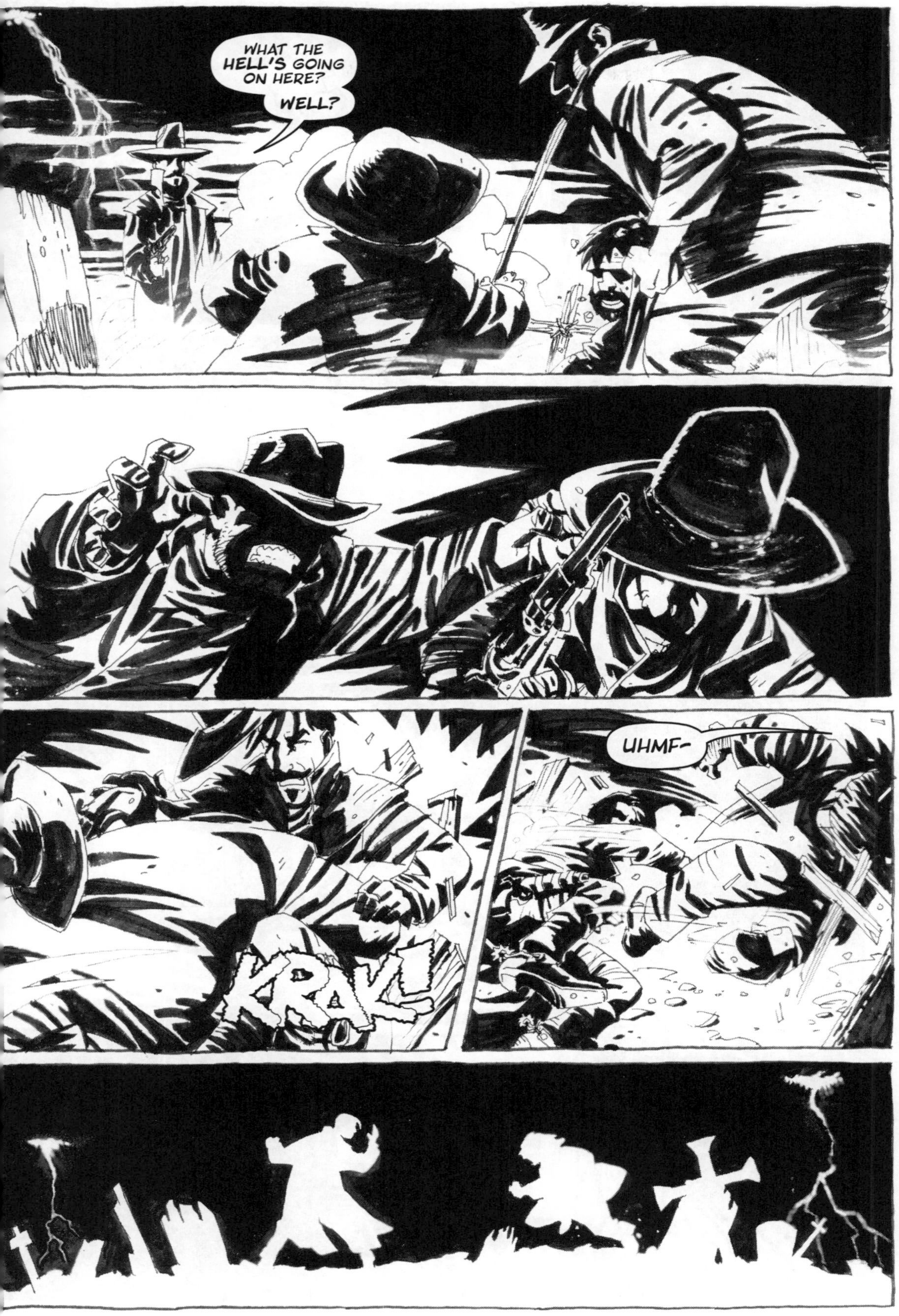
WHAT THE HELL'S GOING ON HERE?
WELL?
KRAK!
UHMF-

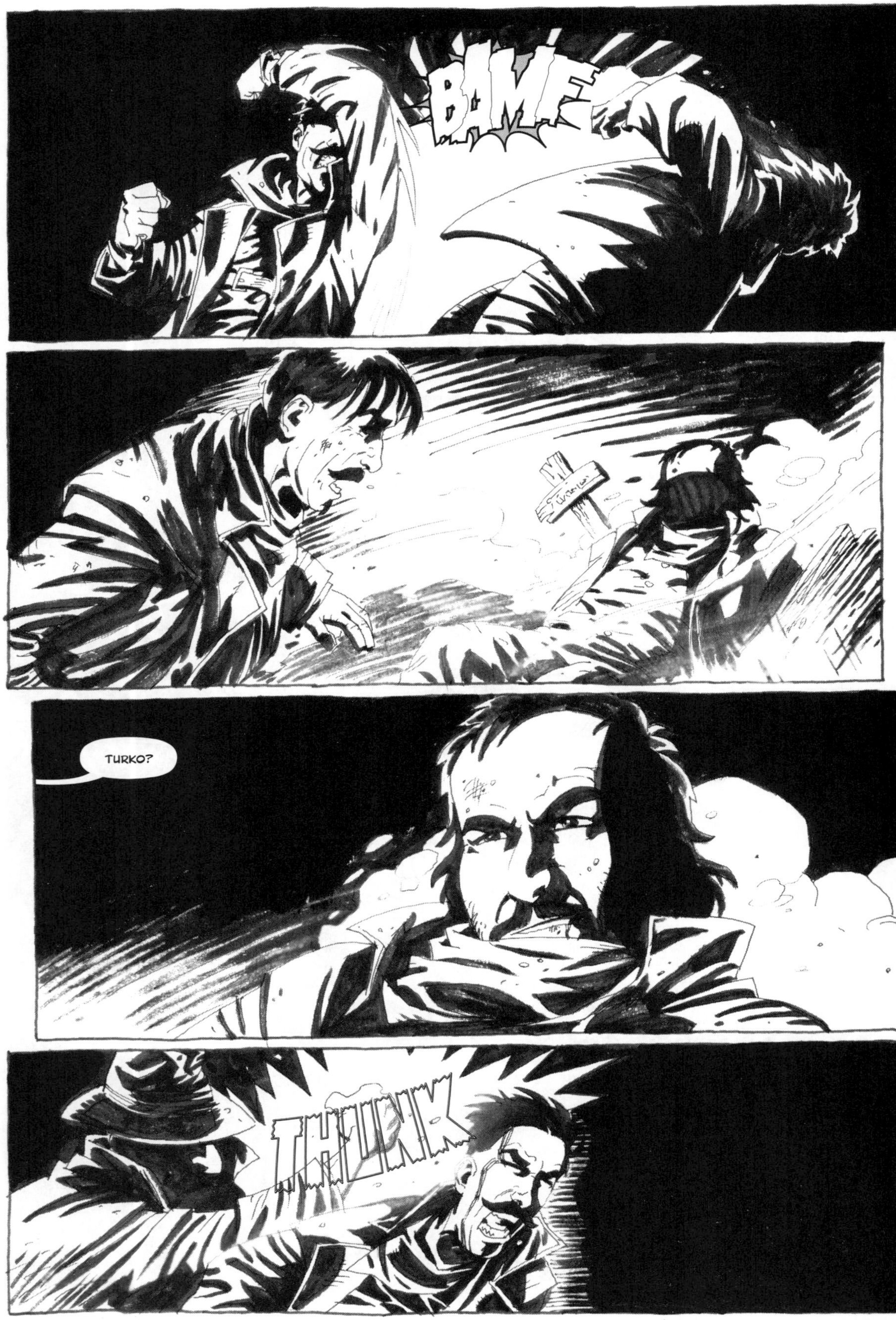
BAMF
TURKO?
THUNK

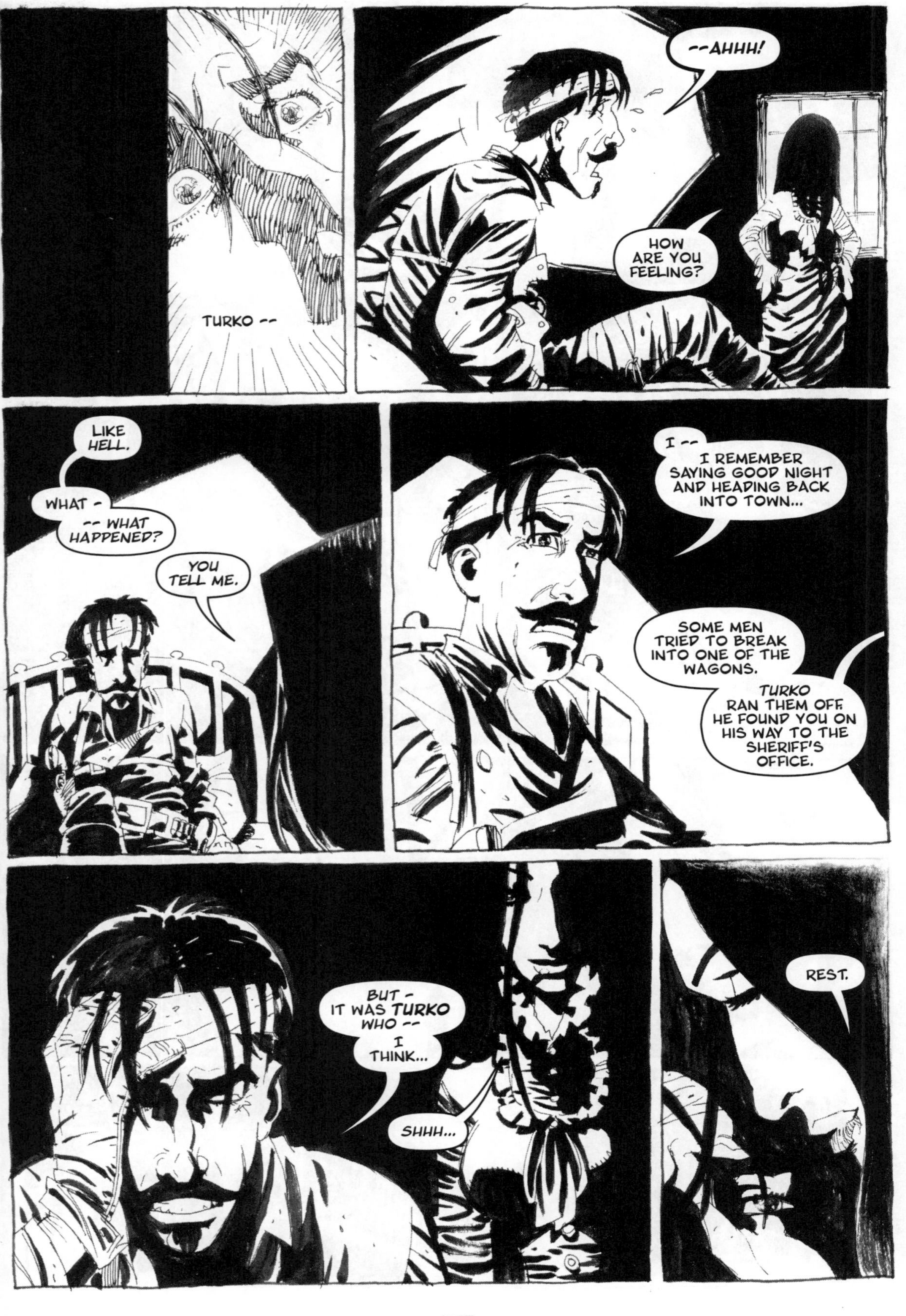
TURKO --
--AHHH!
HOW ARE YOU FEELING?
LIKE HELL.
WHAT -
-- WHAT HAPPENED?
YOU TELL ME.
I --
I REMEMBER SAYING GOOD NIGHT AND HEADING BACK INTO TOWN...
SOME MEN TRIED TO BREAK INTO ONE OF THE WAGONS.
TURKO RAN THEM OFF. HE FOUND YOU ON HIS WAY TO THE SHERIFF'S OFFICE.
BUT - IT WAS TURKO WHO --
I THINK...
SHHH...
REST.

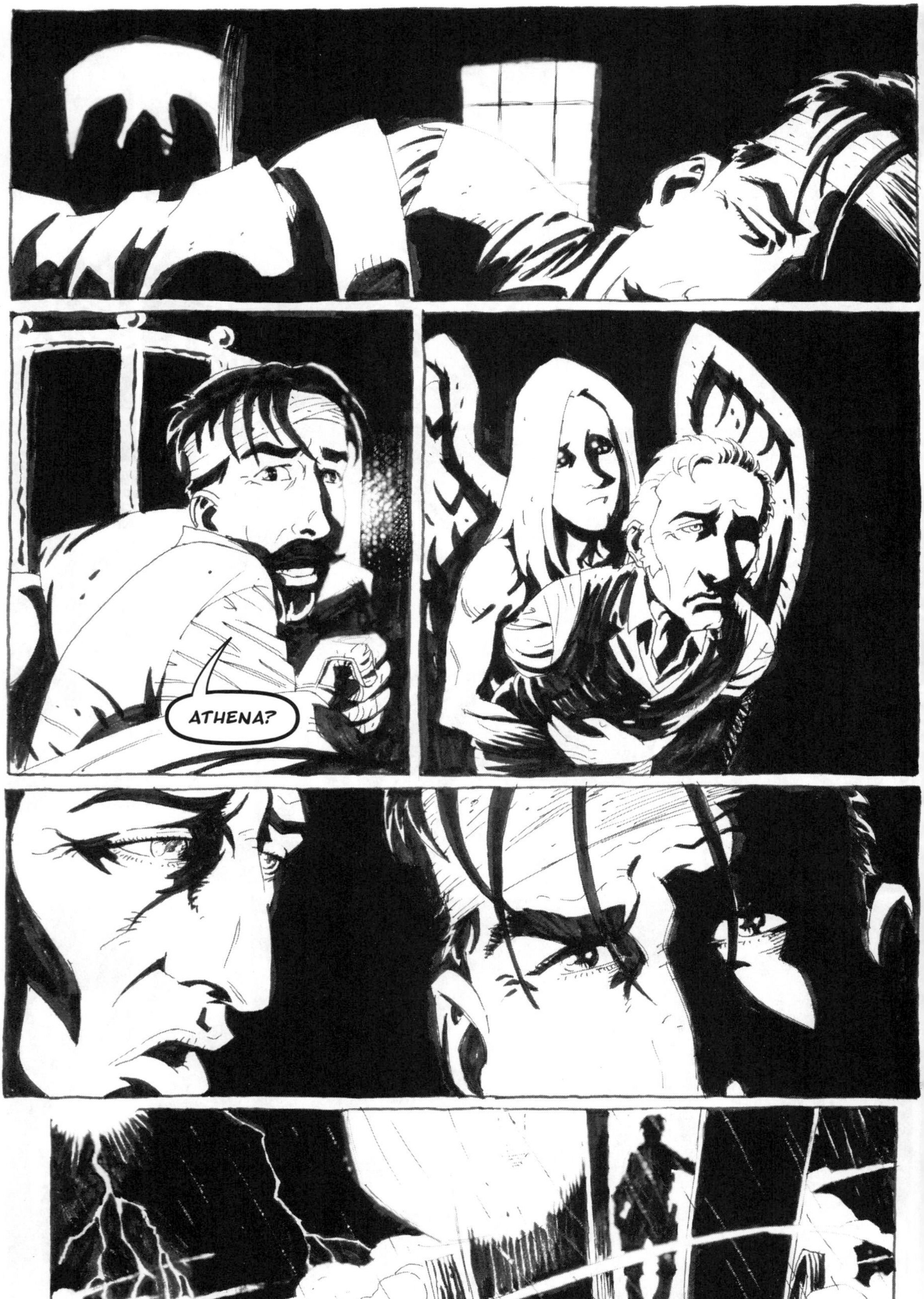
ATHENA?

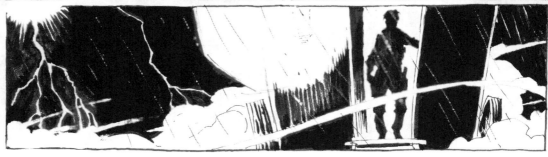

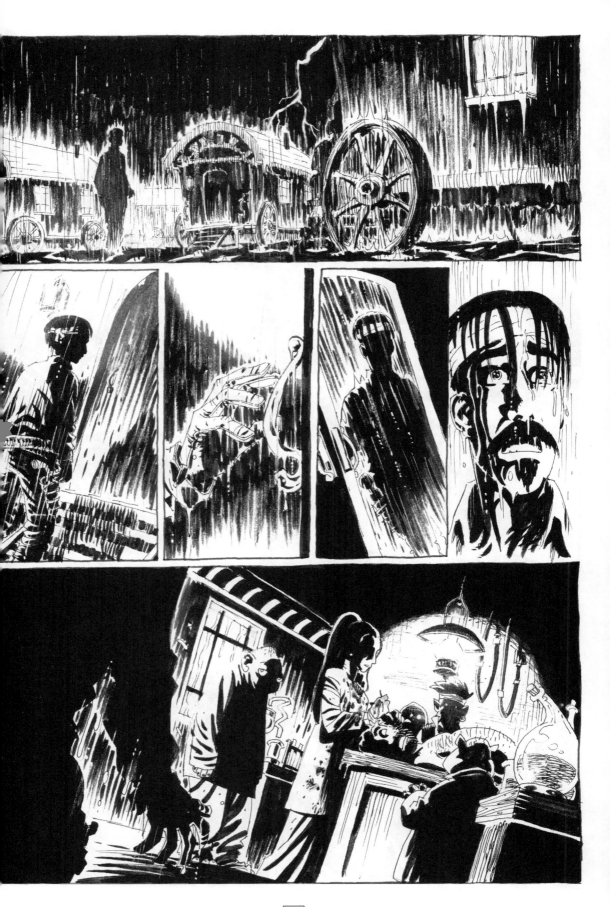

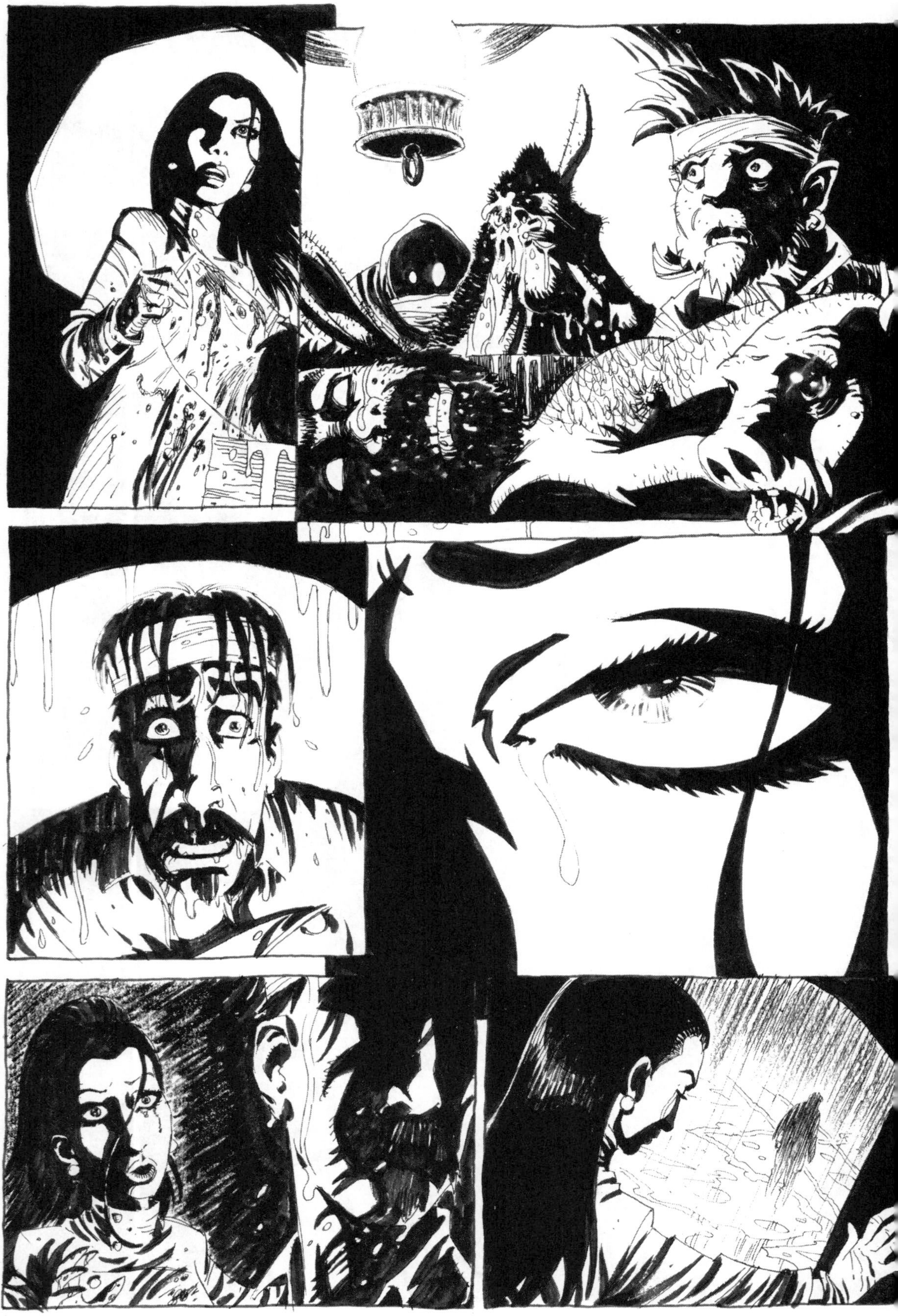

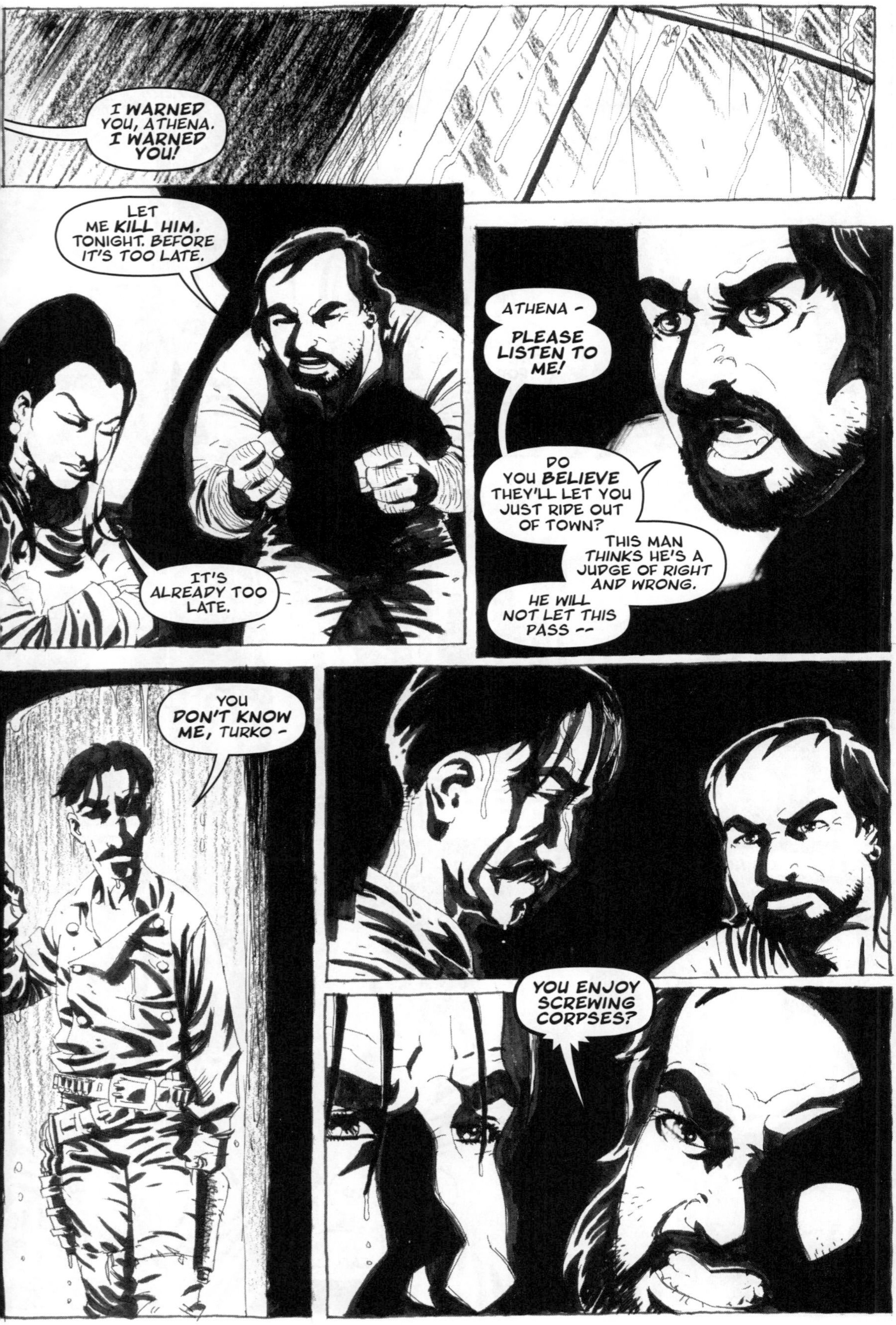

I WARNED YOU, ATHENA. I WARNED YOU!
LET ME KILL HIM. TONIGHT. BEFORE IT'S TOO LATE.
IT'S ALREADY TOO LATE.
ATHENA -
PLEASE LISTEN TO ME!
DO YOU BELIEVE THEY'LL LET YOU JUST RIDE OUT OF TOWN?
THIS MAN THINKS HE'S A JUDGE OF RIGHT AND WRONG.
HE WILL NOT LET THIS PASS --
YOU DON'T KNOW ME, TURKO -
YOU ENJOY SCREWING CORPSES?

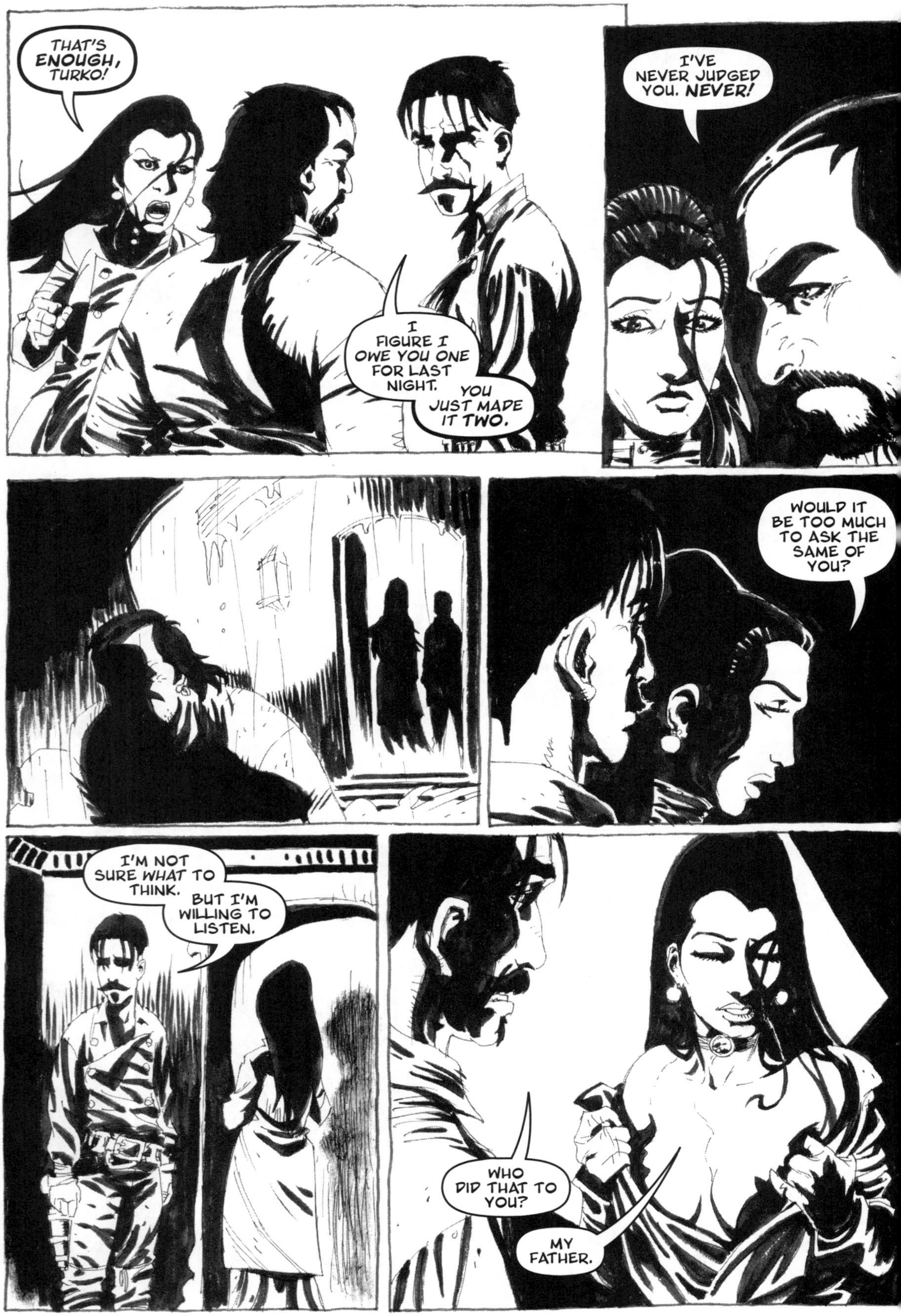
THAT'S ENOUGH, TURKO!
I FIGURE I OWE YOU ONE FOR LAST NIGHT.
YOU JUST MADE IT TWO.
I'VE NEVER JUDGED YOU. NEVER!
WOULD IT BE TOO MUCH TO ASK THE SAME OF YOU?
I'M NOT SURE WHAT TO THINK.
BUT I'M WILLING TO LISTEN.
WHO DID THAT TO YOU?
MY FATHER.

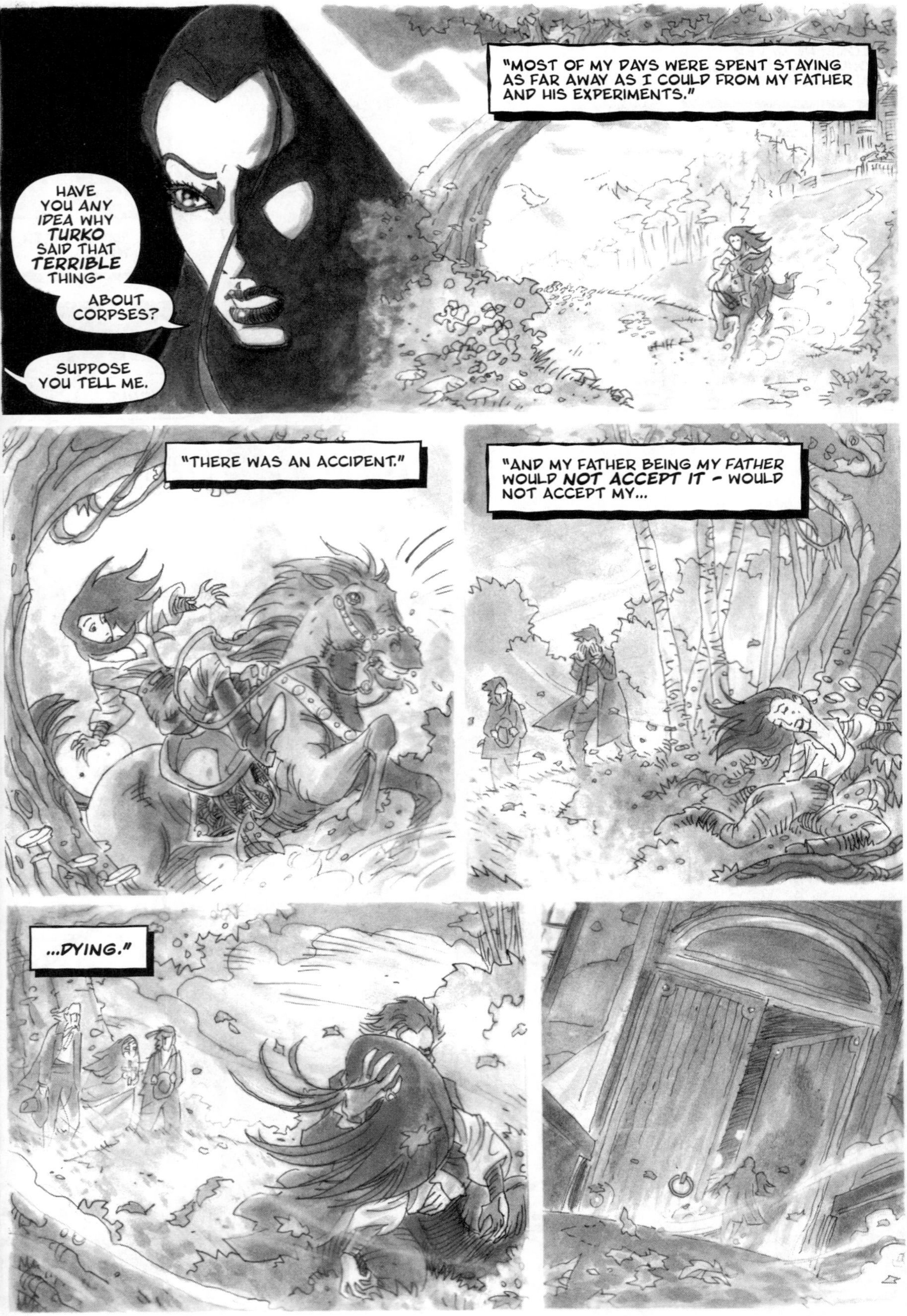
"MOST OF MY DAYS WERE SPENT STAYING AS FAR AWAY AS I COULD FROM MY FATHER AND HIS EXPERIMENTS."
HAVE YOU ANY IDEA WHY TURKO SAID THAT TERRIBLE THING-
ABOUT CORPSES?
SUPPOSE YOU TELL ME.
"THERE WAS AN ACCIDENT."
"AND MY FATHER BEING MY FATHER WOULD NOT ACCEPT IT - WOULD NOT ACCEPT MY...
...DYING."

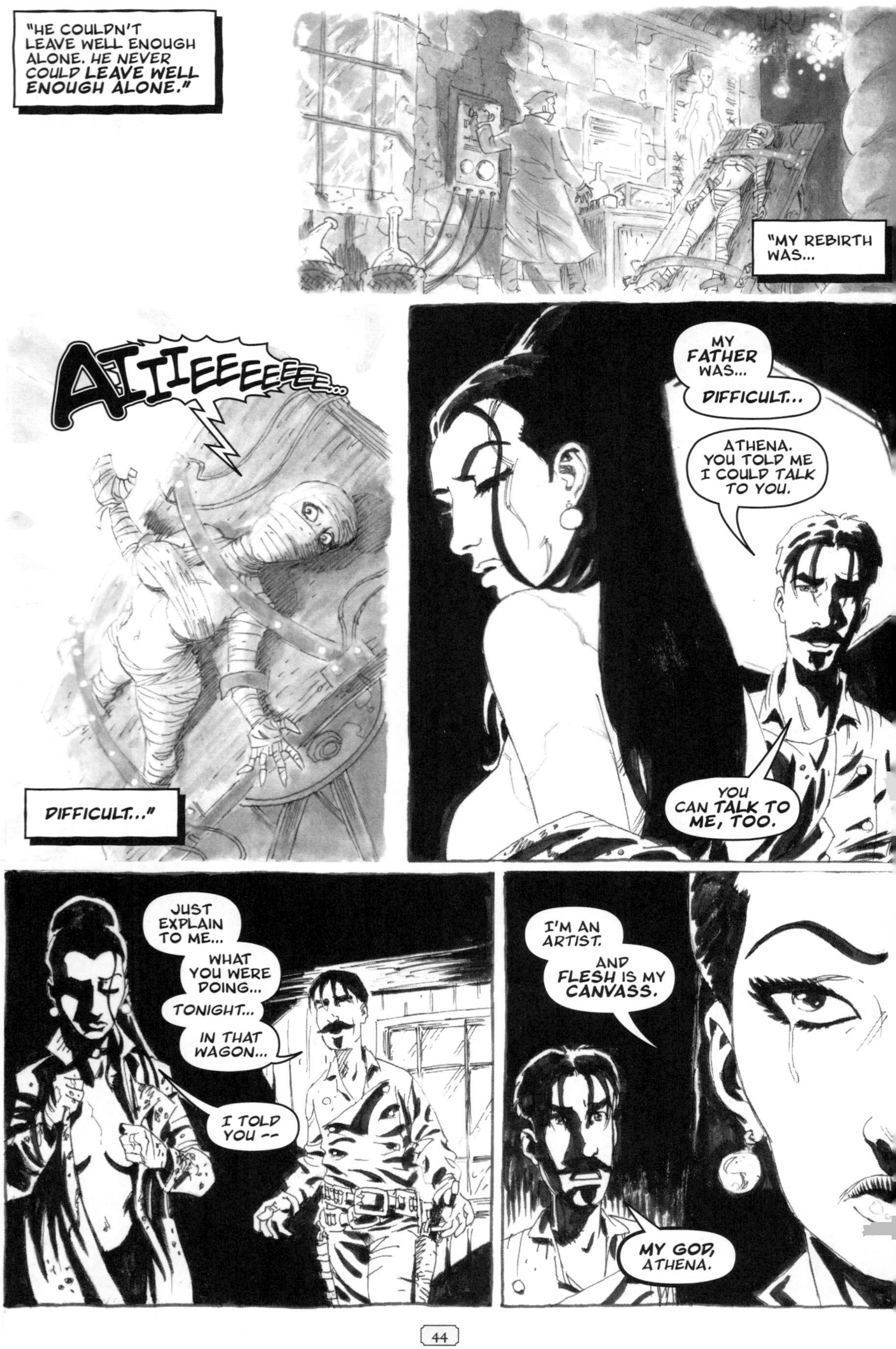
"HE COULDN'T LEAVE WELL ENOUGH ALONE. HE NEVER COULD LEAVE WELL ENOUGH ALONE."
"MY REBIRTH WAS...
AIIEEEEEEE...
DIFFICULT..."
MY FATHER WAS...
DIFFICULT...
ATHENA. YOU TOLD ME I COULD TALK TO YOU.
YOU CAN TALK TO ME, TOO.
JUST EXPLAIN TO ME...
WHAT YOU WERE DOING...
TONIGHT...
IN THAT WAGON...
I TOLD YOU --
I'M AN ARTIST.
AND FLESH IS MY CANVASS.
MY GOD, ATHENA.

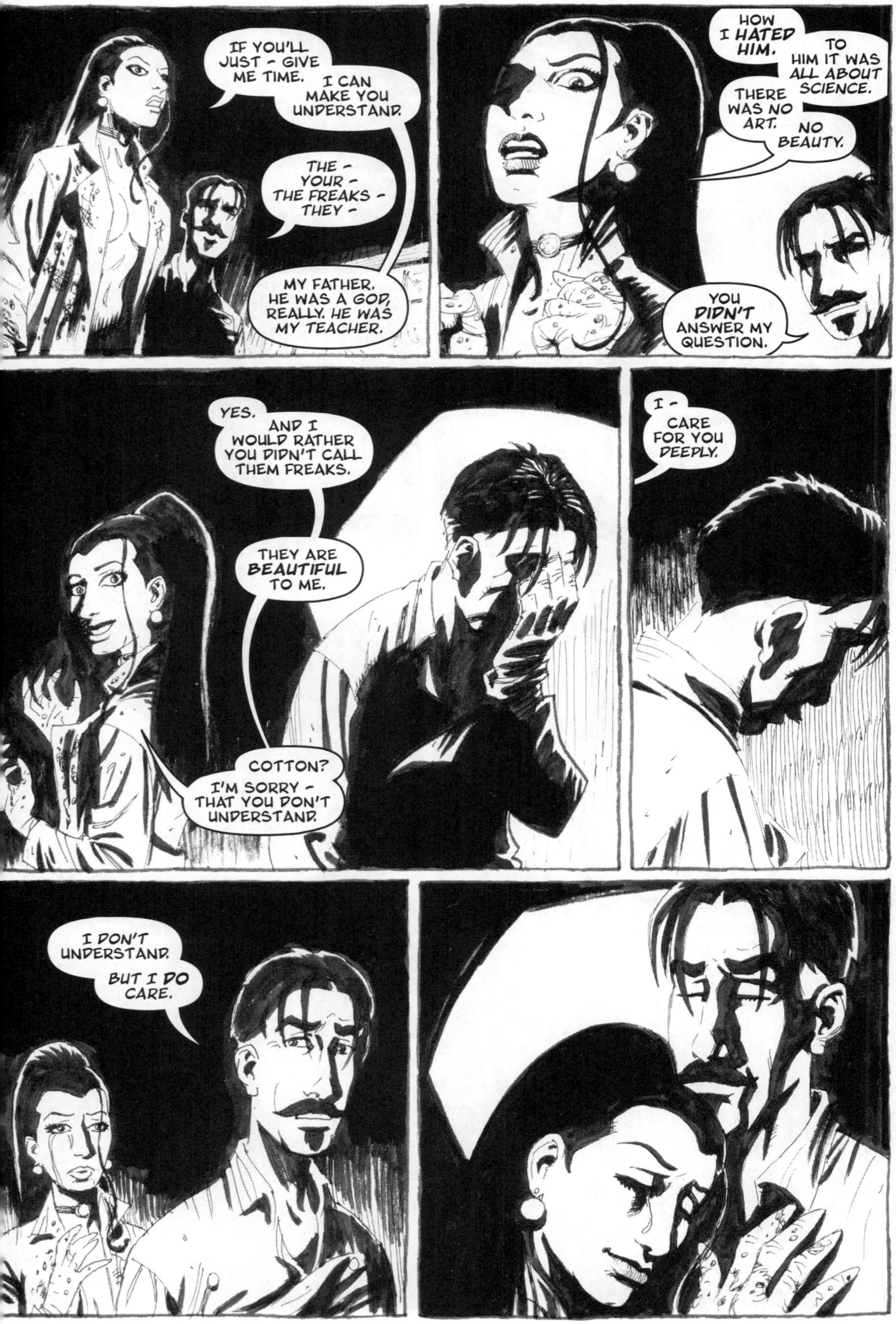

IF YOU'LL JUST - GIVE ME TIME.
I CAN MAKE YOU UNDERSTAND.
THE - YOUR - THE FREAKS - THEY -
MY FATHER. HE WAS A GOD, REALLY. HE WAS MY TEACHER.
HOW I HATED HIM.
TO HIM IT WAS ALL ABOUT SCIENCE.
THERE WAS NO ART.
NO BEAUTY.
YOU DIDN'T ANSWER MY QUESTION.
YES.
AND I WOULD RATHER YOU DIDN'T CALL THEM FREAKS.
THEY ARE BEAUTIFUL TO ME.
COTTON?
I'M SORRY - THAT YOU DON'T UNDERSTAND.
I -
CARE FOR YOU DEEPLY.
I DON'T UNDERSTAND.
BUT I DO CARE.

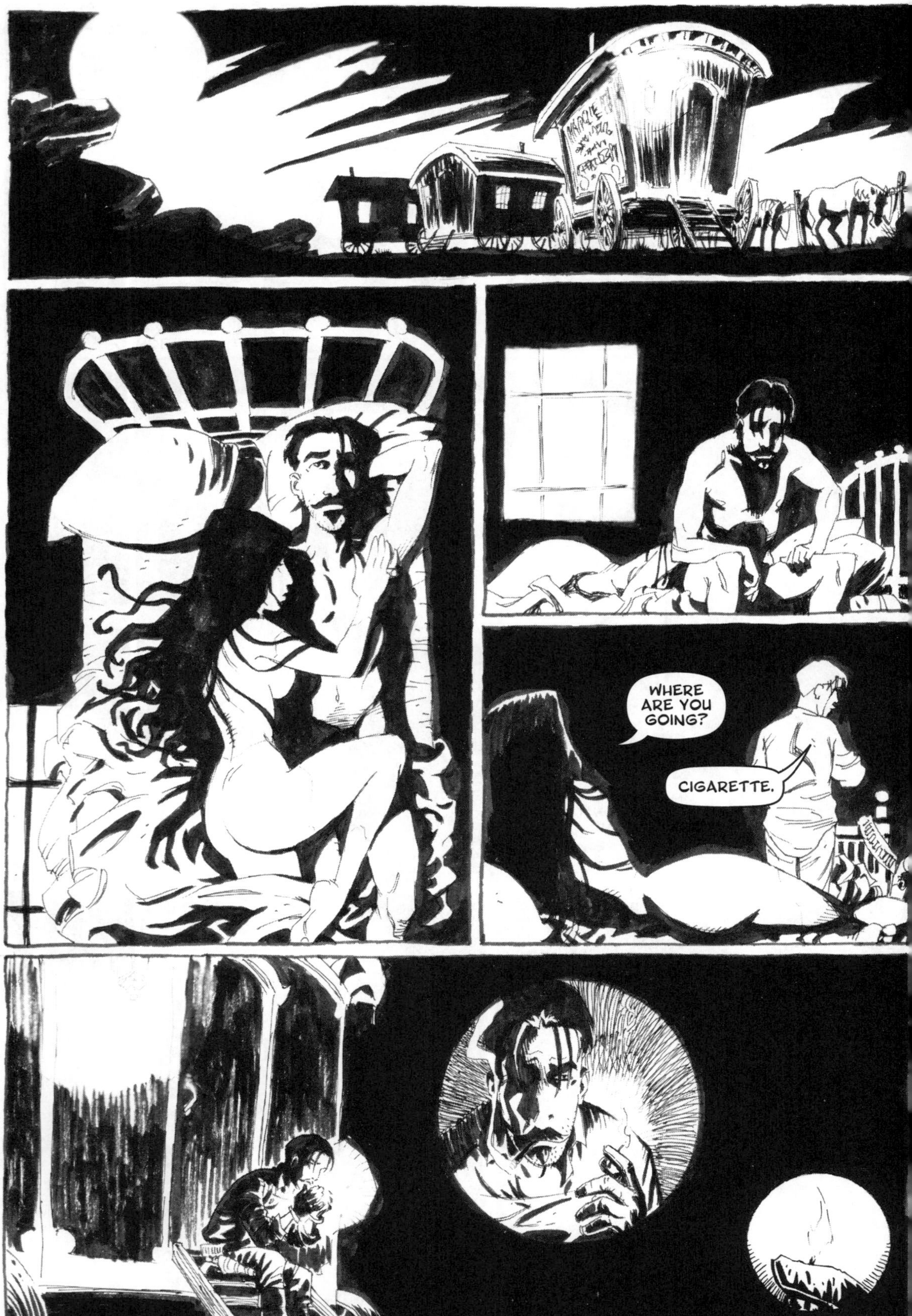
WHERE ARE YOU GOING?
CIGARETTE.

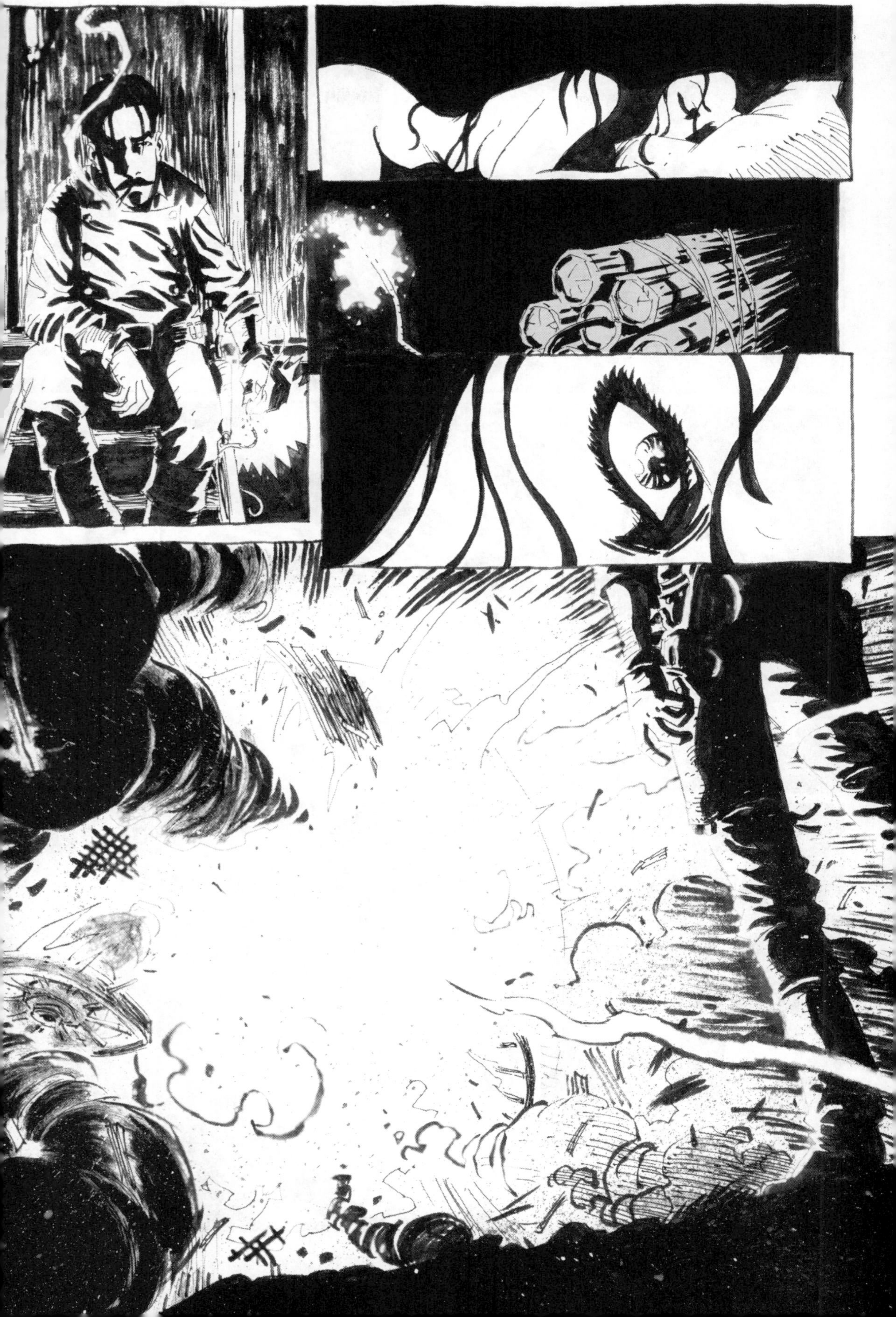

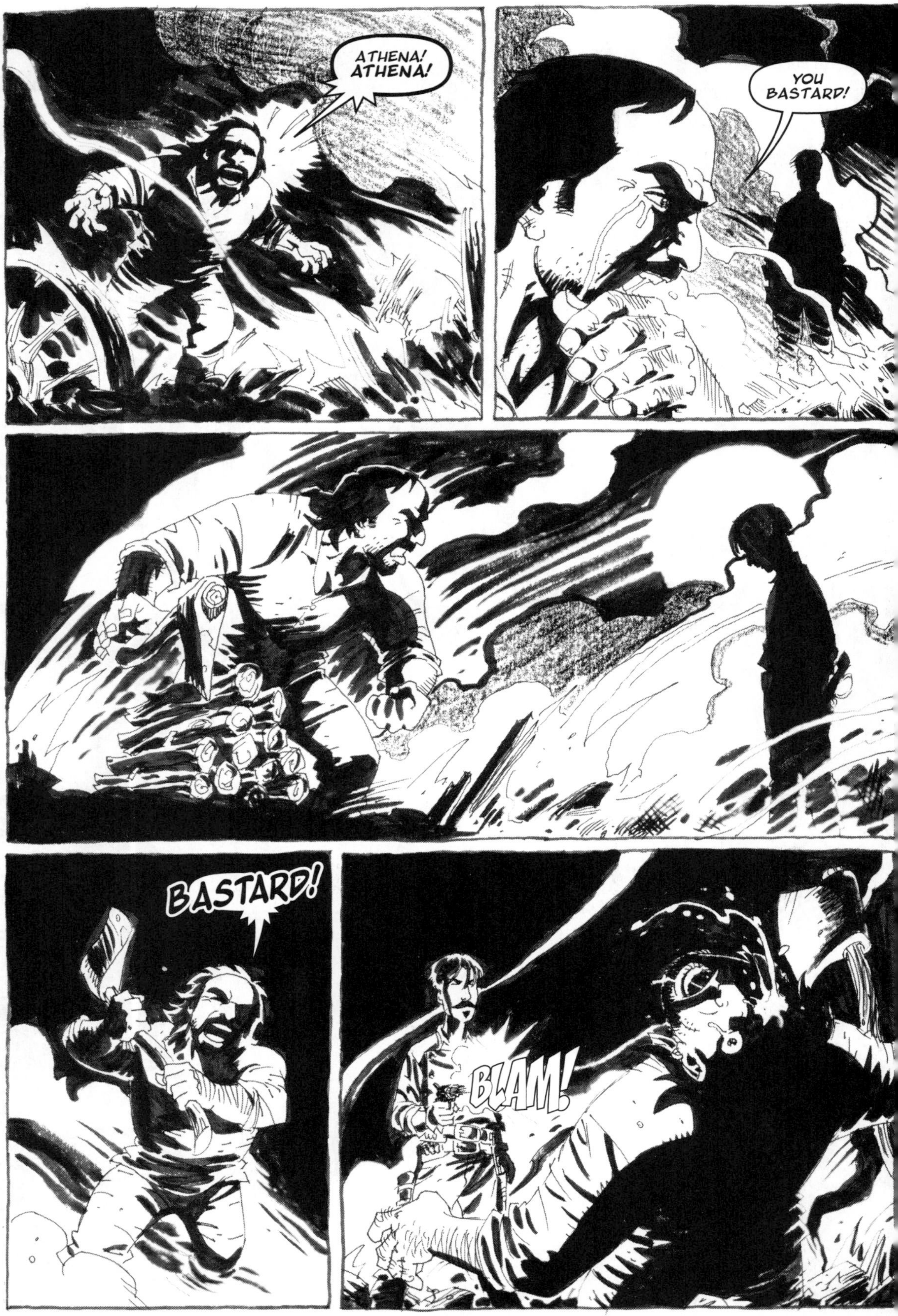
ATHENA!
ATHENA!
YOU BASTARD!
BASTARD!
BLAM!

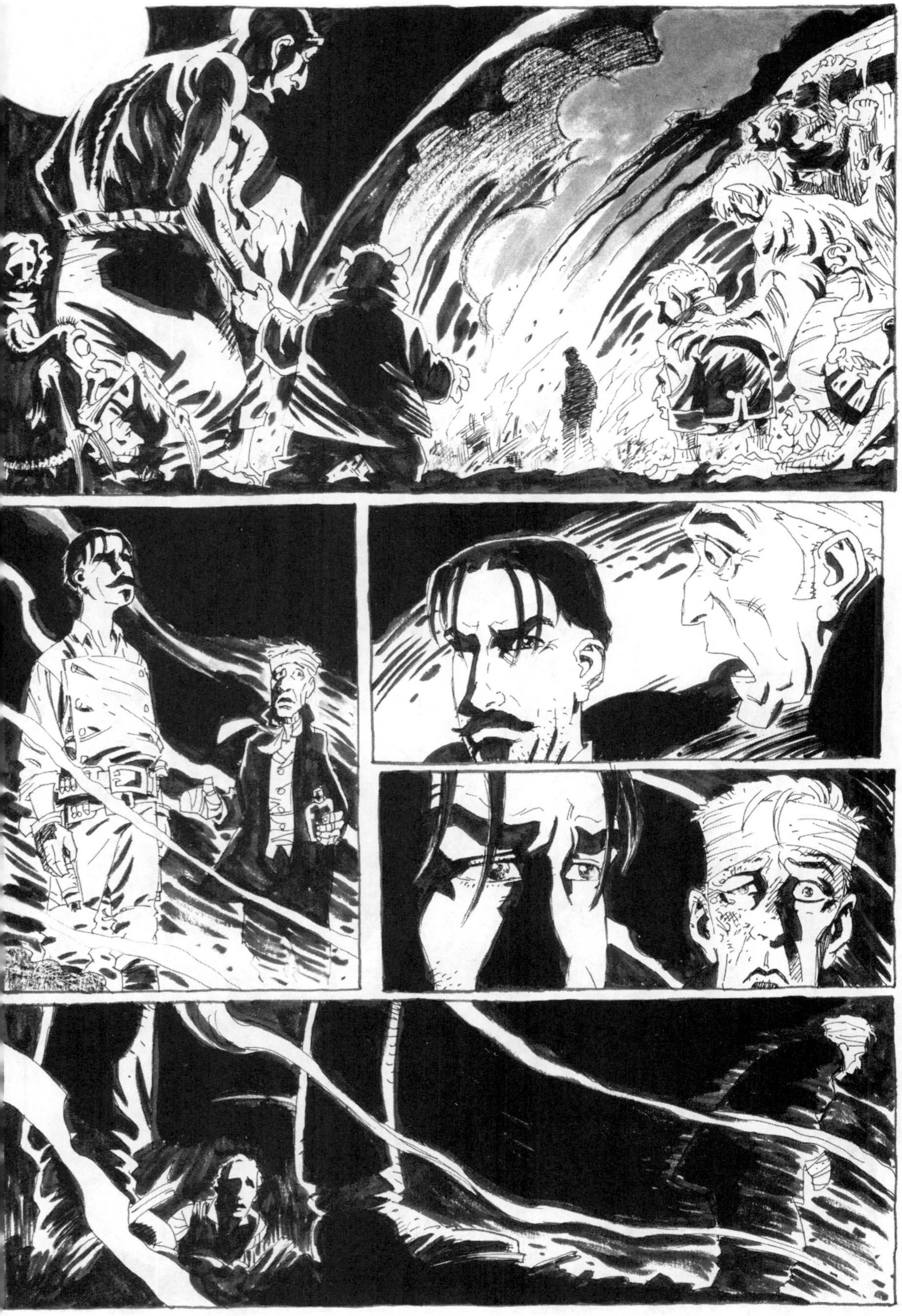

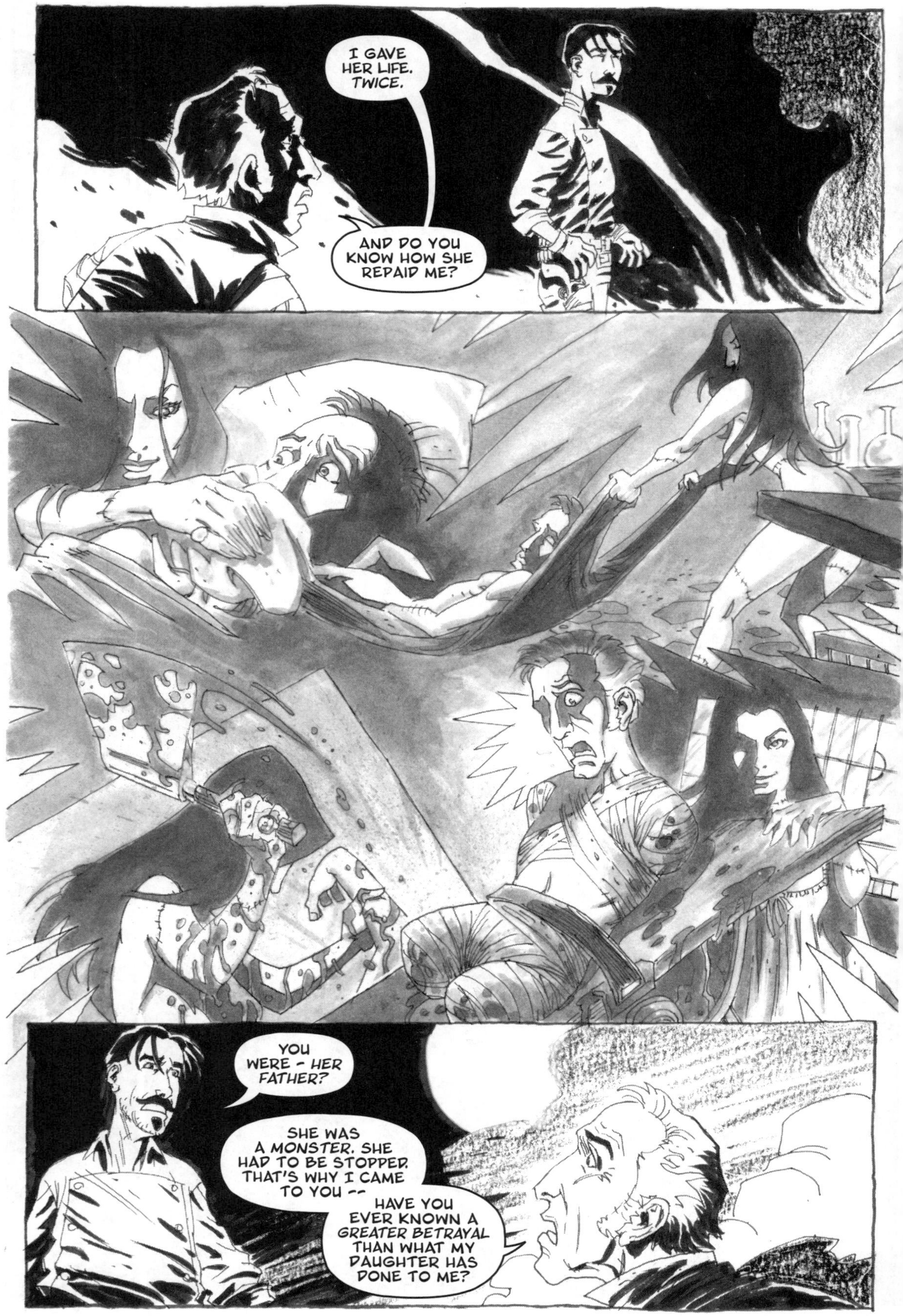
I GAVE HER LIFE. TWICE.
AND DO YOU KNOW HOW SHE REPAID ME?
YOU WERE - HER FATHER?
SHE WAS A MONSTER. SHE HAD TO BE STOPPED. THAT'S WHY I CAME TO YOU --
HAVE YOU EVER KNOWN A GREATER BETRAYAL THAN WHAT MY DAUGHTER HAS DONE TO ME?

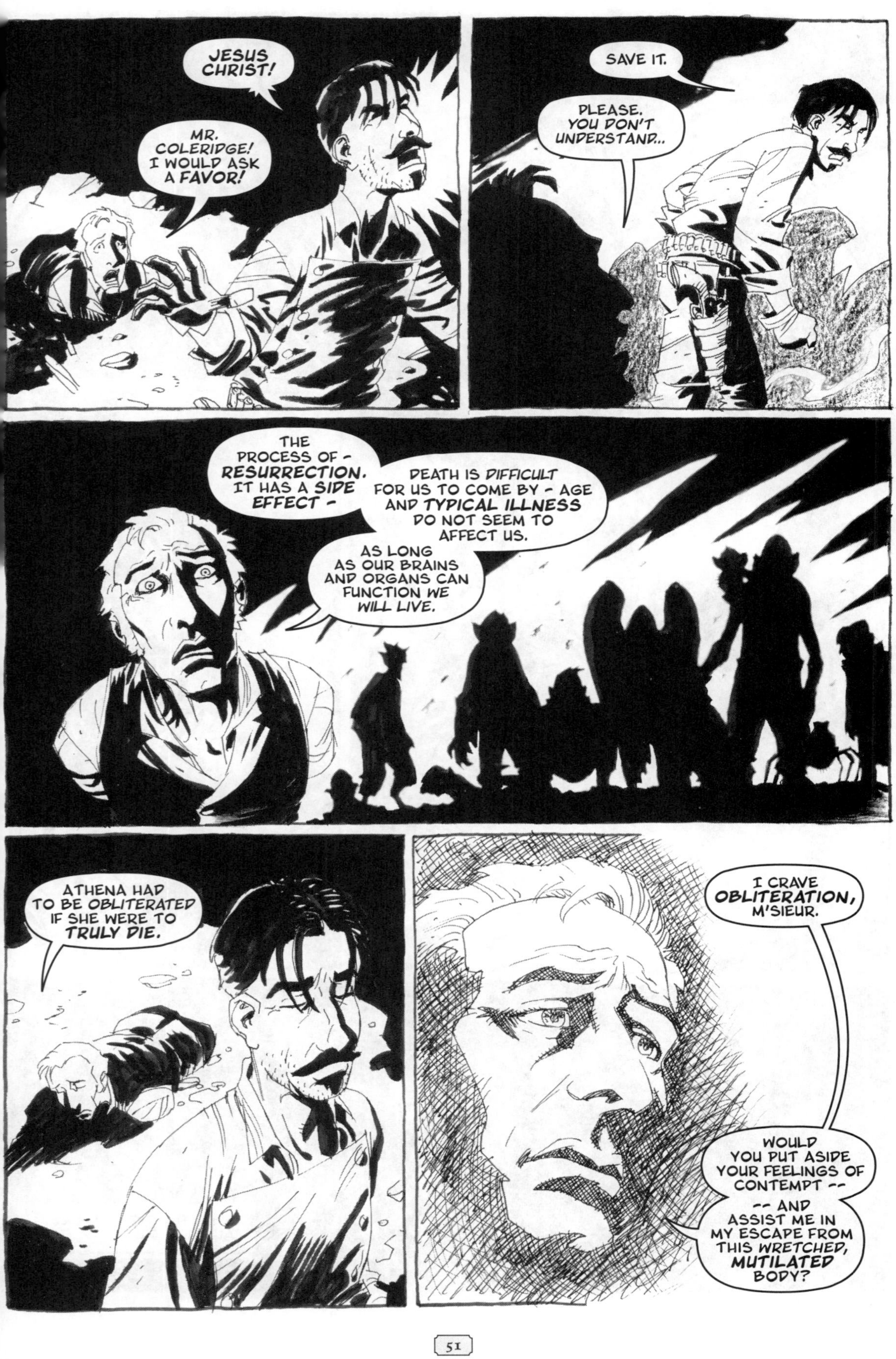

JESUS CHRIST!
MR. COLERIDGE! I WOULD ASK A FAVOR!
SAVE IT.
PLEASE. YOU DON'T UNDERSTAND...
THE PROCESS OF - RESURRECTION. IT HAS A SIDE EFFECT -
DEATH IS DIFFICULT FOR US TO COME BY - AGE AND TYPICAL ILLNESS DO NOT SEEM TO AFFECT US.
AS LONG AS OUR BRAINS AND ORGANS CAN FUNCTION WE WILL LIVE.
ATHENA HAD TO BE OBLITERATED IF SHE WERE TO TRULY DIE.
I CRAVE OBLITERATION, M'SIEUR.
WOULD YOU PUT ASIDE YOUR FEELINGS OF CONTEMPT --
-- AND ASSIST ME IN MY ESCAPE FROM THIS WRETCHED, MUTILATED BODY?

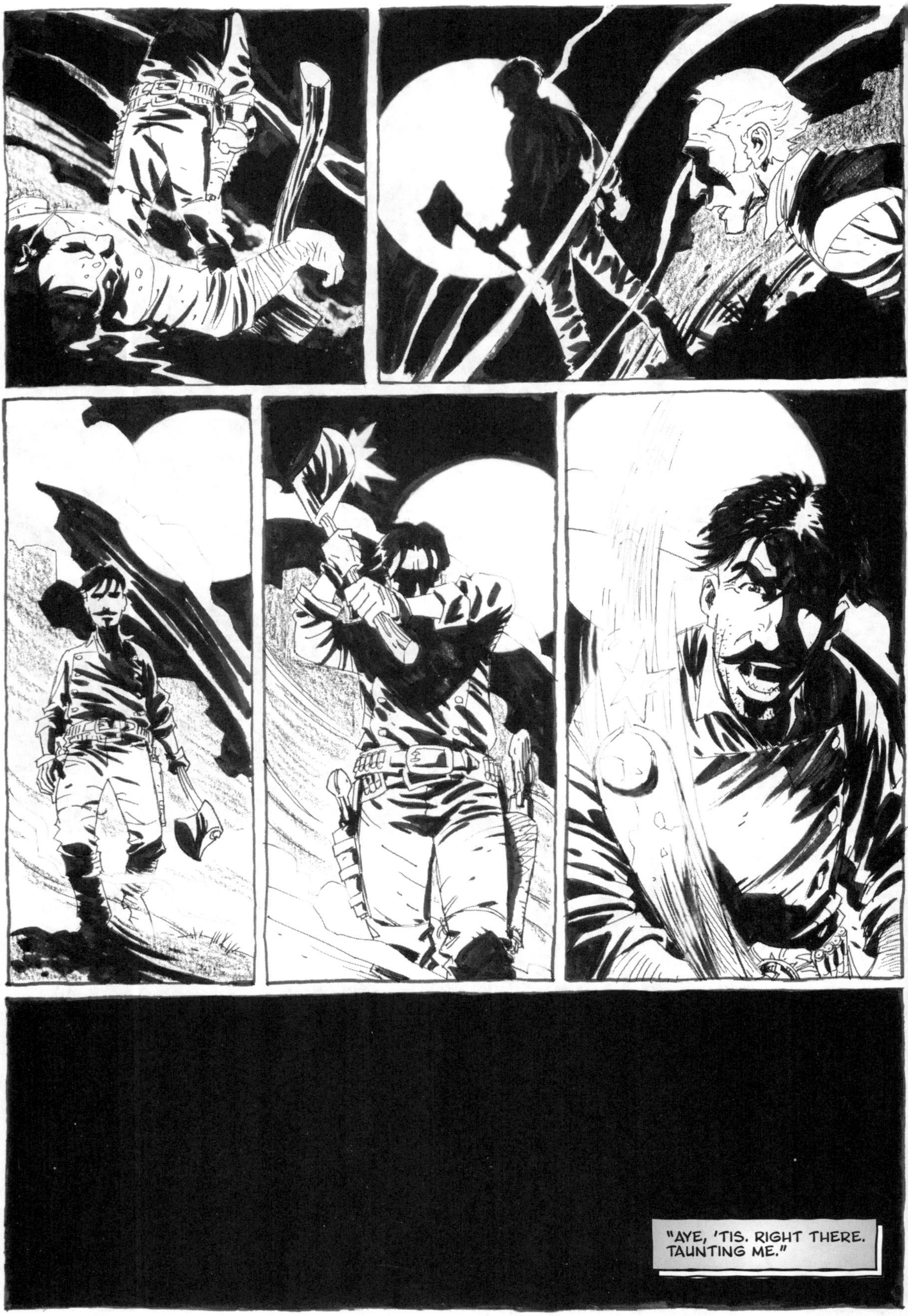
"AYE, 'TIS. RIGHT THERE. TAUNTING ME."

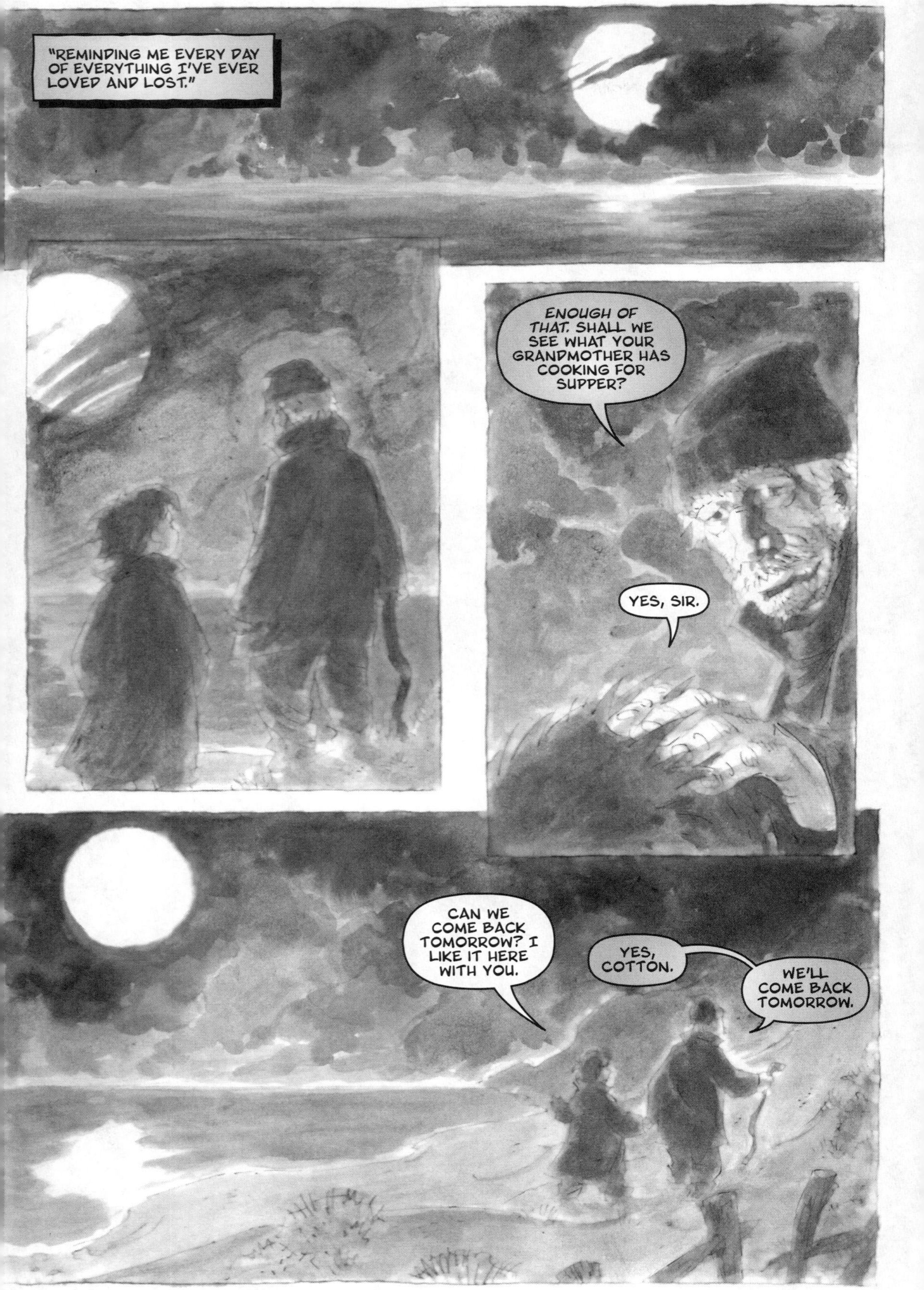
"REMINDING ME EVERY DAY OF EVERYTHING I'VE EVER LOVED AND LOST."
ENOUGH OF THAT. SHALL WE SEE WHAT YOUR GRANDMOTHER HAS COOKING FOR SUPPER?
YES, SIR.
CAN WE COME BACK TOMORROW? I LIKE IT HERE WITH YOU.
YES, COTTON.
WE'LL COME BACK TOMORROW.

SEVEN DISAPPEARANCES IN TWO WEEKS.

THAT'S TOO HARD TO IGNORE.

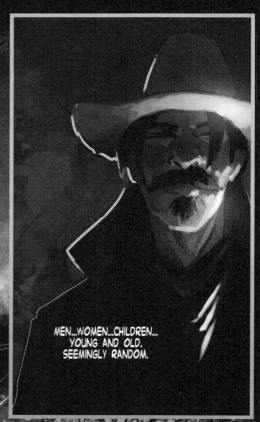

MEN...WOMEN...CHILDREN... YOUNG AND OLD. SEEMINGLY RANDOM.

THE TOWNFOLK THINK IT'S THE WORK OF ANGRY GHOSTS

THAT'S PROBABLY WHY THEY DIDN'T GO ANY FURTHER THAN THIS.

DIDN'T WANT TO DISTURB ANY SHOSHONE SPIRITS.

The WICKED WEST
The Usual Suspects

Story by
Todd Livingston

Illustrated & Lettered by
Scott Keating

I DON'T HAVE THAT PROBLEM

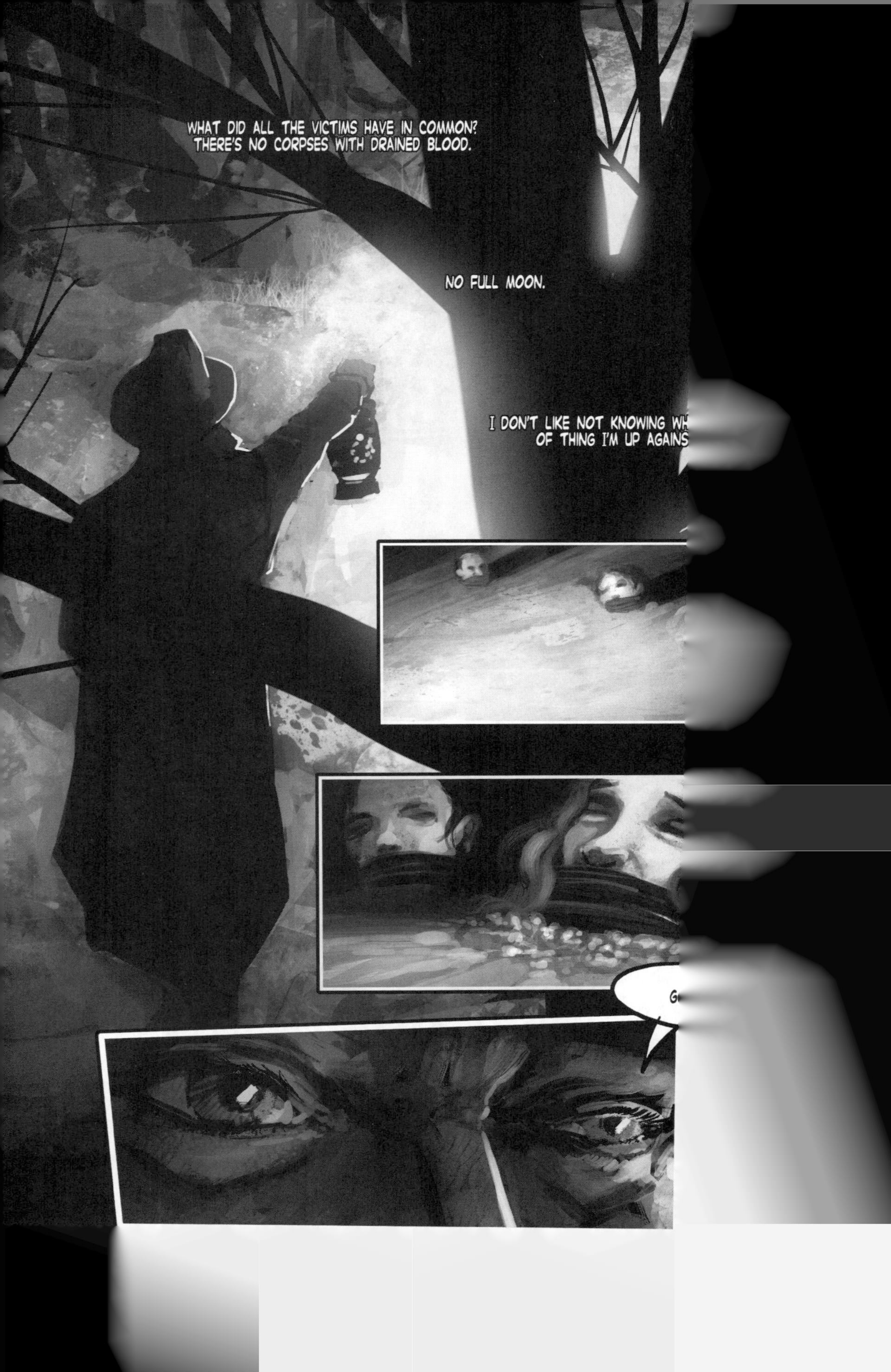
WHAT DID ALL THE VICTIMS HAVE IN COMMON? THERE'S NO CORPSES WITH DRAINED BLOOD.
NO FULL MOON.
I DON'T LIKE NOT KNOWING WH
OF THING I'M UP AGAINS

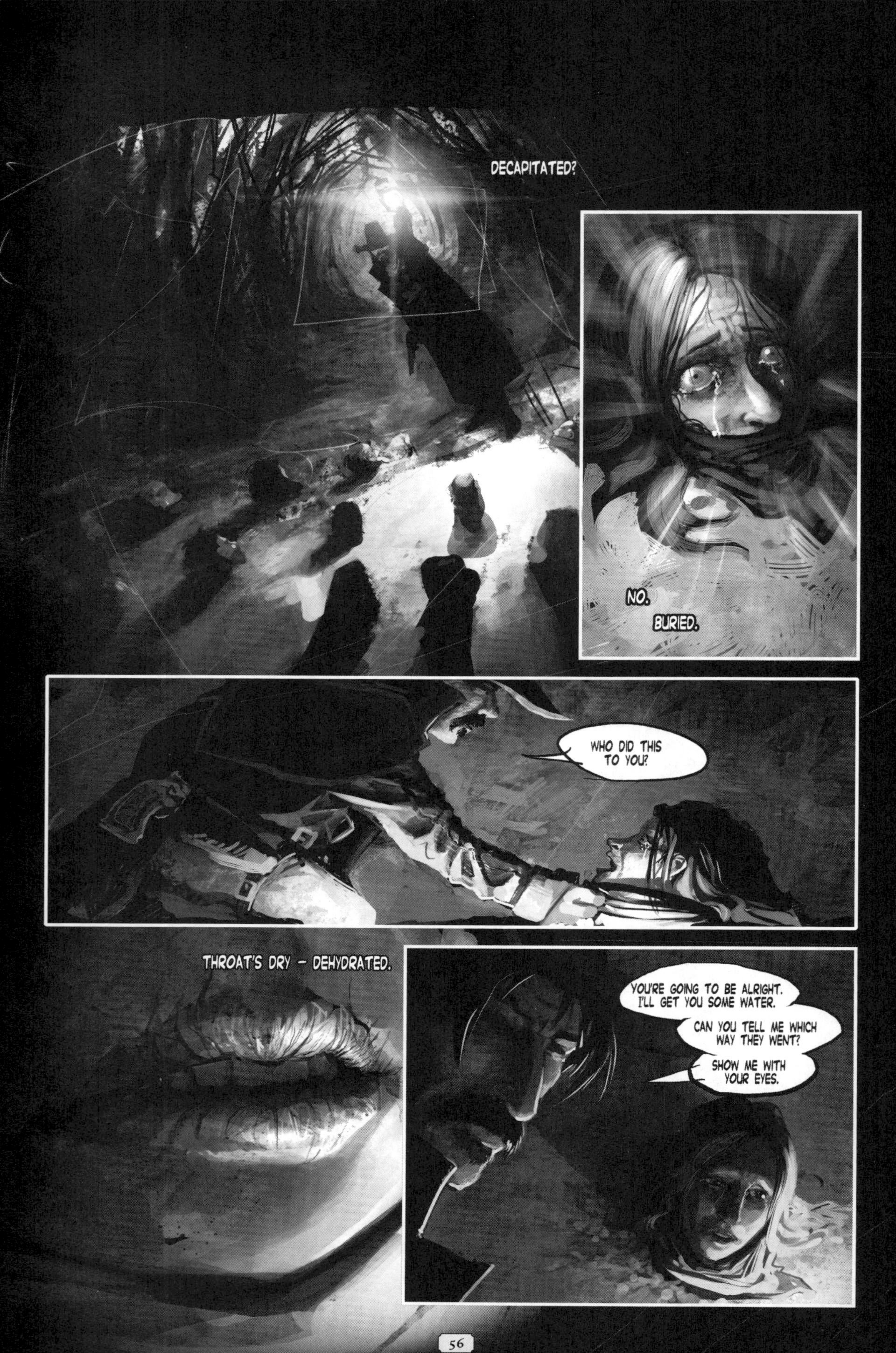
DECAPITATED?
NO.
BURIED.
WHO DID THIS TO YOU?
THROAT'S DRY - DEHYDRATED.
YOU'RE GOING TO BE ALRIGHT. I'LL GET YOU SOME WATER.
CAN YOU TELL ME WHICH WAY THEY WENT?
SHOW ME WITH YOUR EYES.

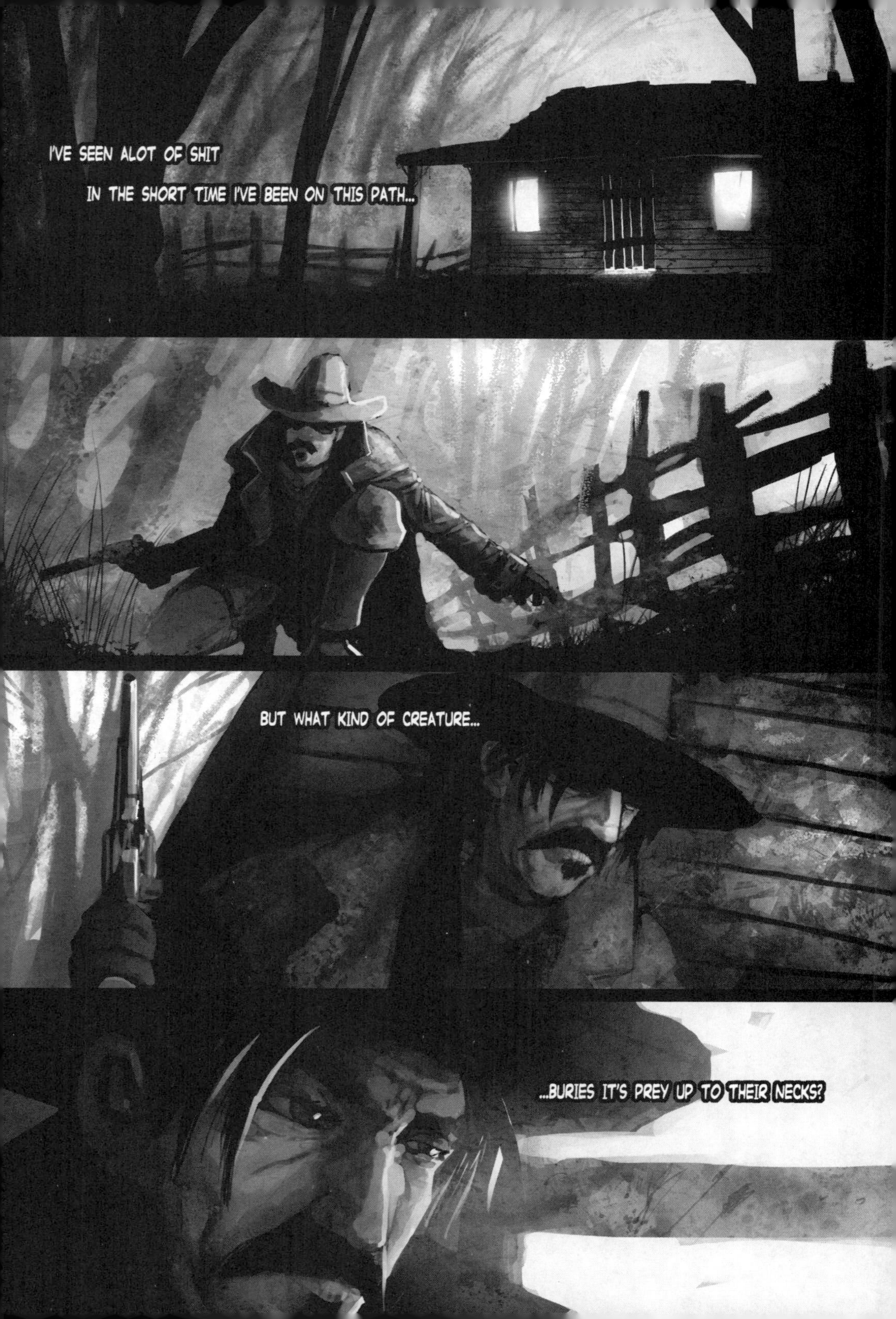
I'VE SEEN ALOT OF SHIT
IN THE SHORT TIME I'VE BEEN ON THIS PATH...
BUT WHAT KIND OF CREATURE...
...BURIES IT'S PREY UP TO THEIR NECKS?

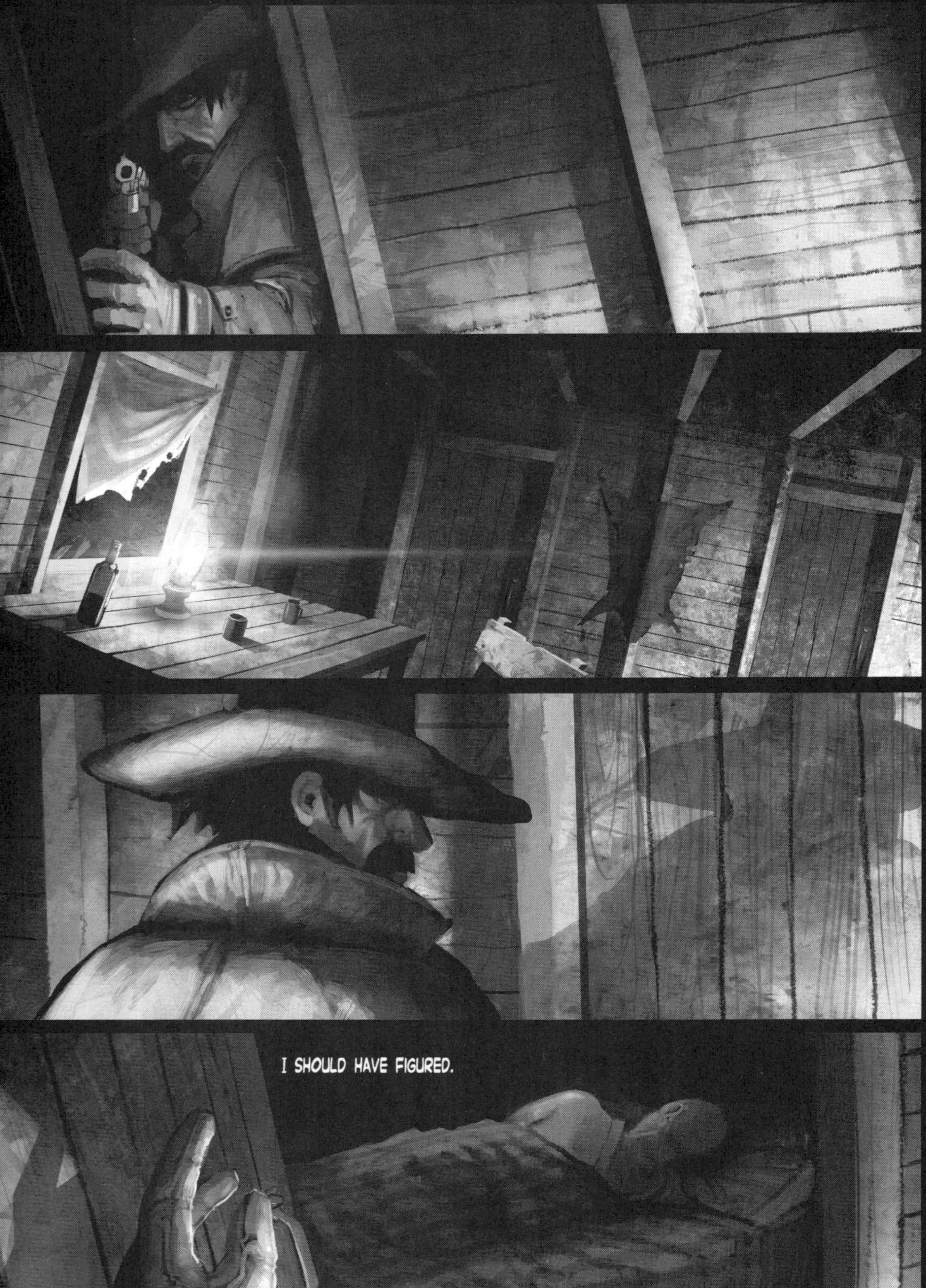
I SHOULD HAVE FIGURED.

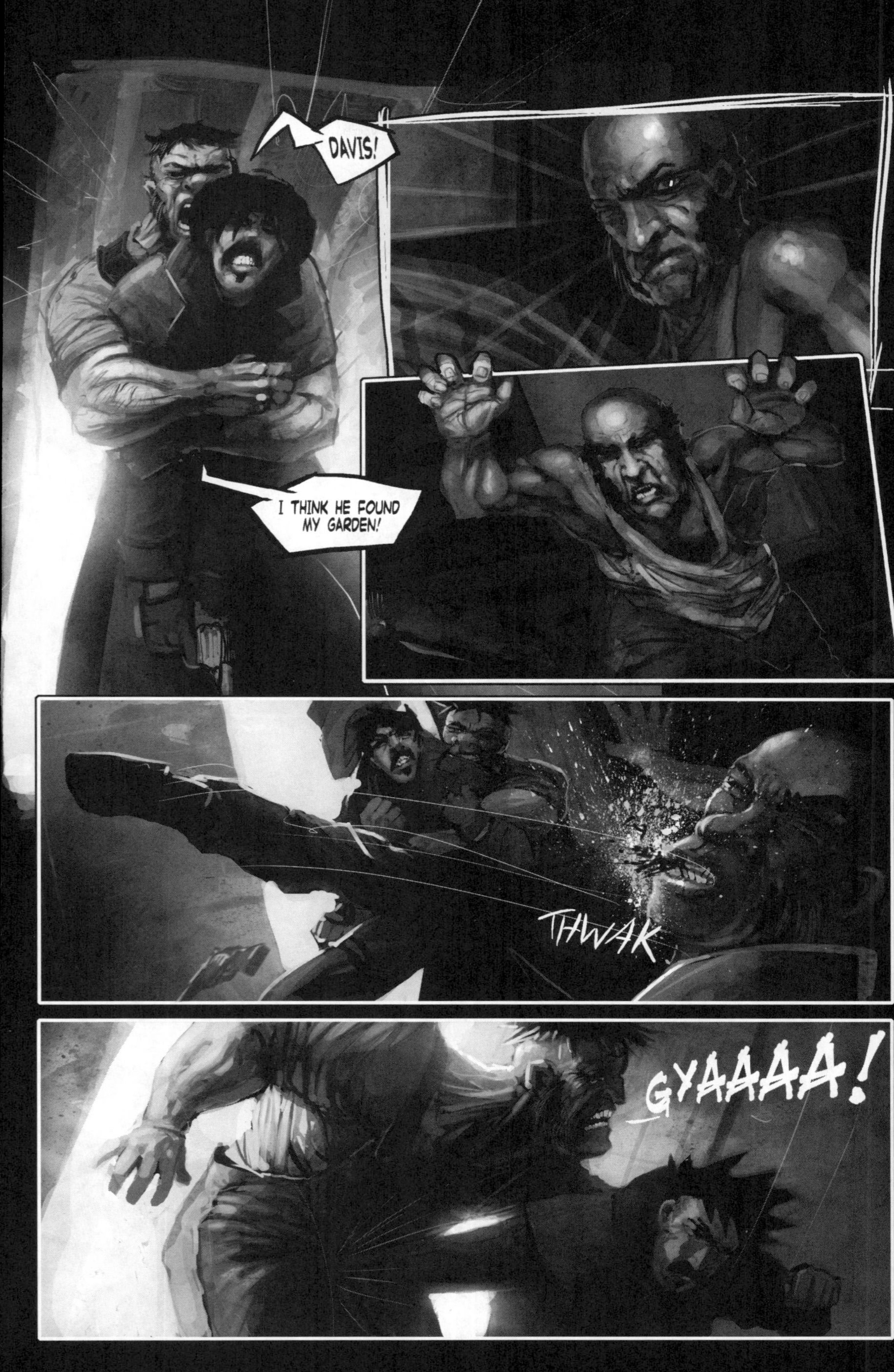
DAVIS!
I THINK HE FOUND MY GARDEN!
THWAK
GYAAAA!

A GARDEN.

JESUS.

THWUMP

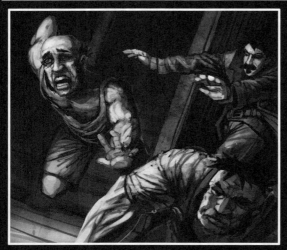

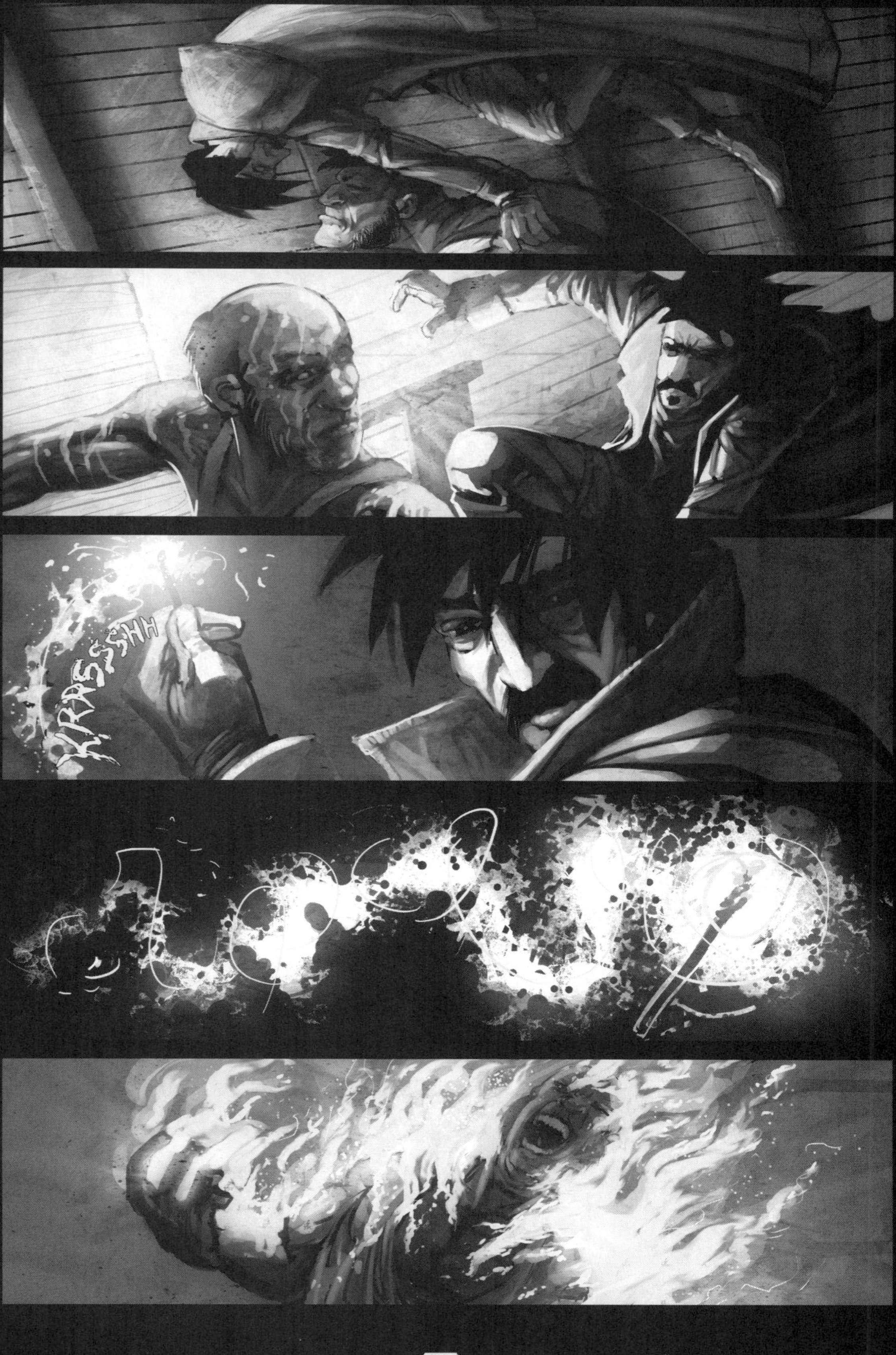
KRASSSSHH

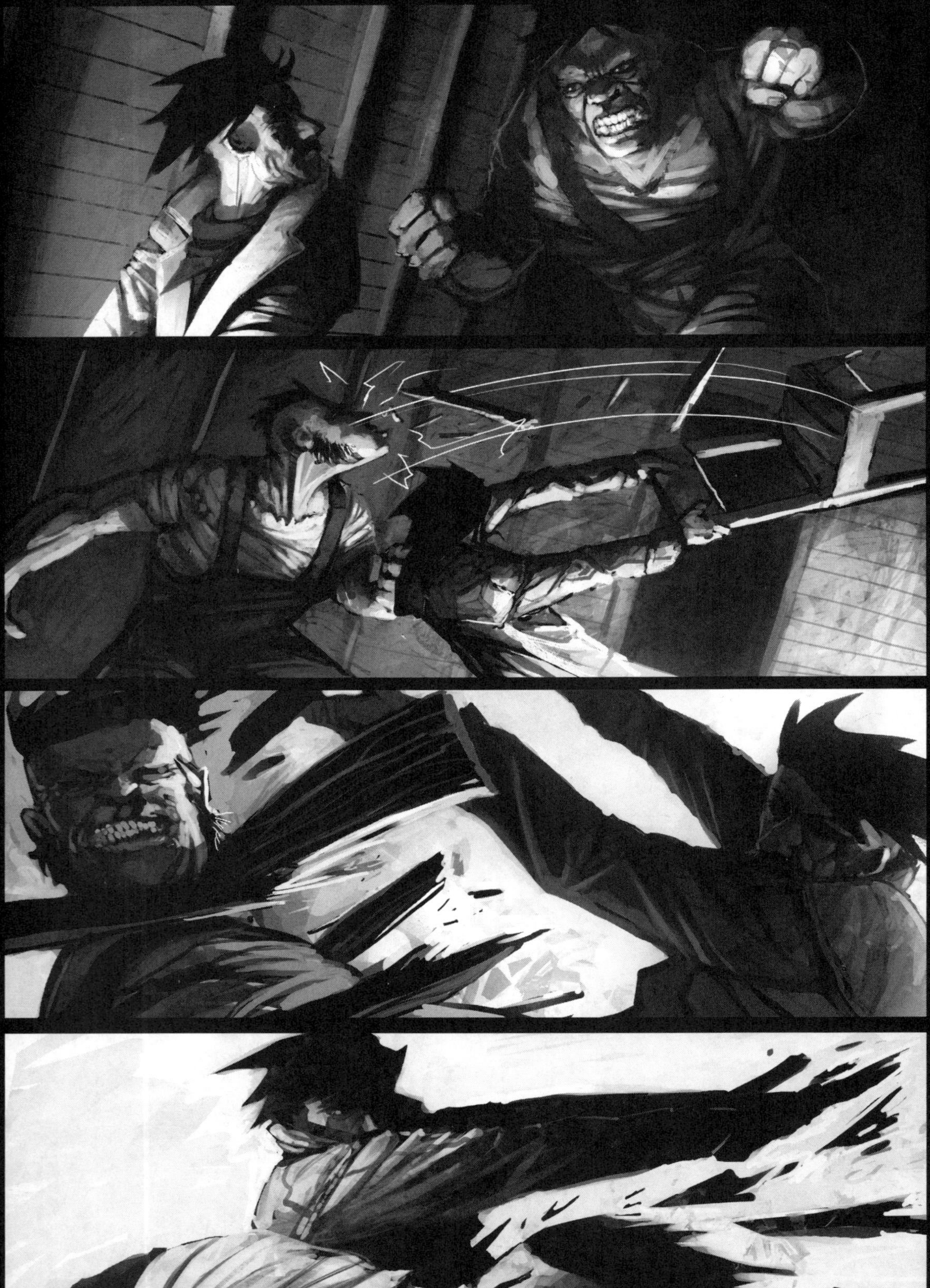

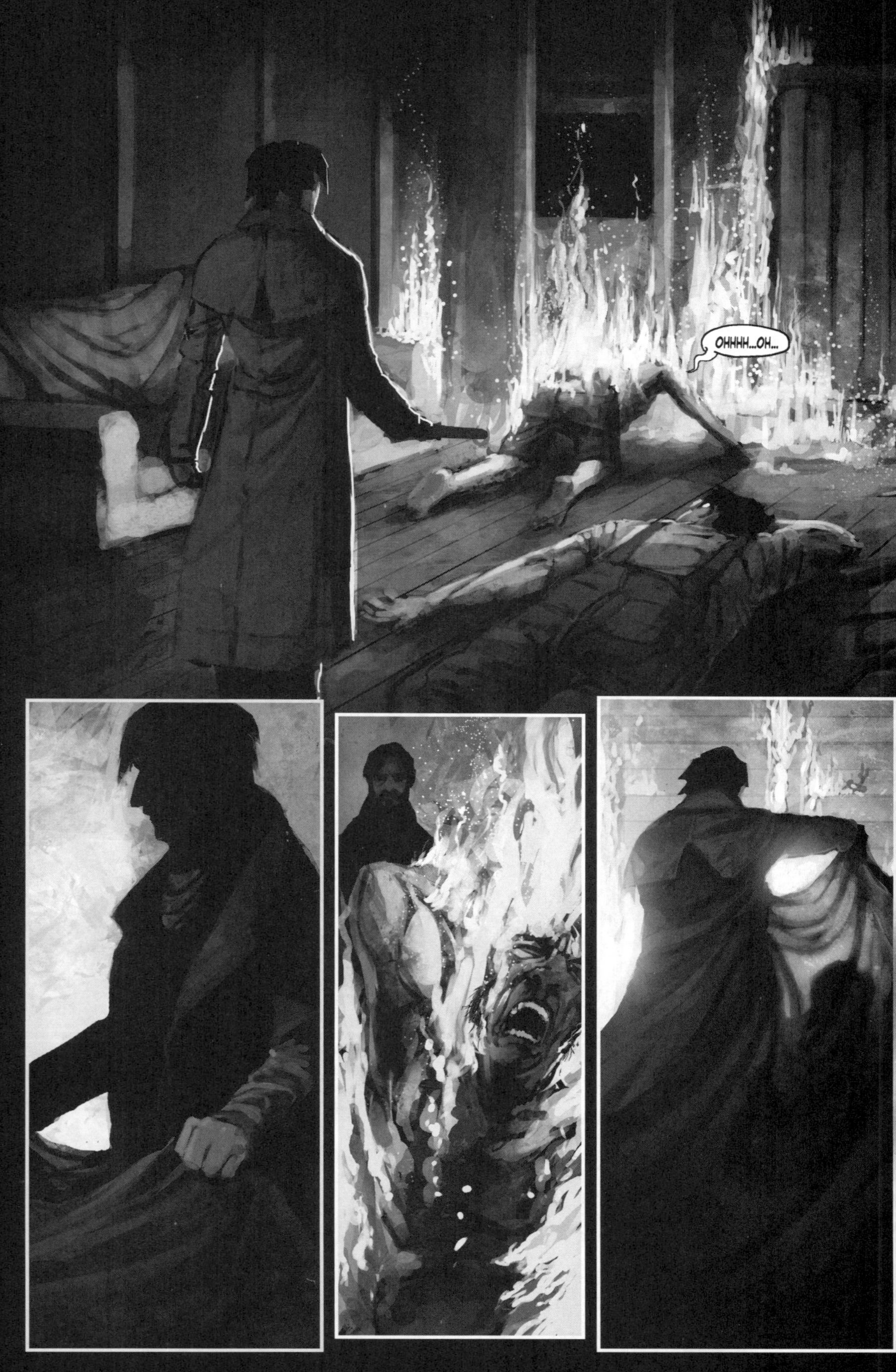
OHHHH...OH...

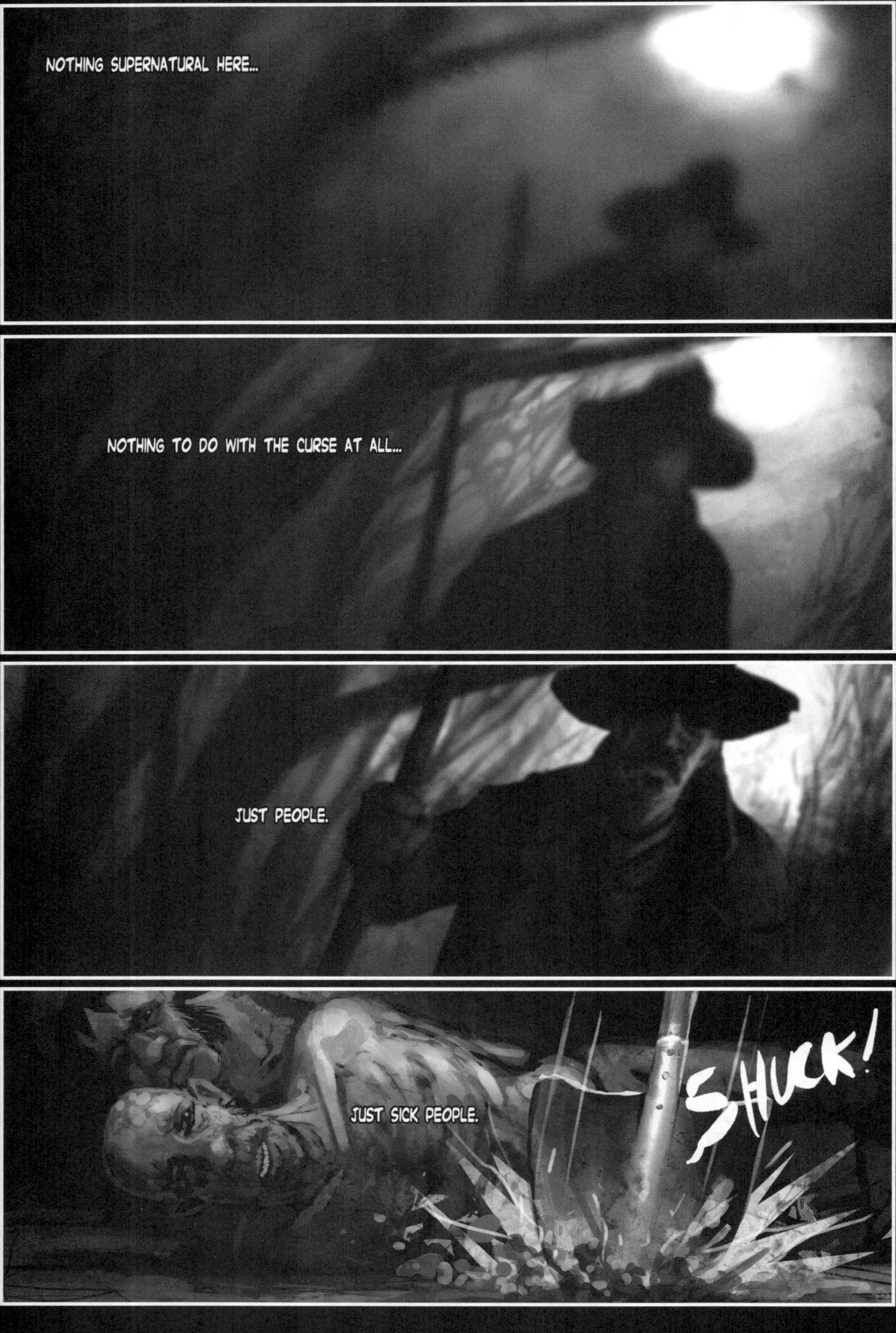
NOTHING SUPERNATURAL HERE...
NOTHING TO DO WITH THE CURSE AT ALL...
JUST PEOPLE.
JUST SICK PEOPLE.
SHUCK!

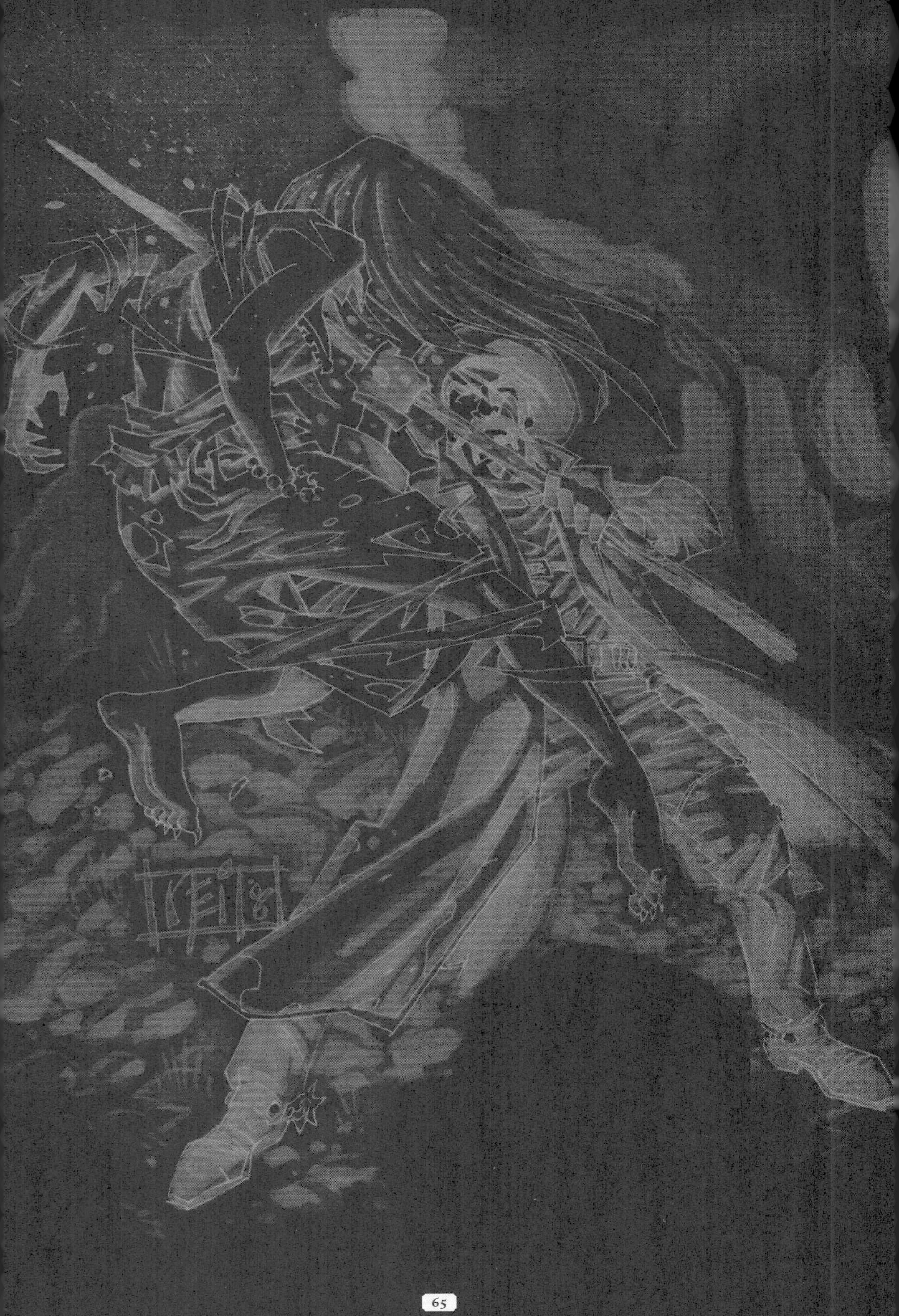

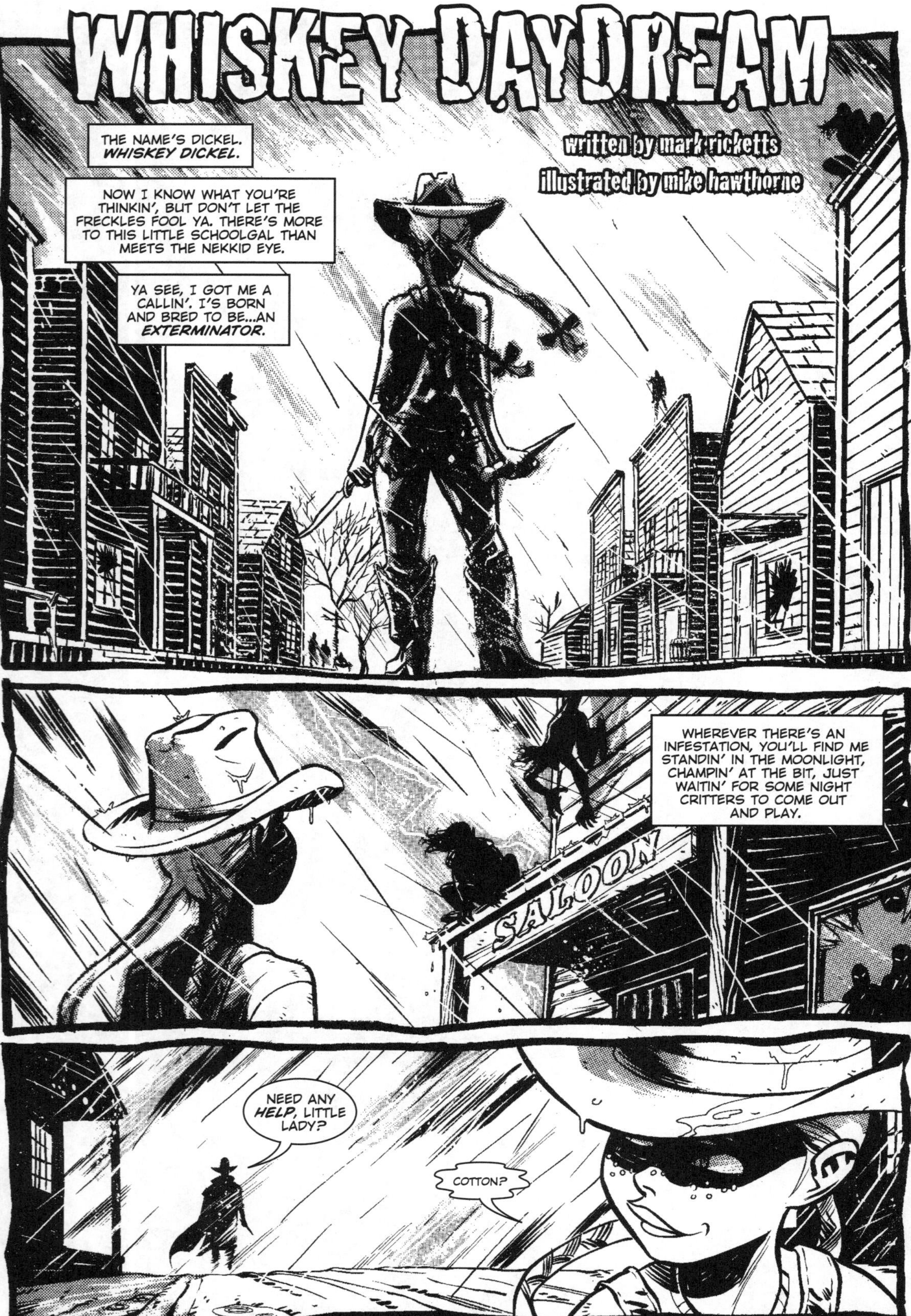
WHISKEY DAYDREAM
written by mark ricketts
illustrated by mike hawthorne
THE NAME'S DICKEL. *WHISKEY DICKEL.*
NOW I KNOW WHAT YOU'RE THINKIN', BUT DON'T LET THE FRECKLES FOOL YA. THERE'S MORE TO THIS LITTLE SCHOOLGAL THAN MEETS THE NEKKID EYE.
YA SEE, I GOT ME A CALLIN'. I'S BORN AND BRED TO BE...AN *EXTERMINATOR*.
WHEREVER THERE'S AN INFESTATION, YOU'LL FIND ME STANDIN' IN THE MOONLIGHT, CHAMPIN' AT THE BIT, JUST WAITIN' FOR SOME NIGHT CRITTERS TO COME OUT AND PLAY.
SALOON
NEED ANY *HELP*, LITTLE LADY?
COTTON?

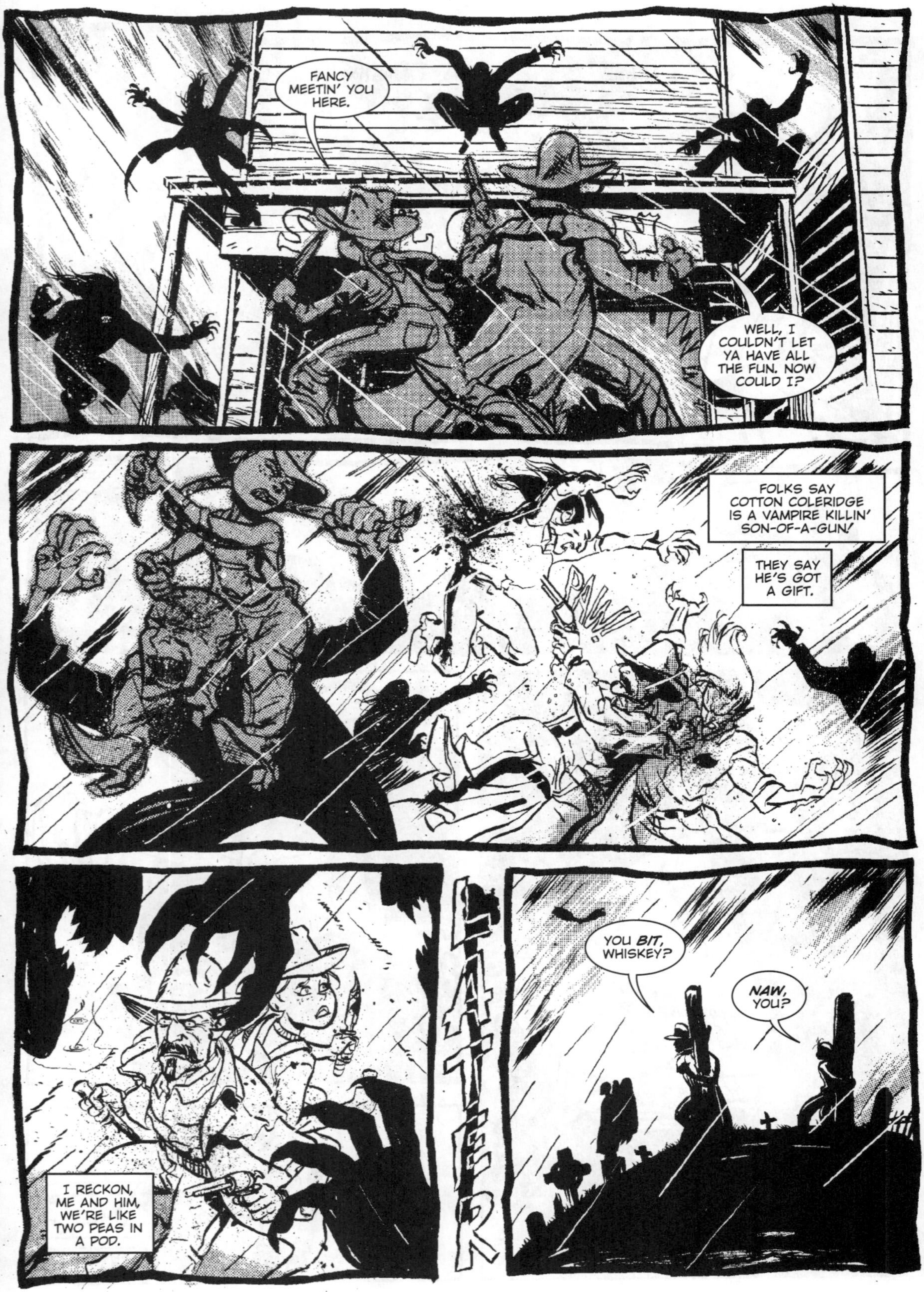
FANCY MEETIN' YOU HERE.
WELL, I COULDN'T LET YA HAVE ALL THE FUN. NOW COULD I?
FOLKS SAY COTTON COLERIDGE IS A VAMPIRE KILLIN' SON-OF-A-GUN!
THEY SAY HE'S GOT A GIFT.
I RECKON, ME AND HIM, WE'RE LIKE TWO PEAS IN A POD.
LATER
YOU *BIT*, WHISKEY?
NAW, YOU?

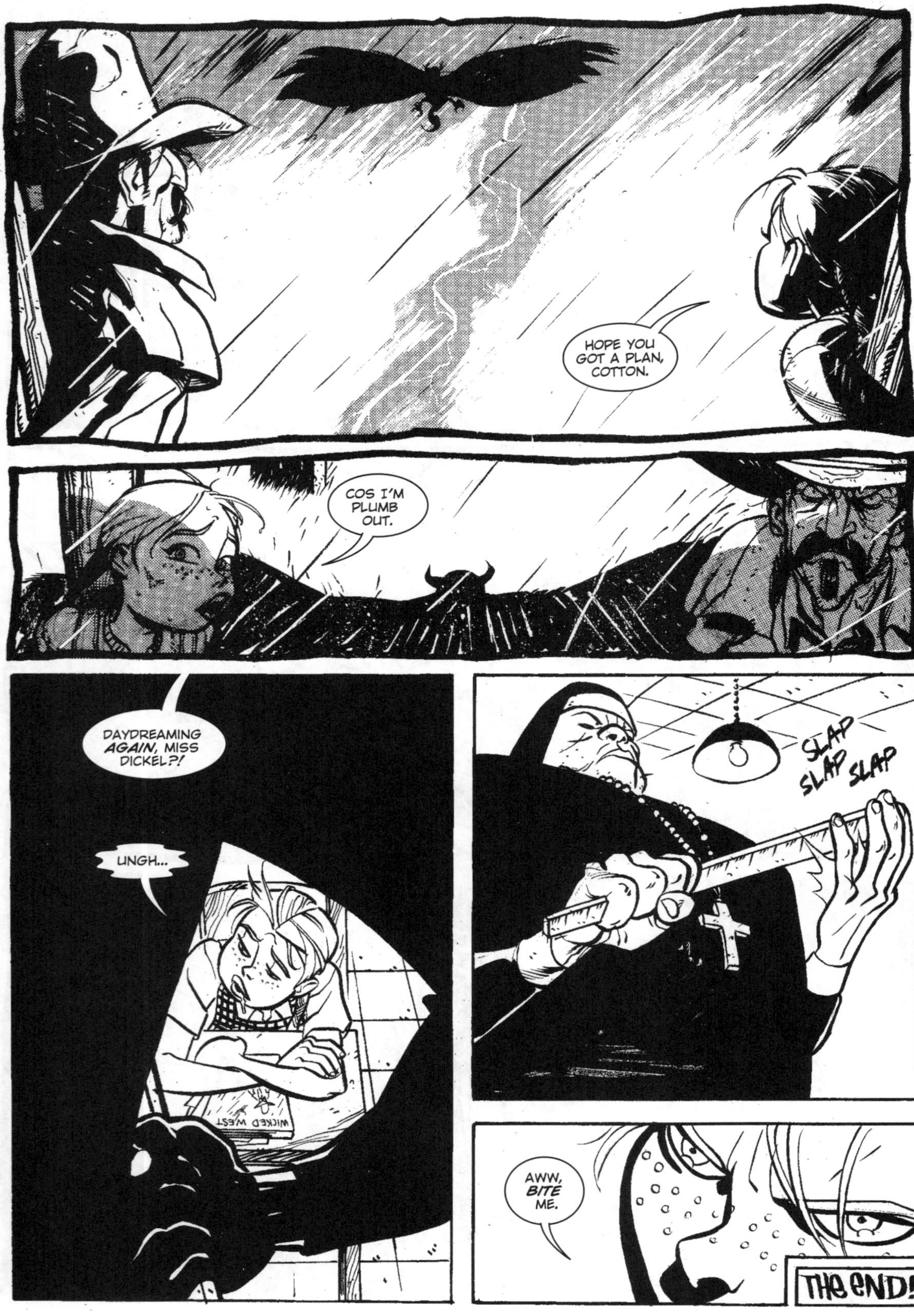
HOPE YOU GOT A PLAN, COTTON.
COS I'M PLUMB OUT.
DAYDREAMING *AGAIN*, MISS DICKEL?!
UNGH...
WICKED WEST
SLAP SLAP SLAP
AWW, *BITE* ME.
THE END!

THE
Assay
Office

StoryBy **Mike Baron**

Illustrations by
Dan Gallagher, Jr.

Sandler had a clear view of the Wallachian Assay Office from his stool in the Greek Palace, a saloon on LaMonte Street in Fort Collins. Two hand-carved Doric columns framed the bar, but the painting over the mirror wasn't Greek. It was French. The kind men liked. Sandler had perched on the bar stool for four days cultivating an image as an amiable cow puncher blowing his wages on booze and Chinese whores. But look closer and Sandler wasn't all that drunk. In fact he wasn't drunk at all. He kept an empty bottle of Old Moose Drool in his pocket and substituted it for the full bottle every time the bar dog served him.

In that time he observed the comings and goings at the Assay Office. The clerk, a cadaverous middle-aged gentleman in a boater and banker's suit, arrived precisely at noon, Monday through Friday, attended by a hulking Pinkerton. Sandler assumed he was a Pinkerton. He had that look—worsted suit, cowboy boots, flinty eyes and a Bisley hog leg tied to his massive thigh.

From noon until nine, when they closed for the day, the Assay Office was busier than a tick on a dog.

They'd found gold in the Mummy Range bringing a flood of humanity. They surged up the Poudre and the Big Thompson spreading to tributaries and creeks like blood filling capillaries. Some outfit called Wallachian Securities owned the Assay Office. Sandler watched men go in with bulging gunnies and emerge unburdened, clutching paper money. He wanted the paper money. After four days he was ready to act. Would have done it already if he hadn't forgotten Easter.

The only problem apart from the Pinkerton was the ranny at the other end of the bar with his face buried in the Fort Collins Coloradoan. Reading about the three hoot owls they'd found west of town Easter morning hanging from their heels from an oak tree, bodies drained of blood. The breathless newspaper account blamed it on bloodthirsty Indians. The whole town was talking about it. Local ministers, of whom there were a multitude, inveighed against the devil's insult against Our Lord and Savior Jesus Christ on His Most Holy of days. Further proof that the land was godless and apocalypse was nigh, as if more were needed.

Friday night was shaping up boisterous. A gang of surveyors from Northwest and Pacific had taken over four tables and were buying drinks and pinching whores like the world was going to end. Every now and then one of them would troop upstairs with a girl. The piano player was killing "Buffalo Gals" and the piano. The street outside was a cacophony of dogs, drunks, jingling wagons and the occasional gunshot. The joint became so crowded Sandler couldn't see the window. He checked his watch. It was nine-thirty. He looked down the bar. The ranny studied his paper. Maybe he just liked that spot.

Sandler gave up his bar stool. He'd scarcely stood when a doxie with cleavage to rival the Black Canyon of the Gunnison plopped down, blasting him with a whiff of lavender. "Thanks, honey!" she growled, swinging her legs out and patting her lap for a skinny man in a string tie. "Right here, honey. We could try it the other way around but I might hurt ya."

Sandler eased his way toward the door. Light in the street was what spilled through doors and windows, and the occasional torch mounted on a wall. Dust hung in layers. Sandler walked the uneven boards to the livery stable down the street. He entered the open door and walked down the stalls to where he'd left Hershey. The horse was glad to see him but its tongue was dry. Sandler stared in disgust at the empty water bucket. He found the Mex who ran the place sleeping in the loft and delivered a stiff kick to his ribs.

"My horse ain't got no water you dumb sumbitch," he snarled. "And here I done paid you five bucks in advance."

The Mex scrambled to his feet. A silver cross hung from a leather thong against his sunken chest in stark contrast to his impoverished appearance. "Sorry, senor! It must have kicked the bucket over. Which horse is yours?"

Sandler shoved the kid toward the edge of the loft. "The sorrel in the last stall. That's why I paid you five bucks in advance! And don't tell me she kicked the bucket over. That bucket's dry as a pyramid. Ahmina be back for my horse in fifteen minutes. You think you can get her watered and saddled for me? That's another five bucks."

The kid smiled. "Sure, senor. You bet!"

"Good. I don't enjoy kickin' ya. See you in fifteen."

Sandler stepped into the slow-moving river of humanity. He was the kind of man your gaze would sweep over without snagging. Middle-sized, middle-aged, with a mustache and a shapeless felt hat he'd bought from a butcher in St. Louis. His sheepskin coat covered his Colt Dragoon. The Closed sign hung in the assay office door, but gas light gleamed

Not being of a religious bent, Sandler had spent Easter at a blind pig off the Overland Trail where he sipped whiskey and watched Parishioners roll by in their Sunday best. It had not always been thus. Once, Sandler had believed in God and observed religious ceremonies. But the frontier had a way of coarsening a man. At least that's what Sandler told himself.

The ranny had been reading the same page all day. He had the upright posture of a former military man, eyes like an ironclad's gun slots, handlebar mustache, strapped like a gunfighter. The ranny too had been watching the Assay Office. What to do. Sandler'd had it in his craw to lift that Assay Office since passing through last fall. He could beat the ranny to the punch and hope for the best. He could make the ranny an offer. Or he could take the ranny out before he made his move. Sandler needed a three-sided coin. He was no good slapping leather. Taking out the ranny looked to be more trouble than it was worth. If he approached the man, the ranny might become suspicious or decide he didn't need Sandler. Then Sandler ran the risk of being back shot. Nope. His best bet was stick to the plan. He'd hit the office at ten while they were still counting.

behind the drawn muslin. Dust hung two feet deep so you could hardly see your boots. A sizeable mob churned through the gully-dry street in search of drink, sex, food, warmth, love, redemption. Sandler wanted money. It was pay day.

At the end of the block he hooked back through the alley dividing a wood frame dry goods store from a red brick bank. He patted the bank wall affectionately, his right boot landing in something soft and squishy. A cur looked up from its bone and snarled.

Sandler held his hands up in a placating gesture. "Easy now." He'd always had a way with animals. He planned to buy a ranch up Montana way, bring up a passel of those tough little Mustangs from Oklahoma, breed them, sell them to other ranchers. Get some dogs. Maybe some mules.

Sandler slipped out the back of the alley quiet as a cat, clung to the shadows of the wall, his piercing eyes sweeping up and down the weed-filled high desert that stretched north and west to the foothills. The lights from a few ranches glowed in the distance. A million stars gleamed, outlining the dragon's backbone of the Front Range.

As Sandler approached the back of the assay office he withdrew his Colt, holding it tight against his head. Five feet from the office the rear door opened and the Pinkerton came out whistling a Stephen Foster tune. Sandler leaped forward and brought the barrel of his Dragoon straight down on the man's bowler with tree splitting force. The impact rang up Sandler's arm all the way to his tailbone. He stepped back, pulling back the hammer.

The Pinkerton turned toward him with an expression of surprise. A trickle of blood ran from beneath the creased bowler and the Pinkerton fell to the earth with a thump, sending up a cloud of dust. Sandler leaped over the prostrate detective and confronted the startled clerk just inside the door. The man wore a banker's vest, a string tie, and glass spectacles. He was as bald on top as Pike's Peak and his mouth hung open in a nearly perfect circle.

"Ah…ah…ah…" he said.

Sandler leveled the Dragoon at the clerk's head. "Hand over the paper money, sir."

The clerk looked with alarm at the heavy canvas sack he held. Keeping the gun pointed at the man's chest, Sandler jerked the bag from the clerk's grip. Sandler could feel the rustle of paper money, but something else too. Something heavy. And there were only two heavies you put in a sack in these parts: gold or silver.

"Now you keep shet and I won't have to lay my barrel across your skull. Ahmina have to tie you up and then I'll be on my way."

The tinkle of broken glass resonated from the front of the store. The clerk started, afraid to move, afraid to turn away. A dark shape entered the corridor behind the clerk and grew larger, an artillery shell headed Sandler's way.

Sandler lifted his right leg, planted his boot in the center of the clerk's chest and shoved him backward into the man running toward them. He didn't wait to see the results. He was out the door and sprinting for the stables, the heavy canvas sack jingling in his hand.

"Stop!" a strange voice echoed from the back of the shop. But Sandler wasn't stopping until he'd put hill and range between himself and whomever had taken it upon themselves to bust up his party. It was the ranny. Sandler knew it. He wasn't about to share his loot or take a bullet in the noggin from some low-rent thief. Sandler had worked too long on this one. As he ran he worried that the horse wouldn't be ready.

But the horse was ready, the grinning Mexican cinching the saddle as Sandler hot-footed it into the stable. Sandler slapped a Liberty gold coin into the boy's hand, didn't catch the look of wonder as he fastened the canvas sack over Hershey's rump, tying it to the saddle bags on either side. He boosted himself into the saddle, cantered out of the livery and threaded among wagons and knots of slow-moving cow pokes north and west, toward the Poudre.

Hershey was fresh and eager to hit the trail. They followed the Poudre past ranches and the military outpost, keeping wide of the sentry. Starlight was more than sufficient to see the hoof and wheel-worn trail. An hour out of town Sandler topped a slight rise and stopped to reconnoiter. He dismounted, pulled the folding brass eyeglass from its leather case, and lay on the dry sandy soil, propping the scope between two rocks. He hadn't expected trouble, but that fool smashing in the front door was bringing it. Someone was bound to notice the broken window and alert the sheriff.

And here came the fool on a white horse, a perfect target for a man with rifle. Sandler was no bushwhacker. He'd creased skulls before and never killed a man. No, he would simply out run the man. Wasn't a horse alive could match pace with Hershey, part Mustang himself. Horse couldn't do much more than twenty-five miles at a stretch. Not in this country. Not if you wanted your horse to live. The same held true for his lone pursuer. Sandler remounted and pressed on at a steady rate. Past Ted's Place where the Poudre slowed and spread some parties had set up camp. Sandler kept going.

An hour later he decided to lay up for the night. There were only a few hours of darkness left. Sandler led Hershey on foot up a gentle canyon trail, out of sight of the main trail, and made a cold camp. He gave Hershey a rub-down before turning in.

Sandler was up at first light, Hershey grazing mountain clover. Sandler remounted the saddle and canvas bag, filled his water bag from the trickle of cold mountain water, and headed back down the trail. Rounding a bend, he stopped in his tracks. Three hundred yards away on the other side of a stand of aspen at the base of a pile of scree came the ranny in ten gallon hat and duster. The ranny stopped when he spotted Sandler. The ranny used his hat to wave, as if greeting a long-lost uncle. The ranny held up his hands to indicate he meant no harm. The ranny wanted to parlay.

Sandler dismounted, unsheathed his Hawken, packed it with powder and ball, settled down behind a chest-high rock and drew a bead on the ground about a foot in front of the ranny's horse and cocked the heavy hammer. The shot echoed off the canyon walls and reverberated. The ball split the earth two feet in front of the white horse which hardly deigned to toss its head. The ranny stared for a minute, slowly shook his head and kept coming. He entered the aspen and was no longer visible.

Sandler's backbone prickled like the devil had stepped on his grave. This wasn't natural. The ranny had to know Sandler could wait for him on this end of the forest and put a hole through his chest big enough to mount a flag. Sandler had got a good look at the ranny's horse. Big. Bigger than Hershey, with hooves the size of Clydesdales. No mountain horse. Sandler looked up, toward the southwest. The trail wound through boulders but seemed passable. Sandler would simply outpace the ranny. No Clydesdale could follow Hershey up a mountain.

Sandler sheathed his Hawken, got in the saddle and leaned forward, close to Hershey's neck. "Onward and upward," he said, holding on to the mane, feeling Hershey's powerful muscles slide beneath his hand. Up the trail they scrambled, sometimes next to a rushing rivulet, sometimes amid the ponderosa and ground hugging juniper. The sun rose. The rocks heated. By midday both horse and rider were sweating profusely. Sandler dismounted, removed his duster. Hershey was breathing heavily, sweat evaporating in the hot dry wind as soon as it appeared. Crisp mountain water pooled nearby. Sandler let Hershey drink, once again swung himself into the saddle, leaned forward until his mouth was at the horse's ear.

It was slow, rugged going, and Sandler frequently had to dismount and lead Hershey up a particularly rocky incline. It was only by chance Sandler spotted the nest of rattlers beneath a rocky overhang of a table rock that otherwise would have made a perfect picnic spot. The trail twisted and turned so often it was no longer possible to see the ranny, but Sandler had no doubt he was still there. The man had that look of inevitability. Sandler hoped the rattlesnakes would get him, or at least spook his horse.

All afternoon they climbed, stopping often to let Hershey catch his breath. As dusk fell they found themselves on the east slope and were soon plunged into shadow, a foretaste of the darkness to come. They stopped at a high mountain meadow rife with crocuses and Spanish bayonet. Sandler rubbed down his exhausted horse. It wasn't until he'd laid up on a bed of pine needles, Hawken at the ready, that Sandler realized he had yet to look in the bag. He pulled it close, undid the heavy leather snaps and poured the contents out on his saddle blanket. Several smaller cotton bags filled with paper money: tens, twenties, fifties and hundreds. And a cotton bag containing something made of metal, stitched shut with sail twine.

Sandler used his Arkansas toothpick to cut the twine. He upended the bag. Out tumbled an eight inch silver crucifix. It gleamed softly with a dull patina of age, inlaid with Latin. It made no sense. The assay office dealt in raw ore. But nothing about the assay office had made sense since Sandler made his move.

Night rose. A wolf howled from a nearby ridge. Hershey whinnied. Sandler's keen ears picked up the snap of a twig. With a sigh, he loaded and primed the Hawken, his hands moving by rote in the dark. The ranny wasn't hard to spot—not on that white horse. Sandler waited until the ranny had completely entered the meadow before drawing back the Hawken's hammer with an ominous click.

"That's far enough," Sandler said in a hard voice.

The man held his hands up. "I'm not lookin' for a gunfight. I'm lookin' to save your life."

"How's that?" Sandler said from concealment.

"You robbed the assay office. You took something—a big silver cross, right?"

"What about it?"

"They were holding the cross for someone. That someone is now after you."

Sandler laughed out loud. "That's a pile of horse manure, mister. Only one knows I'm here is you. Maybe they was holding that cross for you, is that it? Why don'tcha just come out and say so?"

"No." The stranger got off his horse, walked toward Sandler.

"Stop right there," Sandler said.

The stranger stopped. "They were holding the cross for Osterrich Vilknap. He is a demon, a creature of the night. He follows that silver cross the way a cur follows a gut wagon. He can smell it. He knows exactly where it is. He comes on wings."

"You're mad," Sandler barked. "Mister, I've had about enough of your foofaraw. Give me one good reason why I shouldn't put a bullet through your skull."

"Vilknap's a vampire."

Sandler hooted. "You are crazy.""You heard about those bad men found drained of blood."

"Injuns. That's why they call 'em bloodthirsty."

"Wasn't Indians. Sir, I'm going to toss you one of my cartridges. I want you to take a look at it and tell me what you see."

Sandler hunkered down where he didn't present a clear shot. The man pulled a bullet from his belt and with an easy underhand motion pitched it over the jumble of rocks. It landed next to Sandler. Without taking his eyes off the stranger Sandler scooped the cartridge up. It gleamed silver in the moonlight.

"Silver cartridges?" Sandler said.

"You know why?"

"I heard that tale, alongwith Pecos Bill and the Side Hill Hodag." This time as the man approached Sandler let him.

"Name's Cotton Coleridge. I've been on the trail of this particular bloodsucker for six months. Osterrich Vilknap wants the cross to kill another vampire

named Kristof. Kristof killed those three outlaws and a lot more we don't know about."

"But you ain't after him."

"I sure as hell am. That's why I need that cross. But first I have to stop Vilknap. I'm looking to make a double play."

"Well hell," Sandler said. "If you're fixin' to join the party, I might as well build a fire."

"Don't do that. It'll hurt our night vision and we're going to need it." Sandler hunkered down, removed a deerskin quiver from his back. The quiver was covered with a button-down flat and appeared to hold a long metal object about the size of a branding iron.

Sandler removed a plug of chewing tobacco from his coat pocket, bit off a chunk, offered it to Coleridge, who took it. "How'd you find me?"

"I've been on your trail since you creased that Pinkerton. Wouldn't blame you if you'd bushwhacked me, no more'n I blame you for being a thief and a robber."

"That's mighty white of you, Mr. Coleridge. Way I look at it, that assay office was cheating honest miners. I'm just cheating the assay office."

Coleridge's eyes turned to gun slits. He cocked his head to the sky, bending the broad rim of his had to form a curve behind his ear. "The cross!" he hissed. "Where is it?"

Coleridge's fear was contagious. Sandler scanned the sky, hands rummaging for the bag with the cross. He placed it at Sandler's knees. Sandler removed the cross and held it up. "Do you see the inscription? It was put there by Pope Alexander II in 1124 to end Kristof's reign of terror. The Knights Templar pursued him for centuries."

"Kristof's still around, you're saying."

"Yes," Coleridge spoke in a low, urgent voice. "But he's not our problem. He won't go anywhere near this cross. Our problem is Vilknap, Kristof's sworn enemy." Coleridge tossed the cross into a circle of starlight on the meadow. He withdrew his six-shooter, cocked it, and laid it on the ground next to him. He opened the deerskin quiver and removed a silver branding iron ending in a six-pointed star.

Wolves howled in concert. Dozens of them, more than any pack of wolves Sandler had ever heard. They fell silent. The night held its breath. A leathery snap fell to earth, followed by another, and another, the beating of great wings. They grew loud as a tornado bearing down. Sandler grabbed his Hawken and stood aiming wildly at the heavens.

"Where are you, damn you?"

The blow came from behind, knocking Sandler off his feet and sending the Hawken tumbling into the brush. Sandler's skull thumped off a rock. Spots crowded the edge of his vision. An enormous raptor,

Coleridge raised his revolver and fired three silver bullets into Vilknap's chest. Vilknap staggered, regained his balance and smiled. "Ouch. These you call bullets?"

Coleridge leaped at Vilknap swinging the silver branding iron in both gloved hands like a baseball player. The silver club caught the vampire in the side of the thigh knocking him to his knees. Vilknap grasped the earth and looked up with red eyes lit from within, his face no longer human. He lunged. Coleridge stood his ground and stamped the business end of the brand into the vampire's forehead. The thing fell back screaming in multiple frequencies causing the horses to feather-foot nervously and the wolves to cry despair.

Coleridge bore down on the brand forcing the vampire's head against the ground. Vilknap's flesh began to sizzle. The sizzling spread to his extremities. Vilknap's claws, hair, and clothes went up in flame accompanied by an overpowering stench of sulfur. Coleridge bent to his task, staring unblinking into the face of evil. Not until the creature had been reduced to a smoldering pile of ash did Coleridge relent.

Sandler sat up, head spinning. "Mister Coleridge, my apologies. You done put paid to one of Satan's creatures and saved my life for sure."

Coleridge retrieved the silver cross from beneath the ashes of the demon's foot. "I need the cross myself, for the same reason he did—to destroy Kristoff."

Sandler picked himself up and dusted himself off. He got the bottle of whiskey he kept in his saddlebags. "I reckon this calls for a drink." He availed himself of a hefty slug and handed the bottle to Coleridge, who gratefully accepted.

"Tell me something," Sandler said. "If you and him was after the same vampire, why not let him take the cross and do your dirty work for you?"

"They are liars. He would have killed us just the same. Do you not know what night it is?"

"It's Monday."

"It's the first day of Passover. A Jew vampire like Osterich Vilknap must feast on that night when all devout Jews are protected by the blood of the lamb."

Sandler swallowed. Then a strange thing happened. Deep within his belly where his soul resided he felt a rekindling, a lone Lucifer in the darkness that flamed and roared and filled him with a sense of warmth and belonging, as long forgotten words swam their way to his lips.

"Sh'mah Y'israel…" he began.

wings sixteen feet apart, struck the earth, steel in its shoes sparking off flint. The black wings cantilevered up and disappeared, a sorceror's trick. The creature put one gleaming black leather boot on the silver cross and turned to face Coleridge with a snarl, two inch canines gleaming like ivory in moonlight. The creature became a man wearing a black wool suit, his skull covered with a tight cap of black curly hair that extended along his jawline. The black vest buttoned right up to the blazing white of his shirt, neatly tied four-in-hand around his neck. He curled his claws toward Coleridge. Obsidian nails the size and shape of an eagle's beak protruded from every finger.

"Why do you oppose me, cowboy," the creature hissed in a European accent. "Why" sounded like "Vhy." "Give me the cross and I'll leave you intact. Cross me and I'll take your blood, his," the thing pointed at Sandler, "and the horses'."

❧ THE END ❧

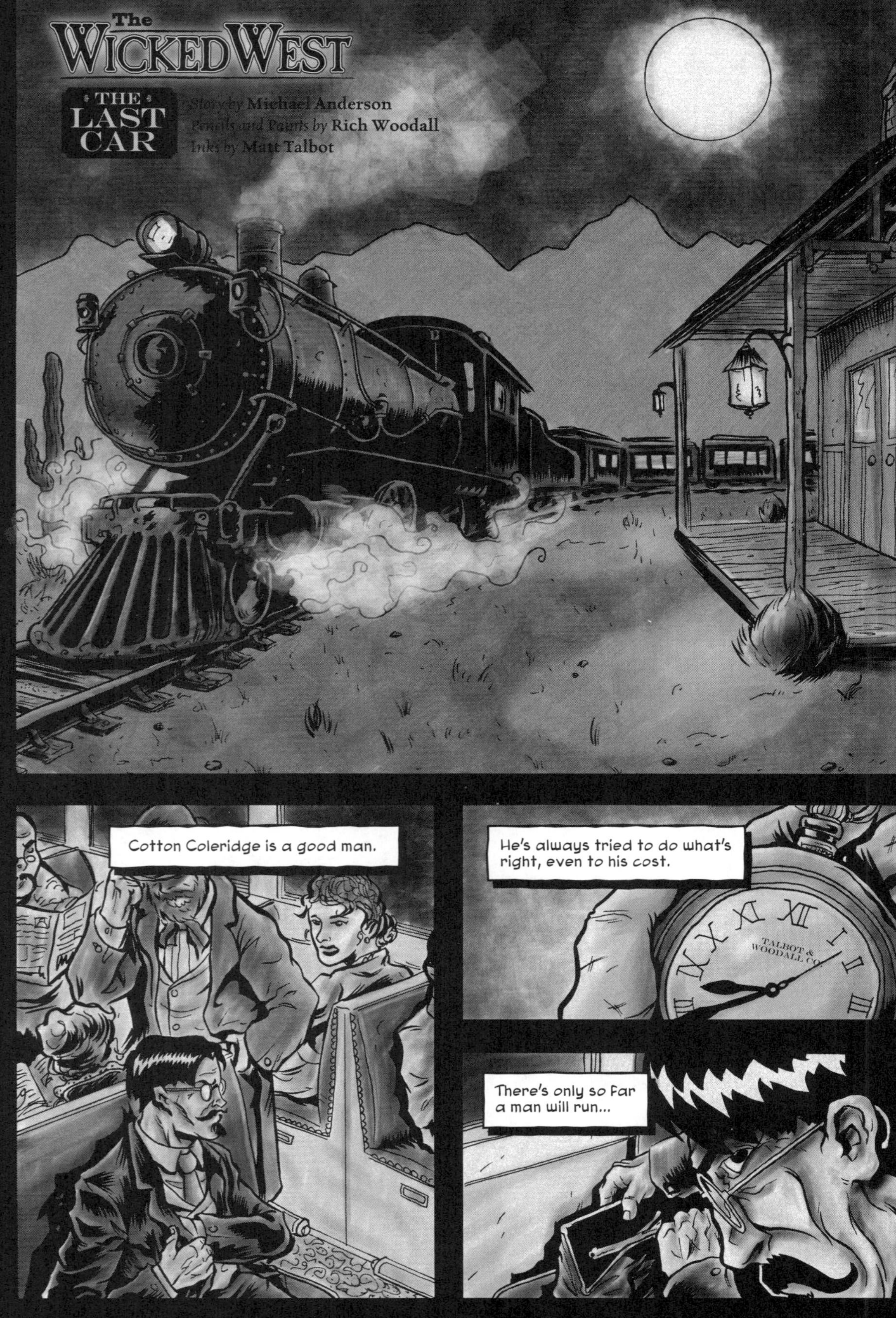
The Wicked West
THE LAST CAR
Story by Michael Anderson
Pencils and Paints by Rich Woodall
Inks by Matt Talbot
Cotton Coleridge is a good man.
He's always tried to do what's right, even to his cost.
TALBOT & WOODALL CO.
There's only so far a man will run...

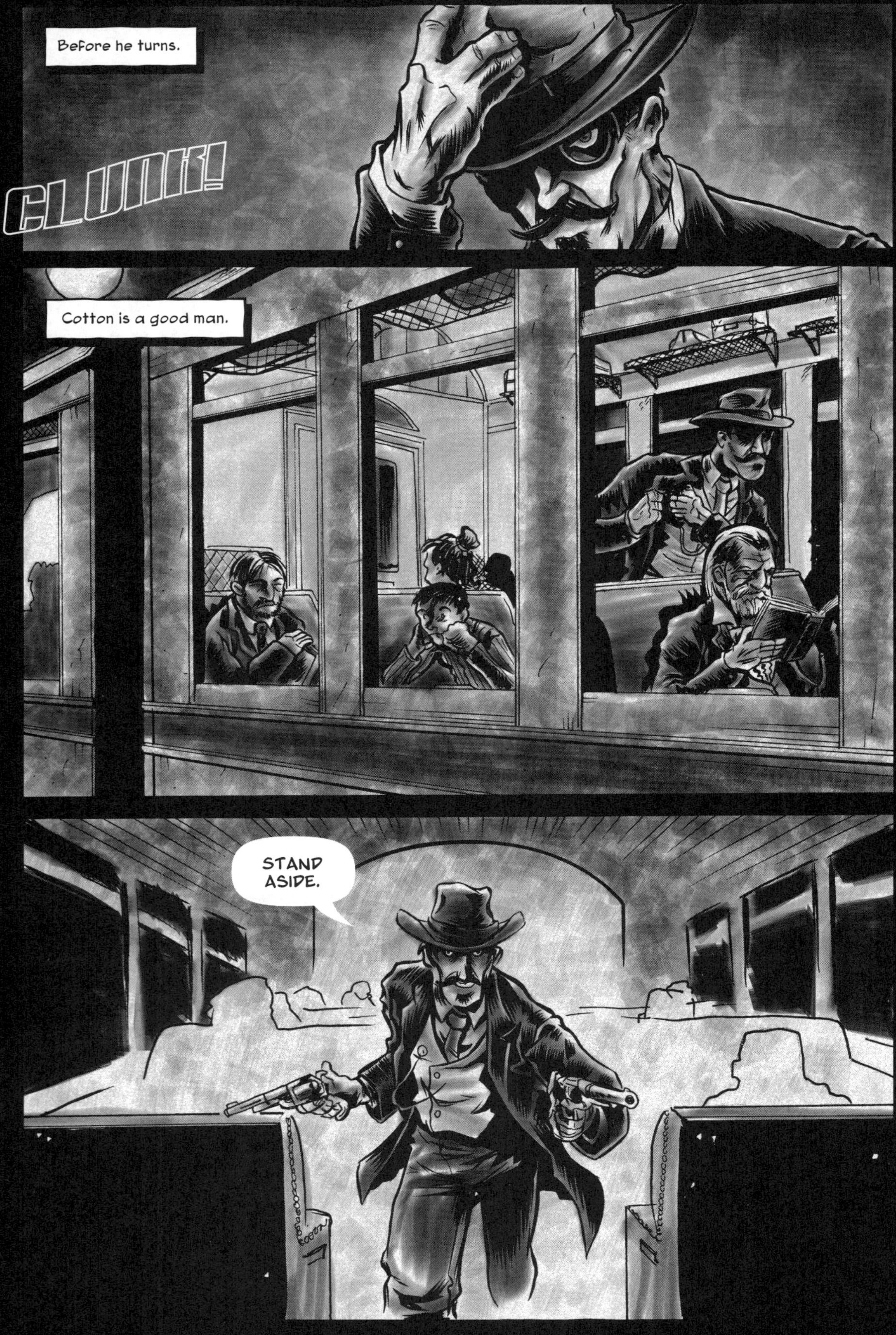
Before he turns.
CLUNK!
Cotton is a good man.
STAND ASIDE.

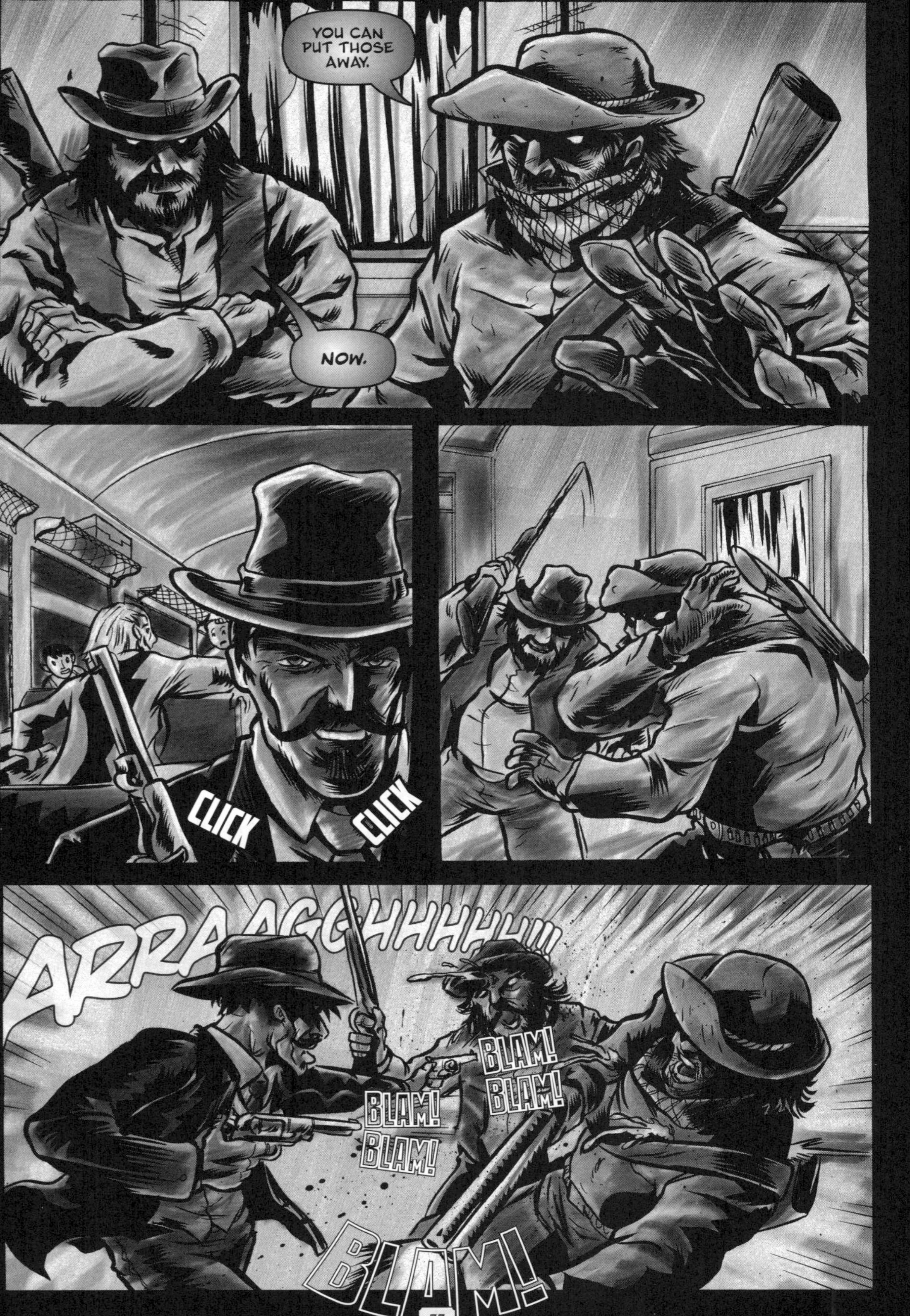
YOU CAN PUT THOSE AWAY.
NOW.
CLICK
CLICK
ARRAAGGHHHHH!!!
BLAM! BLAM!
BLAM! BLAM!
BLAM!

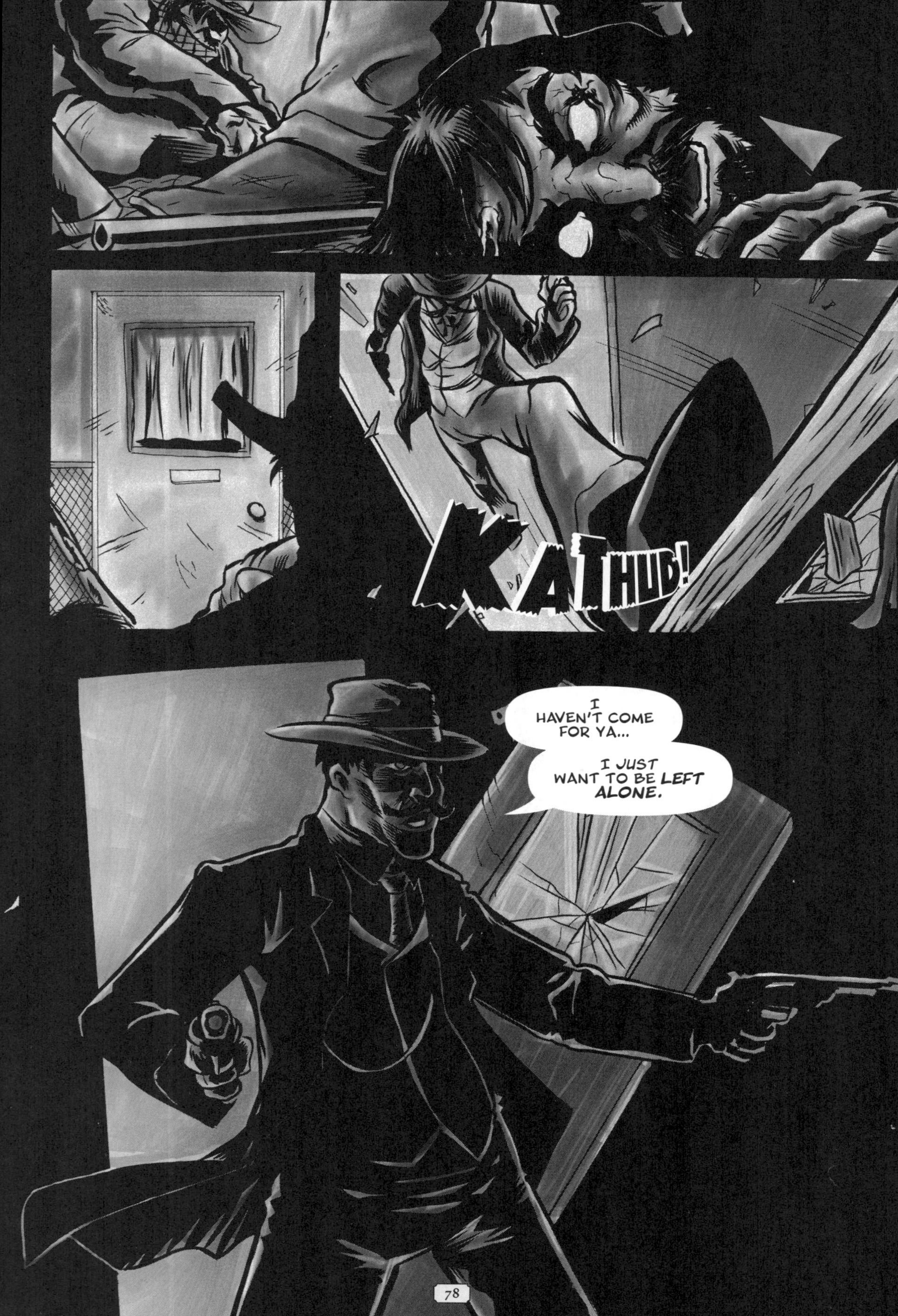
KATHUD!
I HAVEN'T COME FOR YA...
I JUST WANT TO BE LEFT ALONE.

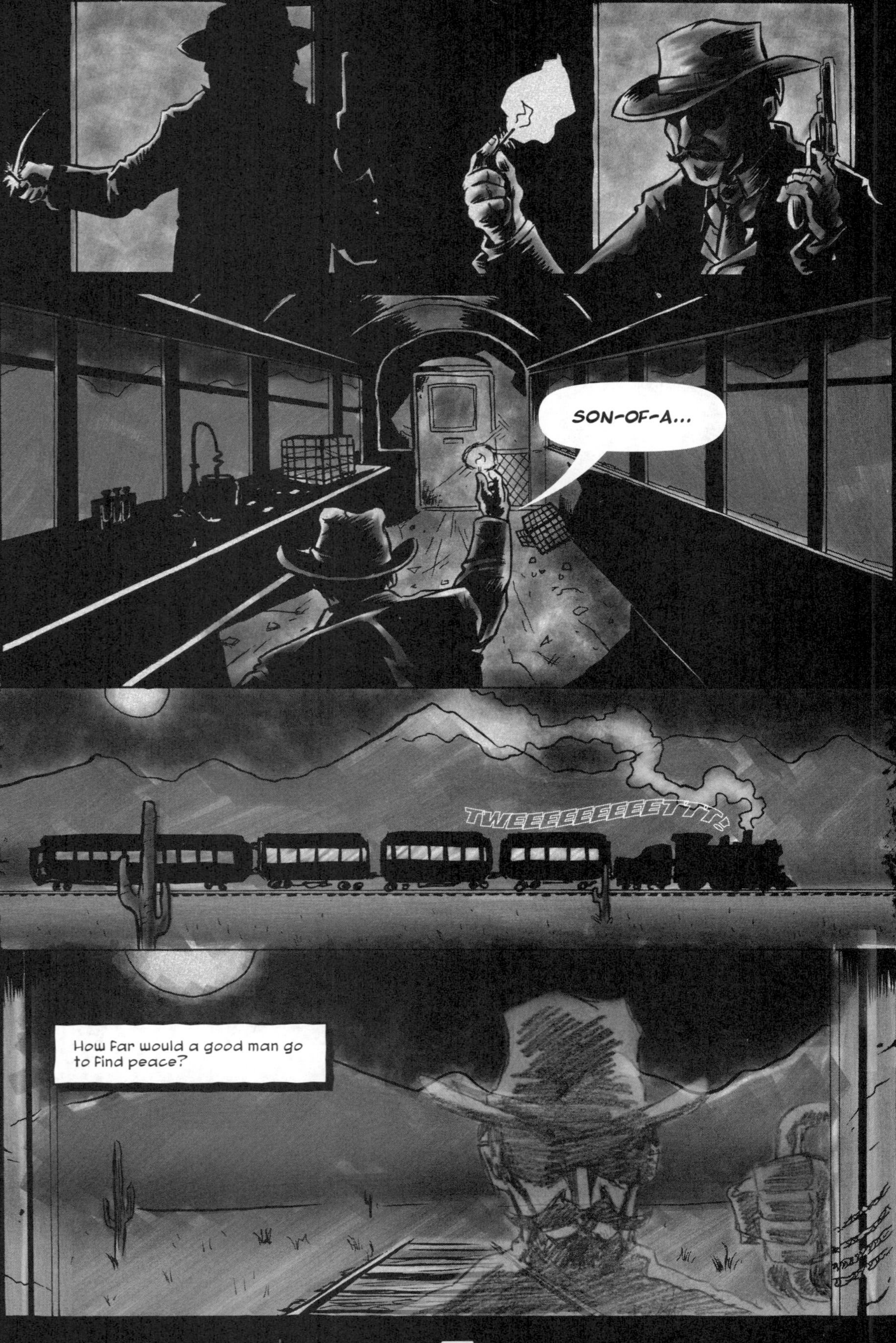
SON-OF-A...
TWEEEEEEEEEETTTT!
How far would a good man go to find peace?

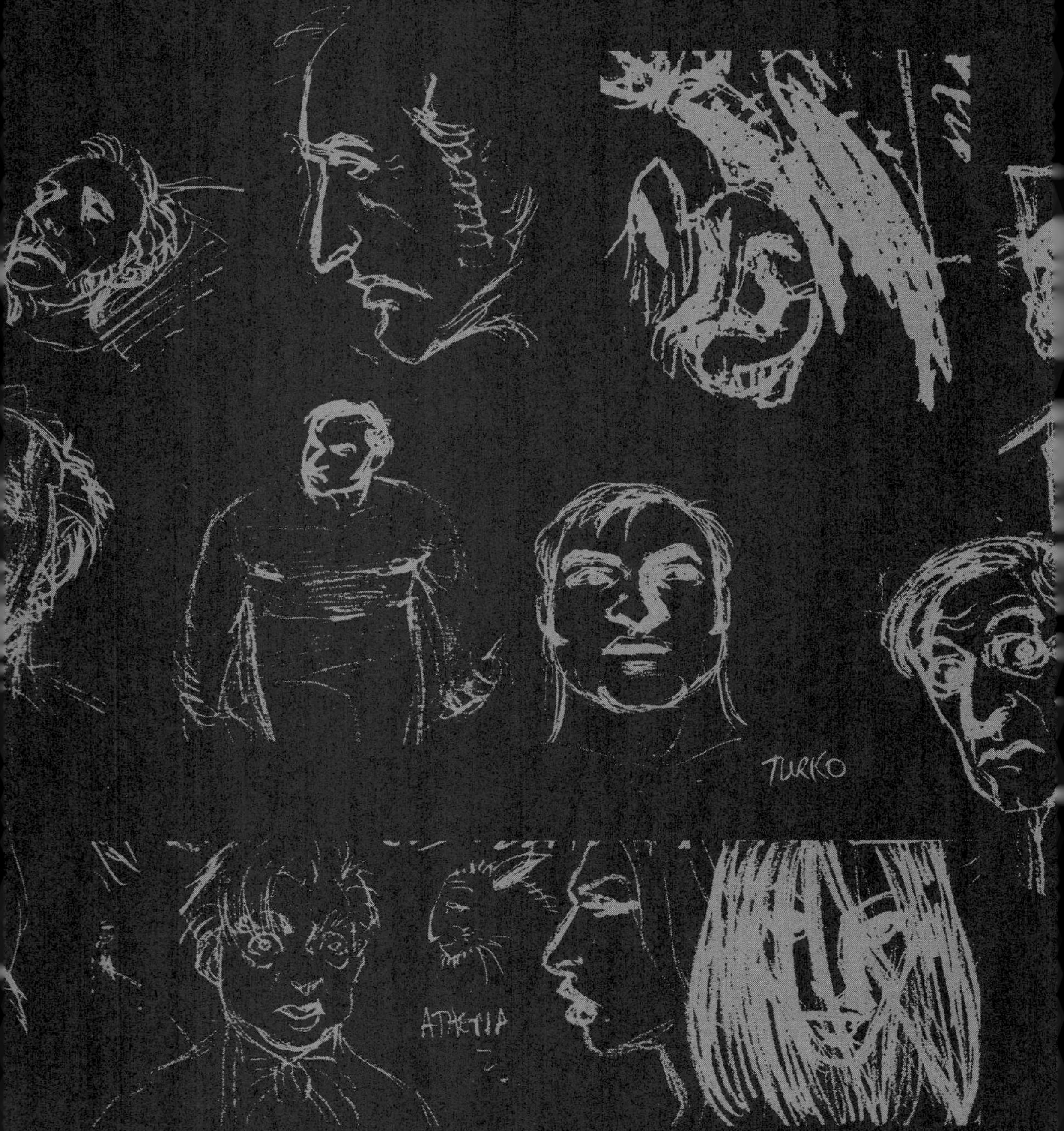
TURKO

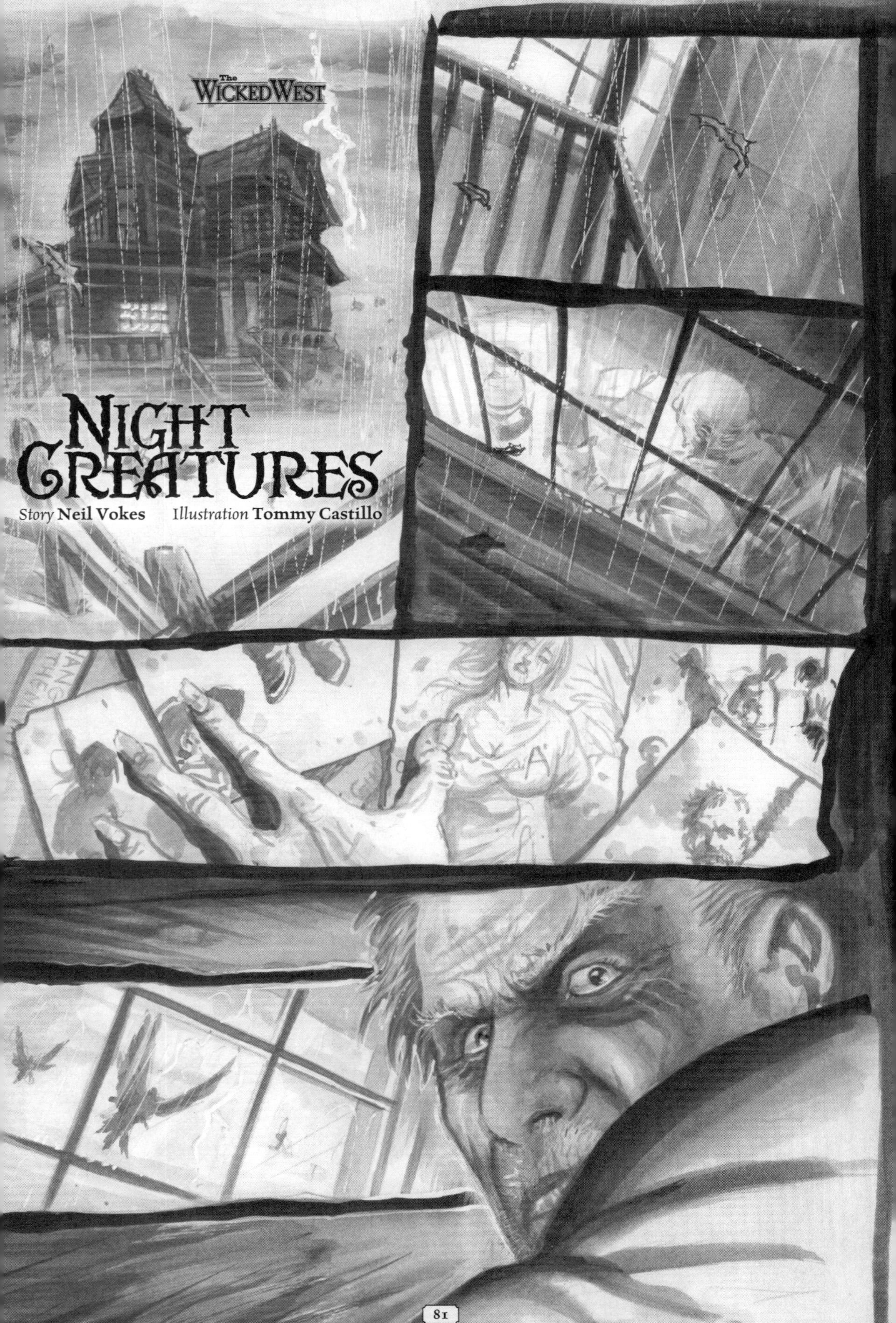
The WICKED WEST
NIGHT CREATURES
Story Neil Vokes Illustration Tommy Castillo

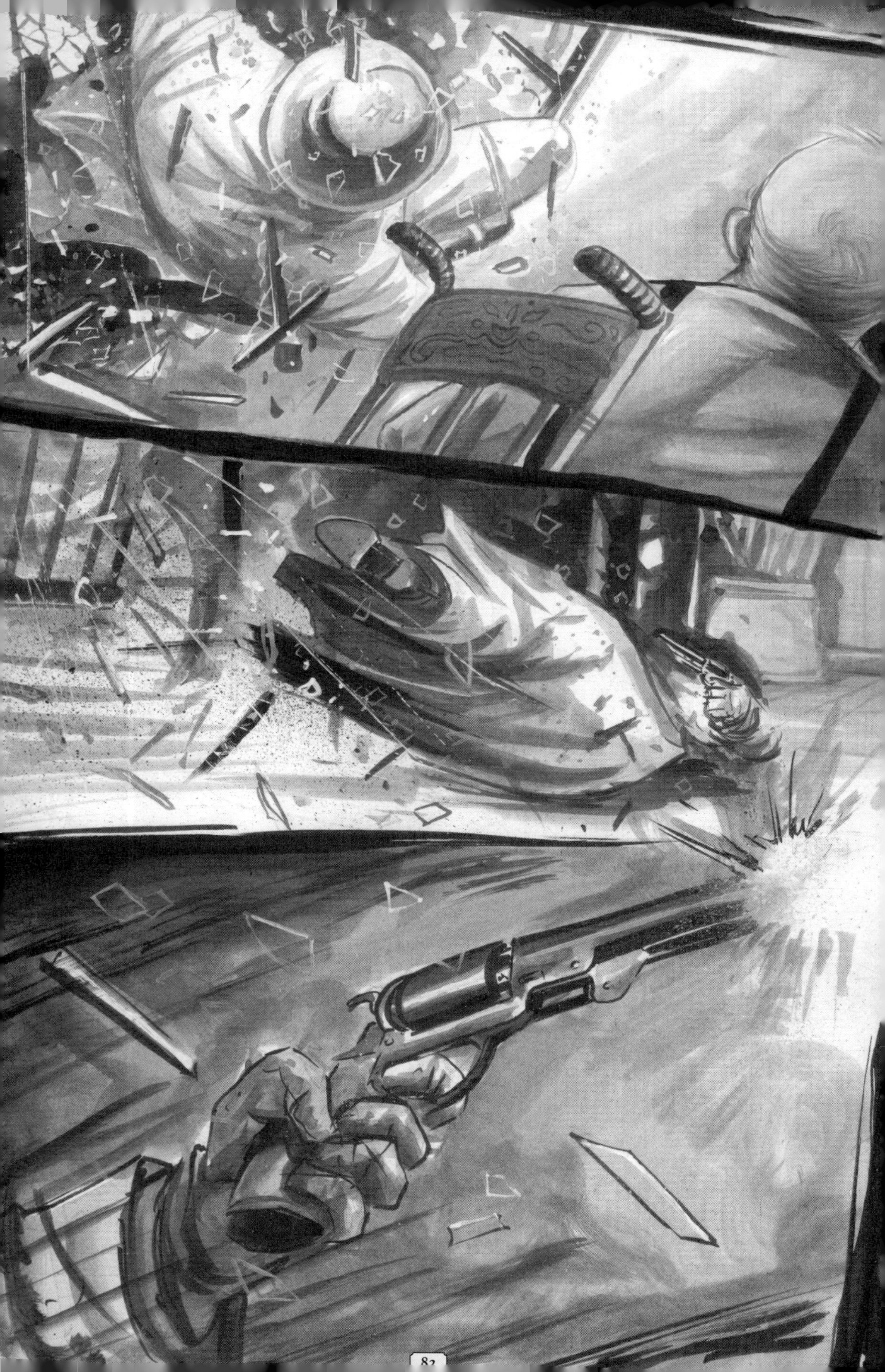

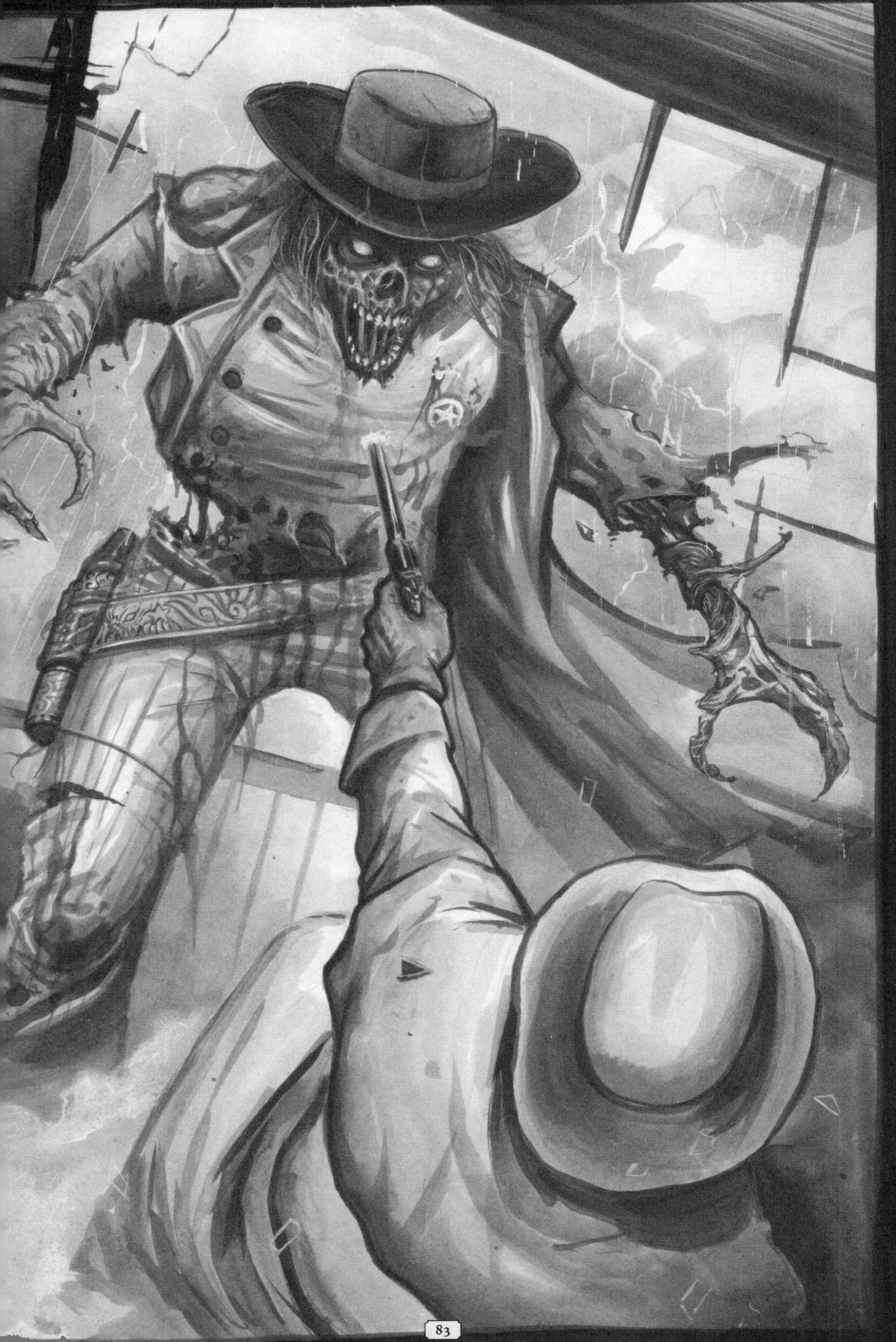

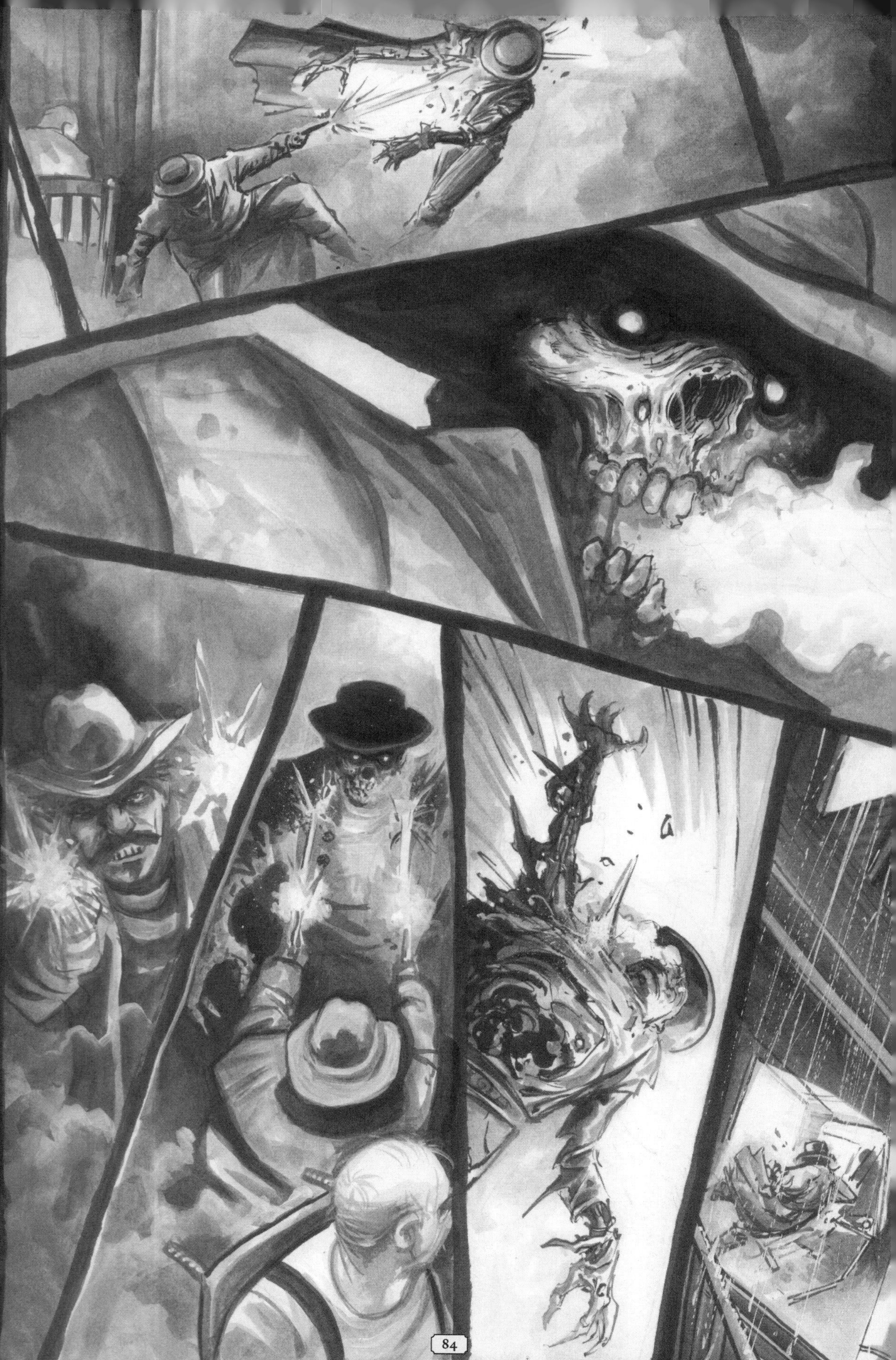

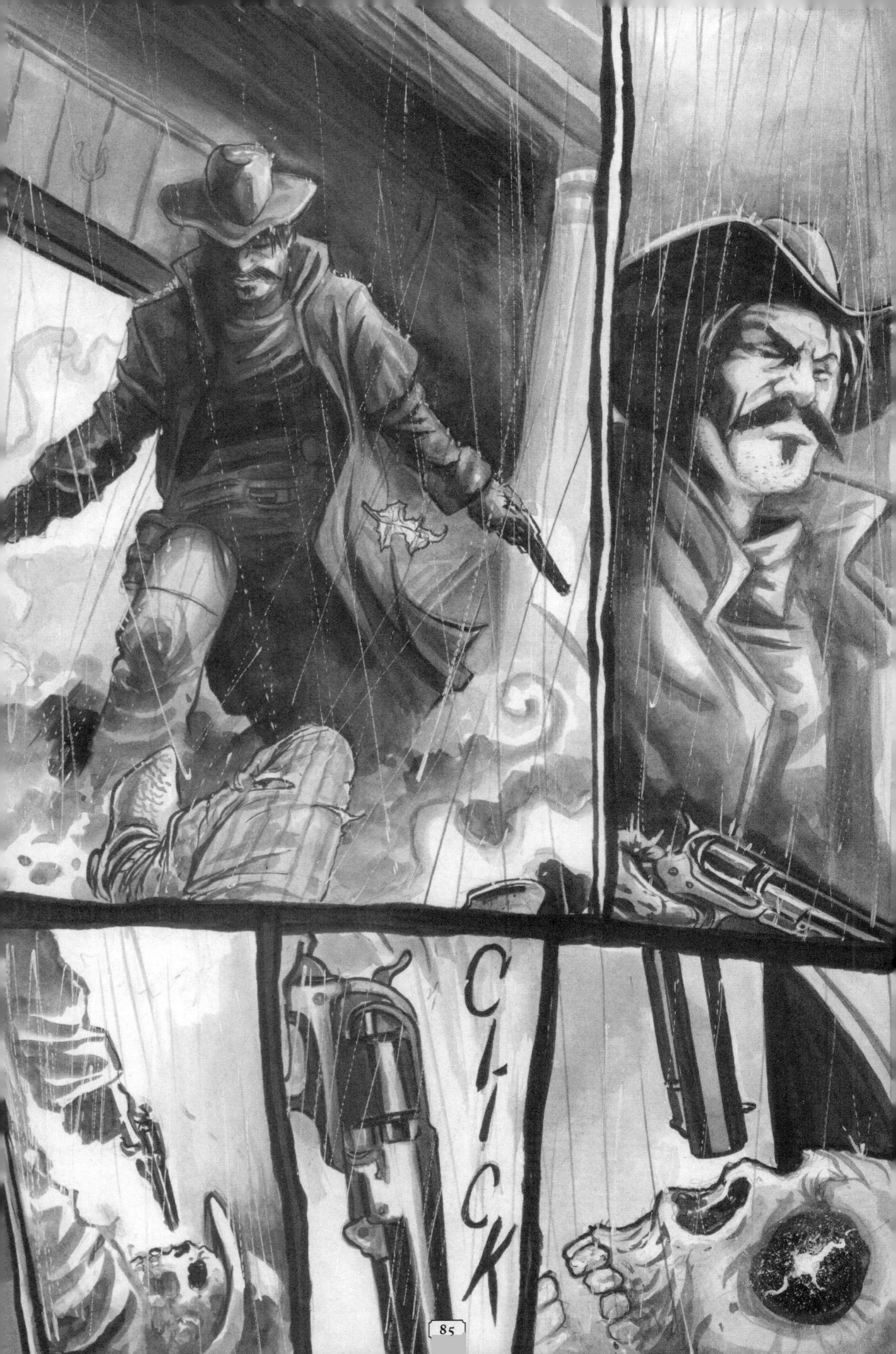
CLICK

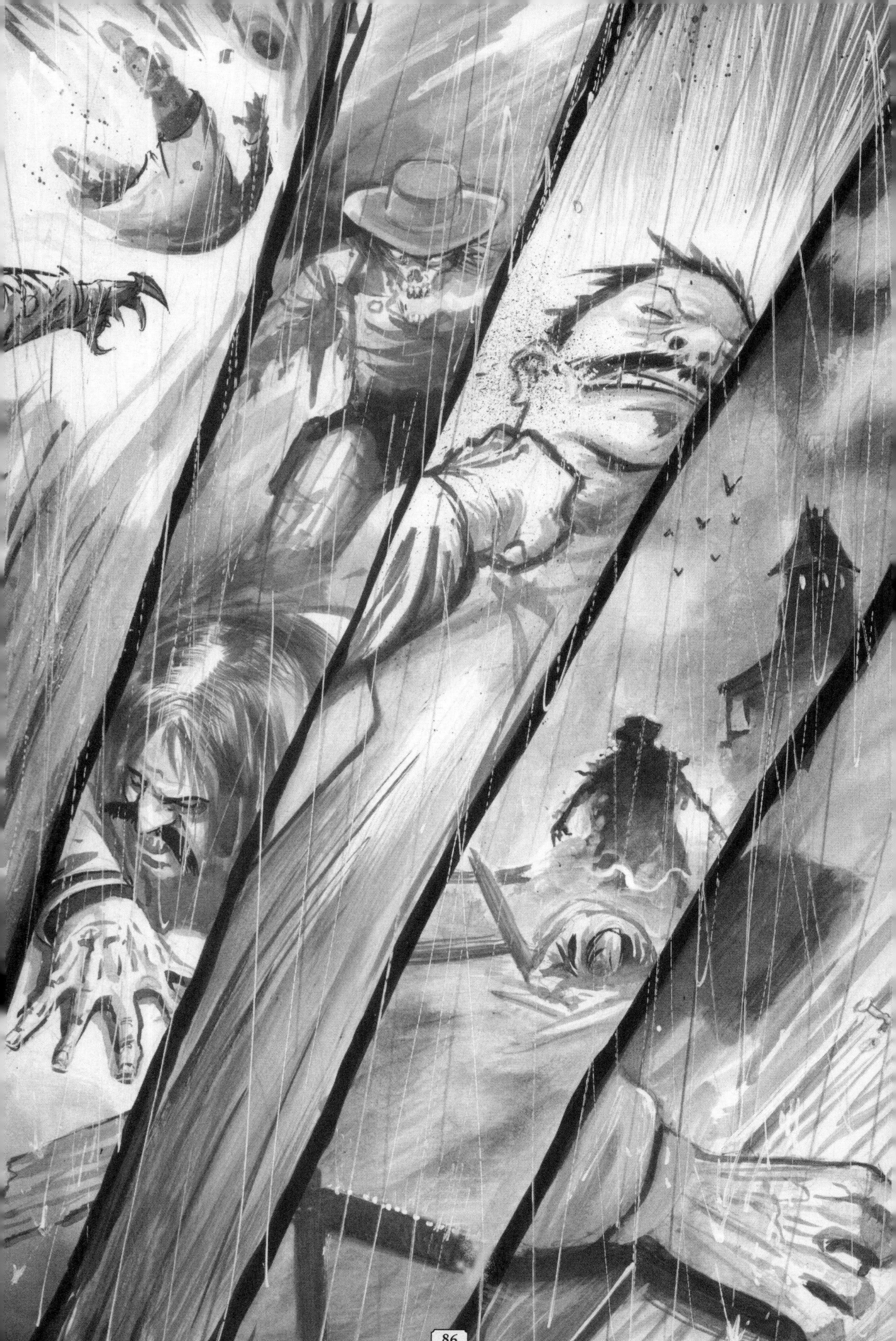

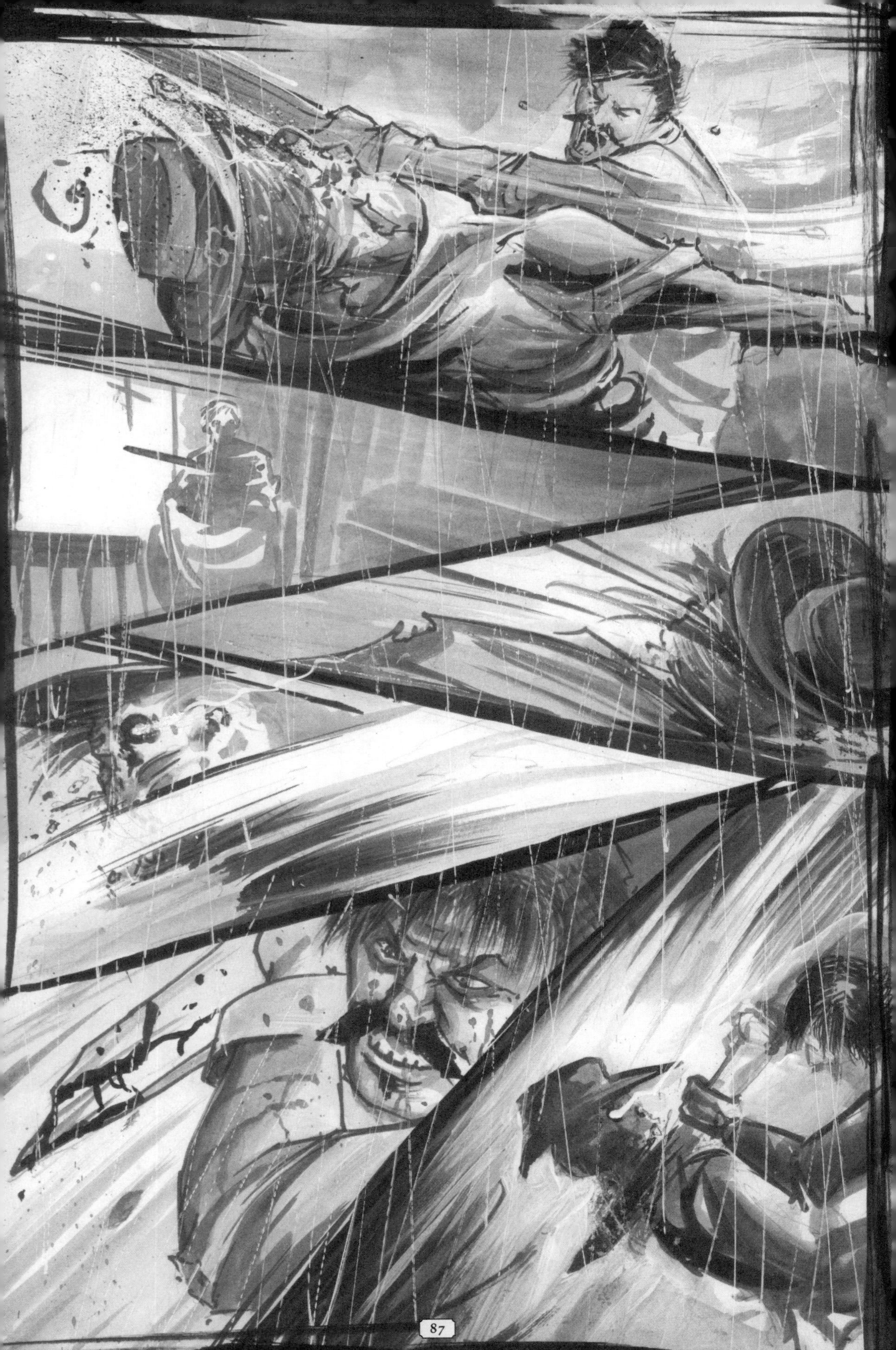

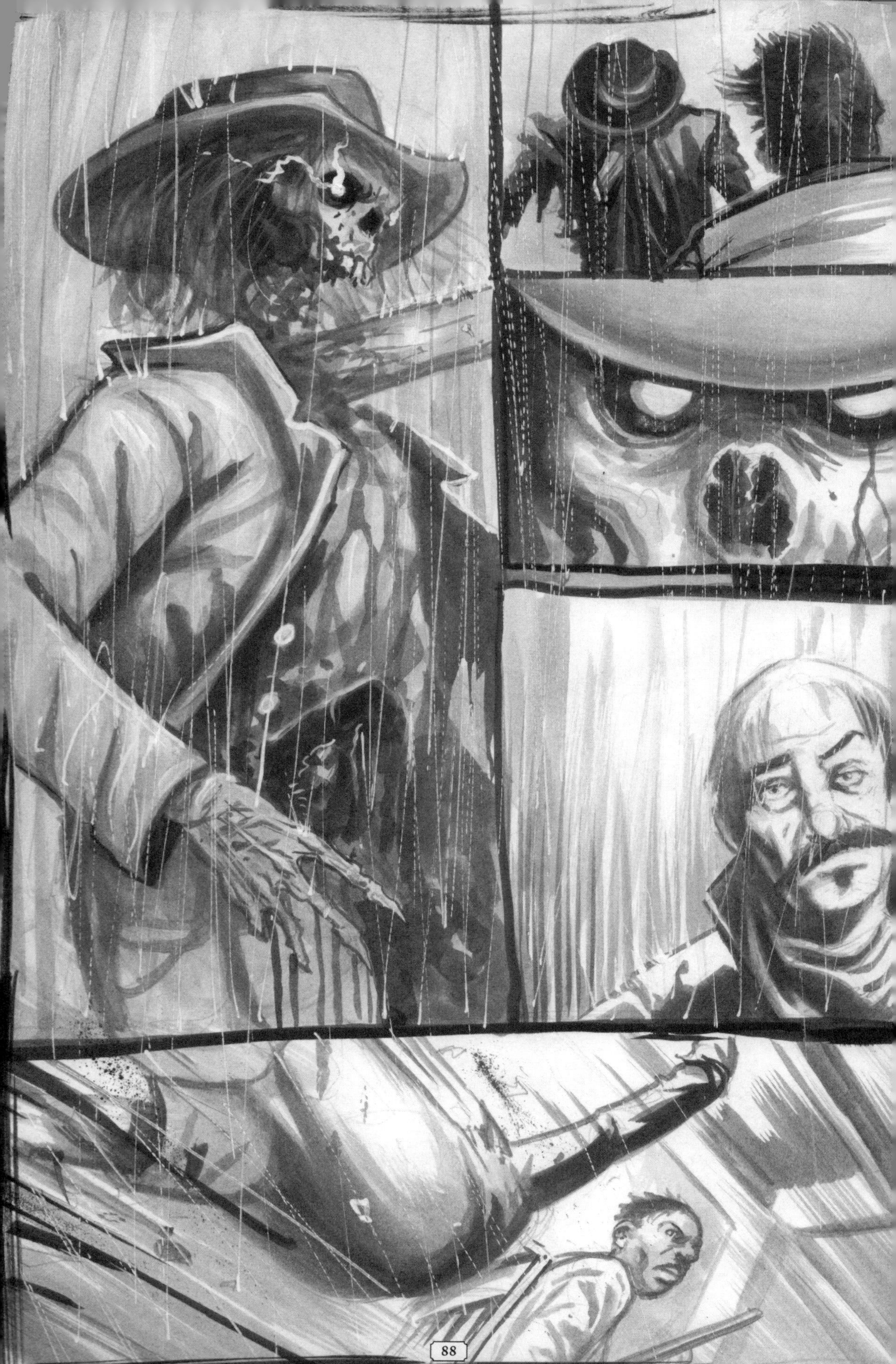

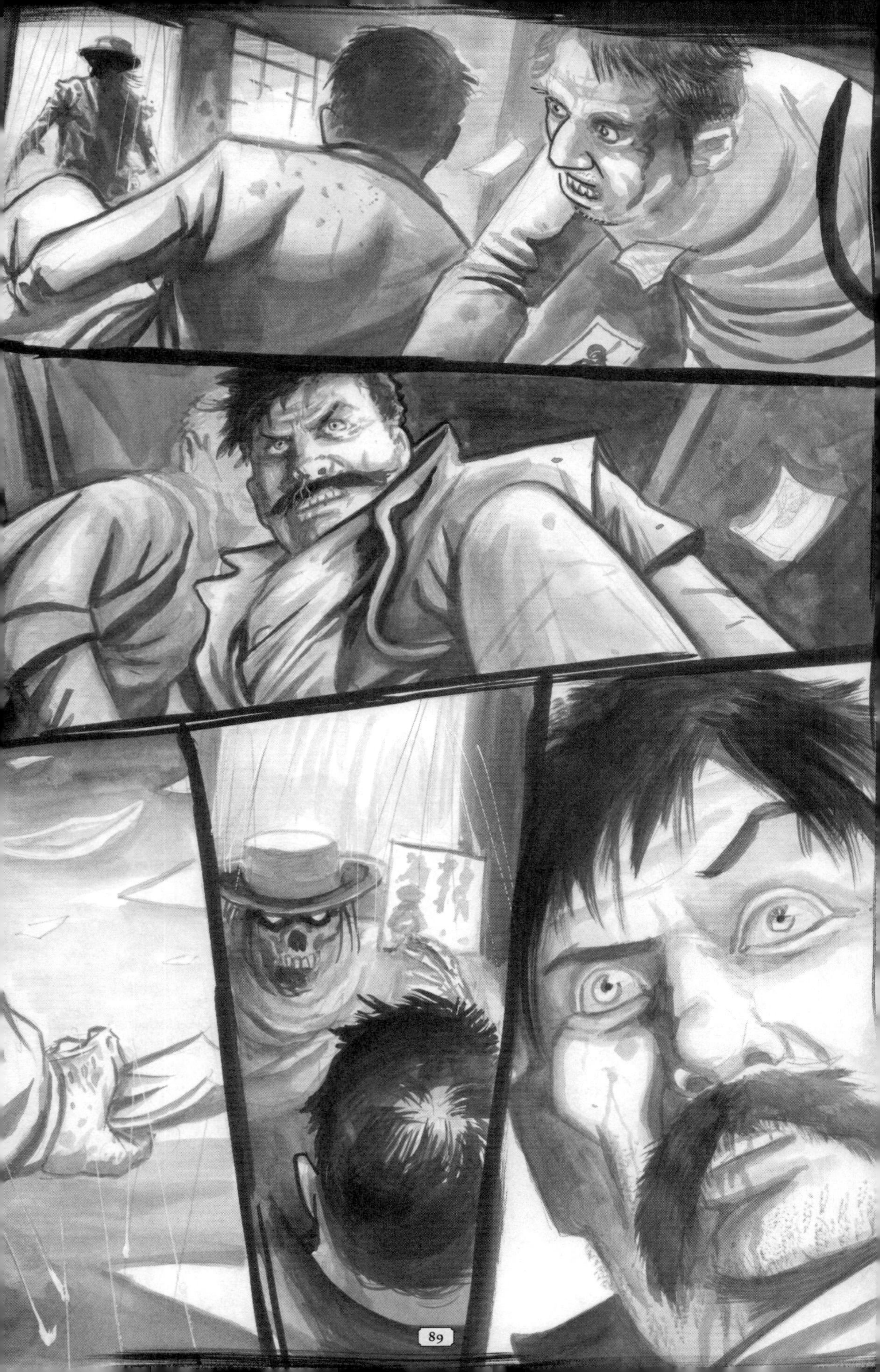

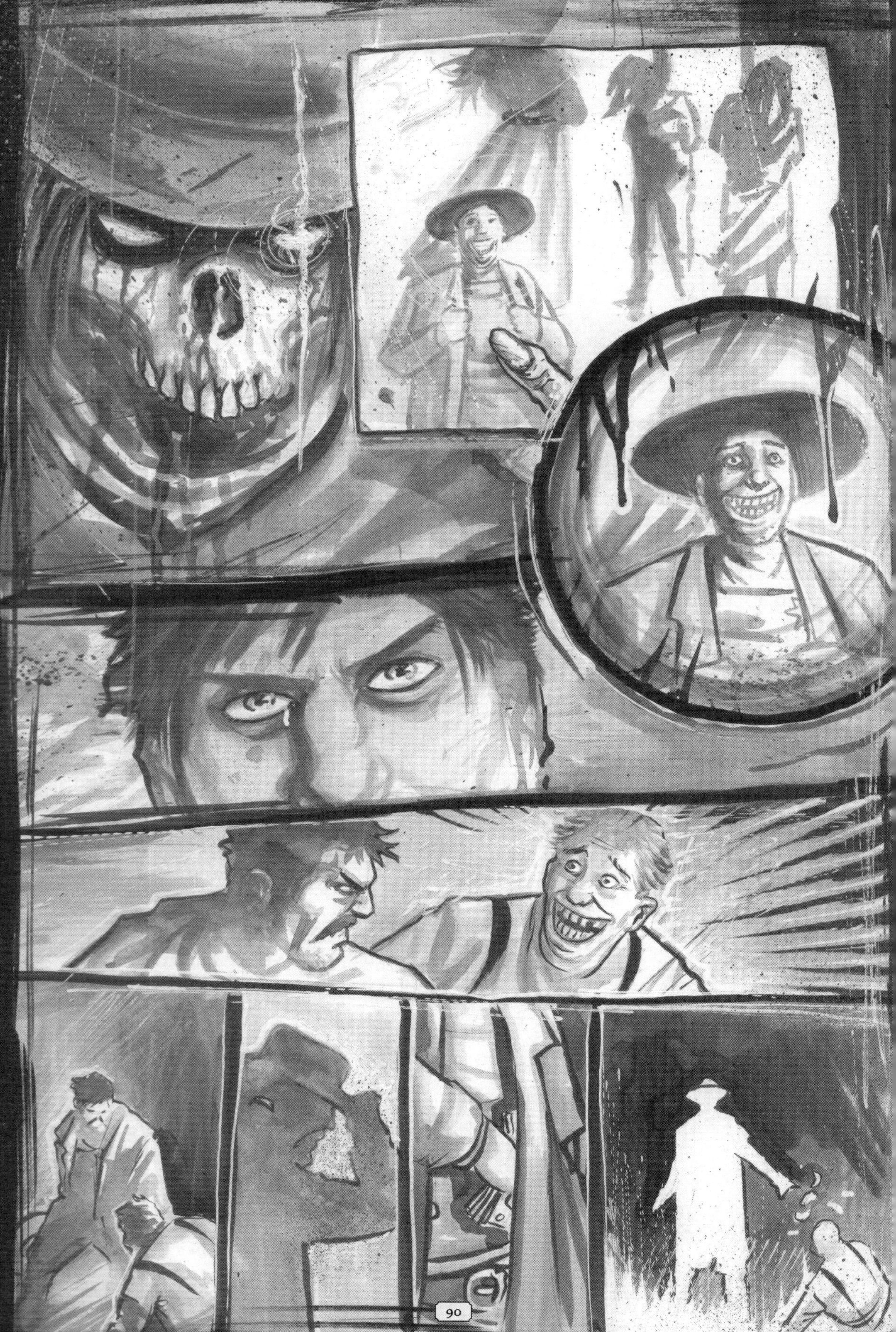

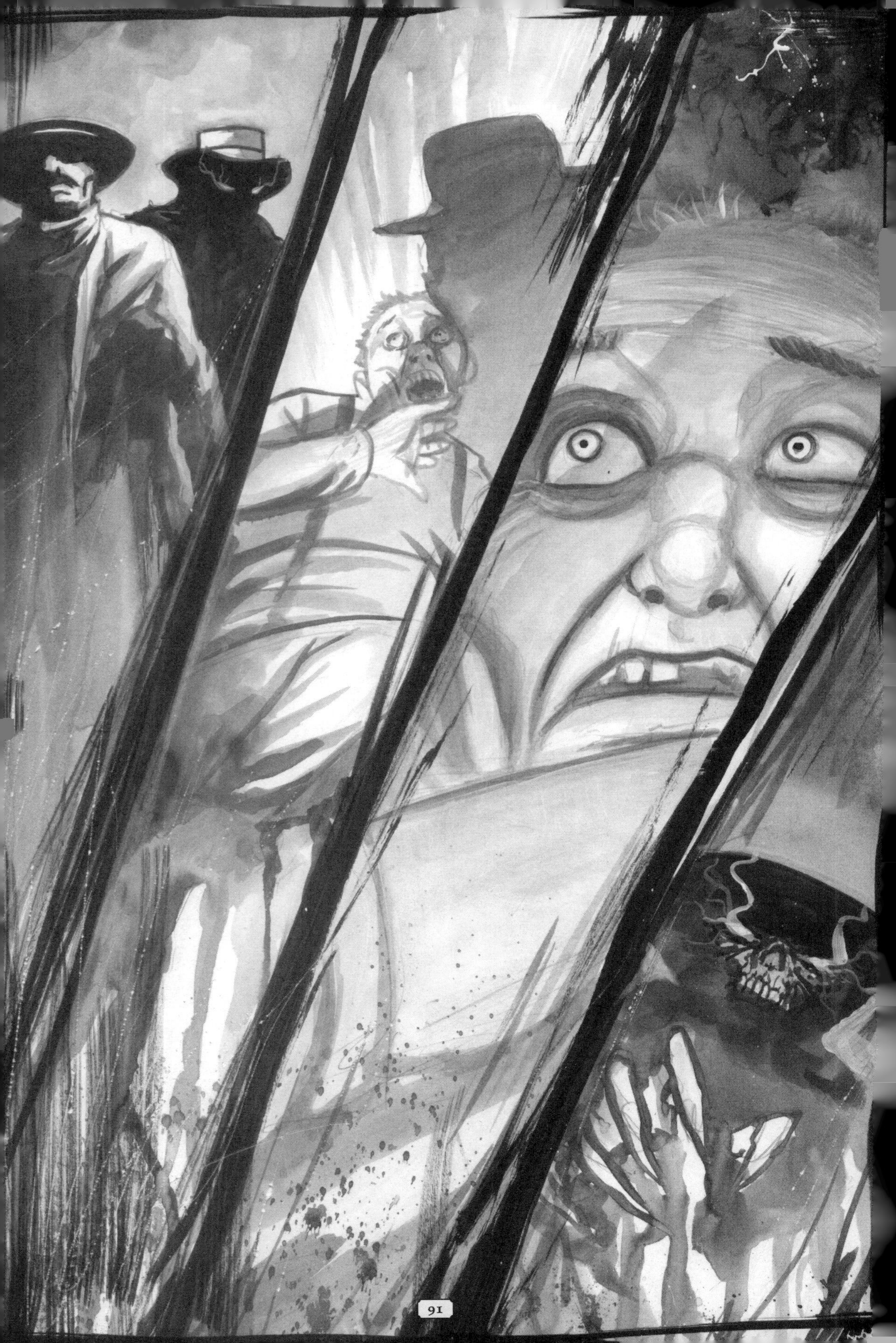

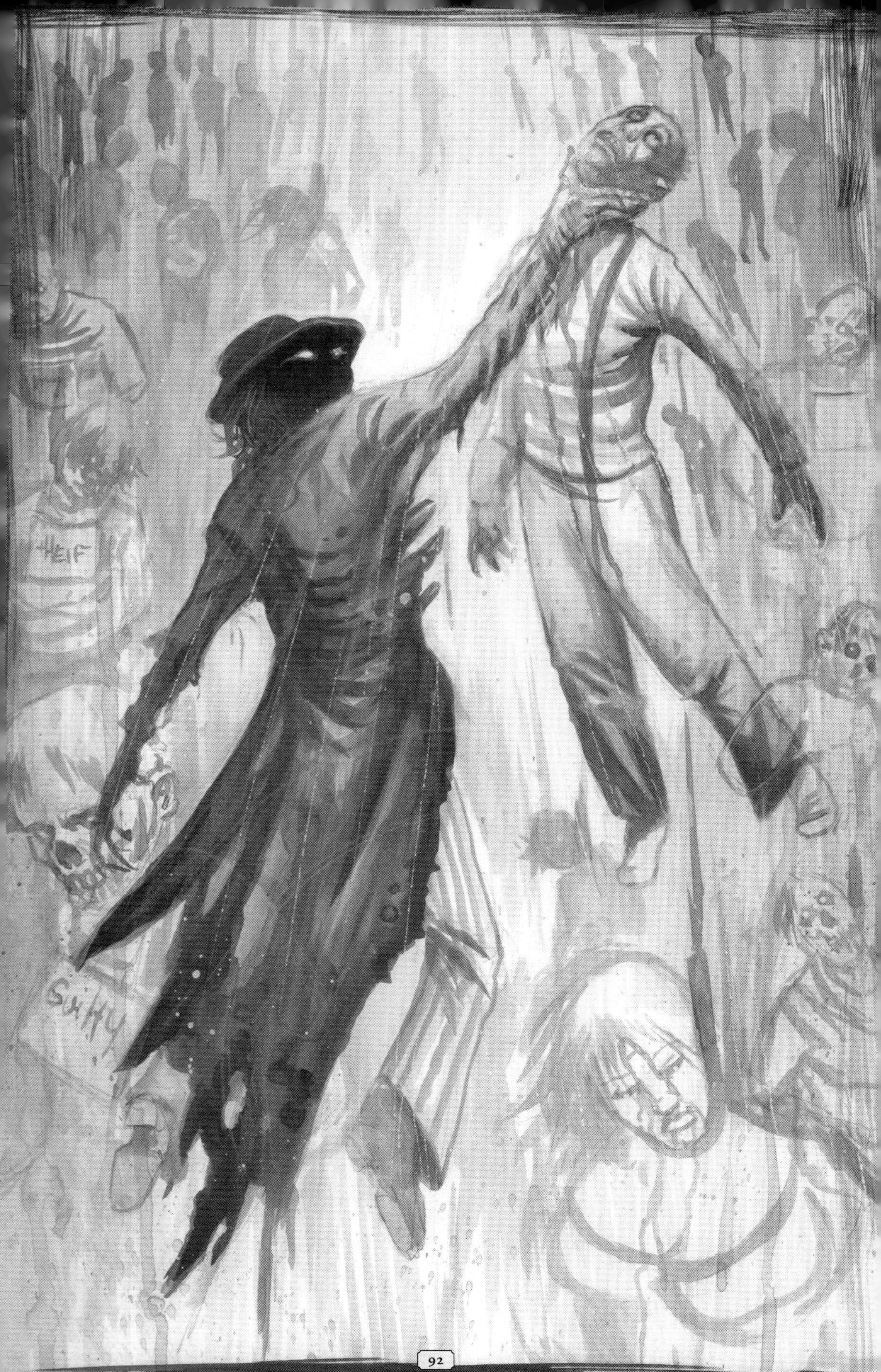

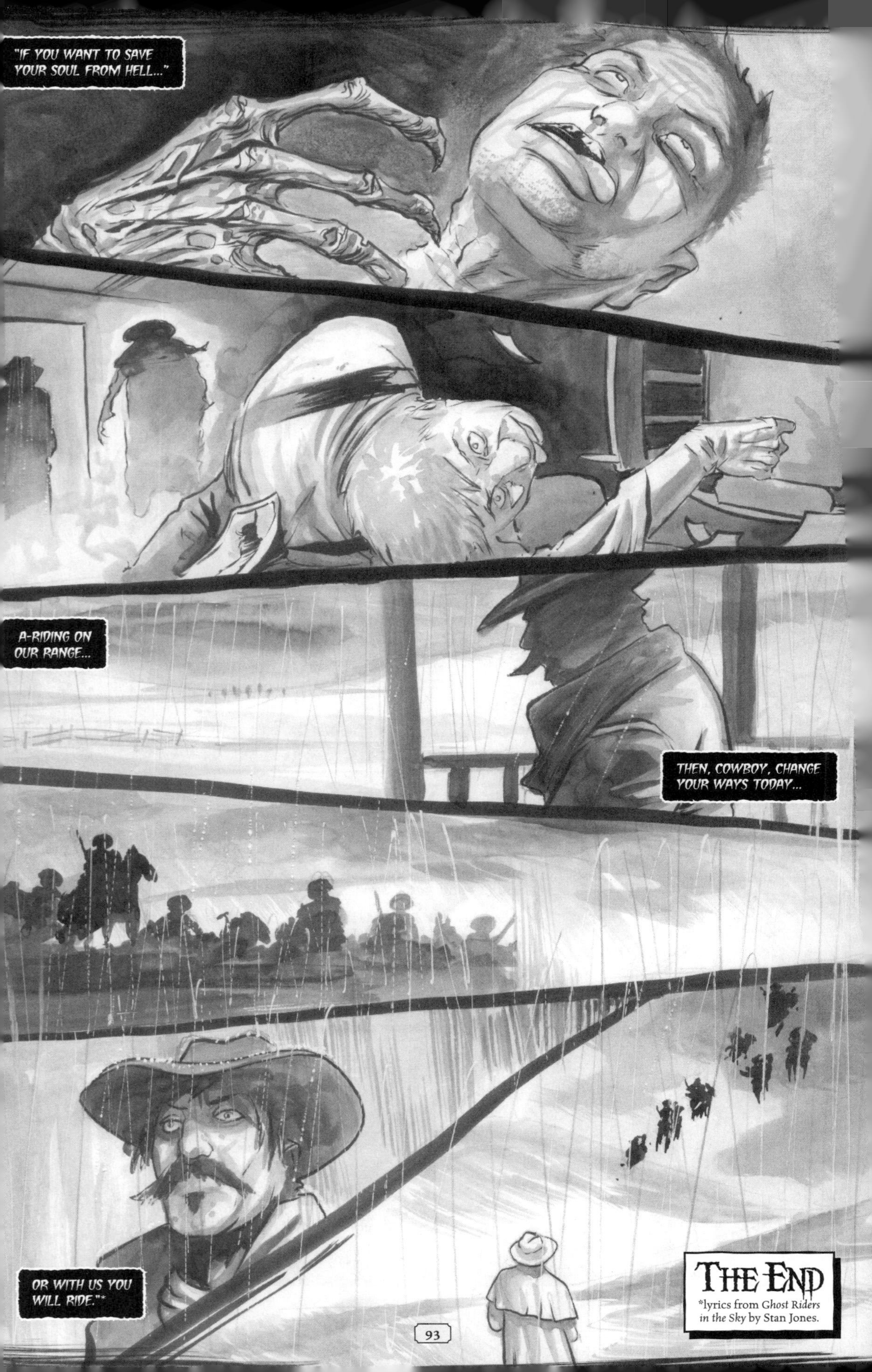
"IF YOU WANT TO SAVE YOUR SOUL FROM HELL..."
A-RIDING ON OUR RANGE...
THEN, COWBOY, CHANGE YOUR WAYS TODAY...
OR WITH US YOU WILL RIDE."*
THE END
*lyrics from Ghost Riders in the Sky by Stan Jones.

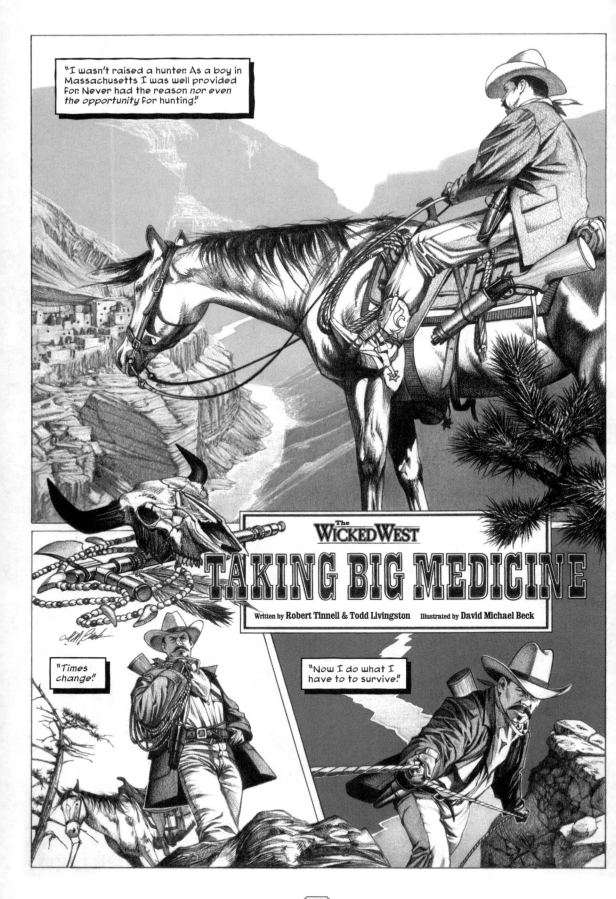

"I wasn't raised a hunter. As a boy in Massachusetts I was well provided for. Never had the reason *nor even the opportunity* for hunting!"

The
WICKED WEST
TAKING BIG MEDICINE

Written by **Robert Tinnell & Todd Livingston**   Illustrated by **David Michael Beck**

"Times change!"

"Now I do what I have to to survive!"

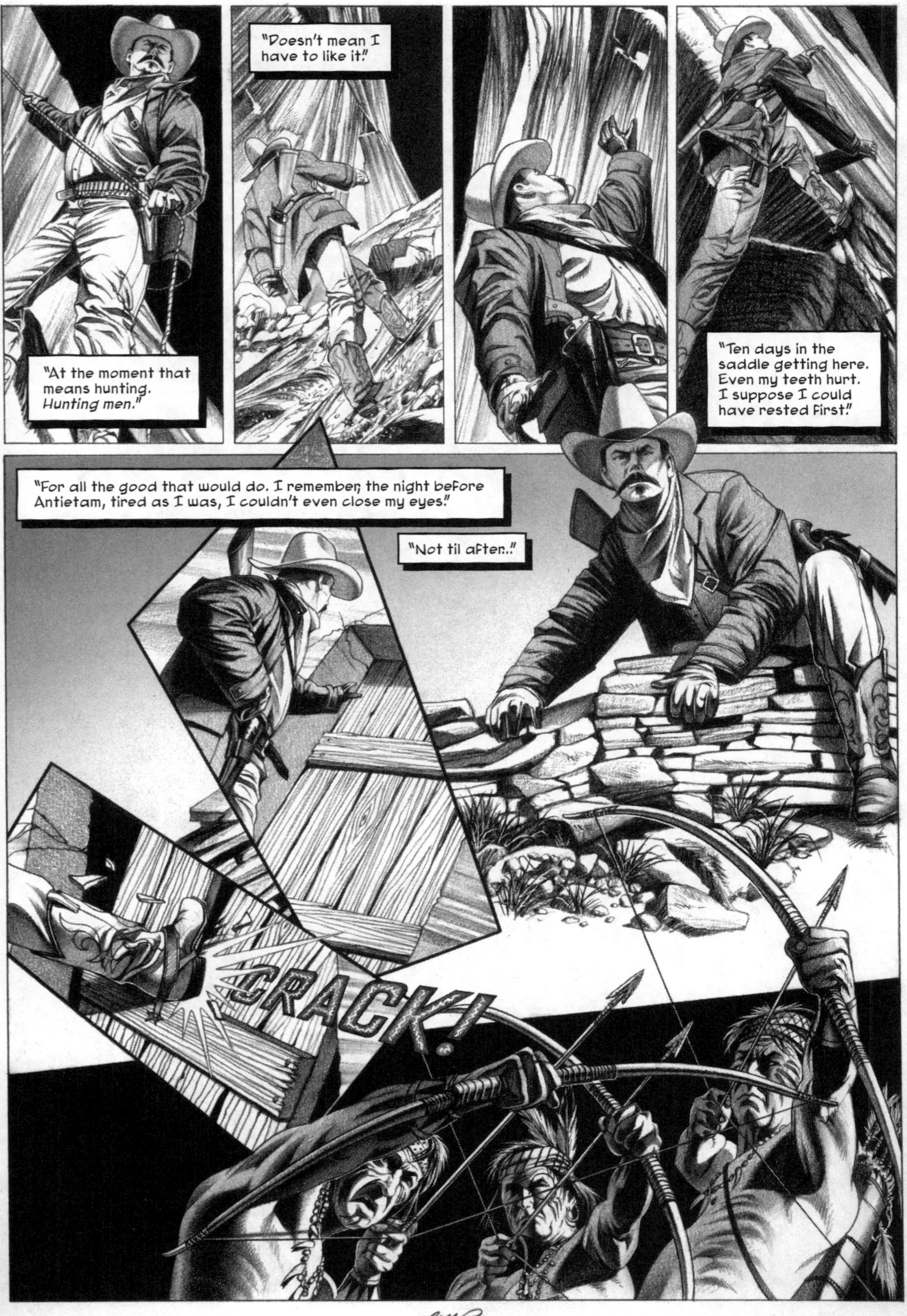
"At the moment that means hunting. Hunting men."
"Doesn't mean I have to like it."
"Ten days in the saddle getting here. Even my teeth hurt. I suppose I could have rested first."
"For all the good that would do. I remember, the night before Antietam, tired as I was, I couldn't even close my eyes."
"Not til after..."
CRACK!

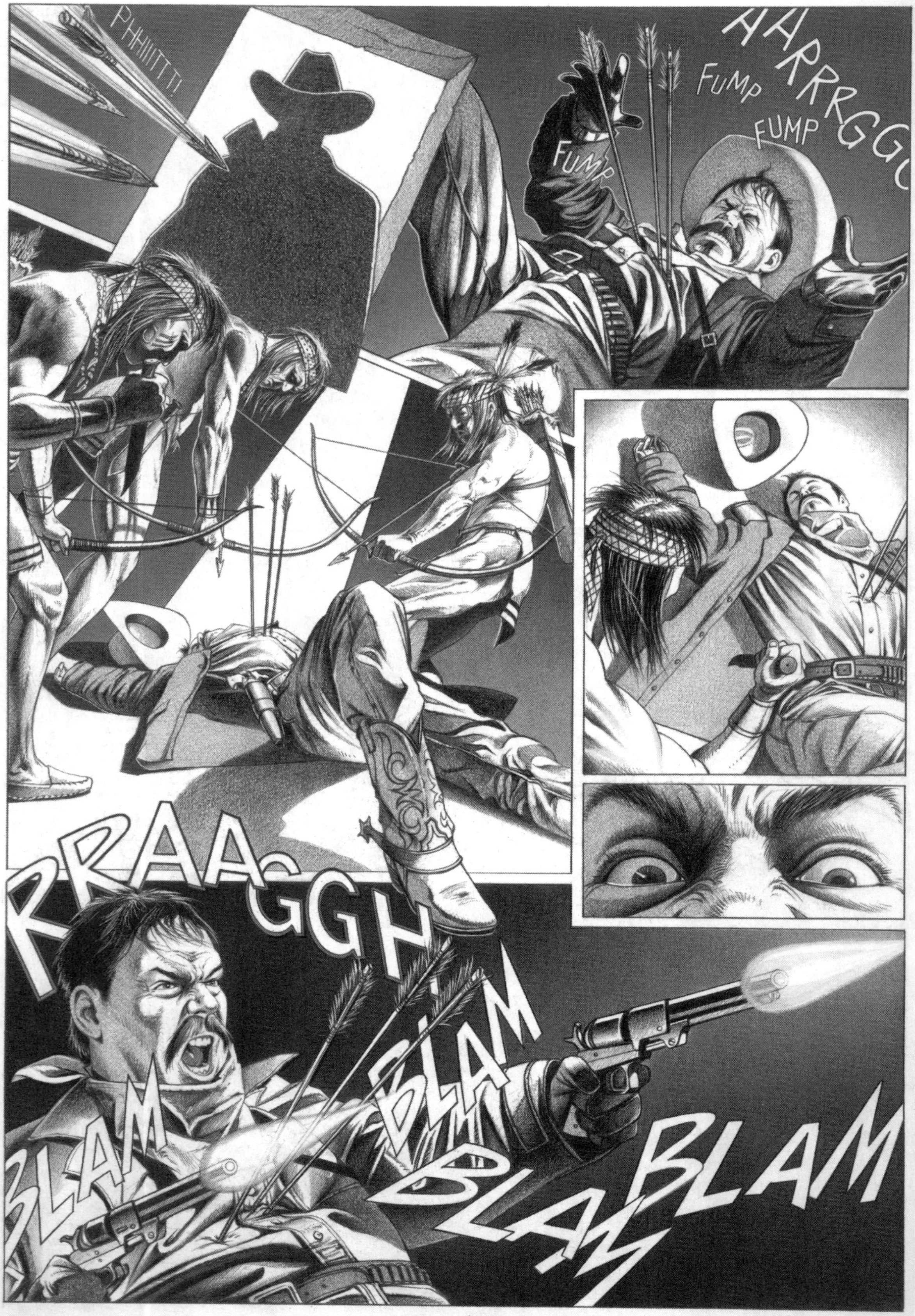
PHHHTTT!
HARRRGGG
FUMP
FUMP
FUMP
RRAAGGH
BLAM
BLAM
BLAM
BLAM
BLAM

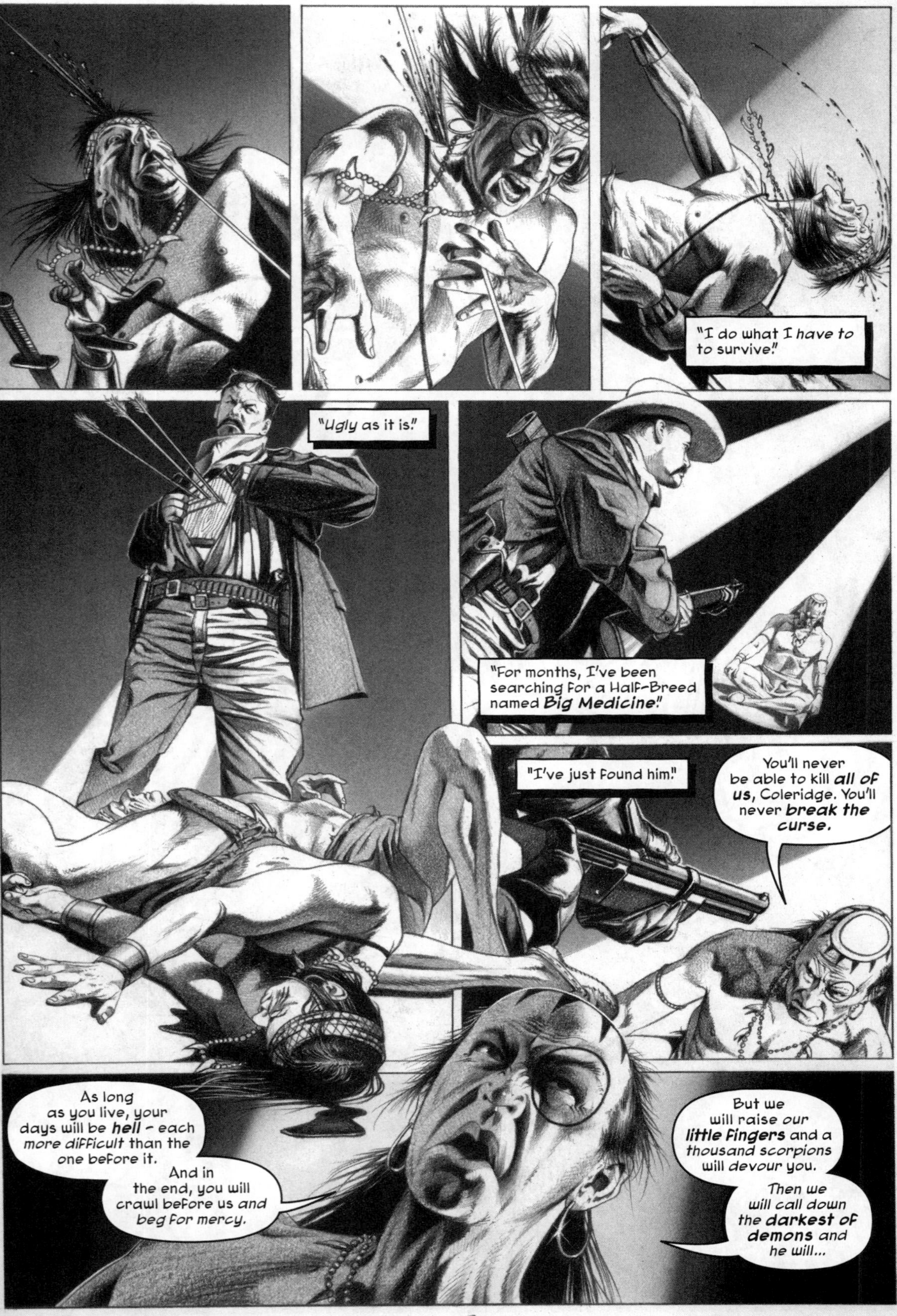
"I do what I have to to survive."
"Ugly as it is."
"For months, I've been searching for a Half-Breed named Big Medicine."
"I've just found him."
You'll never be able to kill all of us, Coleridge. You'll never break the curse.
As long as you live, your days will be hell - each more difficult than the one before it.
And in the end, you will crawl before us and beg for mercy.
But we will raise our little fingers and a thousand scorpions will devour you.
Then we will call down the darkest of demons and he will...

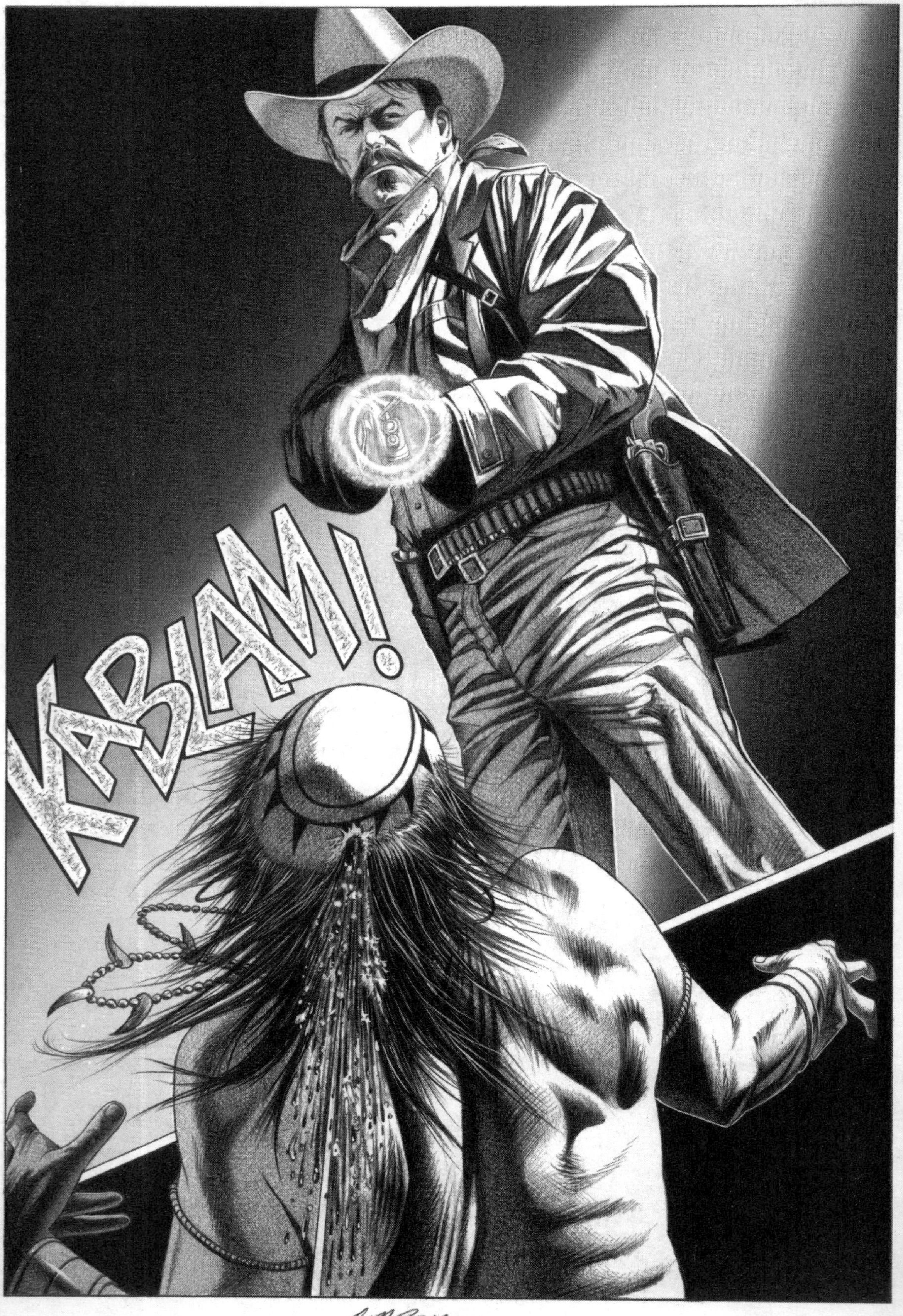
KABLAM!

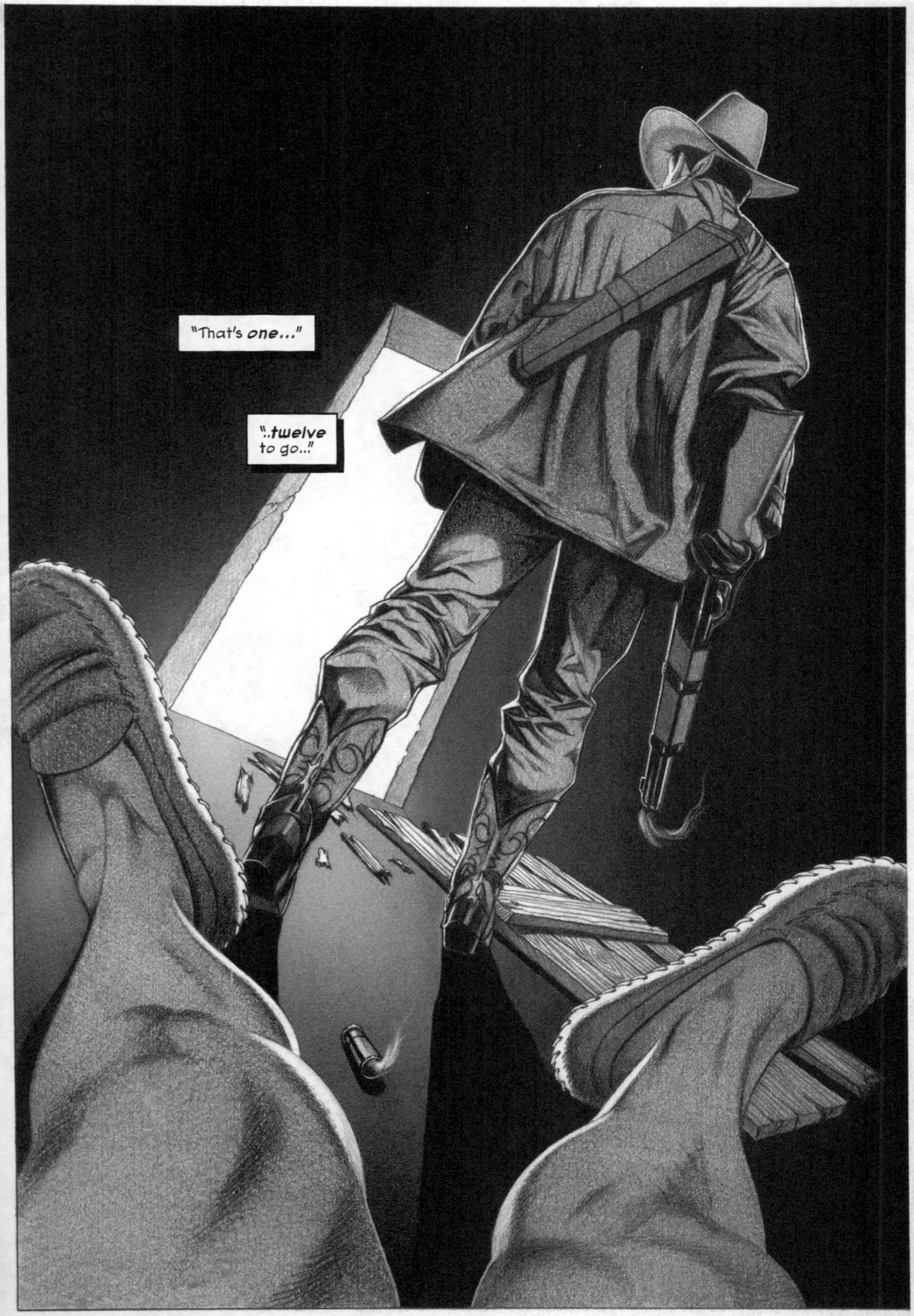
"That's one..."
"..twelve to go..."

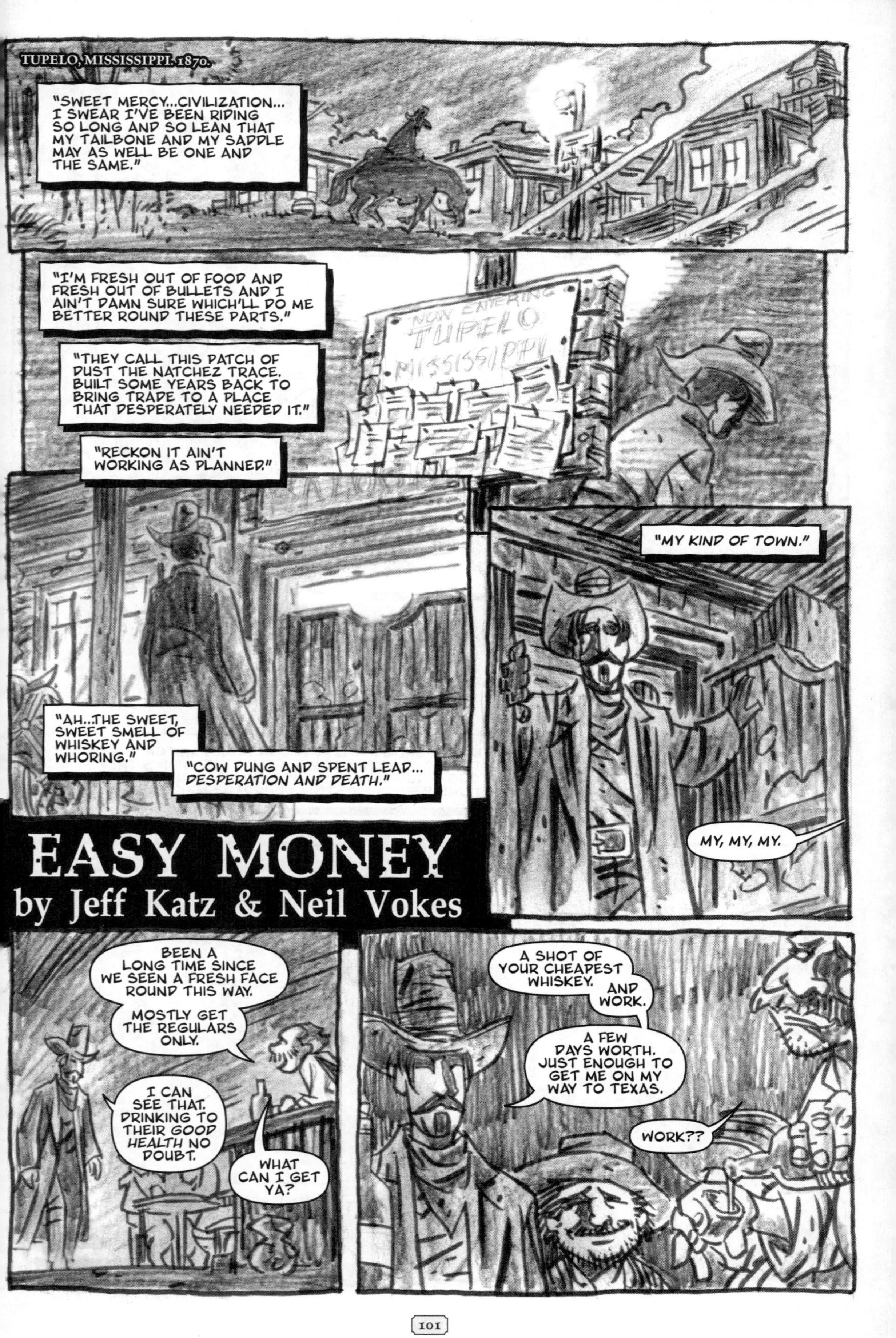
TUPELO, MISSISSIPPI. 1870.
"SWEET MERCY...CIVILIZATION... I SWEAR I'VE BEEN RIDING SO LONG AND SO LEAN THAT MY TAILBONE AND MY SADDLE MAY AS WELL BE ONE AND THE SAME."
"I'M FRESH OUT OF FOOD AND FRESH OUT OF BULLETS AND I AIN'T DAMN SURE WHICH'LL DO ME BETTER ROUND THESE PARTS."
NOW ENTERING TUPELO MISSISSIPPI
"THEY CALL THIS PATCH OF DUST THE NATCHEZ TRACE. BUILT SOME YEARS BACK TO BRING TRADE TO A PLACE THAT DESPERATELY NEEDED IT."
"RECKON IT AIN'T WORKING AS PLANNED."
"AH...THE SWEET, SWEET SMELL OF WHISKEY AND WHORING."
"COW DUNG AND SPENT LEAD... DESPERATION AND DEATH."
"MY KIND OF TOWN."
MY, MY, MY.
EASY MONEY
by Jeff Katz & Neil Vokes
BEEN A LONG TIME SINCE WE SEEN A FRESH FACE ROUND THIS WAY.
MOSTLY GET THE REGULARS ONLY.
I CAN SEE THAT. DRINKING TO THEIR GOOD HEALTH NO DOUBT.
WHAT CAN I GET YA?
A SHOT OF YOUR CHEAPEST WHISKEY.
AND WORK.
A FEW DAYS WORTH. JUST ENOUGH TO GET ME ON MY WAY TO TEXAS.
WORK??

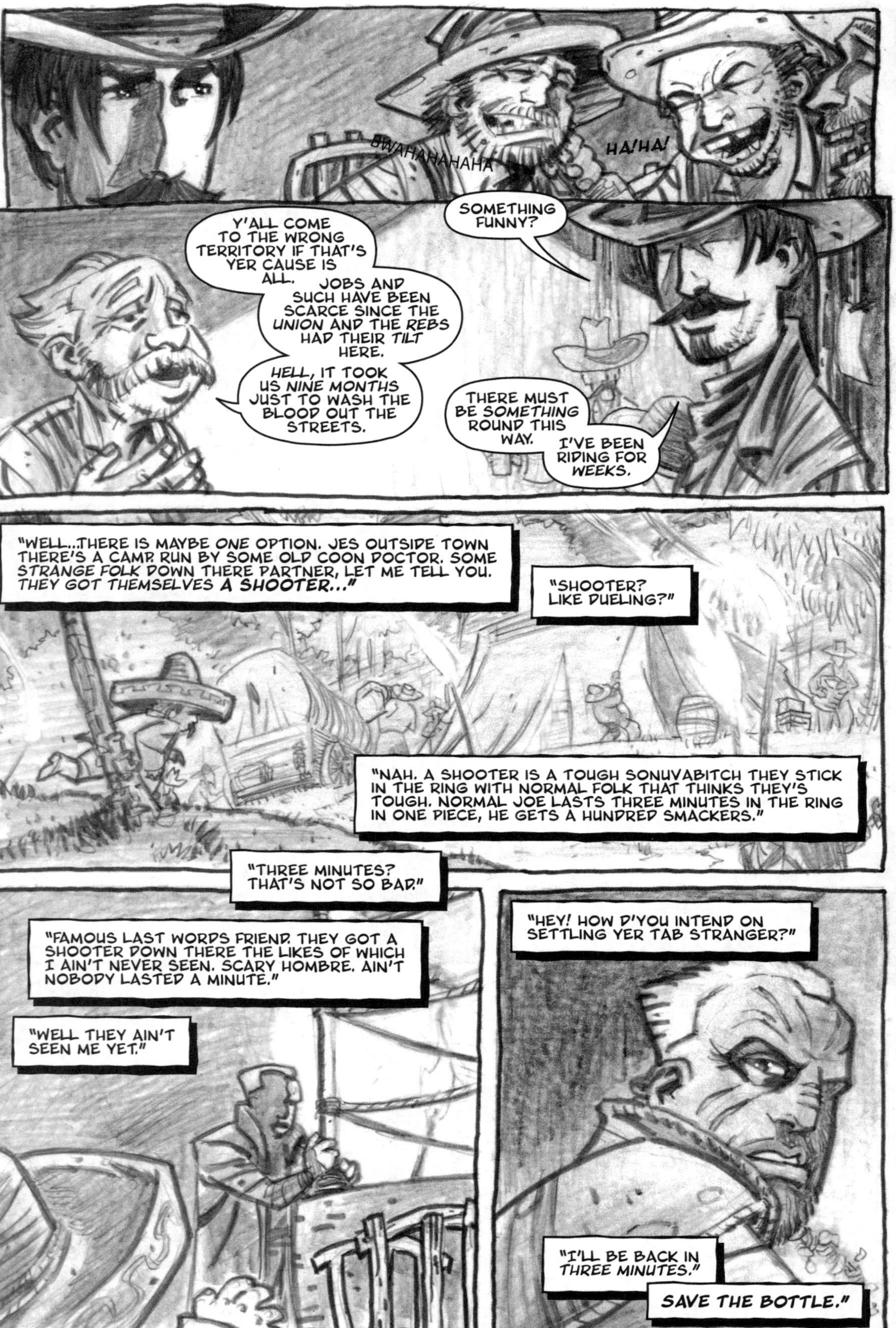

BWAHAHAHAHAHA
HA!HA!
SOMETHING FUNNY?
Y'ALL COME TO THE WRONG TERRITORY IF THAT'S YER CAUSE IS ALL.
JOBS AND SUCH HAVE BEEN SCARCE SINCE THE UNION AND THE REBS HAD THEIR TILT HERE.
HELL, IT TOOK US NINE MONTHS JUST TO WASH THE BLOOD OUT THE STREETS.
THERE MUST BE SOMETHING ROUND THIS WAY.
I'VE BEEN RIDING FOR WEEKS.
"WELL...THERE IS MAYBE ONE OPTION. JES OUTSIDE TOWN THERE'S A CAMP. RUN BY SOME OLD COON DOCTOR. SOME STRANGE FOLK DOWN THERE PARTNER, LET ME TELL YOU. THEY GOT THEMSELVES A SHOOTER..."
"SHOOTER? LIKE DUELING?"
"NAH. A SHOOTER IS A TOUGH SONUVABITCH THEY STICK IN THE RING WITH NORMAL FOLK THAT THINKS THEY'S TOUGH. NORMAL JOE LASTS THREE MINUTES IN THE RING IN ONE PIECE, HE GETS A HUNDRED SMACKERS."
"THREE MINUTES? THAT'S NOT SO BAD."
"FAMOUS LAST WORDS FRIEND. THEY GOT A SHOOTER DOWN THERE THE LIKES OF WHICH I AIN'T NEVER SEEN. SCARY HOMBRE. AIN'T NOBODY LASTED A MINUTE."
"WELL THEY AIN'T SEEN ME YET."
"HEY! HOW D'YOU INTEND ON SETTLING YER TAB STRANGER?"
"I'LL BE BACK IN THREE MINUTES."
SAVE THE BOTTLE."

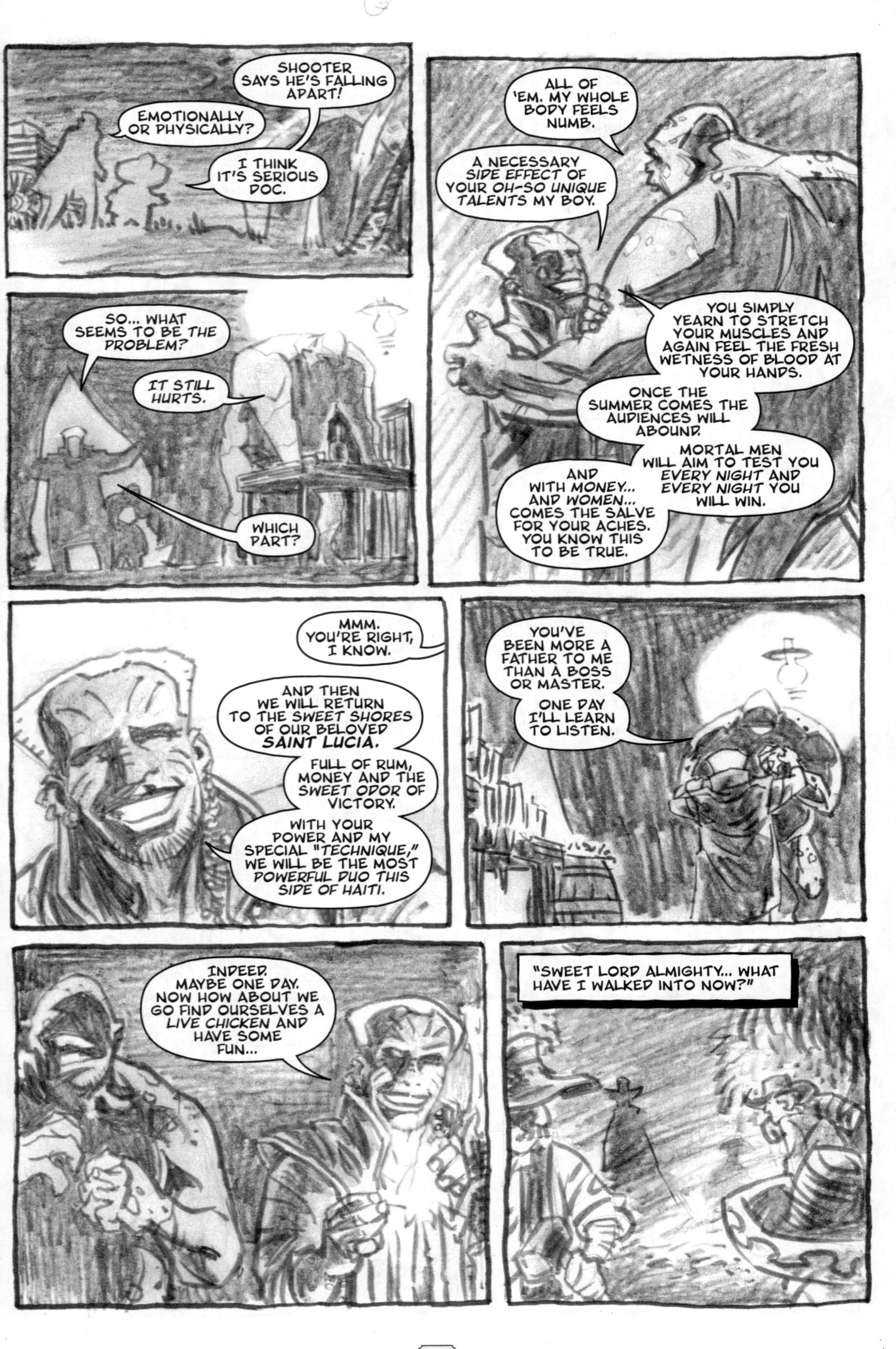
SHOOTER SAYS HE'S FALLING APART!
EMOTIONALLY OR PHYSICALLY?
I THINK IT'S SERIOUS DOC.
SO... WHAT SEEMS TO BE THE PROBLEM?
IT STILL HURTS.
WHICH PART?
ALL OF 'EM. MY WHOLE BODY FEELS NUMB.
A NECESSARY SIDE EFFECT OF YOUR OH-SO UNIQUE TALENTS MY BOY.
YOU SIMPLY YEARN TO STRETCH YOUR MUSCLES AND AGAIN FEEL THE FRESH WETNESS OF BLOOD AT YOUR HANDS.
ONCE THE SUMMER COMES THE AUDIENCES WILL ABOUND.
MORTAL MEN WILL AIM TO TEST YOU EVERY NIGHT AND EVERY NIGHT YOU WILL WIN.
AND WITH MONEY... AND WOMEN... COMES THE SALVE FOR YOUR ACHES. YOU KNOW THIS TO BE TRUE.
MMM. YOU'RE RIGHT, I KNOW.
AND THEN WE WILL RETURN TO THE SWEET SHORES OF OUR BELOVED SAINT LUCIA.
FULL OF RUM, MONEY AND THE SWEET ODOR OF VICTORY.
WITH YOUR POWER AND MY SPECIAL "TECHNIQUE," WE WILL BE THE MOST POWERFUL DUO THIS SIDE OF HAITI.
YOU'VE BEEN MORE A FATHER TO ME THAN A BOSS OR MASTER.
ONE DAY I'LL LEARN TO LISTEN.
INDEED. MAYBE ONE DAY. NOW HOW ABOUT WE GO FIND OURSELVES A LIVE CHICKEN AND HAVE SOME FUN...
"SWEET LORD ALMIGHTY... WHAT HAVE I WALKED INTO NOW?"

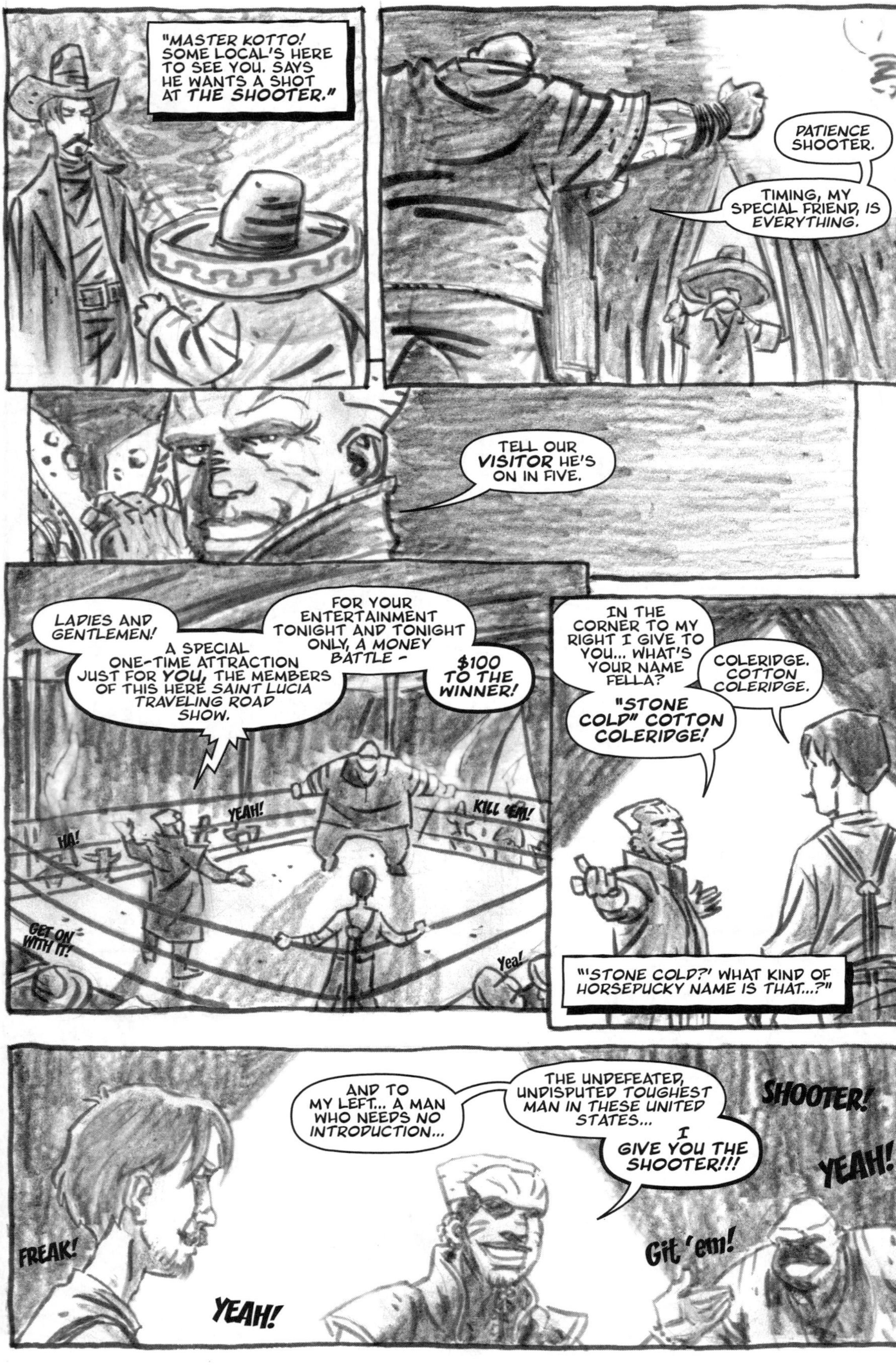
"MASTER KOTTO! SOME LOCAL'S HERE TO SEE YOU. SAYS HE WANTS A SHOT AT THE SHOOTER."
PATIENCE SHOOTER.
TIMING, MY SPECIAL FRIEND, IS EVERYTHING.
TELL OUR VISITOR HE'S ON IN FIVE.
LADIES AND GENTLEMEN!
FOR YOUR ENTERTAINMENT TONIGHT AND TONIGHT ONLY, A MONEY BATTLE -
A SPECIAL ONE-TIME ATTRACTION JUST FOR YOU, THE MEMBERS OF THIS HERE SAINT LUCIA TRAVELING ROAD SHOW.
$100 TO THE WINNER!
YEAH!
KILL 'EM!
HA!
GET ON WITH IT!
Yea!
IN THE CORNER TO MY RIGHT I GIVE TO YOU... WHAT'S YOUR NAME FELLA?
COLERIDGE. COTTON COLERIDGE.
"STONE COLD" COTTON COLERIDGE!
"'STONE COLD?' WHAT KIND OF HORSEPUCKY NAME IS THAT...?"
AND TO MY LEFT... A MAN WHO NEEDS NO INTRODUCTION...
THE UNDEFEATED, UNDISPUTED TOUGHEST MAN IN THESE UNITED STATES...
I GIVE YOU THE SHOOTER!!!
SHOOTER!
YEAH!
FREAK!
Git 'em!
YEAH!

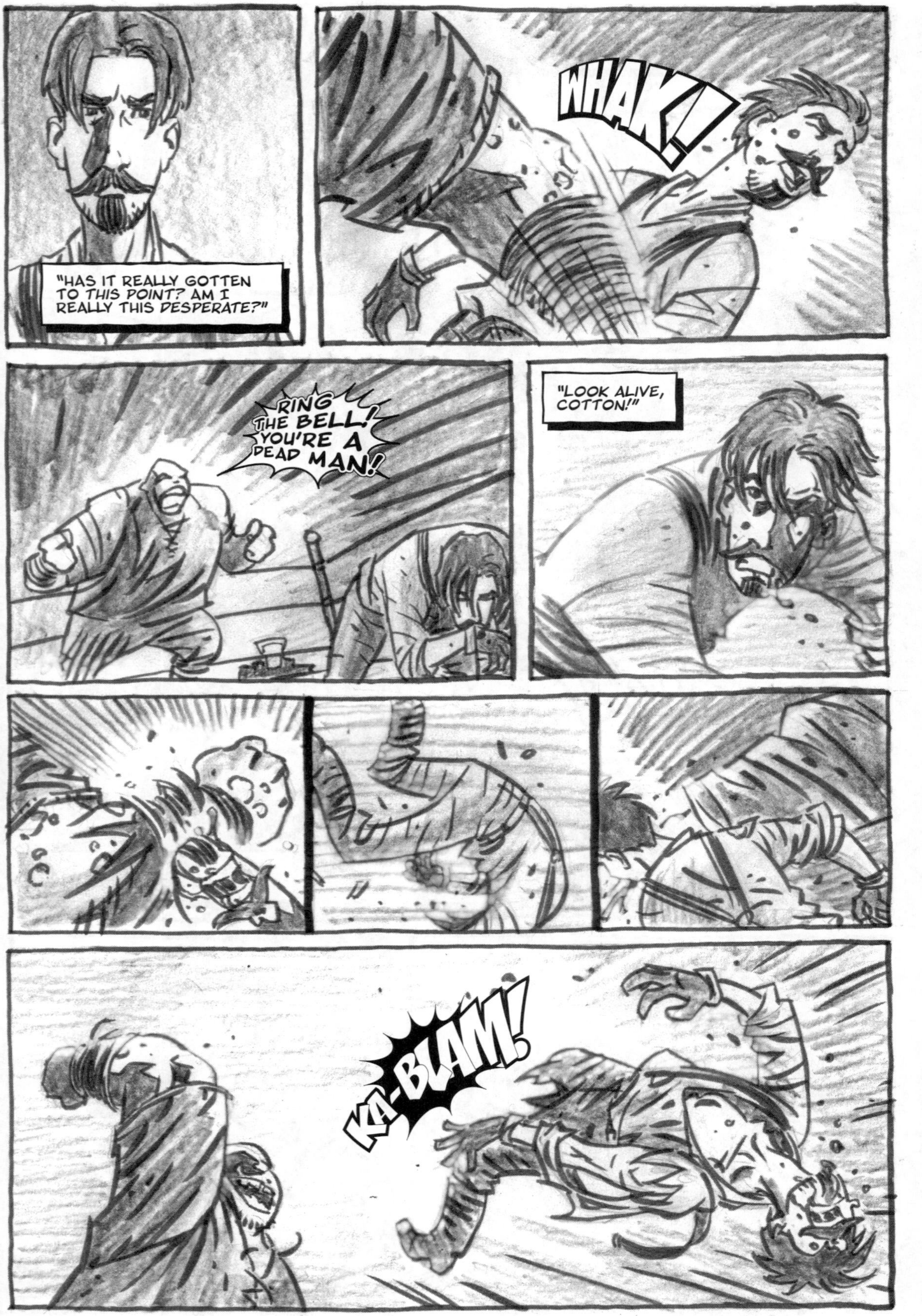
"HAS IT REALLY GOTTEN TO THIS POINT? AM I REALLY THIS DESPERATE?"
WHAK!
RING THE BELL! YOU'RE A DEAD MAN!
"LOOK ALIVE, COTTON!"
KA-BLAM!

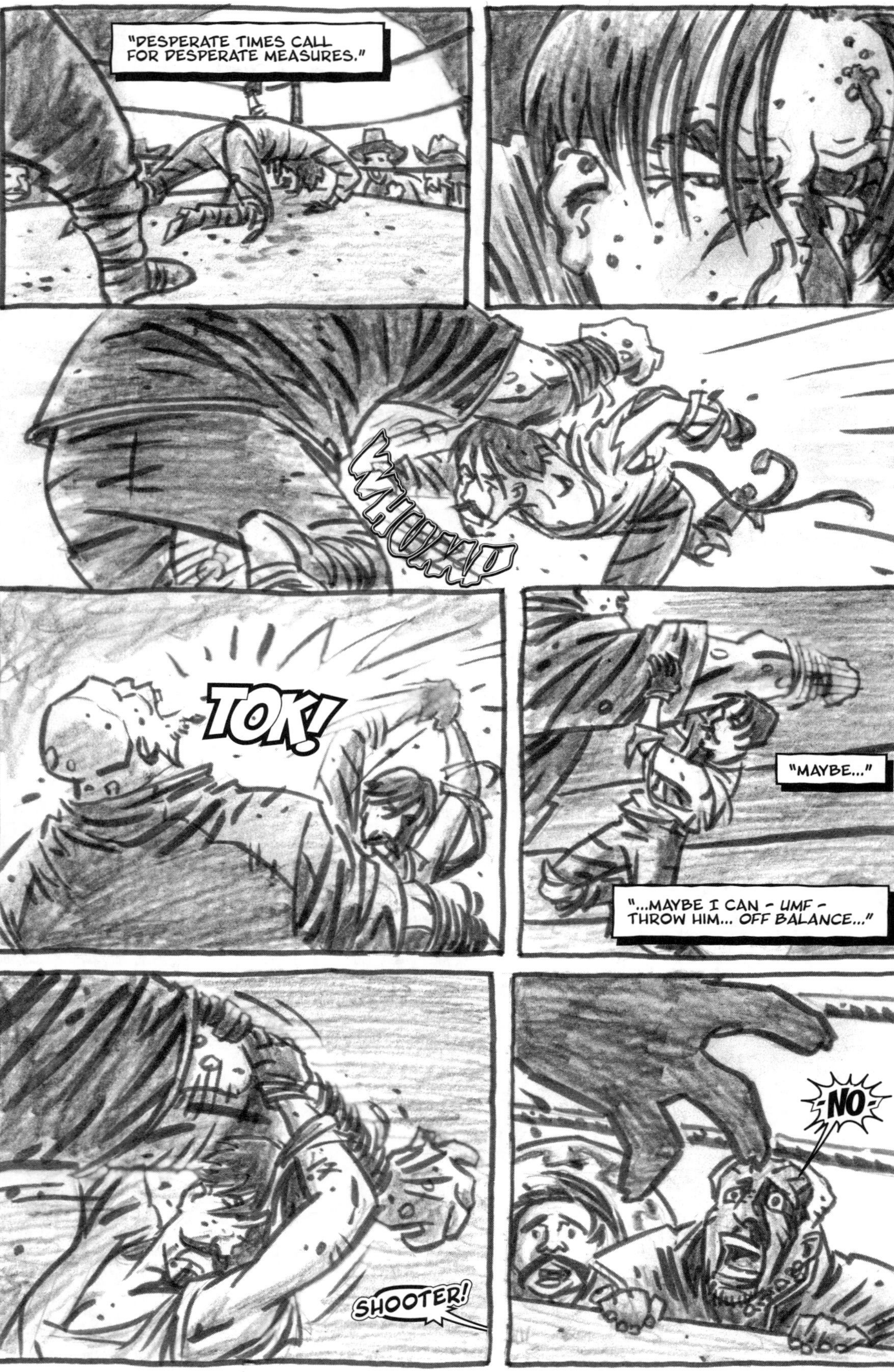
"DESPERATE TIMES CALL FOR DESPERATE MEASURES."
WHUMP
TOK!
"MAYBE..."
"...MAYBE I CAN - UMF - THROW HIM... OFF BALANCE..."
SHOOTER!
NO

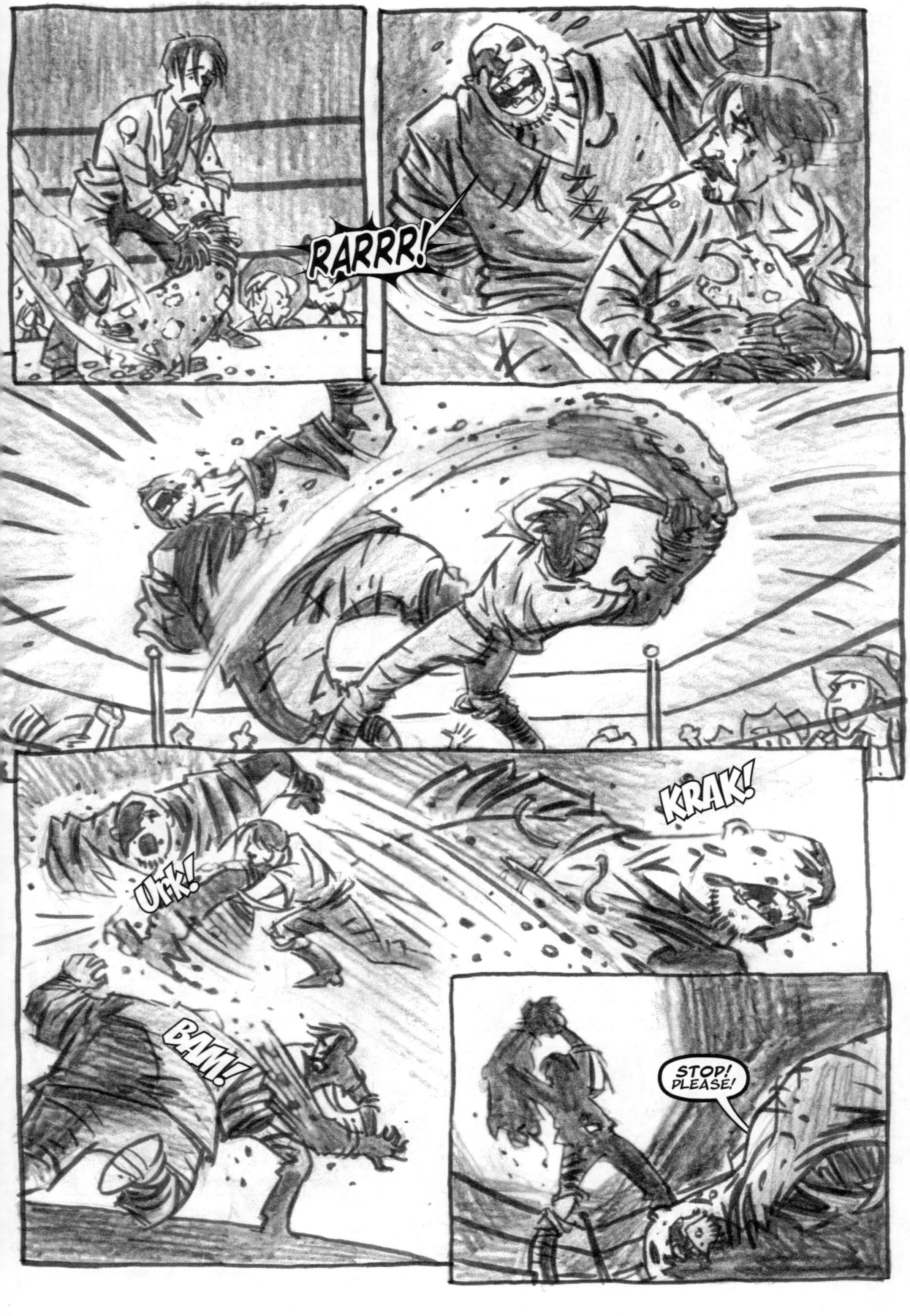
RARRR!
KRAK!
URK!
BAM!
STOP! PLEASE!

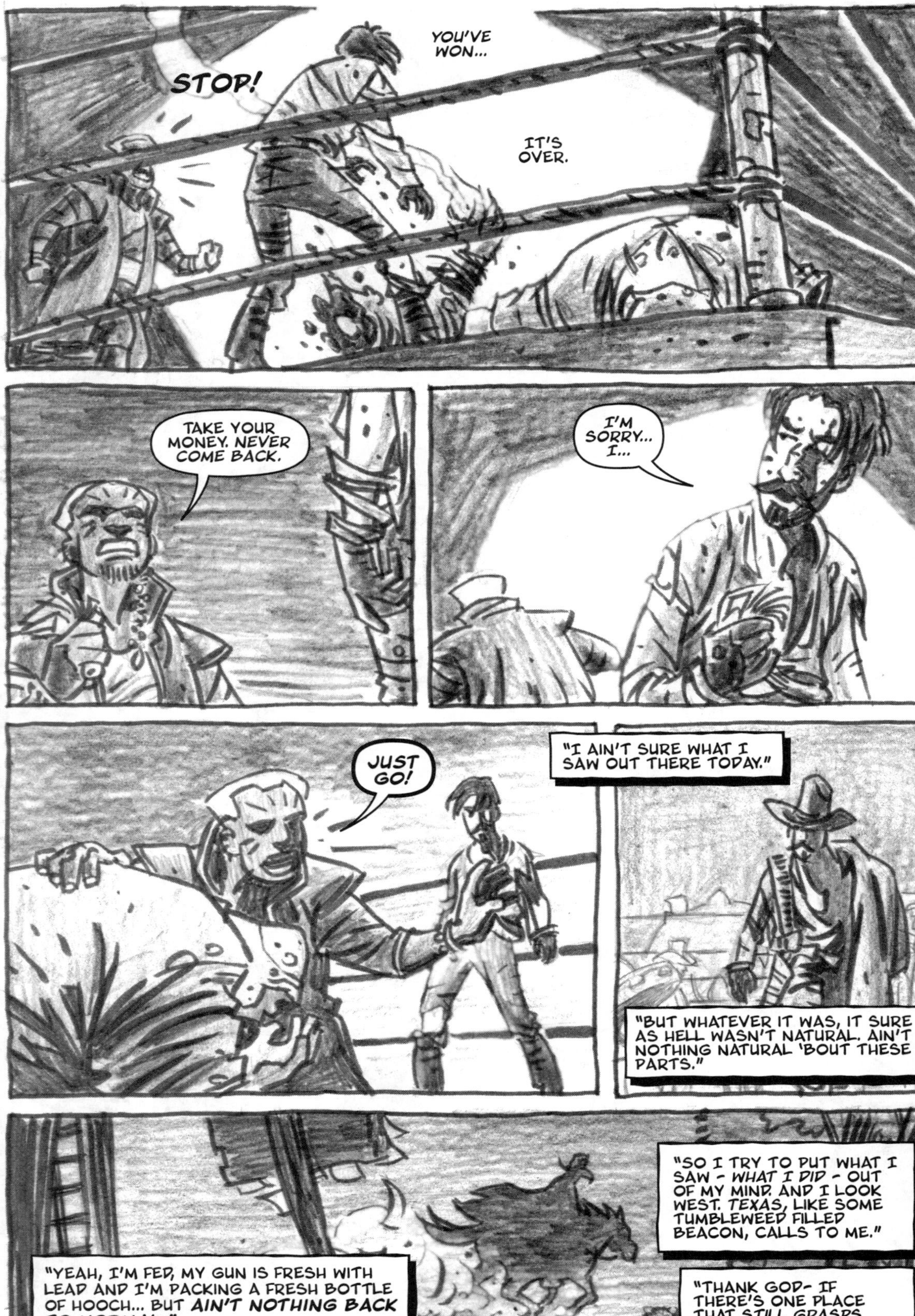

YOU'VE WON...
STOP!
IT'S OVER.
TAKE YOUR MONEY. NEVER COME BACK.
I'M SORRY... I...
JUST GO!
"I AIN'T SURE WHAT I SAW OUT THERE TODAY."
"BUT WHATEVER IT WAS, IT SURE AS HELL WASN'T NATURAL. AIN'T NOTHING NATURAL 'BOUT THESE PARTS."
"YEAH, I'M FED, MY GUN IS FRESH WITH LEAD AND I'M PACKING A FRESH BOTTLE OF HOOCH... BUT AIN'T NOTHING BACK TO NORMAL."
"SO I TRY TO PUT WHAT I SAW - WHAT I DID - OUT OF MY MIND. AND I LOOK WEST. TEXAS, LIKE SOME TUMBLEWEED FILLED BEACON, CALLS TO ME."
"THANK GOD- IF THERE'S ONE PLACE THAT STILL GRASPS NORMAL, IT'S TEXAS..."

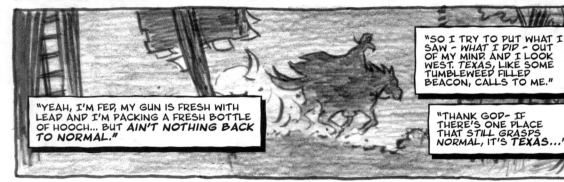

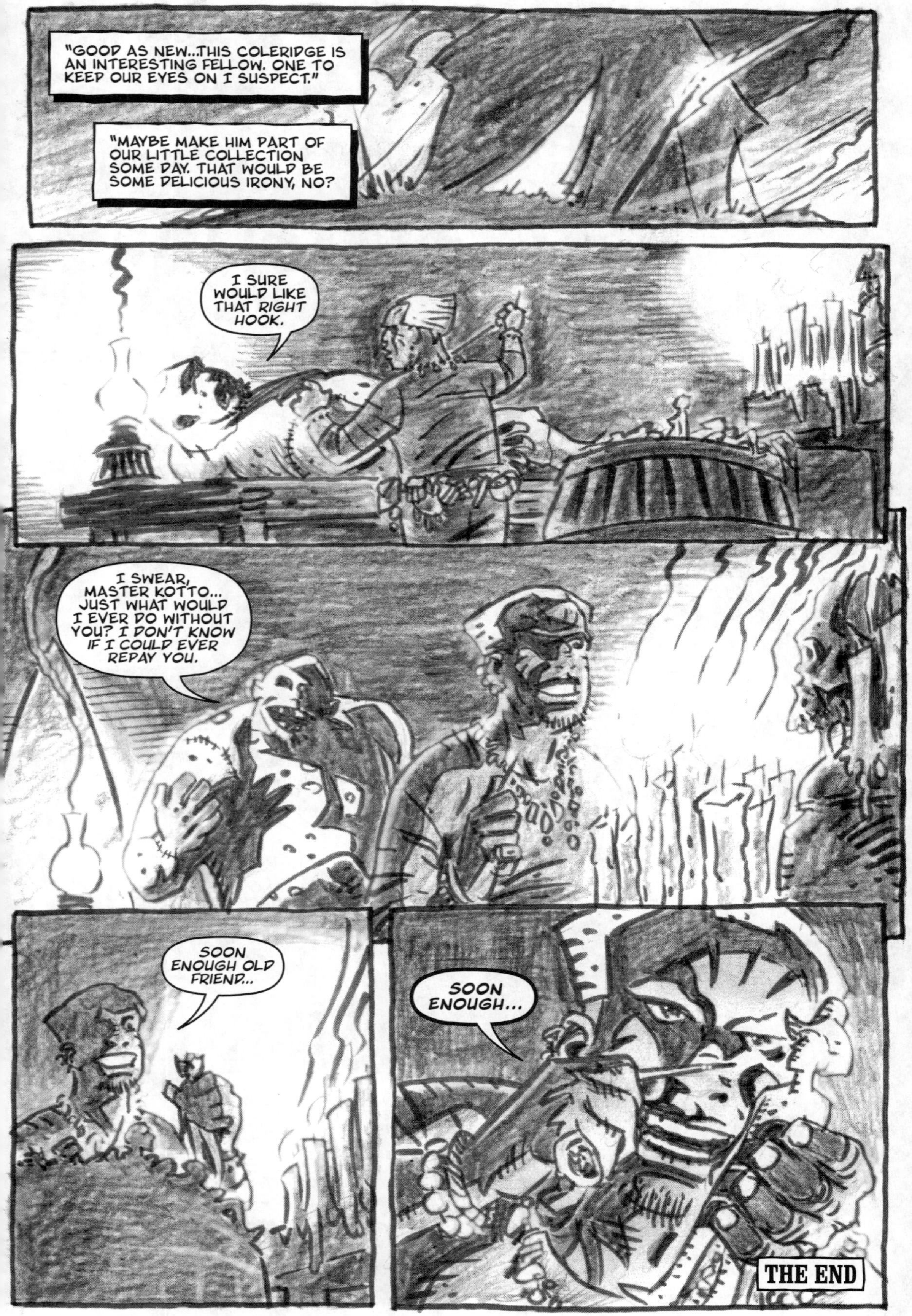
"GOOD AS NEW...THIS COLERIDGE IS AN INTERESTING FELLOW. ONE TO KEEP OUR EYES ON I SUSPECT."
"MAYBE MAKE HIM PART OF OUR LITTLE COLLECTION SOME DAY. THAT WOULD BE SOME DELICIOUS IRONY, NO?
I SURE WOULD LIKE THAT RIGHT HOOK.
I SWEAR, MASTER KOTTO... JUST WHAT WOULD I EVER DO WITHOUT YOU? I DON'T KNOW IF I COULD EVER REPAY YOU.
SOON ENOUGH OLD FRIEND...
SOON ENOUGH...
THE END

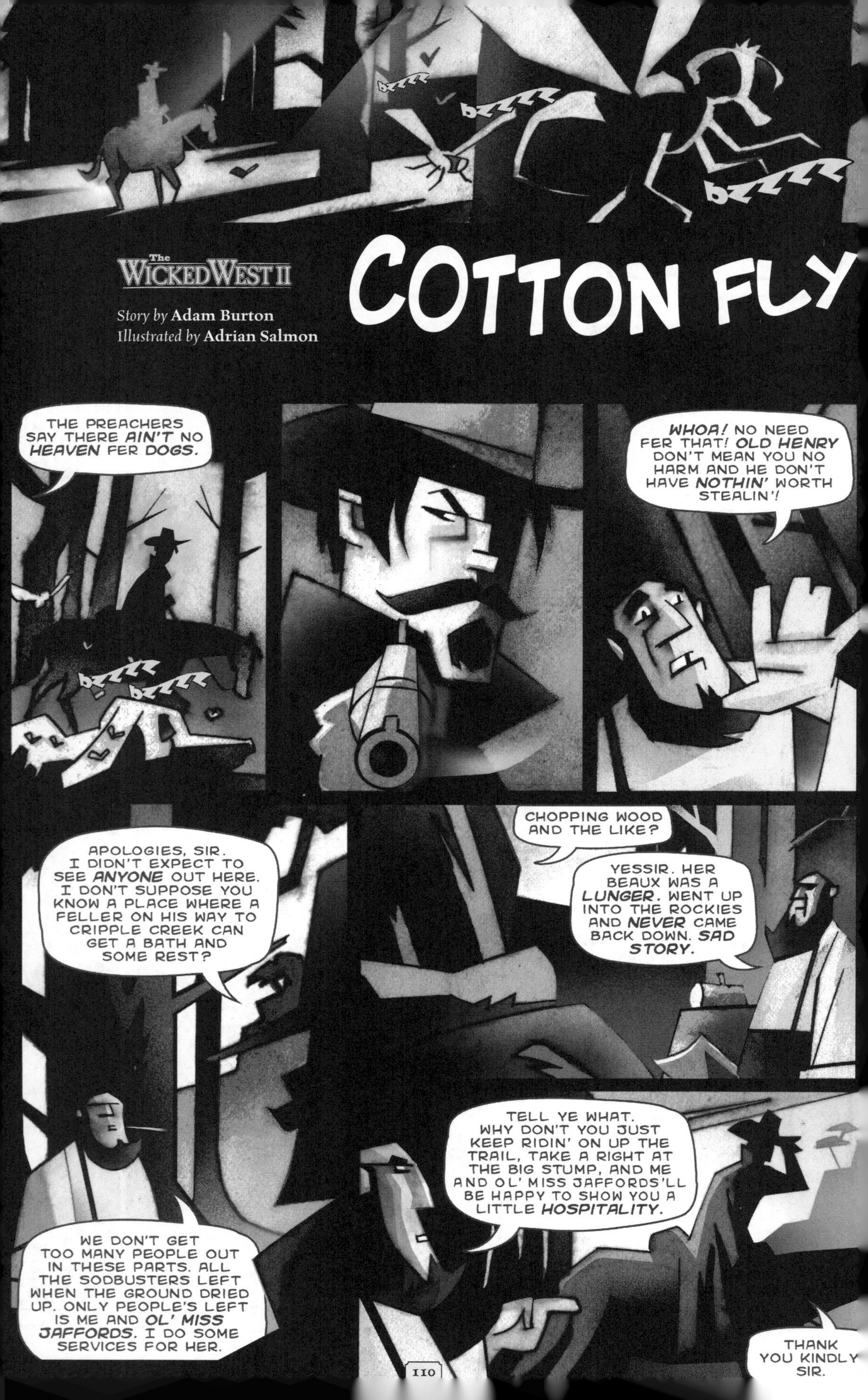
The WICKED WEST II
Story by Adam Burton
Illustrated by Adrian Salmon
COTTON FLY
THE PREACHERS SAY THERE AIN'T NO HEAVEN FER DOGS.
WHOA! NO NEED FER THAT! OLD HENRY DON'T MEAN YOU NO HARM AND HE DON'T HAVE NOTHIN' WORTH STEALIN'!
APOLOGIES, SIR. I DIDN'T EXPECT TO SEE ANYONE OUT HERE. I DON'T SUPPOSE YOU KNOW A PLACE WHERE A FELLER ON HIS WAY TO CRIPPLE CREEK CAN GET A BATH AND SOME REST?
WE DON'T GET TOO MANY PEOPLE OUT IN THESE PARTS. ALL THE SODBUSTERS LEFT WHEN THE GROUND DRIED UP. ONLY PEOPLE'S LEFT IS ME AND OL' MISS JAFFORDS. I DO SOME SERVICES FOR HER.
CHOPPING WOOD AND THE LIKE?
YESSIR. HER BEAUX WAS A LUNGER. WENT UP INTO THE ROCKIES AND NEVER CAME BACK DOWN. SAD STORY.
TELL YE WHAT. WHY DON'T YOU JUST KEEP RIDIN' ON UP THE TRAIL, TAKE A RIGHT AT THE BIG STUMP, AND ME AND OL' MISS JAFFORDS'LL BE HAPPY TO SHOW YOU A LITTLE HOSPITALITY.
THANK YOU KINDLY SIR.

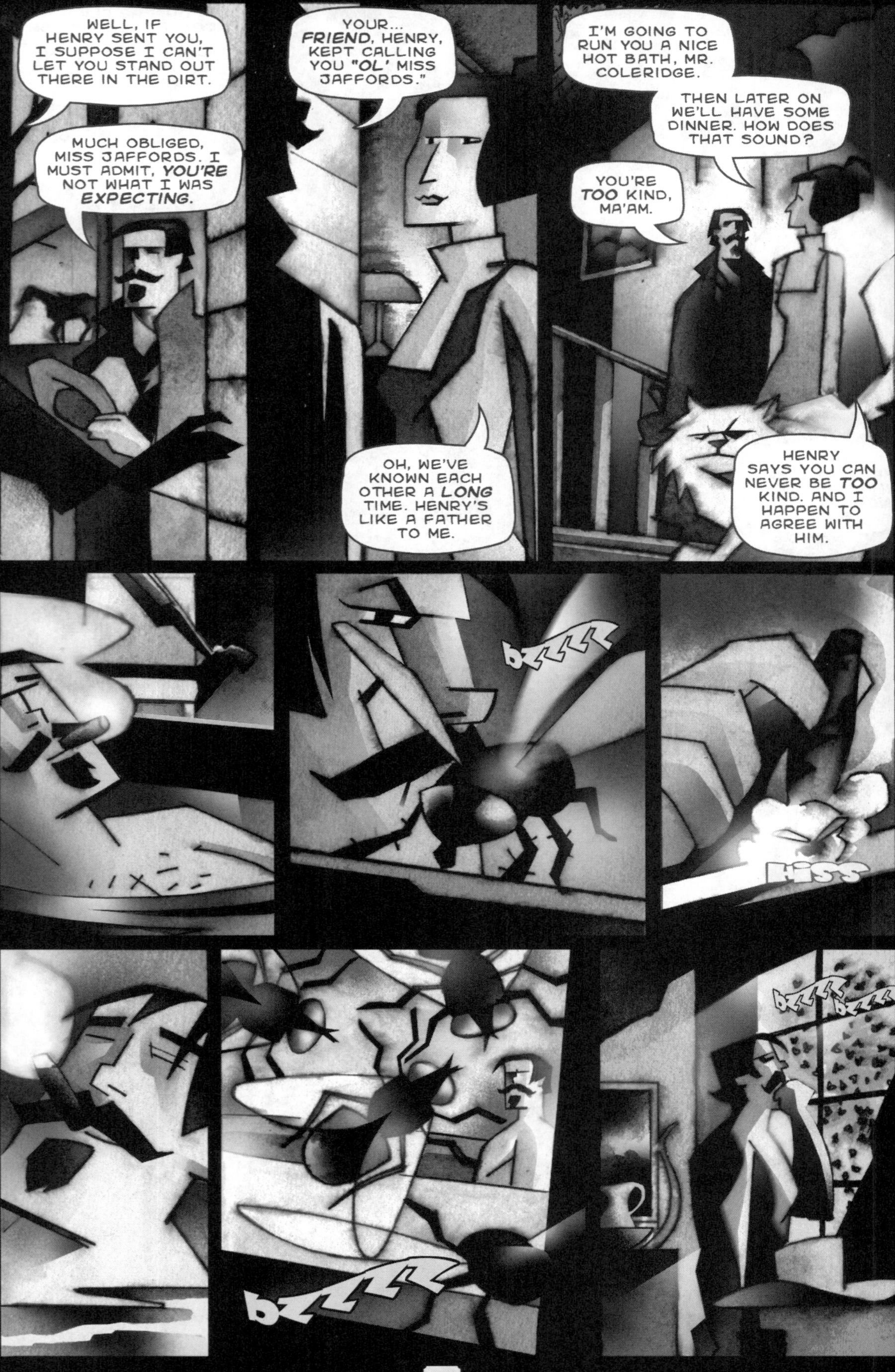
WELL, IF HENRY SENT YOU, I SUPPOSE I CAN'T LET YOU STAND OUT THERE IN THE DIRT.
MUCH OBLIGED, MISS JAFFORDS. I MUST ADMIT, YOU'RE NOT WHAT I WAS EXPECTING.
YOUR... FRIEND, HENRY, KEPT CALLING YOU "OL' MISS JAFFORDS."
OH, WE'VE KNOWN EACH OTHER A LONG TIME. HENRY'S LIKE A FATHER TO ME.
I'M GOING TO RUN YOU A NICE HOT BATH, MR. COLERIDGE.
THEN LATER ON WE'LL HAVE SOME DINNER. HOW DOES THAT SOUND?
YOU'RE TOO KIND, MA'AM.
HENRY SAYS YOU CAN NEVER BE TOO KIND. AND I HAPPEN TO AGREE WITH HIM.
BZZZZ
HISS
BZZZZ
BZZZZ BZZZZ

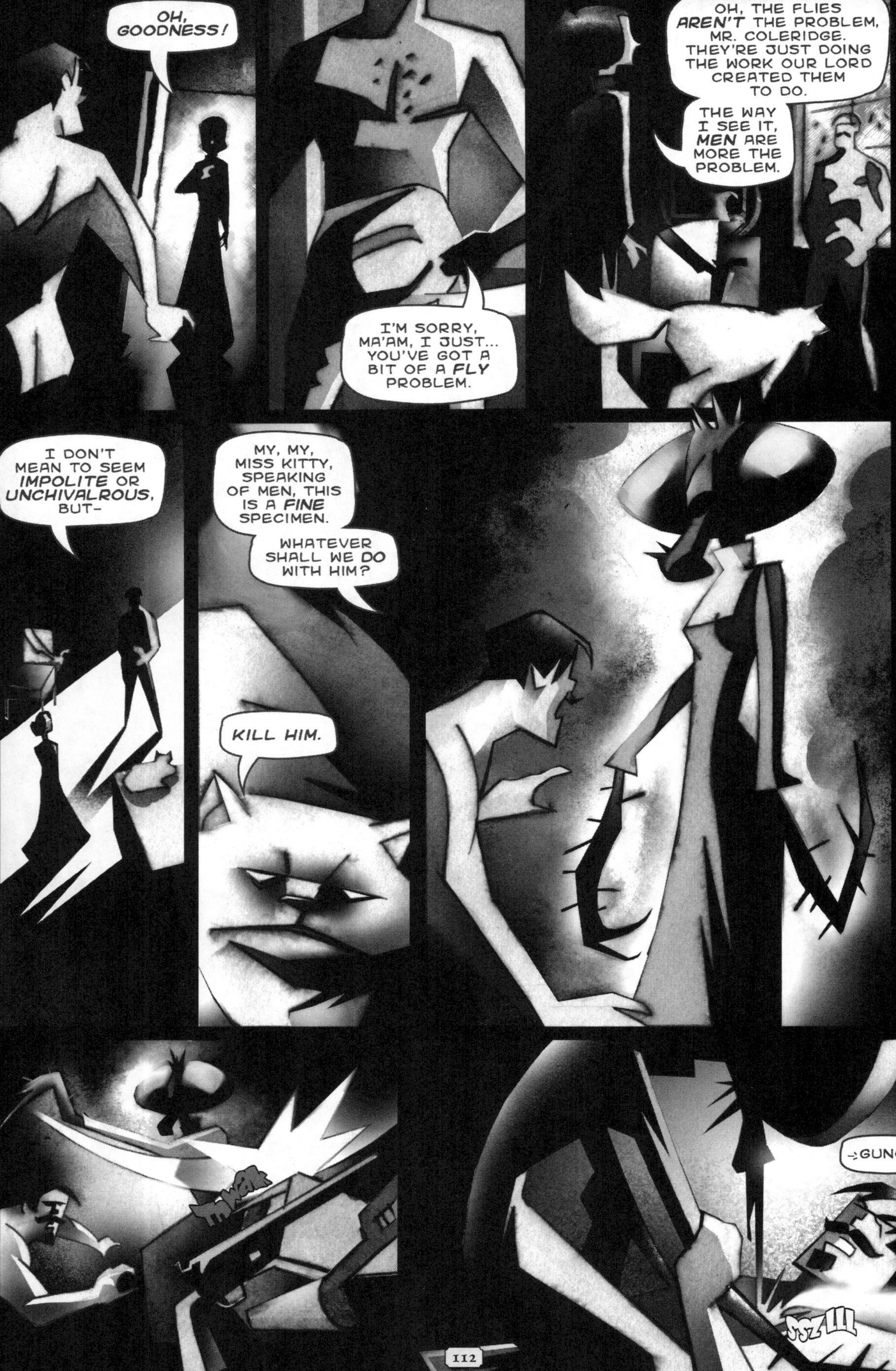
OH, GOODNESS!
I'M SORRY, MA'AM, I JUST... YOU'VE GOT A BIT OF A FLY PROBLEM.
OH, THE FLIES AREN'T THE PROBLEM, MR. COLERIDGE. THEY'RE JUST DOING THE WORK OUR LORD CREATED THEM TO DO.
THE WAY I SEE IT, MEN ARE MORE THE PROBLEM.
I DON'T MEAN TO SEEM IMPOLITE OR UNCHIVALROUS, BUT–
MY, MY, MISS KITTY, SPEAKING OF MEN, THIS IS A FINE SPECIMEN.
WHATEVER SHALL WE DO WITH HIM?
KILL HIM.
THWAK
–GUNGH
SSZLLL

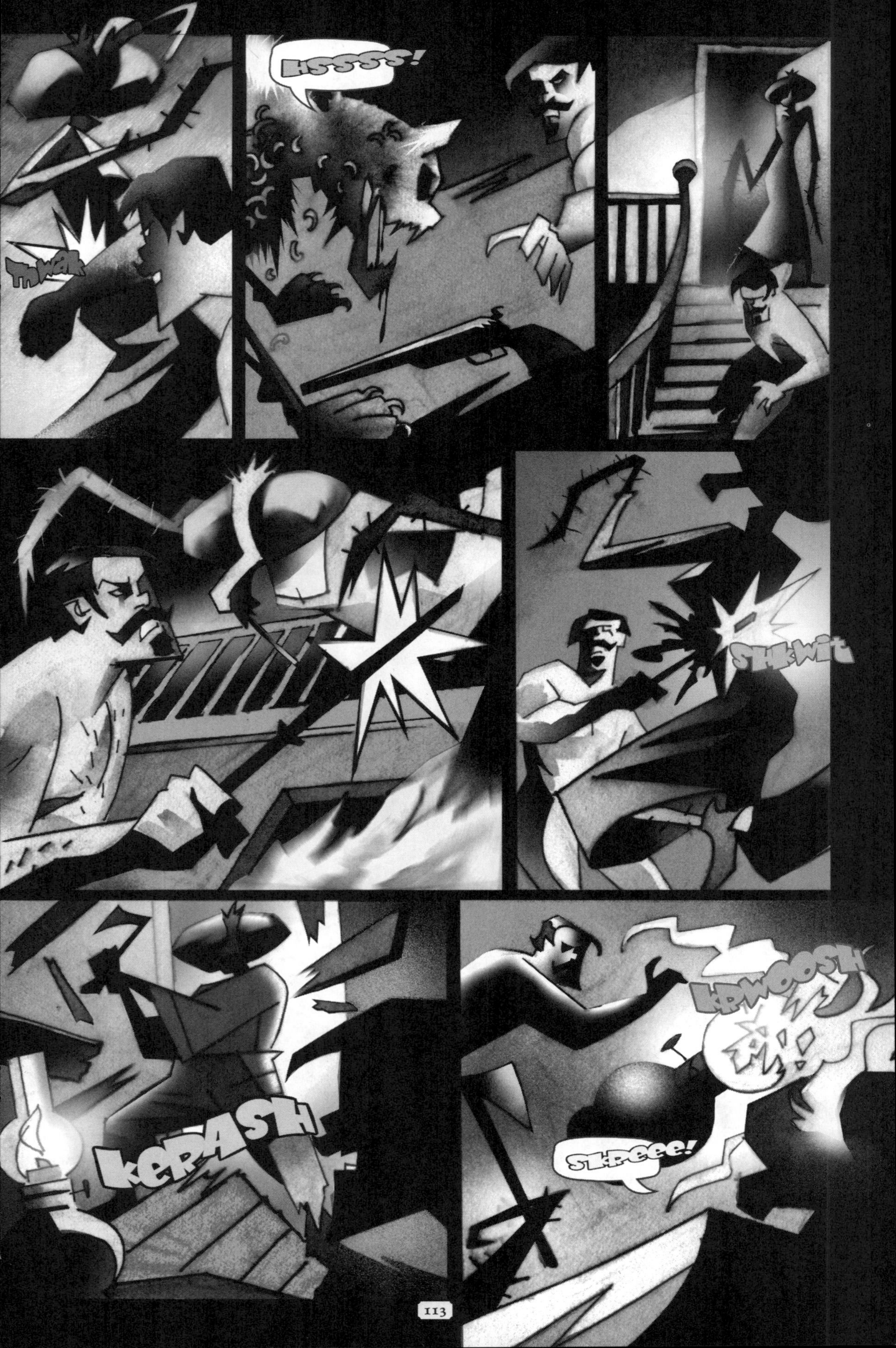
THWAK
HSSSSS!
SHKWIT
KERASH
KPWOOSH
SKREEE!

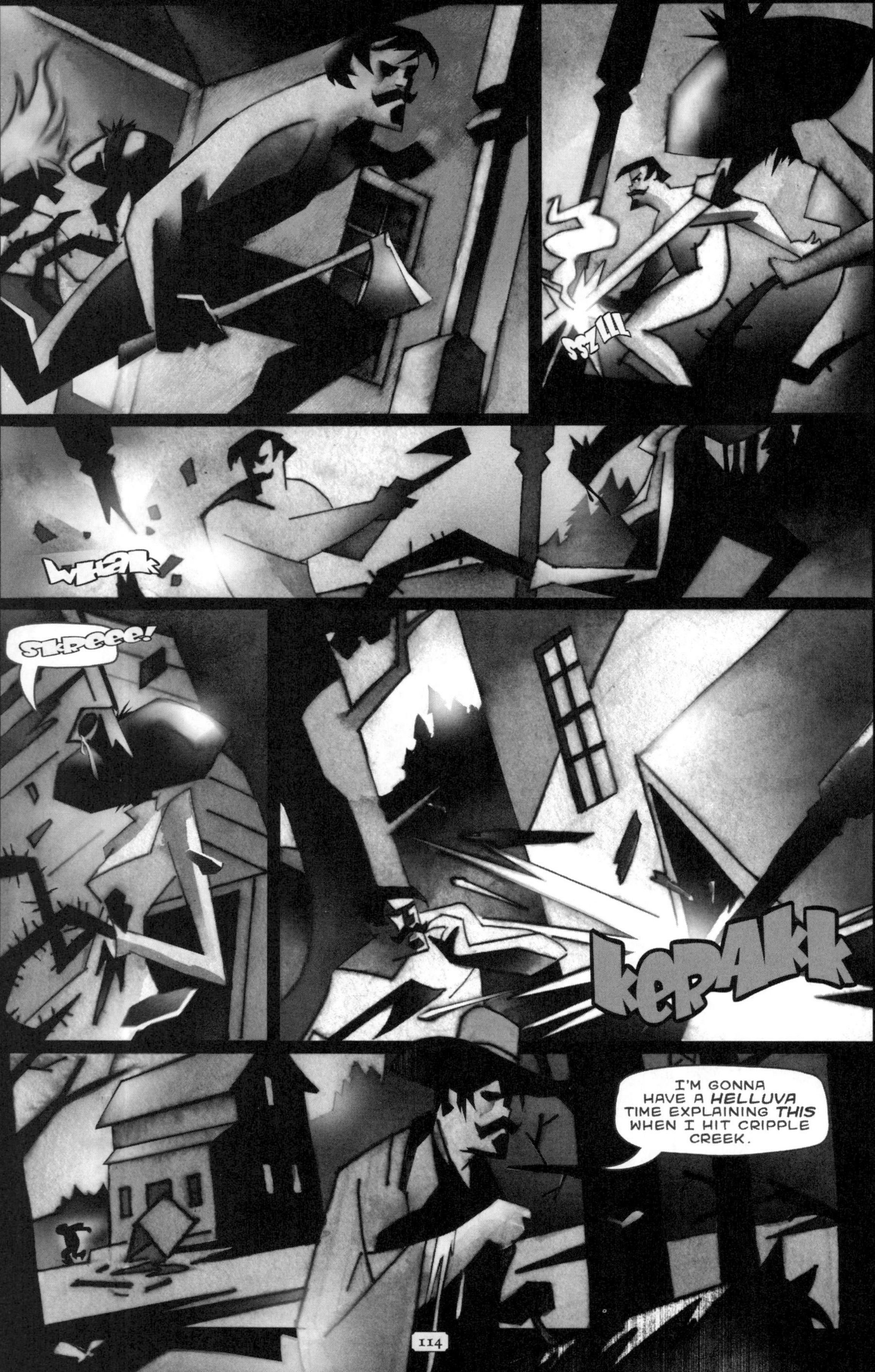
SSZLLL
WHAK!
SKREEE!
KERAKK
I'M GONNA HAVE A HELLUVA TIME EXPLAINING THIS WHEN I HIT CRIPPLE CREEK.

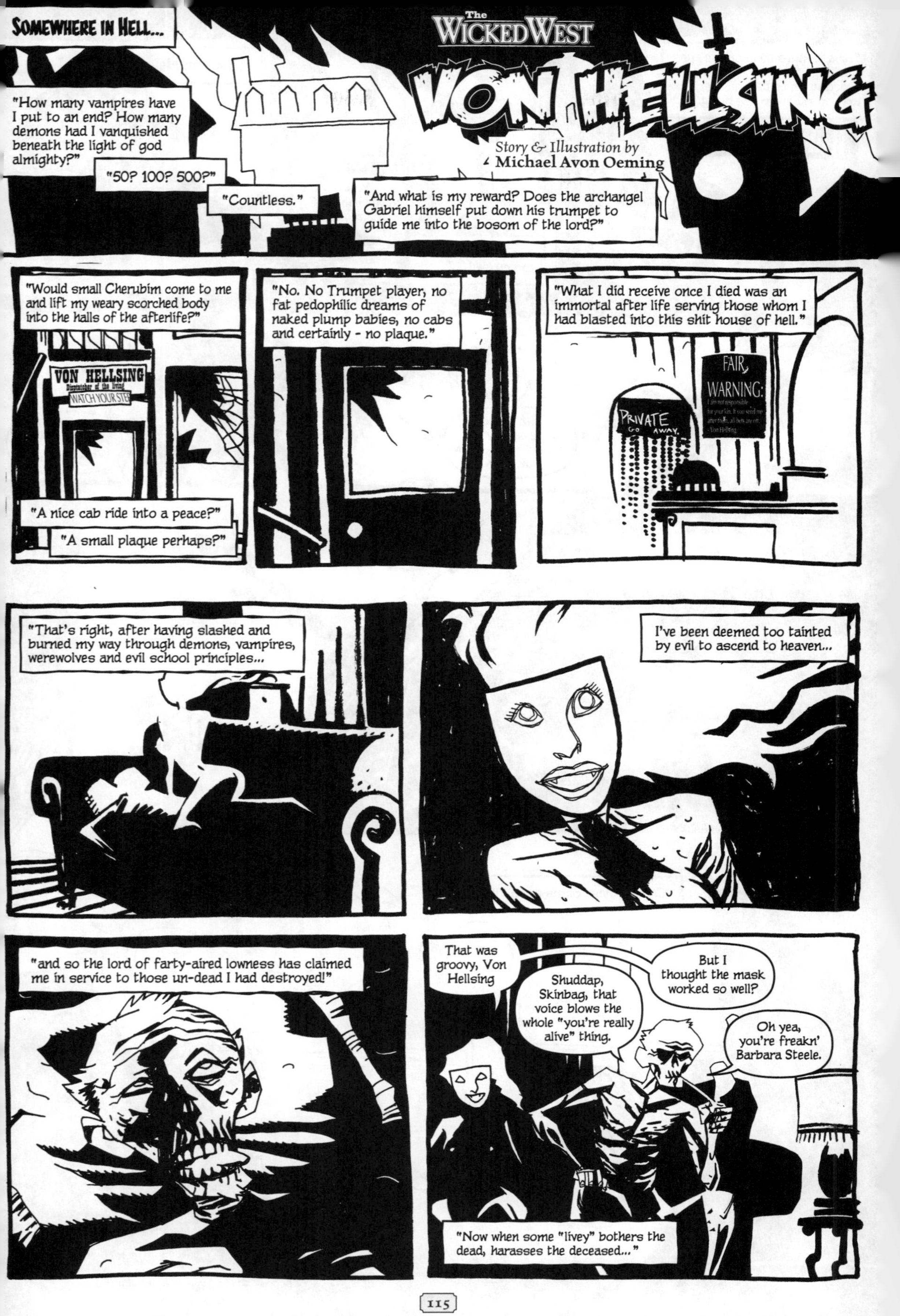

Somewhere in Hell...
The Wicked West
Von Hellsing
Story & Illustration by
Michael Avon Oeming
"How many vampires have I put to an end? How many demons had I vanquished beneath the light of god almighty?"
"50? 100? 500?"
"Countless."
"And what is my reward? Does the archangel Gabriel himself put down his trumpet to guide me into the bosom of the lord?"
"Would small Cherubim come to me and lift my weary scorched body into the halls of the afterlife?"
VON HELLSING
WATCH YOUR STE
"A nice cab ride into a peace?"
"A small plaque perhaps?"
"No. No Trumpet player, no fat pedophilic dreams of naked plump babies, no cabs and certainly - no plaque."
"What I did receive once I died was an immortal after life serving those whom I had blasted into this shit house of hell."
PRIVATE
GO AWAY.
FAIR, WARNING:
"That's right, after having slashed and burned my way through demons, vampires, werewolves and evil school principles...
I've been deemed too tainted by evil to ascend to heaven...
"and so the lord of farty-aired lowness has claimed me in service to those un-dead I had destroyed!"
That was groovy, Von Hellsing
Shuddap, Skinbag, that voice blows the whole "you're really alive" thing.
But I thought the mask worked so well?
Oh yea, you're freakn' Barbara Steele.
"Now when some "livey" bothers the dead, harasses the deceased..."

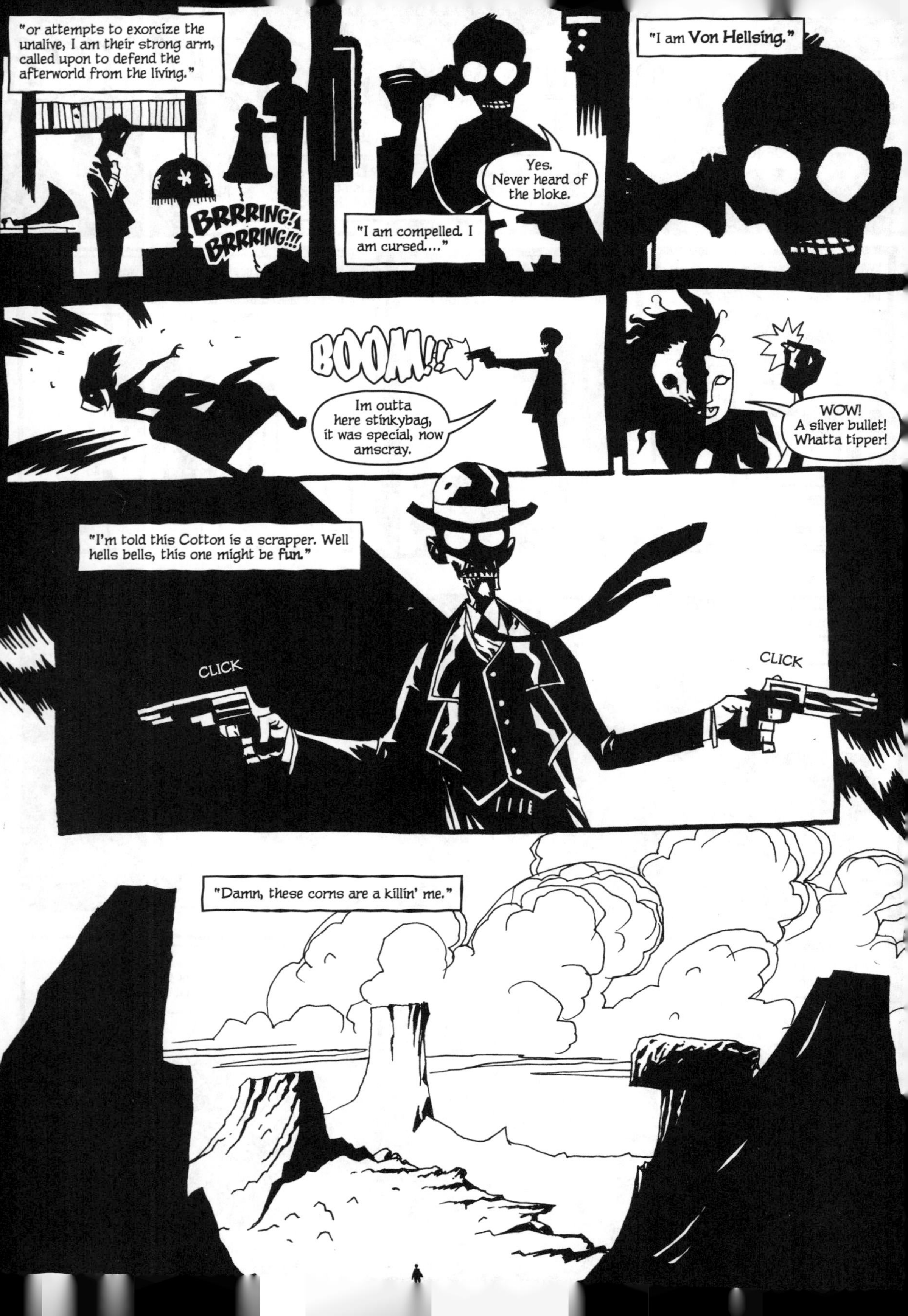

"or attempts to exorcize the unalive, I am their strong arm, called upon to defend the afterworld from the living."
BRRRING!! BRRRING!!!
Yes. Never heard of the bloke.
"I am compelled. I am cursed...."
"I am Von Hellsing."
BOOM!!
Im outta here stinkybag, it was special, now amscray.
WOW! A silver bullet! Whatta tipper!
"I'm told this Cotton is a scrapper. Well hells bells, this one might be fun."
CLICK
CLICK
"Damn, these corns are a killin' me."

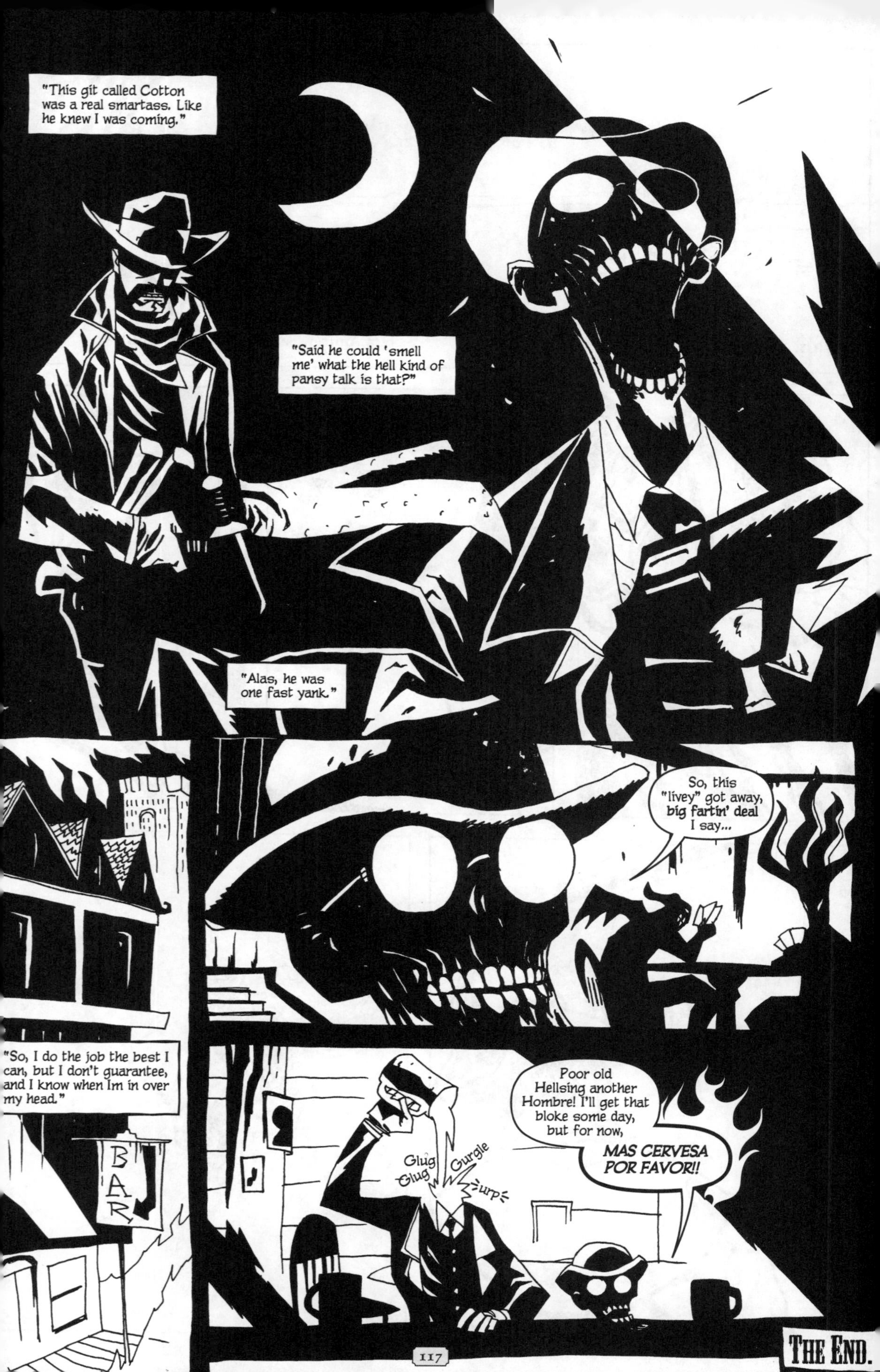
"This git called Cotton was a real smartass. Like he knew I was coming."
"Said he could 'smell me' what the hell kind of pansy talk is that?"
"Alas, he was one fast yank."
So, this "livey" got away, big fartin' deal I say...
"So, I do the job the best I can, but I don't guarantee, and I know when Im in over my head."
BAR
Poor old Hellsing another Hombre! I'll get that bloke some day, but for now,
MAS CERVESA POR FAVOR!!
Glug Glug Gurgle
urp
THE END.

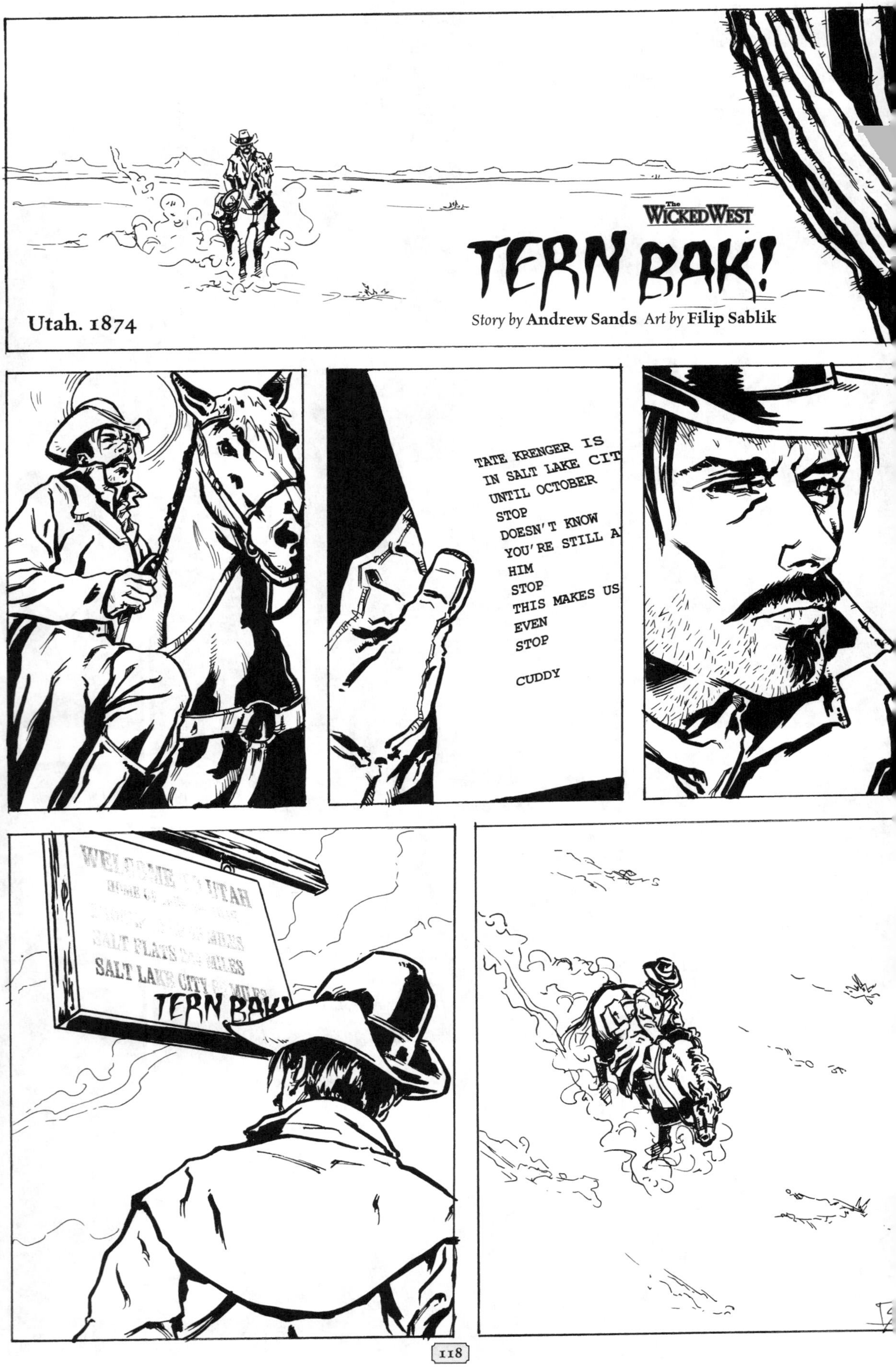
The WICKED WEST
TERN BAK!
Utah. 1874
Story by Andrew Sands Art by Filip Sablik
TATE KRENGER IS
IN SALT LAKE CIT
UNTIL OCTOBER
STOP
DOESN'T KNOW
YOU'RE STILL A
HIM
STOP
THIS MAKES US
EVEN
STOP
CUDDY
UTAH
SALT LAKE CITY
TERN BAK!

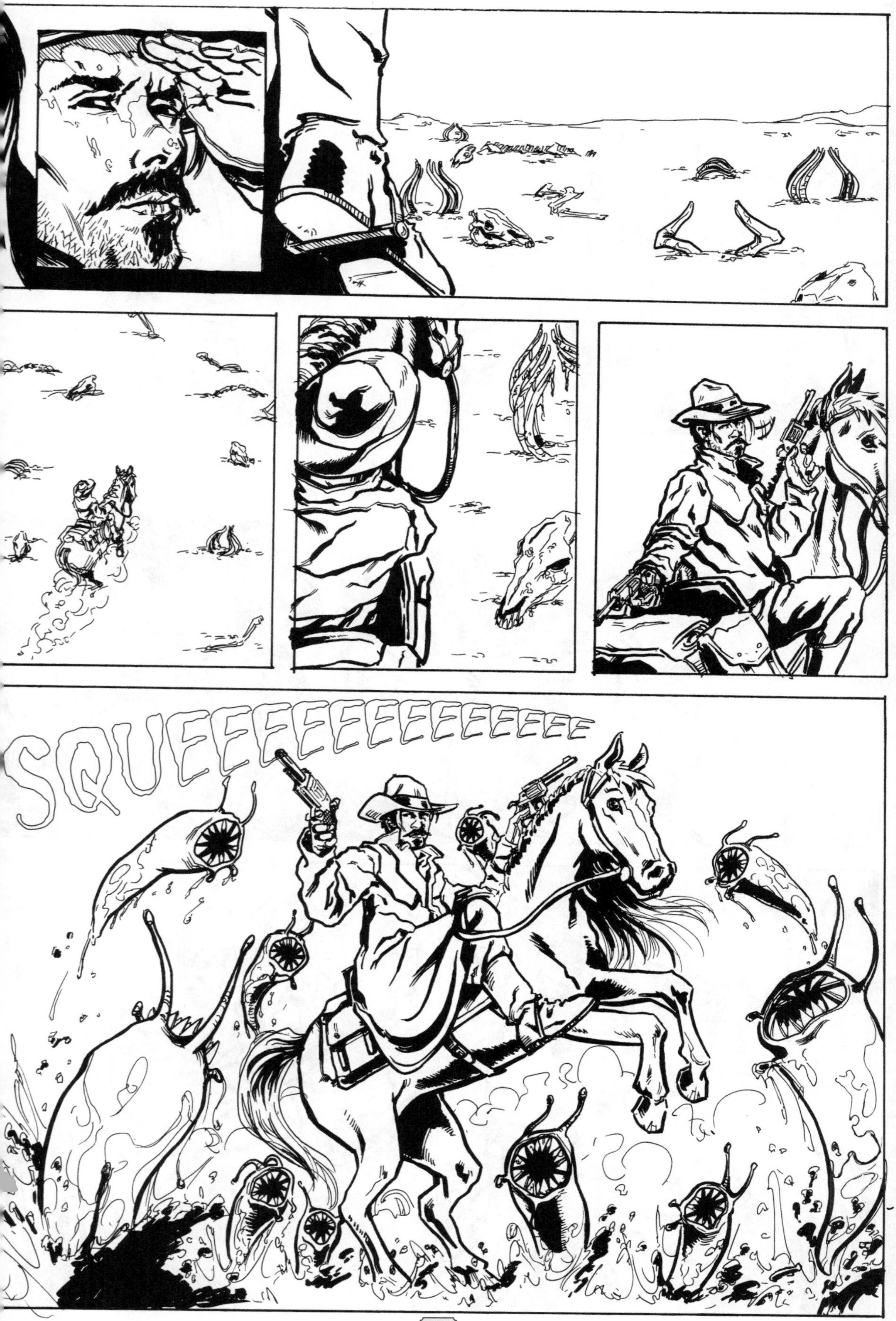
SQUEEEEEEEEEEEEEEE

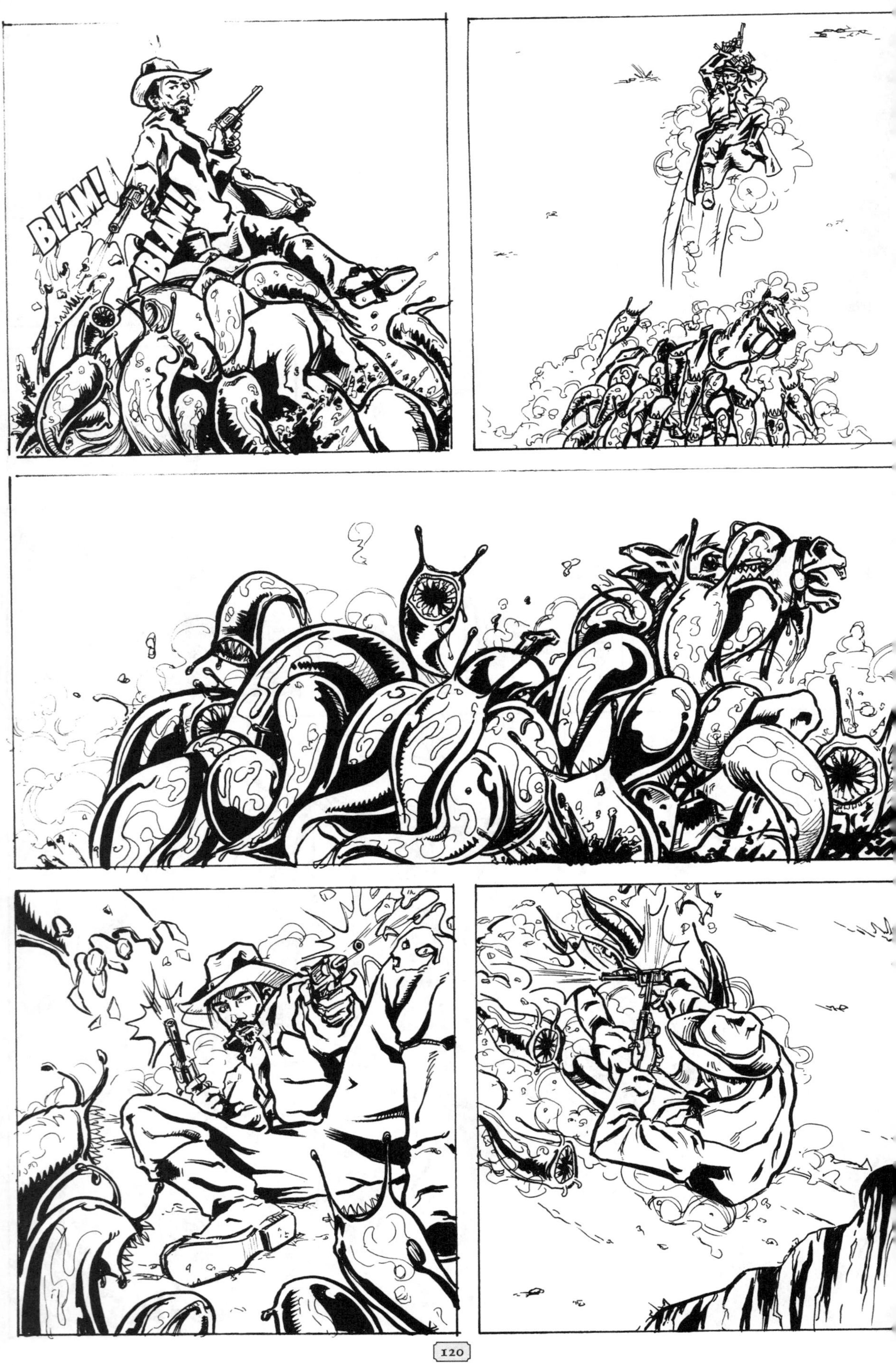
BLAM!
BLAM!

BLAM!
BLAM!
BLAM!
BLAM!
SALT FLATS
NEXT 14 MILES
CITY

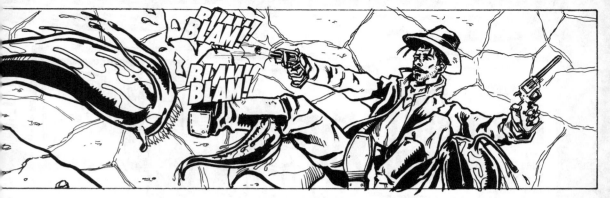

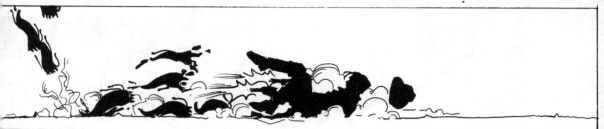

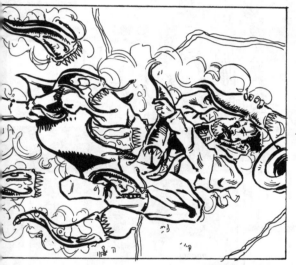

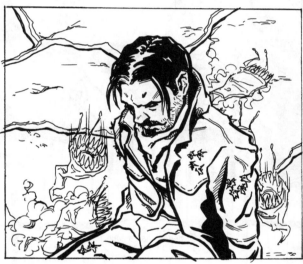

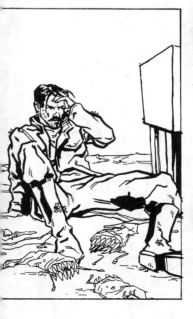

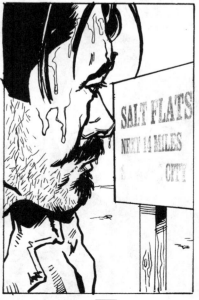

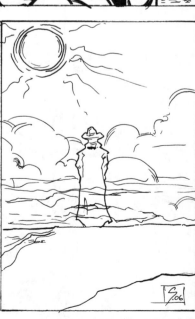

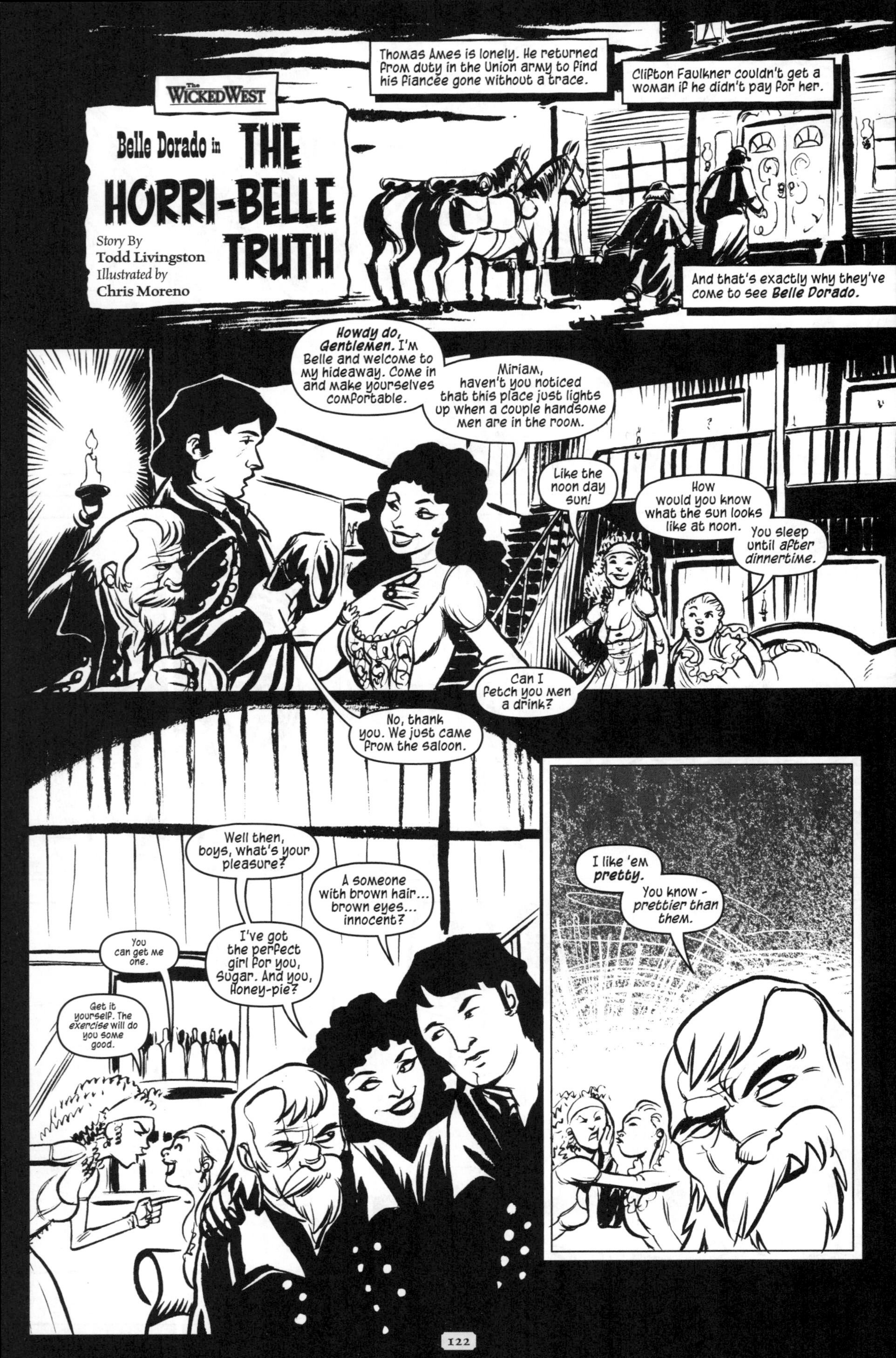
The WICKED WEST
Belle Dorado in THE HORRI-BELLE TRUTH
Story By
Todd Livingston
Illustrated by
Chris Moreno
Thomas Ames is lonely. He returned from duty in the Union army to find his fiancée gone without a trace.
Clifton Faulkner couldn't get a woman if he didn't pay for her.
And that's exactly why they've come to see Belle Dorado.
Howdy do, Gentlemen. I'm Belle and welcome to my hideaway. Come in and make yourselves comfortable.
Miriam, haven't you noticed that this place just lights up when a couple handsome men are in the room.
Like the noon day sun!
How would you know what the sun looks like at noon.
You sleep until after dinnertime.
Can I fetch you men a drink?
No, thank you. We just came from the saloon.
Well then, boys, what's your pleasure?
A someone with brown hair... brown eyes... innocent?
I've got the perfect girl for you, Sugar. And you, Honey-pie?
You can get me one.
Get it yourself. The exercise will do you some good.
I like 'em pretty.
You know - prettier than them.

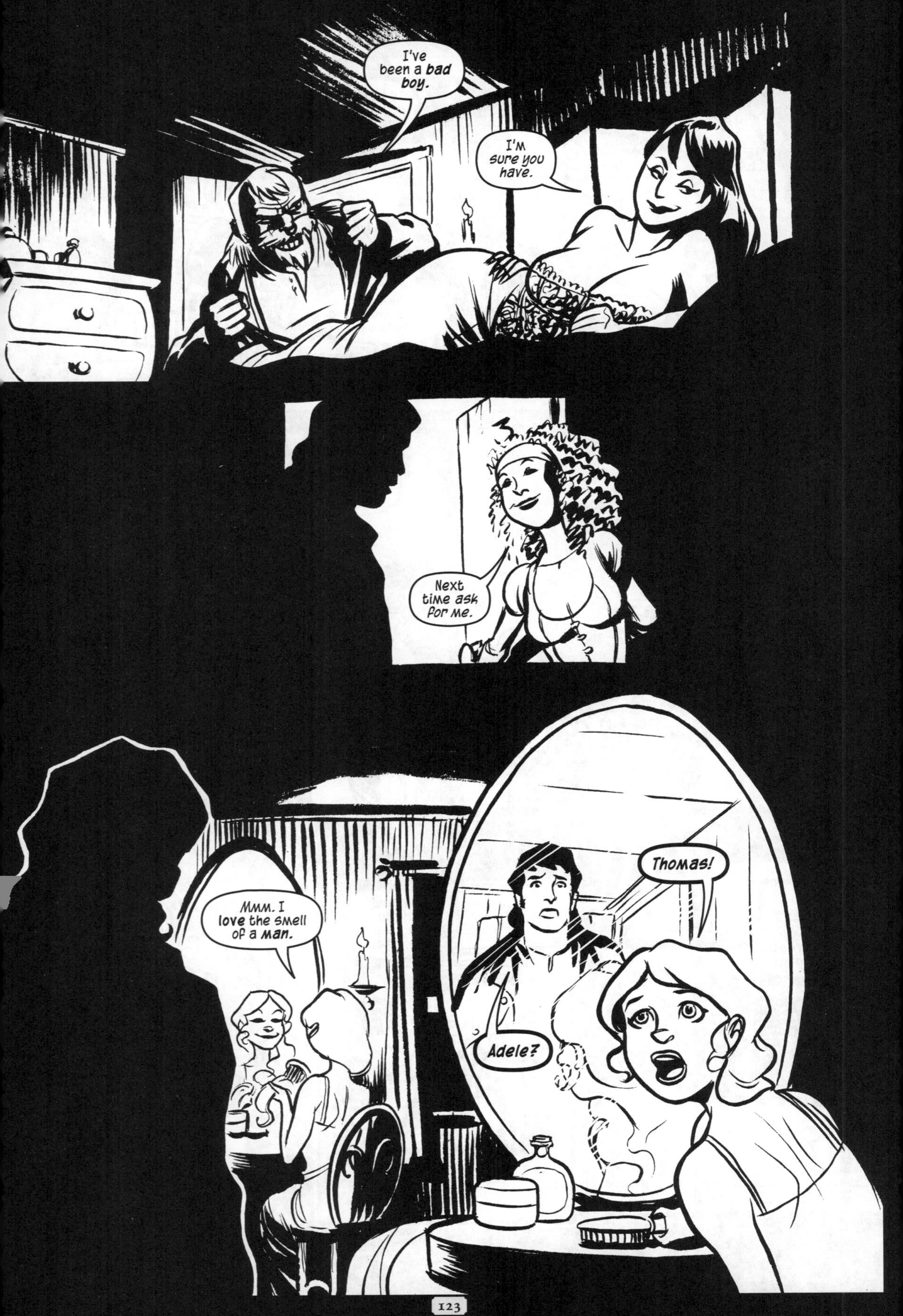
I've been a bad boy.
I'M sure you have.
Next time ask for me.
MMM. I love the smell of a man.
Thomas!
Adele?

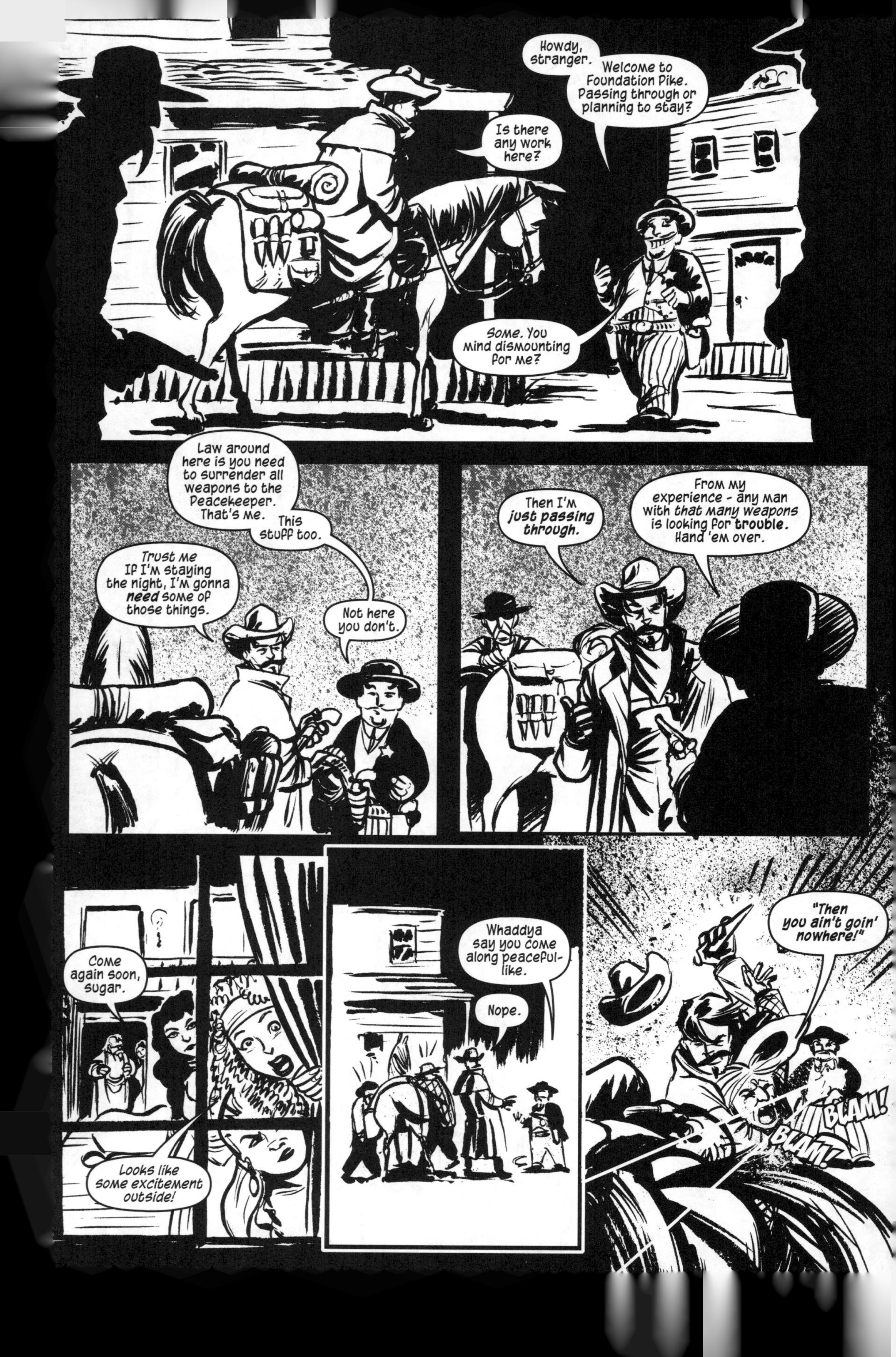
Howdy, stranger.
Welcome to Foundation Pike. Passing through or planning to stay?
Is there any work here?
Some. You mind dismounting for me?
Law around here is you need to surrender all weapons to the Peacekeeper. That's me.
This stuff too.
Trust me If I'm staying the night, I'm gonna *need* some of those things.
Not here you don't.
Then I'm *just passing through.*
From my experience - any man with *that many weapons* is looking for **trouble.** Hand 'em over.
Come again soon, sugar.
Looks like some excitement outside!
Whaddya say you come along peaceful-like.
Nope.
"Then you ain't goin' nowhere!"
BLAM!
BLAM!

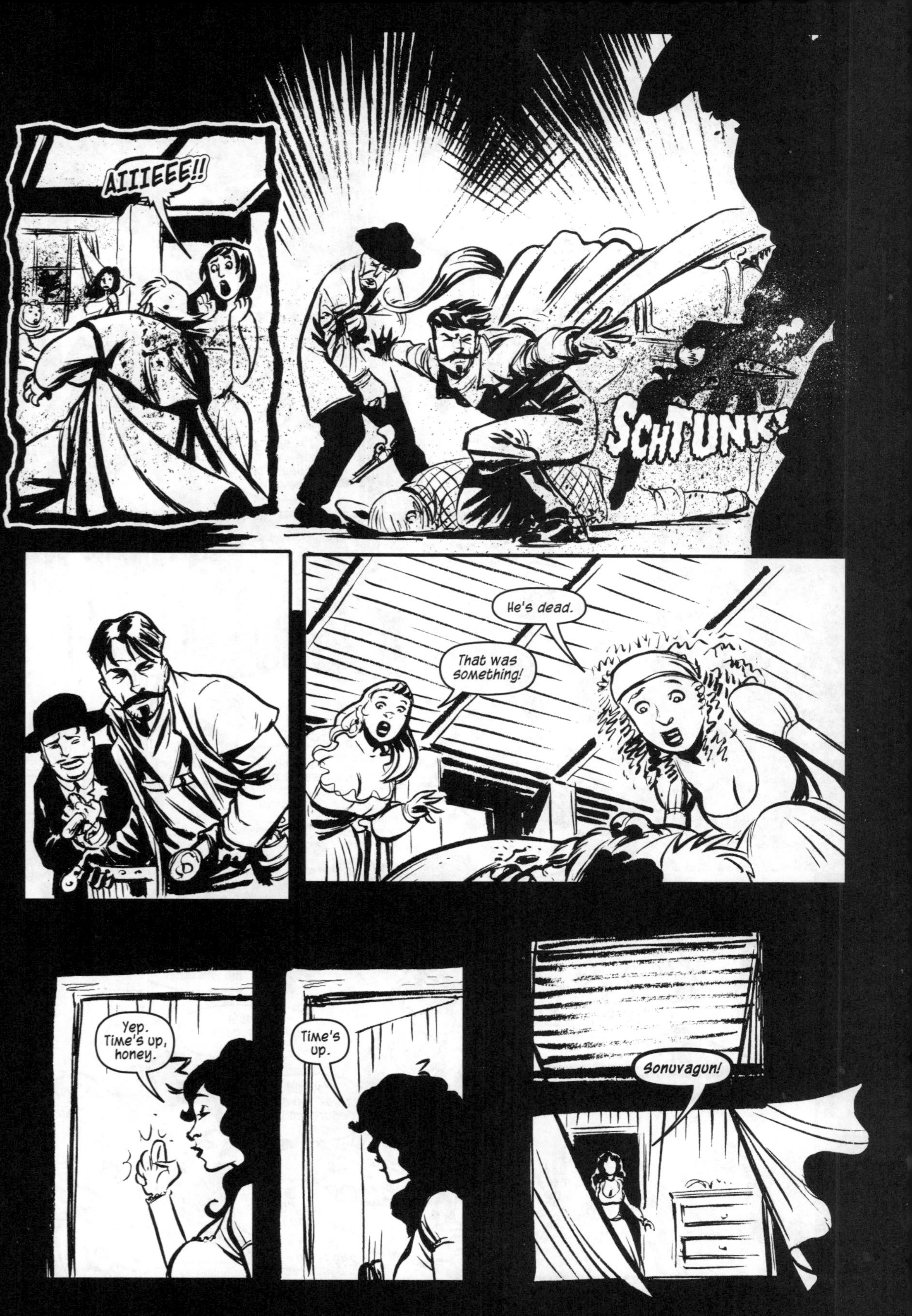
AIIIEEE!!
SCHTUNK!
He's dead.
That was something!
Yep. Time's up, honey.
Time's up.
Sonuvagun!

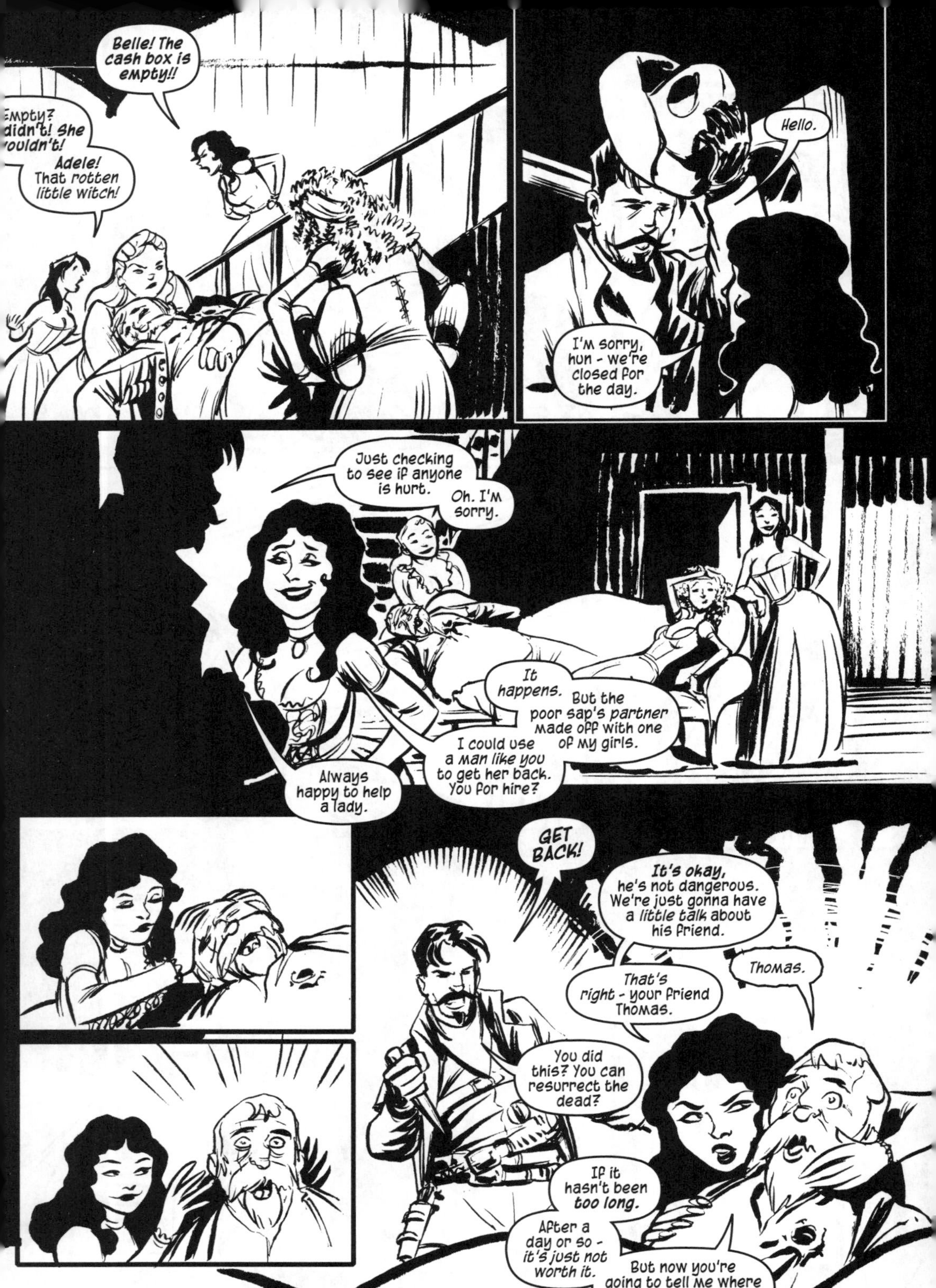

Belle! The cash box is empty!!
Empty? didn't! She wouldn't! Adele! That rotten little witch!
Hello.
I'm sorry, hun - we're closed for the day.
Just checking to see if anyone is hurt.
Oh. I'm sorry.
It happens.
But the poor sap's partner made off with one of my girls.
I could use a man like you to get her back. You for hire?
Always happy to help a lady.
GET BACK!
It's okay, he's not dangerous. We're just gonna have a little talk about his friend.
Thomas.
That's right - your friend Thomas.
You did this? You can resurrect the dead?
If it hasn't been too long.
After a day or so - it's just not worth it.
But now you're going to tell me where Thomas might have run off to.

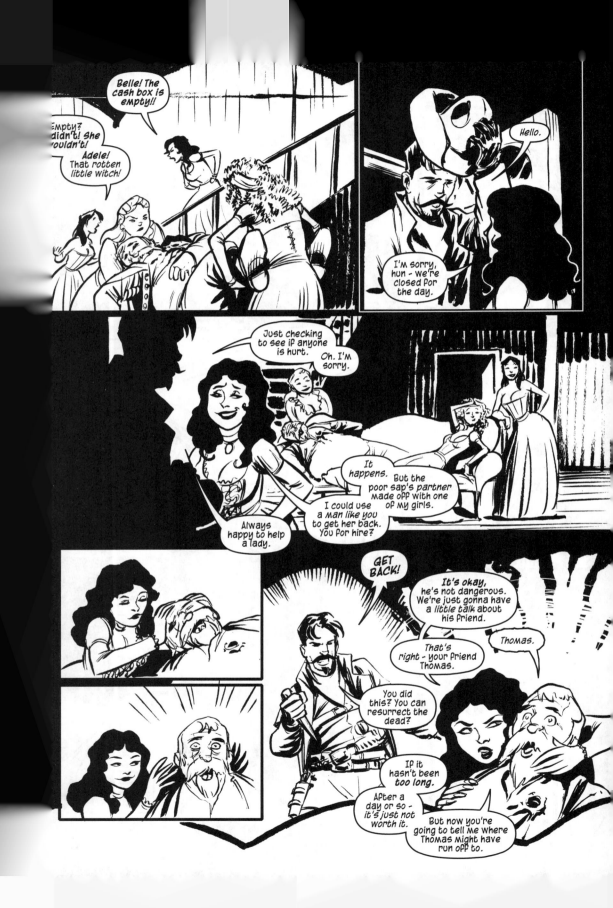

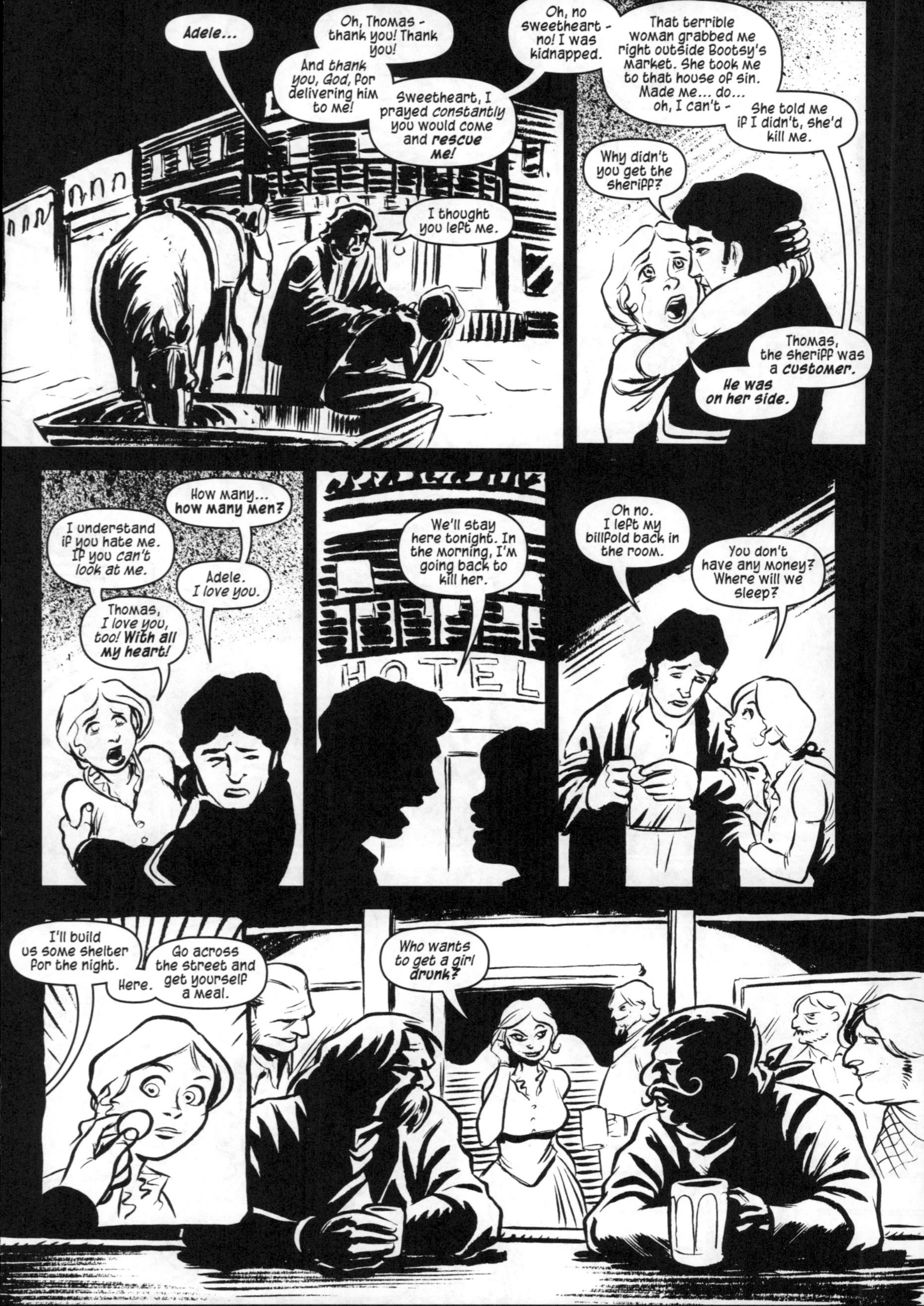
Adele...
Oh, Thomas - thank you! Thank you!
And thank you, God, for delivering him to me!
Sweetheart, I prayed constantly you would come and rescue me!
I thought you left me.
Oh, no sweetheart - no! I was kidnapped.
That terrible woman grabbed me right outside Bootsy's Market. She took me to that house of sin. Made me... do... oh, I can't -
She told me if I didn't, she'd kill me.
Why didn't you get the sheriff?
Thomas, the sheriff was a customer.
He was on her side.
How many... how many men?
I understand if you hate me. If you can't look at me.
Adele. I love you.
Thomas, I love you, too! With all my heart!
We'll stay here tonight. In the morning, I'm going back to kill her.
HOTEL
Oh no. I left my billfold back in the room.
You don't have any money? Where will we sleep?
I'll build us some shelter for the night.
Here.
Go across the street and get yourself a meal.
Who wants to get a girl drunk?

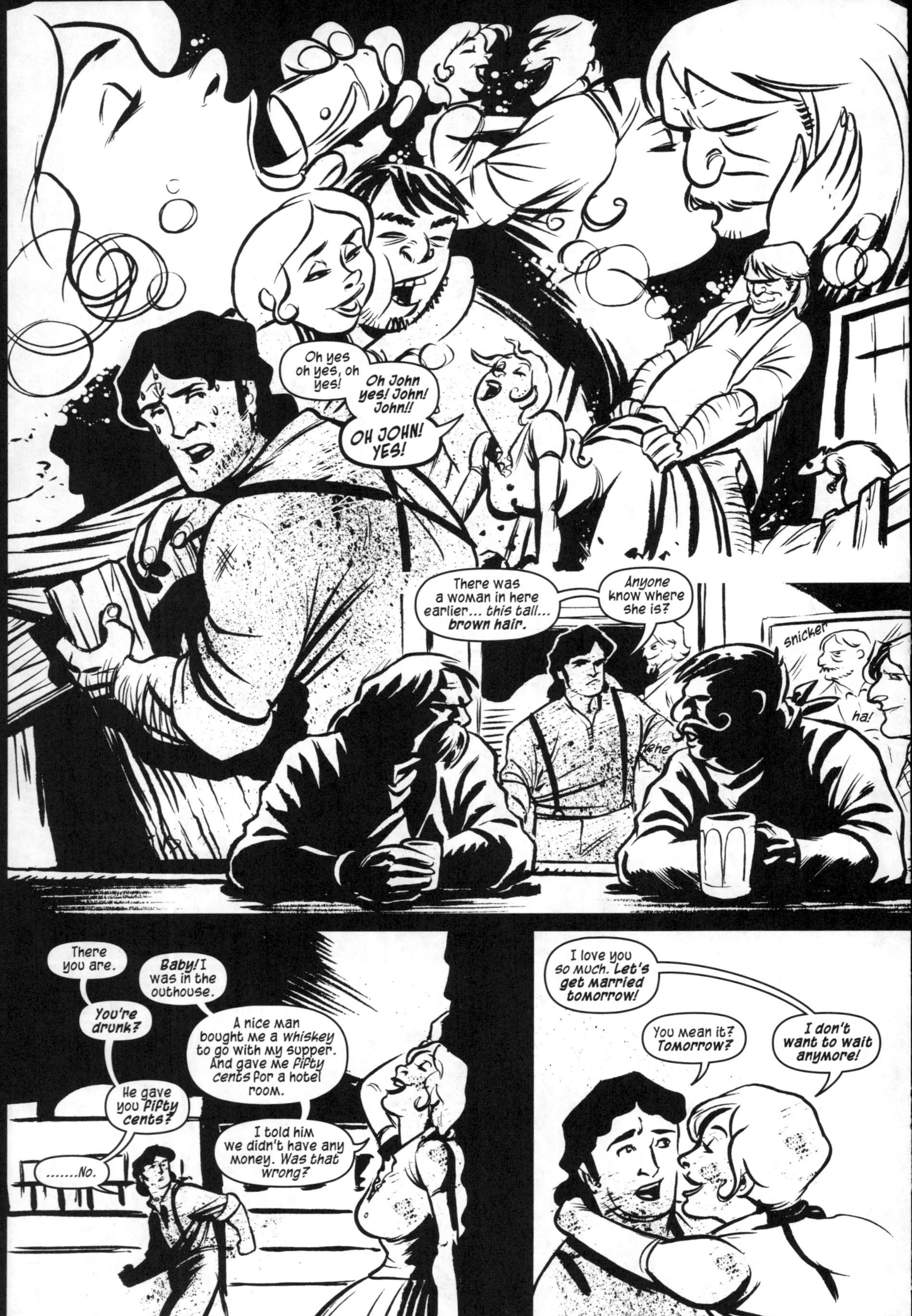
Oh yes oh yes, oh yes!
Oh John yes! John! John!!
OH JOHN! YES!
There was a woman in here earlier... this tall... brown hair.
Anyone know where she is?
snicker
ha!
hehe
There you are.
Baby! I was in the outhouse.
You're drunk?
A nice man bought me a whiskey to go with my supper. And gave me fifty cents for a hotel room.
He gave you fifty cents?
I told him we didn't have any money. Was that wrong?
.......No.
I love you so much. Let's get married tomorrow!
You mean it? Tomorrow?
I don't want to wait anymore!

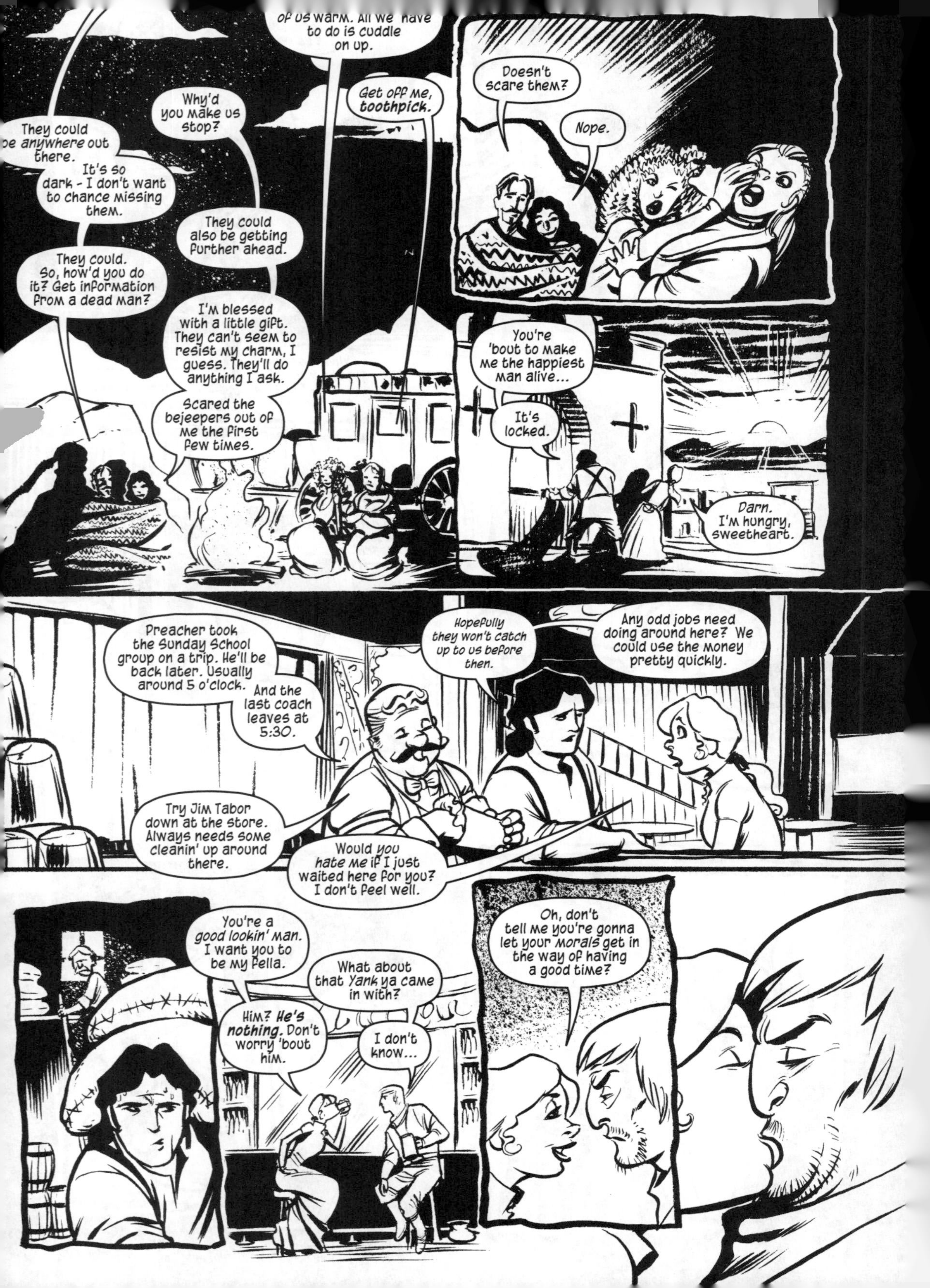

of us warm. All we have to do is cuddle on up.
Get off me, toothpick.
They could be anywhere out there.
Why'd you make us stop?
It's so dark - I don't want to chance missing them.
They could also be getting further ahead.
They could. So, how'd you do it? Get information from a dead man?
I'm blessed with a little gift. They can't seem to resist my charm, I guess. They'll do anything I ask.
Scared the bejeepers out of me the first few times.
Doesn't scare them?
Nope.
You're 'bout to make me the happiest man alive...
It's locked.
Darn. I'm hungry, sweetheart.
Preacher took the Sunday School group on a trip. He'll be back later. Usually around 5 o'clock.
And the last coach leaves at 5:30.
Hopefully they won't catch up to us before then.
Any odd jobs need doing around here? We could use the money pretty quickly.
Try Jim Tabor down at the store. Always needs some cleanin' up around there.
Would you hate me if I just waited here for you? I don't feel well.
You're a good lookin' man. I want you to be my fella.
What about that Yank ya came in with?
Him? He's nothing. Don't worry 'bout him.
I don't know...
Oh, don't tell me you're gonna let your morals get in the way of having a good time?

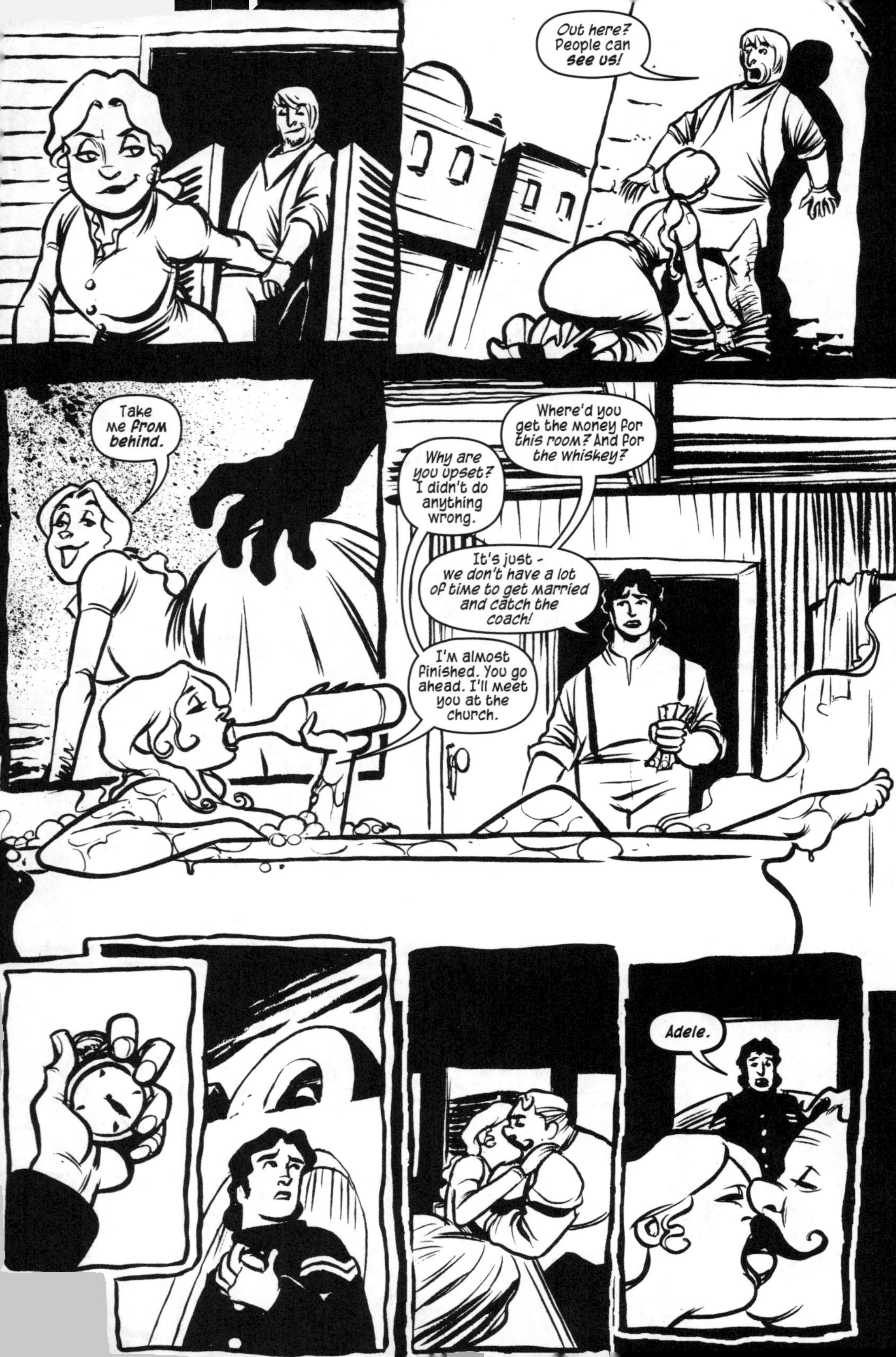
Out here? People can see us!
Take me from behind.
Where'd you get the money for this room? And for the whiskey?
Why are you upset? I didn't do anything wrong.
It's just - we don't have a lot of time to get married and catch the coach!
I'm almost finished. You go ahead. I'll meet you at the church.
Adele.

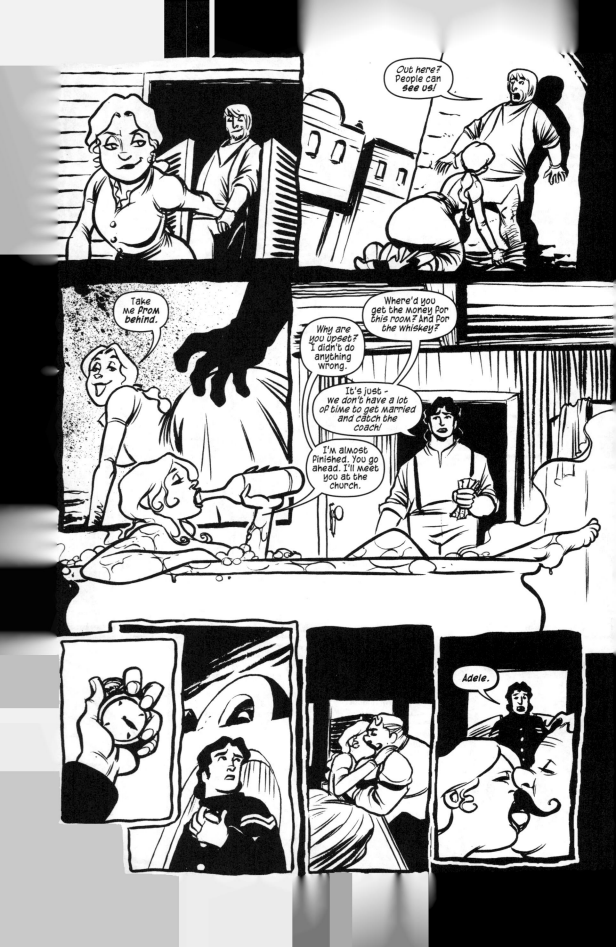

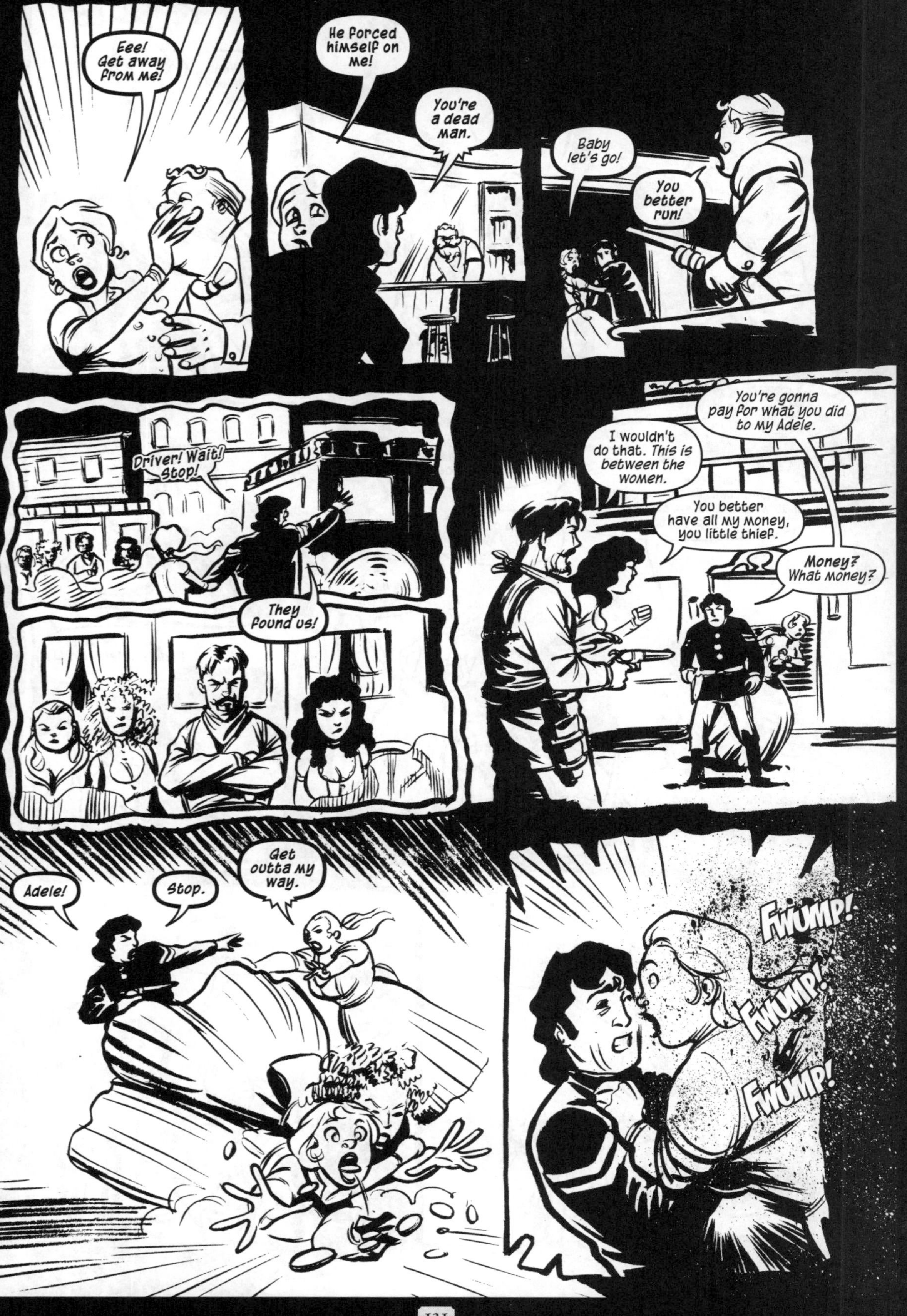
Eee! Get away from me!
He forced himself on me!
You're a dead man.
Baby let's go!
You better run!
Driver! Wait! Stop!
They found us!
I wouldn't do that. This is between the women.
You're gonna pay for what you did to my Adele.
You better have all my money, you little thief.
Money? What money?
Adele!
Stop.
Get outta my way.
FWUMP!
FWUMP!
FWUMP!

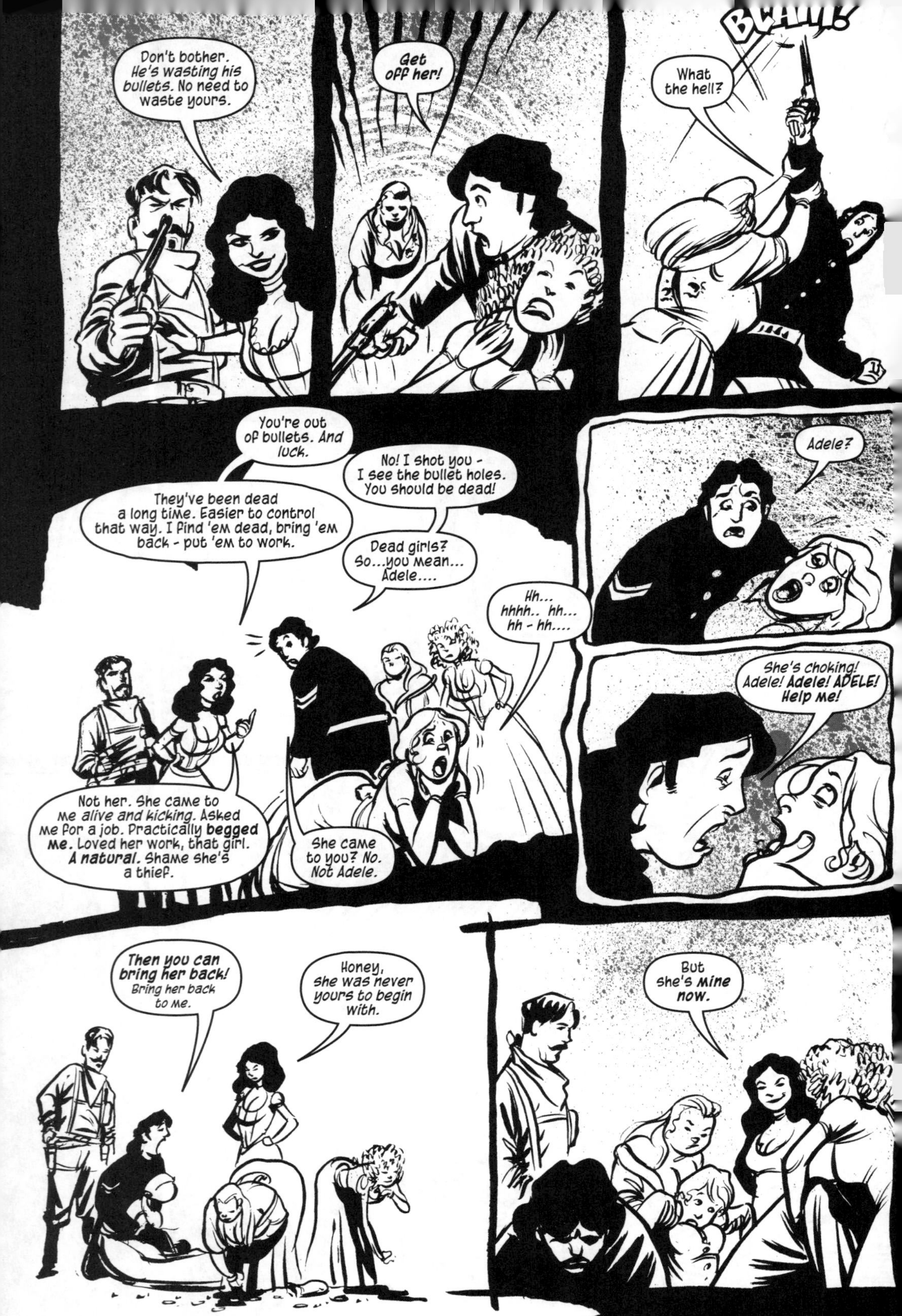
Don't bother. He's wasting his bullets. No need to waste yours.
Get off her!
BLAM!
What the hell?
You're out of bullets. And luck.
No! I shot you - I see the bullet holes. You should be dead!
They've been dead a long time. Easier to control that way. I find 'em dead, bring 'em back - put 'em to work.
Dead girls? So...you mean... Adele....
Hh... hhhh.. hh... hh - hh....
Not her. She came to me alive and kicking. Asked me for a job. Practically begged me. Loved her work, that girl. A natural. Shame she's a thief.
She came to you? No. Not Adele.
Adele?
She's choking! Adele! Adele! ADELE! Help me!
Then you can bring her back! Bring her back to me.
Honey, she was never yours to begin with.
But she's mine now.

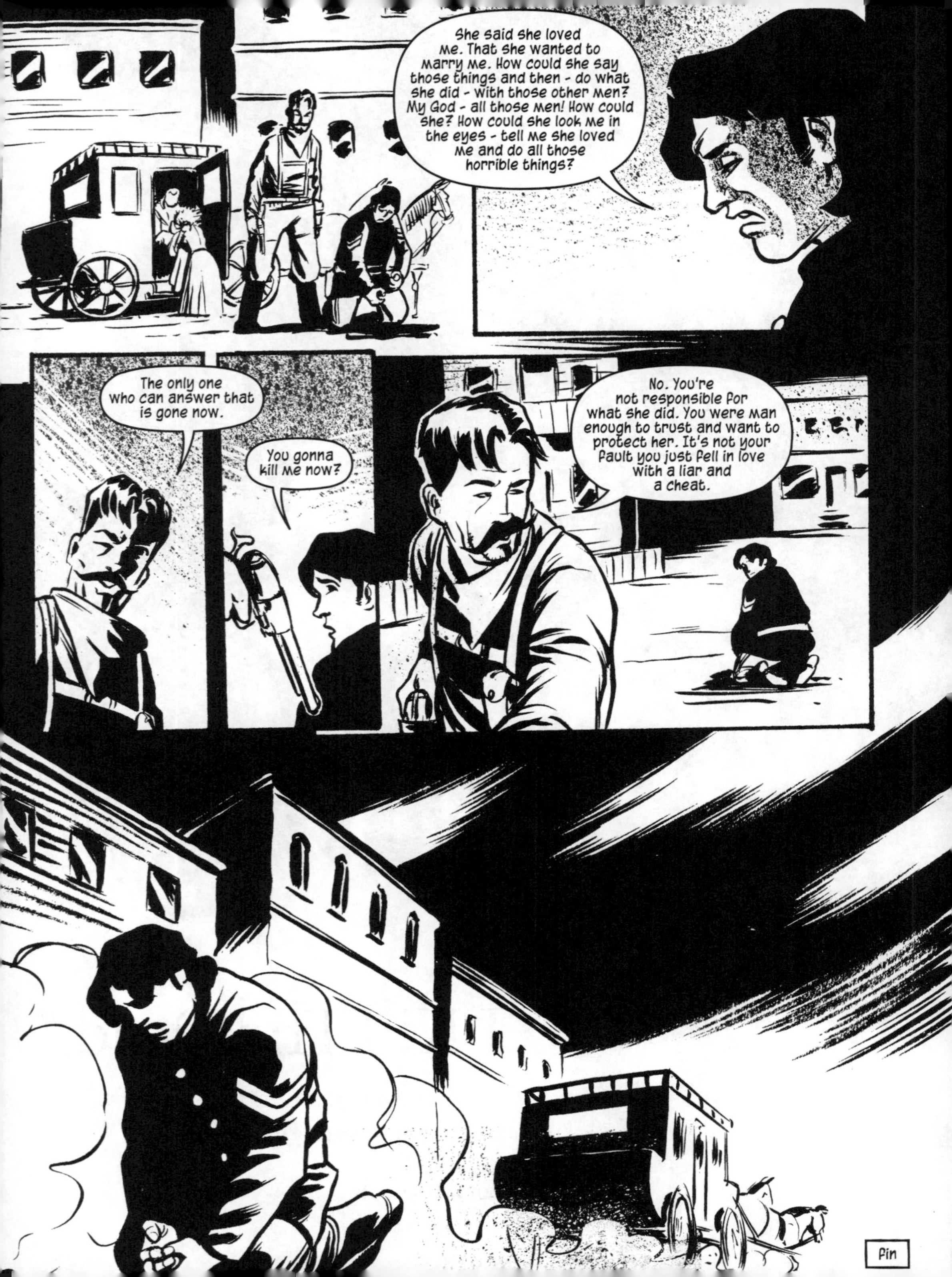
She said she loved Me. That she wanted to Marry Me. How could she say those things and then - do what she did - with those other Men? My God - all those Men! How could she? How could she look Me in the eyes - tell Me she loved Me and do all those horrible things?
The only one who can answer that is gone now.
You gonna kill Me now?
No. You're not responsible for what she did. You were Man enough to trust and want to protect her. It's not your fault you just fell in love with a liar and a cheat.
fin

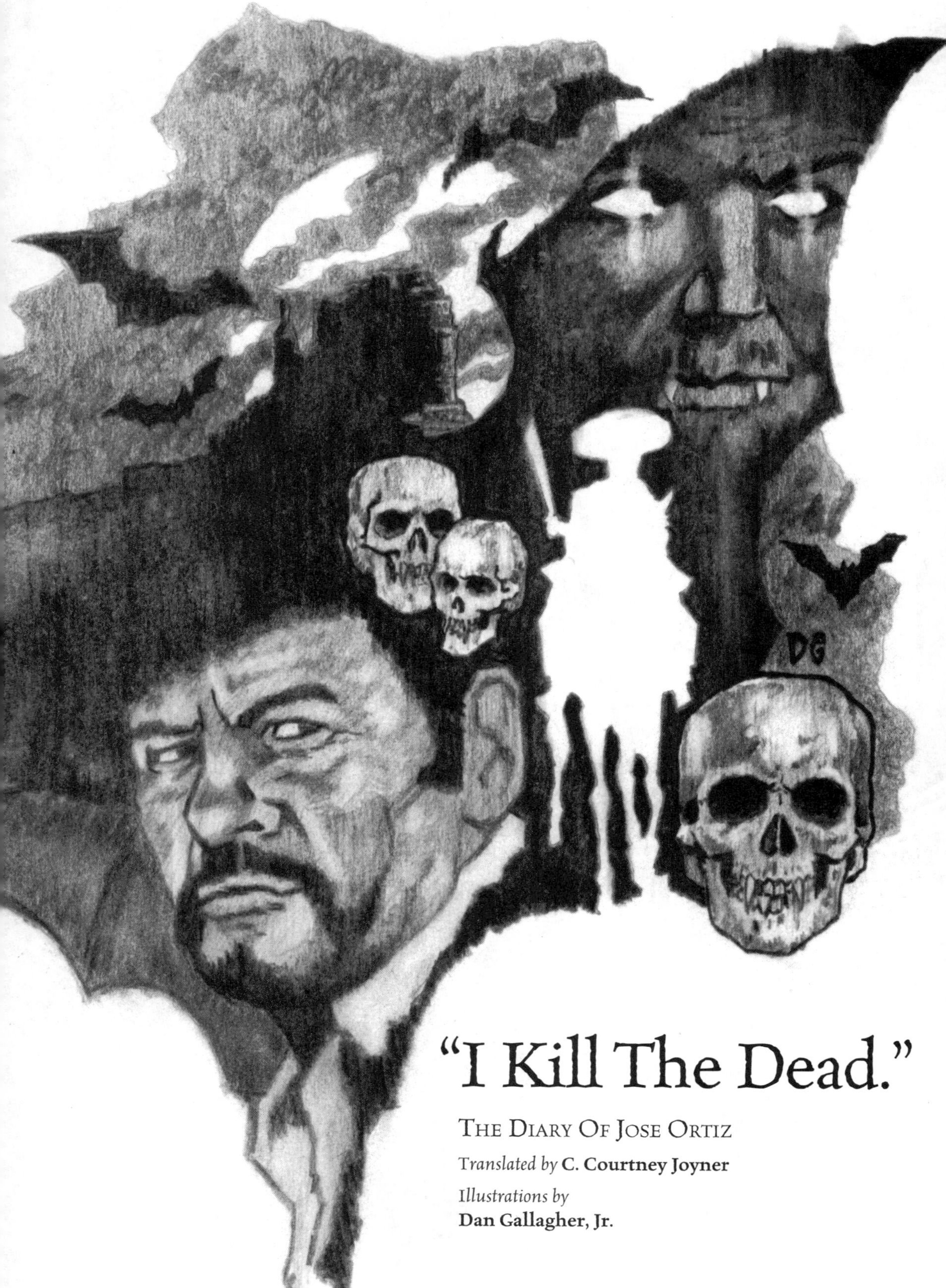
DG

"I Kill The Dead."

The Diary Of Jose Ortiz

Translated by **C. Courtney Joyner**

Illustrations by
Dan Gallagher, Jr.

TRANSLATOR'S NOTE: *The following pages were taken from a diary discovered in an unmarked grave near the Texas/Mexico border. The diary had been sewn into a canvas bag with its author, Jose Estaban Ortiz. Ortiz was convicted of conspiracy in the 1870 murder of Miss Temperance Jones, and sentenced to twenty years at hard labor in the territorial prison in McLennon, Texas. Because of his insistence at trial that he "never killed the living, only the vampire dead," Ortiz earned the nickname El Carnicero de Dios ("God's Butcher"). After his release, Ortiz wandered the border towns, handing out pamphlets about "El Vampyros." Records show he was arrested six times for desecrating graves and twice for body snatching. Each time he claimed he was "protecting the living from the dead." Ortiz vanished in 1893, and his death was a mystery until paleontology students from Rice University unearthed him this year. His diary was clutched in his hands, and a wooden stake had been driven through his chest. Although some of the pages were unreadable, Jose Estaban Ortiz's vivid fears about "El Vampyros" remain intact.*

=AUGUST 15, 1850

I am not a murderer, but I am a killer.

I write these words as my best friend lies beside me, demanding I cut his throat. I have the machete, but not the courage. I need the warmth of my wife and children because I don't know if God will forgive me for what I've done this last day, or what I still must do. I know I won't be able to forgive myself.

If a lawman rode up now, he would see the slaughter and shoot me between the eyes. Heaven would smile at that; and I would rather take a bullet or a knife then face what comes from the dessert after the sun bleeds away.

Chango isn't afraid of the dark, but he's dying. Instead of giving comfort I must write. He says I have to tell what happened, before I kill him. That is his wish. Chango says I owe him a blessed death. Yesterday, all I owed him was a small share of gold from the Rio Grande.

We had started well: Chango brought me into a deal with two gringos, Burke, and a smiling coward who called himself "Tabano" (Horsefly). Chango was mi amigo; the other two were mule-skinners who knew the inner curves of the Rio Grande, and claimed there was a gold shelf that fed into the river and could be panned at the shallows. They needed partners to work the river before someone else beat them to it. For that, quarter shares.

For three sunsets we rode hard, but we found the spot where the Rio cut into the land and left it ribbonned with streaks of brown. I know enough about prospecting to know this is good, and we made camp. Berke and Chango pitched a lean-to and I found wood to make a small run-off channel. Tabano drank, but only whiskey, not "piss-tequila." He angered me.

We were saddle-worn, but too excited to sleep. Chango built a work fire and Berke and I began to pan the channel. The orange light made the gold hard to see, but you don't see gold with your eyes, you feel it between your fingers. The touch tells you the truth. We brought a full ounce from the Rio Grande that night, while Tabano bragged about what he would do with his fortune. I worked, thinking of my family. Tabano yelled about the Chinese whores he would buy in San Francisco.

That's when the bat covered the moon.

It was a black shadow, five buzzards across. We watched as it dove, screeching, out of the moon. I ran for my Kentucky rifle. Berke just ran. But the bat was faster.

A shower of blood soaked me and my black powder. Berke's screams were choked as the bat pulled his legs from his body, ripping through him like paper. I froze as it settled on the ground, lapping his blood with a darting tongue and feeding on wet muscle. I saw that the bat had a man's face; twisted, with fangs over the lips, but a man just the same. The wings were arms ending in claws, with great folds of skin

hanging down. And even though they were covered with hair, the body and legs were Humano.

I knew I was looking into Hell.

I didn't see it slash Chango, but he went down screaming and I fired. The bat-thing moved for Tabano. I re-loaded. The powder was sticky with blood and fouled the breech. When I looked up, Tabano was caught and being lifted into the sky like an owl grabs a rat. I threw a rope and snared Tabano's ankles. I held him fast as the thing tried to fly; the air from his wings swirling the dust like a small twister. I held on. It dragged me, and I lashed the rope to my saddle horn. My mare bucked, pulling Tabano to us. I pulled the trigger and the powder only sizzled, then sparked.

The bullet tore the bat's neck and it swiped at the rope, cutting it clean. It flew for the blue-black hills, its catch in its claws. In a moment, the bat-thing and Tabano were gone. That's what I remember of the first attack; and what I won't forget for the rest of my life.

As I write this, Chango holds out the machete and asks me to do my duty to defeat Tezcatliposa (The God of Hell). El Vampyros has existed in my country since the Conquistadors, and I was raised to fear something I had never seen; just the whispers of old people. Now I have seen it, and I must kill my friend to destroy the vampire.

That is why I will cut Brother Chango's throat.

(Translator's note: *The following two pages were saturated with blood and crumbled when the diary was re-opened. The next entries begin on* August 16th, 1850.)

Morning. The sun's risen and by a miracle I am still here. Not dead-alive, but really alive. I'm sitting on Chango's grave, knowing he'd want me to put down these words. This isn't a confession for the law; most say I was born to be hung anyway. I want my family to know what Brother Chango did for me. For everyone.

My old friend was a monk from the mission of San Rafael. To Tabano and Berke, Chango was just a greedy peasant working for piss-ant shares. But all of his gold was for the mission, not himself. Let the gringos think what they want, we knew the truth. But after the night of the bat, the gold didn't matter. Only blood did. And mi amigo told me what to

do with it.

I prepared all day for the bat. I had black powder bombs and Brother Chango's own silver cross heating in the fire, but he said it wasn't enough. I opened the gold channel, forming a small pool. Chango blessed the Rio Grande, and our souls. He told me what I had to do. The wound from the bat was killing him, and if he died, he'd be damned forever. He swore that was not going to happen. I pulled him to the edge of the pool, and took the machete. I asked for all his strength and he nodded before I laid the blade against his neck and whipped it back. The blood fountained into the water, and Brother Chango went to sleep.

The sun was dying as I dug the grave. As mi amigo wanted, I pounded a tent stake into his heart. I shoveled the last bit of sand onto him when the bat broke from the clouds. I kept my back to it, letting him dive for me. I lit a bomb, waited a few heartbeats, and threw it directly at the thing. The blast sent it spinning to the ground.

I slashed the wings with the machete, then hog-tied its arms to its legs. It twisted wild as my mare and I hauled it to the pool. Bile poured from its mouth as I pushed it in. The scream didn't last five seconds as Chango's blessed blood-water churned, par-boiling the bat-thing to its bones. El Diablo was dead -

And Tabano grabbed me by the throat. He wasn't a mule-skinner or gold-hunter now. He was El Vampyro. The corpse's fingers dug deep as he lifted me into the air. His turning flesh stank, and his tongue and gums were black as he opened his mouth, revealing fangs. I jammed my blade into his gut, opening him. Insects burst from the wound and Tabano hurled me

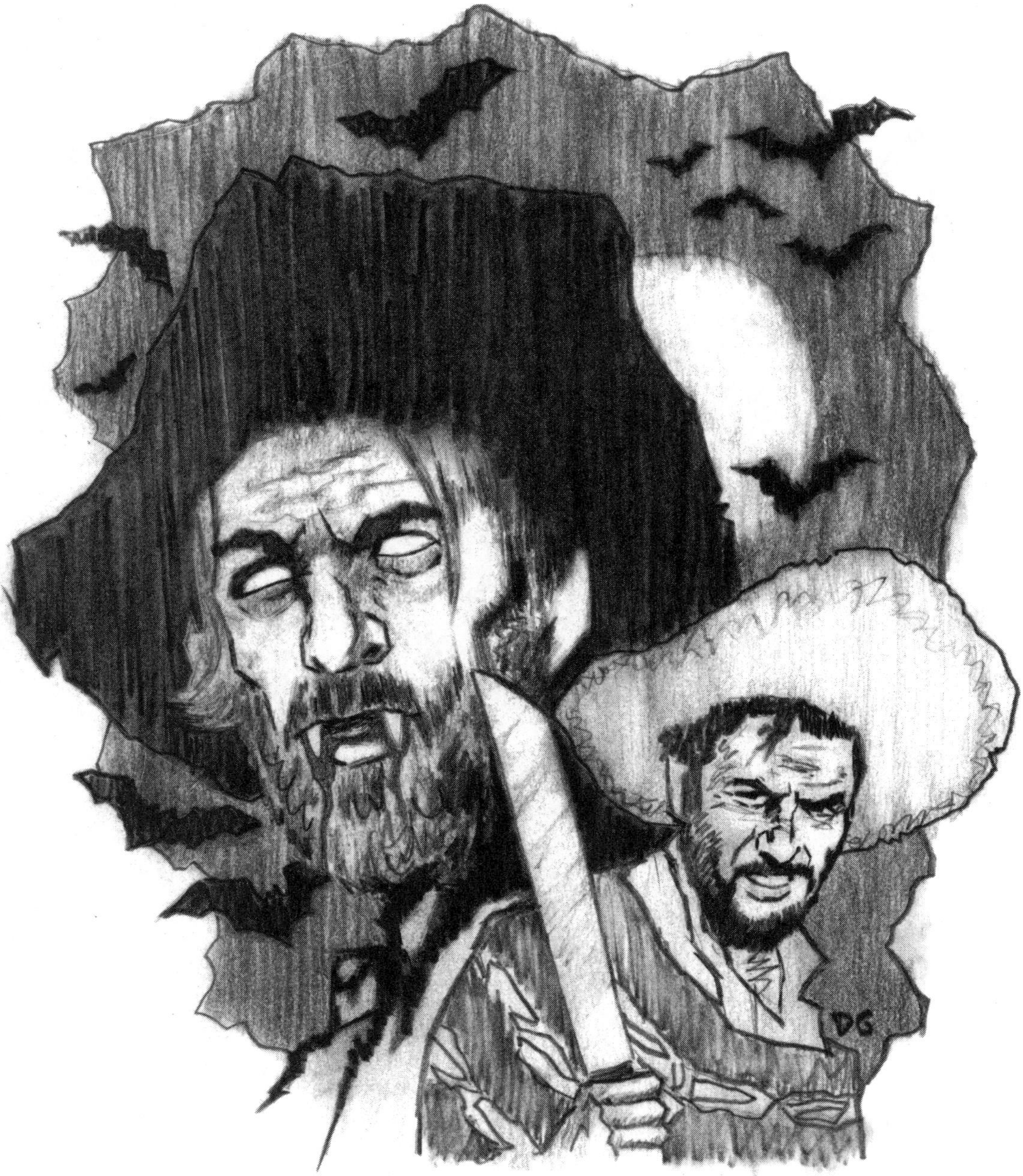
DG

onto the camp fire.

Pain ripped me and I thought I was dead. Or damned.

Came the dawn and Tabano was gone. I woke next to the coals, Brother Chango's silver cross branded into my chest. He had saved me again. I cried. Now Chango's grave is smooth, and the bloody pool is being washed by the Rio Grande. It's the quiet time before more death; my flesh and my mind are scarred forever; Tabano will come back. He is El Vampyro and the night belongs to him. And to me.

I see my future; riding the desserts and climbing the mountains, killing the dead-alive before they can kill. I was just a peasant, but now I have a mission: Mi amigo will not have died for nothing, and I swear I will make sure that El Vampyro dies forever.

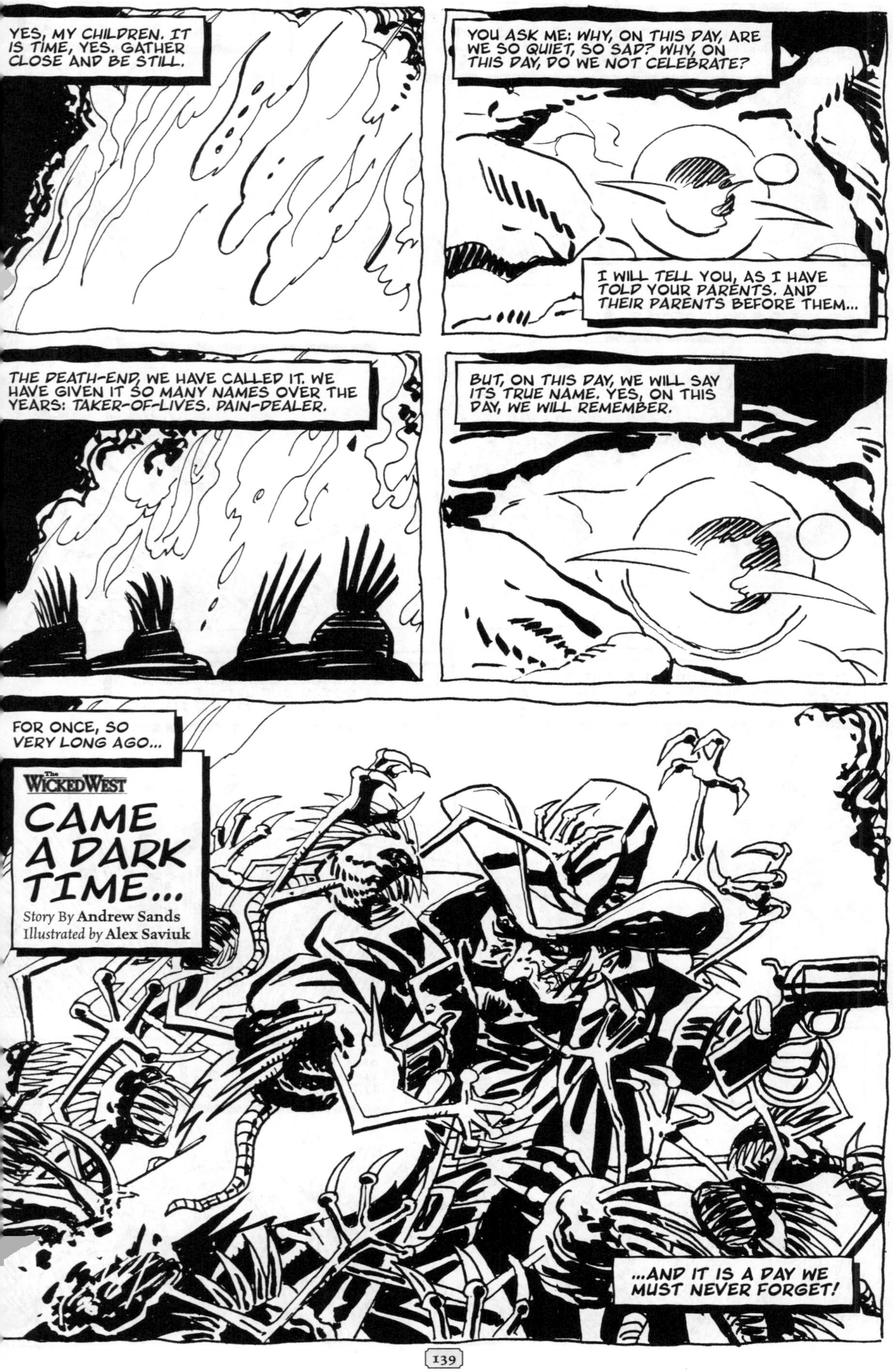
YES, MY CHILDREN. IT IS TIME, YES. GATHER CLOSE AND BE STILL.
YOU ASK ME: WHY, ON THIS DAY, ARE WE SO QUIET, SO SAD? WHY, ON THIS DAY, DO WE NOT CELEBRATE?
I WILL TELL YOU, AS I HAVE TOLD YOUR PARENTS. AND THEIR PARENTS BEFORE THEM...
THE DEATH-END, WE HAVE CALLED IT. WE HAVE GIVEN IT SO MANY NAMES OVER THE YEARS: TAKER-OF-LIVES. PAIN-DEALER.
BUT, ON THIS DAY, WE WILL SAY ITS TRUE NAME. YES, ON THIS DAY, WE WILL REMEMBER.
FOR ONCE, SO VERY LONG AGO...
The WICKED WEST
CAME A DARK TIME...
Story By Andrew Sands
Illustrated by Alex Saviuk
...AND IT IS A DAY WE MUST NEVER FORGET!

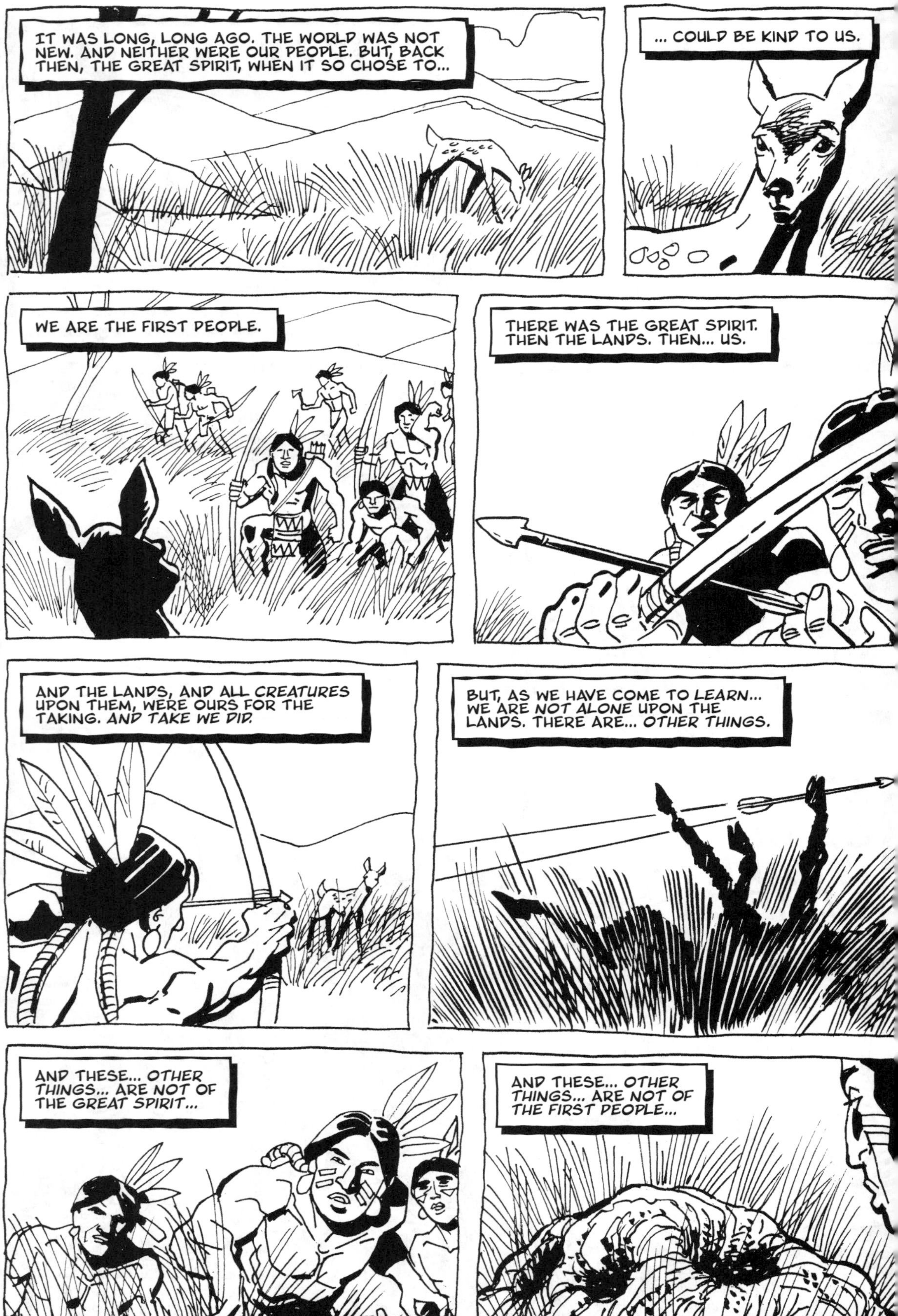
IT WAS LONG, LONG AGO. THE WORLD WAS NOT NEW. AND NEITHER WERE OUR PEOPLE. BUT, BACK THEN, THE GREAT SPIRIT, WHEN IT SO CHOSE TO...
... COULD BE KIND TO US.
WE ARE THE FIRST PEOPLE.
THERE WAS THE GREAT SPIRIT. THEN THE LANDS. THEN... US.
AND THE LANDS, AND ALL CREATURES UPON THEM, WERE OURS FOR THE TAKING. AND TAKE WE DID.
BUT, AS WE HAVE COME TO LEARN... WE ARE NOT ALONE UPON THE LANDS. THERE ARE... OTHER THINGS.
AND THESE... OTHER THINGS... ARE NOT OF THE GREAT SPIRIT...
AND THESE... OTHER THINGS... ARE NOT OF THE FIRST PEOPLE...

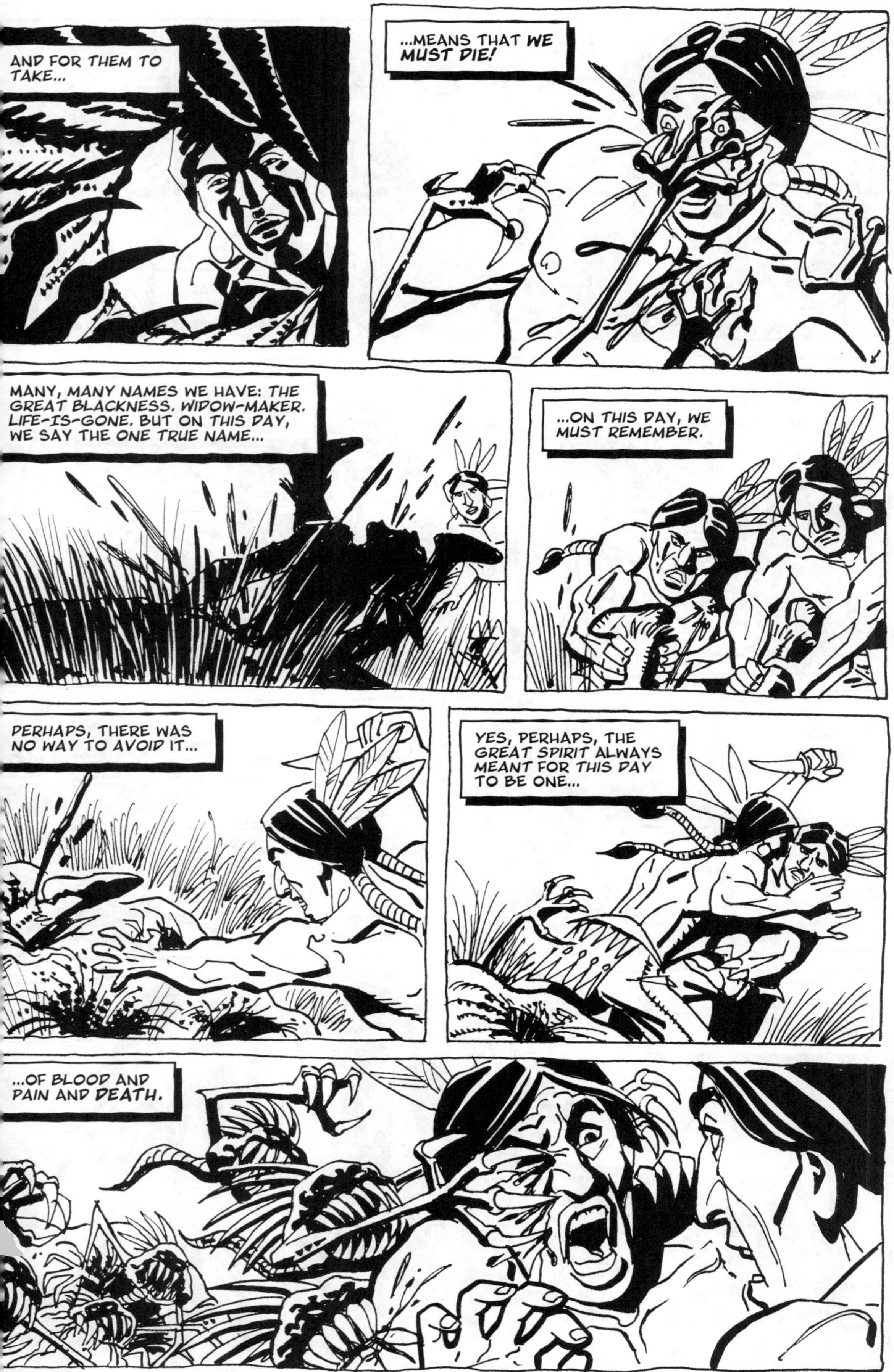
AND FOR THEM TO TAKE...
...MEANS THAT WE MUST DIE!
MANY, MANY NAMES WE HAVE: THE GREAT BLACKNESS. WIDOW-MAKER. LIFE-IS-GONE. BUT ON THIS DAY, WE SAY THE ONE TRUE NAME...
...ON THIS DAY, WE MUST REMEMBER.
PERHAPS, THERE WAS NO WAY TO AVOID IT...
YES, PERHAPS, THE GREAT SPIRIT ALWAYS MEANT FOR THIS DAY TO BE ONE...
...OF BLOOD AND PAIN AND DEATH.

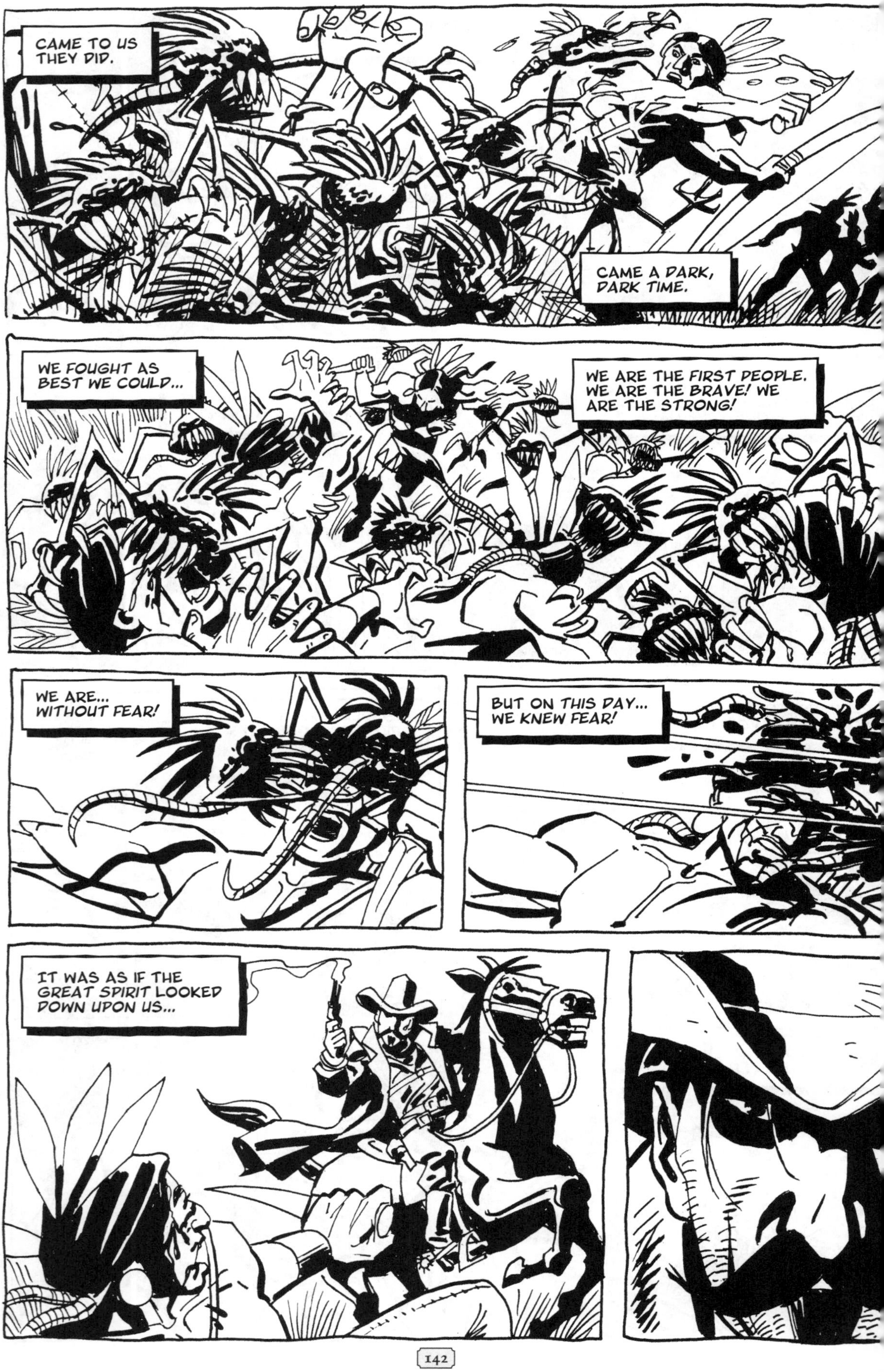
CAME TO US THEY DID.
CAME A DARK, DARK TIME.
WE FOUGHT AS BEST WE COULD...
WE ARE THE FIRST PEOPLE. WE ARE THE BRAVE! WE ARE THE STRONG!
WE ARE... WITHOUT FEAR!
BUT ON THIS DAY... WE KNEW FEAR!
IT WAS AS IF THE GREAT SPIRIT LOOKED DOWN UPON US...

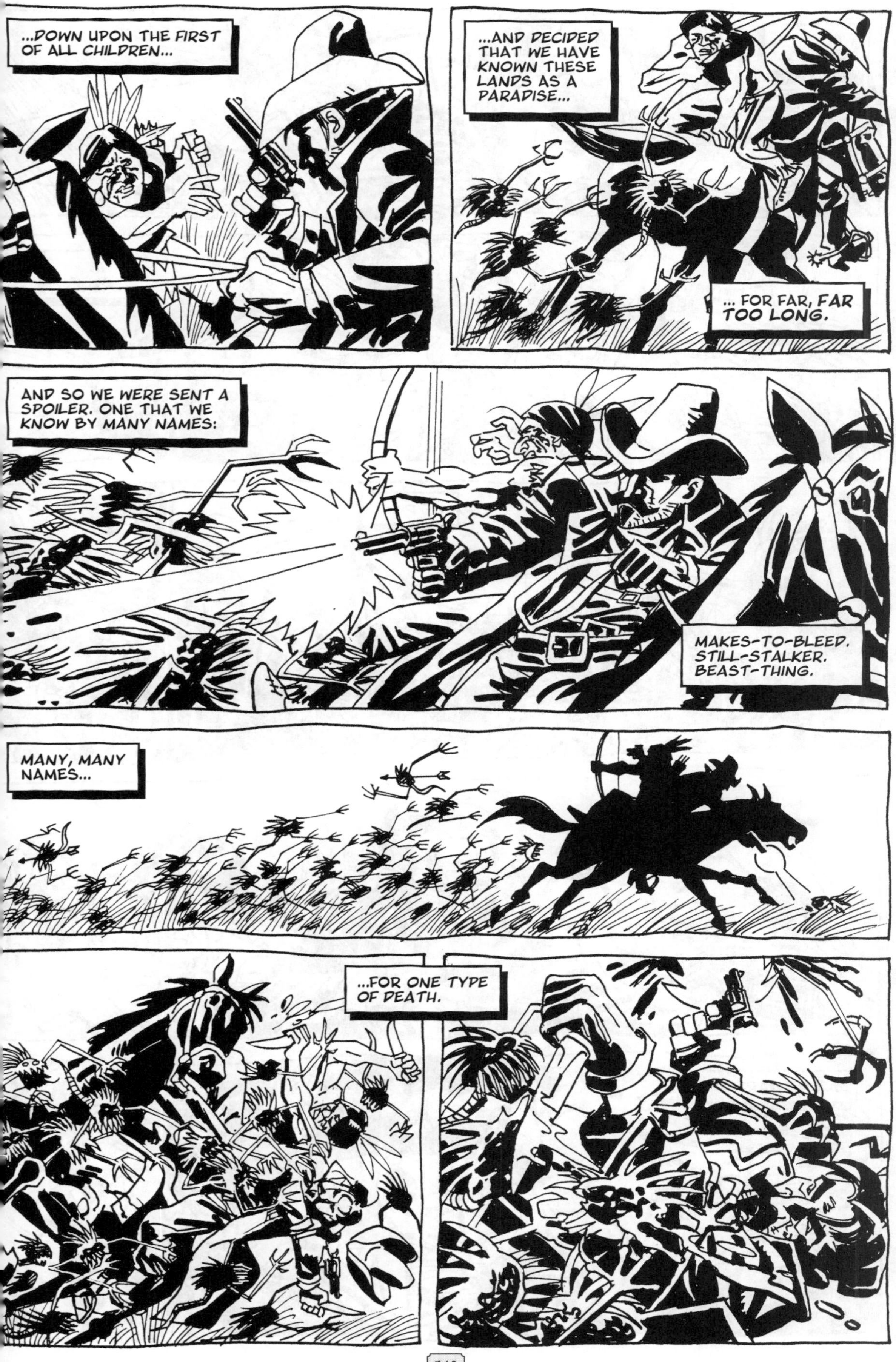

...DOWN UPON THE FIRST OF ALL CHILDREN...
...AND DECIDED THAT WE HAVE KNOWN THESE LANDS AS A PARADISE...
... FOR FAR, FAR TOO LONG.
AND SO WE WERE SENT A SPOILER. ONE THAT WE KNOW BY MANY NAMES:
MAKES-TO-BLEED. STILL-STALKER. BEAST-THING.
MANY, MANY NAMES...
...FOR ONE TYPE OF DEATH.

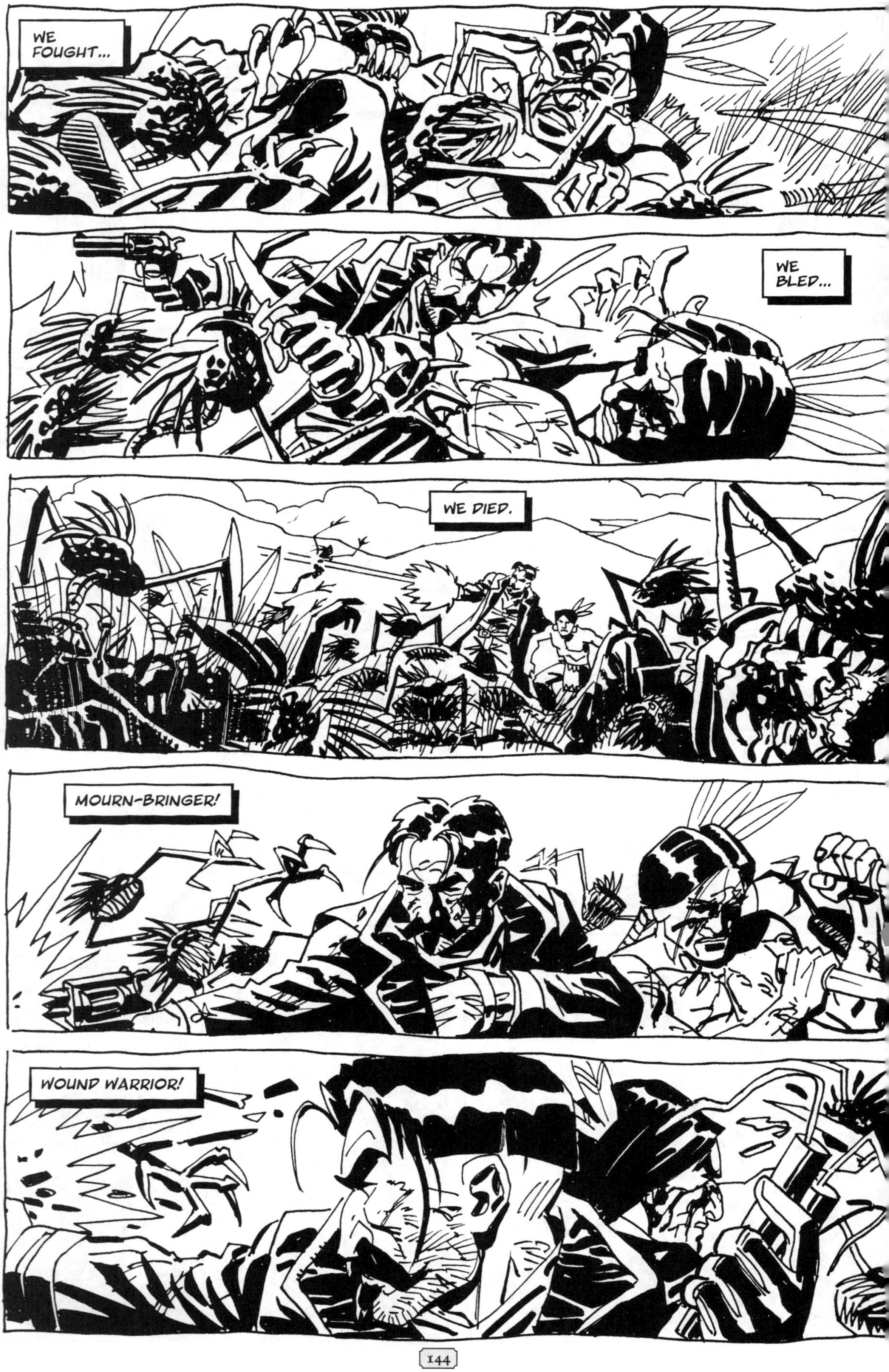
WE FOUGHT...
WE BLED...
WE DIED.
MOURN-BRINGER!
WOUND WARRIOR!

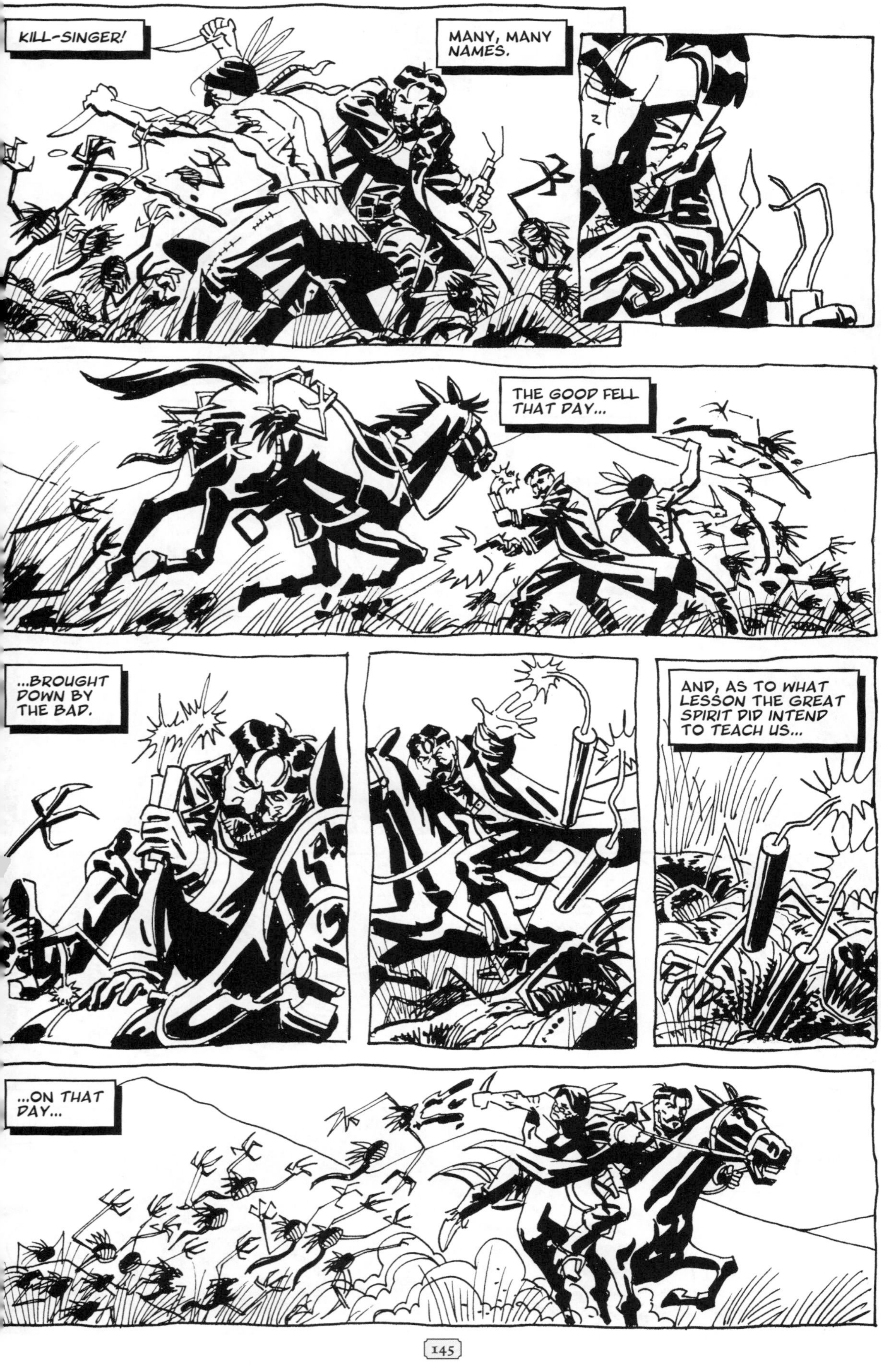
KILL-SINGER!
MANY, MANY NAMES.
THE GOOD FELL THAT DAY...
...BROUGHT DOWN BY THE BAD.
AND, AS TO WHAT LESSON THE GREAT SPIRIT DID INTEND TO TEACH US...
...ON THAT DAY...

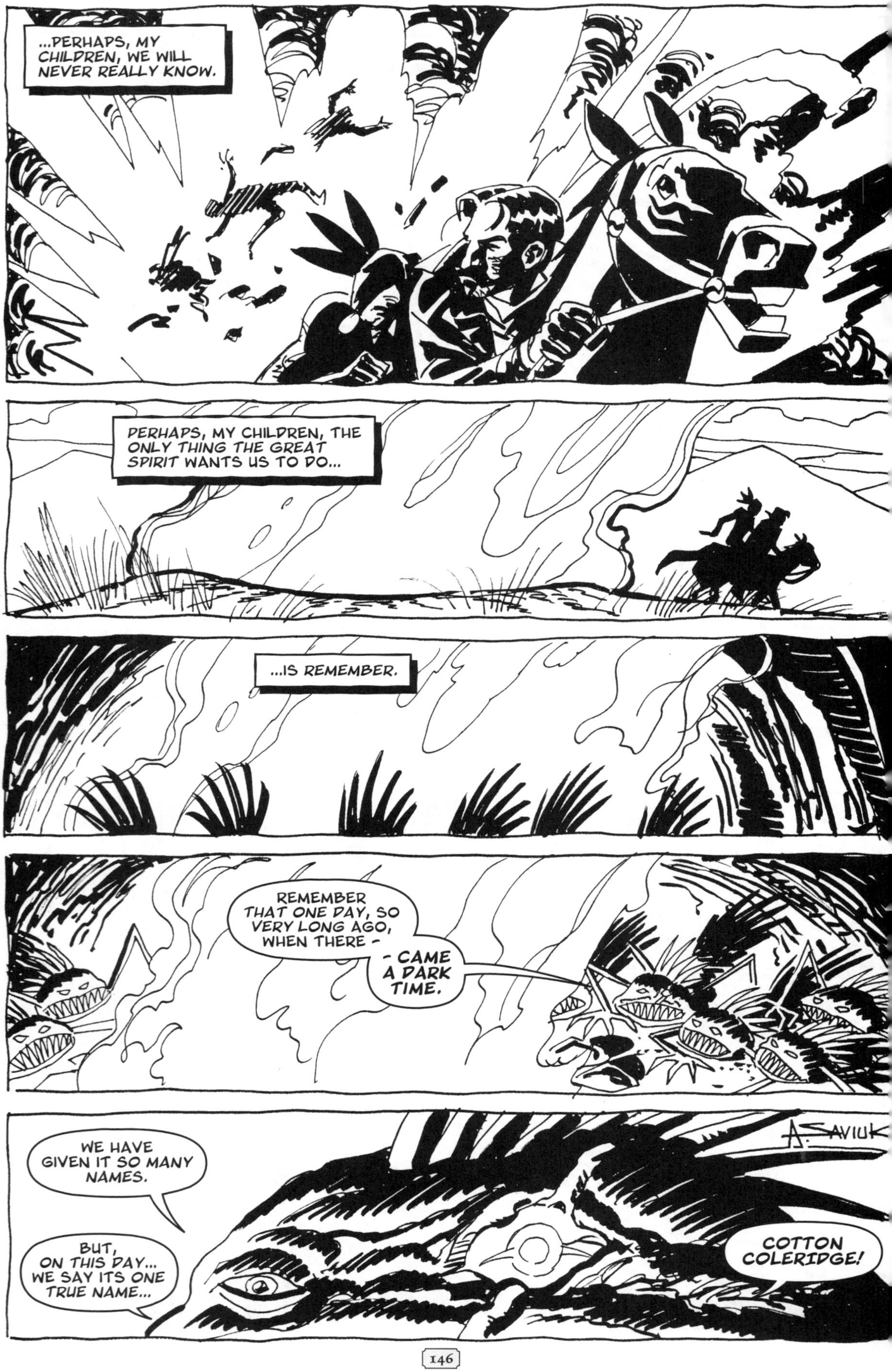
...PERHAPS, MY CHILDREN, WE WILL NEVER REALLY KNOW.
PERHAPS, MY CHILDREN, THE ONLY THING THE GREAT SPIRIT WANTS US TO DO...
...IS REMEMBER.
REMEMBER THAT ONE DAY, SO VERY LONG AGO, WHEN THERE -
- CAME A DARK TIME.
WE HAVE GIVEN IT SO MANY NAMES.
BUT, ON THIS DAY... WE SAY ITS ONE TRUE NAME...
COTTON COLERIDGE!
A. SAVIUK

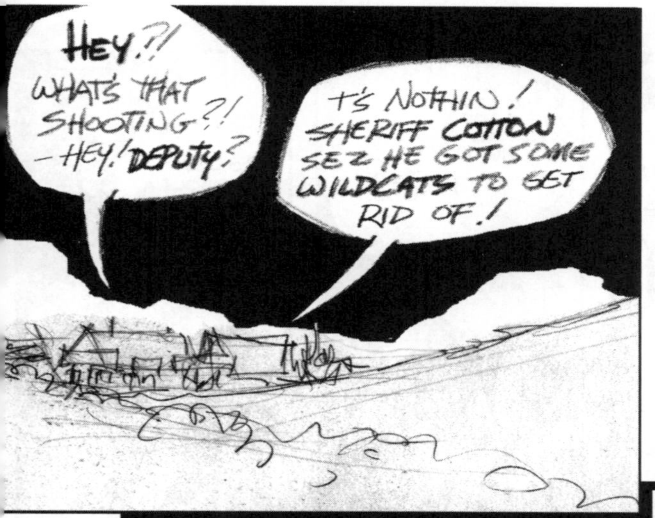
HEY?! WHAT'S THAT SHOOTING?! - HEY! DEPUTY?
T'S NOTHIN! SHERIFF COTTON SEZ HE GOT SOME WILDCATS TO GET RID OF!

Story & Illustration by
Nick Cardy

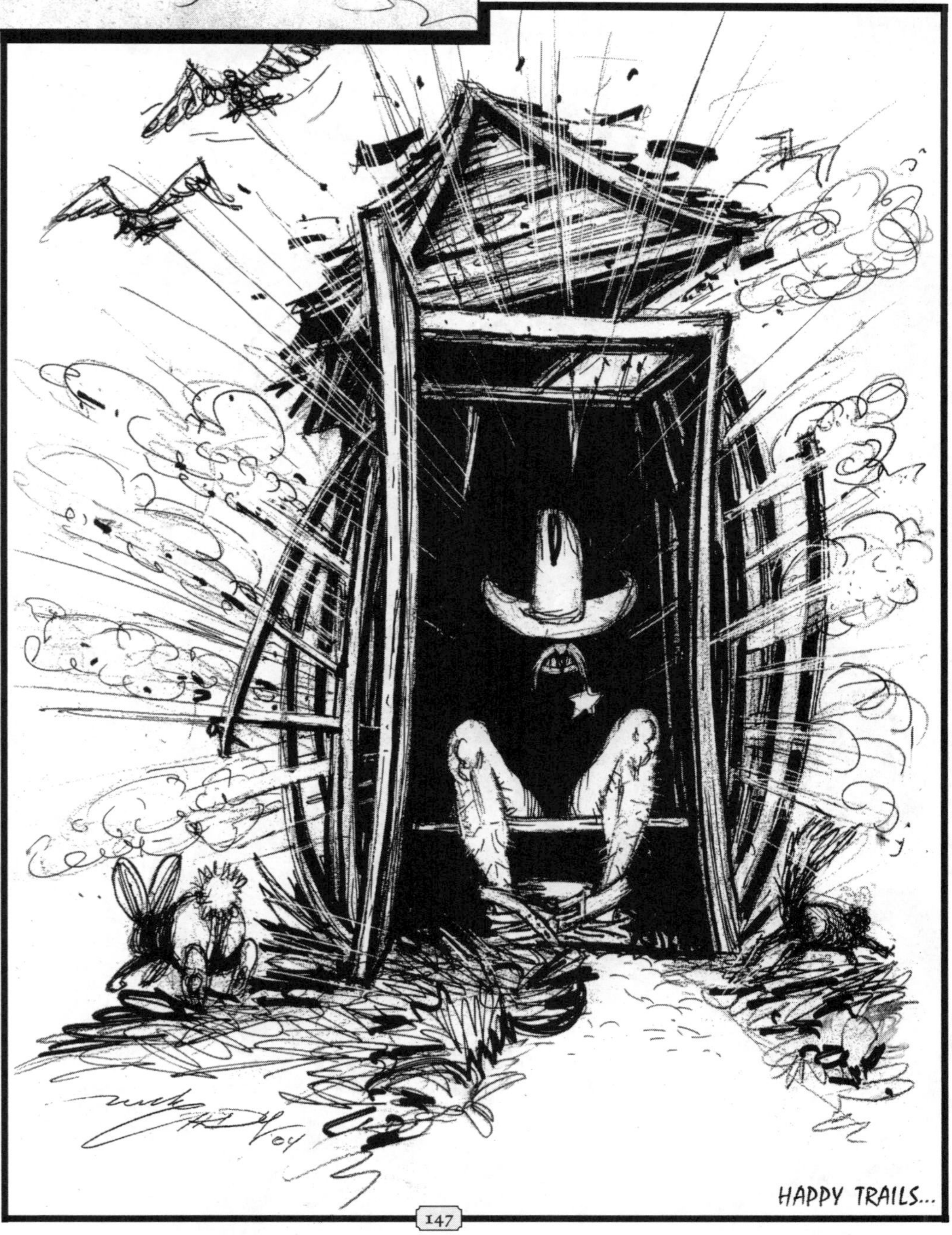
HAPPY TRAILS...

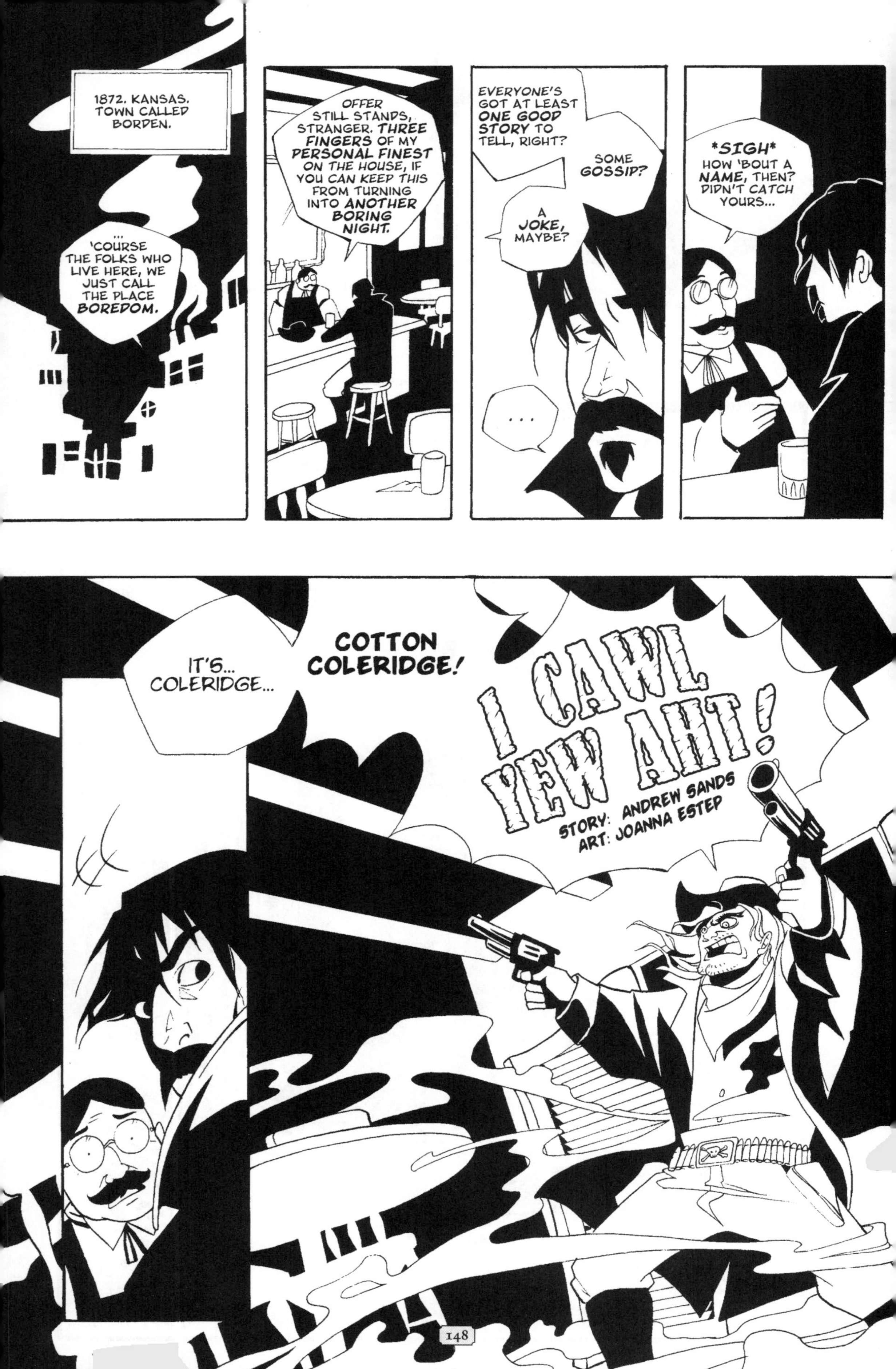

1872. KANSAS. TOWN CALLED BORDEN.
... 'COURSE THE FOLKS WHO LIVE HERE, WE JUST CALL THE PLACE BOREDOM.
OFFER STILL STANDS, STRANGER. THREE FINGERS OF MY PERSONAL FINEST ON THE HOUSE, IF YOU CAN KEEP THIS FROM TURNING INTO ANOTHER BORING NIGHT.
EVERYONE'S GOT AT LEAST ONE GOOD STORY TO TELL, RIGHT?
SOME GOSSIP?
A JOKE, MAYBE?
...
SIGH HOW 'BOUT A NAME, THEN? DIDN'T CATCH YOURS...
IT'S... COLERIDGE...
COTTON COLERIDGE!
I CAWL YEW AHT!
STORY: ANDREW SANDS
ART: JOANNA ESTEP

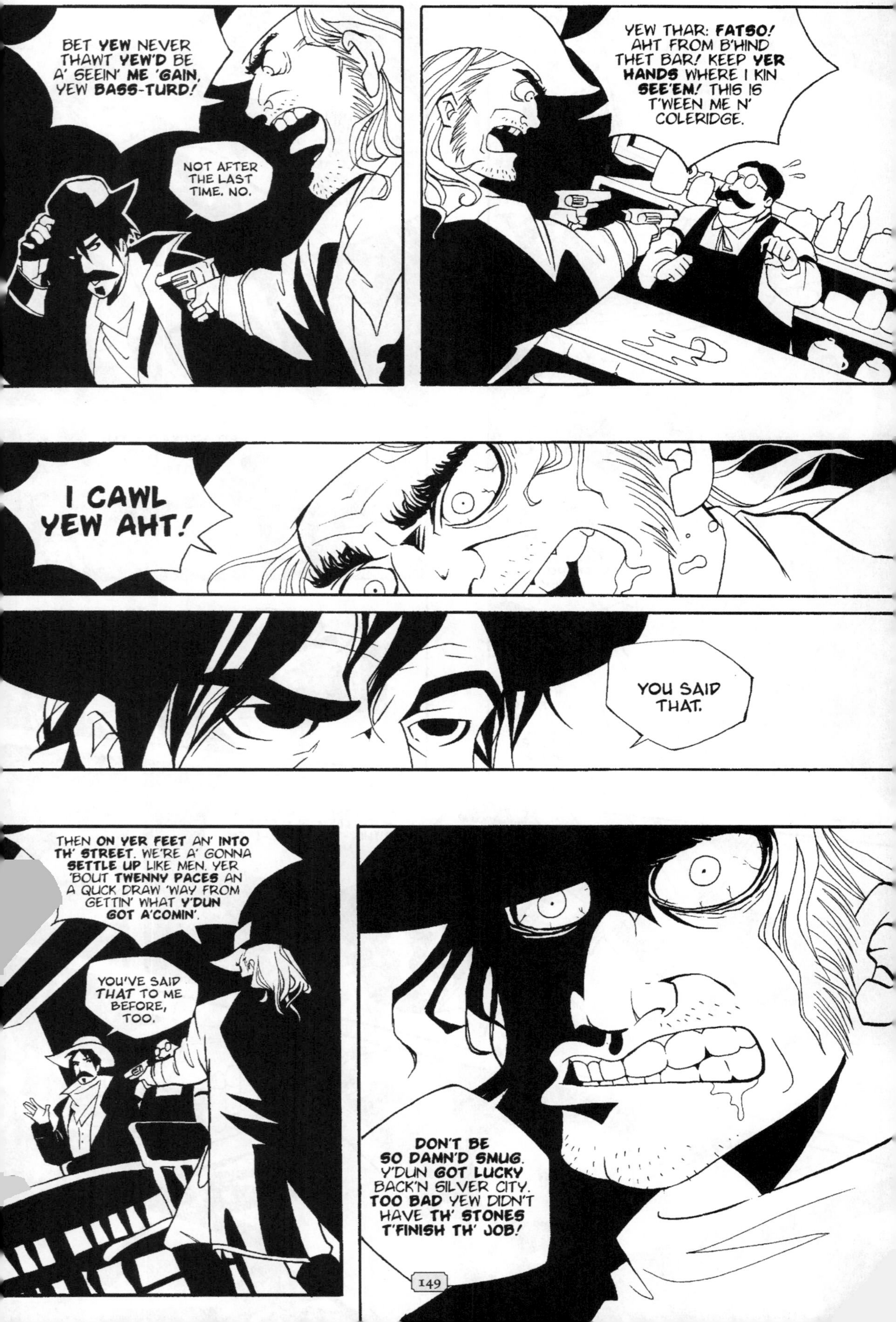

BET YEW NEVER THAWT YEW'D BE A' SEEIN' ME 'GAIN, YEW BASS-TURD!
NOT AFTER THE LAST TIME. NO.
YEW THAR: FATSO! AHT FROM B'HIND THET BAR! KEEP YER HANDS WHERE I KIN SEE'EN! THIS IS T'WEEN ME N' COLERIDGE.
I CAWL YEW AHT!
YOU SAID THAT.
THEN ON YER FEET AN' INTO TH' STREET. WE'RE A' GONNA SETTLE UP LIKE MEN. YER 'BOUT TWENNY PACES AN A QUICK DRAW 'WAY FROM GETTIN' WHAT Y'DUN GOT A'COMIN'.
YOU'VE SAID THAT TO ME BEFORE, TOO.
DON'T BE SO DAMN'D SMUG. Y'DUN GOT LUCKY BACK'N SILVER CITY. TOO BAD YEW DIDN'T HAVE TH' STONES T'FINISH TH' JOB!

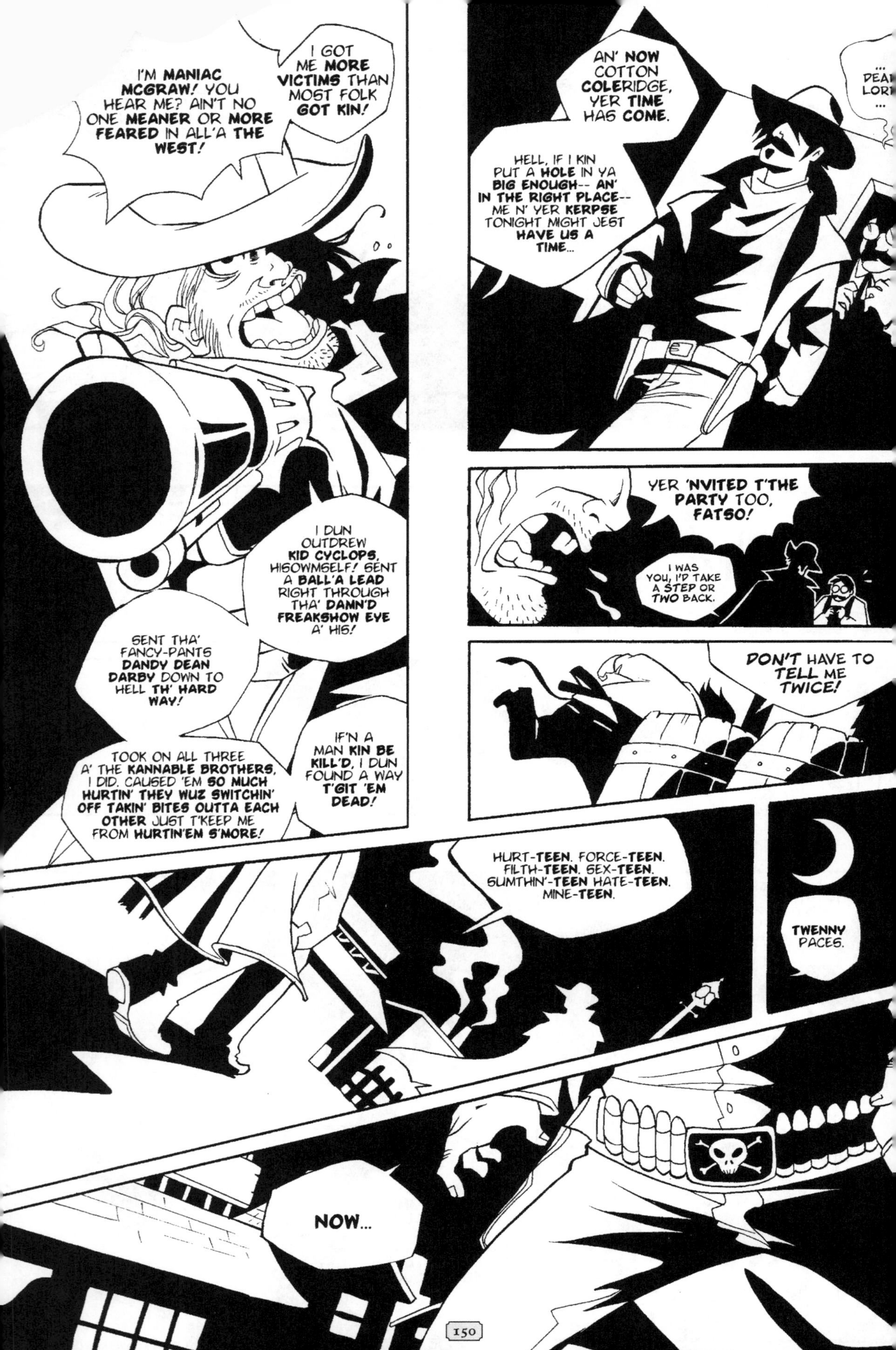
I'M MANIAC MCGRAW! YOU HEAR ME? AIN'T NO ONE MEANER OR MORE FEARED IN ALL'A THE WEST!
I GOT ME MORE VICTIMS THAN MOST FOLK GOT KIN!
I DUN OUTDREW KID CYCLOPS, HISOWMSELF! SENT A BALL'A LEAD RIGHT THROUGH THA' DAMN'D FREAKSHOW EYE A' HIS!
SENT THA' FANCY-PANTS DANDY DEAN DARBY DOWN TO HELL TH' HARD WAY!
TOOK ON ALL THREE A' THE KANNABLE BROTHERS, I DID. CAUSED 'EM SO MUCH HURTIN' THEY WUZ SWITCHIN' OFF TAKIN' BITES OUTTA EACH OTHER JUST T'KEEP ME FROM HURTIN'EM S'MORE!
IF'N A MAN KIN BE KILL'D, I DUN FOUND A WAY T'GIT 'EM DEAD!
AN' NOW COTTON COLERIDGE, YER TIME HAS COME.
HELL, IF I KIN PUT A HOLE IN YA BIG ENOUGH-- AN' IN THE RIGHT PLACE-- ME N' YER KERPSE TONIGHT MIGHT JEST HAVE US A TIME...
YER 'NVITED T'THE PARTY TOO, FATSO!
I WAS YOU, I'D TAKE A STEP OR TWO BACK.
DON'T HAVE TO TELL ME TWICE!
HURT-TEEN. FORCE-TEEN. FILTH-TEEN. SEX-TEEN. SUMTHIN'-TEEN HATE-TEEN. MINE-TEEN.
TWENNY PACES.
NOW...

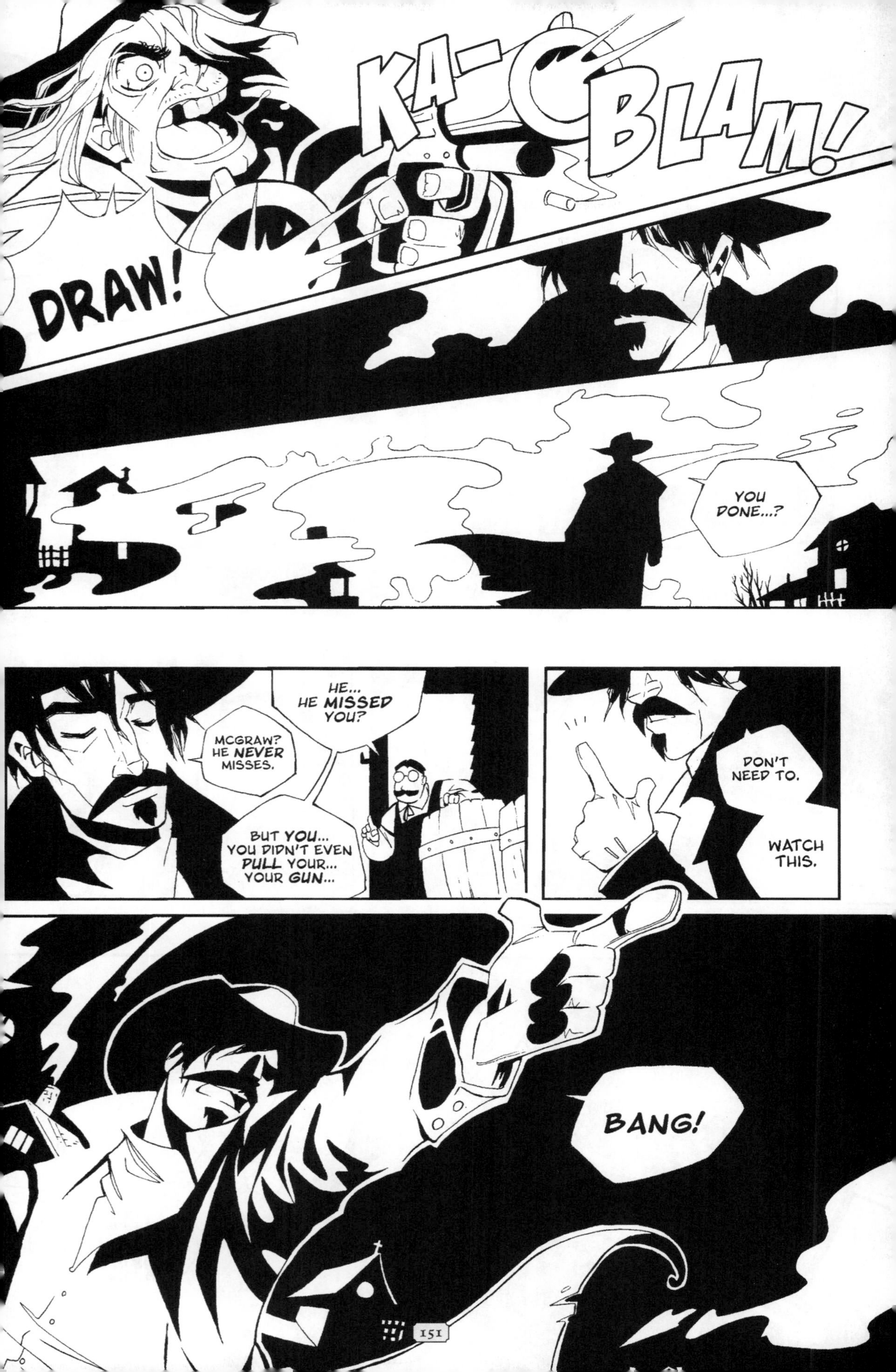
KA-BLAM!
DRAW!
YOU DONE...?
MCGRAW? HE NEVER MISSES.
HE... HE MISSED YOU?
BUT YOU... YOU DIDN'T EVEN PULL YOUR... YOUR GUN...
DON'T NEED TO.
WATCH THIS.
BANG!

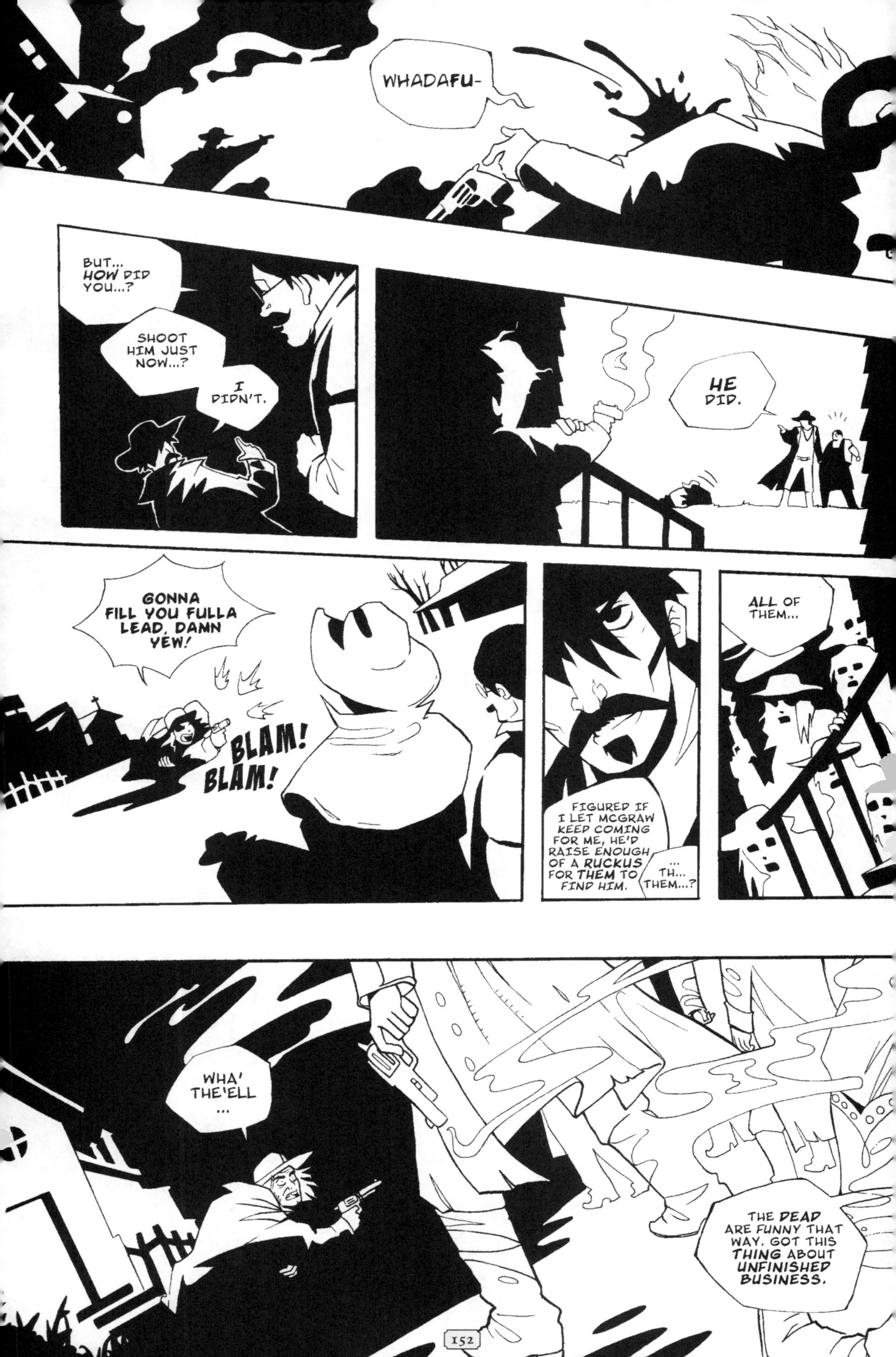
WHADAFU-
BUT... HOW DID YOU...?
SHOOT HIM JUST NOW...?
I DIDN'T.
HE DID.
GONNA FILL YOU FULLA LEAD, DAMN YEW!
BLAM! BLAM!
FIGURED IF I LET MCGRAW KEEP COMING FOR ME, HE'D RAISE ENOUGH OF A RUCKUS FOR THEM TO FIND HIM.
... TH... THEM...?
ALL OF THEM...
WHA' THE'ELL ...
THE DEAD ARE FUNNY THAT WAY. GOT THIS THING ABOUT UNFINISHED BUSINESS.

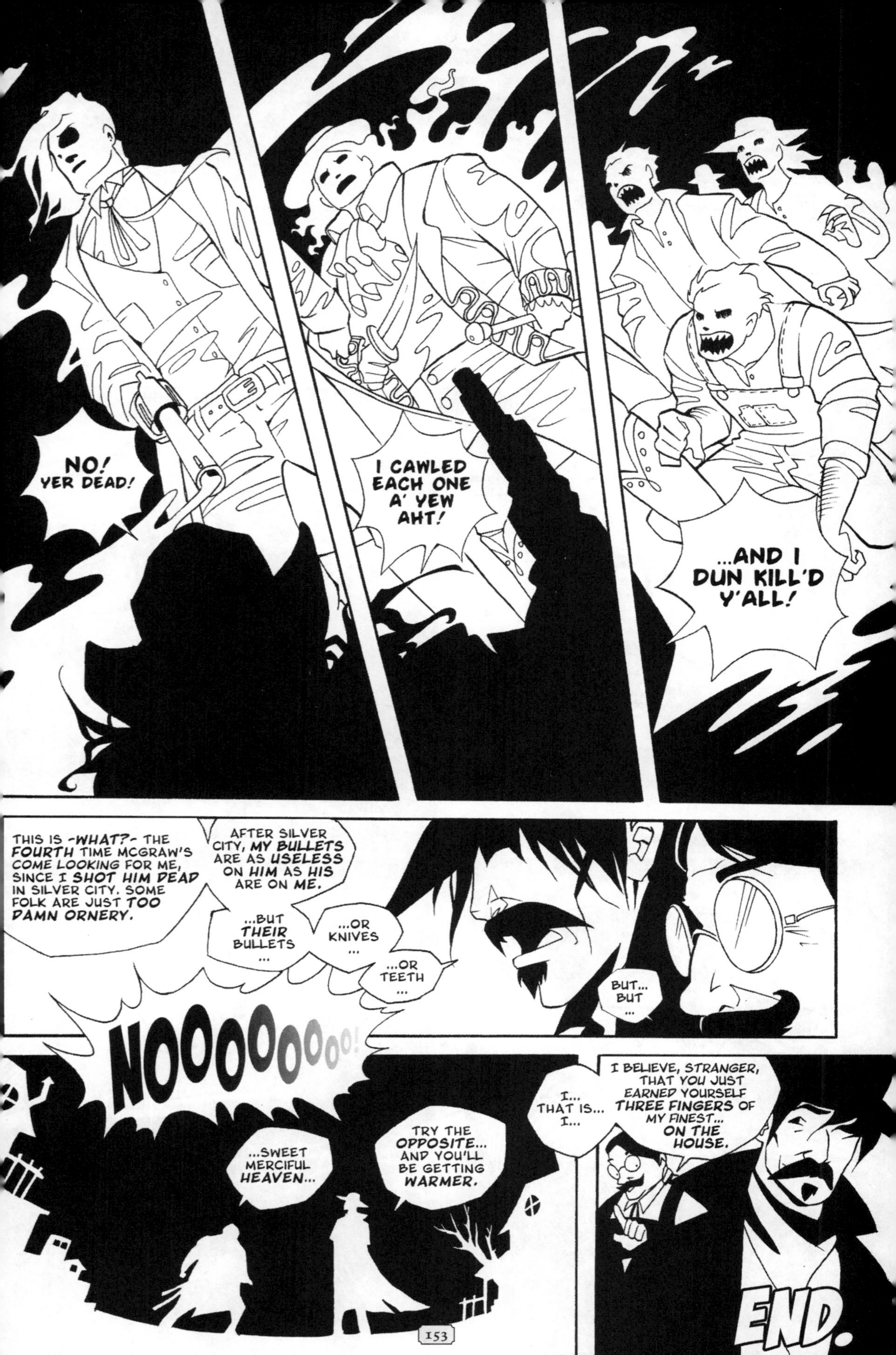
NO! YER DEAD!
I CAWLED EACH ONE A' YEW AHT!
...AND I DUN KILL'D Y'ALL!
THIS IS -WHAT?- THE FOURTH TIME MCGRAW'S COME LOOKING FOR ME, SINCE I SHOT HIM DEAD IN SILVER CITY. SOME FOLK ARE JUST TOO DAMN ORNERY.
AFTER SILVER CITY, MY BULLETS ARE AS USELESS ON HIM AS HIS ARE ON ME.
...BUT THEIR BULLETS ...
...OR KNIVES ...
...OR TEETH ...
BUT... BUT ...
NOOOOOOOO!
...SWEET MERCIFUL HEAVEN...
TRY THE OPPOSITE... AND YOU'LL BE GETTING WARMER.
I... THAT IS... I...
I BELIEVE, STRANGER, THAT YOU JUST EARNED YOURSELF THREE FINGERS OF MY FINEST... ON THE HOUSE.
END.

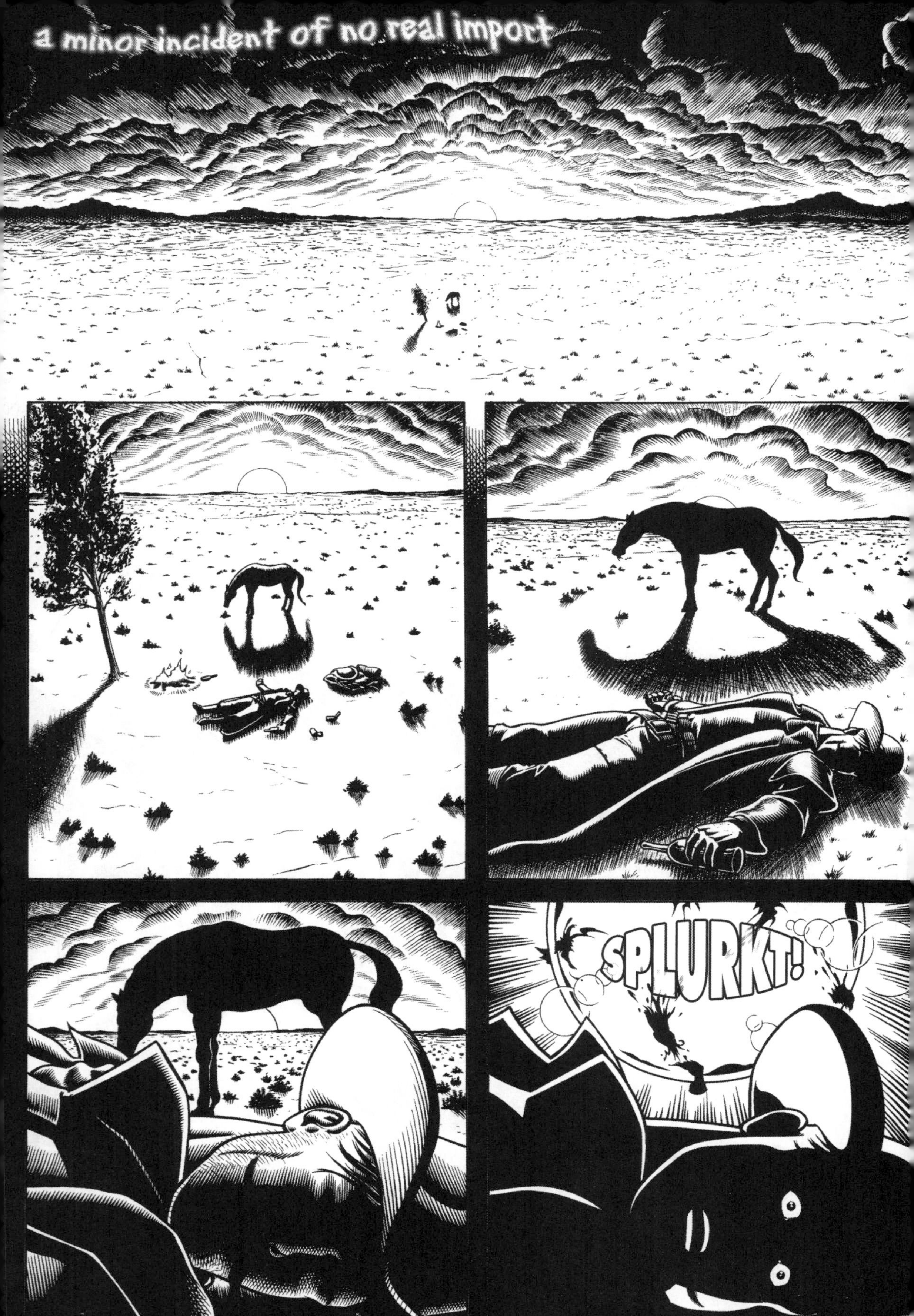
a minor incident of no real import
SPLURKT!

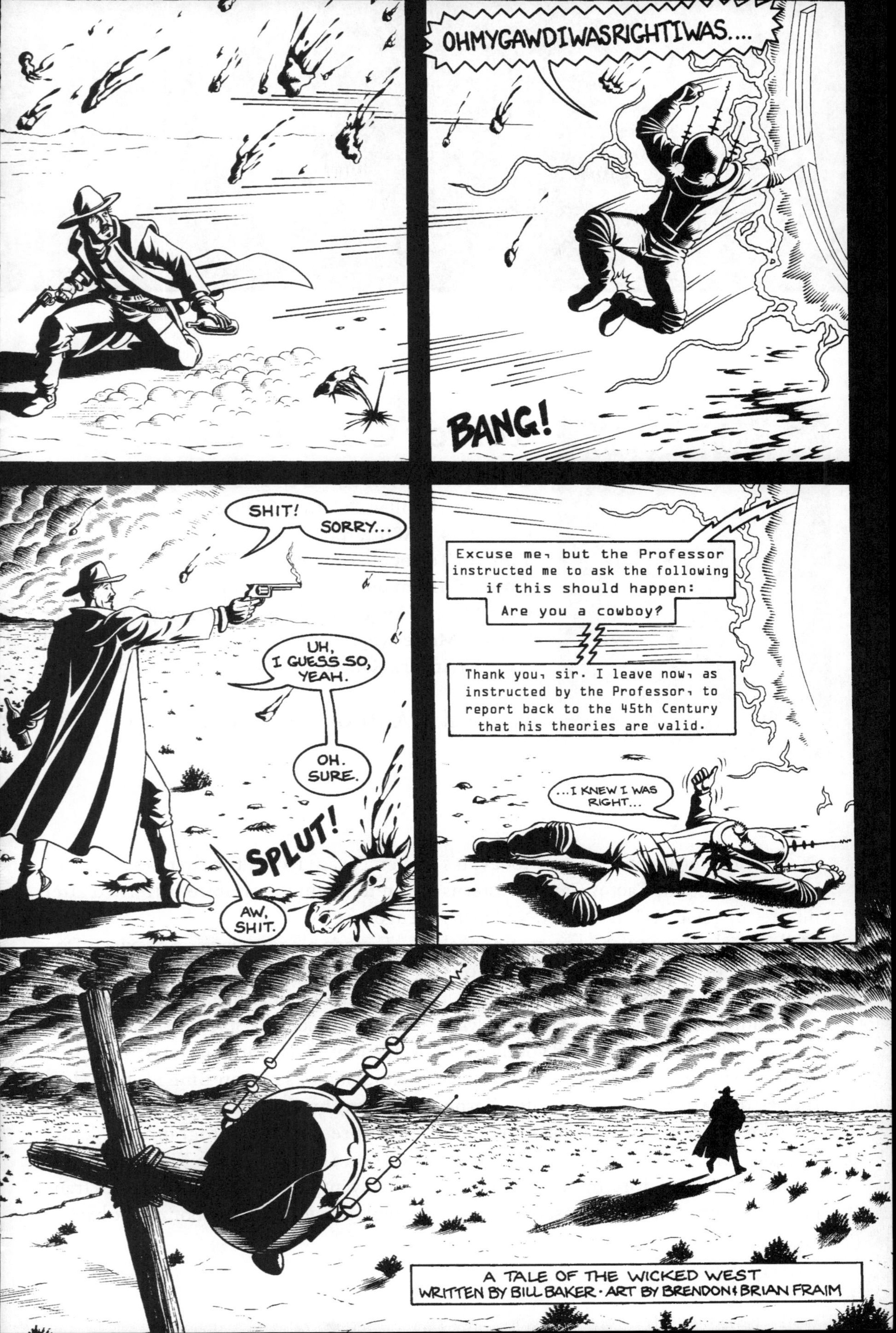
OHMYGAWDIWASRIGHTIWAS....
BANG!
SHIT!
SORRY...
UH, I GUESS SO, YEAH.
OH. SURE.
SPLUT!
AW, SHIT.
Excuse me, but the Professor instructed me to ask the following if this should happen:
Are you a cowboy?
Thank you, sir. I leave now, as instructed by the Professor, to report back to the 45th Century that his theories are valid.
...I KNEW I WAS RIGHT...
A TALE OF THE WICKED WEST
WRITTEN BY BILL BAKER · ART BY BRENDON & BRIAN FRAIM

"Response to TERROR OVER TEXAS - the "movie within the book" in THE WICKED WEST - was really positive. Pure and simple, people loved it and the whole storytelling device. Being as it is an integral part of the first story and the TWW universe we decided to turn some folks loose and reenter the ToT world. So, sit back and enjoy the next four stories as they mine that famous 1932 cinematic vampire classic!"

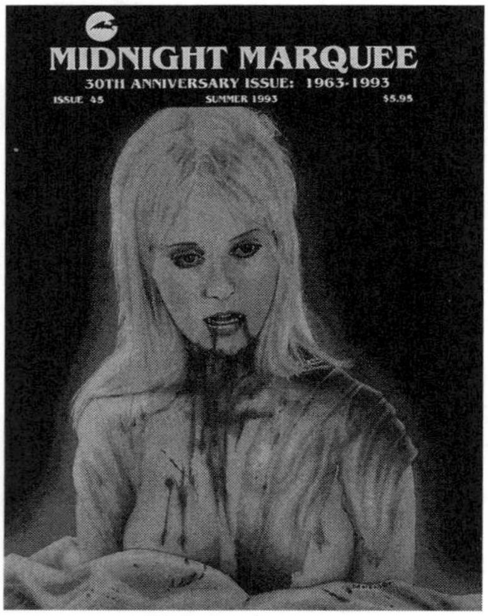
MIDNIGHT MARQUEE
30TH ANNIVERSARY ISSUE: 1963-1993
ISSUE 45
SUMMER 1993
$5.95

Terror Over Texas (1932).

Parmer Pictures (USA) *62 min.*

D: Lambert Miller. **P:** Jeffrey Scott. **S:** Robert Todd, from Cornelius T. Winterpocket's novel Massacre at Javer's Tanks or Terror over Texas.

Cast: Biff Baxter (Cactus Carter); Charles Westfall (Doc Miller); Angela Harbert (Irene Temple); Chester "Buzzy" McGee (Homer Longfeather); Dexter Randall (Lot Derringer); Ramon Vasquez (Don Alessandro).

Reviewed by **Anthony Ambrogio**

If Biff Baxter is remembered today, it's for his series of Cactus Carter westerns directed by Lambert ("All-Thriller, No-Filler") Miller, each distinguished by its unusual storyline, often borrowed from famous sources—e.g., Sandstorm in Sonora (1933), an unauthorized Beau Geste adaptation, with Indians subbing for Arabs and young John Wayne playing Carter's brother; Pirates of the Pacific (1932), a western Jules Verne pastiche, wherein Captain Noman (Ramon Vasquez) in his fantastical "diving boat" shanghais Carter, forcing him to herd a pack of giant wild sea horses; and Terror over Texas (1932), the first post-Dracula film to feature a vampire patterned after Lugosi's Count.

Terror's bloodsucker is a Mexican Don (Vasquez, who like Lugosi, began as a Valentino-like matinee idol; he supported Garbo in Queen of Spies [1927], the silent version of Mata Hari [1931]). This undead conquistador's screen time is short (like the film) but memorable: he revives (in an impressively photographed scene), preys on a child (Stephen King says Terror partially inspired 'Salem's Lot), invades Irene Temple's boudoir and hypnotizes the hapless heroine, and finally is staked in a scene that tops Dracula's bloodless conclusion. (Carter stabs the vampire below frame, but the Don disintegrates on screen, courtesy of some crudely effective stop-motion dissolves which substitute a rotting carcass, then a skeleton for the man-monster before the bones burst into flames and are consumed.)

This sagebrush Dracula-on-a-budget (greatly aided by the moody cinematography of Lien Sekov, a Russian émigré who had shot Eisenstein's state-ordered version of Chekov's play, The Cherry Collective [1926]) goes Universal one better—maybe two better. Miller surpasses Tod Browning in the creepy-animal department. Browning featured one armadillo; Miller gives us a dozen—attacking reformed drunken Indian Homer Longfeather in a feeding frenzy. And Terror expands upon Dracula's vampirized-heroine scenario. Dracula's entranced Mina almost nips her fiancé before Van Helsing's timely crucifix intervention prevents her. Terror's undead Irene approaches Carter by the campfire and nearly bites him before Doc Miller drives a crucifix wedge between the clinching couple. (Admittedly, the source novel supplies the inspiration for this scene in both films, but Terence Fisher's staging and camera set-ups for Lucy's assault on Arthur in Horror of Dracula [1958] suggest that he conducted a thorough study in Terror before shooting that sequence.)

Did Miller see Universal's Spanish Dracula? Angela Harbert's Irene-as-vampire resembles George Melford's sexy, aggressive Lupita Tovar rather than Browning's somnolent, stately Helen Chandler, as illustrated by an earlier campfire scene that, once seen, cannot be forgotten: Irene emerges, as if from the flames, to confront villain Lot Derringer. "What are you looking for, woman?" Lot asks. In chilling close-up, Irene (dead eyes reflecting the campfire light), utters, "Death"—and the camera cuts to a reaction shot of Derringer retreating, fear in his eyes, futilely firing his six-shooter. Three years before Mark of the Vampire's Luna, four years before Dracula's Daughter, Miller gave us the first full-blooded filmic vampiress, an active menace not seen again in cinema until the advent of Hammer's golden horrors.

All-Thriller Miller couldn't avoid some filler in Terror. Biff had to sing at least one extraneous song per film, and Terror was no exception. And every Baxter picture required an unrequited love affair: Carter would meet a woman in reel one and lose her by reel six. Here, he loses the schoolmarm to vampirism. At least Terror scripter Todd made this unattainable object of Carter's affection germane to the plot.

Chimera Video's Terror DVD (part of Michael Price's "Forgotten Horrors" series) offers a pristine print, with some speckling, unavoidable in a film of this vintage. Filmmakers Bob Tinnell and Todd Livingston and comic-book artist Neil Vokes, great admirers of the picture, provide the witty, informative commentary track. Tinnell and Livingston talk so wisely about Robert Todd's script you'd think they wrote it, while Vokes praises the invaluable contribution of cinematographer Sekov.

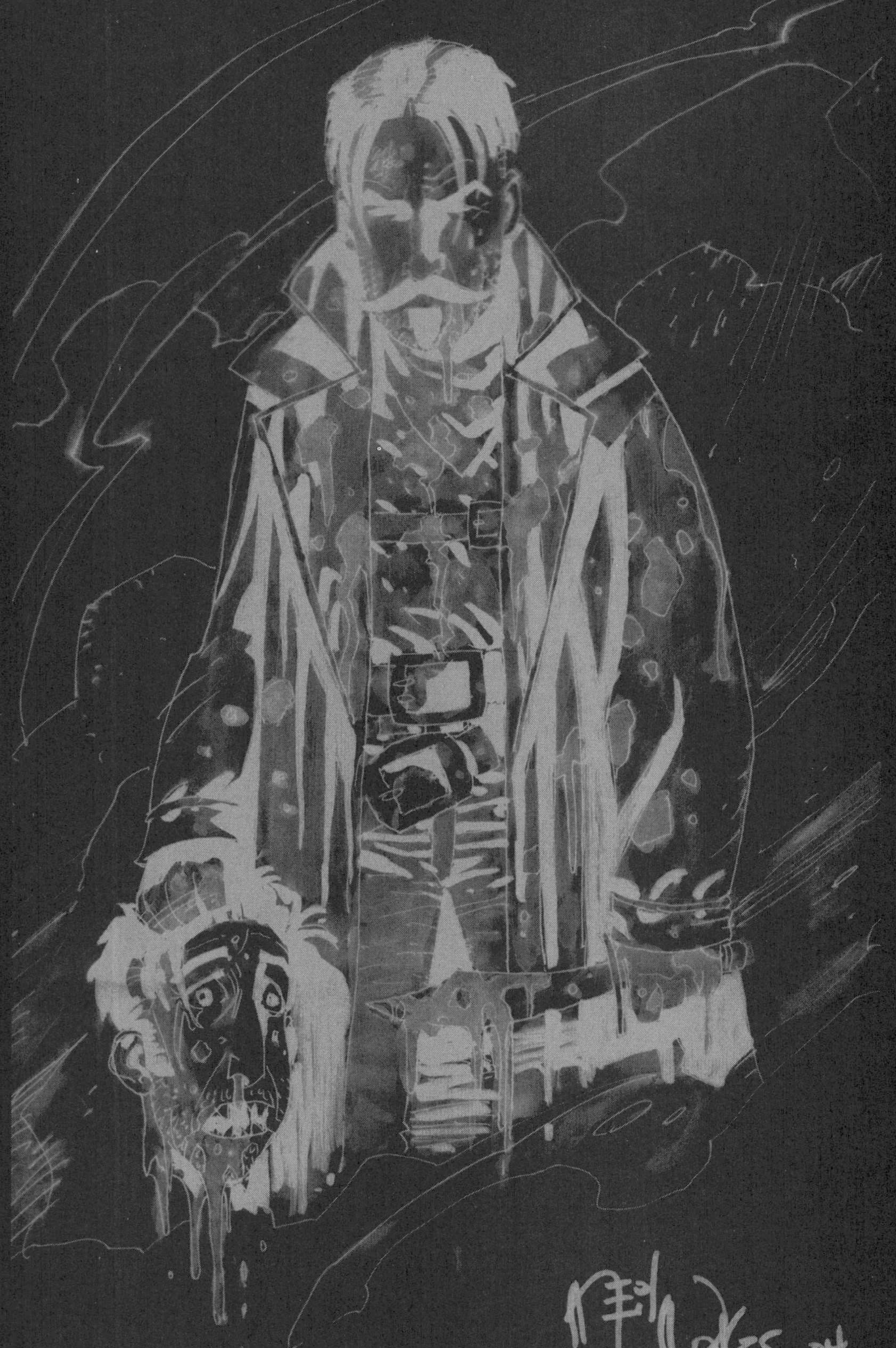

The Wicked West II

Biff Baxter de Bergerac

Story by **Todd Livingston**
Illustrated by **Scott Wegener**

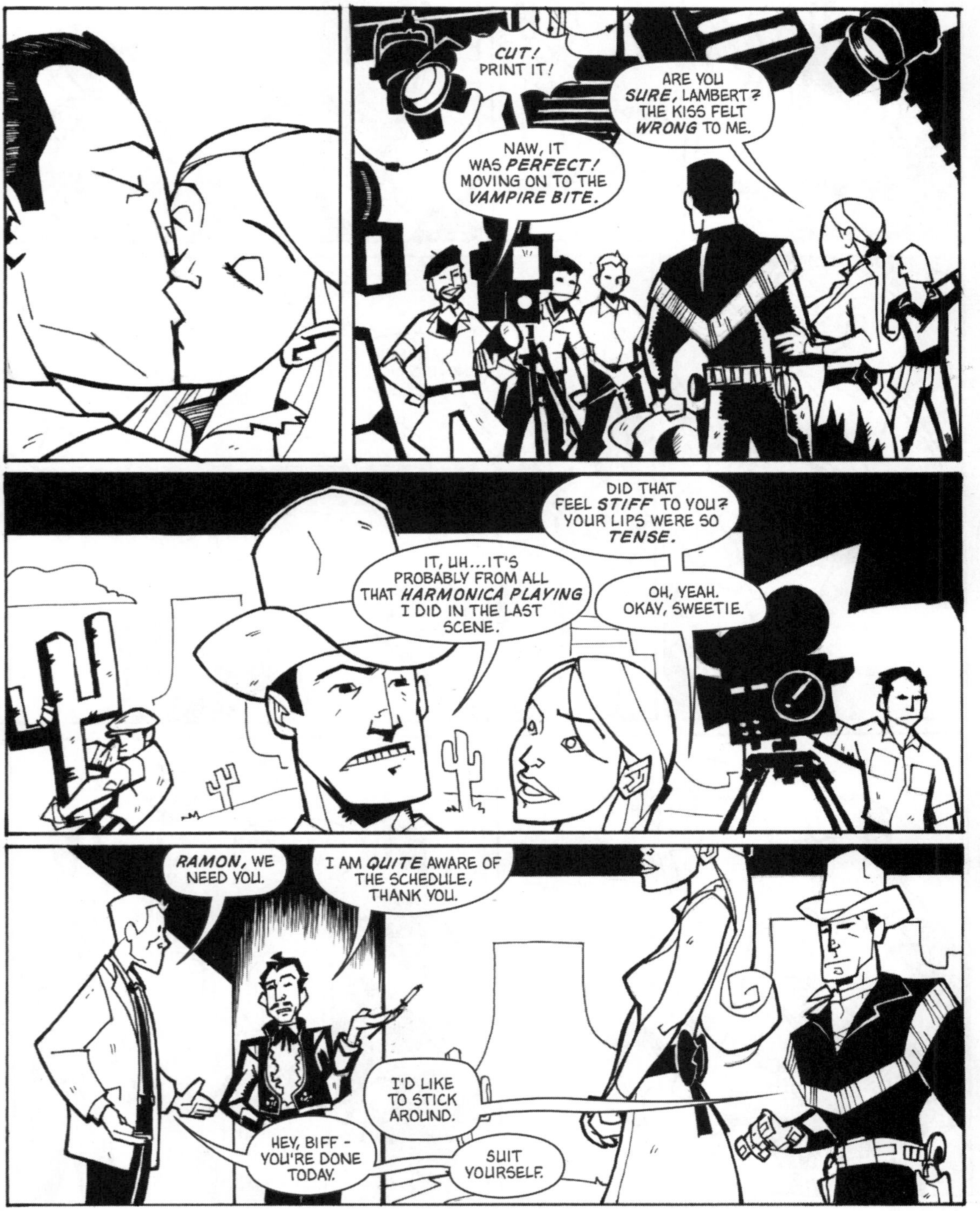
CUT! PRINT IT!
ARE YOU SURE, LAMBERT? THE KISS FELT WRONG TO ME.
NAW, IT WAS PERFECT! MOVING ON TO THE VAMPIRE BITE.
DID THAT FEEL STIFF TO YOU? YOUR LIPS WERE SO TENSE.
IT, UH...IT'S PROBABLY FROM ALL THAT HARMONICA PLAYING I DID IN THE LAST SCENE.
OH, YEAH. OKAY, SWEETIE.
RAMON, WE NEED YOU.
I AM QUITE AWARE OF THE SCHEDULE, THANK YOU.
HEY, BIFF - YOU'RE DONE TODAY.
I'D LIKE TO STICK AROUND.
SUIT YOURSELF.

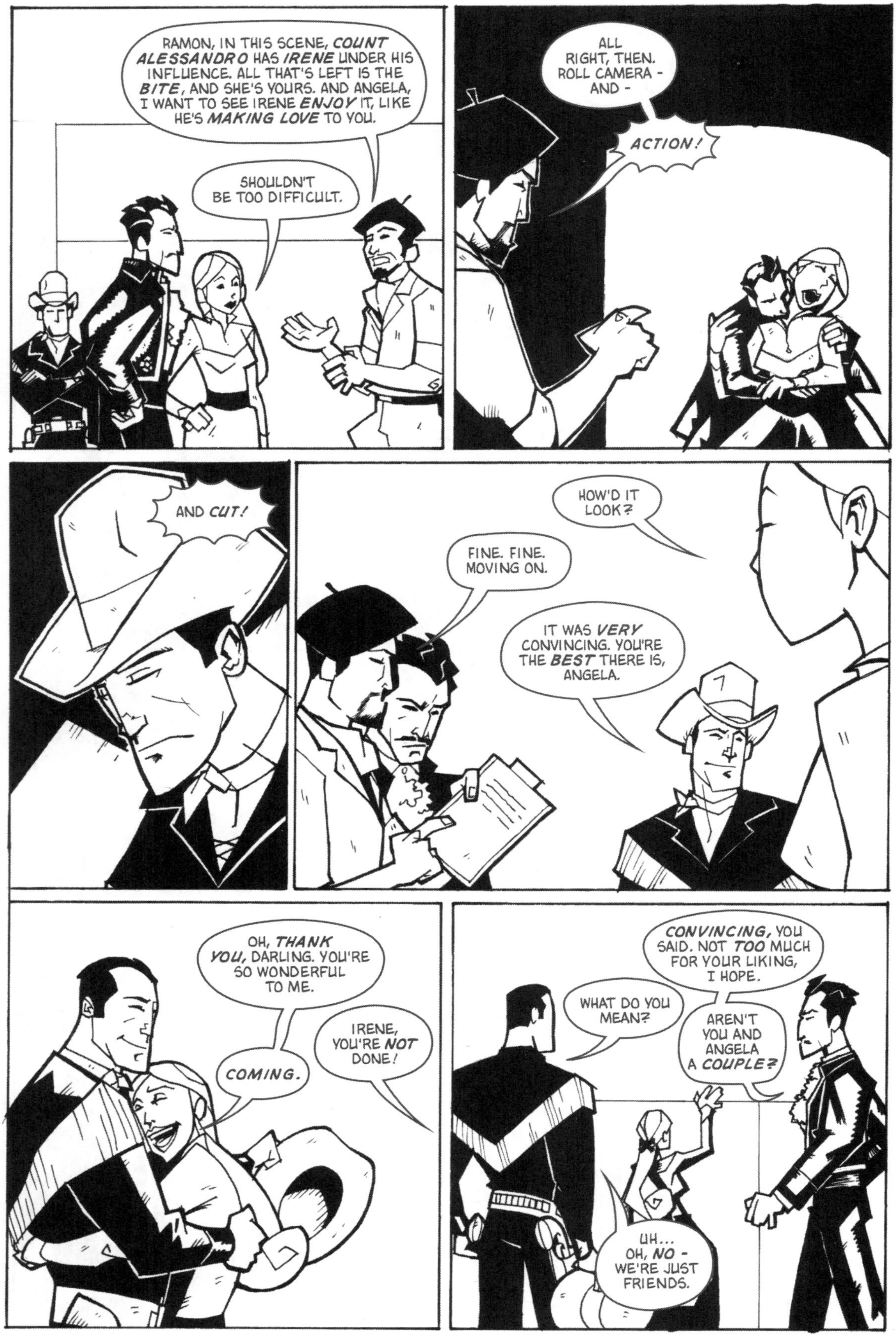
RAMON, IN THIS SCENE, COUNT ALESSANDRO HAS IRENE UNDER HIS INFLUENCE. ALL THAT'S LEFT IS THE BITE, AND SHE'S YOURS. AND ANGELA, I WANT TO SEE IRENE ENJOY IT, LIKE HE'S MAKING LOVE TO YOU.
SHOULDN'T BE TOO DIFFICULT.
ALL RIGHT, THEN. ROLL CAMERA - AND -
ACTION!
AND CUT!
HOW'D IT LOOK?
FINE. FINE. MOVING ON.
IT WAS VERY CONVINCING. YOU'RE THE BEST THERE IS, ANGELA.
OH, THANK YOU, DARLING. YOU'RE SO WONDERFUL TO ME.
IRENE, YOU'RE NOT DONE!
COMING.
CONVINCING, YOU SAID. NOT TOO MUCH FOR YOUR LIKING, I HOPE.
WHAT DO YOU MEAN?
AREN'T YOU AND ANGELA A COUPLE?
UH... OH, NO - WE'RE JUST FRIENDS.

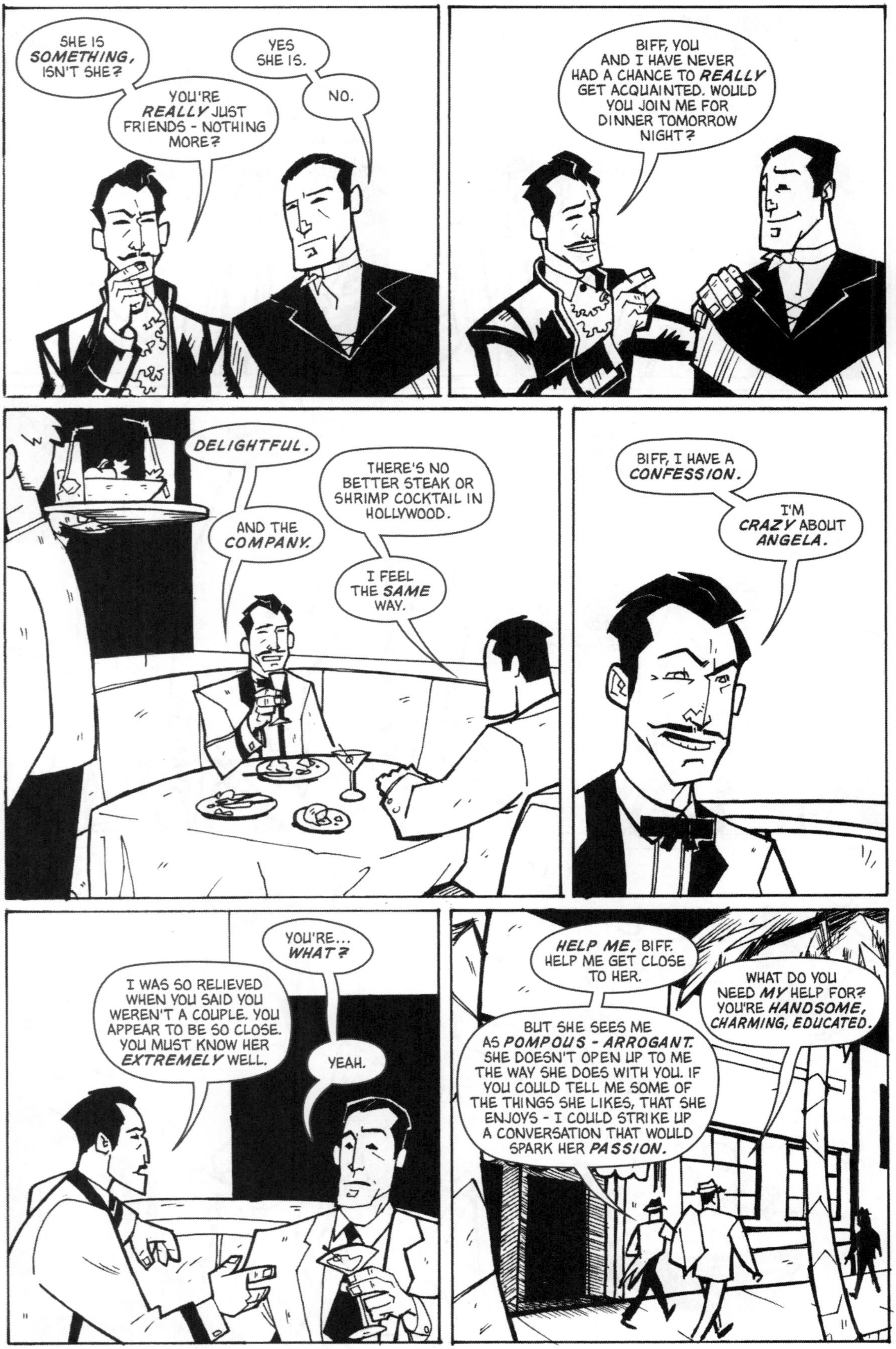
SHE IS SOMETHING, ISN'T SHE?
YES SHE IS.
YOU'RE REALLY JUST FRIENDS - NOTHING MORE?
NO.
BIFF, YOU AND I HAVE NEVER HAD A CHANCE TO REALLY GET ACQUAINTED. WOULD YOU JOIN ME FOR DINNER TOMORROW NIGHT?
DELIGHTFUL.
AND THE COMPANY.
THERE'S NO BETTER STEAK OR SHRIMP COCKTAIL IN HOLLYWOOD.
I FEEL THE SAME WAY.
BIFF, I HAVE A CONFESSION.
I'M CRAZY ABOUT ANGELA.
YOU'RE... WHAT?
I WAS SO RELIEVED WHEN YOU SAID YOU WEREN'T A COUPLE. YOU APPEAR TO BE SO CLOSE. YOU MUST KNOW HER EXTREMELY WELL.
YEAH.
HELP ME, BIFF. HELP ME GET CLOSE TO HER.
WHAT DO YOU NEED MY HELP FOR? YOU'RE HANDSOME, CHARMING, EDUCATED.
BUT SHE SEES ME AS POMPOUS - ARROGANT. SHE DOESN'T OPEN UP TO ME THE WAY SHE DOES WITH YOU. IF YOU COULD TELL ME SOME OF THE THINGS SHE LIKES, THAT SHE ENJOYS - I COULD STRIKE UP A CONVERSATION THAT WOULD SPARK HER PASSION.

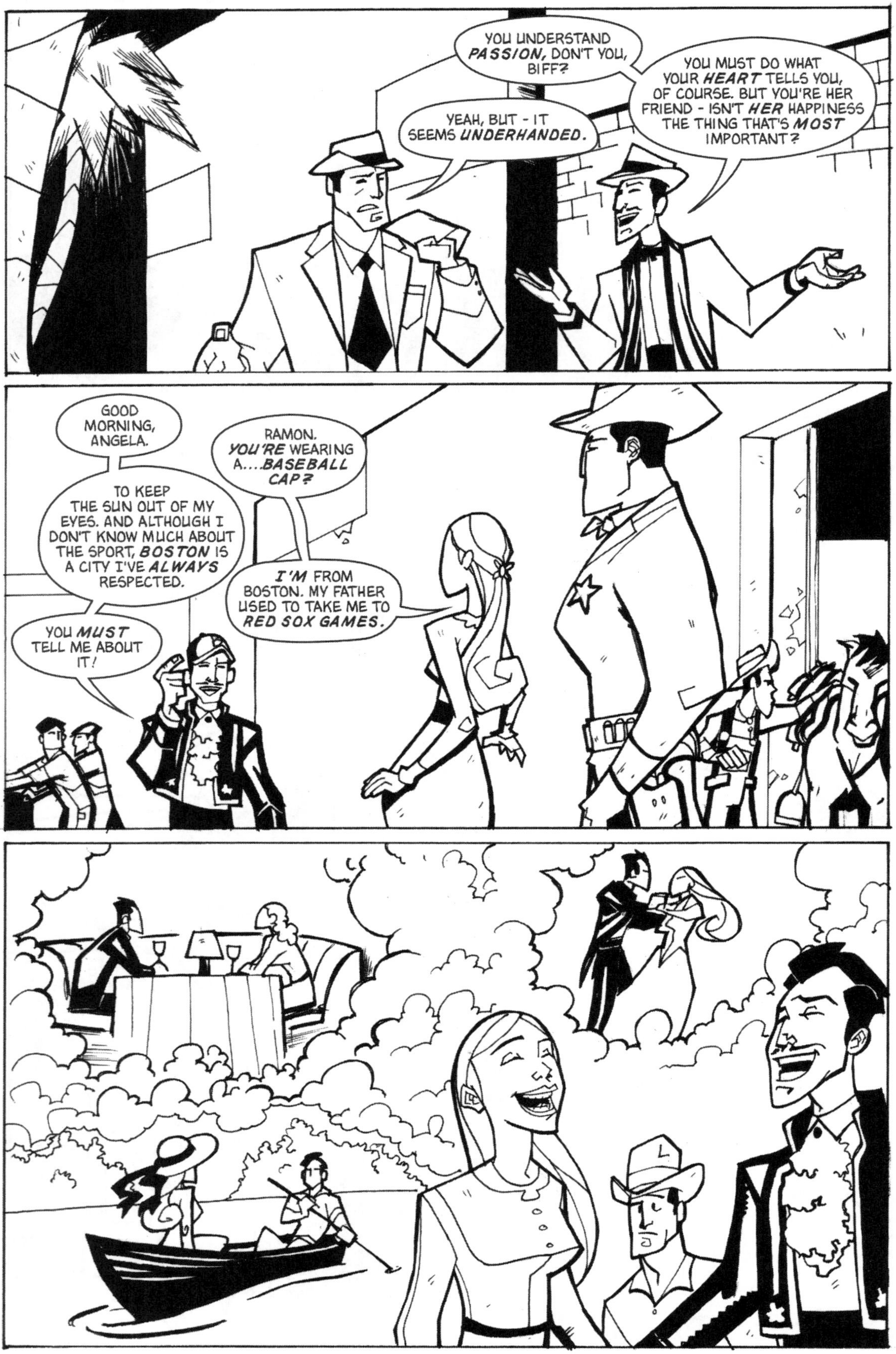
YOU UNDERSTAND PASSION, DON'T YOU, BIFF?
YEAH, BUT - IT SEEMS UNDERHANDED.
YOU MUST DO WHAT YOUR HEART TELLS YOU, OF COURSE. BUT YOU'RE HER FRIEND - ISN'T HER HAPPINESS THE THING THAT'S MOST IMPORTANT?
GOOD MORNING, ANGELA.
RAMON. YOU'RE WEARING A....BASEBALL CAP?
TO KEEP THE SUN OUT OF MY EYES. AND ALTHOUGH I DON'T KNOW MUCH ABOUT THE SPORT, BOSTON IS A CITY I'VE ALWAYS RESPECTED.
I'M FROM BOSTON. MY FATHER USED TO TAKE ME TO RED SOX GAMES.
YOU MUST TELL ME ABOUT IT!

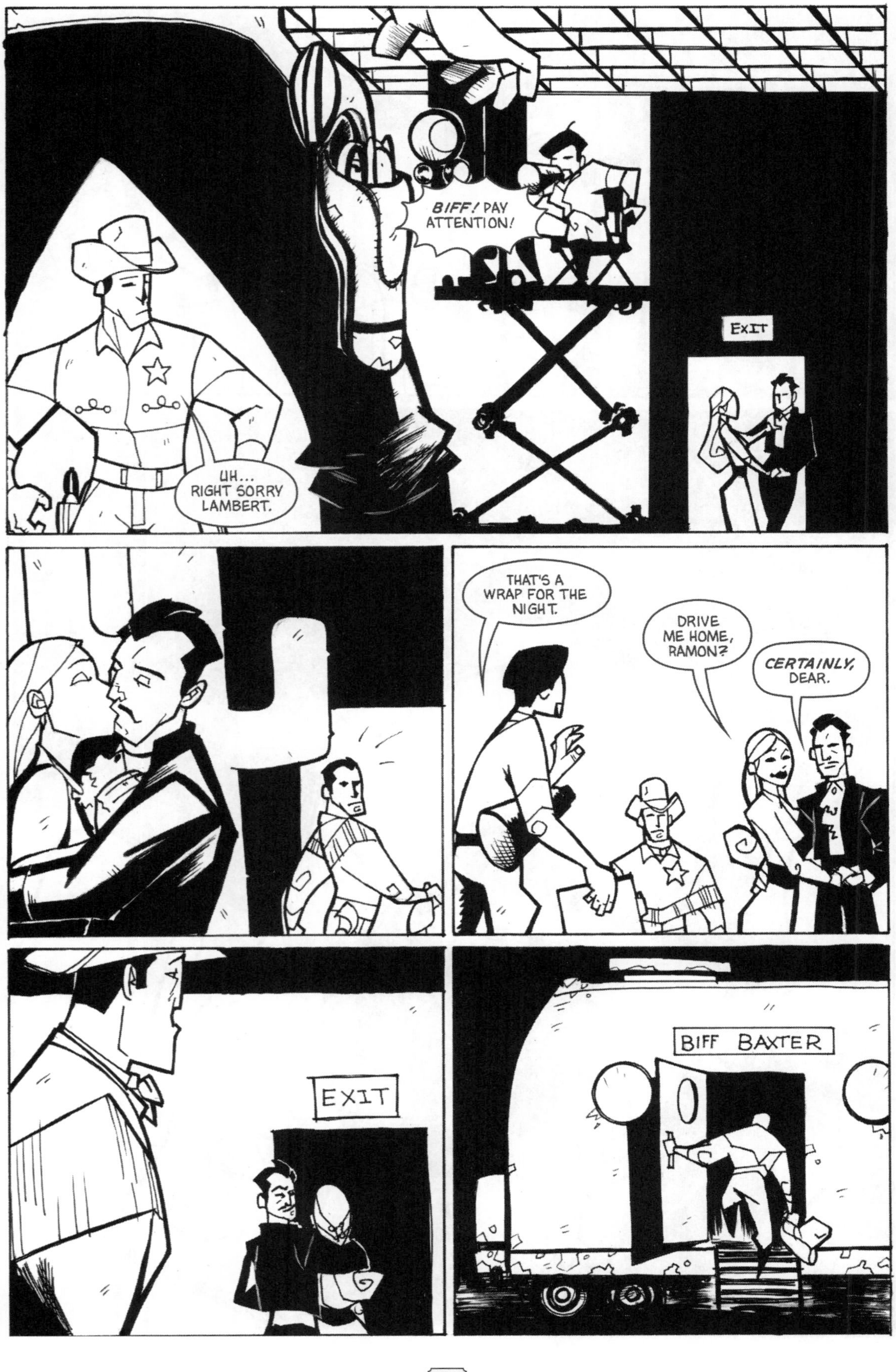
BIFF! PAY ATTENTION!
UH... RIGHT SORRY LAMBERT.
EXIT
THAT'S A WRAP FOR THE NIGHT.
DRIVE ME HOME, RAMON?
CERTAINLY, DEAR.
EXIT
BIFF BAXTER

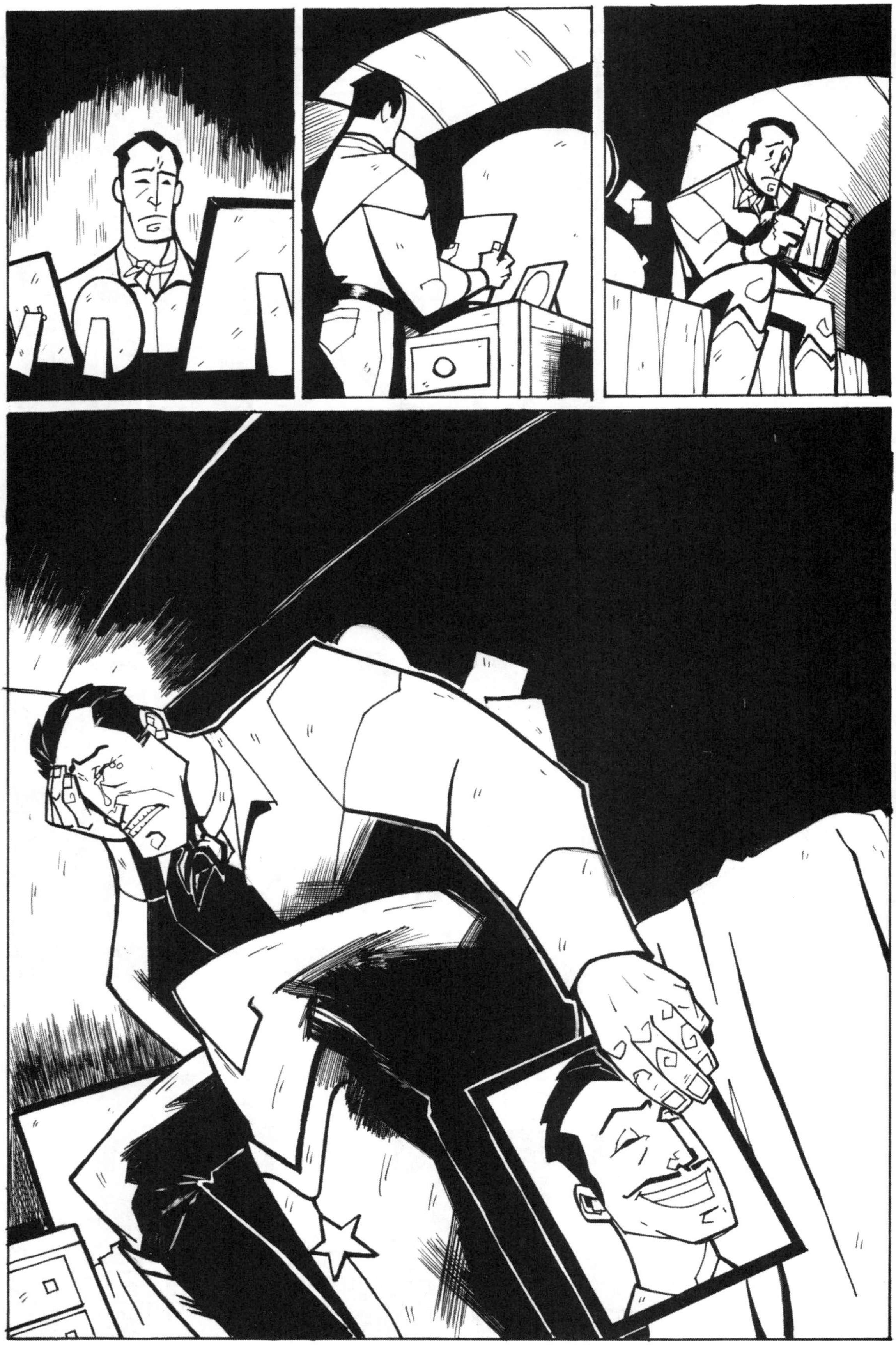

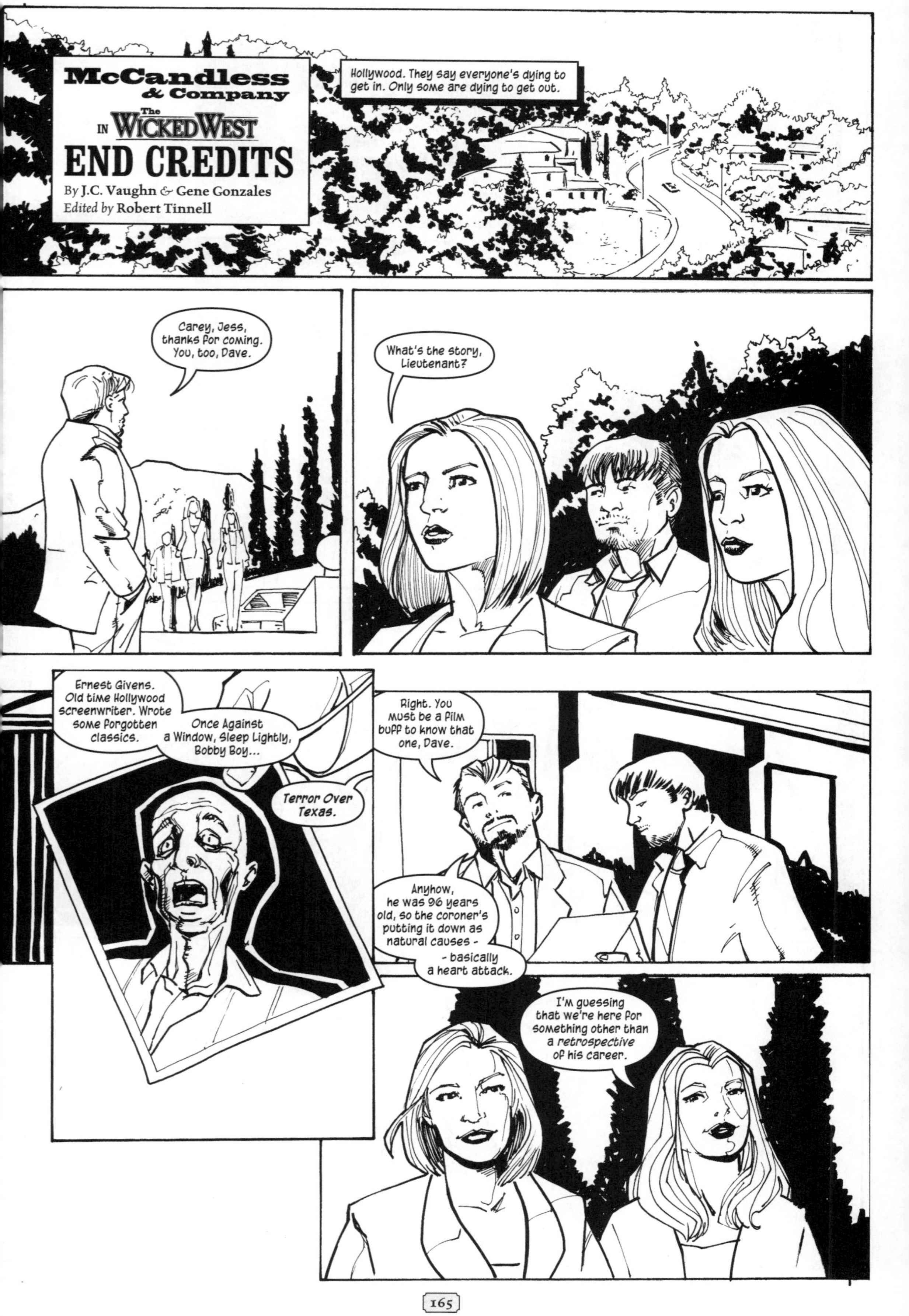
McCandless & Company
in The Wicked West
END CREDITS
By J.C. Vaughn & Gene Gonzales
Edited by Robert Tinnell
Hollywood. They say everyone's dying to get in. Only some are dying to get out.
Carey, Jess, thanks for coming. You, too, Dave.
What's the story, Lieutenant?
Ernest Givens. Old time Hollywood screenwriter. Wrote some forgotten classics.
Once Against a Window, Sleep Lightly, Bobby Boy...
Terror Over Texas.
Right. You must be a film buff to know that one, Dave.
Anyhow, he was 96 years old, so the coroner's putting it down as natural causes -
- basically a heart attack.
I'm guessing that we're here for something other than a *retrospective* of his career.

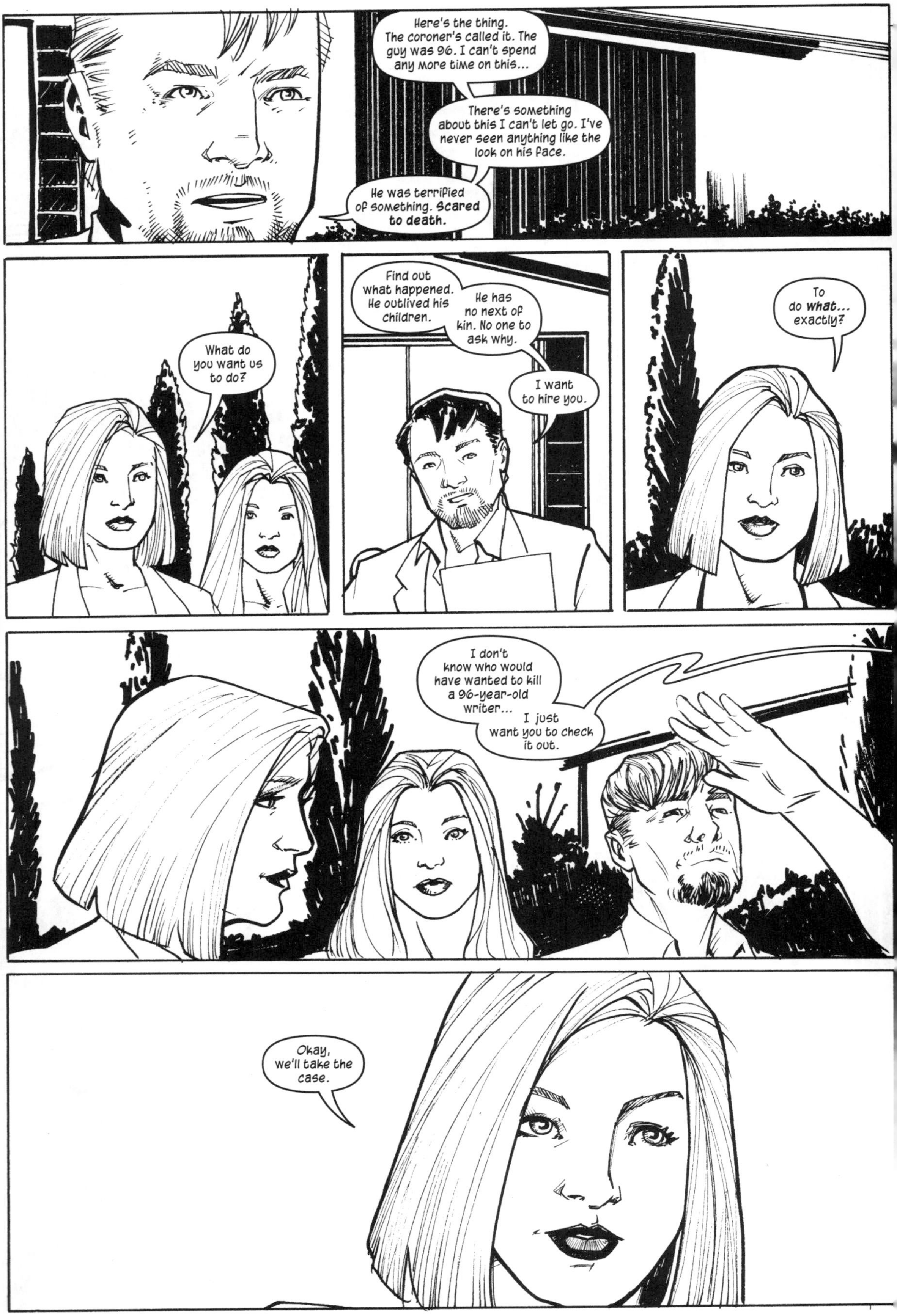
Here's the thing. The coroner's called it. The guy was 96. I can't spend any more time on this...
There's something about this I can't let go. I've never seen anything like the look on his face.
He was terrified of something. **Scared to death.**
What do you want us to do?
Find out what happened. He outlived his children.
He has no next of kin. No one to ask why.
I want to hire you.
To do **what...** exactly?
I don't know who would have wanted to kill a 96-year-old writer...
I just want you to check it out.
Okay, we'll take the case.

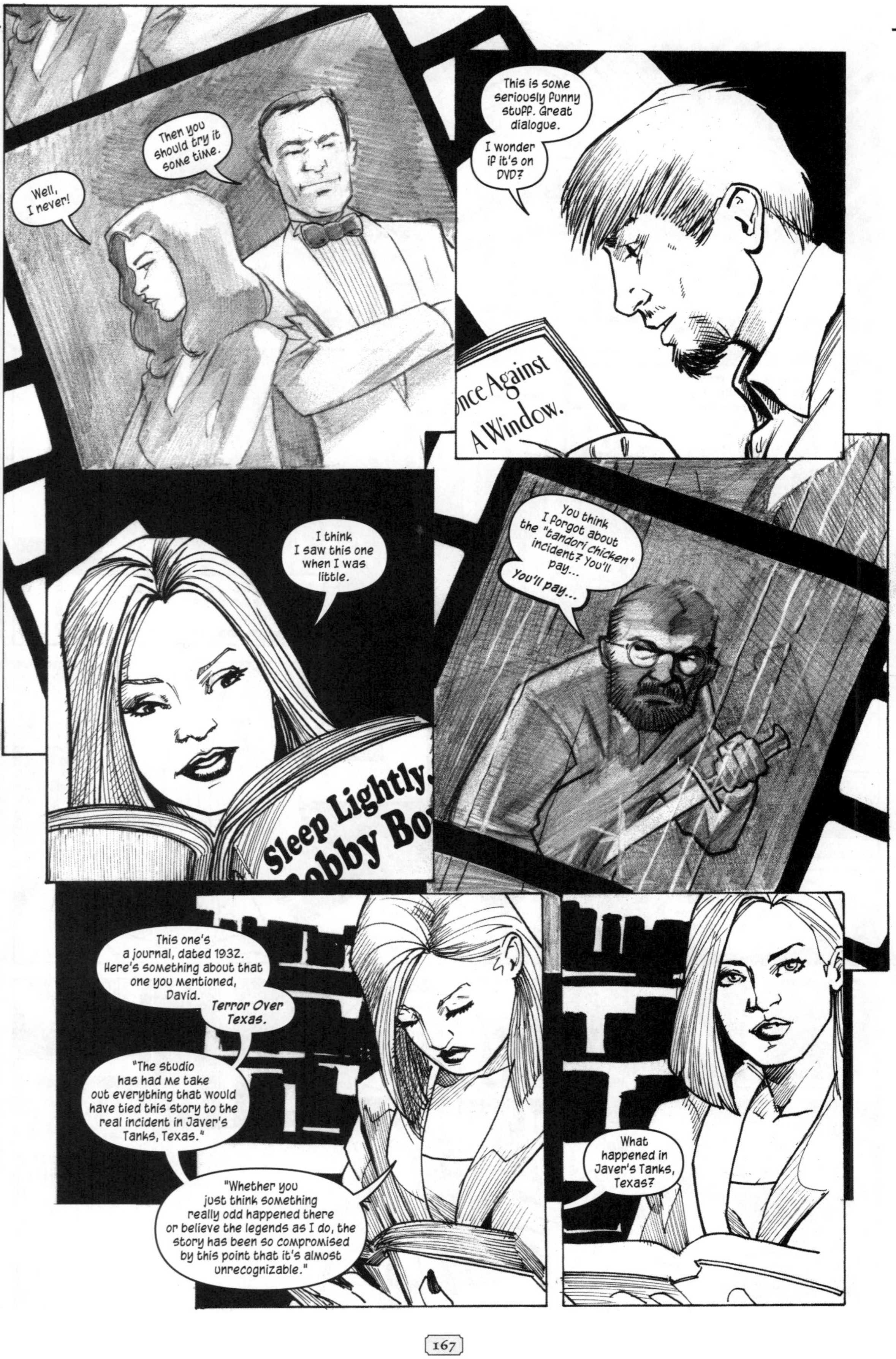
Well, I never!
Then you should try it some time.
This is some seriously funny stuff. Great dialogue.
I wonder if it's on DVD?
Once Against A Window.
I think I saw this one when I was little.
Sleep Lightly,
You think I forgot about the "tandori chicken" incident? You'll pay...
You'll pay...
This one's a journal, dated 1932. Here's something about that one you mentioned, David.
Terror Over Texas.
"The studio has had me take out everything that would have tied this story to the real incident in Javer's Tanks, Texas."
"Whether you just think something really odd happened there or believe the legends as I do, the story has been so compromised by this point that it's almost unrecognizable."
What happened in Javer's Tanks, Texas?

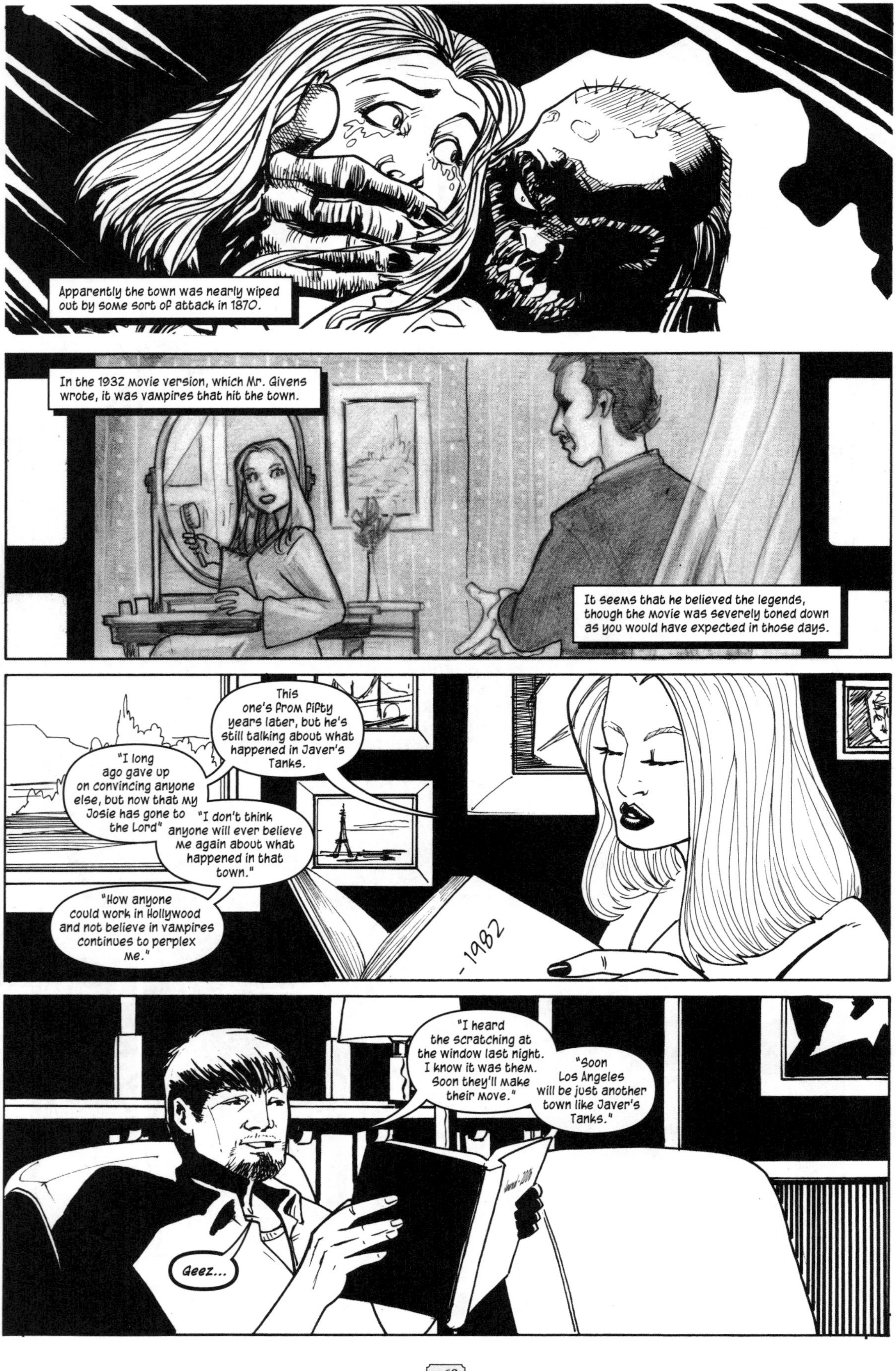
Apparently the town was nearly wiped out by some sort of attack in 1870.
In the 1932 movie version, which Mr. Givens wrote, it was vampires that hit the town.
It seems that he believed the legends, though the movie was severely toned down as you would have expected in those days.
This one's from fifty years later, but he's still talking about what happened in Javer's Tanks.
"I long ago gave up on convincing anyone else, but now that my Josie has gone to the Lord"
"I don't think anyone will ever believe me again about what happened in that town."
"How anyone could work in Hollywood and not believe in vampires continues to perplex me."
-1982
"I heard the scratching at the window last night. I know it was them. Soon they'll make their move."
"Soon Los Angeles will be just another town like Javer's Tanks."
Geez...

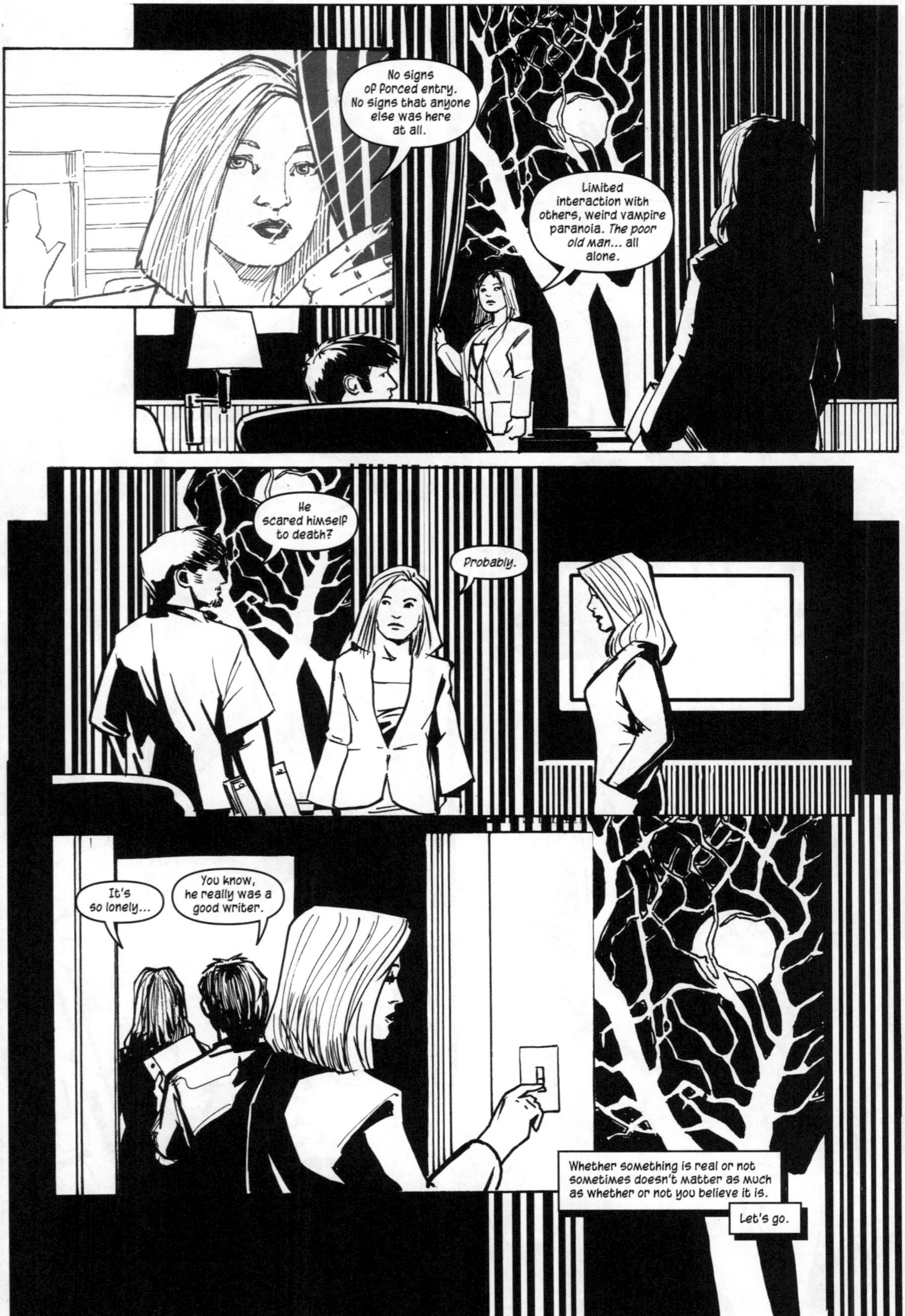
No signs of forced entry. No signs that anyone else was here at all.
Limited interaction with others, weird vampire paranoia. *The poor old man...* all alone.
He scared himself to death?
Probably.
It's so lonely...
You know, he really was a good writer.
Whether something is real or not sometimes doesn't matter as much as whether or not you believe it is.
Let's go.

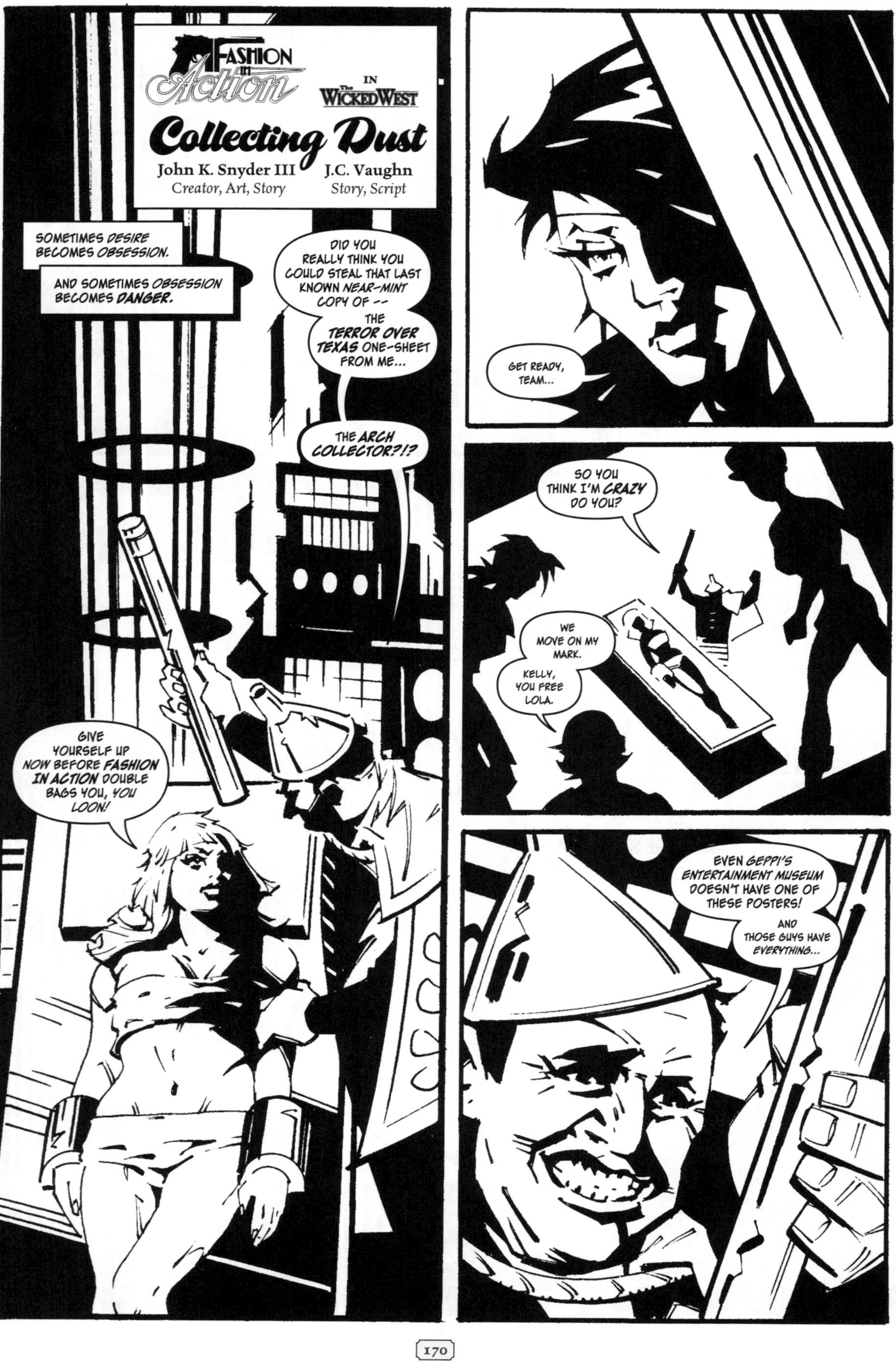
FASHION IN ACTION
IN The WICKED WEST
Collecting Dust
John K. Snyder III
Creator, Art, Story
J.C. Vaughn
Story, Script
SOMETIMES DESIRE BECOMES OBSESSION.
AND SOMETIMES OBSESSION BECOMES DANGER.
DID YOU REALLY THINK YOU COULD STEAL THAT LAST KNOWN NEAR-MINT COPY OF --
THE TERROR OVER TEXAS ONE-SHEET FROM ME...
THE ARCH COLLECTOR?!?
GIVE YOURSELF UP NOW BEFORE FASHION IN ACTION DOUBLE BAGS YOU, YOU LOON!
GET READY, TEAM...
SO YOU THINK I'M CRAZY DO YOU?
WE MOVE ON MY MARK.
KELLY, YOU FREE LOLA.
EVEN GEPPI'S ENTERTAINMENT MUSEUM DOESN'T HAVE ONE OF THESE POSTERS!
AND THOSE GUYS HAVE EVERYTHING...

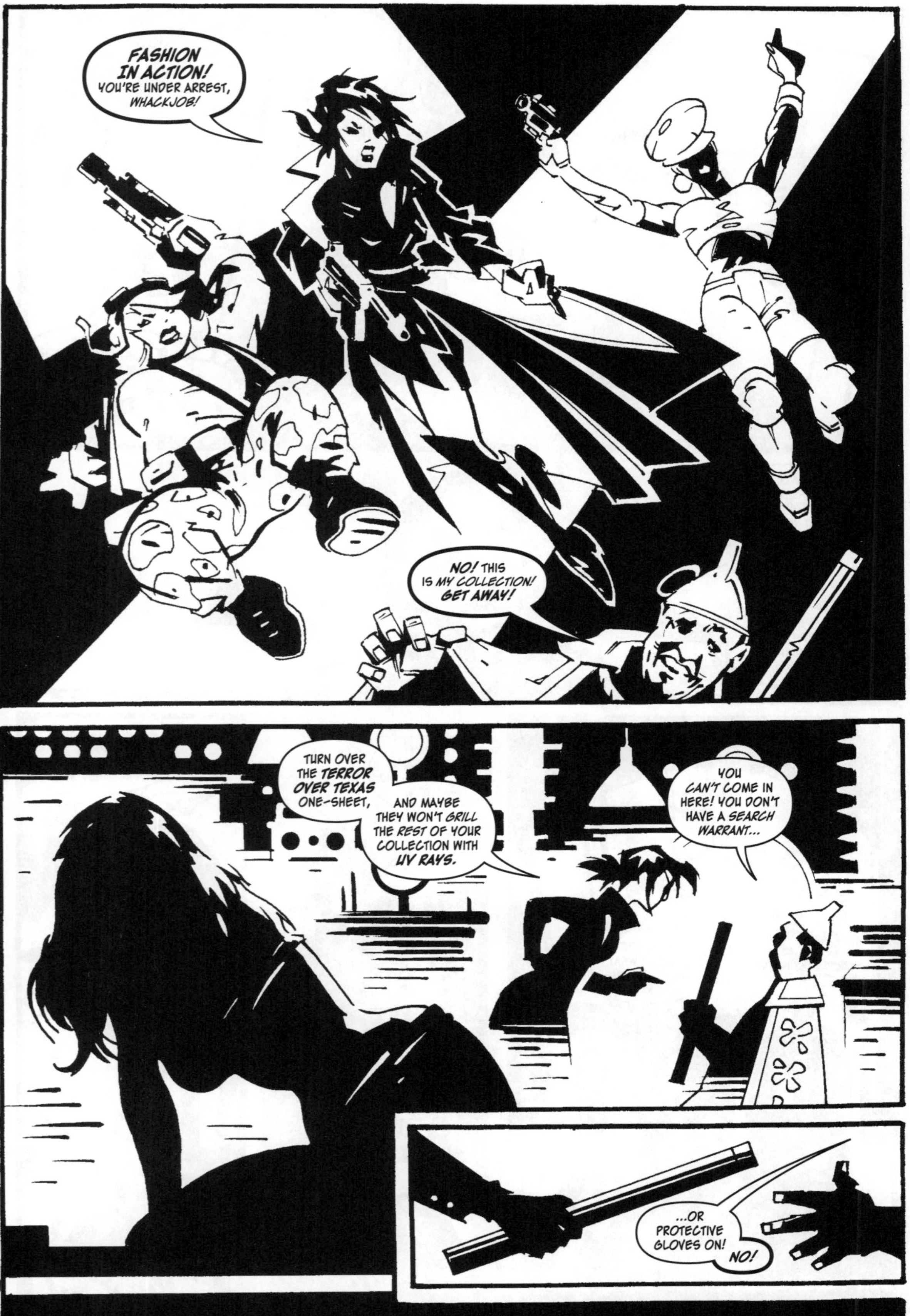
FASHION IN ACTION! YOU'RE UNDER ARREST, WHACKJOB!
NO! THIS IS MY COLLECTION! GET AWAY!
TURN OVER THE TERROR OVER TEXAS ONE-SHEET,
AND MAYBE THEY WON'T GRILL THE REST OF YOUR COLLECTION WITH UV RAYS.
YOU CAN'T COME IN HERE! YOU DON'T HAVE A SEARCH WARRANT...
...OR PROTECTIVE GLOVES ON!
NO!

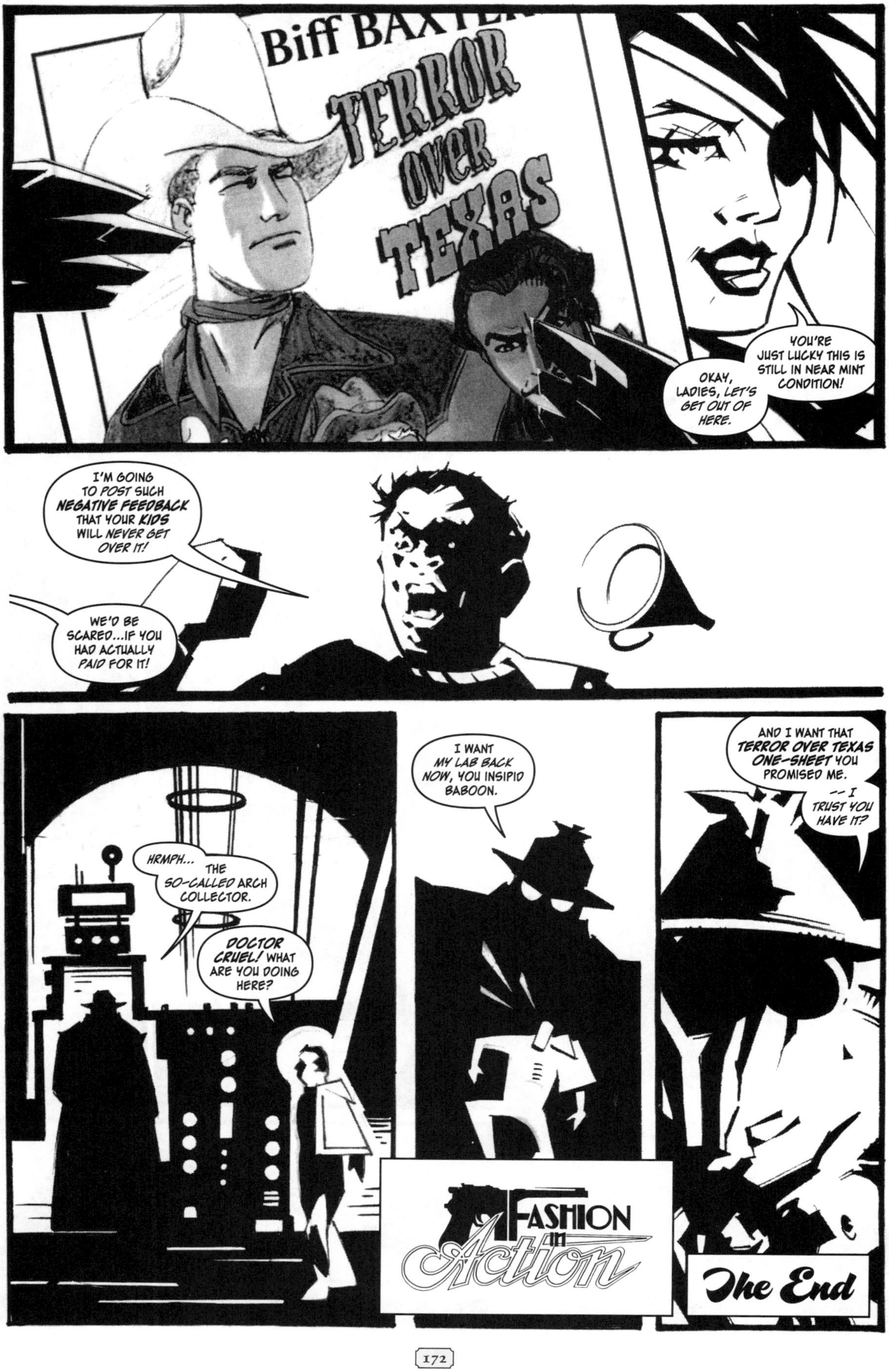
Biff BAXTER
TERROR OVER TEXAS
YOU'RE JUST LUCKY THIS IS STILL IN NEAR MINT CONDITION!
OKAY, LADIES, LET'S GET OUT OF HERE.
I'M GOING TO POST SUCH NEGATIVE FEEDBACK THAT YOUR KIDS WILL NEVER GET OVER IT!
WE'D BE SCARED...IF YOU HAD ACTUALLY PAID FOR IT!
HRMPH... THE SO-CALLED ARCH COLLECTOR.
DOCTOR CRUEL! WHAT ARE YOU DOING HERE?
I WANT MY LAB BACK NOW, YOU INSIPID BABOON.
AND I WANT THAT TERROR OVER TEXAS ONE-SHEET YOU PROMISED ME.
-- I TRUST YOU HAVE IT?
Fashion in Action
The End

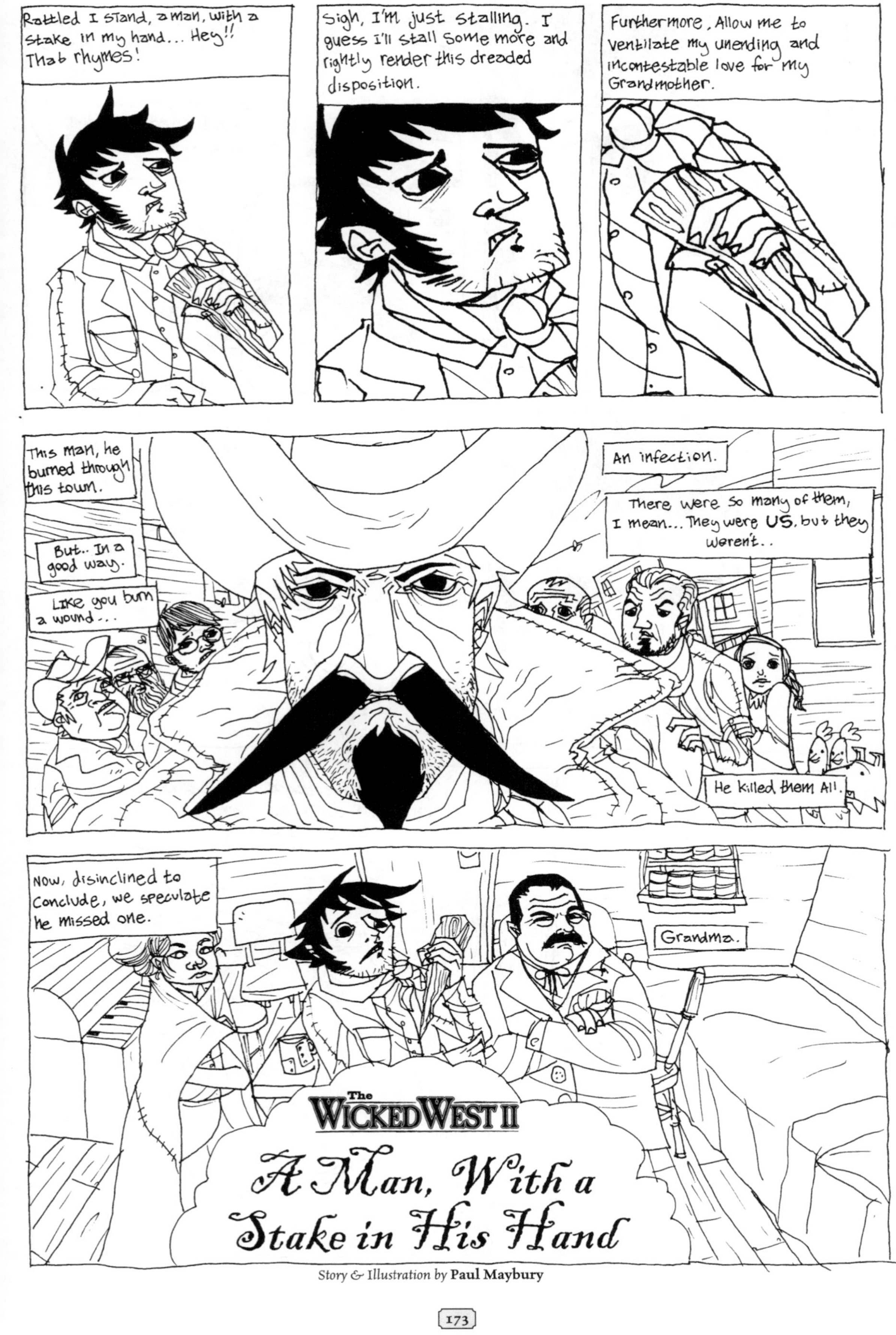
Rattled I stand, a man, with a stake in my hand... Hey!! That rhymes!
Sigh, I'm just stalling. I guess I'll stall some more and rightly render this dreaded disposition.
Furthermore, Allow me to ventilate my unending and incontestable love for my Grandmother.
This man, he burned through this town.
But.. In a good way.
Like you burn a wound...
An infection.
There were so many of them, I mean... They were US, but they weren't..
He killed them All.
Now, disinclined to conclude, we speculate he missed one.
Grandma.
The WICKED WEST II
A Man, With a Stake in His Hand

Story & Illustration by **Paul Maybury**

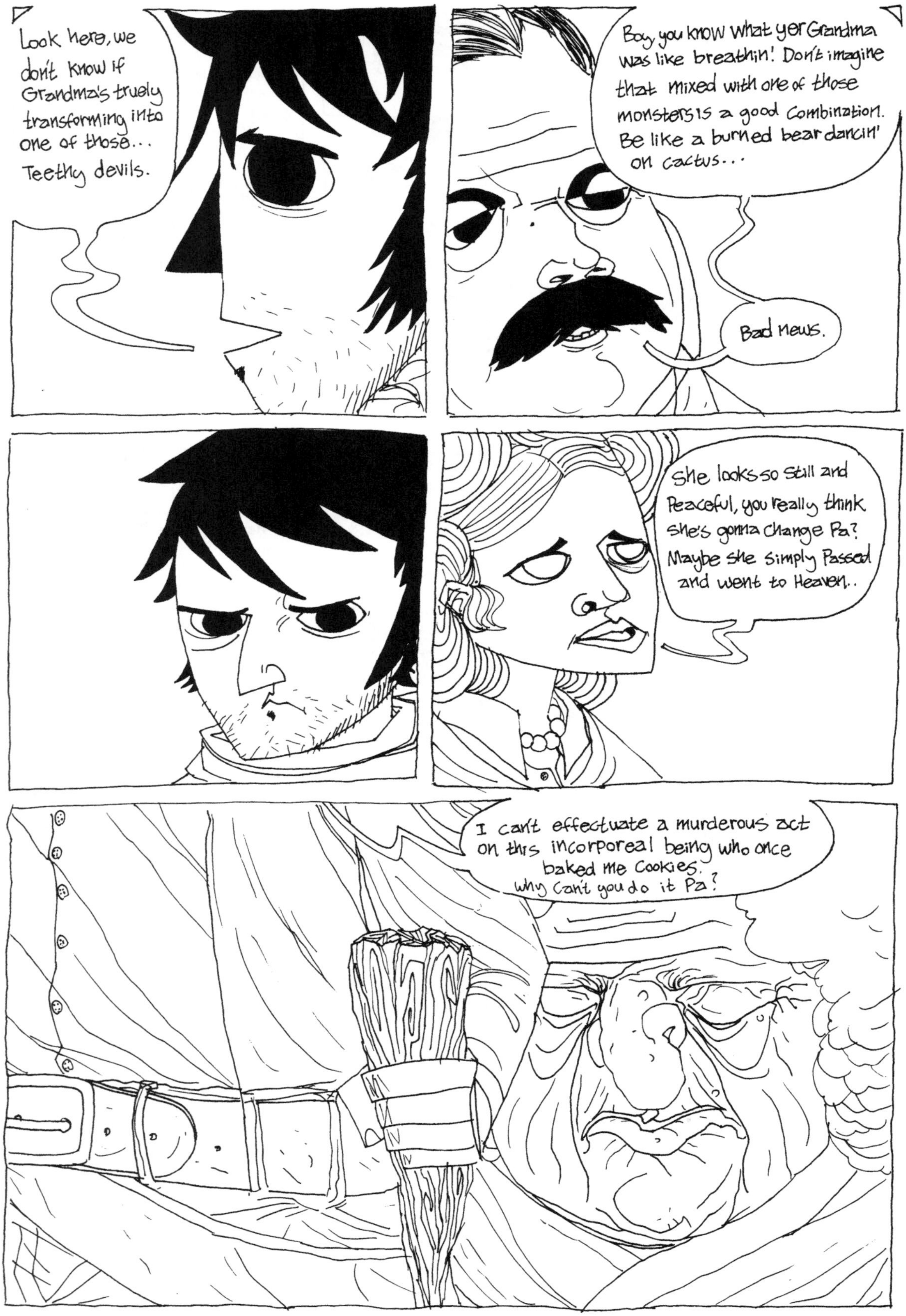
Look here, we don't know if Grandma's truely transforming into one of those... Teethy devils.
Boy you know what yer Grandma was like breathin! Don't imagine that mixed with one of those monsters is a good combination. Be like a burned bear dancin' on cactus...
Bad News.
She looks so still and Peaceful, you really think she's gonna change Pa? Maybe she simply Passed and went to Heaven..
I can't effectuate a murderous act on this incorporeal being who once baked me cookies.
why can't you do it Pa?

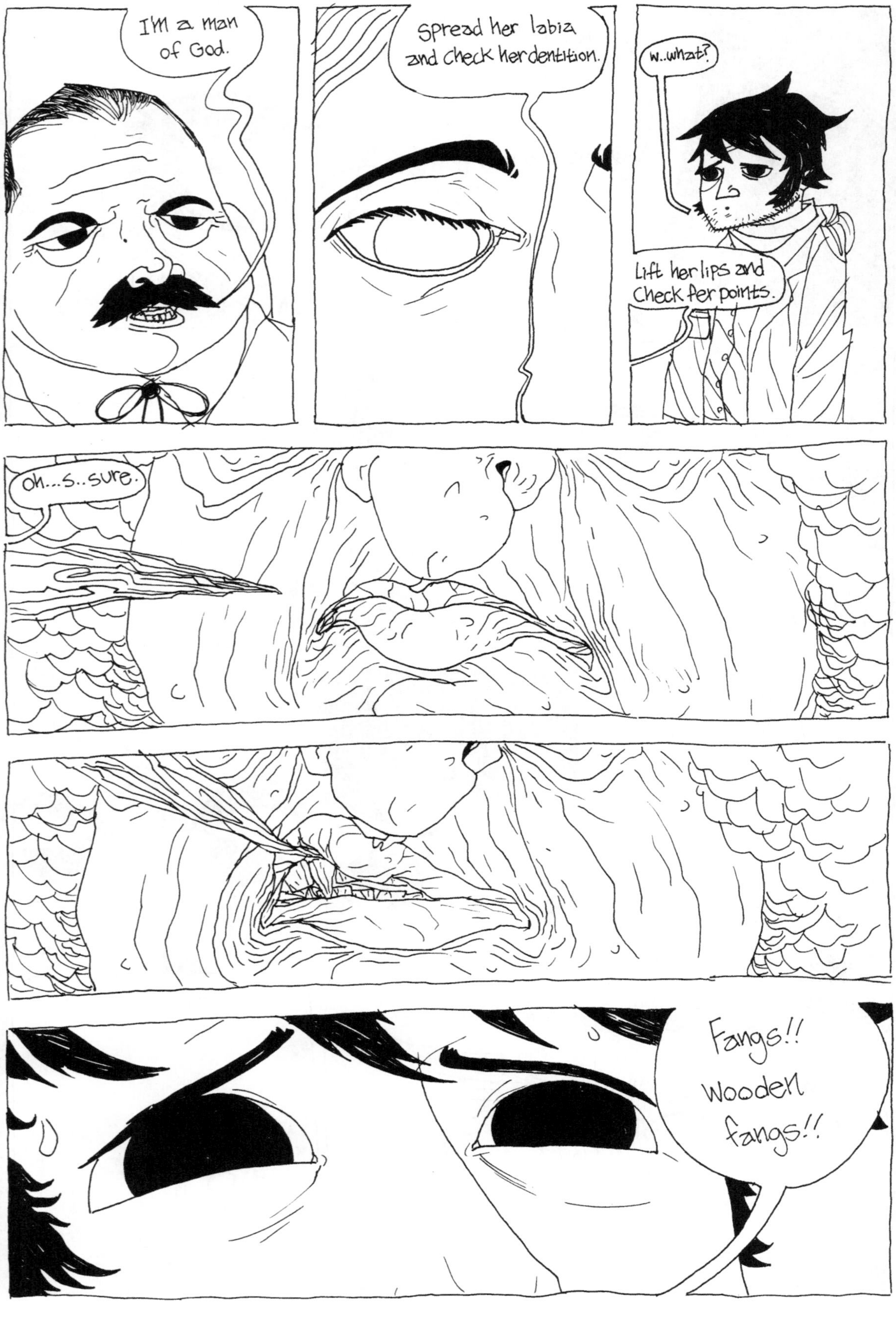
I'm a man of God.
Spread her labia and check her dentition.
w..what?
Lift her lips and check her points.
oh...s..sure.
Fangs!! wooden fangs!!

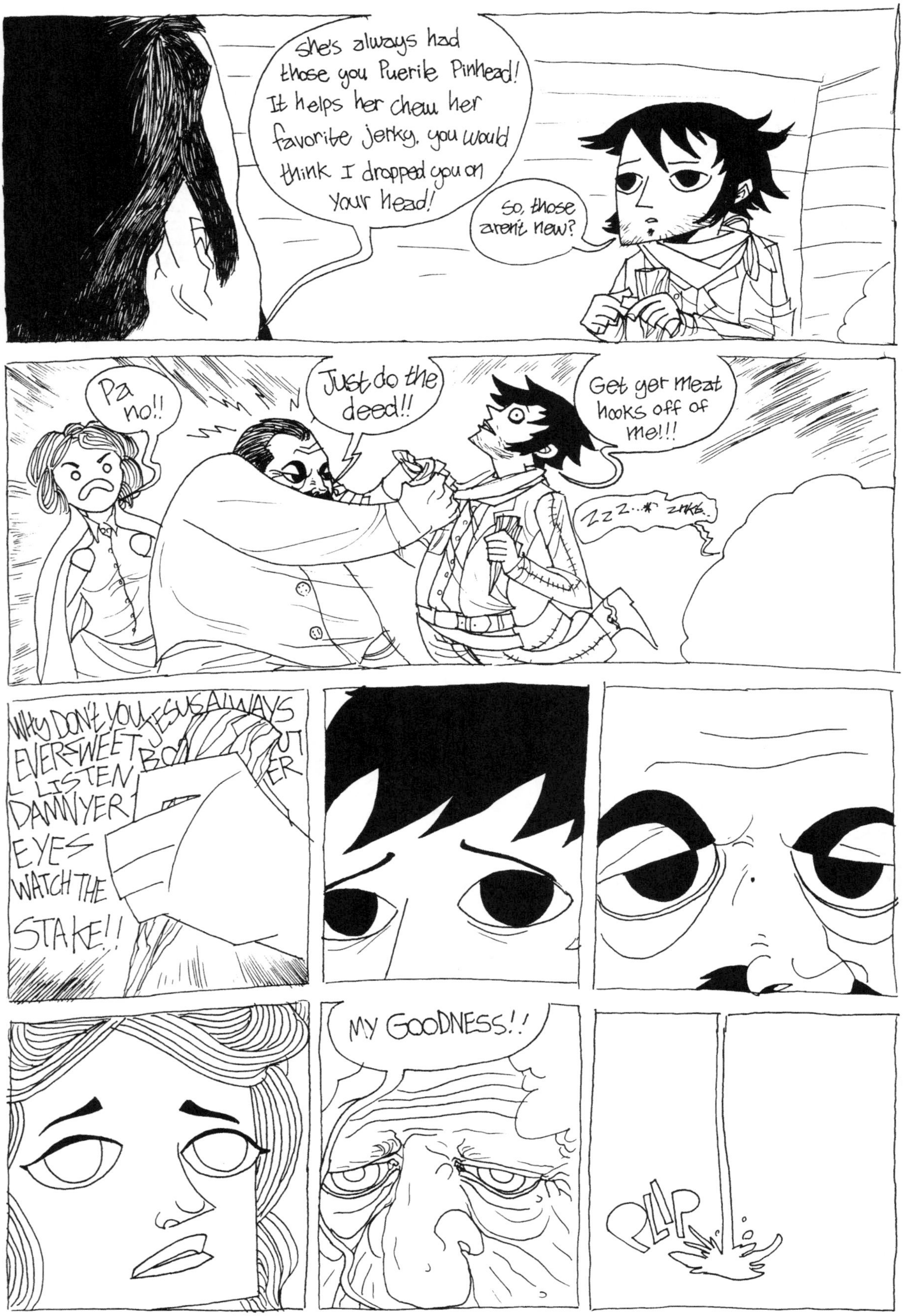
She's always had those you Puerile Pinhead! It helps her chew her favorite jerky. you would think I dropped you on your head!
So, those aren't new?
Pa no!!
Just do the deed!!
Get yer meat hooks off of me!!!
WHY DON'T YOU EVER LISTEN DAMN YER EYES WATCH THE STAKE!!
JESUS ALWAYS
MY GOODNESS!!
PLIP

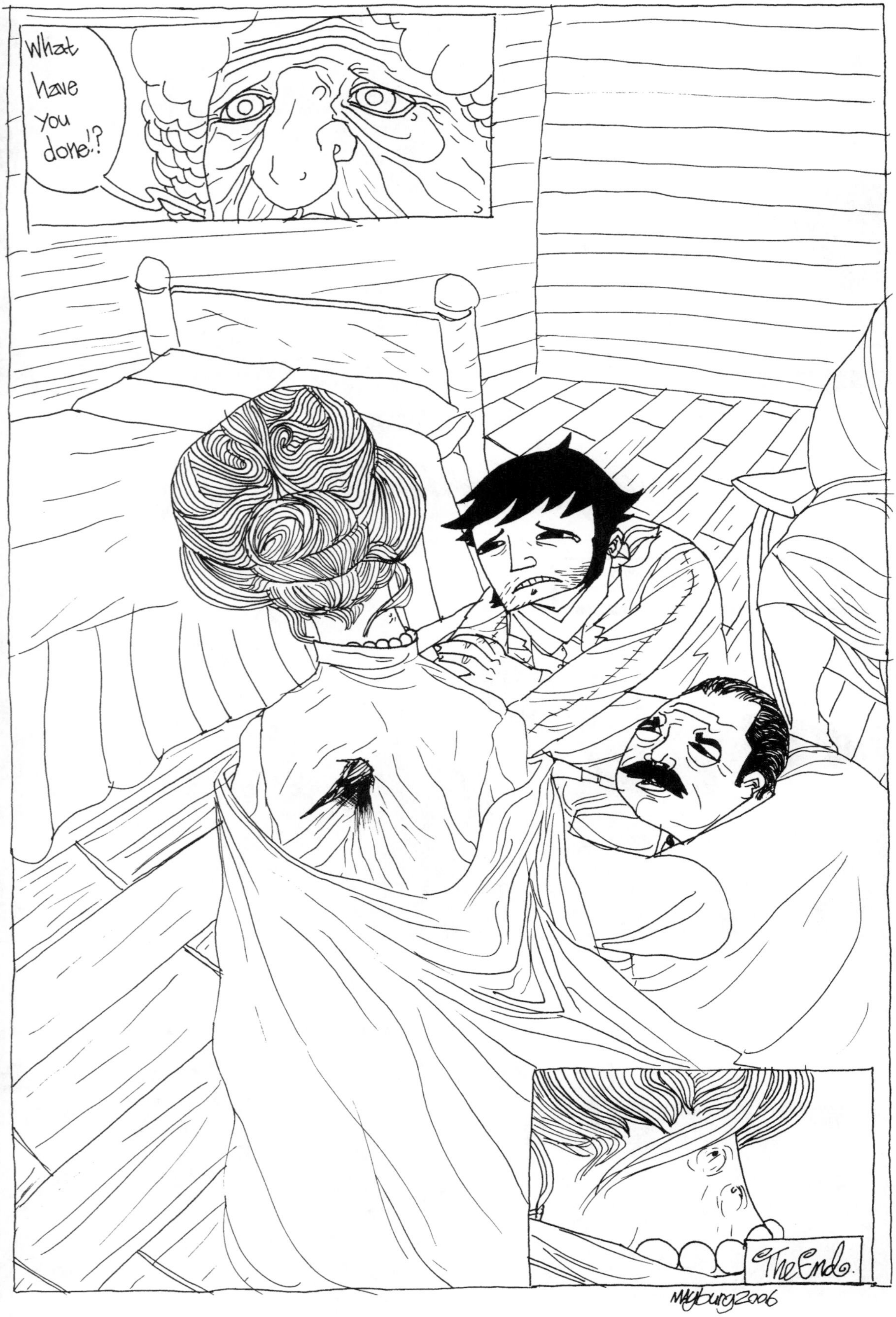
What have you done!?
The End.
MAYBURG 2006

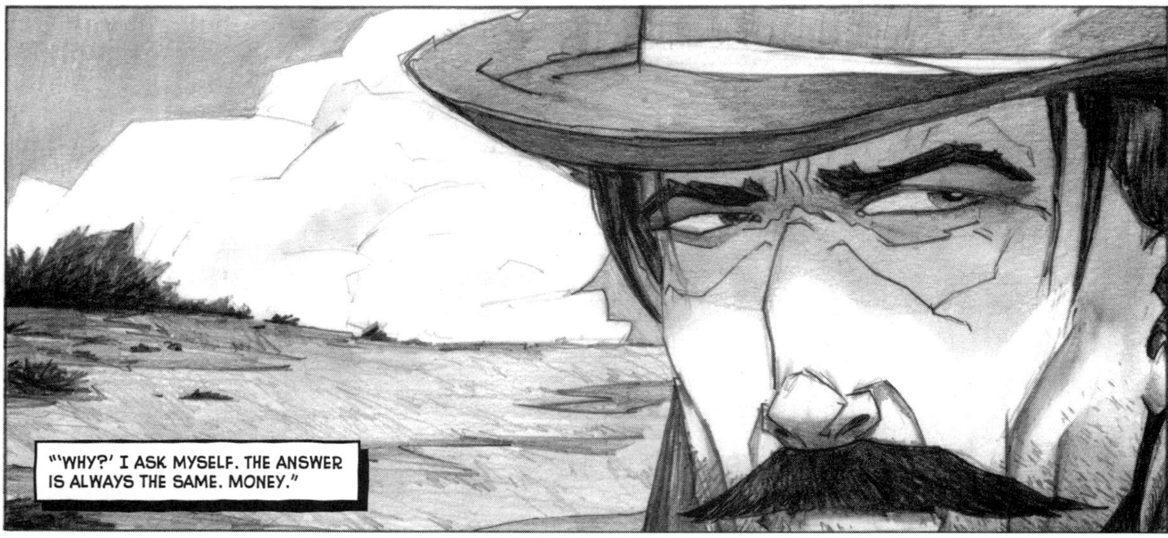
"'WHY?' I ASK MYSELF. THE ANSWER IS ALWAYS THE SAME. MONEY."

Written by **Robert Tinnell** The WICKED WEST *Illustrated by* **Micah Farritor**

Nothing Behind but Sky...*

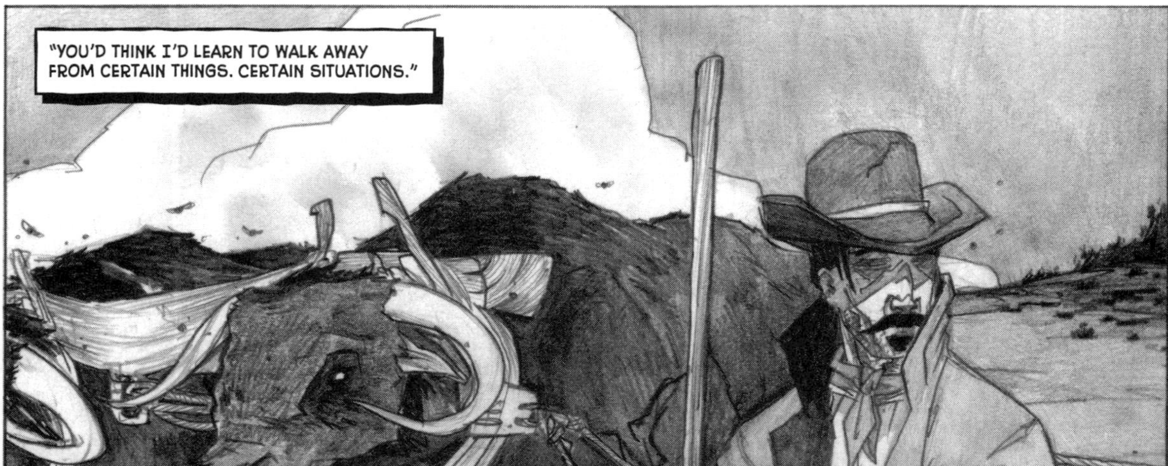
"YOU'D THINK I'D LEARN TO WALK AWAY FROM CERTAIN THINGS. CERTAIN SITUATIONS."

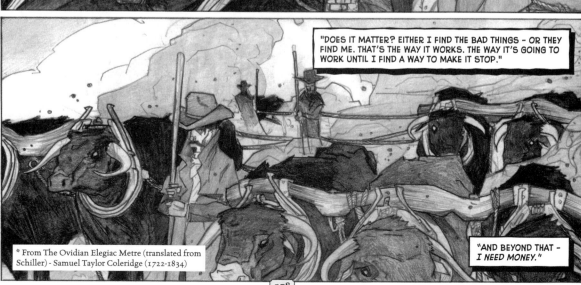

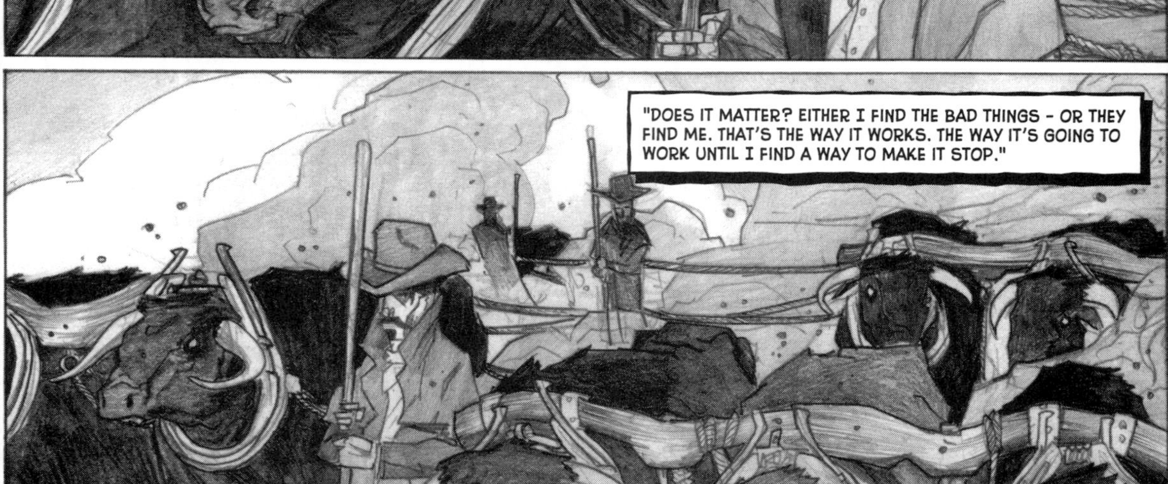
"DOES IT MATTER? EITHER I FIND THE BAD THINGS - OR THEY FIND ME. THAT'S THE WAY IT WORKS. THE WAY IT'S GOING TO WORK UNTIL I FIND A WAY TO MAKE IT STOP."
"AND BEYOND THAT - *I NEED MONEY.*"

* From The Ovidian Elegiac Metre (translated from Schiller) - Samuel Taylor Coleridge (1722-1834)

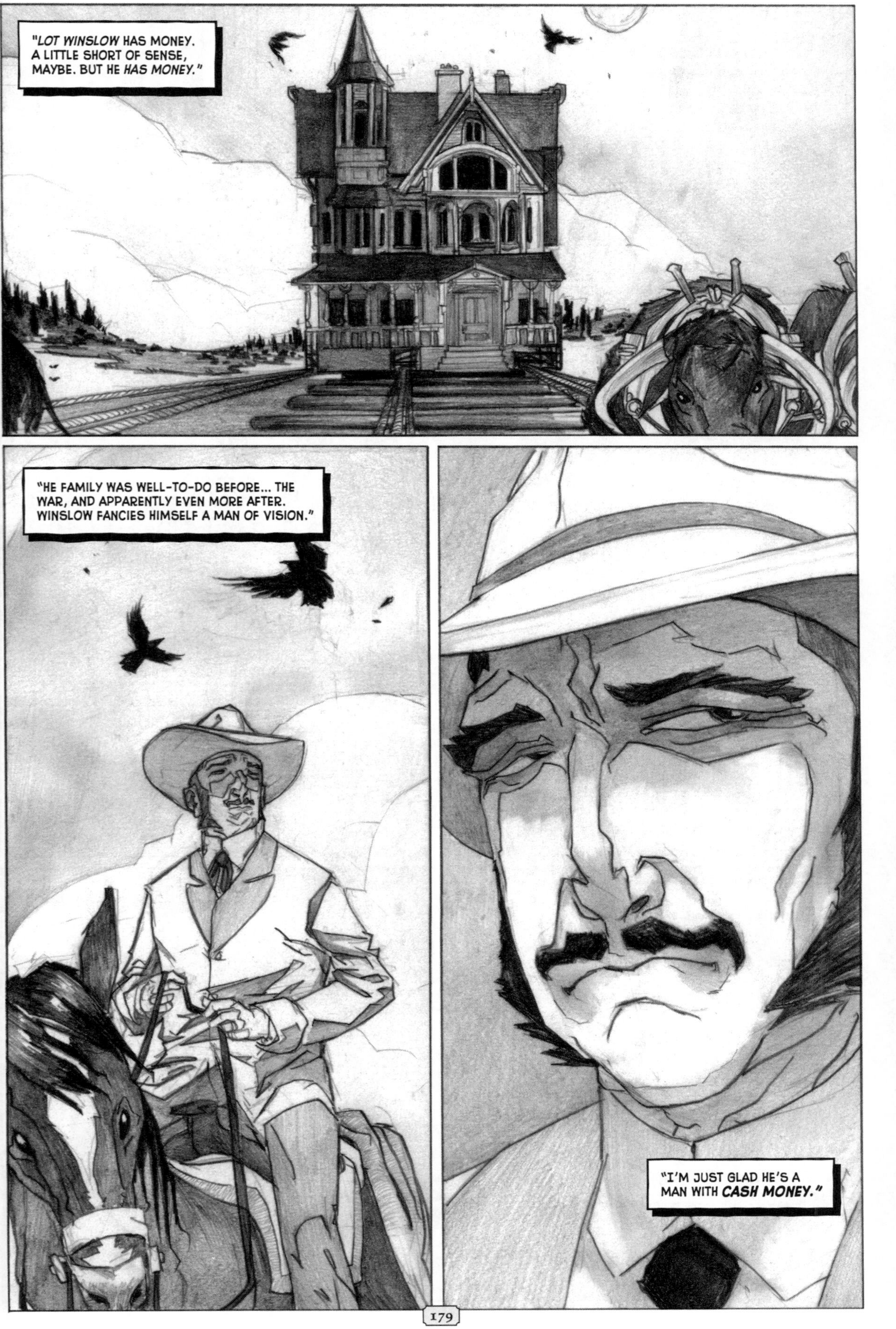
"LOT WINSLOW HAS MONEY. A LITTLE SHORT OF SENSE, MAYBE. BUT HE HAS MONEY."
"HE FAMILY WAS WELL-TO-DO BEFORE... THE WAR, AND APPARENTLY EVEN MORE AFTER. WINSLOW FANCIES HIMSELF A MAN OF VISION."
"I'M JUST GLAD HE'S A MAN WITH CASH MONEY."

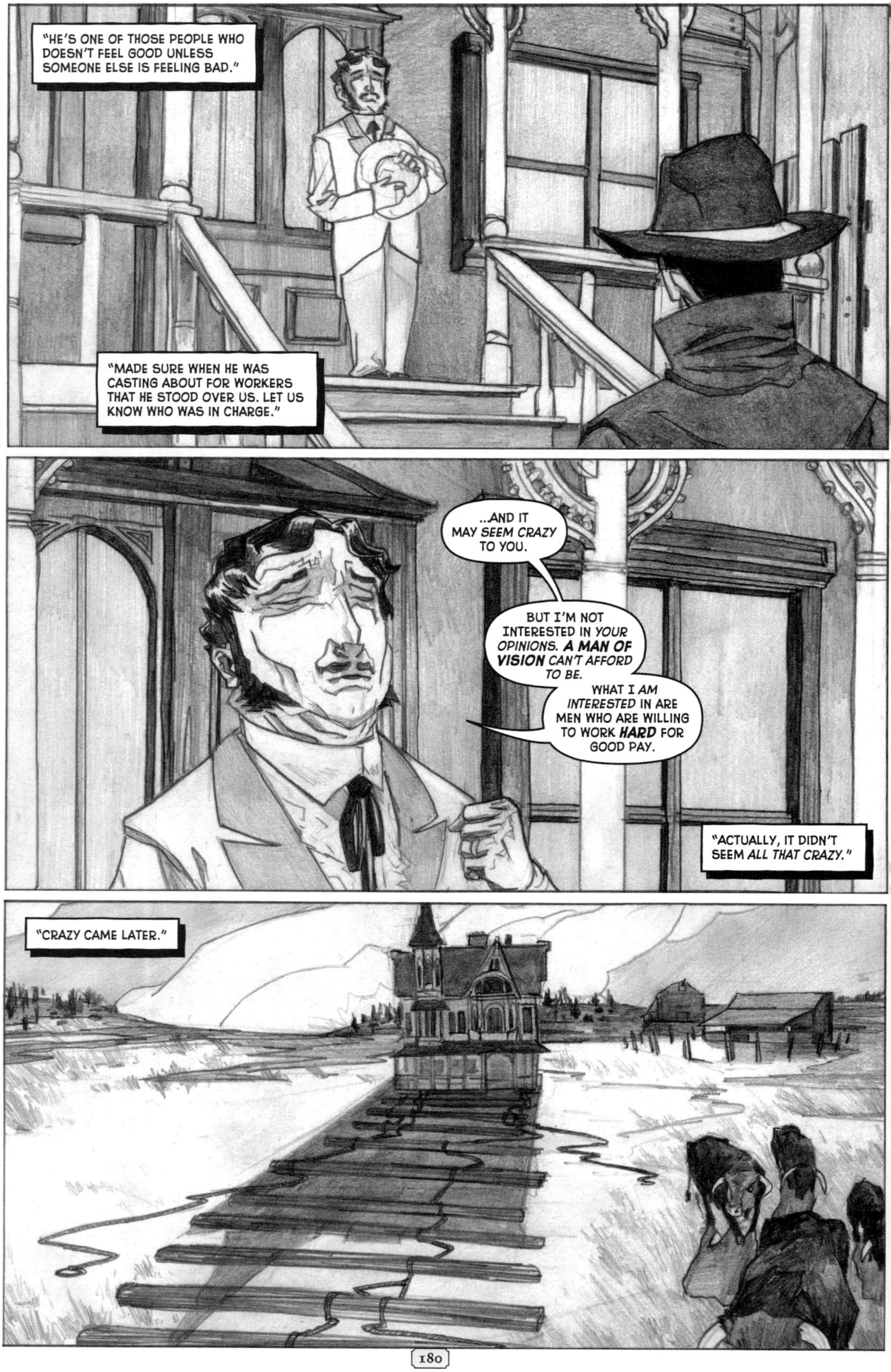
"HE'S ONE OF THOSE PEOPLE WHO DOESN'T FEEL GOOD UNLESS SOMEONE ELSE IS FEELING BAD."
"MADE SURE WHEN HE WAS CASTING ABOUT FOR WORKERS THAT HE STOOD OVER US. LET US KNOW WHO WAS IN CHARGE."
...AND IT MAY SEEM CRAZY TO YOU.
BUT I'M NOT INTERESTED IN YOUR OPINIONS. A MAN OF VISION CAN'T AFFORD TO BE.
WHAT I AM INTERESTED IN ARE MEN WHO ARE WILLING TO WORK HARD FOR GOOD PAY.
"ACTUALLY, IT DIDN'T SEEM ALL THAT CRAZY."
"CRAZY CAME LATER."

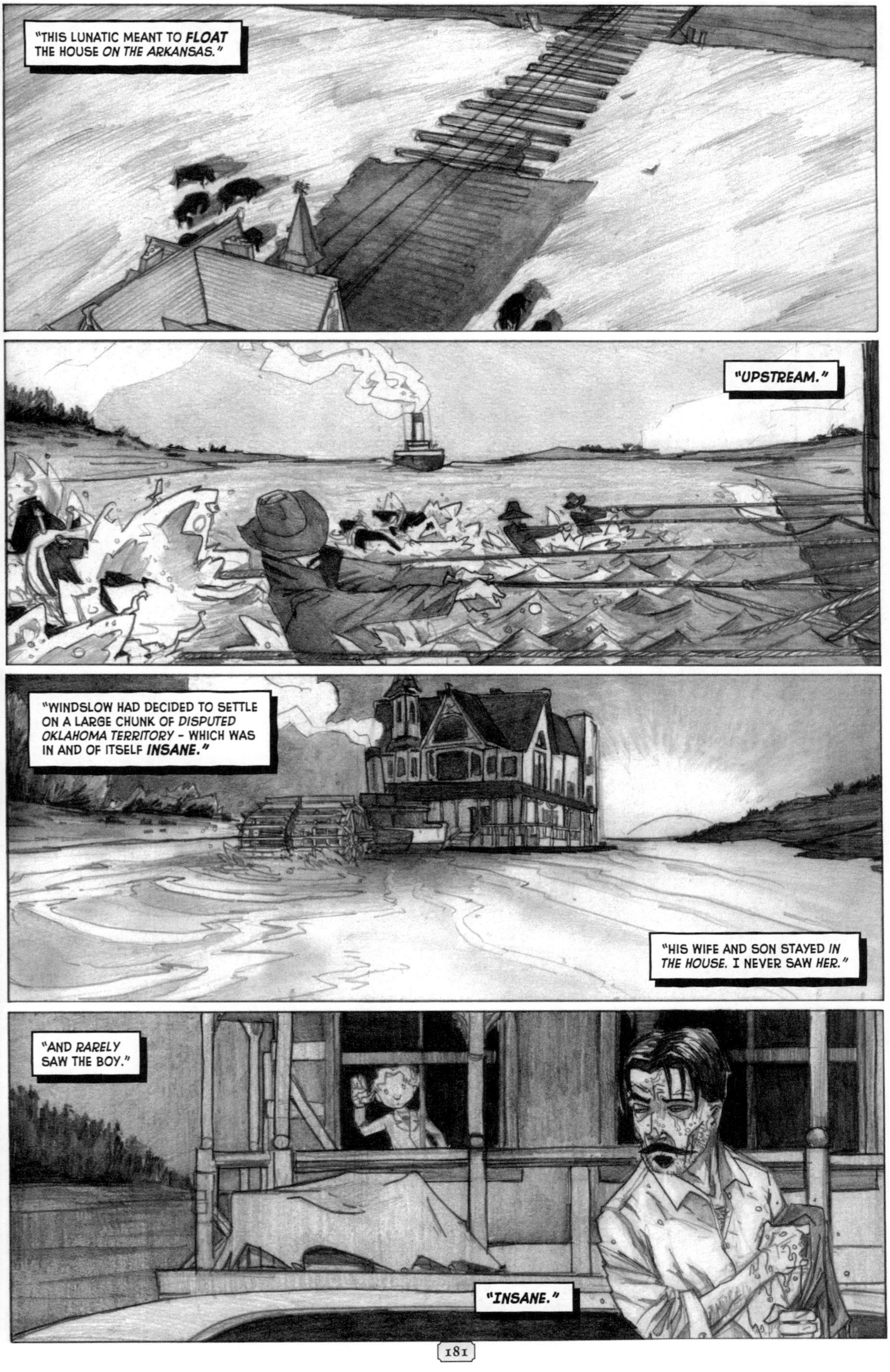
"THIS LUNATIC MEANT TO FLOAT THE HOUSE ON THE ARKANSAS."
"UPSTREAM."
"WINDSLOW HAD DECIDED TO SETTLE ON A LARGE CHUNK OF DISPUTED OKLAHOMA TERRITORY - WHICH WAS IN AND OF ITSELF INSANE."
"HIS WIFE AND SON STAYED IN THE HOUSE. I NEVER SAW HER."
"AND RARELY SAW THE BOY."
"INSANE."

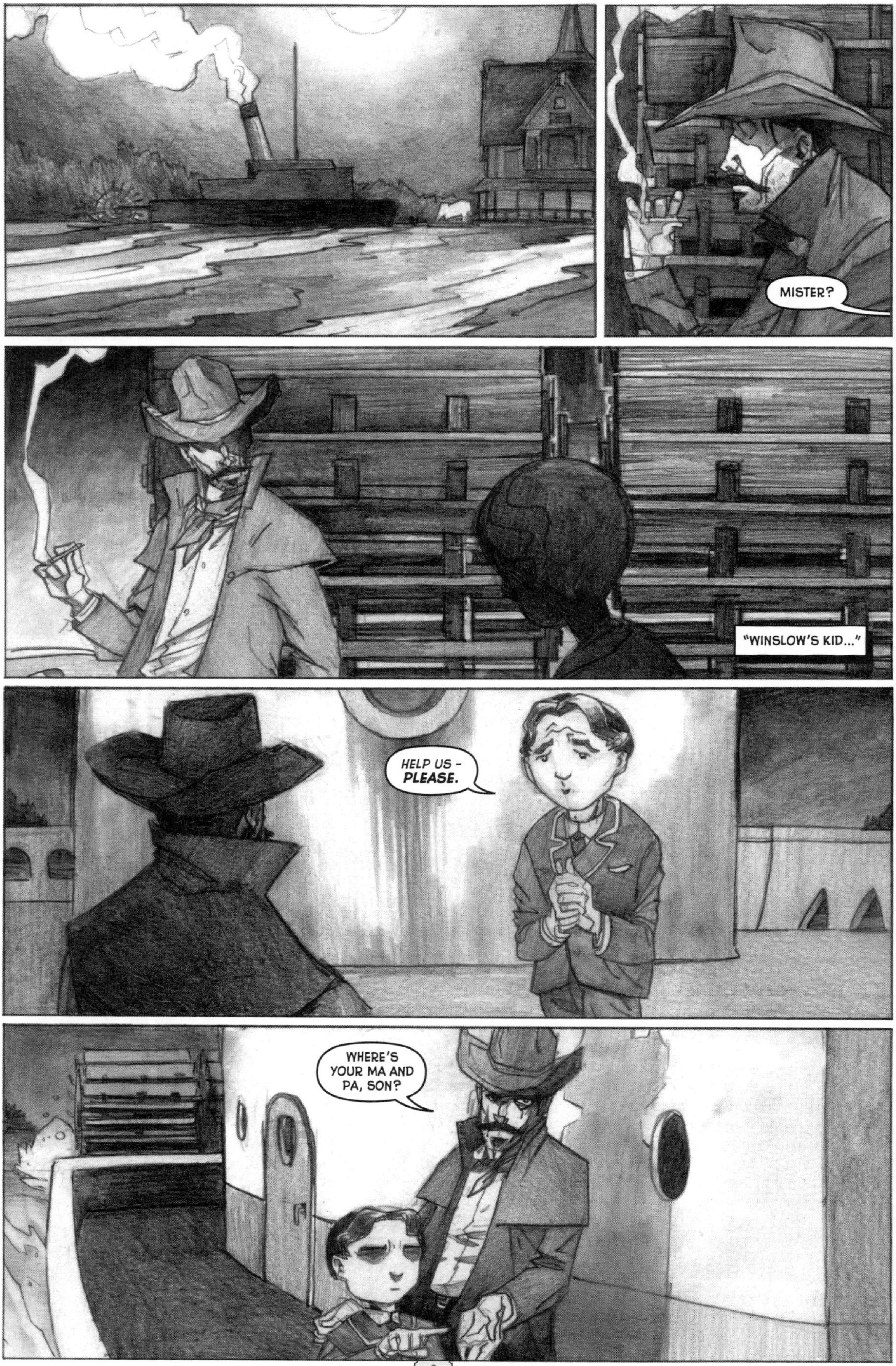
MISTER?
"WINSLOW'S KID..."
HELP US - PLEASE.
WHERE'S YOUR MA AND PA, SON?

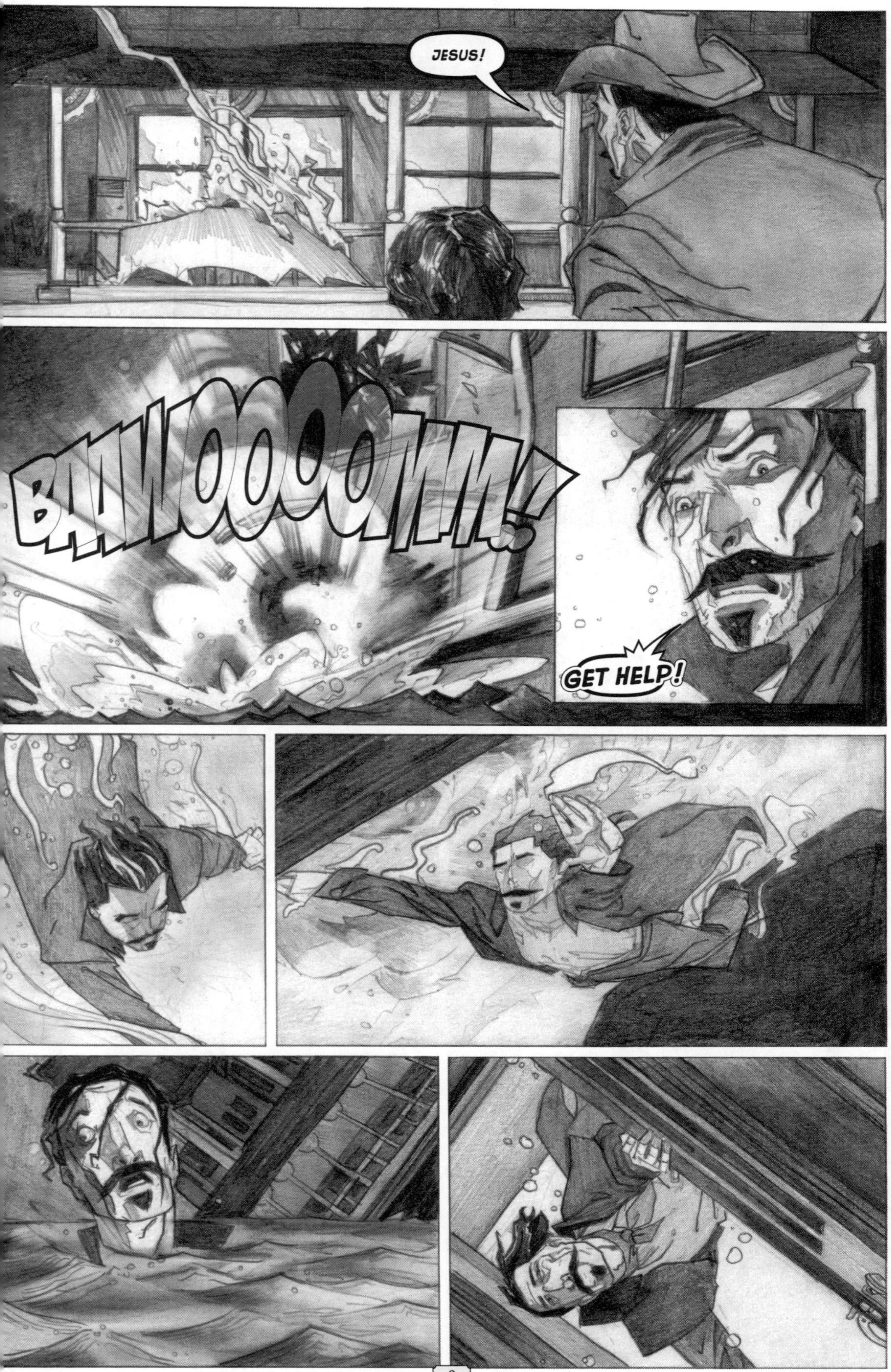

JESUS!
BAAWOOOOOMM!!
GET HELP!

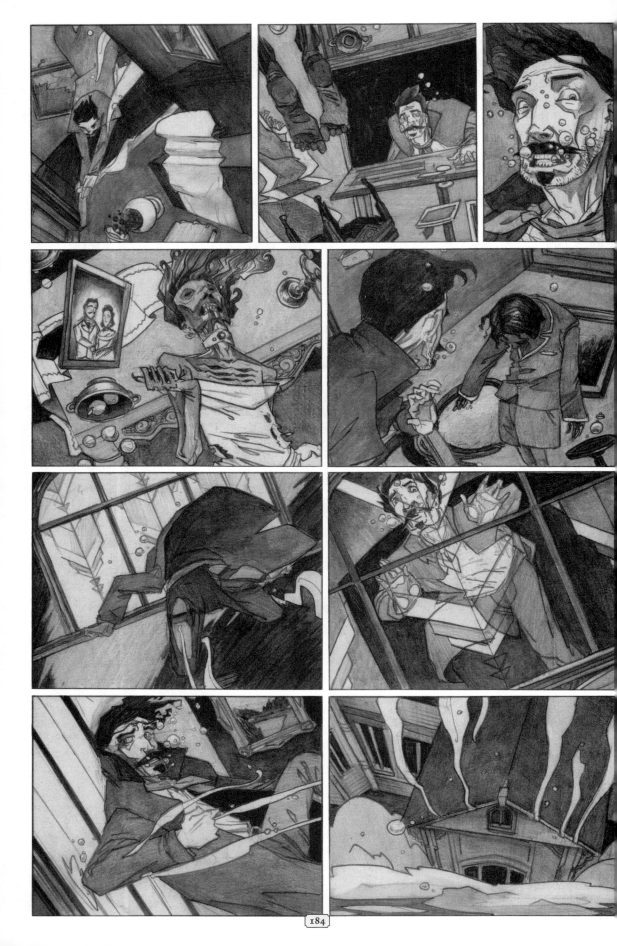

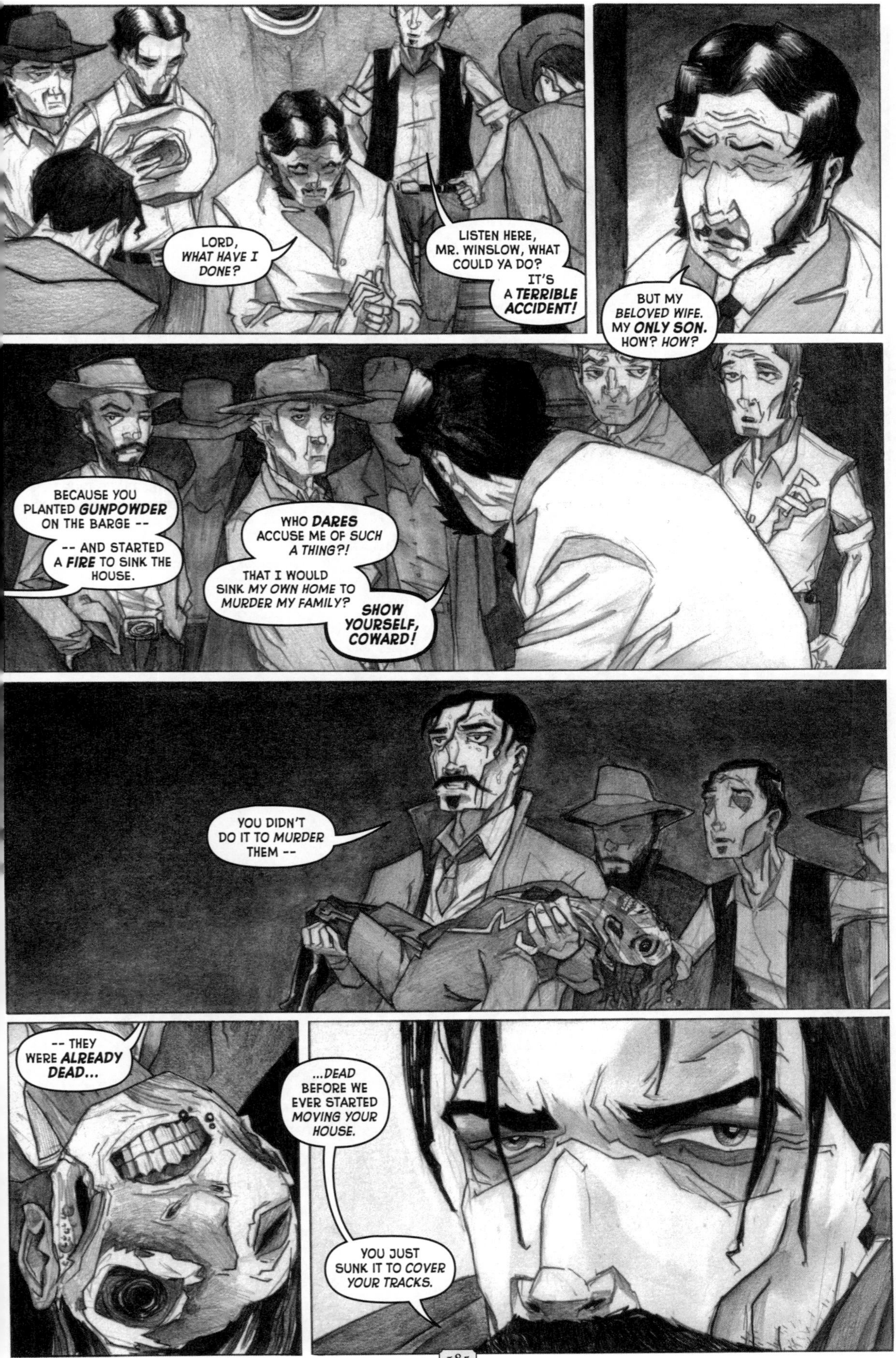
LORD, WHAT HAVE I DONE?
LISTEN HERE, MR. WINSLOW, WHAT COULD YA DO?
IT'S A TERRIBLE ACCIDENT!
BUT MY BELOVED WIFE. MY ONLY SON. HOW? HOW?
BECAUSE YOU PLANTED GUNPOWDER ON THE BARGE --
-- AND STARTED A FIRE TO SINK THE HOUSE.
WHO DARES ACCUSE ME OF SUCH A THING?!
THAT I WOULD SINK MY OWN HOME TO MURDER MY FAMILY?
SHOW YOURSELF, COWARD!
YOU DIDN'T DO IT TO MURDER THEM --
-- THEY WERE ALREADY DEAD...
...DEAD BEFORE WE EVER STARTED MOVING YOUR HOUSE.
YOU JUST SUNK IT TO COVER YOUR TRACKS.

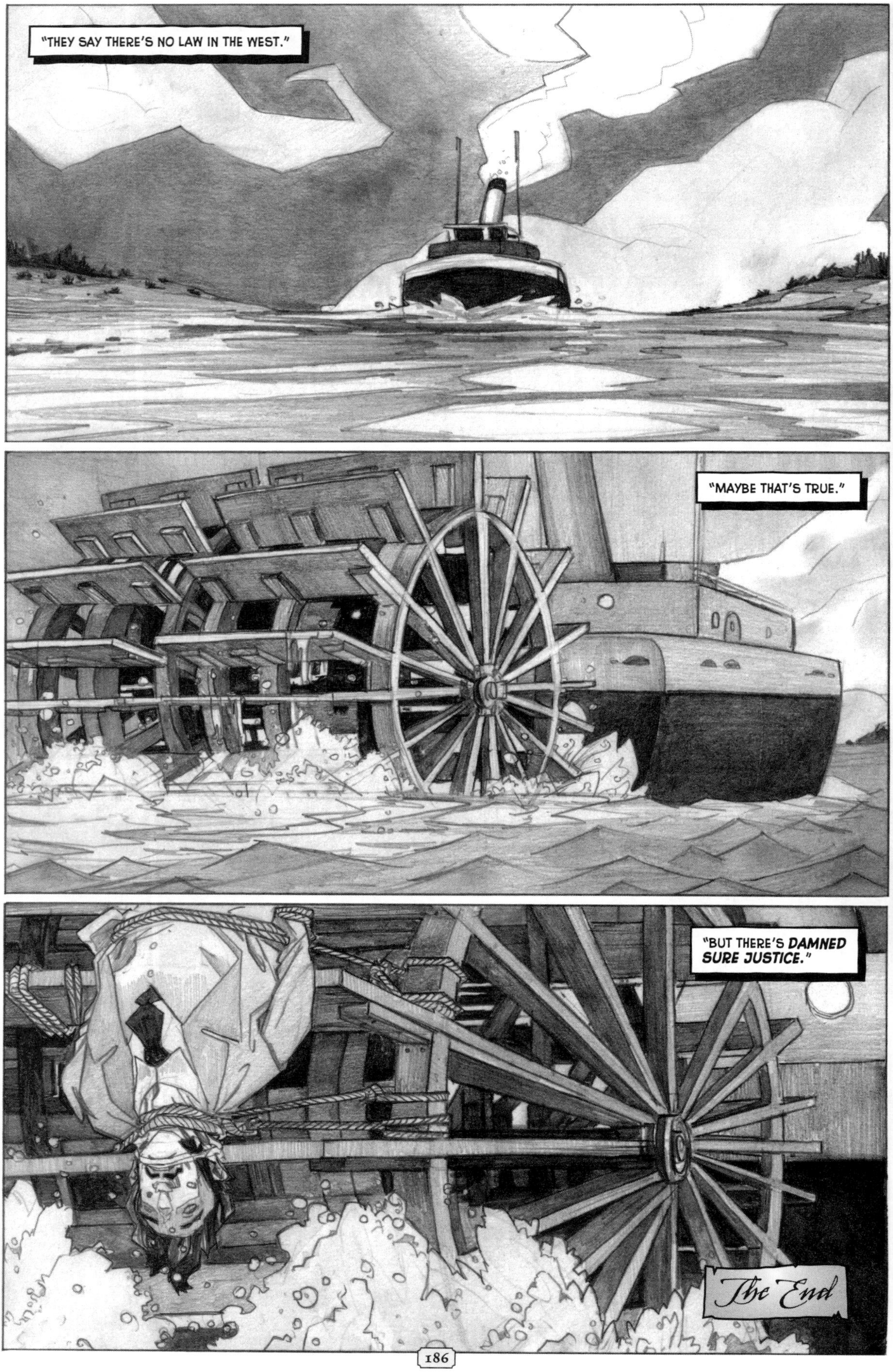
"THEY SAY THERE'S NO LAW IN THE WEST."
"MAYBE THAT'S TRUE."
"BUT THERE'S DAMNED SURE JUSTICE."
The End

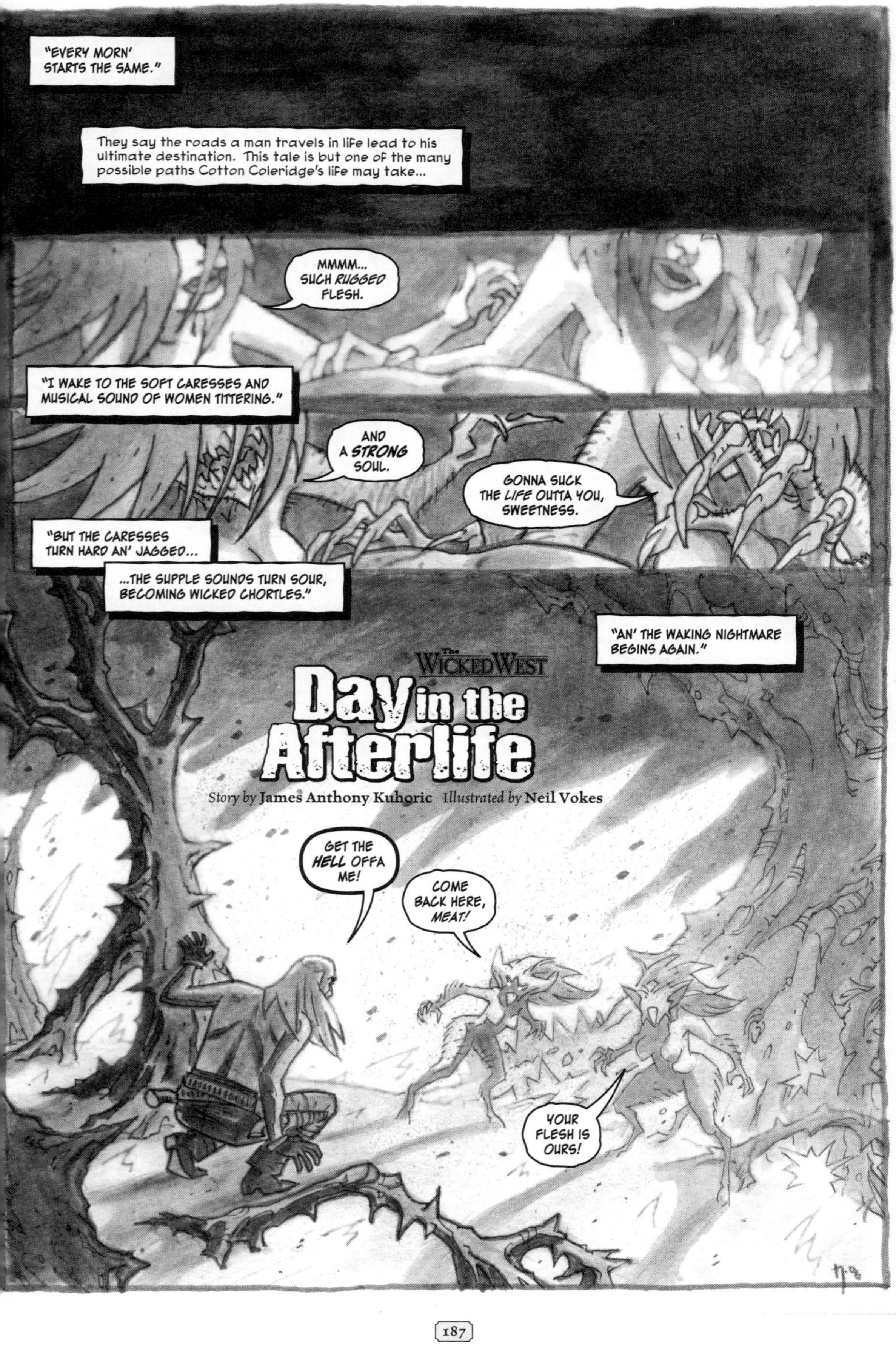
"EVERY MORN' STARTS THE SAME."
They say the roads a man travels in life lead to his ultimate destination. This tale is but one of the many possible paths Cotton Coleridge's life may take...
MMMM... SUCH RUGGED FLESH.
"I WAKE TO THE SOFT CARESSES AND MUSICAL SOUND OF WOMEN TITTERING."
AND A STRONG SOUL.
GONNA SUCK THE LIFE OUTTA YOU, SWEETNESS.
"BUT THE CARESSES TURN HARD AN' JAGGED...
...THE SUPPLE SOUNDS TURN SOUR, BECOMING WICKED CHORTLES."
"AN' THE WAKING NIGHTMARE BEGINS AGAIN."
The Wicked West
Day in the Afterlife
Story by James Anthony Kuhoric Illustrated by Neil Vokes
GET THE HELL OFFA ME!
COME BACK HERE, MEAT!
YOUR FLESH IS OURS!

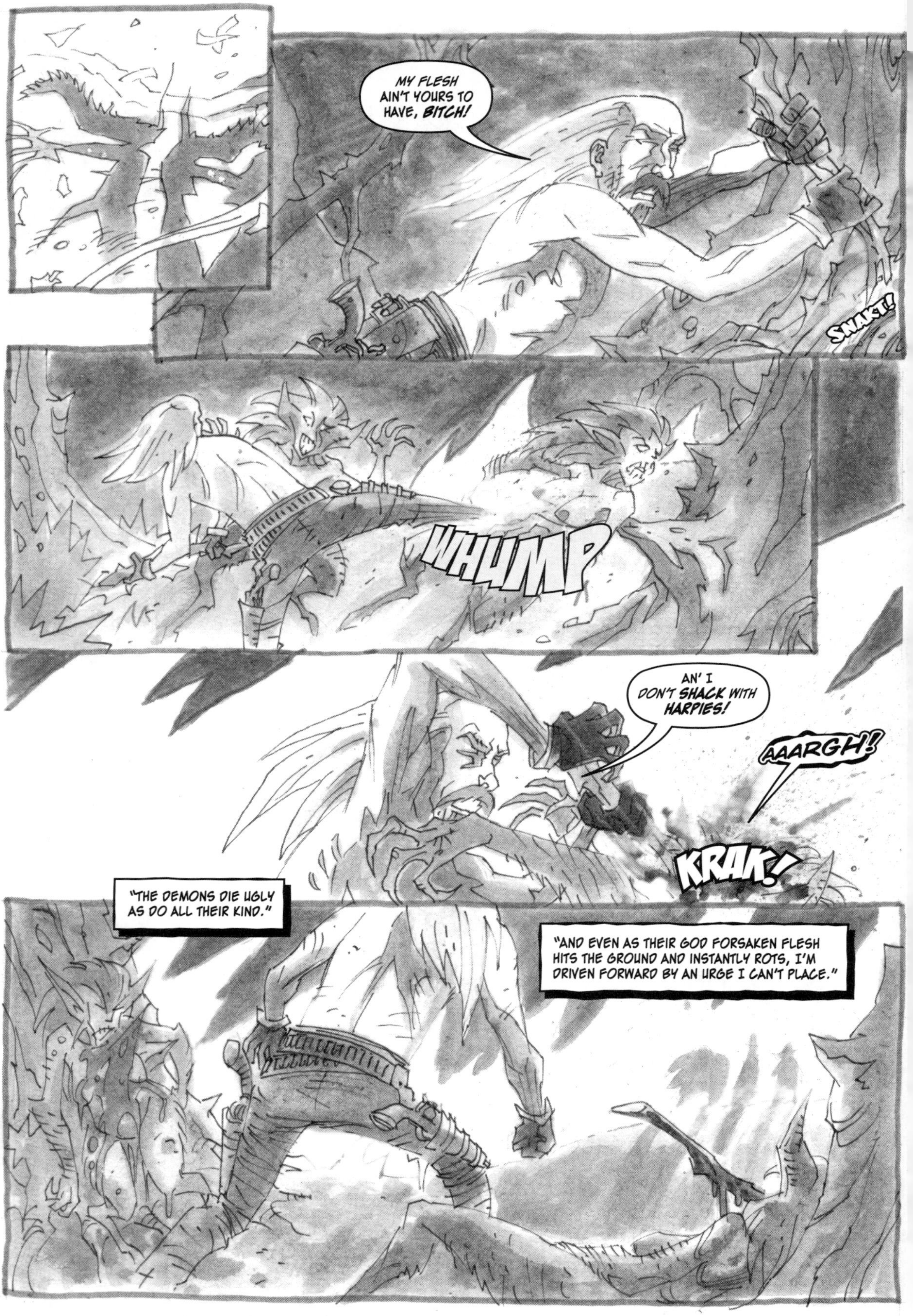
MY FLESH AIN'T YOURS TO HAVE, BITCH!
SNAKT!
WHUMP
AN' I DON'T SHACK WITH HARPIES!
AAARGH!
KRAK!
"THE DEMONS DIE UGLY AS DO ALL THEIR KIND."
"AND EVEN AS THEIR GOD FORSAKEN FLESH HITS THE GROUND AND INSTANTLY ROTS, I'M DRIVEN FORWARD BY AN URGE I CAN'T PLACE."

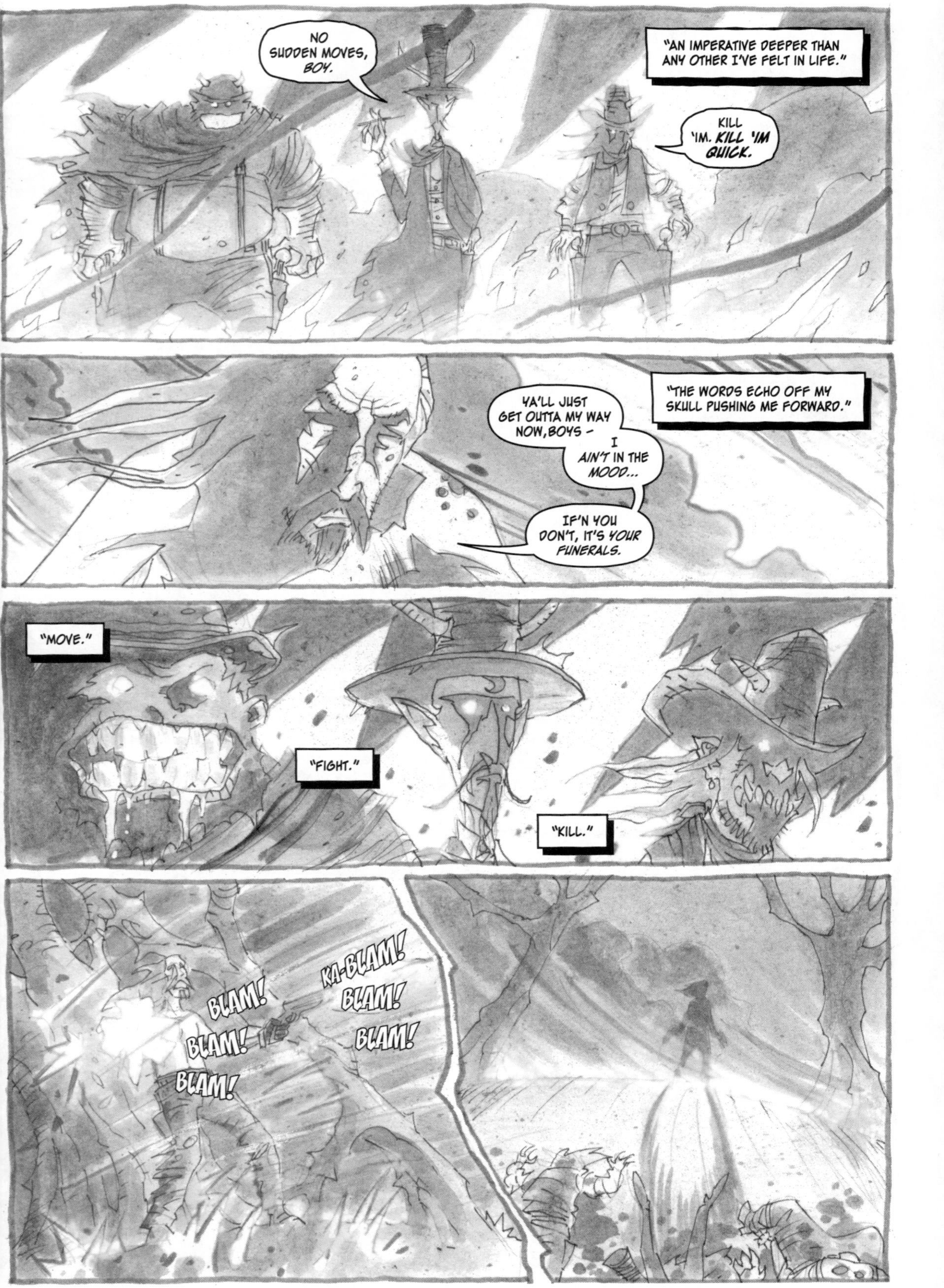
NO SUDDEN MOVES, BOY.
"AN IMPERATIVE DEEPER THAN ANY OTHER I'VE FELT IN LIFE."
KILL 'IM. KILL 'IM QUICK.
"THE WORDS ECHO OFF MY SKULL PUSHING ME FORWARD."
YA'LL JUST GET OUTTA MY WAY NOW, BOYS -
I AIN'T IN THE MOOD...
IF'N YOU DON'T, IT'S YOUR FUNERALS.
"MOVE."
"FIGHT."
"KILL."
BLAM!
BLAM!
BLAM!
KA-BLAM!
BLAM!
BLAM!

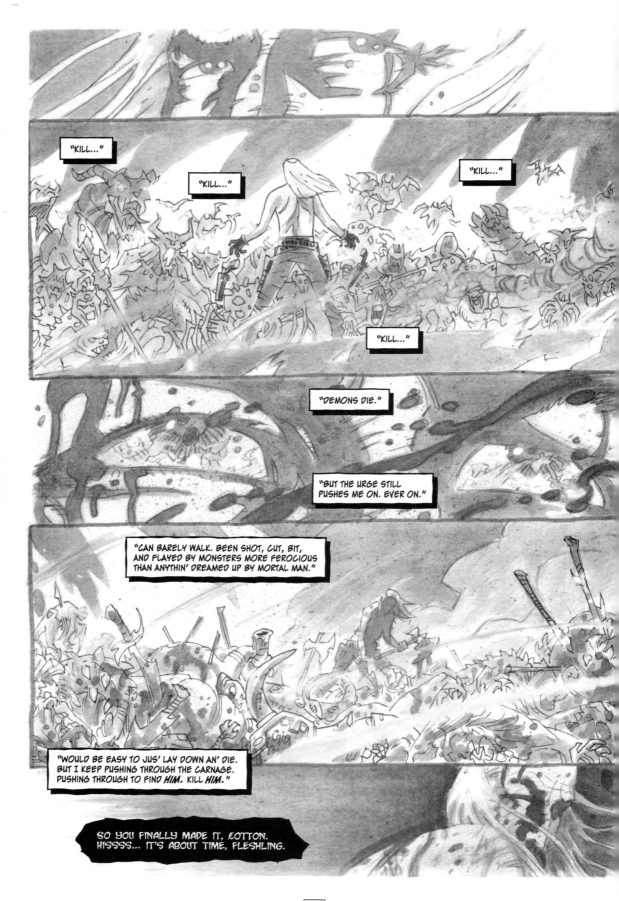

"KILL..."

"KILL..."

"KILL..."

"KILL..."

"DEMONS DIE."

"BUT THE URGE STILL PUSHES ME ON. EVER ON."

"CAN BARELY WALK. BEEN SHOT, CUT, BIT, AND FLAYED BY MONSTERS MORE FEROCIOUS THAN ANYTHIN' DREAMED UP BY MORTAL MAN."

"WOULD BE EASY TO JUS' LAY DOWN AN' DIE. BUT I KEEP PUSHING THROUGH THE CARNAGE. PUSHING THROUGH TO FIND *HIM*. KILL *HIM*."

SO YOU FINALLY MADE IT, COTTON. HISSSS... IT'S ABOUT TIME, FLESHLING.

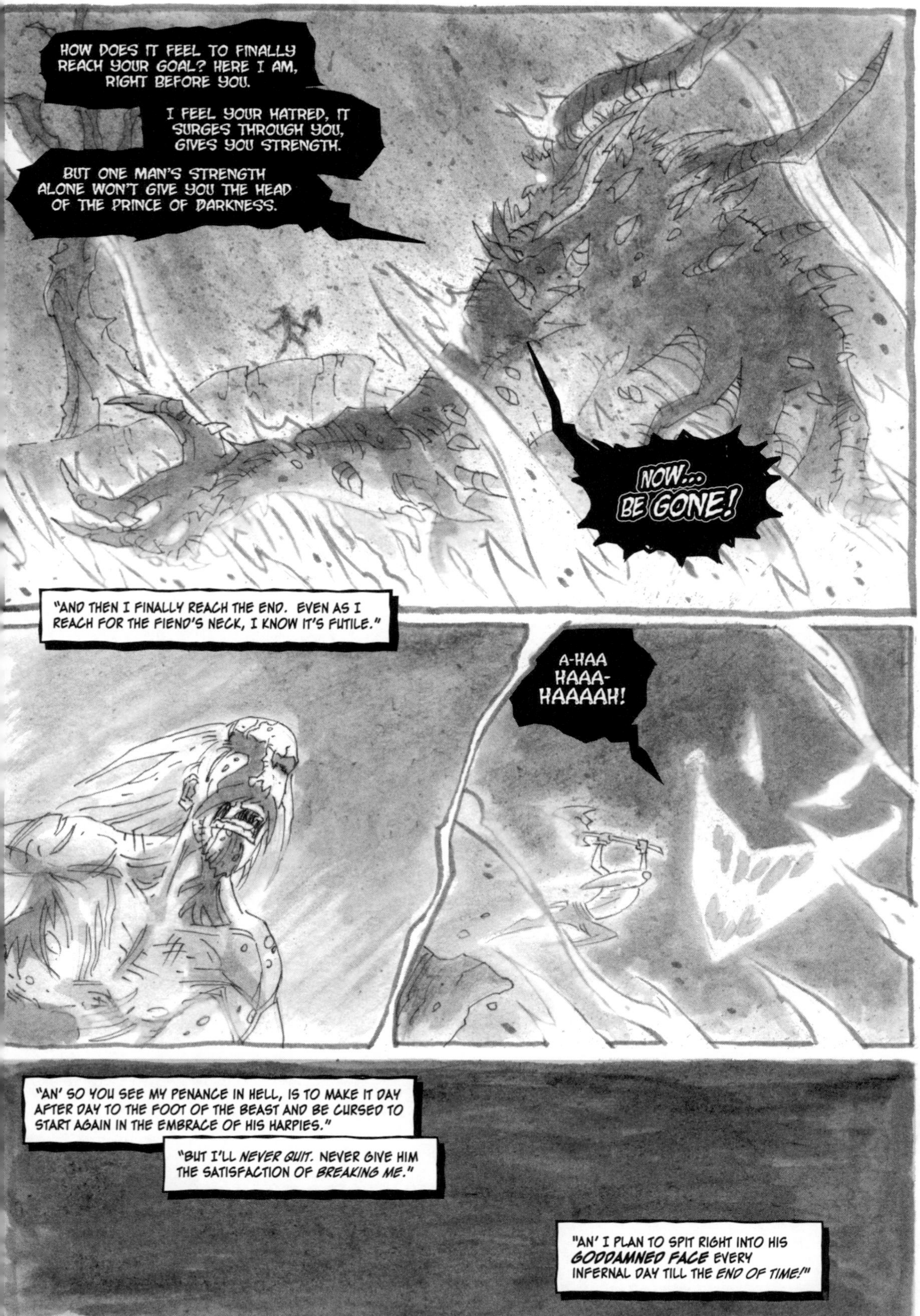
HOW DOES IT FEEL TO FINALLY REACH YOUR GOAL? HERE I AM, RIGHT BEFORE YOU.
I FEEL YOUR HATRED, IT SURGES THROUGH YOU, GIVES YOU STRENGTH.
BUT ONE MAN'S STRENGTH ALONE WON'T GIVE YOU THE HEAD OF THE PRINCE OF DARKNESS.
NOW... BE GONE!
"AND THEN I FINALLY REACH THE END. EVEN AS I REACH FOR THE FIEND'S NECK, I KNOW IT'S FUTILE."
A-HAA HAAA-HAAAAH!
"AN' SO YOU SEE MY PENANCE IN HELL, IS TO MAKE IT DAY AFTER DAY TO THE FOOT OF THE BEAST AND BE CURSED TO START AGAIN IN THE EMBRACE OF HIS HARPIES."
"BUT I'LL *NEVER QUIT.* NEVER GIVE HIM THE SATISFACTION OF *BREAKING ME.*"
"AN' I PLAN TO SPIT RIGHT INTO HIS ***GODDAMNED FACE*** EVERY INFERNAL DAY TILL THE *END OF TIME!*"

SKETCHES / AUTOGRAPHS

Cellular Wisdom
for Women

Also by Joan C. King
Cellular Wisdom-
Decoding the Body's Secret Language

Cellular Wisdom
for Women

An Inner Work Book

JOAN C. KING

Word Keepers, Inc.
Published by Bibliocast
Fort Collins, Colorado

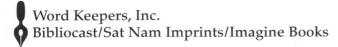

Word Keepers, Inc.
Bibliocast/Sat Nam Imprints/Imagine Books

Books are available at specialty quantity discounts for bulk purchases for sales promotions, premiums, fund-raising, and educational needs.

For details, write or telephone:

Word Keepers, Inc.
5151 Boardwalk Drive, Suite Q-2
Fort Collins, CO 80525
Tel. 970.225.8058
Fax 877.445.1007

Copyright © 2008 by Joan C. King

Interior and Cover Design: Fleur de Lis Design
Cover Image: Gavriel Jecan/CORBIS
Library of Congress Cataloging-in-Publication Data

King, Joan C.
  Cellular wisdom for women: an inner work book /
Joan C. King
    P. cm.
    Includes bibliographical references.
  ISBN-13: 978-0-9785393-8-2
  ISBN-10: 0-9785393-8-9
1. Personal growth workbook—Problems, situations, contemplations, exercises, etc. 2. Self-actualization (Psychology)—Problems, exercises, etc. 3. Body's wisdom (Principles of Biology and Physiology)— how the body's wisdom mirrors the wisdom of our larger lives, models, and principles, etc. 4. Spirituality (Metaphysics)—Creative problem solving through awareness of the body's signals and symbols, etc.
I. Title

Printed in the United States of America

10 9 8 7 6 5 4 3 2 1

Dedicated . . .

. . . to all women who, from the beginning of time,
delve into the depths of their wisdom
to nurture and sustain us all . . .

. . . to all the men who recognize
and revere them . . .

. . . to my husband, Stuart A. Tobet,
whose unfailing, loving support succors and nourishes me.

Author's Note

Cellular Wisdom™ reveals how fundamental truths for living an authentic, fulfilling life are coded in the elegantly complex dance of chemical and energetic interactions within and between our cells. Just as a single human cell is orchestrated from a nucleus at its center, for example, an individual must live life from their core essence to be healthy and whole. Only when cells connect with other cells do they fulfill their potential; in the same spirit, we achieve our grandest purposes in relationship with others. Over thousands of years of evolution, the human body has identified principles such as moderation, diversity, and compassion as essential to its survival. When we learn to appreciate and apply these same principles to our every-day lives, we learn to live a more balanced, focused, exuberant life. Cellular Wisdom™ shows us how to interpret the truths that our bodies teach and how to apply them to our physical, mental, emotional, social and spiritual lives.

Contents

Foreword

With her rare combination of solid scientific knowledge and profound wisdom, Dr. Joan King, has given us a rich and eminently useful book in *Cellular Wisdom for Women: An Inner Work Book*. Dipping into her own life experience and healing journey, she shows us how to peel back layers of inhibiting beliefs so that we can expand into our fullest potential and thrive. I trust that you will emerge from her pages as I did: encouraged, challenged and supported to move forward in your life with your unique gifts.

Full of exercises which provide tools that actually work, the organization of the book allows a personal pace. It is as if a teacher arrived at your house and sits with you, fully attentive, fully engaged, and seeming to know the exact places where insight and encouragement are needed. I experienced joyful energy as I progressed deeper and deeper into the book. That evolved into an exhilarating sense of freedom. Space is provided for notes that will remind you of your own progress and journey when you thumb back through earlier chapters.

Truly a companion and a guide, Dr. King's book shows you how to tap your innate, deeply inner wisdom. The sections titled: 'Our Bodies Model the Teachings' is fascinating and unique to this book. We are shown a template for thriving that is inherent in our bodies. The internal journey, anchored in our cells, then prepares us to create an external plan for flourishing.

Here is a guide book in which you will find clear advice and proven patterns to address anything that might deter your progress toward a productive and exciting life. I emerged from the journey with action plans that took me into my next steps, joyful and soaring with anticipation. I trust you will find your own true wind of genius and fly with brilliance as you engage with this gift of a book.

–Joyce Whiteley Hawkes, Ph.D.,
author of *Cell-Level Healing: The Bridge from Soul to Cell*

Part One
Who am I?

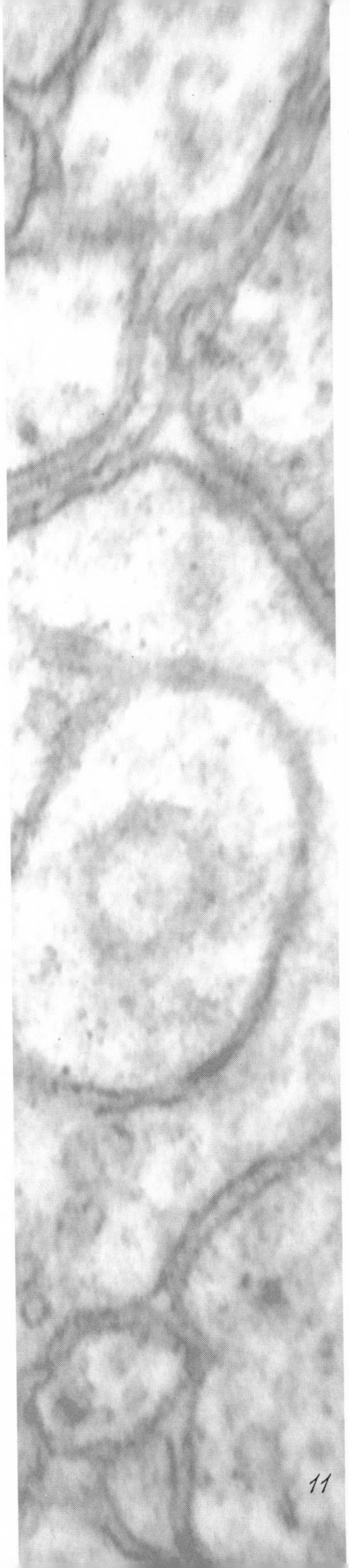

Not Good Enough

I'm five!
It's my birthday.
Why didn't I grow today?

Everybody said,
You're going to be
a "big girl"
when you're five!

Why didn't I grow
this morning?
My birthday's almost over.
I'm not a "big girl."

Something's wrong
with me.

Why, Daddy?
Why did you leave me?
Why did you leave me
with Mother?
I'm only 10.

Yesterday, you were on the ladder
with your hammer
working on the apartment.
At supper last night
you were laughing!

This morning
they told me . . .
you died.
I didn't believe them.
I kept shaking my head and said,
"No, no, it can't be true.
My daddy can't be dead!"

When?
When did you die?
Why did you die?
Why did you leave me?
You wouldn't have left
if I was good enough!

My mother found me in the corner on the floor, sobbing, on the evening of my fifth birthday. My pretty party dress, which she made for me, was getting wetter and wetter as I sobbed. She attempted to console me, but the piercing pain continually erupted in my volient sobs. I sobbed until I was exhausted and fell asleep.

I was very small and eagerly looked forward to growing up on my fifth birthday. But, as my birthday came to a close, I was the same size. I couldn't understand. Why? Wasn't I going to start growing in the morning and be tall by the end of the day? Why didn't I grow? I knew that something was terribly wrong. Everyone in the grocery store, my family, my friends, would rub the top of my head and tell me that I was going to be a "big girl" when I was five. Feelings of disappointment and failure rang through every chamber of my being. I could not talk to my mother. I could only sob.

The pain of loss I experienced five years later, when my father died, pierced my being and seemed to rip me apart. The night before, he was on a ladder, building the addition onto our grocery store and living quarters behind the store. He was laughing and joking with my mother and me at supper. Later, I learned he had a heart attack that evening after I had gone to bed. I heard nothing as he was taken to the hospital. In the morning, they told me he died. The words ripped my heart out. "No, no, no!" I repeatedly screamed, as I shook my head from side to side, "He can't be dead. He can't be dead. Why, why, why did he leave me?" This experience catapulted me into a new realization about life. Life wasn't what I thought it was, and he left me at ten years old to face it all alone. I wasn't worth staying for. I wasn't good enough.

Message to the Reader

These events took place when I was five and ten years old, but they influenced the next fifty years of my life. While I didn't actually hear the words, "not good enough," I felt their message often, echoing throughout my being. I responded by actively pursuing accomplishments. I was going to prove to myself that I was okay, that I was good enough! Even though I accomplished great things: taking on the roles of a Catholic sister, teacher, chemist, electron microscopist, experimental psychologist, neuroscientist, faculty of a major medical school in the northeast, head of my research lab, Chair of the department, Director of a research center, my childhood echoed the belief, "I'm not good enough."

Tired of pushing to achieve more and more, exhausted from running on my continually accelerating treadmill of accomplishment, I became ill. I stopped. I stepped down as Chair, Center Director, researcher and teacher. I took a six-month sabbatical. Not ready to return after six months, I took a year leave of absence, and then early retirement, leaving academia with all its obligations behind.

Who was I underneath all the accomplishments? I stopped trying. I took time to be still—to listen. Writing courses on Monhegan Island, off the coast of Maine, and then courses in Hawaii, on the Big Island helped me look deeply within and find my inner self. Slowly I began to uncover memories. As the memories surfaced, so did the pain, but I continued to write. My gift to myself was in the allowing. I gave myself permission todiscover who I was again. I no longer had the need to prove myself. As I was writing

Cellular Wisdom™, over a year and a half period, I began to view the body and its systems from a completely different perspective—as an inner teacher of how to live. Exploring who I was, underneath everything external, allowed me to touch and then come to know an inner truth, bigger than anything I had ever known before. That's when my knowing began to reveal a whole new kind of work for me.

In this workbook I will guide you through processes to help you touch, and then come to know your inner Cellular Wisdom, and to bring it from your inner world into your outer world. You have the potential to experience greater awareness, exuberant living, further discovery, transcending transitions, and sparkling clear authenticity, the foundation for living from your greatness. It is with this intention focused in our minds and fixed in our hearts that we work together.

When did your "not good enough" messages start? Often they begin, as mine did, in the infancy of our discovery of ourselves and our world. As adults, we tend to internalize what is said about us. We review critical remarks, over and over again, judging ourselves and, most frequently, condemning ourselves, until they take root in our being. What others think of us seems to carry more weight than our experience of our essence. Could it be that we spend little time allowing ourselves to enter the inner depths of our being and come to know the magnificence of who we really are?

Fear of what we might find stops us from entering the inner landscape within us. As you engage in self-discovery, actively participating in the exercises of this inner workbook, you will be guided. I will provide you with a clearly marked, step-by-step path to lead you to a place where you will become aware of remarkable aspects of yourself. The more you allow yourself to engage in these activities and contemplations, the more information and knowledge you gain about yourself. As awareness arises within, the exercises will help you express your truth to your outer world. I honor your choice to participate in these exercises to the level and degree you choose.

I believe you're reading this because your inner navigator is offering you your next step. This is the wisdom we carry within us. Create a new reality—one based upon a strong foundation—the authentic, essential you. It will take time. See the exercises as an investment in yourself, in your life. Doing them, you will lift the veils that hide the glorious, authentic you! Remnants of misperceptions hide your radiance. Now is the time to begin. Recognize the misperceptions! Shed the veils. Choose to begin to live now from your magnificence.

It will require courage! I am confident, beyond a shadow of a doubt in

Message to the Reader

the results you will produce. The rewards of coming to know and experience your essential being will far outweigh the effort you invest. In these exercises, you will be asked to remember times that may be uncomfortable or even painful. Remember, however, that you are on the journey to your greatness. Choose a place to read and do the exercises that is special to you, one that makes you feel safe, secure and nourished. You have all the resources, internal and external, to support you in uncovering and experiencing your greatness.

Are you ready? If so, then let's begin!

The proclamation "I'm not good enough" drips with judgment. It rips through our minds and hearts and ravages any sense of self-worth. The echoes reverberate through the chambers of our being. They come in waves, each one taking away what remains of our sense of self.

Directions to the Reader

Find a comfortable spot, turn off the phone, maybe get a cup of coffee or tea.

We'll begin by reflecting on your childhood, a time when we form foundational beliefs about who we are. Reread the poems at the beginning of this chapter. Is there a memory of a specific event when you felt "not good enough" that emerges? Don't struggle with finding the right memory. Allow your heart to gently show you the scene. Sit back. Let it unfold. Once it has emerged, take your time and describe it here.

"

From this same scene, what specific words or thoughts trigger your response "I'm not good enough?"

Message to the Reader

We become exquisitely aware of our role in creating and manifesting as early as puberty. Later we recognize the multifaceted aspects of our creativity and ability to manifest. However, the belief "I'm not good enough" stops the flow of creative energy, of translating concept and dreams into solid reality.

Directions to the Reader

Where in your life does this belief stop or diminish your creativity? Where in your daily life does this belief stop you from accomplishing dailly sucess? Describe what arises for you as you reflect on these questions.

"

"

Directions to the Reader

Take one of the situations you just described above and recreate the history of the event. Allow it to play out differently. In this version write it freed from the belief "I'm not good enough?" Imagine what you could experience!

"

"

Message to the Reader

Do you want to begin shifting your focus from the belief "I'm not good enough" to one that supports you in creating the life you are beginning to discover? How does one do that?

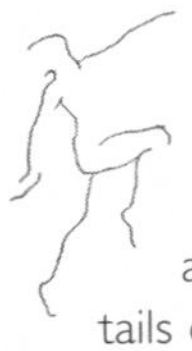

Our Bodies Model the Teachings

The body models how this shift occurs in evolution, in human development, and in our adult lives. In evolution, when a structure is no longer useful to a plant or animal, it's simply left behind. For example, you do not see the long tails of alligators present in birds, which evolved later.

In human development, the fetus in utero actually has a tail that later degrades.

As adults, muscles we do not use become atrophied—they simply waste away. Notice the legs of someone who's been in a wheelchair for some time, with no physical exercise. Deprived of the stimulating influence of neurons, the muscles, no longer nourished, shrink.

Message to the Reader

Turning our focus away from a belief mimics depriving a muscle of exercise, in its effects. Each time we choose to no longer focus on a belief that negatively impacts our life (such as "I'm not good enough"), the belief begins to atrophy, or waste away.

Deprived of the nutrients of neurons, muscles begin to atrophy. Our negative beliefs, embedded in our conscious and subconscious minds for years, will come up over and over again, until they lose energy and atrophy. Each time that the negative belief arises and we choose to turn our focus away from it, it wastes away a bit more.

HOW WILL YOU <u>KNOW</u> THIS?

> Your outside world will begin to reflect your changed beliefs in many simple ways. You may become more tolerant of other people's opinions, ones that previously upset you. Or you may begin to soften toward a situation or person who previously created an emotional charge for you. Watch for the signs. They will emerge.

It's difficult to *not* think of something. For example, right now, try not to think about your negative belief. It is much easier to turn away our focus from a negative belief, if we have something to shift our focus to.

Herein lies the power of articulating a different, nurturing belief. Just as birds developed wings to fly, we can create supportive beliefs that let us fly. Focusing on supportive beliefs helps us turn attention away from negative beliefs. Eventually they will completely waste away. Then, they will no longer impact our lives. Supporting beliefs help us create a life aligned with the deeper truth of who we really are.

Creating and developing a supporting belief is easy for us, as women, when it involves someone else. How many times have we comforted our significant others, children, friends, and co-workers, reminding them of their strengths, encouraging them that they, indeed, could do it? Yet when it comes to ourselves, we seem to be particularly vulnerable to negative rather than supporting beliefs.

Can you afford yourself the same generosity that you offer others? Can you doubt your creative, feminine capacity? You may ignore it, because you take it for granted. You fail to see its magnificence. How many costumes have you made for your children? How many dinner parties have you put together for your husband, significant other or friends? How many times have you helped a friend see another way around a challenge? Or develop a different perspective?

Let's put that feminine creative process to use now. Begin the process that will lead you to create supportive beliefs, atrophy the negative beliefs and empower a supportive truth of who you really are—a being of incredible internal resources.

STEP 1   AWARENESS Become aware of any time that the belief begins to form in your mind and heart. No longer do you want "I am not good enough" to automatically emerge as a response to any situation. For one entire day, observe each time the old belief arises.

Our negative beliefs are embedded in our subconscious, as well as our conscious minds. Sometimes, uncomfortable feelings, not thoughts, arise from these sources. Feelings first emerge as pre-verbal and not as clear, articulated thought. Your feelings may resemble what you described as a child, in the beginning of this chapter, when the feelings were imprinted. Observe when these feelings arise. Become aware of your feelings when they arise. Are they feelings of tightness in your chest, a knot in your pelvic area, a headache? They may emerge in a way that allows you to name them. Are you feeling anger, separation, isolation, sensitivity or something else that is nameable?

Directions to the Reader

Record your observations and feelings here.

”

STEP 2

LIVING Take action! Immediately, once you recognize the feelings associated with or thoughts of your negative belief emerging, you must take action to stop it.

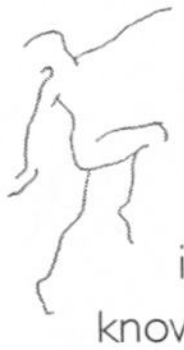

Our Bodies Model the Teachings

Understanding how the emotional brain intensifies activity and impacts emotional tone can help us with this process. When an irritating thought arises it is accompanied by emotion that occurs within the limbic system, commonly known as the emotional brain. The limbic system consists of a number of structures that are interconnected in a circuit or loop. Activity within one structure is then transmitted to the next and the next. Each time the neuronal activity completes a loop, it recruits more and more neurons to join in the process. You experience this as heightened negative emotion. It recruits exponentially. Clearly, it is much more difficult to stop the activity of hundreds of thousands of neurons than of only a few.

This scenario will help you witness the recruitment that occurs within the emotional, limbic brain. Watch how the thoughts and emotions escalate. Your significant other is late. You have the underlying negative belief that "I'm not good enough." You quickly conclude he's late because other people are more interesting to him than you are. Of course, this is not a very empowering thought. At this point in time only a few neurons are activated.

As time passes, your negative belief that "I'm not good enough" goes into full gear and the negative thoughts multiply. "Who is he with?" triggers the response. You begin to think of all the times that he was interested in talking with other women, women who are more beautiful, women who are more accomplished, women who are not stuck at home with a sick child.

Guess how many neurons are activated now?

The story continues. "This isn't the first time he's been late," you announce verbally. Now the emotion truly escalates. You recall every time in the last week, the last month, the last year, he's been late. Before long you've constructed a story. He's having an affair with that new secretary who was hired this year.

Guess how many neurons are activated now?

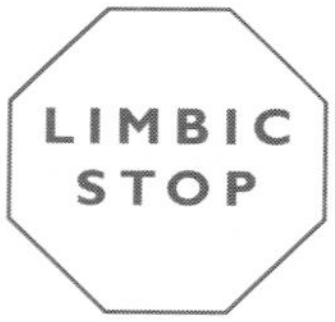
LIMBIC
STOP

Time passes. Your partner opens the door. You greet him with a cold shoulder. When he begins to explain, you say you don't care to listen. It no longer matters to you. You're considering a divorce. He doesn't understand what's happened, but he doesn't want to be around your energy. He decides to leave. His leaving confirms everything you were just thinking. Now you're really convinced that you're "not good enough."

How easily do you think you can stop your emotions at this point?

Our Bodies Model the Teachings

The key is to understand that if you want to stop the escalating vortex, you cannot wait until millions of neurons are recruited into the circuit. You must stop the process as soon as you become aware of your negative feelings or thoughts. I call this process the "Limbic Stop." If you envision the red hexagonal stop sign simply add the word Limbic. Visualizing this stop sign can help you break this escalating emotional circuit.

Let's go back to the exercise, now that you know how to put the brake on with the Limbic Stop. As soon as you observe or feel the effects of your negative belief "I'm not good enough," imagine the Limbic Stop sign. Stop the Limbic circuit. You will get better and better at this as you practice it.

Directions to the Reader

Record here when you were successful, and not successful, in recognizing the emerging belief and responding by engaging the "Limbic Stop."

“

”

STEP 3

DISCOVERY Discover a new, empowering belief. The negative belief lies embedded in your conscious and subconscious mind, because of something someone said or did at some point in your life. The new empowering belief lies much deeper in your being, in the essence of life itself.

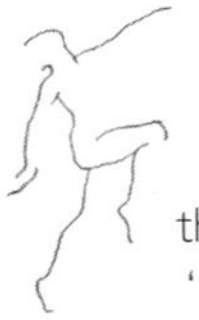

Our Bodies Model the Teachings

Moment by moment we live because an energy infuses each of our cells with the elixir of life! This ancient, yet ever new life force energy, I refer to as "Cellular Wisdom™," the title of my book, published in 2004. It infuses life into every cell——every moment we are alive. This is our origin. Each of us, individually, gives unique expression to this energy. Our beings arise from an energy that is creative and expansive. The very same energy lies at the heart of the first formation of cells from molecules and of organisms from cells. Yes, we are birthed and live because of this very same energy. It is always accessible to us. We do not have to earn it. It is our birthright. This is our truth!

Message to the Reader

This deeper perspective allows us to construct a new empowering and supporting belief—one steeped in truth, not in falsehood. Who are you? An expression of a quietly explosive energy of life! How could you possibly "not be good enough?" Consider your heritage.

In this process, we will be going deeper into our inner world, pre-verbal, and then bringing forth that energy into thought, belief and action in the outer world. This process will, in a step-by-step fashion, lead to an unshakable "knowing" of who you are. Your life will begin to unfold its tapestry of authenticity from that knowing. As you make daily choices, from the most mundane to the life altering, you will begin to make better choices centered in your new state of being.

To reach the deeper level and articulate your new empowering belief, rooted in truth, you must reach a place of stillness, openness and receptivity to an energy that lies close to the interface between energy and matter. It is not a place of words, but a place of feelings. The unfolding of the feelings will lead to thought, belief, action and, ultimately, an unshakable knowing, a new state of being.

To begin this exercise, think of a time that you felt absolutely wonderful, deeply satisfied and resonant with your truth. What were you thinking at the time? This may provide the key to help you articulate the belief that you would like to have about yourself, even if it is not at a level of belief at this time.

Consider how the following examples, which emerge from the depths of one's being, are reflected in action-behavior.

INNER SUPPORTING BELIEF : *"I am one with all life."*
Some outer behaviors that would emanate from this belief—a sense of ease in life and in relationships, relationships characterized by integrity, support and open communication without concern.

INNER SUPPORTING BELIEF: *"I am a unique expression of life energy."*
Some outer behaviors that would emanate from this belief—a celebration of one's own strengths and talents and those of others, with no sense of competition or superiority.

INNER SUPPORTING BELIEF: *"I have access to my own inner wisdom."*
Some outer behaviors that would emanate from this belief—decision making from this inner wisdom with confidence and clarity, without worry about the outcome of the decision.

You may find these statements too lofty, however, they reflect the essence of life and who we really are. If you cannot honestly articulate such a statement, because you can't really believe it, choose a declaration of some way of being that you wish to be.

An articulation could be, for example, "I know I will be able to meet any challenge adequately." Small daily successes build a foundation of positive confidence.

In this case, even if you feel this is not true, you could begin to act as though it is true. This is not duplicity or hypocrisy, if it is something that you want to be true in your life. In this case, you would approach an upcoming challenge in the following way. How would I act if I knew I could meet this challenge? This is a coaching technique widely used, because it allows you to envision possible ways of acting as you approach the challenge that might not have been available to you previously.

With this in mind, take time now to articulate a new belief—one that is rooted in truth or one that you want to be true in your life. This statement should be one that you can easily remember. What is your statement?

Directions to the Reader

"

"

| **STEP 4** | TRANSITION Replace the old false belief with a new belief rooted in truth. |

Here's an example from my life. I was asked to give a talk to a group of women physicians. The talk was scheduled in the evening, after dinner with wine, and after the presentation of awards. Further, it was held in a sterile convention center in the middle of the week, when people were beginning to get tired.

As I began to prepare my talk, I found myself thinking I'm not good enough to keep their attention under the circumstances. Is it any wonder that I found it difficult to create my talk? Fortunately, I caught myself and said, "I won't be able to create or deliver a talk of value with that thought in my mind."

I turned my attention away from myself and toward what I wanted to offer the audience. I wanted to bring something of value to each participant. It was also important that I talk for only a short amount of time. As this circulated through my mind and heart I was easily able to create a powerful talk: "Are you the CEO of your life?"

I walked up to the podium. Standing there, I looked around the room and made eye contact with everyone there. I was setting my intention to bring value to each person. The first words out of my mouth, "I'm setting my watch buzzer for twenty minutes. I'll stop talking when the buzzer goes off." I held up my watch to prove my intention. Everyone laughed. I knew that they would be more likely to listen intensely if they knew I would speak for a short time. As I began, I paced my words slowly. I used simple slides and fewer words to support my thoughts. Within minutes, you could hear a pin drop in the room. I stopped just as the timer went off. The applause was loud and long. Many came up to thank me when the talk was over telling me that they really needed to hear what I had to say.

Message to the Reader

Had I stayed in the mindset that I was not good enough, I would've been unable to offer anything of value.

It is important for us to relinquish our old negative and destructive beliefs, because they prevent us from making our contribution to the world.

If we fail to make our unique contribution, the world will miss something of value. Therefore, steeped in truth, we can claim a new belief about ourselves.

For example, if the old belief "I'm not good enough" arises as "What makes me think I can do this?"
STOP

Now, articulate the true belief!
I have access to my own inner wisdom. Now is the time to begin to live, freely. I may not do this perfectly. But that's okay. I will have done it. I will get better and better at this.

AUTHENTICITY Feel the delight of liberation and the joy of true expression.   **STEP 5**

In preparing my talk, when I changed my thought from "I'm not good enough" to "I want to bring value" I was liberated. My creativity soared. I looked forward to the presentation and delighted in delivering it. Everything changed. I won't forget that event. It was a powerful teacher with two potentially different outcomes. Coming from a truth that I wanted to bring value rather than from an old belief that I was not good enough liberated me from my self-made prison and allowed me to make a contribution and to enjoy true self-expression.

The memory of this event serves me well. I catch myself whenever I begin to imprison myself with my old beliefs. I realize that if I allow the old belief to reign I will not be able to make the contribution that I could make to myself and others. I lose. Everyone loses. Living from the deeper essence of truth allows us access to a greater range of possibilities. As we act from truth, we bring value to ourselves and others. We all win.

Practice will help you do this.

Our Bodies Model the Teachings

Initially, each cell performed all activities as required, such as taking in nutrients, discarding waste products, reproducing, etc. However, there was a great price to pay for this. Cells stayed independent of each other. In order for complex organisms to arise from single cell organisms, which took over one billion years, things had to change. Cells began to differentiate. For example, some cells became reproductive cells, muscle cells, bone cells, etc.... No longer did each cell have to do everything. The reproductive cells' function is to sustain reproduction, not to digest food into nutrients that cells can use. Once specialized, it was important for cells to cooperate with each other, each performing their specific function, for the organism to thrive. Just walking across the room requires that one hundred seventy or so muscles on each side of the body have to flex and contract in synchrony, moving bones so that we can walk. Specialization, cooperation and integration were important to the development of multicelled organisms.

Similarly in our lives, we must be true to ourselves, our essence, in every aspect of our lives. Whenever we fragment a piece of our lives from our essential selves, we no longer resonate with the fullness of who we are. The fragmentation will increase and leave us feeling empty and unsatisfied.

As women, we are exquisitely aware of the cycles of our bodies, the times of our lives. We lead integrated lives and understand when our physical bodies, emotions, mental activity and spiritual energy are out of alignment. Every time we choose a behavior from a faulty inner belief, we are fragmenting ourselves. If this continues, we will feel more and more dissatisfied and empty. Reinstating the truth of who we are internally and externally allows us to realign all the aspects of our lives and live in resonance with our essence.

Message to the Reader

Are you ready now to replace your old, unsupportive belief and bring your new belief, expressing the truth of who you are, into center stage?

If so, keep alert for the emergence of your old belief. As soon as you detect it raising its head, stop and say your new belief.

Now, with that new belief, rooted in truth, circulating in your mind and heart, determine what actions you want to take. In the beginning this will seem difficult. However, the rewards liberate, and freedom is exhilarating.

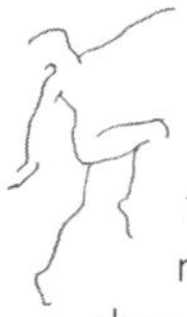

Our Bodies Model the Teachings

New patterns take a while to be established in the body. For example, it takes approximately three weeks for new synapses, connections between neurons, to become established. Keeping the focus for at least twenty-one days is the key to success.

Red blood cells are replaced every ninety days in the body, because they have no nucleus to sustain them. Your empowering and supporting belief, which arises from your inner core like the nucleus sustains a cell, sustains you in the outer world.

In committing to this process you are establishing a new template in your life. Commit to doing this now.

At sixteen, my grandmother, Katherine, married my grandfather, a ship captain, in the "old" country, Dubrovnik, Yugoslavia. They promptly sailed to New Orleans. She never returned. My grandfather was much older than she—he was thirty-six. Soon after arriving, Grandma became pregnant with twins, Peter and Paul. Grandpa sailed back to Yugoslavia, leaving my grandmother alone. She did not even speak English. The twins died shortly after they were born. Grandpa was not there. He sailed from New Orleans to Dubrovnik, every six months or so. Mammaw, my grandmother, spoke eleven other languages, but learned English as her six children went to school. Never did I hear her complain. A fabulous cook, she always remembered what each of her children, and her children's children, liked to eat.

Although she had a life she had not anticipated, she was always laughing and telling jokes, even naughty ones, at the holiday table. Her energy was infectious. She seemed to meet every challenge from a place of deep calm, as though she knew she would be able to handle whatever arose. She was a model of success to me.

Directions to the Reader

Keeping the focus on your success is like playing many videos, each constituting a step on your path, creating a "Template for Success." After a three-week period, record the instances in which you successfully replaced the old negative and destructive belief with the new empowering and supporting belief. These will help you strengthen the habit of living from a deeper presence—accessing your inner teacher and using the information in action in the outer world. You are building your "Template for Success."

"

"

As women, we're acutely aware of the changes in our bodies from the time that we enter adolescence through pregnancy and menopause. Intimately connected with the energies of our bodies, it should be easy for us to access its teachings. Caring for our bodies is a responsibility equal to caring for our mind and spirit. Clearing out the old and making room for the new is a template our bodies use to remain vital and strong.

As hybrids of spirit and matter, everything in one domain necessarily influences the other. In this chapter we are learning the lessons of matter to create from the inside out. Just as cells generate all of their activities from the blueprints in their DNA, we too generate our outer lives from the truths in our inner depths. When we are in alignment of body, mind and spirit we experience the flow of energy.

It's important to become familiar with the feelings of freedom and liberation that come from the deeper essence of the truth of who you are.

I was attempting to prepare a talk for the Theological Opportunities Program (TOP) group at Harvard Divinity School. I couldn't. I tried over and over again with no success. The day of my talk came. I knew only to take a few books and poems with me. I was in the room being introduced. I relaxed. Somehow, I had relied on my intuition to bring the books and poems. As I began to talk the words just flowed. My eyes sought the eyes of everyone in the room, as I spoke. From time to time I would read a poem I wrote or one from the books I brought. I kept contact with the audience throughout the entire talk. Finishing, at first there was silence. Then, they began to stand, one by one, until the whole room was standing and clapping. Afterwards, a woman came up to me and said that was the most organized talk she had heard. She requested my notes. Of course I had none. Fortunately, someone overheard us and told us she had recorded it. The feelings of freedom from fear about what I would say, and liberation, founded on trust, soared through me. I felt I could fly.

Directions to the Reader

Take time now to record here feelings of freedom and liberation you experience as you act in accordance with your authenticity, the deeper empowering and supporting belief of who you are.

"

FOUNDATION Celebrate your success! You are now ready to anticipate situations before the negative and destructive belief has a chance to arise. This will allow
you to be truly liberated to live from the truths of who you are, in all circumstances.

STEP 6

Our Bodies Model the Teachings

The body is continually in the state of discarding the old and embracing the new. During the times in our lives when we're ovulating, estrogen secreted from the ovary supports the development of an egg or ovum over a couple of weeks. When it is fully developed the egg is expelled from the follicle, so that it can be potentially fertilized. The follicle, from which the egg was released, collapses into another structure the corpus luteum, which begins to secrete the hormone progesterone. After a couple of weeks the corpus luteum dies away. Then another follicle will begin to develop and the cycle will repeat once again. A similar cycle occurs in the lining of the uterus to prepare for the implantation of a fertilized egg. If implantation does not occur, the wall of the uterus is shed during menstruation.

In contrast, the majority of our neurons come into being during fetal development. They do not turn over, or divide, but stay with us for the remainder of our lives.

Message to the Reader

Recognizing what needs to be shed, to be replaced, and what needs to remain stable because it is part of our essence is a key to understanding how to live exuberantly.

If the old is not shed, the new cannot appear. If the stable elements, like neurons, essential to our continued competency, are not nourished, they will die.

Knowing the difference between elements that require replacement and those that must be nourished, permanently constitute the foundation of living from the essence of our being.

You've learned how to recognize situations where your old beliefs arise and replace them with new beliefs. You've tasted the glorious feelings of freedom and liberation when you live from your new beliefs. The final step is to anticipate and prepare for circumstances that could challenge your new beliefs. Focus on what you want.

When you've learned to do this you will easily anticipate potentially challenging circumstances and anticipate feelings that would result if they were the primary influence. You will replace the old constrictive story readily, and nourish your essential self.

Our Bodies Model the Teachings

If the follicle remained active, secreting estrogen, after the egg was expelled, the corpus luteum would not form and progesterone would not be available to nurture a newly implanted fertilized egg. Neurons are dependent upon nutrients provided by the blood moment by moment as, unlike other cells, they do not store nutrients for future use. They live completely in the present.

Directions to the Reader

Identify a potentially challenging circumstance.

Play out how the scene would emerge if your thoughts and actions flowed from your old negative and destructive beliefs. This is your Constrictive Story.

"

"

Now you anticipate entering a challenging situation, ready to quickly recognize the constrictive story and release it. You're preparing for the challenge such that you will be primed to release the old and replace it with the new and nourish the stable essential you. You finish building the foundation by envisioning the scene as if you were acting from your inner essential self in the outer world.

Directions to the Reader

See yourself in this challenging situation behaving in the outer world from your new true empowering belief and your essential self. How does the scene emerge now? This is your Expansive Story.

"

This is the reality of who you are, even if you are yet to realize it. As you progressively, step by step, live from the deeper truths you will experience the magnificence of who you are. A drop of water continually hitting a rock erodes the solid stone.

Experiencing the feelings of living in the integration of mind, body and spirit is the Expansive Story. Become familiar with the feelings because they are your guideposts.

When you feel constricted you are living the Constricted Story, which does not emerge from the depths of your being. Recognizing the feelings as coming from your true self in the Expansive Story helps you create the "foundation to live exuberantly, in alignment with your essential self."

What feelings did you experience as you envisioned living from your true essential self

in the "Expansive Story?"

Directions to the Reader

"
_____

_____

_____

_____

_____

_____

_____

_____

_____

_____

_____

_____

_____

_____

_____

_____

_____
"

As you establish the foundation of recognizing what needs to be released and replaced and living from the bigger story, you will feel more energy. Your creativity will abound. You will become eager to make your unique contribution to the world.

Directions to the Reader

Allow some time to stabilize your foundation. Let your thoughts about what contribution you could potentially make in the world begin to emerge over the next few days. See how you could begin to live your "Expansive Story." Do not censor any of your possibilities, but record them here.

"

Before concluding this chapter, let's review the central theme of the six steps:

AWARENESS Be aware of any time that your negative belief emerges.	**STEP 1**
LIVING Take action. Use the Limbic Stop and choose.	**STEP 2**
DISCOVERY Discover an empowering and supporting belief.	**STEP 3**
TRANSITION Replace the negative, destructive belief with an empowering, supportive belief.	**STEP 4**
AUTHENTICITY Feel the delight of liberation and the joy of true expression.	**STEP 5**
FOUNDATION Celebrate your success! And live from the truth of your essence in flow and harmony!	**STEP 6**

You've identified some major "keys" that unlock your magnificence. When we "know" the fullness of our being, we can live expansively and contribute to the universe in our unique feminine way. We are creators, nurturers who hold the vision of the Universe. The knowledge of our essence is necessary for us to perform this function, for we are to remain unshakable regardless of outer circumstances. This is one fundamental "key" to living a feminine life of wholeness in which mind, body and spirit are fully aligned. Authenticity and integrity radiate from our being when we reach this state. We become models of how the world could be.

In doing these exercises you have uncovered the essential you through awareness, taking action in your life, discovering your essence, transitioning from old beliefs to new ones, living authentically from the foundation that you have built. A second "key" is the blueprint you have through these processes—your "Template of Success!" Use it! Come to know the power of your inner being in living your outer life.

As long as we hold the negative and destructive belief of "not being good enough," we are unable to touch the genius within and bring it to the world. We must know our powers in order to be able to use them to gently and lovingly create the essence of the world.

 Please join Joan in a further discussion on using your "Template of Success."
http://www.cellular-wisdom.com

Want to ask questions? Go to Joan's blog
blog.beyond-success.com *and pose your question. Joan will answer you.*

Can't, until . . .

He knew, that very night,
their wedding night
It was a mistake.

But, what could he do?
He was a good Catholic,
and so was she.

Ecstasy waited
until this night,
their wedding night.

And then
the children came,
a girl
a boy.
He couldn't leave,
not now,
can't, until . . .

. . . kindergarten,
primary school,
high school,
college.
He must be there
for them.

Thirty years after
the mistake,
he left
to create another life
of meaning,
of love.

When I first heard this story, my heart ached for my dear friend and the pain he experienced throughout the empty years—thirty years. How could he stand living in a marriage without love for so many years?

But then I thought about myself. How could *I* have stayed in the convent eleven years? I realized that the lump sum of years doesn't happen all at once, but over time, year by year. The first six years in the convent, I was determined to be the best possible Dominican Sister. That focused determination and my strong will to make it so left me no alternative perception, until my own body told me a truth about my choice. My body knew something I was unwilling to look at. I should've known something was wrong, when I became ill. I fell on the floor, for no apparent reason, unable to move, unable to get up, but hearing everything said around me. "What's wrong?" they asked. I couldn't answer. I couldn't talk. Finally, after what felt like an eternity, but was really less than ten minutes, I moved and stood up.

At first I thought the incident was an anomaly. But then, it happened over and over again: once a week, three or four times a week, progressing in strength and frequency. A Chilean neurologist, a very wise man, examined me. I was to take final vows five years after I first entered the convent. That time was quickly approaching and I was determined to take those vows. The convent had its own assessment—was I well enough to carry out the duties of the Dominican Sisters?

I struggled to be well. What could I do about this? How could I keep from falling down? It seemed like there was nothing I could do to will myself well. I heard the words, "Leave the convent and you'll be fine." Dr. Garcia Ole was asking me to give up everything I had believed was my life, my purpose, and me. I thought, *I can't, until. . . .* So I continued to struggle with my "familial paralysis." And I thought I'd won! I took my final vows.

Six years after taking my final vows I left the convent. Dr. Garcia Ole had known something, had seen something, and had heard something my body was telling him and me. He listened. For him, the answer was simple. But I chose to stay because I believed I couldn't leave until something had to be finished. It just took me six more years to know that "the until" had already happened. My body was telling me that I had already finished and needed to move on. I have not had a falling down episode since leaving the convent.

Why could I not hear the words of the neurologist and spare myself the years of striving to be someone I clearly did not want to continue to be? Why couldn't my friend acknowledge his mistake early in his marriage instead of spending thirty more years with emptiness?

Once we become free of the misperceptions we hold about circumstances that bind us, preventing action, we can slip into sadness at our own inability to better navigate the course of our lives. We can wallow, go even deeper into a misperception and feel saddened about the length of time it took us to get to the place of action. It's natural to experience feelings of sadness, but the important thing to remember is not to stay stuck in the guilt or self-incrimination. We change when we're ready to change. Allow the feelings to flow through you and out from you. This scenario and others like this, staying too long, is an example of one of the body's teachings.

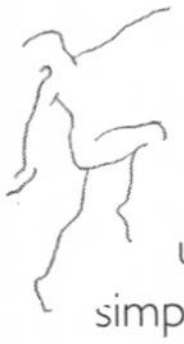

Our Bodies Model the Teachings

Although specialized for communication, not every stimulus causes a neuron to fire and conduct an impulse. Each neuron has a specific threshold. A stimulus must exceed the threshold to induce the neurons to fire. Some stimuli are simply not strong enough, individually, to reach the threshold and cause the neuron to fire. Stimuli may accumulate over time. The accumulation reaches the threshold. The neuron fires. Communication with another neuron ensues. The message passes on. Action results.

Message to the Reader

Have you been in a situation, at work or at home, in which you stayed for what seemed like too long a time before leaving or changing it? The sequence of events leading to leaving or changing the situation holds gems of knowledge.

One of the things I've learned in reviewing my eleven years in the convent was the benefit and detriment of a strong sense of focus. Focused upon being the best Dominican Sister, worthy of life-long "final" vows, and the best chemistry teacher in the college, did not allow me to pay attention to anything else—even my own illness. Locked into my determination to be the best, I almost lost myself.

One evening I was speaking with a group of my colleagues, complaining about the rigidity of the rules in the convent that arose over a specific controversy, and the loss of the spirit of the rules. Many contributed to the conversation. I was particularly vocal that night. A colleague turned to me and said, "If you don't like it so much here, why don't you leave?" That shook me to my core. I struggled all night with those words echoing through all levels of my mind. I awoke to a new realization—I did not belong in the convent any more. Then I stumbled onto another, more profound awareness—I could leave! Finally, I recognized the signal. I was free to go.

Focus is important to sustain energy and commitment, but excessive focus, focus on performance and not a state-of-being, can so narrow your perspective that it prevents you from recognizing important messages that lie outside of your peripheral vision. Your blinders give you a limited vision of what's going on around you. You never want to paint yourself into a corner. That locks you into a belief that you "can't, until ____________________." The reality is, you always have choices.

Directions to the Reader

When the time is appropriate for you to do this exercise, go to a place where you will not be disturbed, and create circumstances of feeling safe.

Describe a situation in which you know you stayed too long. It could be a relationship, a job, an activity, or a place. What were the external signals that told you that you were staying too long? What were the internal feelings that repeated the same message?

"

"

What was it about the situation that made you believe you *had* to stay?

"

"

Is staying longer than you need to, a pattern in your life? Do you know you need to leave someone or something, but stay anyway?

What was your perceived benefit for staying so long? What was the detriment?

STEP 1	RECOGNIZE Having sustained a certain condition for an extended period of time, signals may arise to alert you to make a decision to leave that condition.

Directions to the Reader

What was created in your life to activate you to leave? Or was there one thing that forced you to finally look at the situation and leave? Or were there a series of symbols (messages or events) that prompted you to leave or change the situation? Note here the process that led you to change.

"

_____

_____

_____

_____

_____

_____

_____

_____

_____

_____

_____

"

Hopefully, this situation allowed you to grow in your awareness about personal timing, letting go, embracing change, etc. What have you learned about yourself from this situation?

"

_____

_____

_____

_____

”

The circumstance in which we seemed to remain too long may have been an unfolding process that could not have been rushed. A rose unfolds its petals, from a tightly closed bud to a fully opened state, revealing its center. This process has its own inherent, internal timing. It cannot be rushed.

Message to the Reader

STEP 2

DISTINGUISH An unfolding process to change takes its own timing. This is different from the everyday pattern of limiting possibilities by statements such as "can't, until. . . ."

In contrast, we engage in imposing limits and negate “ripe” possibilities with almost every thought of our internal brain chatter. We say, “I can’t, until ____________.” Here are some examples of negative thinking that limits possibilities.

I can't write my book until I leave this job.
I can't buy the clothes I like until I lose weight.
I can't explore new opportunities while I live in this town.
I can't ask for a raise until I have another great accomplishment.

The examples are endless.

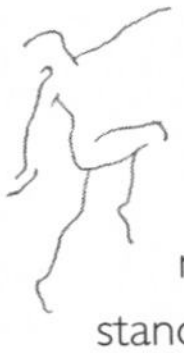

Our Bodies Model the Teachings

Neurons are the only cells in the body that do not expend energy storing nutrients. The price for not doing so is considerably high. Neurons that do not receive adequate blood flow become deprived of nutrients. If the circumstances persist, the sustained deprivation will eventually cause the neurons to die. This appalling risk allows the neurons to remain totally present to the moment at hand. The advantage that offsets the risk allows neurons to detect stimuli as soon as they occur and respond in a timely fashion.

Message to the Reader

What are your "can't, until _____" statements? Sometimes, we become aware of these kinds of statements when we're talking to someone else. We hear the words tumble out of our own mouths.

"Can't, until _____" statements limit what is possible in our lives. Therefore, it's important to recognize them and discover the concealed possibilities.

Directions to the Reader

In this exercise, you have another opportunity to become aware of your own self-imposed limited thinking. Find a quiet, alone space to contemplate and review conversations with significant others: family, friends, colleagues and associates. As you replay these conversations in your head, listen for any words such as, "I can't, until. …"

Note any "I can't, until …" statements here. Write down any noticeable patterns. Are your conversations focused on one "I can't, until …" statement, with a specific subject matter, or several statements, with several things you can't, until?

*Message to
the Reader*

Within each of your "can't, until ..." statements, lie concealed great possibilities. For example, within the statement, "I can't write my book until I leave this job," lies concealed the possibility of writing your book. Or within the statement, "I can't buy the clothes I like, until I lose weight," lies concealed your appreciation of beauty and the desire to dress yourself in beautiful garments. The same is true for these statements:

Statement
"I can't explore new opportunities until I leave this town."

Possibility
"I can explore new opportunities now."

Statement
"I can't ask for a raise until I have another great accomplishment."

Possibility
"I can ask for a raise now."

DISCOVER Inherent in the problem is the solution. Seek the hidden possibilities within your "can't, until ..." statements.	**STEP 3**

*Directions to
the Reader*

Discover the possibilities hidden within your "can't, until ..." statements. Write your "can't, until ..." statements. Under each one, write the possibilities concealed within the statement. Note the example offered above.

| **STEP 4** | DETERMINE   Choose action steps that will transform possibility into reality. |

Do you want to transcend the limitations of your "can't, until . . ." statements? Do you want to take one or more actions toward making the revealed possibility a reality?

If your answer is "Yes," write the possibility and under it write one or more actions that you can take now to begin to transform the possibility into reality. Make sure you make the action(s) real and doable for you. Even the smallest act moves you forward toward transforming some aspect of your life. You just dropped a pebble into a still pond and the ripples will move into every phase of your being.

"

_____

_____

_____

_____

_____

_____

_____

_____

_____

_____

_____

                                                                    "

Directions to the Reader

As you consider each of the action steps, you will have a response: physical, mental or emotional. Often one of these is dominant. Review the action steps from the last exercise, attending to the response that you feel, whether it is physical, mental or emotional. A physical response may be a tightening in your solar plexus or around your heart, or a sense of deep relaxation. A mental response might be one of experiencing

disconnection with or distance from, or conversely, an alignment with, a thought. You may experience an emotional response, such as a recoiling from, with distaste or a feeling of expansiveness and excitement, or maybe exhilaration.

List the actions that you outlined above. Without concern for your "can't, until . . ." statements, what physical sensations, thoughts, or emotions are preceding your putting these steps into action? Determine how you can best navigate to ensure that you will take the proper actions to move you forward. Describe for yourself a safe and doable plan of action.

"

_____

_____

_____

_____

_____

_____

_____

_____

_____

_____

_____

"

NOTICE Become aware of your responses to the action steps you have specified.	**STEP 5**

HOW WILL YOU _KNOW_ THIS?

A plan of action allows you to begin the opening process for yourself. It is incremental, developmental, one step at a time. You may begin to see options, other choices, that didn't exist before. You open yourself up to new choices; you go deeper into the knowing of who you are. You might begin to see how each step is lining up with what you know as your authentic blueprint. You'll remember you had dreams, dreams you may still want to create. How will you know when you've stopped waiting . . . until your partner, your spouse, your children, your parents, your move, your bigger pocket book, your job, give you the green light to proceed with your life? You'll allow change to happen within you first, then the rest of the world will move . . . to accommodate and adjust to your very real needs and wants and dreams. You will know when the letting go allows the shift within you to no longer be a process, but becomes a new state of being.

STEP 6   ACTION Make a commitment to live your life in action. Set a deadline and announce your commitment to someone else.

Directions to the Reader

Note the action steps that evoked positive responses, whether they were physical, mental or emotional. List those here.

Should you begin to feel overwhelmed by looking at the details of the entire plan with deadlines, step back and view your plan from a different perspective. Get above the plan as an observer, almost as though you are positioned in a hot air balloon rising into the sky. Know that your commitment, an expression of your essential being, will lead the way, unfolding your path, step by step. Make it easy. Be attentive to the signals and signposts in your environment. They are there to help you identify the directions of the unfolding process.

Our Bodies Model the Teachings

Timing regulates many physiological processes. Specific neurons in the region of the brain called the hypothalamus function as "clock" timers.

Their activity drives a whole host of processes that regulates our sleep-wake cycle, secretions of hormones, tendency to greater or lesser activity, etc. Each component of the body responds in an appropriate way to the signals received either directly from the neurons in the hypothalamus, or from other systems in the loop. In spite of the complexity, that host of systems must be regulated, and when it is there is no "overwhelm." Each component responds in its own way when it receives a relevant signal. The harmony that results constitutes the symphony of life in our bodies.

When I first left academia, I turned away from everything scientific, because I identified science with the pain of constriction that I had felt the last few years before I left. As weeks and months passed, I found myself returning to scientific principles, but viewing them from a much broader perspective. I began to deliberate about writing a book from this broader perspective. Just as this idea was incubating, a colleague, who had been an editor with a major publisher for twenty years, mentioned to me that if I decided to write a book, she would "midwife it." That same week I became aware of voice recognition software that would allow me to "speak" my book. My concern that my writing would reflect the sterile scientific strategy dissolved. I knew it was time to write *Cellular Wisdom*™.

Before concluding this chapter, let's review the central theme of the six steps:

RECOGNIZE Signals arise to alert you that something is changing and it is time to make a decision to let go and allow the change. **STEP 1**

DISTINGUISH An unfolding process takes time and differs from an everyday pattern of limiting possibilities by statements such as "can't, until. . . ." **STEP 2**

DISCOVER Hidden possibilities are within your "can't, until . . ." statements. **STEP 3**

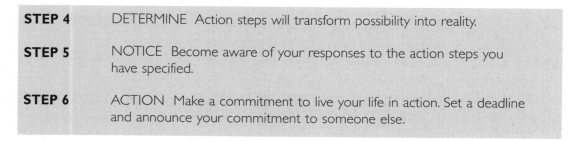

STEP 4   DETERMINE Action steps will transform possibility into reality.

STEP 5   NOTICE Become aware of your responses to the action steps you
                 have specified.

STEP 6   ACTION Make a commitment to live your life in action. Set a deadline
                 and announce your commitment to someone else.

These steps constitute a path, a trajectory to create from possibility.
Slightly shifting perspective, alert to significant signals, with the thread
of commitment, transforms your life. Being mindful that the process can
be easy and that the mental/emotional feelings of being overwhelmed
need not emerge. These incremental steps develop confidence to allow
the unfolding, taking action at just the right time. Know that all is well.

*Please join Joan in a further discussion of your creating a life of possibility
at* http://www.cellular-wisdom.com

Want to ask questions? Go to Joan's blog
blog.beyond-success.com *and pose your question. Joan will answer you.*

Why Me?

The Void engulfs me:
a dark swirling mass.
I see no bottom.
I'm falling . . .
falling . . .
falling. . . .

It lasts for hours.
Timeless.
Falling with no end
in sight.
Falling with no sense
of me
ending or beginning.

Why, why is this
happening
to me?

The black hole engulfs me.
I can do nothing.
I think of nothing . . .
I am nothing . . .
known.

I let go . . .
allowing.
It draws me in,
further,
deeper,
darker.

Finally, exhausted,
I rest,
at the bottom
of
my surrender.

Friday... I decided ... I would leave academia. I would leave the laboratory that was my exploratory haven; leave the medical students and their awakening to the functioning of the nervous system; leave a lifestyle of travel, achievements and acknowledgments. Academia had grown too small for me.

How did I know this? I was fragmented. My professional life and my personal life were splintered expressions of someone I no longer recognized as authentically me. I needed room to grow into my next phase of Joan. I didn't know what was ahead of me. That didn't matter, because on this Friday, I decided to embark, to shift, to change, to move forward, to act and that intention propelled me onward. The something that knew the time was ripe to act, also knew I'd be safe, even in the unknown, even without my academic identity, even if I didn't consciously know it. At least that's all I knew on Friday.

Saturday, my husband and I drove almost two hours northeast of Boston to our house in the countryside in Middleton, New Hampshire. Entering the calm embrace of the hundred and fifty year old Cape house made me feel safe—I let go. Like a cosmic black hole in space, I began to slip into its pull, sinking down into sadness, stumbling on to the sofa. I lay there, held together by only the loss, the deeply depleting loss of self and sadness; falling down into the Void, unsure of who I was, where I would land, or whether I would land. The hours passed with no recognition of time. I was somewhere in-between myself. When I could finally stir, I was completely spent, but I could move my fingers and toes. I could feel my body. I was still alive. I pushed up off of the sofa alone, then stood straight up, found my husband and said, "I'll be all right."

I didn't understand what had accumulated inside of me in such a wave of transition that would manifest this happening to me. Why couldn't I just fit in? Why couldn't I just make it work? I was accomplished. I was successful. But whose definitions did I have to follow in order to be accomplished? Successful? What roles was I having to play that created an appearance of wholeness on the outside, while splintering my interior self into fragments, causing unhealthy coping mechanisms to become my prevalent way of being. I was acting in what felt like someone else's life to continue a lifestyle that no longer served me. Why me? Other people seemed to do it so easily, to even envy my polished life.

Message to the Reader

Change, major change, occurs more and more frequently today. Everything in our lives has sped up. No longer are companies expected to keep a "family" relationship with employees. The speeding up of our lives has also created short-term experiences. Employees who would have normally worked for a company their whole lives are being let go during mergers and acquisitions. Bottom line corporate issues displace many. Marriages dissolve. Families disperse. Catastrophes wipe out shorelines, communities, and lives. The pace quickens. We find ourselves, as I did, unable to maintain our old paradigm, having to shift, to change, while not knowing anything about the new paradigm. For me, "the new" remained shrouded in the darkest shadows that I came to know later

as my way of bridging the transition—the dying away and mourning of the familiar toward the creating and birthing of the undiscovered new.

Naturally, sadness and grief ensues as our world collapses.

In these scared times of "not knowing" it is essential that we flow with what we do know—the truth of who we are. What is this truth of who you are? You are more than your physical surroundings that dress your identity. You are more than your mental thoughts that name and define you. You are more than your emotions that fuel your intentions. That part of you that is constant, unchangeable, foundational, in and through-out all things: this is you—Spirit expressing itself in form. But eager to exit this "in-between time," this present pain, and get on with our lives, we lose that sacred breath moment between our inhale and our exhale. Allow the richness of staying with the unknown to reverberate through every aspect of your physical, mental, emotional and spiritual being. It is a time pregnant with meaning, even in the unknowing.

Have you experienced such a collapse in your life? Are you in the midst of one now? Do you have a sense that such a collapse lurks around the corner?

Find a comfortable place and adorn it in a way that makes you feel safe and secure, and open your heart to this next experience of self-discovery.

Directions to the Reader

Allow your breathing to slow and your mind to calm. If music or chanting takes you inward to a place of stillness, give it to yourself. Use outside props that support you in this process.

First, acknowledge yourself quietly, with all the affirmation of knowing, by quickly review-ing some of your past experiences. *Your life is a journey of change* and significant change is a part of all life. You know this. You witness this every day in the mundane—global weather patterns, for example.

As disrupting as change might be, it holds the elements of alchemy to transform your life.

Describe here any disruption or change that *has occurred, is occurring* or *is likely to occur.* Don't struggle or hide. Simply allow your thoughts and the accompanying feelings to emerge from that deep well of stillness within.

"

"

In doing this exercise, you are acknowledging, allowing and accepting, at a very deep level, change. You are moving through a process that takes you to your center place of magnificence.

Elisabeth Kübler-Ross, M.D. (1926-2004) in her classic work *On Death and Dying*, published in 1969, describes the "Five Stages of Grief." They are: denial and isolation, anger, bargaining, depression, and acceptance. These stages often mirror significant events of change in our own lives, because something is dying away, transitioning from one form of expression into another form of expression.

In acknowledging that a major disruption has occurred, you effectively dispose of the dysfunction of denial.

STEP I   ACKNOWELDGE When you note that a disruption has occurred in your life, you eliminate denial.

What were your first thoughts around this disrupting change? For example, did you think, *This couldn't be happening to me. Things like this don't happen to good people.* Did you struggle with the thoughts that you were all alone in this struggling transformation? *Who can I talk to about this? Is there anyone out there who would understand me?* Did these thoughts move into your physical body significantly, so that you felt discomfort, pain or change? What immediate emotions surfaced? Fear? Abandonment? Or did something move beyond those initial thoughts, physical sensations, and emotions to embrace the oncoming change? Was there a moment you recognized as surrender?

Can you name what part of you fought it? Tried to stop it from happening? Finally, what allowed you to let go and surrender to it? As best as you can remember, or if it's a current situation, write down your awareness of the process you went through. Try to remember and name your thoughts surrounding the event, how your body felt, and what emotions played out in the initial awareness of your significant life change until you surrendered into the **change**.

Directions to the Reader

"

_____

_____

_____

_____

_____

_____

_____

_____

_____

_____

_____

_____

_____

_____

_____

_____

_____

_____

_____

_____

_____

"

During my times of transition, I had no appreciation for the depth and breadth or benefit I would derive from surrendering into the unknown to navigate from a place in the Void. I could not sense that I would ever escape the Void. I had no awareness, while in the process of transitioning, that if I could just get out of my own way, I was making my way easier, I was simply allowing my future to emerge in its own perfect timing.

Looking back at those times of great upheaval, I acknowledge these benefits and the meaning they brought me. A deep compassion for others undergoing similar transitions infused me with understanding the process and knowing the need to allow change. It committed me to an intention to assist and guide others who might be floundering in their "how-do-I-allow-change?" I wanted to support their passage into and through change, evoking their greatness through it. My own experiences with significant change integrated compassion for others and their struggles with change. As a result of my changes, I grew in my awareness and consciousness of the human condition.

I also experienced a shift in self-realization by standing in my integrity, making decisions I knew were important to make for me, in spite of their unpopularity. By doing this again and again, by embracing and being ready to accept any consequences, I came to trust my ability to stay in integrity in the midst of chaos.

I will not forget what I experienced in the process of my emergence.

STEP 2   EMERGE   Find the meaning that can emerge in the disruption or collapse of your world.

If your world has/is/might collapse from some significant change or disruption, begin now to look at the meaning embedded in the change. You are about to discover meaning; even if you are in the midst of this experience, or you are anticipating the collapse of your world, some process has already begun.

When you allow yourself the opportunity to step back from your reactive self and see the events that are playing out in front of you from the vantage point of the observer, meaning begins to emerge. You see the scattered dots of people, events, and situations connect into some type of pattern that has meaning for you. *Oh, that's why. Aha, I'm not going crazy, it's happening for a reason.* Out of the breaking down rubble of your world, something is already calling you to go forth, even if you are not yet willing. It is the grander scheme of your life, playing itself out to expand your small life, into a grander purpose.

Your ability to find meaning creates enormous power as described by Viktor Frankl in his classic work of 1959, *Man's Search for Meaning*. His own search for meaning allowed Frankl to develop a completely new approach to psychiatry, while being incarcerated for three years during World War II at Auschwitz, Dachau and other Nazi concentration camps.

If we can see the meaning in the collapse of our world, we can transcend it.

Find that place both physically and synergetically, that opens you to explore and reflect on changes in your life, whether you were able to embrace them as your world collapsed, or pushed back against them in denial. Here is your place and time to reflect your own process.

Write your reflections here.

Directions to the Reader

"

"

Our Bodies Model the Teachings

We take for granted the continual shedding of skin, which happens daily and renews the body's largest organ, which prevents water loss and helps us live in the dry environment of terra firma. The renewal of skin helps us heal wounds that penetrate it and threaten infection. This is the daily dynamic of life.

The birth of a child through the uterine canal culminates a lengthy process characterized by dramatic significant change, evident in fertilization, implantation, the growth of the fetus during pregnancy and its final release from the womb in birth.

Message to the Reader

Notice that our response to birthing a child is not "Why, me?" The discomfort of pregnancy and the pain experienced during labor are quickly eclipsed by the deep joy of birthing a new human being. The result of the period of incubation, so palpable, commands the new perspective of joy, replacing pain. The pain is temporary and the joy buoyant.

Understanding this unfolding sequence brings a broader perspective should we once again be plunged into the depths of "not knowing."

Have you avoided making a decision because in making it and acting on the steps to follow, you might disrupt your life's status quo and be thrown into the black hole of "unknowing?"

Change, significant change, remains inherent in the dynamic of life. Holding back so as not to plunge into the stream of change does not benefit you. Growth, shedding the old and embracing the new, reflects the vitality of life.

Our Bodies Model the Teachings

Imagine if we never shed the outer layer of skin or never birthed the child. An ever-growing exterior/interior shell would burden us, growing in weight, each day. Our prison would grow and grow, inhibiting movement, the ability to exchange gases and liquid with the external environment or secrete hormones in the normal, cyclic fashion—ultimately compromising our health.

STEP 3   LISTEN Your interior stillness is where awareness helps you to identify what you already know.

Directions to the Reader

Choose a quiet place and time that will allow you to listen to your inner promptings.

Settle in with ease, knowing that regardless of appearances, "All is well." This knowing supports you as you explore the inner promptings of change. What do you know that you have yet to identify that you know?

Take this sacred time to write what you discover in this exploration.

"

"

It was 1966 and my last night in West Virginia. I had left Poor Bottom, Kentucky, where I was serving as a Volunteer In Service to America (VISTA), earlier in the day, to spend an evening in Charleston, West Virginia, before taking a flight home. The discovery of a lump in my breast prompted me to return to my hometown of New Orleans for diagnosis and treatment. I was sad to leave. As a community organizer I had come to know the people in Appalachia, their big hearts and their overwhelming difficulties in negotiating political matters. Their request for a road up the hollow met with an unambiguous, "No." The citizens of Poor Bottom took this answer as a final one. They were completely deflated. Washed by a stream on both sides, the current road was less and less navigable as you drove up the hollow of the mountain. They really needed the road. My contribution was to strategize with them creating alternative approaches. I left before I knew if they ever got the much-needed road. Leaving made me feel that I was abandoning them.

In New Orleans, the diagnosis was favorable. The lump was simply a cyst of fluid. It was easily removed. Though my work in Appalachia was replaced by the discovery of the lump, I felt a calling to go to medical or graduate school to learn more about the dynamics of people and how I might be of greater service. That fall I entered graduate school and began to study psychology, to learn more about motivation, learning, etc. This led to my obtaining a Ph.D. in neuroscience and physiological psychology a few years later.

The discovery of the lump led me on a trajectory that prepared me for the work that I do today. I'm very grateful for the entire sequence of events beginning with serving as a VISTA volunteer and ending with my graduation from graduate school and the obtaining of my Ph.D. My life turned in a different direction because of the appearance of the lump in my breast.

STEP 4	KNOW Allow yourself to know that regardless of appearances, "All is well."

Message to the Reader

What if you knew, really knew, that regardless of the risk and the potential demise of elements of your life, the process would lead you to a place grander than you ever imagined?

How would knowing that change your perspective with regards to making decisions that risk destroying parts of your life?

Directions to the Reader

Sit with these questions for a while. Let them infuse you. Steep in their energy. Write what emerges.

"

"

STEP 5   REDISCOVER What was lost can be recaptured in set-aside dreams and forgotten possible futures.

Message to the Reader

Look beyond the pain associated with change and the unknown to the vision of a possible future. What dreams have you held beneath the surface consciousness for fear of how they would transform your life? Inherent in these dreams are the clues to your life's assignment and purpose—your life's theme. Release the dreams into your consciousness. Allow them to empower you to do whatever is necessary to realize them. Take time now to remember the dreams of your childhood, the dreams of your adolescence, the dreams of young adulthood. Your dreams came from the substance of you and reflect possible trajectories.

Directions to the Reader

Use this space to write down your dreams. Collect them. Gather them here again for your review. You are not committing to them; you're simply *re-member-ing* them.

Directions to the Reader

Did one of your remembered dreams stir you deeply? Or did fragments from many dreams weave together into a single fabric and stir you deeply?

Write the dreams that stirred your soul.

"

"

Once I returned to New Orleans and learned that the lump in my breast was not a problem, I was excited about pursuing graduate school. In the convent I could only attend graduate courses at universities during the summer, because of my heavy teaching load. Released from that obligation and no longer concerned about my health, I worked during the day as a chemist and applied to graduate programs in psychology. Finally, I would be able to explore "what makes people tick." I had wanted to do that since I first entered the convent. I found graduate school exhilarating and exhausting, simultaneously. However, I knew that my future would be different because of my graduate education.

Message to the Reader

What would activating any element of your dream bring to you and your life now? Would the joy of experiencing the realization of some part of your dream motivate you and infuse you with energy? Are you ready to commit to decisions that would allow you to move closer toward realizing your dream?

Directions to the Reader

If you are ready to make a commitment to move forward, spend some time now writing the decisions that you would have to make. Remember, at this point, you are not committing to any one decision.

HOW WILL YOU *KNOW* THIS?

If you were to stay, lingering in the arms of catastrophe as a victim, you would not arrive at this place of surrender knowing that "All is well," regardless of the external appearances—Step 4. You would be incapable of rediscovering your dreams—Step 5 or moving forward to Step 6. Once we make the decision to leave the arms of catastrophe, surrender to the reality of the disruption and accept responsibility for moving forth, it is as though an announcement is made to the universe. People will show up in your life. People will talk to you about your dreams, or groups will light your path. You will be led. You will find a book that gives the information that will help you activate your decisions and continue on your journey.

COMMIT By activating any aspect of your dreams, you are showing up for the possibility of their fulfillment.   **STEP 6**

NOW review the decisions you just identified. Which of these will you commit to making? By when? Sometimes it is important to ask someone to witness our commitment to change. This should be a person you trust; someone who honors you and the changes you are about to make; and someone who will support you through the process of change by listening, observation and witnessing. If you know who that person is now, please write down a name here. There is power in naming. List your reasons for choosing this individual to support you in your transition.

Directions to the Reader

Before concluding this chapter, let's review the central theme of the six steps:

STEP I   ACKNOWLEDGE   A disruption in your life occurred or is anticipated. Acknowledge the disruption or change that has occurred or is likely to occur.

STEP 2   EMERGE   Meaning can be found in the midst of disruption or collapse of your world. It provides the substantive energy that allows you to transcend the difficulties. Look for the meaning.

STEP 3   LISTEN   There is much within you that you know and are not aware of. Listen to your interior stillness where awareness helps you to identify what you already know.

STEP 4   KNOW   Allow yourself to know that regardless of appearances, "All is well."

STEP 5   REDISCOVER   Rediscover your dreams and your possible future.

STEP 6   COMMIT   Commit to making some specific decisions, taking action and activating your dreams.

With this series of steps lie the keys to creativity and freedom. You have responded proactively and creatively to disrupting circumstances. Life now holds new possibilities, new dreams. Importantly, you've avoided casting yourself as a victim.

This series of exercises may be particularly challenging, because we are not given the skills to approach disrupting change in this way. However, the effort that you expend in stretching to do the exercises will be enormously beneficial to you.

Like Kubler-Ross's "Five Stages of Grief,"—denial, anger, bargaining, and depression—lead to acceptance, this series of steps that you have taken in doing these exercises allows you to acknowledge the disruption, find the meaning in it, listen to your inner promptings, know that "all is well," rediscover your dreams, and commit to decisions and actions. This leads you to claim the fullness of life, not avoiding its tragedies or being lost in catastrophe as a victim.

Responsibility for our lives lies with no one else but ourselves, not our circumstances and not what others think that we should do. The essence of life lies in the depths of your own being. Collaborations with others, connections with others represent extremely valuable resources; yet, the

responsibility for our lives lies within us. Use your power to create your life—one of great possibility.

Please join Joan in a further discussion of using this set of steps to create an abundant life of great possibility at http://www.cellular-wisdom.com

Want to ask questions? Go to Joan's blog blog.beyond-success.com *and pose your question. Joan will answer you.*

"What's Wrong?"

I dialed
and waited for her
to answer.
I knew
what I would hear.

She didn't
expect
my call.
I would
take her
by surprise.

She answered.

"Hi, Anna,"
I said.
I heard
what I
expected.

"What's wrong?"
Each time I hear
the words,
they cut
my heart.
Again.

She can't say,
"Good to hear from you."
Or,
"I was thinking about you."

She has to ask,
"What's wrong?"

I don't remember the first time I heard my mother ask, "What's wrong?" The words cut my heart every time I heard them.

I heard the stories of how during the Great Depression the family lost their business and with it the family wealth. I heard the stories of how she walked to "Normal School," where she trained to be a teacher, with only a dime in her pocket for lunch. She didn't have enough money for the streetcar. Before the Depression, she, her two brothers and three sisters sat at their restaurant table every night of the week, each ordering whatever they would like to eat. I often wondered: Did my mother's loss create the fear I felt emanated from her, as she asked, "What's wrong?"?

A prickly energy like fear seemed to prompt my mother's expectation that something would go wrong. Her many rituals, locking my car door as soon as I sat down, or moving my purse to a safe location wherever I was—in restaurants, in department store fitting rooms, in the theater, etc. —seemed to stay the prickly energy of fear for the moment. Each time she enacted one of her rituals, it cut my heart. She was not always fearful. There were times we had a lot of fun. But the stream of palpable fear was never far away.

Watching my mother build her own prison, seeing the effects of living from fear etched into my mind, I had to decide. Was I going to live as she did, close to this stream of fear, or was something else possible? Risk, unwelcome in our home, held opportunities, great possibilities for me. I chose risk. Risking "not leading a normal" life, I entered the convent at seventeen. Risking loss of my "safe haven" at twenty-eight I left the convent, joined VISTA (Volunteers in Service to America), and worked in Poor Bottom Kentucky. After twenty-seven years of teaching, scholarly research and administration, I left my tenured position in academia. Each of these risks contributed to my personal and professional growth.

*Message to
the Reader*

Did I feel afraid as I made those decisions and took those risks? Of course, but I put fear aside and walked into the energy of risk, convinced of the opportunities that lay beyond the fear. I knew without a shadow of doubt that if I did not put aside my fear or walk through it, it would capture me and hold me prisoner for the rest of my life.

*Directions to
the Reader*

Find a comfortable place where you feel safe and secure. Read again the poem at the beginning of this chapter. What do you experience as you read the poem? Does it remind you of a similar event or theme played out by someone in your life? Even if nothing comes to mind immediately, allow some time for something to rise to conscious awareness. Identify it. Describe it here.

"

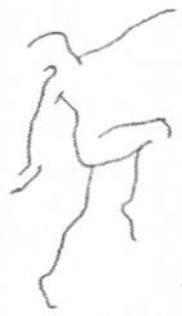

Our Bodies Model the Teachings

Our bodies continually survey our internal and external environments for influences that might be foreign and, therefore, potentially harmful to the body. As soon as the presence of foreign molecules is detected, our body systems instantly respond. Invaders are encapsulated, deactivated or destroyed, precisely because they do not belong within the body. They are not part of the body.

Message to the Reader

In response to my mother's palpable fear as she echoed, "What's wrong?" I chose to face my own fears and to take risks that could open up new possibilities for me. I knew deep within that this response reflected my truth, my essence and was vital to my continued growth. Her fear would not become my fear.

Directions to the Reader

What was your response to the event that you remembered as you read the poem? Did you assimilate the energy of that event into yourself? Does the event influence your patterns of behavior or values, even now? Or, as in my case, did the event trigger a different response in you—as my mother's words triggered my choice to put aside fear and take risks?

Describe your responses.

"

*Message to
the Reader*

*Living the fullness of who you are—with conscious awareness, from your life pur-
pose, making your contribution to the world—requires that you recognize what is
inconsistent within your very being, your essence, and remove it from your life
repertoire, promptly, before it imprisons you and blinds you to possibility.*

Once you've identified something inconsistent within the essence of you,
and have become aware of your response to it, you're primed to make the
choice to overcome the foreign influences in your life. As we've learned,
the body encapsulates, deactivates or destroys foreign invaders to prevent them from compromising vital bodily functions.

How do you conquer foreign influences that threaten the vitality of who
you are, your spirit? Sometimes, it is necessary to physically leave a toxic
situation, particularly if the influences constitute a constant threat to your
vitality, to who you are and how you express who you are in the world. My
decisions to leave the convent and to leave academia provided enormous
possibilities for me that were not present while I remained in either clois-
tered situation. Certain aspects of both of those external environments
crippled me and hampered full expression of who I am, although they had
been, for some years, very valuable in my development.

However, the restrictive influence does not always arise from outside
environments but, rather, resides inside.

Due to my exposure to my mother's questioning, "What's wrong?" fear stealthily took
up residence in my internal environment. For many years I did not realize that I continually anticipated that something would likely go wrong in any situation. I eventually realized that this pattern operated in my life. I would picture an upcoming event as a beautiful painting representing the scene of the event. If something went awry with a planned
event—such as rain on the day of a picnic or someone being late for an event, or someone canceling a date—the scene in my perfect painting would decompose. The previously vibrant colors and coherent elements of the scene decayed into a raw jumble of
sharp edges of garish colors with no identifiable pattern of people's faces or of scenes.

The painting reflected my experience. The event was ruined. The sharp edges of my distorted internal painting inflicted much prolonged pain. Not only did I not enjoy the planned event, if it occurred, but I became psychologically and physically spent.

My internalization of the fear symbolized by my mother's habitual questioning, stopped me from tapping into the joyous energy of the altered event and the people I was with. Finally, I grew tired of living in pain. Once aware of this disempowering pattern, I made the decision to be happy, internally, independently of whatever occurred in the external world. I wanted my feelings to reflect the wholeness of who I am, the deep joy of being alive. No longer would I swing from anticipated joy to pain because of what was occurring in the world. I announced my decision to my husband with conviction. In the first few weeks of living this decision, I created a process to establish my essential internal environment and live from it, rather than from the ever-changing external one. This is my process.

Message to the Reader

RECOGNIZE when you *begin* to slide down the emotional slope of disappointment, before your internal painting decomposes and the event is ruined.

STEP 1

AFFIRM that you want to enjoy the event, regardless of how the circumstances might go awry.

STEP 2

CHOOSE happiness. Instead of focusing on "What's wrong?" ask, "What's right about the altered situation? How can I make it beneficial to myself and others?" This shift in perspective changes the prevailing energy of the situation.

STEP 3

Are you currently experiencing a negative situation that could benefit from the process of choosing happiness?

Directions to the Reader

Briefly identify your current negative situation.

"

Name the negative pattern that you want to remove from your life (such as my expecting something would go wrong).

"

"

Describe what you experience, inside, when you begin to slide down the emotional slope of disappointment. How can you begin to recognize this in its early stages? Is there a physical sensation by which your body signals to you? Do your thoughts shift to a specific theme? Do the physical and mental bodies signal something before the emotional body begins its slide?

"

"

What do you want to affirm (similarly to my choosing that I wanted to enjoy the events

of my life and the people with me)?

"

_____

_____

_____

_____

_____

_____

_____

_____

_____

_____

_____ *"*

Ask "What's right about this?" "How can I make it enjoyable for myself and others?"

What other questions will you ask to choose happiness in this previously negative cir-

cumstance?

"

_____

_____

_____

_____

_____

_____

_____

_____

_____

_____

_____ *"*

Message to the Reader

List the influences that you want to change in your life, regardless of their origins. Remember that you choose the way you respond to any given circumstance. If your habitual response does not support your essence, you can choose to respond differently.

This process can be applied to anything that causes you emotional distress. The questions may differ, but this three-step process is the same: 1) **Recognize** that you are beginning to slide down that emotional hill; 2) **Affirm** that you want something different; 3) **Choose** happiness and ask the questions which will help you achieve that.

For example, you may have a friend who often calls you to recount her troubles in full detail. Have you learned how to experience compassion without internalizing the troubles of others? If you experience emotional pain with them, you may want to use this process to mitigate this influence. As soon as you recognize that you are sliding down the emotional slope, listening to your friend's tales of woe, create a pause. Find an excuse to leave the conversation for a moment. If you're on the telephone, you can ask the person to hold on for a moment as the doorbell is ringing, or you must go to the bathroom. In person, you could find similar excuses to remove yourself temporarily from the circumstance that would normally lead you into emotional distress. You have now accomplished Step 1 of the process.

In the time away from the situation, affirm what you want to happen rather than what is happening. Do you want your friend to not expect you to listen to her troubles for hours and hours? Do you want to distract your friend from her worries by beginning to talk about possibilities, choices or possible adventures? Think through what you want to affirm. Affirm it. You've completed Step 2.

Finally, choose happiness. You may inform your friend that you cannot listen to her woes for long periods of time. Or, you can begin to ask your friend about what she could do for herself to help her feel better. Encourage her to make decisions to implement appropriate actions by asking her whom would she enjoy doing activities with, or offering to do something with her yourself. Asking her to participate with you in different kinds of activities—possibly seeing a show, joining a book club—may facilitate her happiness as well as yours. You've done Step 3.

Directions to the Reader

Now, repeat the previous exercise from this new perspective. Repetition facilitates mastery. The value of the exercise lies in its extreme effectiveness in transforming negative influences into ones that support you in living from your essence.

Briefly identify the negative situation and the person with whom it arises.

Briefly identify the negative internal pattern you experience in this situation.

Identify what you experience when you begin to slide down the emotional slope of negativity. How can you recognize this feeling in its early stages?

What do you want to affirm in this situation and with this person?

What questions will you ask in order to allow yourself to choose happiness in this specific negative circumstance?

"

"

Message to the Reader

Gaining facility in this three-step process evokes a centeredness and groundedness in the strength of your own being. You may want to repeat this process for several of the circumstances to increase your ease in implementing the three steps. Growth, however, is rarely linear. Particularly in times of stress, you may find that you take one or many steps backward. As disconcerting as this is, it is important to learn from those times and strengthen your resolve to continue the process. Keeping the focus regardless of failures constitutes a major secret of success. A "failure" is just an opportunity to learn, to refine your process. Each time you effectively engage in this exercise you liberate yourself from negative emotional patterns that can imprison you, and awaken to the possibilities inherent in every situation, if you can only see them.

Looking for possibilities represents a skill greatly lacking in our society and our educational process, yet possibilities represent the doors to thriving in life.

Mimi (not her real name), a faculty member in one university, wanted to leave that university and go back to the one from which she had received her Ph.D. However, the university she wanted to be associated with had not advertised an open faculty position. She told me about her desire to move to the other university and the fact that no position had been advertised. I suggested to Mimi that she contact people she knew at her target university, from doing her Ph.D. studies there, and make them aware of her desire. After several such conversations, Mimi spoke to the person heading the department she wanted to join. Although no position was available, the department head so valued Mimi's expertise that he actually created a position, specifically for her. Within six months, she moved to the new university with a significant increase in her salary.

What allowed Mimi to proceed in this fashion, when she did not see an obvious opportunity, and create the opportunity she wanted?   *Message to the Reader*

KNOW you will need to have a clear understanding of what you want.	**STEP 4**

Mimi knew exactly what she wanted, in this case. However, in other situations, it may take some time of reflection and discussion with friends, mentors, colleagues or coaches for you to clearly define what it is you want.

LOCATE RESOURCES Locate people you know who exemplify the circumstances and opportunities you desire. If you don't know anyone, talk to others who may know someone with whom you could speak.	**STEP 5**

ACCESS INFORMATION Do some research and find out who the leaders are in your desired field. Request an informational interview.	**STEP 6**

Unsure about whether I wanted to become a practicing Personal/Professional Coach, I identified four prominent coaches and contacted them for twenty–minute informational interviews. Three of the four responded favorably. In the telephone interviews I asked them the questions plaguing me. What did they enjoy about coaching? What challenges did they face in coaching? What preparation did they have to enter the field of coaching? If they were to enter the field today, what preparation would they want to have? What did they see as the future of coaching? Did they recommend gaining certification and accreditation? What were the advantages of doing this? Did they have a lucrative coaching practice? How long did it take them to develop an active and lucrative coaching practice? Did they engage in coaching full-time or part-time?

Their answers provided important input to help me decide whether and how I wanted to go about transitioning from academia into creating my own coaching practice. Having been in academia almost my entire adult life, I was not interested, initially, in going into a coach training program. Through a mutual friend, I learned of a career coach, Cheryl Gilman. I contacted Cheryl and worked with her for several months in a coaching relationship as I considered leaving academia. When I decided to start my own coaching business, Beyond Success, in 1998, I asked Cheryl to work with me in a supervisory role, similarly to how postdoctoral fellows work with their sponsors. Cheryl asked me to outline my expectations and how I wanted to work with her. I would tell my clients they would have two coaches rather than one, me in the foreground and Cheryl in the background. This one-year arrangement worked effortlessly, and gave me an opportunity to see my potential as a coach.

Later, I entered a formal coaching program I found particularly attractive: Success Unlimited Network Program®. This program appealed to me as it encompassed one-on-one training in the Boston area, where I was living, and included spirituality as a component of the coaching program. The one-on-one training appealed to me as I could spend time learning what I did not know rather than what I had learned through my varied experiences as a faculty member, Lab Director, Department Chair and Center Director. In-person training appealed to me because of its intimacy. Finally, spirituality constituted a fundamental theme for the coaching I wanted to do.

Message to the Reader

Had I looked only at traditional coaching programs available at the time, held in groups in faraway places, or over the telephone, I would not have had the rich experiences of working with Cheryl Gilman for one year and of one-on-one training with Teri-E Belf, head of the Success Unlimited Network® Program.

Had Mimi not contacted the university where she wanted to work merely because they had not advertised any available positions, she would not have achieved her goal of moving there.

Our Bodies Model the Teachings

Cells relentlessly scan for chemicals of import, such as nutrients, hormones, and neurotransmitters. We learned previously about the cells and systems of the body scanning for foreign molecules. Vigilant for possibilities, cells and systems also continuously scan for biochemical substrates that help them maximize their functions. Sensing pain, neurons communicate with other neurons which have the appropriate receptors to permit signals to travel long distances across the body, such as from your toe to your brain, in fractions of a second and provide relevant information, so that you quickly remove your toe from that sharp object it barely touched. Single neurons receive as many as 10,000 synapses, inputs, per unit area of their membranes, and integrate them to make a decision, such as whether to stimulate a muscle and ultimately move bones in our arms and legs so we can pick up a cup or walk across the room.

Similarly, gathering information relevant to an upcoming decision provides input to help you make a decision that truly reflects who you are. Particularly difficult decisions benefit greatly from the information you acquire from others who have experienced what you are facing and can provide a perspective on the process.

Message to the Reader

As before, find a comfortable place where you feel safe and secure. Reflect. What opportunities have been calling you? Maybe you have not listened to their previous calls. Now listen deeply. Is there a decision that moves you in the direction of alluring possibility? Describe it here.

Directions to the Reader

List some people who could serve as resources for you, providing information relevant to your decision.

From the above list, whom will you contact? What information do you want that person to provide? Timing is important in everything, so when you get a sense that the time is right, make the initial contact.

What relevant information have you acquired from drawing on your resources above? How has this process helped you make your decision?

"

What decision have you made?

"

"

Before concluding this chapter, let's review the central themes of the two basic processes.

The first process, directed to our choosing happiness, involves three separate steps.

STEP 1   RECOGNIZE when you begin to slide down the emotional slope of disappointment, before your internal painting decomposes and the event is ruined.

STEP 2   AFFIRM a positive outcome, such as your enjoying the altered event, regardless of how the circumstances may have gone awry.

STEP 3   CHOOSE happiness. Instead of asking "What's wrong?" ask, "What's right about the altered situation? How can I make it beneficial to myself and others?" This shift in perspective changes the prevailing energy of the situation.

This process frees us from a disabling emotional state and helps us create an empowering, insightful state. Whether you want to uproot an old negative emotional pattern, resolve conflicts, or create empowering initiatives, you will find this process useful.

The second process expands the first by helping you see possibilities and acquire information to allow you to make impactful decisions. It also has three steps.

STEP 4   KNOW you will need to have a clear understanding of what you want.

STEP 5   LOCATE RESOURCES Locate people you know who exemplify the circumstances and opportunities you desire. If you don't know anyone, talk to others who may know someone with whom you could speak.

STEP 6   ACCESS INFORMATION Do some research and find out who the leaders are in your desired field. Request an informational interview.

Please join Joan in a further discussion on the two processes, your successes and difficulties or questions about how to proceed at
http://www.cellular-wisdom.com

Want to ask questions? Go to Joan's blog
blog.beyond-success.com *and pose your question. Joan will answer you.*

Too Emotional

Run, Lassie, run!
I cried as I sobbed
watching Lassie
run from danger.

"It's only a movie,"
my mother would say.
"Why are you
so emotional?"

The large eyes in
a small dark face
looked through me
from the TV screen.

The child looked hungry
and afraid.
The ad requested money
to feed her.

I could not reach her,
feed her.
Tears rolled down my face.
Why am I so emotional?

Is something wrong with me because I am so emotional? For years, that question plagued me, when I was in the convent, when I was Chair of the Department and Director of the Research Center. Why was I so emotional?

Only in the last few years have I begun to understand my emotional nature in general, and specific capacities in particular. My compassion and empathy give birth to my connection with people, animals and nature. I am acutely aware of what other people feel. This capacity to literally stand within another person's shoes, and understand their thoughts, feelings and behaviors from their own perspective, defines "empathy." Originally derived from the Greek word for "affection", today, empathy is defined as a process whereby one person imagines the thoughts, feelings and emotions of another, so as to be standing in their shoes. Empathy involves the flexing of perspectives from ourselves to others. Clearly, different people are able to emphasize with those in specific circumstances to differing degrees. Becoming aware of our beliefs about ourselves and others, and of our capacities to understand ourselves and others, represent significant components of the foundation of our emotional beings. It is difficult, for instance, for me to emphasize with perpetrators of injustice, as I am unwilling to step into their shoes. On the other hand, I quickly and easily stand in the shoes of the hungry child yearning for the comfort of food, alone and unsure of when she will eat. Often, with such understanding, we can predict what another person might feel and do in this or that circumstance.

While empathy constitutes the basis whereby we can understand people from different cultures and developmental experiences, actually experiencing another person's emotions or other pain represents a distortion of empathy. This distortion burdens us and strangles the flow of energy into our beings. Actors who have played Hamlet and intensely enter into the character's emotional state, for example, report becoming depressed and taking on Hamlet's worldview.

Sympathy is distinguished first by being an emotion rather than the awareness of empathy. Often the emotions of sadness or pity arise in response to viewing the condition of another person. Sympathetic persons, in contrast to empathetic ones, do not stand in the other's shoes, but view the other from their own perspectives. The emotions of sorrow or pity are directed toward the other person. Those receiving pity, on the other hand, often feel condescended to, or "less than" , as if they are seen as unable to handle whatever circumstances prevail.

Both empathy and sympathy can form the basis of the transcendent capacity of compassion, a sense of shared suffering in the human condition characterized by kindness and a desire to alleviate suffering with no element of judgment. Usually compassion leads to action, internal or external, directed specifically to alleviating suffering.

In the words of the Dalai Lama: "Compassion makes one see the picture clearly; when emotions overtake us, the lack of seeing clearly clouds our perception of reality and hence the cause of many misunderstandings leading to quarrels (even wars)." American Buddhist Monk Bhikkhu Bodhi wrote: "compassion … springs up by considering that all beings, like ourselves, wish to be free from suffering, yet despite their wishes continue to be harassed by pain, fear, sorrow, and other forms of *dukkha* (suffering)."

Are we too emotional? What do we readily express in our lives: empathy, sympathy, compassion, pity, or a bit of all of them? It is vital to know in order to move yourself beyond the limits of making choices about your life from an emotionally based platform.

Empathy appears to be an ancient capacity that promotes social cohesion. Recent research with mice reveals that even they demonstrate behavior consistent with empathy. Mice writhe as they witness pain inflicted on other mice, but only those they have associated with in the past. The communication has been analyzed even more recently and appears to require that the mice actually "see" each other in order to demonstrate evidence of empathy. Even plants display a response to potential harm directed to another plant approached with a scissors, detected by a change in electrical activity: the galvanic skin response.

Could capacities and emotions, including those as complex as empathy, have their roots early in the emergence of life?

I do not believe it is *what* we feel, or even *how much* or *how quickly* we feel, such as my descriptions in the poem, that constitutes a problem. Emotions, feelings dwell within the substance of physical life. Rather, it's the way we choose to respond to our feelings—the beliefs we form and the actions we take—that shapes our lives.

Our Bodies Model the Teachings

Among our cells, neurons specialize in detecting information, every kind of information. Some detect pain, others the stretch of a muscle, or the movement of an object, or changes in temperature, each appropriate to its specific function. Immediate information about a specific original stimulus, however, remains useless to the organism. Additional input from other modalities or senses must be obtained and integrated for a human to operate as a complete organism, responding to a complex environment containing many sources of stimulation. The process of integration weaves together input from multiple sources—information from neurons detecting specific kinds of stimuli—into a whole. This integrated information provides what we need to determine an appropriate response.

For example, in a restaurant one evening, a tottering waiter crashes a complete place setting of dishes and glasses from the adjacent table. Rushing to his assistance, other waiters help him clean the debris as unobtrusively as possible. A few minutes later, you get up from your table and walk toward the restroom. A large fragment of a wine glass undetected in cleanup rips through your skin close to your ankle. You feel the blood oozing out and dripping down your foot. Sensing the pain, you quickly move to the restroom to rinse the wound and bind it. The information relaying pain gained higher priority than information about the colors of the carpet, the people you were passing as you walked from your table, the lighting in the room, etc. Its relevance superseded the relevance of other incoming information.

Message to the Reader

Each cell senses that which is relevant to it and transfers that information to an integrating site. Emotion, like yeast, leavens the bread of life. Imagine the sterility of life with no emotion. Equally abhorrent would be a rollercoaster life of drama and crises, in which you live totally subservient to the waxing and waning of your emotions. The nervous system is hard-wired to detect specific kinds of information, transmit its information and integrate it with information from other sources to create a whole "picture." In contrast, we must learn to regulate and integrate our capacities and emotions into the warp and weft of a stable life.

Let's examine your style of regulating your emotions.

Directions to the Reader

Locate your comfortable place for reflection.

Recall recently experiencing a strong emotion. Name the emotion: happiness, anger, surprise, fear, love, sadness, exuberance, jealousy, joy, envy, enthusiasm, guilt, gratitude, embarrassment, shame, pride, etc. Describe what you felt in that situation.

What action did you take in response to your feelings? For example, did you integrate your anger with the respect you feel for that individual and the level of trust you have for each other? Did you respond immediately, with no attempt to regulate or integrate your emotion—contact the person and proceed to scream at him or her? Or did you stuff down your feelings and tell yourself they are irrelevant? Describe your action.

Did your actions reflect the authentic, essential you? Did they help you create something that supports the authentic, essential you?

If the answer was "No" to the above, what was the impact of your actions in your life?

If you were to relive that situation now, feel the same emotions, what actions would you take?

IDENTIFY Discern your style, or different styles, of regulating your emotions.	**STEP 1**

Pure emotion arises quickly and decays quickly—as, for example, mine do as I watch a television advertisement and see the beautiful eyes in the face of a starving child. This dynamic feature characterizes the "feelings" part of emotion. In addition, we are familiar with emotions sustained over hours, days, weeks, months, years—even a lifetime. How does this happen? In addition to feelings, emotions evoke thoughts and build beliefs that sustain feelings through time. Regulating our emotions requires that we understand the dynamic aspect of pure feelings, allowing them to arise and then recede and, if sustained, seek the underlying thoughts and beliefs that continue to feed the emotion.

Message to the Reader

Once again, review a situation in which you experienced a strong emotion. Describe your feelings.

Directions to the Reader

How long did you stay in the emotional state? What circumstance(s) or person(s) supported you in staying in that emotional state?

What actions did you take?

What thoughts sustained your emotion?

"

What beliefs underlay the sustaining thought patterns?

"

"

If you were to relive that identical situation now, what actions would you take?

"

"

What thoughts would support you in taking that action?

"

_____

_____

_____

_____

_____

_____

_____

_____   ”

STEP 2   DISCOVER Become aware of the thoughts that sustain your emotions.

Shocked by the apparent suicide of Denise Denton, 46-year-old Chancellor of the University of California Santa Cruz, her colleagues, faculty and friends mourned their loss. An accomplished MIT-trained electrical engineer, the first female Dean of Engineering at a major research university, Denton worked to recruit and retain women in science and engineering. A recent recipient of the Maria Mitchell Women in Science Award, Denton used the power of her leadership to raise the visibility of obstacles faced by women in science and engineering. I served with Denise on the advisory board of a grant to recruit and retain women in science and engineering at the University of Wisconsin, her alma mater. A trailblazer and declared lesbian, Denton was hailed by students for her openness and advocacy. Others criticized her for employing her female partner in the UC system and for the considerable amount of money spent in renovating her living quarters on campus.

Message to the Reader

· *A woman with more accomplishments than you can imagine, leaps from the 44th floor of an apartment building in San Francisco, apparently taking her own life at 46 years of age. What was she experiencing that required such drastic ending of her life? The complexity and compelling nature of our emotions can delude and deceive us about possible options. One cannot help but imagine that this woman— intelligent, creative, and vibrantly alive—could have found some other way to handle her emotions instead of leaping to her death.*

Philosophers and psychologists debate now, and have debated for more than a century, the origin and nature of our emotions. How much of our emotional repertoire have we learned from our parents, siblings and friends?

Directions to the Reader

Review the previous two exercises, then name and describe the emotions you experienced.

"

"

Recall emotional times in your family as a child. What specific emotions do you recall being expressed by your mother, father, siblings or close friends? Describe the strongest ones.

"

"

Can you see any relationship between the emotions you described in the first exercises and those played out in your family? Write your insights.

"

STEP 3   EXPLORE   Traverse the emotional landscape you witness in your family setting.

Message to the Reader

Appreciating the learned components of our emotions can cause us to blame those from whom we learned them, or those who elicited the emotional response. When we are children, we almost automatically take on those beliefs and associated emotions projected toward us by family and others with whom we frequently interact. Such beliefs continue to operate on an out-of-awareness level and to shape out lives and influence our feelings and actions, until such time as we detect them and discard or reprogram them to be more appropriate for the adults we have become. Even as adults, we can react from those automatic response programs we learned as children, and can pick up emotions implanted in us by others. If, however, a component of emotions is learned, it can be unlearned and replaced with new, stronger emotional beliefs. A major step in disconnecting our past from our present is to forgive ourselves for taking on the influences and learned emotions of our family or others close to us. As stated earlier, we choose our responses to any given circumstance, so there is no blame to be laid. We were doing the best we knew how at the time, but now we know better. Regardless of others' or our past actions, there is no need for us to remain stuck in the past. Self-forgiveness allows us to release the emotional baggage and sets us free to open to new possibilities.

Directions to the Reader

In a very safe and calm place, relax and recall emotionally intense times of your childhood. Do not engage in this activity if you sense an extreme emotional response as you begin the exercise. You can participate by choosing a less emotionally intense interaction, one that does not cause you distress.

Imagine a specific scene and allow it to play out. Whom do you identify, recognizing the strong, and still present emotions brought forward from this individual?

What would you say to yourself to forgive yourself for taking on those emotions and

beliefs?

Sometimes the degree of offense does not permit forgiveness unless one receives support in going through the process. If this is the case, please do take advantage of a counselor, therapist or friend to work through the pain and release it. Only when you free yourself of such burden of blame will you be able to regulate your emotions and engage in those that promote the expression of your authentic, essential self.

Message to the Reader

The simple exercise above is likely to be insufficient to fully release the past, even if it was not traumatic. Research has demonstrated that writing about painful emotions, especially those that are difficult to talk about, allows the writer to release the pain. You begin the process of removing the emotional charge of situations, and of those people associated with the circumstances, to gain new insights into your emotional beliefs.

Directions to the Reader

What else calls to you for expression about the previous exercise involving forgiveness?

"

"

STEP 4 FORGIVE Absolve yourself of any wrong choices or actions in your past.

Message to the Reader

We can create a state of emotional well-being. I find researcher Barbara Fredrickson's "Broaden and Build" process of expanding positive emotions particularly potent. Fundamentally, positive emotions, such as "joy, interest, contentment, pride and love," help us broaden our beliefs, our routine ways of thinking and acting, into more expansive ones. Doing this, we develop new personal resources, new ways of responding, which can help us when we are faced with adversity. How does this work? For example, we experience joy and feel the urge to expand that experience into activities, such as playing, pushing against limits—not just physical and social limits, but also intellectual and creative limits. These might not be routine activities for us. Experiencing additional positive emotions, such as contentment, we incrementally build our resiliency, our ability to recover more quickly from adverse circumstances and negative emotions.

An analogy might be useful in understanding this process. The keyboard of the piano contains seven octaves (groups of eight). Suppose you learn to play on a mini-piano with only two octaves. Clearly, the range of expression would be restricted and the richness of the sound minimized. Suddenly, you discover a piano with four octaves. Now you can play music you could not have played on the two-octave piano. Delighted with the new sound, you then hear someone playing a piano with all seven octaves. Now the range of expression and richness of the sound exceeds everything else you have experienced or imagined. Learning to play with seven octaves, you have gained the ability to play more complex and interesting music, which is more exciting and fulfilling. You have expanded your repertoire beyond that which you initially experienced using only two octaves.

The continued experience of positive emotions, such as love, enhances our ability to find positive meaning in our circumstances and conditions. The accumulated benefits of experiencing positive emotions generate a sustained condition of positive outlook, demeanor and emotional well being, support our growth as individuals, and improve the quality of our relationships with others. Positive outlook and demeanor alter our mindsets, widen the scope of our attention, and increase our intuition, creativity and resilience to adversity. Lowered levels of cortisol, reduced inflammation in response to stress, resistance to viruses, reductions in stroke, and greater longevity are just some of the documented physical consequences of sustained emotional positivity. In general, we flourish: experience satisfaction with our lives, use flexible and broad thought and action patterns, engage in personal growth and development, and are resilient in the face of adversity.

Let's practice how to develop emotional well-being by experiencing positive emotions.

Describe a positive emotion that you have experienced recently.

Directions to the Reader

What activities did you engage in while you were experiencing the positive emotion?

How can we promote experiencing positive emotions? We cultivate positive emotions indirectly by looking for the positive meaning in current circumstances.

For the next day, observe your emotions. Do not try to alter them; simply observe them. What did you observe?

For the next day, consciously intend to find some positive meaning in the current circumstances that you face throughout the day. What did you do? What was the effect?

"

"

What would your life look like if you were "flourishing?"

"

"

CREATE Formulate a specific intention to experience positive emotions, finding uplifting meaning in your experiences.

STEP 5

Review what you have written above and identify what aspect of your flourishing life you want to create first. Be specific in identifying a goal, such as "I want to finish writing this workbook by the end of the month" or "I want to create a closer relationship with my friends in the next two months." Describe your goal.

Directions to the Reader

"

"

What positive meaning underlies your goal?

"

"

What positive emotions might you experience when you achieve your goal?

Once you've completed these exercises, write your commitment to accomplish your goal, including the designated time.

LINK Connect specific goals with positive emotions in order to flourish. **STEP 5**

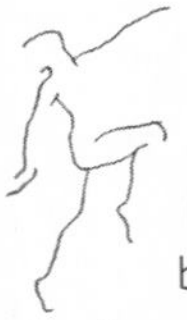

Our Bodies Model the Teachings

Each neuron senses its relevant stimuli, those that have "meaning" for it. The information from multiple neurons, each sensing different kinds of information, becomes integrated and transmitted to the command centers in the brain. We then make decisions.

Authenticity marks the activity of all the neurons, spiking in their own rhythms, recognizing their unique signals, transmitting information and interacting with others to create the "big picture." Meaning emerges at each level of activity.

Message to the Reader

Programmed to act in total alignment with their function, neurons model living from meaning, creating a sustained state of emotional well-being. This is their default program. In contrast, we must learn to live in a state of emotional well-being, some as adults, others, fortunately, as children.

Before concluding this chapter, let's review the central theme of the six steps:

STEP 1   IDENTIFY Discern your style, or different styles, of regulating your emotions.

STEP 2   DISCOVER Become aware of the thoughts that sustain your emotions.

STEP 3   EXPLORE Traverse the emotional landscape you learned from your family.

STEP 4   FORGIVE Absolve yourself of any wrong choices or actions in your past.

STEP 5   CREATE Formulate a specific intention to experience positive emotions, finding uplifting meaning in your experiences.

STEP 6   LINK Connect specific goals with positive emotions in order to flourish.

Following this step-by-step process, you will use your emotions to leaven the bread of your life and transform it. You will flourish. I'm not saying that you will never feel sad, angry or upset. I am saying that you will slowly see a shift from a pervasive feeling of not knowing what your life is about, experiencing emotions in isolation, to one in which you will fully engage in life, weaving your emotions into all aspects to create a life worth living, meaningful and, at times, even joyous.

Please join Joan in a further discussion of creating a flourishing life
http://www.cellular-wisdom.com

Want to ask questions? Go to Joan's blog
blog.beyond-success.com *and pose your question. Joan will answer you.*

Part Two
Process of Change-An Awakening

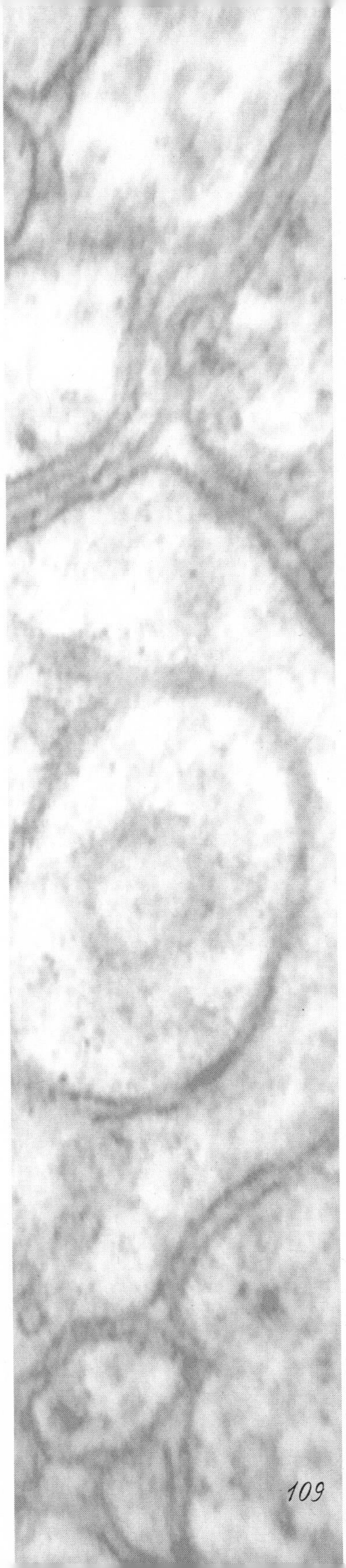

Who's There?

Who's there
behind the illusion?
Who are you
to be so afraid
of revealing yourself?
I see you hiding
behind me.
I want to know
you!

Won't you come out?
I will not judge
your brightness,
your cleverness,
your talents.

I yearn to know
the power
of your being,
the vastness
of your spirit,
the beauty
of your love.

Won't you come out?
Light the shadow
of my façade?
Find out where I hide?
Free the prisoner?

You are Spirit,
moving in and throughout,
freeing me to know
the One who's there.

We are wives, mothers, daughters, granddaughters, grandmothers, engineers, scientists, writers, painters, business owners, professionals, academics, nuns, leaders, followers, etc., etc., etc. Our roles have often defined us. They do not accurately define "*who* we are." Nonetheless, when our roles are stripped away or slip away, we find ourselves more or less "lost." It feels as though some part of ourselves has been lost when the role has disappeared.

When I left academia, I left behind all the dimensions of academic life, including my office and research laboratory. No longer would I frequent lecture halls, and teaching labs, or travel to review or site-visit grant applicants. All that was gone. In that moment, when I drove my packed car out of the medical school parking lot, that long-term career was over.

For others, the loss of a spouse, a position, a business, or a hometown drops our identity into a void. Such loss strips away our knowing of who we are.

We have so identified with our roles that we are unaware of the substance of who we truly are. We have lived most of our lives immersed in the dimensions of the roles we play, while the inner essence of our being has claimed little attention.

Directions to the Reader

"

With what roles in your life do you currently identify? Name and describe them here.

_____

_____

_____

_____

_____

_____

_____

_____

_____

_____

_____

_____

"

Directions to the Reader

How do your roles define you? For example, who are you as a wife? As a professional? As a daughter? As a business owner? Describe here how you see yourself in each of your multiple roles.

" "

Identifying with specific roles often leads to continually assessing how well we're doing in fulfilling our roles. If assessment leads to personal growth, it represents a valuable tool. For many of my coaching clients—and, for a time, for me as well—the continual assessment provided opportunities for critical self-judgment and condemnation of performance. So involved are we in analyzing, judging and criticizing our various role-performances that we literally lose our essential selves.

That happened to me after my years of serving as Chair, Center Director, Laboratory Leader, and more. My critical self almost suffocated my essential self. Fortunately, after leaving academia I was able to take the time to get to know myself, my essential self. The poem at the beginning of this chapter expressed my desire to leave the critical self behind and get to know the essential Joan King, the spiritual being devoid of any role, yet whole and integrated in every role I embraced. If the roles become our identities, as mine did, we subsume ourselves into the roles and lose the essential whole self. Then we must ask ourselves, "Who's there?"

Message to the Reader

Has your critical self eclipsed your essential self? Are you so busy analyzing and judging your performance in your roles that you are not living from your essential self?

HOW WILL YOU KNOW THIS?

When your critical self dominates, a sense of anxiety about how you're measuring up permeates whatever you do. You continually compare your role-performances to those of others. Are you the best manager? Are you the best mother? Your critical self most often answers, "No, you must do more and better and then maybe you'll measure up to the *others*."

Such judgment creates a feeling of "less than." This feeling literally blocks you from living from your essential self, from bringing your unique set of talents, capabilities and passions to particular activities and projects—to your life!

Comparison rules when your critical self dominates your essential self. Questions such as "How does my car compare with their car?" or "Is my office as large as hers?" or "Am I as well positioned to move up in the company as he or she is?" This internal critique creates duality in your world of self-assessment. You can never be like all those "others" out there and still be your authentic self. You lose the esssence of you when your critical self dominates. It's a hungry monster with an insatiable appetite. There is no meaning in this game. There will always be someone better than you in some aspect in your life. Furthermore, even if you were to become the best in all your roles, something would be significantly lacking. The phrase "Comparisons are odious," in use since the 14th century, encapsulates the futility of comparing yourself to others.

Directions to the Reader

What recording does your critical self play in your head? Does it ask questions you can't answer? Make you feel guilty or inadequate? Can you capture that critical voice's words and relate them here? Recognize that this is an exercise, and that you are naming the critical voice in order to bring awareness of who you are to the surface.

"

Comparisons completely distract us from the essence of our lives. They clog our mental energy, drain our emotional energy and conceal the magnificence of who we are.

Message to the Reader

Re-read the poem at the beginning of this chapter. Even if you do not think of yourself as a poet, go sit in a quiet place and use images to reveal messages to yourself. Then take those images and thoughts and put them down in a new way—the poet's voice. Can you write your own poem of "Who's there?" Do your best. Remember, this is a perfect example of not comparing. This is private, just for you, not for anyone else. Allow yourself some poetic license to know yourself, your true essence, in lines and phrases.

Directions to the Reader

”

STEP 1 CEASE COMPARING Comparisons hold us in bondage, as we continually measure who we are and what we do against others.

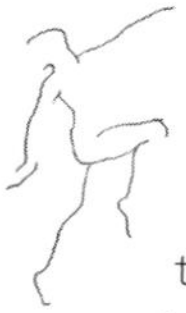

Our Bodies Model the Teachings

Cells and systems of our bodies continually sense and respond to our internal and external environments. Receptors for specific molecules embedded in the outer membranes of our cells inform the cells about the internal/external environments. Most importantly, the cells and systems of our bodies respond appropriately. This means that they respond in a fashion consistent with the nature of each specific cell or specific system. For example, in the visual cortex there are some neurons that only respond to an obliquely moving line. Others respond only to color. Some respond only to certain levels of light intensity. In each case the cells and systems respond in ways consistent with their essences, analogous to our essential selves.

Message to the Reader

Writing became a way for me to explore who I am. Reflecting on my ideas, feelings, experiences, and models, I opened to the fact that no one in the entire universe duplicates me. The opening question on my Web site www.beyond-success.com is "Who are you to deprive the world of your genius?"

This might at first glance appear arrogant. I chose this question as an opening because it expresses a universal truth we often ignore or deny. Each of us hums with a combination of tones and undertones of energy expressed as talents, interests, skills, and experiences. When we fail to express this energy because we are distracted by comparing ourselves to others or attempting to act or be like others, the whole world misses out on *our* tones. A hole results in the energetic fabric of the universe. "Who are you to deprive the world of your genius?" Have you ever thought it might be your unique expression that is the last piece of the puzzle to make some picture in the universe whole? Don't underestimate the importance of your presence in the world. Your uniqueness is required.

Let's get to know the essential you. Our natural propensities can be revealed by reflecting on things we loved as children.

Set up space in a room, on a table, with fun objects, such as play dough, yarn, a sketchbook, colored pens, anything that is attractive to you.

As you reflect on these questions answer them in creative ways. For example, you might first draw an answer in your sketchbook, before you craft words to reveal your thoughts, feelings and experiences.

I remember as a young child giving my cousins saltine crackers if they would sit down and let me stand up in front of them and talk to them. Truly, this constituted one of the things I most loved to do as a child, and it demonstrates my penchant for articulating concepts and having others listen to them. When I was standing in front of them I felt joyous, confident and grateful to be able to speak. I was standing at the center of my universe, at the center of my unique self.

Think back to your childhood. What activities did you love? What did you feel almost compelled to do because it took you toward the center of your being? Was it dress-up? Creating undersea communities in the yard? Dancing? As you think back, try to name three things that significantly stay at the top of your awareness. Name those three activities and how you chose to express them to family, friends, and maybe even strangers.

Directions to the Reader

Directions to the Reader

Describe how you felt when you engaged in each of these activities. If any one of the activities stood out for you, please name it here and describe why it dominated your childhood loves.

"

"

STEP 2 REMEMBER What you loved doing as a child, and how it made you feel, are clues to your authentic self.

Message to the Reader

Embedded in the desires we expressed as children lie some important clues to our essential selves. Particularly, our desires reveal fundamental values we hold dear.

I clearly value expressing ideas and communicating them to others by both the written and the spoken word. This value underlies the deep joy I experience in working in a coaching relationship with others as I articulate a value not previously recognized by my client, but revealed to me by their actions. The value, once articulated, brings clarity to a challenge or dilemma and allows the client to move more effectively through it to resolution in a way that is consistent with her essential self.

The following list of values, taken from the Coach Training and Certification Manual of Success Unlimited Network® http://www.successunlimitednet.com, is not exhaustive but is presented to stimulate your thinking about values.

Adventure

Aesthetics

Affection

Altruism

Appearance

Balance

Challenge/risk

Commitment

Community

Cooperation/teamwork

Control of time/immediate environment

Creativity

Flexibility

Friendship

Good working/living conditions

Holism

Home life

Independence

Inquiry

Integrity

Leadership

Mastery/achievement

Meaningful work

Money

Ownership

Personal discovery and development

Physical health

Pleasure (enjoyment, satisfaction, fun)

Privacy (solitude)

Quality

Recognition and feedback

Security

Service

Spirituality

Stability

Wisdom

Which of these values can you recognize in the activities you loved as a child? Is there one value that was dominant? Is that value dominant for you today?

Directions to the Reader

"

"

STEP 3   VALUE Your childhood desires emerged from values which were important to you. Become aware of these values.

Directions to the Reader

Recall times, regardless of the stage of life, when you felt deeply satisfied, as though you could say, with regard to what you were being or doing, "This is really me."

Go to a place that is particularly tranquil, and where you will not be disturbed. Quiet your conscious mind and do not let it lead this exploration. Imagine you are in a boat, floating on a cloud, drifting in a hot air balloon, or some favorite or fanciful mode of transportation. Give the command to land at any time in your life when you experienced being really you. Allow your heart to move your vehicle across the domain of your life.

Recall at least five such instances. Describe here who you were being and what you were doing at this time of deep satisfaction. Focus only on the positive aspects of these instances. Do not allow any negative aspects to intrude. Should they appear, simply dismiss them, and focus on the positive aspects of your feeling that "This is really me." It is best to do this exercise in one sitting.

Instance 1

"

_____

_____

_____

_____

_____

_____

_____

_____

_____

_____

_____

"

Instance 2

"

"

Instance 3

"

"

Instance 4

"

Instance 5

"

Look over these experiences once again. Describe how you feel as you recall them as a group. What is the common thread linking them?

Directions to the Reader

"

As you examine how you were being and what you were doing that made you feel so deeply satisfied in this group of five instances, describe what emerges about your essential self.

Directions to the Reader

"

| STEP 4 | KNOW What is deeply satisfying, deeply meaningful in your life, brings awareness of who you are. |

Sometimes, others witness our personal qualities and recognize them, while we do not. Interview three to five people who know you very well, and ask them these questions:

"What personal qualities do you see evidenced in my behavior?"

"Can you give me an example?"

"Under what circumstances would you ask me for help?"

"Why would you come to me for help in those circumstances?"

This list of personal qualities taken from the Coach Training and Certification Manual of Success Unlimited Network® http://www.successunlimitednet.com, is not exhaustive. The list may be helpful to those you interview in identifying your personal qualities. You may want to check off those they perceive as yours.

loyal	assertive	idealistic	logical
persistent	conscientious	resourceful	thrifty
determined	cooperative	intuitive	ambitious
objective	stable	thorough	inspiring
subjective	firm	centered	conceptual
reliable	optimistic	team player	quiet
personable	tactful	autocratic	stubborn
committed	tolerant	decisive	naive
permissive	honest	astute	fast learner
realistic	truthful	calm	courteous
analytical	modest	risk-taking	patient
reticent	courageous	empathetic	people oriented
positive	attentive to detail	generous	focused
articulate	sensitive	organized	individualistic
pensive	understanding	sincere	willing
dogmatic	unyielding	versatile	alert
confident	compatible	perceptive	authentic
punctual	instinctive	powerful	candid
cultured	helpful	self-controlled	curious
cheerful	forthcoming	purposeful	expressive
energetic	supportive	responsible	dynamic
fun	intelligent	results-oriented	playful
blunt	talkative	persuasive	spontaneous
democratic	diplomatic	flexible	sense of humor
outgoing	careful	enthusiastic	

Directions to the Reader

Record their comments here

"

"

Our Bodies Model the Teachings

The specialized function of each distinct system within the body depends upon the performance of other systems. Because of this specialization and cooperation, the organism as a whole thrives. For example, after the follicle in the ovary expels the egg, it collapses. New blood vessels grow into the collapsed follicle, helping to form the corpus luteum, which will secrete progesterone to help create an environment to nourish a fertilized egg. In this case, the endocrine system, including the follicle and corpus luteum within the ovary, depend upon the function of the vascular system to help form the corpus luteum after the ovum is expelled, and to distribute progesterone to needed organs, such as the uterus, to sustain pregnancy. This example of specialization and cooperation between body systems illustrates how important it is for each system to remain true to its function so that the whole organism can thrive. The follicle and corpus luteum in the ovary secrete hormones. Blood vessels transport nutrients. Increases in the number of blood vessels in the collapsed follicle help the corpus luteum to form by bringing needed nutrients so that the cells in the collapsed follicle can change into corpus luteum cells and secrete progesterone. Each system must remain true to its function for specialization and cooperation to operate.

APPRECIATE Honor your personal qualities and claim them as a resource. **STEP 5**

*Message to
the Reader*

*Like cells and systems, when we live from our essential selves we are aligned
with our purpose. As a result, when we live in alignment with purpose, we experience joy and meaning in our lives. The purpose of the endocrine system to
secrete hormones, and that of the blood supply to transport nutrients, are easily evident. We, too, find purpose by examining those times when we have felt
aligned with our essential self, experienced joy, and recognized meaning.*

*Directions to
the Reader*

Now it's time to put together your picture of your values, significant experiences and

personal qualities: to articulate your purpose—the passion that infuses your life with

energy and meaning.

Review all you have written in this chapter.

What themes emerge as interests you had as a child? Themes could be communica-

tion, entertainment, educating, playing, etc. What values ran through these themes?

Name the significant, meaningful experiences. What personal qualities can you see

emerging from this review? Are these life qualities present with you today, or are they

hidden, still waiting to emerge into your life purpose?

"

"

Pursuing purpose leads us to live a larger life. It leads us in directions we may never have anticipated. Inspired by purpose we actualize the potential that lies within.

From the story of my childhood speaking in front of my cousins, my value of leadership emerges. From the death of my father at age 10, a story I told in Chapter 1, the value of spirituality emerged strongly into my life. In significant, meaningful times, I experienced a taste of magnificence, such as when I spoke to the Theological Opportunities Program without knowing what I was going to say. Other significant events involved my using a path such as entering or leaving the convent. Some of my personal qualities are optimism, courage, idealism, empathy, enthusiasm, and expressiveness.

Reviewing this mosaic reveals me as a woman devoted to seeing greatness in others and choosing to help evoke that greatness in myself and in others. This energy fuels me.

With the mosaic in mind, what do your personal qualities tell you about your purpose in life? What and how have you chosen to express those qualities?

Directions to the Reader

Describe what emerges about your purpose here.

" "

PURPOSE Meld the mosaic pieces together and let them inform you of your purpose. **STEP 6**

It may take several reviews to meld the pieces together and allow them to show you the underlying purpose of your life, expressing who you really are, and loving it.

This exercise contains the seeds of meaning that can fuel your larger life.

It may help to review the steps of the process one more time to encourage purpose to come forth.

Before concluding this chapter, let's review the central theme of the six steps:

CEASE COMPARING Comparisons hold us in bondage, as we continually measure who we are and what we do against others. **STEP 1**

REMEMBER What you loved doing as a child, and how it made you feel, are clues to your authentic self. **STEP 2**

STEP 3   VALUE Your childhood desires emerged from values which were important to you. Become aware of these values..

STEP 4   KNOW What is deeply satisfying, deeply meaningful in your life, brings awareness of who you are.

STEP 5   APPRECIATE Honor your personal qualities and claim them as a resource.

STEP 6   CREATE Meld the mosaic pieces together and let them inform you of your purpose.

The single key of purpose is to find it and live it. When you are about your purpose, day by day, moment by moment, your life is painted on the greatest canvas possible. The exercises in this chapter focus your awareness and lead you to discover your purpose. The golden key of purpose opens doors you might never have identified otherwise. It allows you to see what you might never have seen and identify who you are now. Your allies will be drawn to you and your purpose, and will come to be a part of that adventure with you. Never underestimate the power of purpose.

 Please join Joan in a further discussion of using this set of steps to create an abundant life of great possibility at http://www.cellular-wisdom.com

Want to ask questions? Go to Joan's blog blog.beyond-success.com *and pose your question. Joan will answer you.*

Who Am I Becoming?

The hard mouth,
incapable of laughter,
the cold, dark eyes,
scrutinizing me
in the mirror:
Who am I becoming?

The shrill voice,
too loud,
striking out:
Who am I becoming?

My cold heart
withdraws
from people:
Who am I becoming?

Stress exacts its toll. Sustained stress threatens our very being.

The face in the mirror: could that be my reflection? The hard mouth, cold and dark eyes: how could that be me? Did I really speak that way, with shrill voice, too loud, striking out? Was my heart freezing, pushing others away?

The burden of stress pressed on me, squeezing precious life out of my being. I was dying from the pressures of demands. My creative years as Chair complete, I transformed into a mere manager. I managed staff, managed new facilities, managed faculty, and answered to administrators. Staff wanted me to be available for every issue, every problem, every dispute, disregarding the department managers. Faculty wanted me to drive their agendas. The deans of the medical, dental and veterinary schools demanded that I keep each of their agendas in the forefront. When they failed to detect progress they pursued me, relentlessly. The pain of their incessant demands tore into my being. They were the predators, I the prey. By the end of each day, I collapsed into a pile of incoherent, painful shreds. I hated it. The pain grew, the feast of others' needs consuming me continued, and I was becoming someone I did not know.

Message to the Reader

Situations like the one I lived through develop over time. Only after I spent three rather fulfilling years creating new initiatives, programs, etc. did the painful phase of my chairmanship emerge. However, within the next two years, I experienced the transformation described above. Shocked into realizing what I was becoming, I knew I could no longer tolerate the situation. I decided to leave.

Do you recognize any of these elements operating in your life currently?

STEP I RECOGNIZE Address the source of pain in your life.

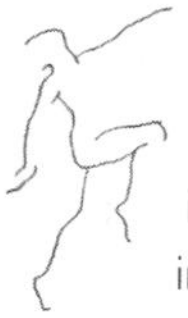

Our Bodies Model the Teachings

Pain signals action in the body. In fact, pain was the first stimulus for action in evolution. Simple cells floating in supportive aquatic environments engaged in all the activities of a cell: nutrition, reproduction, etc. However, harmful, noxious, compounds signaled the cell to move away from its environment and, eventually, to protect itself in many ways.

Pathways capable of transmitting pain signals extend throughout the human body and use different mechanisms to ensure its recognition. Pain communicates dysfunction, disharmony, requiring action. Pathways for sharp pain —such as is experienced when one steps on a nail—engage reflexes to pull the foot away from the dangerous object. Other, evolutionarily older, pathways carry the prolonged ache associated with pain.

The pairing of pain and action reverberates through all species. Retreating from pain constitutes the first action. Pain ignored induces damage to the body.

Consciousness allows us to conceal that which we do not wish to recognize. Not so in the body.

Message to the Reader

Directions to the Reader

Go to a place of comfort to explore your inner landscape. Settle in and know that you can address whatever emerges.

Is there a source of pain in your life? Describe it.

"

"

What impact is that pain having on you now? Who are you becoming?

"

"

APPRECIATE There is value in knowing that pain is a symbol, the messenger, that something in your life needs to change. **STEP 2**

*Directions to
the Reader*

When the body detects pain, it takes action, if possible, to remove the source of pain.

What actions have you taken to remove the source of your pain?

"

_____

_____

_____

_____

_____

_____

_____

_____

_____

_____

_____

_____

_____

"

What actions *could* you take to remove the source of pain?

"

_____

_____

_____

_____

_____

_____

_____

_____

_____

_____

"

IDENTIFY Be specific in naming the actions you could take to remove the source of pain. **STEP 3**

You may have already addressed the major source of continual, sustained stress causing pain in your life. You have gotten the divorce, remarried, left the job, taken the job of your dreams, moved to another highly desired location, etc. Nonetheless, stress remains an integral part of our lives. Some stress enhances performance, while excessive stress diminishes it. Learning to recognize moderate and optimal levels of stress, and using it to create vibrant lives, ushers in a new depth of doing and being.

Message to the Reader

Our Bodies Model the Teachings

The body sustains a balance between activating and calming influences in the body by the complimentary activities of the two divisions of the autonomic (think, automatic) nervous system: the sympathetic and the parasympathetic nervous systems. Walking home alone at night we hear footsteps behind us. Suddenly, we realize that few other people are on the street. The darkness of the patch before us looms large. Our hearts beat faster, our blood pressure rises. We are ready for action. This represents the physiological responses of the sympathetic nervous system. We reach our destination, unlock the door, turn on the lights, relock the door, and sink into our beloved, soft couch. We calm down. This calming response represents the action of the parasympathetic nervous system. The dance of these components of the autonomic nervous system maintains balance in our bodies.

While some stress prepares us for action and increases performance, too much stress or sustained stress induces dysfunction and eventually illness. Learning to recognize the "sweet spot" of just the right amount of stress to enhance our performance underlies our capacity to create a vibrant, exuberant life.

Message to the Reader

WITNESS Notice what creates too little, too much, and optimal stress on you and your life activities. **STEP 4**

In this exercise, you will identify specific circumstances in which you experienced various amounts of stress and recall the impact of those stressors on your performance. *Too little stress* reflects little motivation or arousal and no inducement to take action. Consider a circumstance at work or at home when you planned to perform a certain

Directions to the Reader

action; however, no urgency accompanied your desire, no deadline loomed large and, ultimately, you did not perform the action. Describe your scenario of too little stress.

Describe your internal experience in this circumstance.

Describe the impact of your internal processing on your external productivity.

"

_____

_____

_____

_____

_____

_____

_____

_____

_____

_____

_____
"

Too much stress reduces performance. Recall a different circumstance at work or at home when you experienced a deadline that seemed impossible to meet. You had no access to the materials or other resources you needed, or were blocked from proceeding in some way by your colleagues, family or friends, or whatever other circumstances contributed to the excess of stress.

Message to the Reader

Describe your scenario of too much stress.

"

_____

_____

_____

_____

_____

_____

_____

_____

_____

_____
"

Describe your internal experience in this circumstance.

"

"

Describe the impact of your internal processing on your external productivity.

"

"

Message to the Reader

Optimal stress induces optimal productivity. Recall a circumstance at home or at work when you experienced the "sweet spot"—just the right amount of stress to maximize your productivity. Maybe you were about to give a talk and experienced a tingling of excitement mixed with a bit of anxiety. As you walked on stage and stood before the audience, your excitement infused vitality into your speech. You could feel the audience responding, listening deeply to your ideas. As you ended the speech, you knew it touched your audience. You could feel the positive impact as they began to stand up and applaud.

Identify your experience of optimal stress.

Describe your optimal stress scenario.

"

"

Describe your internal experience in this circumstance.

"

"

Describe the impact of your internal processing on your external productivity.

"

"

Now that you've reviewed circumstances in which each of the three parameters of stress, too little, too much, and optimal stress, were operative, take time to compare your internal experiences.

Directions to the Reader

What do you notice that is different about experiencing optimal stress?

"

"

Can you moderate too little stress and too much stress and transform them into the "sweet spot" of optimal stress? Unequivocally, the answer is YES! Today we do not normally experience raging tigers attacking us unexpectedly, inducing high levels of stress. Most of the stress we experience emerges from our perception of danger, rather than the presence of danger itself.

A gift of a visit with my mother in New Orleans for my birthday delighted me. My duties as Chair of the Department and Director of the Research Center demanded I spend only a few days there. Arriving in New Orleans, we left the airport and stopped at a restaurant for a quick meal. I called to tell my aunt, who was with my mother, that we were in town. "Quickly," she said, "come quickly." Bolting our food, we dashed out and rushed across the Mississippi River Bridge. A slip of a woman now, my mother was hooked to an oxygen tank. Her skeletal face with dark black circles under her eyes revealed undeniably her condition.

Her doctor suggested we call hospice. I hardly noticed how many days passed, as each came and went. She let me rub her back from time to time. The intimacy warmed my heart and, I hoped, hers—until the last day, when she signaled, "No, don't rub my back any more." Later that night, just as I left the room, she died. Burial and funeral arrangements occupied the next few days. In all, I was away for two weeks. How my perception changed! Originally, I thought I could only spare two days away from my busy office.

That experience revealed to me how I had created my own prison of stress. During the two weeks I was away, everything got taken care of back at work. The world did not collapse because I was away for two weeks. Our perceptions create stress.

The understanding that we create stress because of our perception gives us the power to change the perception, resulting in a change in the experience of stress. The first line of action is to determine how much you must do and when can you simply say, "Not now."

Message to the Reader

Think of some times when, after the fact, you realized you could have said "No."

Directions to the Reader

I learn much from observing my husband. "Not a chance," he laughs, when someone asks him to do more than he can handle at the time.

When was the last time you simply said "No" to a request. We women often think we have more energy than ten horses and can do anything. While this is true at inner levels, in the world of observable energy, limitations exist.

Message to the Reader

FORMULATE Learn how you would say "No" to requests that would create conditions of excess stress.   **STEP 5**

Recall here some circumstance in which you agreed to do something, but later realized that someone else could have done it, or that it simply was not necessary that you do it, or do it when requested. Describe one of those times.

Directions to the Reader

Struggling, you accomplished what was requested. However, you also learned something about how you could have said "No" or "Not now, later, or maybe." Describe what you learned.

How would you respond, today, faced with the same request?

A different strategy—Moderating stress by changing your perception.

> CHANGE A small shift in your perceptions can convert conditions of **STEP 6** excess stress into conditions of optimal stress.

How can you go about moderating stress by moderating your perception of it? People have developed many different strategies to change their perception of situations. In one strategy for example you create a plan to meet a stressful deadline and then eliminate as many other activities as possible to allow you to follow the plan and meet the deadline. Focusing my energy on implementing the plan to meet the specific challenge works effectively for me and for many of my clients.

You may have employed strategies to reduce stress, such as consulting with someone, talking over the problems with friends and trusted allies, hiring someone to help you meet the challenge, or obtaining additional training so that you could meet the challenges with appropriate strategies.

Recall a circumstance in which you effectively transformed a stressful circumstance into a less stressful one by taking an action. Describe the action you took. *Directions to the Reader*

Other ways to expand your repertoire of strategies to moderate and transform stress become apparent as you interview other people and find out what strategies they use to deal with excess stress.

Identify three people whom you believe effectively handle stress. Contact them and request a 15-minute interview. Formulate the questions you want to ask before you speak with them. The questions may include ones such as: "How do you handle particularly stressful situations?" "Do you have a strategy to transform particularly stressful situations into less stressful ones?" "What strategies work best for you?" Formulate the questions you plan to ask in the interview.

Identify the three people you will interview and write in the dates and times you will interview them.

What strategies have you discovered from your interviews?

Which of these strategies might you use to modify and transform stress, and how will you adapt them to your unique approaches so that they will work for you?

Armed with these methodologies, how would you meet the challenges of a stressful situation, alter your perception of the stress and create the conditions of optimal stress and maximal productivity?

"

Anchoring our insights, we have discovered how to make optimal stress work for us. We create who we are, moment by moment, by each decision that we make. While we do not control the circumstances occurring in the world, we control our responses to them.

Before concluding this chapter, let's review the central theme of the six steps:

STEP 1   RECOGNIZE Know the sources of pain in your life.

STEP 2   APPRECIATE There is value in knowing that pain is a symbol, the messenger, that something in your life needs to change.

STEP 3   IDENTIFY Name specific actions you could take to remove the source of pain.

STEP 4   WITNESS Be the observer of the impact of too little, too much, and optimal stress on you and your life activities.

STEP 5   FORMULATE Practice saying "No" to requests that would create conditions of excess stress.

STEP 6   CHANGE Shift your perceptions and convert conditions of excess stress into conditions of optimal stress.

Equipped with this information and experiencing this knowledge, you can claim and create a life of *optimal* stress. By practicing these exercises, you will gain great facility in choosing the stresses, changing your perception of them, and creating a life of optimal stress.

Please join Joan in a further discussion of using this set of steps to create an abundant life of great possibility at http://www.cellular-wisdom.com

Want to ask questions? Go to Joan's blog blog.beyond-success.com *and pose your question. Joan will answer you.*

Ask For Help

The deadline looms.
The clock ticks.
I am working
as hard as I can.
Will I make it?

Working from
dawn til midnight,
driving on
into a new day,
everything else
forgotten.
The clock ticks on.
Will I make it?

Anxious,
I push
harder and harder,
bargaining with time
to create
an illusory promise
of more time later.

Will I make it?

As I worked harder and harder, pushed and drove myself, feeling anxious, I did not **think** of asking for help. I was not alone. In a 1999 survey of Women in Neuroscience, I asked women whether they sought help when they knew they needed it. The answer: only 38% responded "Yes," while 35% responded that they **never** request help.

What is it that keeps us from asking for help? I remember reading about "the imposter phenomenon" when I was Chair, and wondered whether I was an "imposter?" High achieving women who feel fraudulent, doubting that their achievements result from their ability, exemplify the "imposter." Are we afraid to ask for help because someone might find out that we are imposters?

Even with my knowledge of how cells continually discard what they no longer need and how diverse cells collaborate to execute functions, I did not recognize the analogy for my own life. My fear of being "not good enough" drove me to work harder and longer and take on more.

Message to the Reader

Fear of failure underlies the imposter phenomenon. The imposter, not believing in her ability to meet challenging situations effectively, conjures up calamitous scenarios in which she will be exposed publicly as incompetent and fraudulent. Regardless of our strengths and skills, we perceive ourselves as lacking in self-efficacy and cringe at the thought of asking for help, which might expose our feared inadequacies.

Directions to the Reader

Find a comfortable space in which you feel safe and secure. Assemble the materials, journal, etc. and reflect on these questions. Have you ever felt like an "imposter," achieving success, but fearing that the success did not result from the use of your abilities and that sooner or later someone would find out that you have "feet of clay"? Describe the circumstance.

What were you thinking and feeling in this circumstance?

"

"

RECOGNIZE Reflect on yourself. Are you living with a belief in the "imposter phenomenon?" **STEP 1**

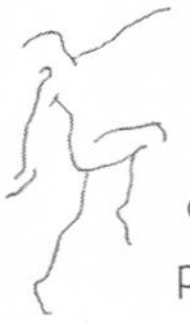

Our Bodies Model the Teachings

Individual cells continually discard that which is no longer useful to them. In development, those neurons that do not connect with other neurons die. This principle of discarding whatever is no longer useful prevails at all levels in the body.

Message to the Reader

Holding an "imposter" attitude, lacking a sense of competence in managing our environment or making effective use of the opportunities that surround us, we can be described as low in "environmental mastery." Should we continue to hold these dis-empowering attitudes, our success remains quasi-stable with failure lurking behind every challenge. Fortunately, we can change. We can discard our dis-empowering attitudes, learn to appreciate our skills and strengths, and take advantage of opportunities in our environment we may not have seen previously, including asking for help*, and increasing our compassion for ourselves.*

How do we go about learning self-compassion?

Self-compassion replaces self-judgment with self-kindness, isolation from others with identification with others—as members of the human race and subject to its frailties—and mindfulness of the whole of one's being versus over-identification with a specific failure.

We increase self-compassion when we relinquish the scathing judgment of our inadequate performance and consider that everyone at some time makes mistakes and fails. In fact, those who enjoy significant success attribute much of their success to learning from their failures.

Directions to the Reader Find a comfortable and safe space and create conditions so that you will not be disturbed for the next period of time. Recall a circumstance in which someone you know and care for experienced failure and you helped her or him in some way. What were your feelings toward that person? Describe them.

_____

_____

_____

_____

_____

_____

_____

_____

_____

_____

_____

What did you do to help that person?

_____

_____

_____

_____

How did the person respond to your help?

❝

❞

Did you feel compassion for the person and her or his experience of failure?

❝

❞

Now recall a failure you experienced. Describe it.

In your imagination assume two roles: you as the person experiencing failure and you

as a friend helping. What do you, the person experiencing failure, want to say?

What's important for you to tell your friend?

What do you, as friend and helper, say to you, the one experiencing failure? What's important for you to tell her, the person experiencing failure?

"

"

People who practice exercises like this for a month develop greater self-compassion. In turn, greater self-compassion reduces anxiety and increases well-being. The misrepresentation of our abilities characteristic of the imposter phenomenon gives way to a realistic appraisal of our strengths and talents.

INCREASE   Self-compassion and self-confidence enhance your well-being and amplify all aspects of your higher self.   **STEP 2**

Understanding our failures, as well as our successes, as part of the larger human condition, promotes self-compassion and connectedness with others. Similarly, connectedness with others promotes self-compassion.

Message to the Reader

As women, we highly value connecting with others. One type of interpersonal relationship—that between more experienced and less experienced individuals, mentors or coaches—can help us (the mentees/coachees) recognize our strengths and talents and realize our potential. In specific circumstances, our mentor or coach may be our mother, friend, business associate, boss or an esteemed leader in our field. Mentors and coaches serve many functions, such as helping us to appreciate our strengths and talents, to expand our perspective, to understand our perfectionism as maladaptive or useful, to construct realistic goals rather than unrealistic ones likely to increase the imposter phenomenon, and to increase our sense of belonging. Mentors may open doors for us, providing opportunities for connections not otherwise available. Coaches help us appreciate our strengths and talents by reviewing with us times when we have been successful, and by offering assessments that confirm specific talents and strengths. Empowered mentoring or coaching provides an opportunity for the collaboration natural to us as women.

Directions to the Reader

Given the documented benefits of mentoring and, recently, of coaching, you may want to identify several people whom you admire and contact them requesting to speak with them about the possibility of their serving you as mentor or coach. Analyzing effective mentor-mentee relationships, trust arises as a very important variable. When talking with a prospective mentor or coach, be aware of whether you feel you could trust this person. Reflect on these questions. Do you have a mentor or coach? If so, do you trust her/him? Is s/he effective in working with you? That is, does s/he listen to your concerns, provide feedback, help you clarify your goals and refine your strategies to reach those goals in ways that are resonant with your authentic self? Write your answers.

If you do not have a mentor or coach, or if your current mentor or coach does not fulfill your expectations, clarify what you are looking for in a mentor or coach, or what you want your mentor or coach to help you with.

"

"

How do you identify a potential mentor or coach? Areas likely to yield a potential mentor include: within your organization, within a professional organization of which you are a member, connected to you by friendship, or someone with whom you could connect through a friend. Coach profiles can be found at the International Coach Federation http://www.coachfederation.org. You can search the database "Find a coach," putting in the parameters that are important for you, such as location, experience, coaching certification, coaching niche, etc. Contact information is provided. The possibilities are endless. Be proactive in looking for someone who could potentially fulfill your expectations. Talk to people about looking for a mentor or coach. Identify several people as potential mentors or coaches. Write their names.

"

Generate the questions you will ask in your informational interview with a potential mentor or coach. Begin the interview by telling your potential mentor what you admire about her or him and why you would want her/him as a mentor. In the case of a coach, describe what about her or him attracted you to request an interview. Clarify what you are looking for in a mentor or coach. Describe the kind of interaction you are looking for—such as meeting on a weekly, monthly, quarterly or yearly basis in person, talking via telephone, communicating via e-mail—and what you want the mentor or coach to help you with.

Directions to the Reader

Write your outline for the informational interviews here, including all the elements above: potential mentors/coaches' names, why you would want each of them to serve as your mentor or coach, followed by what you are looking for in a mentor or coach, the kind of interactions you would like, what you want them to help you with, etc.

Whom will you contact and when?

What was the outcome of your interaction with your potential mentors or coaches?

Did you identify a mentor or coach with whom you want to work? If so, when will your mentoring or coaching relationship begin? How will you be able to tell that the relationship is producing the results you desire? Write the answers to these questions.

"

_____

_____

_____

_____

_____

_____

_____

_____

_____

_____

_____

"

If your first endeavors to find a mentor or coach who resonates harmoniously with you and will work with you fails, do not be discouraged. It may take some time to find the right person, but investing energy in the search will pay off for you in multiple ways. Repeat the identification strategies and exercises above. If you find that your anxiety about your performance and your perfectionism stops you from moving forward in pursuing a mentor or coach, it may be appropriate for you to seek psychotherapy. Unlike in the past, today we understand the value of psychotherapy and its contribution to psychological well-being, so that the stigma of the past no longer exists.

Ask your primary doctor, close friends or family members about recommendations for psychotherapists. Research them to determine whether they might be appropriate to help you. Clarify what you want help with and what results you would like to produce. Find the help you need.

STEP 3   CONNECT We are not islands. We are all connected. From that place of knowing, find your perfect mentor or coach.

WORK As your relationship with a mentor or coach develops, you work from a place of support.	**STEP 4**

Our Bodies Model the Teachings

Cells not only discard what they do not need, they reach out for what they do need, via connection. If you remove cells from the body and put them in a petri dish with nutrients, within minutes they are reaching out to connect with each other. In the body, few results are produced by single cells; most come from cells acting in concert. For example, neurons are supported by non-neural cells, glia, which are ten times more abundant than neurons and nourish them. Neurons connect with other neurons to transmit information from the outside world to allow us to see, taste, smell and, from our intentions, to progress into actual movement. One single neuron is incapable of doing this. Collaboration and cooperation represent hallmarks of our cells' success.

Collaboration and cooperation are also hallmarks of our success, personally and professionally. Collaborations provide opportunities to fuse two different expert perspectives, appreciate each expert's contribution, and expand the knowledge and perspective of each.

Message to the Reader

Have you engaged in collaborative projects in your personal or professional life? If so, describe your most recent collaborations.

Directions to the Reader

"
_____

_____

_____

_____

_____

_____

_____

_____

_____

_____

_____

_____
"

What benefits did you derive from your collaborations?

Message to the Reader *If you have not engaged in collaborations in the last year, now is the time to explore how collaborations could benefit you, personally or professionally.*

Directions to the Reader

Identify an area in your life that could benefit from collaboration with someone else.

What do you want from the collaboration?

Directions to the Reader

Identify someone with whom you would like to collaborate on this initiative. Contact her or him and inquire about the possibility of beginning the collaboration. Whom did you contact, and what did you learn?

"

"

Message to the Reader

What makes collaboration successful? In my experience successful collaborations provide benefits to both parties. If the collaboration lacks reciprocity, it may result in one individual feeling taken advantage of, causing resentment. Avoiding this requires that each person be clear about what she or he wants from the collaboration, but also how she or he wants to work together with the other. Several factors determine successful collaborations. One such factor, personal style, can have enormous impact. People with different styles may find it difficult to work together seamlessly. For example, some people like to make decisions early and proceed with strategy while others would prefer to explore many options and not make decisions until they feel they have exhausted all possibilities. Further, some people think individually and then share what they have conceived. Others cannot sit in a room alone and conceive of new ideas, but must interact with others to develop ideas. Some require deadlines to ensure progress, others resent deadlines, preferring a more open unfolding of the project. Know and appreciate your style and that of the people you are considering as collaborators.

Directions to the Reader

Appreciate your style of collaborating. Describe it.

What is the style of the person with whom you are thinking of collaborating? Describe it. If you do not know her or his style, ask the person about it, then describe it.

Another factor deserving of consideration is how many collaborators you work with most effectively. Given your personal preferences, do you work optimally one-on-one with a single collaborator, or would a team effort offer you greater opportunities, personally and professionally?

STEP 5   APPRECIATE When you value your style of collaboration and that of a potential collaborator, appreciation is the focus that expands your process and results.

Bringing together the results of these exercises, articulate a specific personal or professional collaborative project and the goal of the collaboration.

Directions to the Reader

Identify your collaborator(s) and their styles of collaboration and communication, their skills or experience that complements yours, and what you hope to gain from the project.

Envision the duration of the project and how you will initiate, communicate, proceed and complete the project.

"   How will you evaluate the success of the project?

_____

_____

_____

_____

_____

_____

_____

_____

_____

_____

_____

_____

_____

_____   *"*

| EMBARK Begin a collaboration, cognizant of the goal and all the parameters you have defined to promote a successful collaboration. | **STEP 6** |

Before concluding this chapter, let's review the central theme of the six steps:

RECOGNIZE The "imposter phenomenon" is a misrepresentation of your strengths and talents.	**STEP 1**
INCREASE With self-compassion, expand your realization that you are a part of the larger human condition.	**STEP 2**
CONNECT Your are not alone. Partner with a mentor or coach.	**STEP 3**
WORK With a mentor or coach, you are supported in your inner and outer work.	**STEP 4**
APPRECIATE When you value your style of collaboration and that of a potential collaborator, the focus is in appreciation.	**STEP 5**
EMBARK Begin a collaboration, cognizant of the goal and all the parameters you have defined to promote a successful collaboration.	**STEP 6**

Following this template you will leave behind the "imposter," the anxious person fearing failure. You will increase compassion for yourself and, understanding the larger human condition, connect with and work with a mentor or a coach to clarify your strengths, identify realistic goals and effective strategies, appreciate how you can work most effectively with a collaborator, appreciate your style of collaboration, explore potential collaborators, understand their styles, and embark on an empowering collaboration, cognizant of all the factors that will ensure its success. In this manner you will move from isolation to connectedness to enjoy the richness of connection, and expand your knowledge and perspectives.

 Please join Joan in a further discussion of coming to appreciate your strengths and talents and using them in collaboration with others to create successful projects at http://www.cellular-wisdom.com.

Want to ask questions? Go to Joan's blog blog.beyond-success.com *and pose your question. Joan will answer you.*

Part Three
Claim Your Essence

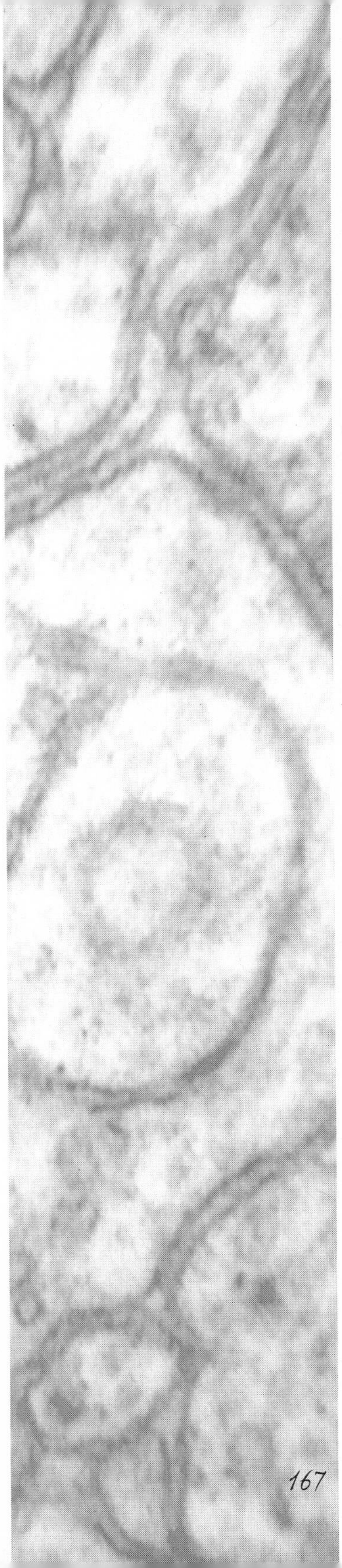

Passion and Purpose

The ocean, vast and blue,
sparkling
in the Hawaiian sunlight
called out to me,
"Yes, you can."

I felt my spirit expand
into the vastness of the ocean
and I knew
I could
swell the passion of my heart
into waves of silent purpose
to become the vastness of
One.

I could choose
who I become.

As a child, I dreamed of many adventures: as a dancer, pianist, teacher, writer and more. In high school, I danced in the carnival ball, sang in the glee club and choir club, served as the business manager of the yearbook, wrote articles for the school newspaper, and acted in the drama club. In the convent, I went to college, learned to teach and do research. Everything evaporated when I left the convent. The vista of my life loomed large before me. Who would I become? What was I passionate about? What was my real purpose?

Curiosity about people led me to a graduate program in psychology. Looking for the neural basis of behavior led me to examine brain structure and function: neuroscience. Research and teaching, once again, filled the years. The challenge and stress of being Chair, however, weighed upon me, and sent me into the depths of my being, looking for my truth, my integrity. When I left behind academia, once again everything familiar evaporated. Once again, the vista of my life loomed large before me. Who would I become? What stirred in me was a passion for something I had not yet named. That passion would lead me to my life's purpose. I was about to step out onto the path that would lead me to both: passion and purpose.

The poem wrote itself as I gazed across the ocean, looking for who I would become. I was taking a writing class on the Island of Hawai'i at Kalani Honua, meaning literally, Earth-Heaven, or more like Heaven on Earth. My first writing class on Monhegan Island off the coast of Maine, and this class in Hawai'i, provided opportunities to explore who I was beneath all the roles I had assumed and, most importantly, who I wanted to become. I wrote a lot about my childhood, the convent and academia. I was suspended in "between time," no longer there but not yet somewhere else.

I knew the qualities I wanted to radiate. I collected quotations about wisdom, strength, peace, love, vastness. Each day I would read one of these to focus my energies upon those qualities, which I wanted to radiate. This process infused me with a deep calm about my future.

Biographies and autobiographies became the substance of my explorations into possible directions for myself. Books by or about women such as Mother Teresa, Eleanor Roosevelt, and Helen Keller were the textbooks where I looked for the answers to my questions: How did they find their future? How did they become who they were? My understanding that we sculpt who we are moment by moment, by every decision we make and every thought we think, slowly unfurled. I could choose who I would become by the focus of my thinking and the decisions upon which I would act. Even with my knowledge of how our cells continually discard what they no longer need and how diverse cells collaborate to execute functions, I was slow to recognize the analogy for my own life, and how my fear of being "not good enough" had driven me to work harder and longer and to take on more.

Understanding that we create who we are brings enormous responsibility for our thoughts and our actions.

Message to
the Reader

What thoughts or decisions have you been entertaining for the last six months? Are these thoughts centered in a passionate desire to do something? Learn about something? Were these thoughts centered around how you have wanted to express yourself to the world? Name those thoughts and passions.

Directions to
the Reader

"

_____

_____

_____

_____

_____

_____

_____

_____

_____

_____

_____

_____

"

What impact did these thoughts and actions create in you, on who you are, now? How do the stirrings within you drive you in your passions to do? To become? Name how that passion looks when clothed in purpose.

Directions to
the Reader

"

_____

_____

_____

_____

”

STEP 1 BE ALERT Pay attention to your thoughts. They are the key to your ability to navigate in life.

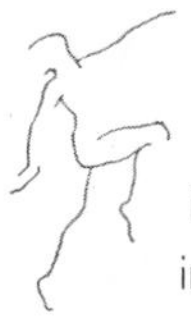

Our Bodies Model the Teachings

A script for development guides how all the different cell types in our bodies divide, migrate and interact with other cells. The environment of the cells interacts with this inner script to create a harmonious community of cells, tissues and organs working together seamlessly. This script is the passionate dance of our cells in their purpose of expressing themselves as our bodies.

Message to the Reader

When we tune into our inner script, we too can find the program that maximizes our potential. The life force within cells constitutes the source of the script. It never abandons us and remains always available. It contains the code of our vastness, the seed of our purpose.

Directions to the Reader

Assemble some tools: a journal, pens or pencils, and retreat into a comfortable space where you will not be disturbed. Who are the people, currently living, historical or mythic, who influence you? What about them do you admire? Do/did they live passionate, purposeful lives? What qualities in their lives demonstrate this?

“

What qualities do you want to radiate from the essence of your being?

Directions to the Reader

*Directions to
the Reader*

Review the earlier exercise of your thoughts and actions of the last six months. Do these align with and reflect the qualities that you want to radiate?

If not, what thoughts and actions would you engage in, in those particular circumstances, to emulate the qualities you want to create?

> IDENTIFY Become aware of the qualities you want to radiate, and
> determine which thoughts and actions reflect those qualities.   **STEP 2**

Our Bodies Model the Teachings

Cells possess all they need to activate their inner script. Rarely do cells deviate from their script. When they do, however, dysfunction, disease, and death result. This occurs when deleterious circumstances alter the script, such as radioactive exposure. In this circumstance, the cells fail to fulfill their potential. Normally, cells enact their inner script uninterrupted.

When we discover that we have deviated from our inner script, we have the opportunity to clarify and define the qualities that would allow us to develop to our full potential. Sometimes, we retreat from or confuse specific qualities or characteristics that attract us.   *Message to the Reader*

The question "Who are you to deprive the world of your genius?" on the homepage of my coaching web site *www.beyond-success.com* reflects my philosophy that each of us possesses an inherent genius that is unique. Expression of our genius may require courageous thoughts and decisions to activate the script. For example, the characteristic "power" can refer to "the ability to do or act; capability of doing or accomplishing something," as defined by Random House Webster's unabridged dictionary. This definition of power aligns with the concept of self-efficacy or personal agency. A very different definition is "the possession of control or command over others; authority," also from Random House Webster's unabridged dictionary. Women often find the nuance of "power" abhorrent, because of the distortion of power into the use of force or might in our society and our world. Unfortunately, resisting the notion of embracing our true inner power undermines our potential to make the contribution that each of us can make and no one else can.

"Freedom" represents the "power to determine action without restraint," again according to Random House Webster's unabridged dictionary. Underlying true power and freedom resides the concept of "personal agency" the ability "...to intentionally make things happen by one's actions." This concept is an active area of research in social psychology. If we do not have the freedom to act, we cannot "make things happen." If we lack true power we cannot conceive of taking the actions to "make things happen." What drives our power? Our passion, which drives our purpose. Through purpose we contribute our unique expression of creation into the world.

If we are to make our contribution to the world and claim our reason for being, we must embrace our personal agency and use our true power freely. In my experience with women friends and clients, and in my own life, I notice how readily we embrace our personal agency when we act for a cause, a cause about which we are passionate. While in Tuscany recently, I visited the home of St. Catherine of Siena, who lived in the 14th century, a woman I hold in great esteem and who continues to influence my life. I chose my name in the convent, Sr. Mary Karen, in honor of St. Catherine. Karen remained the only derivative of Catherine available to me. The youngest of 22 children, Catherine, unable to write, dedicated herself to bringing peace and love into the world. She dictated letters to prelates to stay war. Her letters rebuked, reminded and urged prelates to be stallions of truth. So impressed was Pope Gregory XI, exiled in Avignon, France, and afraid of being poisoned, that he followed Catherine's direction and relocated to Rome, in spite of the opposition of his advisers. Though Pope Gregory died shortly thereafter, Catherine communicated with the new pope, Pope Urban VI, admonishing him to control his temper, relentless in her passion to maintain the unity of the church.

Directions to the Reader

Consider a time when you cared deeply about an issue, a problem or a cause, at any time during your life. What did that passion feel like? How did it align you with your purpose?

What actions did you take in the name of that passion?

In performing those actions, what power did you claim? What freedom did you embrace? Identify any portion of awareness that passion brought you in understanding your life's purpose. Describe the characteristics that shaped your personal agency, your ability to make things happen.

STEP 3   RECOLLECT   Look back to past actions when you were motivated by dedication to a cause.

Message to the Reader

Anytime may prove the optimal time to fire your passion.

The dawning of understanding sweeping across students' faces and the thrill of discovering principles of basic science infused my life with purpose and passion for many years. However, the deteriorating political environment within the department diminished my passions significantly. Leaving academia behind, I searched for the thread that wove together my interests. I discovered that my belief in people's greatness and my desire to help them evoke it inflamed my passion. This now represents the seminal purpose and passion and everything that I do.

In response to queries by former colleagues about whether I miss teaching and doing research, I answer, "I am more creative in my life today than I have ever been. My joy explodes as I watch people create or reconstruct their lives as they become clear about who they are, their purpose and their passion."

Directions to the Reader

What passions or causes shape your actions today? How do these align with your purpose?

What actions do you engage in now, in the name of that cause or path, driven by your passion?

How do you experience your power, freedom and personal agency today?

Directions to the Reader

"

"

CONNECT Bring all your vision, dreams and passion into alignment. **STEP 4**

You may experience a disconnection between the purpose and passion that you feel and your experience of yourself as the agent of change capable of activating your freedom and wielding your power to activate your dream. If this is the case, you are poised to dig deeper within and drink from the well of your own greatness.

Message to the Reader

How can you accomplish this?

Know that your greatness lies in wait for your discovery. This is true for everyone. Fired by the flames of your purpose and passion, you can unearth the resources within you that will facilitate your acting to bring about your purpose.

Athletes make use of the process of mental visualization to enhance their performance. By imagining themselves in an upcoming game and mentally practicing meeting the challenges in the game, their performances improve.

Directions to the Reader   Describe the action that you want to accomplish to further your purpose and passion.

Visualize yourself acting from your true power, freely and with effective personal agency. Describe what you see.

"

Directions to the Reader

Are you unable to visualize yourself effectively acting to promote your purpose and passion? What stops you?

"

"

Message to the Reader

If you cannot imagine yourself promoting your purpose and your passion, it is important to recall that you have access to an unlimited internal resource—the life force that enters your body and enlivens each of your cells moment by moment, every moment.

Directions to the Reader

Find a quiet and comfortable place to engage in reflection and visualization. Imagine that you can see into the depths of each of the trillions and trillions of cells in your body. The spark of light glistening in the center of each cell carries your vital life force. Everything you need resides here in this life force.

What is it you need to act with personal agency to further your purpose and passion?

"

"

Call up, from your own cells, the life force, the energy, that you need to act with personal agency.

See yourself receiving the energy that you need flowing from the center of all your cells, filling your entire being, your mind, your heart, your body.

Now, repeat the visualization you originally attempted. Imagine yourself acting from your true power, freely and with effective personal agency. Describe here what you see.

"

_____
_____
_____
_____
_____
_____

"

IMAGINE Be an actor and see yourself acting in alignment with your passion. **STEP 5**

As you continue to practice the imaginary experience, you will anchor the ener-　Message to
gy that you need to be an effective personal agent. If you do this every day, even　the Reader
for only five to ten minutes at a time, you will begin to see a change as you allow
the energy of life to support you in claiming the fullness of your life.

Stirring the energy of your passion, you will begin to identify specific
actions to birth your contribution into the world and live in alignment
with your purpose.

Take time to describe here some of those actions. Each day pick one action to　Directions to
implement.　the Reader

"
_____
_____
_____
_____
_____
_____
_____
_____
"

ACT All action begins with inner movement. Passions stir. Purpose **STEP 6**
seeks expression. You act.

My absolute confidence that the universe partners with us in bringing forth our purpose and passion springs from my knowing that each of us is here to bring something unique into being. When we act in accordance with our purpose and passion, we can expect to be supported by allies, people we know now and others we will meet to help us unfold our purpose and passion.

Before concluding this chapter, let's review the central theme of the six steps:

STEP 1	BE ALERT Thoughts can hold your life hostage. Look for the impact they have in your life.
STEP 2	IDENTIFY Determine which thoughts and actions best reflect your highest qualities, then radiate those qualities.
STEP 3	RECOLLECT Be mindful of your actions during a time when you were motivated by dedication to a cause.
STEP 4	CONNECT Your passion is the fuel of your dreams.
STEP 5	VISUALIZE See yourself acting in alignment with your passion.
STEP 6	ACT Bring your purpose and passion into the world.

Execute these steps, and you choose who you are becoming. This repetitive process ensures your development in alignment with your purpose and passion. The process can be viewed as an ascending, never-ending spiral, literally the stairway to heaven. Each time you go through the cycle, you will have brought one piece of your purpose and passion into the world. As you do, you will see more opportunities to begin the process again. Being alert to your thoughts, identifying your qualities in new dimensions, and recollecting your actions provides assurance that you can do it once again, connecting with ever deepening dimensions of your passion. Imagining yourself acting from your true power, in alignment with your passion, you will bring yet another piece of your purpose and passion into the world. This glorious process of creating and choosing who you are represents the highest aspect of humanity.

Please join Joan in a further discussion of using these steps at
http://www.cellular-wisdom.com

Want to ask questions? Go to Joan's blog
blog.beyond-success.com *and pose your question. Joan will answer you.*

Yes, I Am

I Am
the energy
of Life,
of the stars in the heavens,
of the trees on Earth.
The life force.

I Am
Cellular Wisdom.

Enlightenment breaks through the fog of our doubt and disbelief to brighten the landscape of our essence. We are life itself. The energy that pulses into our cells brings that life wisdom to us. I experienced this life wisdom before writing of my first book, *Cellular Wisdom*, in 2004.

Message to the Reader

If you have had the privilege of being with someone as they die, you witness the withdrawal of their life force. If you have had the privilege of witnessing a birth, you have seen life burst forth with the baby's first cry.

The peace that accompanies the breakthrough of light illuminating our true essence floods us with a deep joy and love. This does not mean we have overcome our imperfections, but rather that we appreciate them as part of our human condition.

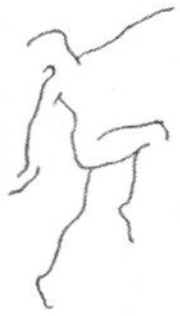

Our Bodies Model the Teachings

The life force enters every cell, and does so indiscriminately, without concern about the cell's perfection.

Message to the Reader

Unconditional love parallels the reality of the life force entering all cells regardless of any condition. Have you given unconditional love to a child, or someone else, or received unconditional love from a parent, or someone else?

Directions to the Reader

Describe your experience of unconditional love.

Have you experienced giving yourself unconditional love? If so, describe it.

Directions to the Reader

"

"

Unconditional love sets us free from judgment and allows us to transcend the expectation of the next moment, to live in the present moment.

Message to the Reader

Beauty opens us into expansiveness of love. Whatever that quality of beauty is that we give to a thing or a person, beauty gives us intense pleasure and deep satisfaction. It can arise from a shape, color or sound, or through observing qualities in a person of high spiritual consciousness. The natural beauty of the earth brings awe. Beauty resides in the witnessing of a friend baring their soul, trusting you with their vulnerability. When we step deeper into the essence of beauty, beyond the surface qualities of time, trend or judgment, we connect with the transcendent quality of beauty—love. We open ourselves wider to the possibility of knowing unconditional love.

A beautiful moment with my husband occurred after we were married about ten years. During those years, I had from time to time doubted his love for me, not because he did anything to cause me doubt, but rather because I did not feel worthy of love and kept looking for the gap, the flaw in his love. After exhausting all my tests of his love, I finally believed in his love for me. As I told him this, tears ran down his face and he said to me, "Finally, you know I love you." This was a moment of expansive love.

*Directions to
the Reader*

When have you experienced transcending the reality of the moment to experience some sort of timeless expansiveness? Describe your experience.

The desire to live vibrantly, sparkling with the energy of life, reflects our longing for the wholeness of who we are. Freed from the shackles of doubt and anxiety, we can mold and sculpt our fullness, bringing forth our greatness. Moments of great clarity, experiencing a heightened awareness of life, often accompany times of inner conflict, the making of difficult decisions, experiencing seething suffering, or tumultuous transition.

*Directions to
the Reader*

If you have had such an experience of heightened awareness, describe it.

The mystery of life unfolds in unexpected synchronicities that burst into our lives and often influence its direction. A compelling sense of wonder accompanies such events.

Have you had such an experience of unexpected synchronicities? If so, describe it.

What sense of *wonder* was brought into your life by this experience?

Directions to the Reader

RECOGNIZE Notice your moments of unconditional love, self-transcendence and expansiveness. In these moments you touch the unseen substance of life.   **STEP I**

Review the above exercises, looking for glimpses of what you're learning about who you are. Write what you learned.

Directions to the Reader

During several years of my leadership as Chair of the Department and Director of a Research Center, I came to understand the strength of my integrity in a way I had never experienced it previously. Maybe because powerful people pulled me in many different directions, I knew I had to stand in the center of my being, strong and clear. I now count "integrity" as a cornerstone in the foundation of my being.

Directions to the Reader

What characteristics, such as integrity, insight, striving toward wisdom, have you experienced, and which constitute components in the foundation of your being?

STEP 2   IDENTIFY   Name the characteristics you have come to know lie at the foundation of your being. The "you" you are coming to know lives in the depth of your essence.

The quality "personal wisdom" refers to a state of consciousness—the point in personality development at which we exhibit a rich insight into our lives; the possible causes of our behavior and feelings, and our relation toward others; a sense of the meaning of our lives, our goals, competencies and emotions; how to express and regulate our emotions, and develop and maintain social relationships; a basic acceptance of ourselves and tolerance for others' values and lifestyles; and finally, a tolerance of ambiguity in the use of strategies to manage uncertainty by being open to experience, trusting and developing flexible solutions. Personal wisdom grows and deepens when we align ourselves with the understanding of the model of our own Cellular Wisdom™. This automatic functioning and interaction of our cells then serves us as a mirror of our larger lives—or vice versa—and being aware of it informs and reinforces our understanding of our actions and interactions in and with the world outside of our "Selves."

Is there a circumstance in your life that could benefit from your personal wisdom?

Describe the circumstance.

Directions to the Reader

What specific aspect of personal wisdom would be particularly useful in this circumstance?

_____

_____

_____

_____

_____

_____

_____

_____
                                                              "

| **STEP 3** | DISCERN Recall a situation which would benefit from your personal wisdom and the aspect of personal wisdom that would be most useful. |

Message to the Reader

How do you tap into Cellular Wisdom™ in order to bring forth this aspect of personal wisdom? Since Cellular Wisdom™ is pre-verbal, the most direct way to connect with it is to meditate—to relax the conscious mind, and clear away all thoughts, judgments and disturbing emotions to create a clear opening to experience Cellular Wisdom™.

Before engaging in meditation, formulate a clear intention about what aspect of personal wisdom you want to bring forth, as you described above. During meditation be attentive to any thoughts and feelings that arise. After meditation, write what has emerged for you.

Prepare to meditate. The quick pace of our lives does not optimize conditions for meditation. Here are a couple of techniques I use to allow me to enter the peaceful, clear space required for meditation.

Sitting in a quiet place, comfortable in your body, close your eyes and begin to pay attention to your breathing.

Technique 1 As a state of calmness begins, allow yourself to imagine going into a beautiful garden of your own making. Entering the garden you may choose to sit in a very beautiful spot, surrounded by flowers and trees, perhaps a languid pond. Sometimes, I choose to sit in the arms of a tree. Often, I will ask permission to merge with the tree. As I do, my body stretches to feel the full extent of the tree. I feel the life force entering the roots of the tree, moving up its trunk and out into its branches. Stay here for the duration of the meditation, if you choose.

Technique 2 As a state of calmness begins, envision a beautiful place in nature, in the mountains or the ocean. Viewing this beautiful landscape,

imagine that you are a bird, your favorite bird, flying over the mountains or the ocean. Feel the freedom of flying. Choose a place where you would like to land. Proceed to land there. Now, see your bird body begin to dissolve so that all of the molecules separate and enter the rock of the mountain or the sands of the ocean. In that state, feel the life force in the rock or the sand. Stay here for the duration of the meditation, if you choose.

If either of these techniques appeals to you, use it, or use another technique that allows you to deeply relax and clear your mind of thought and your body of tension.

After meditation write what emerged for you upon tapping into your Cellular Wisdom™.

Directions to the Reader

Directions to the Reader

With what you have learned in meditation, determine what specific actions you plan to take and describe them.

"

_____

_____

_____

_____

_____

_____

_____

_____

_____

_____

_____

_____

_____

_____

_____

_____

"

STEP 4   ENGAGE Meditate. Open to your Cellular Wisdom™ and decipher actions that are aligned with your personal wisdom.

Imagine yourself in action, in total alignment with the aspects of wisdom you want to exhibit. Areas of the brain activated by imagery overlap considerably with those areas activated by visual perception in real-time. This means you activate much of the same parts of the brain by imagining as by actually witnessing. Imagining a future action may facilitate performing it, because of the similar brain activation. This has been well documented among athletes who employ mental imagery to improve athletic performance.

Describe what you see when you imagine yourself performing the wisdom actions you want to perform.

Directions to the Reader

"

"

Were you effective in imagining yourself performing the wisdom actions you want to perform? If not, I suggest that you repeat the entire process beginning with meditating and follow through to imagining, until you mentally see yourself performing the desired actions.

Once you successfully picture yourself performing your wisdom actions, set a deadline. Write the actions and deadline here.

Directions to the Reader

"

"

Directions to the Reader

What was the impact of your actions on the circumstance or situation you wanted to alter?

"

_____

_____

_____

_____

_____

_____

_____

_____

_____

                                                "

STEP 5   IMAGINE Picture yourself in action until you can see yourself acting from your wisdom, then act.

After serving as Chair of the Department and Director of a Research Center for five years, I knew it was time for me to step down. It became clear to me in meditation that it was also time for me to leave the academic environment. In my case, this would mean taking early retirement. Tufts University School of Medicine had no plan to buy out early retirees. Therefore, I knew that requesting such funds from the Dean of the Medical School would not be productive. I also did not want to hire a lawyer and begin discussion on a litigious note. I felt I really deserved funds for early retirement because of the significant contributions I had made in my roles as Chair of the Department and Director of the Research Center, in addition to my roles as faculty: teaching, research-ing, and promoting the University by serving on national committees, evaluating grants and site-visiting research institutions across the US and Canada. I had no idea about how to make my request in a way that might be productive. Aware of this, I simply chanted my mantra, internally: "Show me." A mantra is a sound or word used to focus intention.

A couple of weeks later, a sales representative at a department store I frequented called to invite me to lunch with a friend she wanted to introduce me to. We met at the sales representative's luxurious condo and proceeded to have lunch at the Four Seasons Hotel, across from Boston Common. The sales representative's friend, Paula Chauncey, a woman who had held senior positions in banking for many years, was now opening her own consulting business. In the middle of lunch, with no preparation, I heard myself blurt, "You wouldn't be the kind of person who could help me write a proposal to Tufts University explaining why they should pay me to retire early, would you?"

Paula responded simply, "Yes."

We began to work together in August, a few weeks after we met. I presented to the Dean a fifteen-page proposal, with a one-page Executive Summary, documenting the contributions I had made. My proposal yielded positive results. Further, Paula and I have become very close friends. I'm so grateful for this unexpected encounter, which not only yielded me funds for early retirement, but also brought a dear friend into my life.

Although I had no idea how to proceed or what actions to take to bring about a positive resolution and receive payment for early retirement, I knew I deserved such, and that there was a way, even if I didn't at first know what it was. It was with utter confidence that I chanted my mantra: "Show me."

Message to the Reader

Is there a circumstance or situation you would like to resolve but you are unable to formulate specific actions that would lead to the preferred resolution?

Describe the circumstance or situation.

Directions to the Reader

Directions to the Reader

How do you want this situation to be resolved?

" "

Do you believe that you deserve this resolution? If the answer is yes, describe the basis of your belief.

" "

If you do not believe you deserve this resolution, is there some resolution that you

do believe you deserve?

"

_____

_____

_____

_____

_____

_____

_____

_____

_____

"

Now is the time to chant my mantra: "Show me." Do it every day for 21 days. This is how long it takes to establish new synapses in the brain or acquire a new habit. During this time, watch, be alert to synchronicities which might arise, so you can take advantage of them, as I did by asking Paula, "Are you the kind of person …"

When ready, come back to this page and write down what has occurred in response

to your plea: "Show me."

"

_____

_____

_____

_____

_____

_____

_____

_____

"

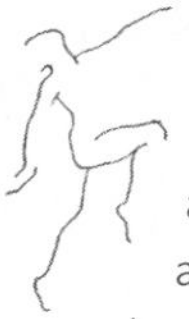

Our Bodies Model the Teachings

As the life force pulses through our cells moment by moment, it directs all the activities of the cell, without the cell needing to know what is going to happen and when. Our cells display a trust that they will always have what they need when they need it.

Message to the Reader

Many times we cannot tell what steps to take until we take the first step, which presents new perspectives of possibilities. This leads to a second step, until eventually we recognize the path and where it is leading. Holding the energy of knowing that at the deepest level of being "all is well," regardless of external appearances, helps us create the opening for possibilities to emerge.

Directions to the Reader

Have you had the experience of not knowing either what you want or how to get it but clarity emerged slowly through an unfolding step-by-step process? Describe the process.

" "

If this has happened to you in the past, you can have confidence that it will happen again. If you have not experienced such a step-by-step unfolding, now is the opportunity to attract such a process. As mentioned previously, tolerance of ambiguity is a hallmark of personal wisdom.

Directions to the Reader

Consider a particular circumstance or situation that you would like to see resolved. Review the meditation exercise.

Directions to the Reader

Meditate on the circumstance or situation, intending to find one step that you can take. Prepare for meditation and allow yourself to let go of all thoughts in your mind and tension in your body. Write what thoughts and feelings emerged from the meditation.

As you reflect on these, what action step can you take toward a resolution?

Know that regardless of whether you can see the resolution or not, if you are moving in the right direction, you can feel it. If you become uncertain or tense anticipating a particular step, then you know it is not the right step to take. Follow your internal compass and you will be moving in the direction that is right for you.

Directions to the Reader

After you've taken the first step, what other step occurs to you?

"

_____

_____

_____

_____

_____

_____

_____

_____

_____

_____

_____

"

In this manner, your action plan will unfold and lead you toward a destination that will become clear as you walk along the path.

STEP 6   ASK   Use the suggested mantra, "Show me" to help you resolve a specific situation in which you cannot decipher how to proceed. Stay attentive to your environments, internal and external. Act when the opportunity arises.

The mystery of life intertwines many elements into pathways that appear to be circuitous, but lead undeniably to an opportunity for you to express the fullness of who you are. Slowly we will come to know the magnificent creatures we are, the embodiment of the life force itself, with all its expansiveness and creativity.

Let's review the steps whereby you ultimately live from your cellular wisdom.

STEP 1	RECOGNIZE . Notice your moments of unconditional love, self-transcendence, and expansiveness. In these moments you touch the unseen substance of life.
STEP 2	IDENTIFY Name the characteristics you have come to know lie at the foundation of your being. The "you" you are coming to know lives in the depth of your essence.
STEP 3	DISCERN Recall a situation which would benefit from your personal wisdom and the aspect of personal wisdom that would be most useful.
STEP 4	ENGAGE Meditate. Open to your Cellular Wisdom™ and decipher actions that are aligned with your personal wisdom.
STEP 5	IMAGINE Picture yourself in action until you can see yourself acting from your wisdom, then act.
STEP 6	ASK Use the suggested mantra, "Show me" to help resolve a specific situation in which you cannot decipher how to proceed. Stay alert to your environments, internal and external. Act when the opportunity arises.

These steps into the depths of life and then out again to bring forth your greatness will allow you to fully engage in life with all its uncertainties, understanding who you truly are at the depths of your being and appreciating your magnificence. You will delight in the process of life, open to its emerging mysteries, freely shifting perspectives, changing energies, as each moment of life presents itself. As a full participant in the unfolding of life you will bring more and more of your deep self into freely choosing courses of action from a sense of knowing what is a true expression of your essence. Along the way, you will make mistakes, but you will treat those mistakes as opportunities to learn, refining your process, and not as catastrophes to be mourned. You know your deep personal wisdom, arising from your Cellular Wisdom™, and you will once again align yourself with it. This is the joy of life, the joy of coming into the fullness of who you are, living completely in the moment. Life becomes meaningful and deeply satisfying as you live, unfolding your greatness moment by moment, trusting that you have that greatness as a part of your life force coming to you in every moment. Celebrate your being and your becoming, every moment spent in the stream of life.

Please join Joan in a further discussion of living from Cellular Wisdom,
evoking your greatness at **http://www.cellular-wisdom.com**

Want to ask questions? Go to Joan's blog
blog.beyond-success.com *and pose your question. Joan will answer you.*

Conclusion

Sssssssssshshshshsh!

Slip into the silent stillness.

Sssssssssshshshshsh!

Let the wonderings of the mind go.
Float in the myriad chambers of your soul's depths.
Sssssssssshshshshsh!

Slip into the presence
of Being.
Sssssssssshshshshsh!

Everything you yearn for
is here.
Sssssssssshshshshsh!

Feel the fullness of
I AM,
in all the dimensions of your being.
Sssssssssshshshshsh!

Experience all your hopes,
all your dreams,
realized.
Sssssssssshshshshsh!

Discover:
You
are the
I AM.
Sssssssssshshshshsh!

I leave you with a few final thoughts as you continue your inner and outer journey toward greater awareness and expanded consciousness to know the wisdom of Self.

Hearing the call to greatness within, understanding the vitality of life that flows through your body's cells and systems, you began this journey. You listened to its call as you moved from the question "Not Good Enough?" through the chapters to the final statement, "Yes, I Am."

In exploring the inner domains of your experiences, you examined foundational beliefs; created new supporting beliefs; built a "template for success"; uncovered your values, personal qualities and life purpose; recognized when you were sliding down the emotional slope; learned to choose happiness; clarified what you want and accessed resources to help you create it; learned to recognize signals about critical changes; discarded patterns that limit possibilities; identified your style of regulating emotions; developed ways to create emotional well-being; increased your compassion for Self; connected with others and engaged in collaboration; visualized yourself acting from your purpose and passion in the world; identified characteristics that lie at the foundation of your being; discovered your personal power; and tapped into your Cellular Wisdom™ to bring your vision into the world.

Like your body's cells whose default condition is to thrive, your journey to greatness expands with every movement emanating from your authentic energy. The process to evoke greatness forever expands as you choose to thrive and grow. Greatness has no limits. The path of deepening your knowledge of Self resembles a spiral staircase. So, how, you ask yourself, will you continue to attend to, listen and hear your call to greatness? How will you know when to take the next step as you engage in your day-to-day activities, once you have completed the exercises in this book?

Whereas your cells have evolved to thrive, you choose to thrive or not to thrive. You must set aside time to listen to the flow of your life. You must become intimate with the continuous nudges or symbols in your life. These are the signals giving you feedback on when and how to take the next step. Re-invigorate your commitment. Consider revisiting this inner type of work once a year. Continue the process of expanding your perspectives and deepening your insights of how *your way of being in the world* is fulfilling your purpose. The expression of your significant contributions to self, partners, family, community and the world, position you right in the middle of your developing greatness from your authentic being. Like your cells invigorate your tissues, by activating stem cells housed there, committing them to a course of development in deepening the knowing of our process, we invigorate our lives. Harmony ensues in body, mind and spirit.

Keep the call to greatness alive by interacting with others who have also heard the call and are committed to revitalizing their sense of Self, wanting to know the fullness of who they are! This interaction may involve your spouse, a family member, business associates or a community of individuals wanting to take this journey together.

If you decide to participate as a group, meet once a month after completing the exercises individually from one chapter. The monthly meetings become a safe haven for you and others to come together to share your insights and changes in personal perspectives. What greater gift could you give yourself and those you care about than an expanded sense of being, keeping alive your call to greatness? Some individuals in the group will likely confront unanticipated challenges. The richness of the diversity of perspectives and insights shared in the intimacy and safety of the monthly meetings provides stabilizing support for those facing crucial challenges. The mirror of this group dynamic is in our body's journey of our cells. Traveling together, our cells move seamlessly from their place of origin to their respective places of performance and function in the body.

Again, we see this same type of support as our cells migrate along structures that support them in moving in the right direction, ensuring they reach their appropriate sites. This is the wisdom of the body.

Some individuals in a group situation will make long-overdue decisions. The collective energy of the group mobilizes that person to recognize the value of her decisions and make the difficulties involved in unfolding the decision easier, as she becomes more aware of her own internal resources and the support of others willing to share her perspectives and insights in the journey.

Interior journeys parallel the unexpected joys, appreciation for different tastes, surroundings, cultures, and worldviews, as well as the challenges of traveling our physical world. Navigating our inner realms or our outer world is still a journey of discovery. Discovery excites and activates our hearts and minds. We reap the richness of understanding and expansive experiences. Adventurers, like Antoine de Saint-Exupery, a pilot and author of the *Airman's Odyssey: A Trilogy* and *The Little Prince*, succinctly articulate the choice to thrive: "Affirm life!" and "Life always bursts the boundaries of formulas." In the words of *The Little Prince*, "One sees clearly only with the heart. Anything essential is invisible to the eyes."

Keep your inner sight acute. Pay attention to that which is invisible to the eyes. Take time now to review what you have discovered along the way of this deepening journey. Anchor your discoveries now by writing a summary of your new perceptions

Directions to the Reader

about who you are, how you see the world and your purpose as a contributor to others.

"

_____
_____
_____
_____
_____
_____
_____
_____
_____
_____
_____
"

Directions to the Reader

With whom will you share this information?

"

_____
_____
_____
_____
_____
_____
_____
_____
_____
"

Directions to the Reader

What *intentions* do you have for expressing your authentic self, bringing forth your greatness?

" "

Do not be dismayed that the journey is never-ending. With each step we see new sights, come to discover new levels, and appreciate more deeply the fullness of our being. Along the path, we *awaken*, an event described by mystics as a unique experience of Oneness, which surpasses any previous sense of unity. Like the cracking of an eggshell, everything changes: your perception of the world, yourself and your relationship to everyone and everything that is alive. Evelyn Underhill describes awakening as a "shifting of the field of consciousness…consciousness has suddenly changed its rhythm and a new aspect of the universe rushes in."

Congratulations! You opened to the teachings of your body's Cellular Wisdom™. Exploring your inner landscape, you searched for truths of who you are. You glimpsed, and then came to know more fully, the vastness of your being. The steps you took, modeled by your body's cells and systems, creating a journey in mind, body and spirit. *You* forged your pathway to evoking your greatness! You. Never forget that you are a magnificent being!

Acknowledgements

Women across the world, across time have inspired me, awed me and fascinated me in their abilities to keep the focus of their lives in the midst of accelerating demands from the workplace and from their families.

My grandmother enthralled us all with her wit, her unique love for us and her indomitable spirit. My mother's determination to become a teacher, to excel and to show her students how much fun learning could be influenced me in indefinable ways.

The women who participated in the Cellular Wisdom™ for Women Workshops always seeking their larger selves, ready to explore, examine and excavate contributed much to my understanding of Cellular Wisdom™ for Women.

My Editor and Publisher, Toni Dianne Holm, led me down the path of ever deeper understanding and articulation. Fleur di Lis Design's contribution to the cover and interior design of the book deserves grateful recognition, as does Editor, George E. Tice and Copy Editors, Laura Daniel and Robert M. Smith.

My teachers, both formal and informal, stamped their spirit on this work in fundamental ways; they have stretched and deepened my understanding of the capabilities of the human spirit.

My students and friends ask the questions that lead me to probe the concepts from myriad perspectives and gather the gold hidden in the depths.

I acknowledge the enormous legacy that all of you have graced me with.

Letter to the Reader

Dear Reader,

I have always enjoyed sharing my ideas as a writer, teacher, speaker, and workshop leader and would love to expand my sharing with you, my reader. For years women have gone unrecognized for our valor, persistence and our greatness! No longer. I support and honor you as the supporters, nurturers and changers of the world. Speaking of support, thank you for reading "Cellular Wisdom for Women." To further support you in your contemplations, discussions, understanding and incorporation of these principles in your life, I invite you and book club participants to contact me so that I can speak with you as you either begin or end your reading of this book. If you are not in a book club, but would enjoy speaking with me or contacting me, please do not hesitate to do so. I welcome the contact. I can be reached at 970-226-5626 or joanking@beyond-success.com .

You are the yeast of the world and I salute you!

Sincerely,

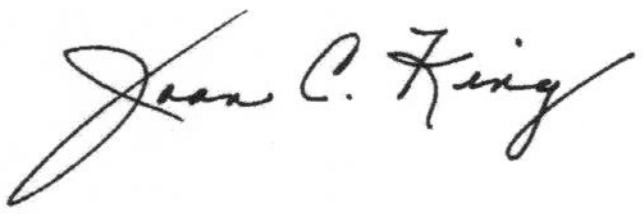

Joan C. King

Author Biography

Joan King's life path embodies the blending of the hard and noetic sciences. At the tender age of seventeen, she stepped into life at the Dominican convent in her hometown of New Orleans, Louisiana. Eleven years later she left that religious training to become a chemist, then received a Ph.D. in neuroscience and psychology. Her twenty-year tenure as a professor at Tufts University School of Medicine, lead her to a dynamic crossroads of personal self-discovery. She left academia. Her new found "inner knowing" ignited the writing of her book *Cellular Wisdom*. It became the foundation in understanding how our bodies model the teachings of our beliefs. Joan King's blending of science and spirituality birthed her professional coaching business, Beyond Success LLC, in 1998. Today, Joan is helping others apply these same dynamics for women and men in relationships and business as a Master Certified Coach. As an author, Joan is finishing her work with cellular wisdom in the forthcoming titles: *Cellular Wisdom at Work – An Inner Work Book, Cellular Wisdom for Relationships – An Inner Work Book, Cellular Wisdom for Men – An Inner Work Book*; and a Second Edition of the foundational book, *Cellular Wisdom – Decoding the Body's Secret Language*.